COMPUTER SCIENCE AND STATISTICS:
Proceedings of the Sixteenth Symposium on the Interface

COMPUTER SCIENCE AND STATISTICS

PROCEEDINGS OF THE SIXTEENTH SYMPOSIUM ON THE INTERFACE

Atlanta, Georgia, March 1984

edited by

L. BILLARD

University of Georgia
Athens, Georgia, U.S.A.

1985

NORTH-HOLLAND – AMSTERDAM · NEW YORK · OXFORD

ISBN: 0 444 87725 8

Published by:
ELSEVIER SCIENCE PUBLISHERS B.V.
P.O. BOX 1991
1000 BZ AMSTERDAM
THE NETHERLANDS

Sole distributors for the U.S.A. and Canada:
ELSEVIER SCIENCE PUBLISHING COMPANY, INC.
52 VANDERBILT AVENUE
NEW YORK, N.Y. 10017
U.S.A.

This work relates to the Department of the Navy Grant Number N00014-84-G-0024 issued by the Office of Naval Reserarch. The United States Government has a royalty-free license throughout the world in all copyrightable material contained herein.

Library of Congress Cataloging in Publication Data

Symposium on the Interface (16th : 1984 : Atlanta, Ga.)
Computer science and statistics.

1. Mathematical statistics--Data processing--
Congresses. I. Billard, L. (Lynne), 1943- .
II. Title.
QA276.4.S95 1984 519.5'0284 85-1587
ISBN 0-444-87725-8 (U.S.)

PRINTED IN THE NETHERLANDS

Preface

The Computer Science and Statistics: Sixteenth Symposium on the Interface was a continuation of what has become an extremely successful symposia series. Statistical and computer science societies each independently hold professional meetings which tend (as is natural) to concentrate on its own particular discipline with the result that a void remains where the interface is concerned. Yet, by their very nature the interface of these two fields is one of great and growing significance and importance. The Sixteenth Symposium held in Atlanta in March 1984 and hosted by the University of Georgia, Athens, provided a unique opportunity for the interaction of professionals and workers who may be primarily trained in either statistics or computer science but whose interests and specializations interface with the other discipline. Thus, these specialists could meet and discuss new and exciting developments in these areas of common interest.

The Keynote Address was presented by Professor George Marsaglia, former chairman, Department of Computer Science, Washington State University. Dr. Marsaglia has made significant contributions to the interface area of statistics and computer science most notably in random number generation. Previous Keynote Speakers have been primarily statisticians with overlap interest in statistical computation. Although well trained in statistics, Dr. Marsaglia is currently in a computer science department. As such he was able to bring fresh and invaluable insights to the Symposium. This shift in emphasis away from having speakers most of whom were essentially statisticians was continued into the selection of speakers for the Symposium's invited workshop sessions. Indeed, a distinguishing feature of the Sixteenth Symposium was the participation of many speakers whose major affiliation is with computer science rather than with statistics.

The format for the Sixteenth Symposium followed that of earlier symposia, specifically, after an opening Keynote Address, there followed twelve invited workshop sessions generally featuring three to five speakers. Two or three sessions ran concurrently over a two day period. In addition, contributed poster sessions were presented during a lunchtime session each day. As best as can be ascertained, the presentations were of high quality with the result that registrants were provided with ample material to stimulate their thoughts and to provide continued motivation and ideas to implement in their own research endeavors.

As Organizing Chairman I would like to express my thanks to all those who assisted me so ably in ensuring the success of this Sixteenth Symposium. In particular, I wish to thank the Office of Naval Research for its financial support; to the Statistical Computing Section and the Atlanta Chapter of the American Statistical Association, the Association for Computing Machinery and the International Association for Statistical Computing who served as cooperating professional societies; to previous Organizing Chairmen who were willing to share the benefits of their experiences; to Jonathan Arnold, Michael Brannigan, Jean Porter, Robert Prince and Jeffrey Smith who constituted the organizing committee; and to Gloria Fondren, Sandra Roberts, Dawn Tolbert and Valerie Watkins for their invaluable secretarial assistance. To all these people, a very special thank you.

Lynne Billard
Athens, Georgia

FINANCIAL SUPPORTERS OF THE SIXTEENTH INTERFACE SYMPOSIUM

U. S. Office of Naval Research

COOPERATING ORGANIZATIONS

American Statistical Association
- Statistical Computing Section
- Atlanta Chapter

Association for Computing Machinery

International Association for Statistical Computing

Contents

1 KEYNOTE ADDRESS

3 A Current View of Random Number Generators
George Marsaglia, Washington State University

11 WHAT'S NEW AND INNOVATIVE IN COMPUTER GRAPHICS
Organizer: *Ingram Olkin, Stanford University*

13 Min/Max Autocorrelation Factors for Multivariate Spatial Imagery
Paul Switzer, Stanford University

17 GEOMETRIC AND SET-VALUED STATISTICS
Organizer: *William F. Eddy, Carnegie-Mellon University*

19 Aspects of Random Sets
Richard A. Vitale, Claremont Graduate School

25 Ordering of Multivariate Data
William F. Eddy, Carnegie-Mellon University

31 DEVELOPING STATISTICAL WORKSTATIONS
Organizer: *L. Billard, University of Georgia*

33 Statistical Software: Progress and Prospects
J. A. Nelder and R. J. Baker, Rothamsted Experimental Station

39 Responsibilities, Problems and Some Solutions for the Profession's Input into Microcomputer Software
Brian P. Murphy, University of Western Australia

45 RELIABILITY OF COMPUTER SOFTWARE AND COMPUTING NETWORKS
Organizer: *Nozer D. Singpurwalla, The George Washington University*

47 A Bayes Empirical Bayes Approach for (Software) Reliability Growth
Michio Horigome, Tokyo University of Mercantile Marine, Nozer D. Singpurwalla, The George Washington University, and Refik Soyer, Tokyo University of Mercantile Marine

57 Bayesian Inference for the Weibull Process with Applications to Assessing Software Reliability Growth and Predicting Software Failures
Jerzy Kyparisis, Florida International University and Nozer D. Singpurwalla, The George Washington University

65 NUMERICAL METHODS
Organizer: *Douglas M. Bates, Queen's University and University of Wisconsin*

67 Computational Methods for Generalized Cross-Validation
Douglas M. Bates, University of Wisconsin and Queen's University

75 Secondary Storage Methods for Statistical Computational Operations
Setrag N. Khoshafian, Douglas M. Bates and David J. DeWitt, University of Wisconsin

83 COMPUTATIONAL GEOMETRY AND STATISTICAL APPLICATIONS
Organizer: *Robert J. Serfling, The Johns Hopkins University*

85 A Class of Problems in Statistical Computation: Generalized L- and Related Statistics
Robert J. Serfling, The Johns Hopkins University

89 Algorithms for Selection in Sets, with Applications to Statistics
Greg N. Frederickson, Purdue University and Donald B. Johnson, The Pennsylvania State University

97 The Application of Voronoi Diagrams to Nonparametric Decision Rules
Godfried T. Toussaint, McGill University, Binay K. Bhattacharya, Simon Frazer University, and Ronald S. Poulsen, McGill University

109 Multidimensional Sorting -- An Overview
Jacob E. Goodman, City College CUNY and Richard Pollack, Courant Institute NYU

115 COMPUTER-SUPPORTED INSTRUCTION: PROSPECTS AND PITFALLS
Organizer: *Lucio Chiaraviglio, Georgia Institute of Technology*

117 Computer-Supported Instruction: Prospects and Pitfalls
Lucio Chiaraviglio, Georgia Institute of Technology

119 OPTIMAL TRANSFORMATIONS IN REGRESSION
Organizer: *John P. Sall, SAS Institute*

121 Estimating Optimal Transformations for Multiple Regression
Leo Breiman, University of California, and Jerome H. Friedman, Stanford Linear Accelerator Center and Stanford University

135 Quantitative Analysis of Qualitative Data
Forrest W. Young, University of North Carolina

159 A Comparison of the ACE and MORALS Algorithms in an Application to Engine Exhaust Emissions Modeling
Robert N. Rodriguez, SAS Institute

169 TIME SERIES
Organizer: *G. C. Tiao, University of Chicago*

171 Computer Investigation of Some Non-linear Time Series Models
Clive Granger, Frank Huynh, Alvaro Escribano and Chowdhury Mustafa, University of California at San Diego

179 Model-Based Treatment of a Manic-Depressive Series
Agustin Maravall, Bank of Spain

189 Seasonality and Seasonal Adjustment of Time Series
Steven Hillmer, University of Kansas

199 GRAPHICAL TOOLS FOR DATA ANALYSIS
Organizer: *R. McGill, Bell Laboratories*

201 Looking at More than Three Dimensions
W. L. Nicholson and D. B. Carr, Pacific Northwest Laboratory

211 STATISTICAL DATABASES
Organizer: *Harry K. T. Wong, Lawrence Berkeley Laboratory*

213 Anti-Sampling for Estimation
Neil C. Rowe, Naval Postgraduate School

215 CONTRIBUTED PAPERS

217 Nonparametric Estimation of the Modes of High-Dimensional Densities
Steven B. Boswell, Georgia Institute of Technology

227 SPIRIT: An Intelligent Tutoring System for Tutoring Probability Theory
Amos Barzilay, University of Pittsburgh and XEROX Palo Alto Research Center, and Jerrold H. May and Harry E. Pople Jr., University of Pittsburgh

233 Interval Estimation of the Noncentrality Parameter of a Gamma Distribution
Paul Chiou and Chien-Pai Han, East Texas State University and University of Texas

237 Fuzzy Set Theory Used to Prioritize Geochemical Nuclear Waste Research
Kenneth S. Czyscinski and William V. Harper, Battelle Memorial Institute

247 Biplot for Exploration and Diagnosis -- Examples and Software
K. R. Gabriel and C. L. Odoroff, University of Rochester

253 Statistical and Data Digitization Techniques Applied to an Analysis of Leaf Initiation in Plants
Colin R. Goodall, Princeton University

265 An Alternative Test for Normality
Thomas R. Gulledge Jr. and Stephen W. Looney, Louisiana State University

269 Computer Generated Distributions for a Random Statistic of Mixtures of Gamma Populations
K. J. Kapoor, Henry Ford Hospital, and D. S. Tracy, University of Windsor

277 Quality Control on Microcomputers
T. Bruce McLean, Georgia Southern College and McElrath and Associates, Inc.

281 Sampling Distribution of Skewness Coefficient for Normal Mixtures
Derrick S. Tracy, University of Windsor and Kunwar J. Kapoor, Henry Ford Hospital

287 Diagnostics for Assessing Multimodality
M. Anthong Wong and Christian Schaack, Massachusetts Institute of Technology

Availability of Proceedings

15th (1983)	North Holland Publishing Company Amsterdam The Netherlands
13, 14th (1981,82)	Springer-Verlag New York, Inc. 175 Fifth Avenue New York, NY 10010
12th (1979)	Jane F. Gentleman Department of Statistics University of Waterloo Waterloo, Ontario Canada N2L 3G1
11th (1978)	Institute of Statistics North Carolina State University P. O. Box 5457 Raleigh, North Carolina 27650
10th (1977)	David Hogben Statistical Engineering Laboratory Applied Mathematics Division National Bureau of Standards U.S. Department of Commerce Washington, D.C. 20234
9th (1979)	Prindle, Weber, and Schmidt, Inc. 20 Newbury Street Boston, Massachusetts 02116
8th (1975)	Health Sciences Computing Facility, AV-111 Center for Health Sciences University of California Los Angeles, California 90024
7th (1974)	Statistical Numerical Analysis and Data Processing Section 117 Snedecor Hall Iowa State University Ames, Iowa 50010
4,5,6th (1971,1972, 1973)	Western Periodicals Company 13000 Raymer Street North Hollywood, California 91605

The Seventeenth Symposium on the Interface will be held March 17-19, 1985, in Lexington, Kentucky. The chair will be David M. Allen of the University of Kentucky.

KEYNOTE ADDRESS

A Current View of Random Number Generators

George Marsaglia
Washington State University

COMPUTER SCIENCE AND STATISTICS:
The Interface, L. Billard (ed.)

A CURRENT VIEW OF RANDOM NUMBER GENERATORS

George Marsaglia

Computer Science Department
Washington State University
Pullman, Washington, 99164

The ability to generate satisfactory sequences of random numbers is one of the key links between Computer Science and Statistics. Standard methods may no longer be suitable for increasingly sophisticated uses, such as in precision Monte Carlo studies, testing for primes, combinatorics or public encryption schemes. This article describes stringent new tests for which standard random number generators: congruential, shift-register and lagged-Fibonacci, give poor results, and describes new methods that pass the stringent tests and seem more suitable for precision Monte Carlo use.

1. INTRODUCTION

Most computer systems have random number generators available, and for most purposes they work remarkably well. Indeed, a random number generator is much like sex: when its good its wonderful, and when its bad its still pretty good. But many of the standard random number generators (RNG's) are not good enough for increasingly sophisticated Monte Carlo uses, such as in geometric probability, combinatorics, estimating distribution functions, comparing statistical procedures, generating and testing for large primes for use in encryption schemes and the like. At least, that is my current view, and I will give reasons for it, by describing new, more stringent tests that standard RNG's fail yet new kinds of generators pass. The more stringent tests are still reasonable, related to the kinds of applications of RNG's that cheap and fast computing power have made feasible, often calling for samples of hundreds of thousands or millions. The kinds of generators that pass the more stringent tests are those that combine simple, standard generators in various ways.

Most of the standard RNG's produce a sequence of elements by means of a linear transformation on some algebraic structure. Three methods dominate: congruential, shift-register and lagged-Fibonacci. These will be called *simple* RNG's; details and properties will be summarized in sections below. Most examples of simple generators pass standard tests for randomness, such as those enumerated in Knuth's volume 2 [6], but may fail spectacularly on one or more of the new, stringent tests described below. Methods that combine two of the simple generators do much better on the stringent tests.

After summary descriptions of the three most common simple RNG's: congruential, shift-register and lagged-Fibonacci (with more detail on the latter two, as, in spite of being considered by various researchers for the past 25 years, they are not as widely known as congruential RNG's), I will give some theoretical justification for combining simple generators, then describe new, stringent tests that simple generators fail but combination generators pass.

2. SIMPLE GENERATORS: CONGRUENTIAL

These generators use a linear transformation on the ring of reduced residues of some modulus m, to produce a sequence of integers:
$x_1, x_2, x_3, \ldots \quad x_n = ax_{n-1} + b \bmod m.$
They are the most widely used RNG's, and they work remarkably well for most purposes. But for some purposes they are not satisfactory; points in n-space produced by congruential RNG's fall on a lattice with a huge unit cell volume, m^{n-1}, compared to the unit cell volume of 1 one would expect from random points with coordinates constrained to be integers. Details are in [9,10]. Congruential RNG's perform well on many of the stringent tests described below, but not on all of them.

3. SIMPLE GENERATORS: SHIFT-REGISTER

These are based on viewing the bits of a computer word as the elements of a binary vector, then using iterates of a linear transformation to generate a sequence of binary vectors, and hence computer words, that may be interpreted as a sequence of uniform random integers. In terms of vectors and matrices, the sequence is $\beta, \beta T, \beta T^2, \beta T^3, \ldots$ with β a 1×n binary vector, T an n×n binary matrix of 0's and 1's, all arithmetic modulo 2 and addition of binary vectors the exclusive-or, $\oplus$, of the two corresponding computer words. Shift-register generators are sometimes called Tausworthe generators.

The binary matrix T is usually chosen so that the product βT may be produced with simple computer operations. A good choice is $T = (I+R^s)(I+L^t)$, where R is the matrix that transforms every vector $\beta = (b_1, b_2, \ldots, b_n)$ into $\beta R = (0, b_1, b_2, \ldots, b_{n-1})$, and $L = R'$ transforms β into $\beta L = (b_2, b_3, \ldots, b_n, 0)$. Thus R is all 0's except for 1's on the principal super-diagonal; L is all 0's except for 1's on the principal sub-diagonal. Then $\beta T = \beta(I+R^s)(I+L^t)$ may be easily produced by forming $\beta \leftarrow \beta \oplus \beta R^s$, with a logical right-shift-s and a $\oplus$, followed by $\beta \oplus \beta L^t$ with a logical left-shift-t and another $\oplus$.

The maximum possible period of a shift-register generator is 2^n-1, the number of non-null $1\times n$ binary vectors. For such a generator, any non-null initial (seed) vector may be used, a desirable property for generators that allow setting the seed value, which to the user becomes any non-zero integer.

Matrix theory provides an easy means to characterize shift-register sequences of maximal period; for a proof, see [11].

THEOREM 1. *Let T be an $n\times n$ non-singular binary matrix. In order that the sequence $\beta,\beta T,\beta T^2,\beta T^3,\ldots$ have period $k = 2^n-1$ for every non-null binary vector β, it is necessary and sufficient that the matrix T have order 2^n-1 in the group of non-singular $n\times n$ binary matrices.*

4. SIMPLE GENERATORS: LAGGED-FIBONACCI

These generators use an initial set of elements $x_1,x_2,\ldots,x_r$, two "lags" r and s with $r > s$, then generate successive elements by the recursion, for $i>r$, $x_i = x_{i-r} \bullet x_{i-s}$, where $\bullet$ is some binary operation. The initial (seed) elements are computer words and the binary operation might be $+,-,*$ or $\oplus$ (exclusive-or). For + or -, the x's might be integers mod 2^n or single- or double-precision reals mod 1. For *, odd integers mod 2^n.

We designate such a generator loosely as $F(r,s,\bullet)$, although each lagged-Fibonacci generator depends on details of the particular binary operation and the finite set of elements it operates on. Examples of generators of maximal period are F(17,5,+) or F(17,5,-) on integers mod 2^n, period $(2^{17}-1)2^{n-1}$; F(17,5,-) on 32-bit reals mod 1, period $(2^{17}-1)2^{23}$ or 64-bit reals mod 1, period $(2^{17}-1)2^{55}$; F(17,5,*) on integers mod 2^n, period $(2^{17}-1)2^{29}$; F(17,5,$\oplus$), period $2^{17}-1$. Other good choices for (r,s) are (31,13),(55,24) plus many others, some of which are listed in Knuth [6], p28.

A lagged-Fibonacci generator is easily programmed, using a circular list and two pointers. For example, a procedure for an F(17,5) generator uses 17 memory locations, initially filled as $L(1)=x_{17}$, $L(2)=x_{16},\ldots,L(17)=x_1$ and pointers I=17, J=5. Then each call to the procedure executes these instructions:

```
L(I) ← L(I)•L(J)
output L(I)
I ← I-1 ; if I=0, I ← 17
J ← J-1 ; if J=0, J ← 17
```

(Decrementing the pointers and testing on 0 is usually faster than incrementing and testing on 17.)

Characterization of maximal period $F(r,s,\bullet)$ generators may be based on the theory of linear recursive sequences of integers:

$$x_i = a_1x_{i-1}+a_2x_{i-2}+\ldots+a_rx_{i-r} \mod m.$$

There is extensive literature on this problem, much more extensive than necessary for our purposes, for it is possible to develop a brief, self-contained treatment for characterizing lagged-Fibonacci generators of maximal period for the most important modulus, 2^n, using only elementary matrix theory. For lagged-Fibonacci generators, the integer recursion reduces to $x_i = x_{i-r} \pm x_{i-s}$, but the theory for the general integer recursion mod 2^n is just as easily established, by considering an initial vector of integers, $\alpha = (x_1,x_2,\ldots,x_r)$ and succesive vectors $\alpha T,\alpha T^2,\alpha T^3,\ldots$ generated by a matrix T of integers. Here is the result; for a proof, see [11].

THEOREM 2. *Let T be an $r\times r$ matrix of integers, with odd determinant. In order that the sequence of vectors*

$$\alpha,\alpha T,\alpha T^2,\alpha T^3,\ldots \mod 2^n$$

have period $(2^r-1)2^{n-1}$ for every $n \geq 1$ and every initial vector of integers $\alpha = (x_1,\ldots x_r)$, not all even, it is necessary and sufficient that T have order $j = 2^r-1$ in the group of non-singular matrices for mod 2, and order 2j for mod 4 and order 4j for mod 8.

To verify that a particular F(r,s,+) or F(r,s,-) generator has maximal period $j = (2^r-1)2^{n-1}$ for integers mod 2^n, one need only call a matrix-squaring routine a few more than r times to verify that T has order j,2j,4j for mod 2,4,8. *This will be true only if $H = T^{2^r}$ is T mod 2, not T mod 4 and H^2 is not T mod 8.* The matrix T has 0's everywhere except for 1's on the principal sub-diagonal and two 1's in the appropriate positions of the last column. For example, the F(3,1,-) generator on integers mod 2^n has $T = \begin{pmatrix} 0 & 0 & 1 \\ 1 & 0 & 0 \\ 0 & 1 & -1 \end{pmatrix}$ and a few calls to a matrix-squaring routine verifies that T^8 is T mod 2, not T mod 4 and T^{16} is not T mod 8. Since T is nonsingular and $j = 2^3-1$ is prime, the order of T for modulus 2 is j. When j is composite, say $j = 2^{55}-1$, it takes a little more work to verify the order of T. Successive squaring will verify that T^{j+1} is T for mod 2 and not T for mod 4, etc., but one must also verify that T^k is not I mod 2 for each $k = j/p$, with p ranging over the prime divisors of j. Even then, a simple computer program will serve to establish– or refute– that a proposed F(r,s,+) or F(r,s,-) generator has maximal period.

To find the period of an F(r,s,*) generator under multiplication of residues relatively prime to a modulus m, one need only express the Abelian group of those residues as a direct product of cyclic groups, then consider the F(r,s,+) generator on the exponents of the generators of the cyclic groups. For example, every odd integer mod 2^n has a unique representation as a product $(-1)^i3^j$ with $i \in \{0,1\}$ and $j \in \{1,2,\ldots,2^{n-2}\}$. Thus the period of F(r,s,*) for odd integers mod 2^n is the period of F(r,s,+) on integers mod 2^{n-1}:

If the F(r,s,+) generator has maximal period, $(2^r-1)2^{n-1}$, for integers mod 2^n then the F(r,s,) generator on odd integers mod 2^n has period $(2^r-1)2^{n-3}$.*

The F(r,s,-) generators on reals are particularly suitable for random number subroutines that return UNI or VNI, continuous random variables on [0,1) or (-1,1). Ordinarily, such subroutines generate a random integer from some set, then divide by the largest integer in the set to get the required UNI or VNI. If initial values $x_1,x_2,\ldots,x_r$ are all binary fractions of the form $k/2^n$, then the binary operation $x\bullet y$ = if $x\geq y$ then $x-y$, else $x-y+1$ in the $F(r,s,\bullet)$ generator will produce a sequence of reals on [0,1), each a binary fraction $k/2^n$ with numerator the integer that would be produced by the corresponding F(r,s,-) generator on integers mod 2^n.

Thus the F(r,s,-) generator using $x-y$ = if $x\geq y$ then $x-y$, else $x-y+1$ on 32-bit reals (having 24-bit fractions) produces real UNI's on [0,1) with period $(2^r-1)2^{23}$ directly, without need for the division operation necessary in conventional generators. The same method will directly produce 64-bit double precision reals with period $(2^r-1)2^{55}$.

Lagged-Fibonacci Generators with ⊕.

The F(r,s,⊕) sequence starts with an initial set of computer words $x_1,x_2,\ldots,x_r$ then generates successive words by the recursion $x_i = x_{i-r} \oplus x_{i-s}$. The tests described below show generators based on this sequence to be some of the worst of all generators. In addition, the maximum possible period is 2^r-1, whatever the word size, far short of the attainable $(2^r-1)2^{n-1}$ for F(r,s,+), F(r,s,-) or $(2^r-1)2^{n-3}$ for F(r,s,*) with words of n bits. The exclusive-or operation, ⊕, is no faster than + or - in most computers, and not available in many high-level languages, so, taken with the poor statistical performance and relatively short periods, one wonders why F(r,s,⊕) generators have ever been given serious consideration. But they have. Called "generalized feedback shift register generators", they have been the subject of several papers [1,2,4,7].

5. COMBINATION GENERATORS

Empirical studies suggest that combining two or more simple generators, by means of a convenient computer operation such as +, -, *, or ⊕ (exclusive-or), provides a composite with better randomness than either of the components. There is interesting theoretical support for such an observation.

Let x be a random variable taking values in a finite set S. To fix ideas, let S = {1,2,3}; the theory is easily extended to any finite set. Let the probability vector for x be (a,b,c), that is,

$P(x=1)=a,\ P(x=2)=b,\ P(x=3)=c.$

We seek uniform distributions on S, i.e., those with probability vector $(\frac{1}{3},\frac{1}{3},\frac{1}{3})$. Let $\delta(x)$ be the distance between the distribution of x and the uniform distribution, defined by

$$\delta(x)=\|(a,b,c)-(\tfrac{1}{3},\tfrac{1}{3},\tfrac{1}{3})\|=[(a-\tfrac{1}{3})^2+(b-\tfrac{1}{3})^2+(c-\tfrac{1}{3})^2]^{\frac{1}{2}}.$$

Let y be some other random variable on S, independent of x, with probability vector (r,s,t). Furthermore, suppose we have a binary operation on S, with operation table forming a latin square, say

•	1	2	3
1	3	1	2
2	1	2	3
3	2	3	1

Then we may use the binary operation • to form a new random variable, $z = x\bullet y$, and the distribution of z will be "closer" to uniform than that of either x or y:

THEOREM 3. $\delta(x\bullet y) \leq \delta(x)$ and $\delta(x\bullet y) \leq \delta(y)$.

The proof is simple for the above S and •, and it generalizes in an obvious way.

$P(x\bullet y=1) = as + br + ct$
$P(x\bullet y=2) = at + bs + cr$
$P(x\bullet y=3) = ar + bt + cs.$

Thus the probability vector for $z=x\bullet y$ is

$$(a,b,c)\begin{pmatrix} s & t & r\\ r & s & t\\ t & r & s\end{pmatrix} = (a,b,c)M, \text{ say.}$$

Then, since $(\frac{1}{3},\frac{1}{3},\frac{1}{3})M = (\frac{1}{3},\frac{1}{3},\frac{1}{3})$,

$$\delta(x\bullet y)=\|(a,b,c)M-(\tfrac{1}{3},\tfrac{1}{3},\tfrac{1}{3})\|=\|(a-\tfrac{1}{3},b-\tfrac{1}{3},c-\tfrac{1}{3})M\|.$$

Thus,

$$\delta(x\bullet y) \leq \|(a-\tfrac{1}{3},b-\tfrac{1}{3},c-\tfrac{1}{3})\| = \delta(x),$$

since, for every probability vector (f,g,h),

$$\begin{aligned}&\|(f,g,h)M\|^2\\ &= (sf+rg+th)^2 + (tf+sg+rh)^2 + (rf+tg+sh)^2\\ &\leq sf^2+rg^2+th^2 + tf^2+sg^2+rh^2 + rf^2+tg^2+sh^2\\ &= f^2 + g^2 + h^2 = \|(f,g,h)\|^2,\end{aligned}$$

using the elementary inequality $E(w)^2 \leq E(w^2)$.

This theoretical result suggests that if two RNG's produce sequences $x_1,x_2,x_3,\ldots$ and $y_1,y_2,y_3,\ldots$ on some finite set S on which we have a binary operation •, then the combination generator, producing $x_1\bullet y_1,x_2\bullet y_2,x_3\bullet y_3,\ldots$ should be better, or at least no worse than, either of the component RNG's. Applications might include + or - for residues of some modulus m, exclusive-or, ⊕, on computer words, or multiplication on the set S of residues relatively prime to modulus m, such as odd integers mod 2^k. The binary operation need only have the property that its operation table forms a latin square; it need be neither commutative nor associative.

Another attractive feature of combination RNG's is that they tend not only to make the results more uniform—they make them more independent. Given $x_1,x_2,x_3,\ldots$ we hope that x_1 is uniform on S, that (x_1,x_2) is uniform on S×S, that (x_1,x_2,x_3) is uniform on S×S×S, and so on. If we combine $x_1,x_2,x_3,\ldots$ and $y_1,y_2,y_3,\ldots$ then (x_1,x_2,x_3) has a certain distribution on the finite set S×S×S, as does (y_1,y_2,y_3), and thus $(x_1\bullet y_1,x_2\bullet y_2,x_3\bullet y_3)$ has a distribution at least as uniform on S×S×S. But that means the combined vector tends to have independent coordinates, since uniformity on a product set S×S×S implies independence of the coordinates.

These remarks apply to any m-tuples $(x_i,x_j,\ldots,x_k)$ and $(y_i,y_j,\ldots,y_k)$; on the product set S^m, the composite vector $(x_i\bullet y_i,x_j\bullet y_j,\ldots,x_k\bullet y_k)$ is likely to be closer to the ideal of having independent, uniformly distributed elements than either of the contributing vectors.

What is the period of a combination generator? The reader may wish to convince himself of the following: If $x_1,x_2,x_3,\ldots$ and $y_1,y_2,y_3,\ldots$ are strictly periodic sequences of elements of S, having periods rd and sd with r and s relatively prime, then the period of $x_1 \cdot y_1,\ x_2 \cdot y_2, x_3 \cdot y_3,\ldots$ is rst, where t is a divisor of d. Thus the shortest possible period is rs, the longest rsd, and it is not difficult to construct composites having periods rst for all divisors t of d.

References [8] and [12] seem to have first urged that simple generators be combined; Brown and Solomon [3] provided theoretical support for such combinations. They gave an elaborate proof that x + y mod m was more uniform than x or y on residues mod m, relying heavily on the techniques of majorization. Marshall and Olkin [13] p. 383 made the result more general in their elegant book on inequalities and majorization. To those not familiar with the powerful techniques of majorization, the above development, using only elementary properties of vector norms, may be preferable.

6. TESTS OF RANDOM NUMBER GENERATORS

A random number generator is supposed to produce a sequence of independent, identically distributed (i.i.d.) random variables $x_1,x_2,x_3,\ldots$. Any function of elements of that sequence may serve as a test, if its distribution is known, or even if its distribution is merely compared with that of other RNG's. In spite of the ease with which tests of RNG's may be created, there are surprisingly few reported in the literature. The same simple, easily passed tests are reported again and again. Such is the power of the printed word.

A few tests were suggested in the early days of making tables of random digits [5], and M. D. MacLaren and I suggested a few more [8]. These, and a few others, have become a *de facto* standard set of tests, enumerated in Knuth's V2, [6]. Knuth's books are such marvels that they sometimes discourage initiative—so well done that many readers take them as gospel, the definitive word on the particular subject treated. And so they are, most of the time. But not, I think, for testing random number generators.

Anyone with a knowledge of probability theory should be able to create his own tests. If the RNG is to be used for a particular problem, one should try to create a test based on a similar problem for which the underlying distributions are known, or, lacking that, at least compared with results produced by widely different RNG's. I will describe several tests that I use. They are called *stringent* tests, because they seem more difficult to pass than the mild tests that have become standard. Most of them were developed as analogues to particular Monte Carlo problems, but with conditions that make finding the underlying distributions possible.

7. OVERLAPPING M-TUPLE TESTS

We illustrate with an example. Consider a sequence of n values such as

5,4,5,0,4,2,7,3,4,1,...,5,3,6,2.

Suppose these are base-8 digits produced by the first 3 bits of n calls to a RNG. A standard test would use Pearson's chi-square, $\sum(\text{OBS-EXP})^2/\text{EXP}$, on the individual digits, on non-overlapping pairs, triples, etc. to see if the observed were satisfactorily close to the expected frequencies. Such are typical tests of RNG's—simple and easily passed.

As a means to test independence as well as uniformity, suppose we first make the sequence circular by adjoining the first two elements to the end, getting

5,4,5,0,4,2,7,3,4,1,...,5,3,6,2,5,4

(this has an asymptotically negligible effect, but it makes deriving the subsequent covariance matrix much simpler.) Then consider the n triples formed by successive elements of that sequence:

(5,4,5),(4,5,0),...,(3,6,2),(6,2,5),(2,5,4).

Let w_{ijk} be the number of times the triple (i,j,k) appears in this sequence of n triples. If n is large, the 256 random variables w_{ijk} should be jointly normal with means $\mu_{ijk} = n/256$ and a certain covariance matrix C. If C^- is any weak inverse of C, $CC^-C = C$, then the quadratic form:

$$\sum(w_{ijk}-\mu_{ijk})c^-_{ijk,rst}(w_{rst}-\mu_{rst})$$

is invariant under choice of C^- and should have a chi-square distribution with degrees of freedom the rank of C, and thus provide a test for both uniformity and independence of successive values produced by the RNG. Of course, any set of three bits other than the first three could serve for the test, or sets of four bits, etc.

The above quadratic form turns out to be remarkably easy to evaluate. Here is the rule: Compute Q_3, the quadratic form one would use if naively applying Pearson's test to the 3-tuples:

$$Q_3 = \sum_{i,j,k} (w_{ijk}-\mu_{ijk})^2/\mu_{ijk}.$$

Then compute Q_2, the naive quadratic form for testing of pairs:

$$Q_2 = \sum_{i,j}(w_{ij}-\mu_{ij})^2/\mu_{ij},$$

where w_{ij} is the number of occurences of the overlapping pair (i,j) in the original sequence. Then the general quadratic form in the weak inverse C^-, above, reduces to $Q_3 - Q_2$, and is asymptotically chi-square with 8^3-8^2 degrees of freedom.

More generally, this is the overlapping 3-tuple test for i.i.d. sequences: Let $v_1,v_2,v_3,\ldots$ be a sequence of independent random variables taking values $1,2,\ldots,b$ with probabilities $p_1,p_2,\ldots,p_b$. If w_{ijk} and w_{ij} are, resp., the number of times the triple i,j,k and the double i,j appear in a circular sequence of n v's, then

$$\sum_{i,j,k} (w_{ijk}-\mu_{ijk})^2/\mu_{ijk}-\sum_{i,j} (w_{ij}-\mu_{ij})^2/\mu_{ij}$$

is asymptotically chi-square distributed with b^3-b^2 degrees of freedom, and is equivalent to the liklihood-ratio test for jointly normal variables with covariance matrix that of the b^3 random variables w_{ijk}.

A similar result holds for testing, say, overlapping 4-tuples: the quadratic form $Q_4 - Q_3$ should be chi-square with $b^4 - b^3$ degrees of freedom, where Q_4 is the $\sum(OBS-EXP)^2/EXP$ value one would get by naive application of Pearson's test to the overlapping 4-tuple counts.
The test results MTUPLE, displayed below, are based on overlapping 3-tuples for bits 1,2,3 then for bits 2,3,4 then 3,4,5 and so on, for each successive three bits of the computer words produced by the RNG being tested.

Another example of the overlapping m-tuple test is based on a circular list $v_1,v_2,\ldots,v_n,v_1$ with the v's the number of 1's in the first six bits of computer words produced by a RNG. Then the v's take values k = 0 to 6 with probabilities $p_k = 2^{-6}6!/(k!(6-k)!)$ and the quadratic form $Q_2 - Q_1$ should be chi-square distributed with 49-7 = 42 d.o.f., where $Q_2 = \sum(w_{ij}-np_{ij})^2/np_ip_j$ and $Q_1 = \sum(w_i-np_i)^2/np_i$. Fibo(r,s,⊕) generators fail such a test.

8. OVERLAPPING-PERMUTATION TESTS

This is an example of an overlapping m-tuple test for which elements of the overlapping m-tuples are not independent, or even successive states of a Markov chain: Let $u_1,u_2,u_3,\ldots,u_n$ be uniform variates produced by a RNG. Each of the overlapping 3-tuples $(u_1,u_2,u_3),(u_2,u_3,u_4),\ldots$ is in one of six possible states:
State 1: x<y<z; State 2: x<z<y; State 3: y<x<z; State 4:y<z<x; State 5: z<x<y; State 6: z<y<x.
Thus overlapping triples of u's lead to a sequence of states such as

3,3,2,5,1,4,3,...,3,2,5

If w_{ijk} = no. of times ijk appears in the state sequence, then

$$\sum(w_{ijk}-\mu_{ijk})c^{-}_{ijk,rst}(w_{rst}-\mu_{rst})$$

provides a chi-square test, if the means and covariance matrix C, and any weak inverse C^- can be found. This test, designated OPERM below, is not very stringent. Most RNG's pass it, except for F(r,s,⊕), which fail most tests anyway. Perhaps using permutations of four or five would be more illuminating. Finding a C^- for the covariance matrix of the 5-permutation case is an interesting challenge.

9. THE OPSO TEST

OPSO means overlapping-pairs-sparse-occupancy, a test devised to overcome the problem of the huge samples necessary for the overlapping-pairs tests, when the number of possible pairs is very large. For example, if we use the first 11 bits of successive words produced by a RNG to give a sequence of integers in the range 1 to 2048, and want to use the overlapping 2-tuple test, we would need some 2^{26} calls to the RNG in order that the counts w_{ij} be satisfactorily close to jointly normal with the derived covariance matrix.

Instead, suppose we envision 2^{22} cells, each associated with a particular pair i,j and consider the generalized occupancy problem– for each successive pair i,j we place a ball in the appropriate cell. If x_0,x_1,x_2 are, resp., the number of cells with 0,1,2 balls then, with very large n, we expect that x_0,x_1,x_2 will be jointly normal with means and covariance matrix to be calculated. With my student, L. H. Tsay, I found the means and covariances some years ago. It turned out, however, that using just x_0 served as a good test of RNG's. Here are a few examples of the resulting OPSO test:

The first 10 bits from each of 2^{21} calls to the super-duper RNG produced a circular list of 2^{21} integers in the range 1 to 1024, and placing balls in cell(i,j) for each overlapping pair i,j yielded 141,711 empty cells. Subtracting the mean, μ = 141909, and dividing by σ = 290.46 produced what should have been a standard normal variate, value -.682. Performing the test four times yielded the values -.682, .32, -1.09, -.84. Quite satisfactory.

But four similarly constructed values for the congruential RNG $x_n = 62605x_{n-1} + 113218009 \bmod 2^{29}$ (the Berkeley Unix Pascal RNG) produced 1.81, 1.92, 2.15, 3.36. Not so good. This congruential generator fails the OPSO test, but not spectacularly. The congruential RNG $x_n = 69069x_{n-1} \bmod 2^{32}$ produced the four values 4.611, 4.682, 4.114, 5.591, a failure bordering on the spectacular for four supposedly standard normal variates. For something really spectacular: the F(17,5,⊕) generator produced ten successive values of 2895.9 standard deviations from the mean.

Here is a short table of the number of bits, the sample size n, the mean μ and standard deviation σ for similar OPSO tests:

No. of bits	n	μ	σ
10	2^{21}	141,909	290.26
11	2^{22}	1,542,998	638.75
11	2^{23}	567,637	580.80

10. PARKING LOT, LATTICE AND RELATED TESTS

These tests are designed to assess the uniformity of points in m-space, when coordinates of the points are successive calls to a RNG. Congruential generators use iterates of a linear transformation on the ring of residues of some modulus, and as a consequence, m-tuples of points produced by the generator fall in a lattice with a relatively large unit-cell [9,10]. Since shift-register generators also use iterates of a linear transformation, there might be some sort of regularity analagous to that for congruential generators, and there is. But the binary vectors produced by a shift-register generator are viewed as base 2 representations of integers in subsequent use, and the regularities get folded over and distorted, much as the original sedimentary layers in the earth are folded and distorted in geological formations viewed eons later. Figure 1 gives an example of such regularities in shift-register generators. On the top is a set of 16000 random points produced by a good random number generator, one that combines two standard generators. The bottom shows 16000 points produced by the very shift-register generator proposed by Whittlesey [14] as a replacement for congruential generators, after discovery of their lattice structure [9]. The proposed shift-register generator uses 31 bit binary vectors and $T = (I+R^{28})(I+L^3)$.

Lagged-Fibonacci generators also use iterates of a linear transformation, but lags such as in F(17,5,-), F(31,13,-) or F(55,24,-) generators seem long enough that no obvious regularities appear in dimensions up to 10 or so.

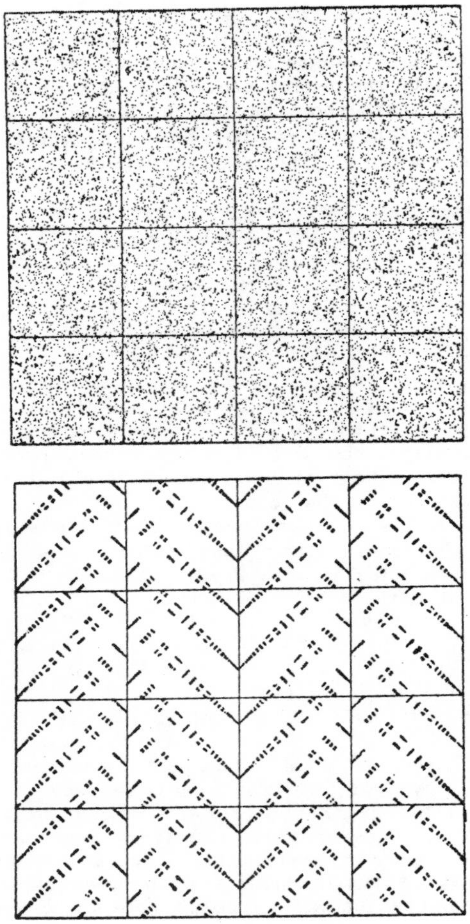

Figure 1.

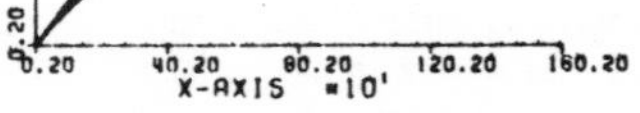

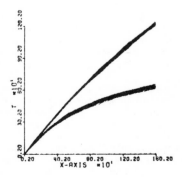

Figure 2.

Visual tests such as in figure 1 are striking, but not feasible in higher dimensions. A quantitative version of the parking lot test goes as follows: Let each point in m-space be the center of a spherical or cubic "car", of specified diameter, and suppose we park "by ear", (as many people do). If $c_1, c_2, \ldots, c_k$ are non-overlapping cars, already parked, we try to park randomly until we succeed with a car that does not hit any of those already parked, then add the new car to the list. Out of n tries, we will have a list of k cars successfully parked. I do not know the distribution of, say, k(2000), but simulation with a good RNG gives the mean and variance accurately enough for comparison with other RNG's. Figure 2 shows the difference in curves k(n), the number of cars parked after n tries, for a combination RNG (top curves) and a shift-register RNG (bottom curves). Clearly the two are different; extensive tries with various combination RNG's suggest the upper curves are those to be expected with a perfect RNG and thus shift-register (and also $F(r,s,\oplus)$) generators fail parking lot tests.

The quantitative parking lot tests can be performed in any dimension; one need only specify the size and shape of "cars", then try m-dimensional parking-by-ear to compare the performance of different RNG's. The random parking of cubes and spheres is an important, unsolved probability problem, and RNG's used for simulating such problems should be beyond reproach.

11. THE BIRTHDAY-SPACINGS TEST

This is the discrete version of what I call the *Iterated-Spacings Test*, which goes like this: Let $S_1, S_2, \ldots, S_n$ be the spacings induced by n-1 uniform random variables on [0,1). If the S's are sorted, to get $S_{(1)} \le S_{(2)} \le \ldots \le S_{(n)}$, then the weighted differences:

$nS_{(1)}, (n-1)[S_{(2)}-S_{(1)}], (n-2)[S_{(3)}-S_{(2)}], \ldots, 2[S_{(n)}-S_{(n-1)}], [1-S_{(n)}]$

form a new set of uniform spacings, to which the KS test may be applied, then the weighted differences of those sorted spacings produce a new set of spacings, and so on, forever: Each set of uniform spacings leads to an infinite sequence of sets of uniform spacings.

In practice, the procedure breaks down after 3 or 4 to perhaps 10 iterations, because of the finite representation of uniform variates in the computer. Degeneracy arises from equal values of spacings, and thus the discrete version of this procedure leads to the *Birthday-Spacings Test*: Let the RNG produce integers $I_1, I_2, \ldots, I_m$ in the range 1 to n. The I's are m birthdays in a year of n days. The famous problem of Von-Mises and Feller on duplicate birthdays is not stringent enough for a test here, but the problem of duplicate spacings is: Sort the I's to get $I_{(1)} \le I_{(2)} \le \ldots \le I_{(m)}$, and let Y be the number of values which appear more than once among the spacings, $I_{(2)}-I_{(1)}$, $I_{(3)}-I_{(2)}, \ldots, I_{(m-2)}-I_{(m-1)}, I_{(1)}+m-I_{(m)}$ Thus Y is m minus the number of distinct spacings, and Y is asymptotically Poisson with parameter λ =

$m^3/(4n)$. A proof, by Janos Komlos, and detailed discussion of the test will appear elsewhere.

The birthday spacings test addresses only the set of integers produced by a RNG, not the order in which they are produced. Congruential generators generally pass the test. Shift-register generators fail it, as do lagged Fibonacci generators using +,- or ⊕. Of the simple generators, only congruential and lagged Fibonacci using multiplication pass the birthday spacings test; most combination generators pass it. Note, however, that the lagged Fibonacci generator with multiplication is on odd integers mod 2^K, so spacings can only take even values. Yet the number of duplicate spacings has the distribution required for RNG's producing both odd and even integers. The same holds for multiplicative congruential generators that only produce odd integers. Strange.

12. RANKS OF RANDOM BINARY MATRICES.

Many Monte Carlo studies, particularly in combinatorics and graph theory, call for random incidence matrices, elements 0 or 1 to represent the absence or presence of some property. It is natural to let the rows of such a random matrix be formed by successive computer words, or portions of words, produced by a random number generator.

Shift-register or $F(r,s,\oplus)$ generators are not suitable for such use. In order that the sequence of 1×n binary vectors $\beta, \beta T, \beta T^2, \ldots$ have a long period, it is necessary that the first n vectors in the sequence be linearly independent. Thus a binary matrix with rows formed by n or fewer successive vectors produced by a shift-register generator will always have full rank, while a truly random m×n binary matrix will have rank m with probability $(1-2^{-n})(1-2^{1-n})\ldots(1-2^{m+1-n})$, about .30 when m = n and n ≥ 10 or so.

More specifically, the rank of a random m×n binary matrix takes the value r = 1,2,...,min(m,n) with probability

$$2^{r(n+m-r)-mn} \prod_{i=0}^{r-1} [(1-2^{i-n})(1-2^{i-m})/(1-2^{i-r})].$$

If the rows of the m×n binary matrix are m successive computer words, or portions thereof, produced by a random number generator, then the rank of the matrix should have the distribution given by the probabilities above. Shift-register generators fail such tests, as do $F(r,s,\oplus)$ generators. Congruential and $F(r,s,\pm)$ usually pass.

13. A SUMMARY OF SOME TEST RESULTS

	LATTICE	PARKING	MTUPLE	OPSO	BDAY	OPERM	RUNS	RANK
Congruential	FAIL	pass	FAIL	FAIL	pass	pass	pass	pass
Shift-Register	pass	FAIL	FAIL	FAIL	FAIL	pass	FAIL	FAIL
Lagged-Fibonacci using ⊕	pass	FAIL	FAIL	FAIL	FAIL	FAIL	FAIL	FAIL
Lagged-Fibonacci using + or -	pass	pass	pass	pass	FAIL	pass	pass	pass
Lagged-Fibonacci using *	pass	pass	pass	pass	pass	pass	pass	pass
Super-Duper	pass	pass	FAIL	pass	pass	pass	pass	pass
COMBO	pass	pass	pass	pass	pass	pass	pass	pass
NCOMBO	pass	pass	pass	pass	pass	pass	pass	pass

14. CONCLUSIONS

The table below indicates how various kinds of RNG's perform in DIEHARD, a battery of stringent tests designed to test RNG's more thoroughly than standard tests do. It uses various overlapping m-tuple and OPSO tests to test for independence as well as uniformity, and tests all parts of a computer word, not only the most significant bits. Choice of starting values seems to make no difference in the tests, and results marked FAIL are spectacular failures—the observed distribution produced by the RNG is nowhere near that called for by probability theory for truly i. i. d. sequences.

The tests show that by far the worst RNG's are those that use exclusive-or: shift-register and $F(r,s,\oplus)$, perhaps not surprising when one considers that a RNG is supposed to scramble the bits of a current computer word, or words, to get a new one, and ⊕, a no-carry add, does little to scramble bits, compared to +,- or *.

The tests on lagged-Fibonacci generators used $F(17,5,\bullet)$, $F(31,13,\bullet)$ and $F(55,24,\bullet)$. The binary operations +,- and * gave good results, except on the birthday-spacings test using + or -, while ⊕ gave almost uniformly terrible results. Note, however, that $F(r,s,\bullet)$ generators with a very long lag r, say $F(607,273,\bullet)$ or $F(1279,418,\bullet)$, passed all tests for every choice of binary operation: +,-,* and even ⊕.

Combination generators do best in stringent tests. The generator COMBO returns $x_i - y_i \bmod 2^{32}$, with $x_n = x_{n-1} * x_{n-2} \bmod 2^{32}$, an $F(2,1,*)$ generator on odd integers, and $y_i = y_{i-3} - y_{i-1} \bmod 2^{30}-35$, an $F(3,1,-)$ generator. It passed all tests, as did NCOMBO, a similar combination except that $y_i = y_{i-3} - y_{i-1} \bmod 2^{32}-5$. These are two combination generators that use only a few computer instructions and have no arrays to access. Thus they are fast. Many other examples are, of course, possible. One should not get too carried away with the promise of combination generators provided by the above theory, however. In combining generators, it seems prudent to use sequences with incompatible algebraic structures, and with the combining binary operation on an incompatible structure as well. The generator Super-Duper, part of the McGill Random Number Package widely used at several hundred locations, combines the congruential generator $x_i = 69069x_{i-1} \bmod 2^{32}$, via ⊕, with the shift-register generator $\beta \leftarrow \beta(I+R^{15})(I+L^{17})$. It fails the MTUPLE test on substrings of low order bits, probably because both of the constituent parts do, and ⊕

is a poor binary operation for scrambling bits. Those who use Super-Duper may want to modify the assembly language instruction, replacing ⊕ by - in the step that combines the two simple generators.

Congruential generators with a prime modulus seem to do better on stringent tests than do those with modulus 2^n. While the latter are easier and faster for computer implementation, they give unsatisfactory results on substrings of low order bits. Multiplication modulo a prime p is more difficult to implement in modern machines with 2's complement integer arithmetic. One of the best ways is to represent integers as double precision reals and use the DMOD function. In that case, the prime modulus $p = 2^{31}-1$, used in a popular IBM generator, seems a poor choice. It gives only 31, rather than 32 bits, and p-1 has too many factors. Better choices are, for example, $p = 2^{32}-209$, which give a full 32 bits, or $p = 2^{37}-45$, which, with a multiplier of 19 or fewer bits, allows full and exact exploitation of double precision arithmetic. For the two latter choices, (p-1)/2 is also prime, so that half of the residues of p are primitive elements and may be used as multipliers giving the full period.

There is not room here for a full development, but a brief description of a step toward a "universal" RNG may be appropriate. It uses an F(r,s,-) sequence, with different entry points for the set up, for the binary operation - on reals mod 1, or on integers mod 2^n. The set up permits choice of r,s and n, with r as large as available memory allows, and the initial computer words $x_1,x_2,\ldots,x_r$ generated bit-by-bit, by means of the parity of elements of an F(3,1,-) sequence on integers mod 32707, a prime still small enough to give exact integer arithmetic in any CPU of 16 or more bits. If r is large, say 607 or 1279, the F(r,s,-) generator is suitable by itself, but, in any case, there is an option to combine with another generator: congruential, or a suitable, different lagged-Fibonacci generator for micro-computers when multiplication is too expensive.

The result is a sequence of satisfactorily random reals or integers that may be made the same for a wide variety of computers using a wide variety of languages, such as IBM PC, Apple, TRS80, Cromemco, PDP11, Vax, HP3000, IBM360/370 or Amdahl V8, thus providing means for exact comparison or duplication of Monte Carlo experiments on different machines.

Based on the above discussion, my current view of RNG's may be summarized with the following bottom line: combination generators seem best; congruential generators are liked, but not well-liked; shift-register and lagged-Fibonacci generators using ⊕ are no good; never use ⊕; lagged-Fibonacci generators using +,- or * pass most of the stringent tests, and all of them if the lag is long enough, say 607 or 1279; combination generators seem best—if the numbers are not random, they are at least higgledy-piggledy.

REFERENCES

[1] Arvillias, A.C. and Maritsas, A.E. Partitioning the period of m-sequences and applications to pseudorandom number generation. *J. ACM* 25, (1978) 675-686.

[2] Bright, H. J. and Enison, R. L. Quasi-random number sequences from a long period TLP generator with remarks on applications to cryptography. *Computing Surveys* 11 (1979) 357-370.

[3] Brown, M. and Solomon, H. On combining pseudorandom number generators, Technical Report No. 233 (1976), Dept. of Statistics, Stanford University.

[4] Fushimi, M. and Tezuka, S. The k-distribution of generalized feedback shift register pseudorandom numbers. *Comm. ACM* 26, (1983) 516-523.

[5] Kendall, D. G. and Babington-Smith, B. Randomness and random sampling numbers, *J. Royal Statist. Soc.* 101 (1938) 146-166. See also *J. Royal Statist. Soc. Supplement* 6 (1939) 51-61.

[6] Knuth, D. E. *The Art of Computer Programming, V2: Semi-numerical Algorithms*, 2nd Edition, Addison-Wesley, Reading, Mass., 1981.

[7] Lewis, T. G. and Payne, W. H. Generalized feedback shift register pseudorandom number algorithms. *J. ACM* 20 (1973) 456-468.

[8] MacLaren, M. D. and Marsaglia, G. Uniform random number generators, *J. ACM* 12 (1965), 83-89.

[9] Marsaglia, G. Random numbers fall mainly in the planes. *Proc. Nat. Acad. Sci.* 61, (1968) 25-28.

[10] Marsaglia, G. The structure of linear congruential sequences, In *Applications of Number Theory to Numerical Analysis*. Z. K. Zaremba, Ed., Academic Press, New York, 1972.

[11] Marsaglia. G. Matrices and the structure of random number sequences. *Linear Algebra and Its Applications*, To appear.

[12] Marsaglia, G. and Bray, T. A. One-line random number generators and their use in combination, *Comm. ACM*, 11, (1968), 757-759.

[13] Marshall, A. W. and Olkin, I. *Inequalities: Theory of Majorization and its Applications*, Academic Press, New York, 1979.

[14] Whittlesey, J. R. B. On the multidimensional uniformity of pseudorandom number generators. *Comm. ACM* 12, (1969) 247.

What's New and Innovative in Computer Graphics

Organizer: *Ingram Olkin, Stanford University*

Invited Presentations:

Min/Max Autocorrelation Factors for Multivariate Spatial Imagery, *Paul Switzer, Stanford University*

COMPUTER SCIENCE AND STATISTICS:
The Interface, L. Billard (ed.)

MIN/MAX AUTOCORRELATION FACTORS FOR MULTIVARIATE SPATIAL IMAGERY

Paul Switzer

Stanford University
Stanford, California

Gridded multivariate data, typical of satellite and other multi-channel remote-sensed data, may be linearly transformed pointwise by a procedure which tends to isolate the noise component of the data. Some properties of this MAF (min/max autocorrelation factors) procedure are explored using simple spatial stochastic structure. An example is given using ten-channel imagery.

INTRODUCTION AND SUMMARY

We present a method for general-purpose processing of multi-channel data on a spatial grid with a view to isolating signal and noise components of the data. At each grid point x in the region of the image we have a p-variate measurement denoted $\underset{\sim}{Z}(x)$. This measurement consists of a p-variate signal $\underset{\sim}{S}(x)$ contaminated by p-variate noise $\underset{\sim}{\varepsilon}(x)$, neither of which is separately observable and for which the separate statistics are not typically available. We will propose a procedure (MAF) which transforms $\underset{\sim}{Z}(x)$ linearly to a new set of p-variates which have the following property: the low-number variates have minimal spatial autocorrelation, identified as mainly noise, and the high numbered variates have maximal spatial autocorrelation, identified as mainly signal.

The proposed procedure differs from naive principal components in that it makes explicit use of some global spatial statistics of the observable data. It also differs from filtering theory in that it does not require separate statistics for the unobservable signal and noise.

The plan of the paper is first to discuss briefly a few shortcomings of procedures based on spatial filtering (local averaging) and standard principal components. Next the MAF procedure is described together with some of its properties in the context of simple spatial models. Finally, an example is presented of 10-channel imagery in which noise separation seems to have been successfully accomplished but which did not yield as well to standard procedures.

SPATIAL SMOOTHING AND SIGNAL BLURRING

Noise separation is conventionally attempted using spatial smoothing algorithms such as moving averages applied separately to each data channel. Such procedures will indeed reduce the variance of the noise but will inevitably create some blurring of the signal. This reduction in local signal contrast may impair subsequent image interpretation and classification.

It is possible to quantify this contrast reduction due to local averaging in the context of certain spatial stochastic models. For example, consider a univariate gaussian signal process with a smooth isotropic autocorrelation function $\rho(\Delta)$, where Δ is the spatial lag. Suppose we create a simple moving average using a circular window of radius δ. The locally averaged signal is then rescaled to have the same variance as the original signal. Let g be the mean absolute gradient of the original signal process and let g_δ be the mean absolute gradient of the locally averaged signal. Then it can be shown that (1)

$$\frac{g}{g_\delta} = 1-\delta^2\left\{\frac{\frac{1}{6}\,\rho^{(iv)}(0) - \frac{1}{4}|\rho''(0)|^2}{|\rho''(0)|}\right\} + O(\delta^4)\ .$$

Suppose further that

$$\rho(\Delta) = [1 + (a\Delta)^2]^{-2}$$

at short distances Δ, and that $\rho(\delta) = 0.8$. Then g/g_δ is $0.76 + O(\delta^4)$, giving a 24% reduction in signal contrast for this example.

As an alternative to the blurring associated with local spatial averaging, attempts have been made (2), (3) to isolate noise in multivariate imagery by operating pointwise on the data for each pixel. The idea is to somehow use the correlation or redundancy in the information provided by different data channels. The common form of this approach is to extract principal component factors of the $p\times p$ covariance matrix $\underset{\sim}{\Sigma}$, computed by treating the pixels as replicates of a p-variate observation. The low numbered factors, having smallest variance, are treated as noise factors and the high numbered factors, having largest variance are treated as signal factors.

It is not immediately obvious why such a variance criterion should distinguish signal from noise. Furthermore, no spatial properties of the image are used to define the factors, i.e., if the pixels were randomly rearranged the factor definitions would not change. But the most serious shortcoming of naive principal components factors are their lack of invariance to rescaling of the data. For example, differential stretching of data channels will alter the factor definitions, as will the reduction of the covariance matrix to a correlation matrix.

Still, application of the naive pointwise procedure does, in some examples, produce a set of factors which seem to show decreasing amounts of spatial structure. Later, we will try to provide a rationale for this outcome using a simple class of spatial stochastic models, in order to indicate when one might expect the naive procedure to succeed.

Of course if one has a full specification of the separate and joint spatial properties of both the disentangled signal and noise components of the multivariate image data, then it is possible to prescribe optimal least squares estimates of the signal itself (4). These estimates will have the form of moving averages, and they operate simultaneously on all the data channels. While such procedures are optimal pointwise for reconstructing the signal, nevertheless the spatial gradient of the estimated signal will show a downward bias in its magnitude which may impair subsequent interpretation.

MIN/MAX AUTOCORRELATION FACTORS

We now propose a noise separation procedure for general purpose processing of multivariate imagery which operates pointwise to avoid the signal blurring introduced through smoothing or spatial averaging procedures. However, the pointwise operator itself is defined using primitive global spatial characteristics of the data. So, in principle, our procedure overcomes the qualitative objections to both spatial smoothing and naive pointwise data processing.

Define p orthogonal linear combinations $\underset{\sim}{Y} = (Y_1, \ldots, Y_p)$ of the original multivariate observation vector $\underset{\sim}{Z} = (Z_1, \ldots, Z_p)$, called MAF (min/max autocorrelation factors), with the following property: Let $Y_i(x) = \underset{\sim}{a}_i \underset{\sim}{Z}(x)$, $i=1, \ldots, p$, and let $r_i(\Delta) =$ correlation $(Y_i(x), Y_i(x+\Delta))$. Then

$$r_1(\Delta) = \min_a \text{ correlation } (a'Z(x), a'Z(x+\Delta))$$

$$r_p(\Delta) = \max_a \text{ correlation } (a'Z(x), a'Z(x+\Delta))$$

$$r_i(\Delta) = \min_a \text{ correlation } (a'Z(x), a'Z(x+\Delta)) \quad \text{and}$$

$$\text{correlation } (a'Z(x), a_j'Z(x)) = 0 \quad \text{for} \quad j < i.$$

If we suppose that the image noise is weakly autocorrelated spatially compared with the autocorrelation of the image signal, then it is reasonable to expect that the low numbered factors will be mainly noise. The MAF procedure would then provide the desired noise separation, leaving the high numbered factors relatively uncontaminated.

An important property of the MAF procedure is its invariance to linear transforms, a property not shared by naive pointwise principal components procedures or its extenstions to spatial or temporal series (5). Specifically, if $\underset{\sim}{Z}^* = \underset{\sim}{B}\underset{\sim}{Z}$ where $\underset{\sim}{B}$ is any $p \times p$ nonsingular matrix, then the MAF solution for $\underset{\sim}{Z}^*$ is the same as the MAF solution for $\underset{\sim}{Z}$. In particular, it is irrelevant whether or not the data have been rescaled so that each frequency band has the same range of observed values, a common practive in satellite image processing. It is also not important to know the instrument gain factors for each of the frequency bands.

The MAF procedure has other formulations which permit the use of standard multivariate routines to extract the factors. Specifically, the factors are obtained as the eigenvectors of a matrix $\underset{\sim}{\Sigma}_\Delta \underset{\sim}{\Sigma}_0^{-1}$ where

$$\underset{\sim}{\Sigma}_\Delta = \text{cov}\{\underset{\sim}{Z}(x) - \underset{\sim}{Z}(x+\Delta)\}$$

$$\underset{\sim}{\Sigma}_0 = \text{cov}\{\underset{\sim}{Z}(x)\} .$$

This formulation is somewhat more convenient than the canonical correlation formulations where $\underset{\sim}{Z}(x)$ and $\underset{\sim}{Z}(x+\Delta)$ are considered to be two sets of p variables observed at each x. Since the canonical factors for the first set of p variables must be identical to the corresponding canonical factors for the second set, it will be necessary in practice to fix up the $2p \times 2p$ covariance matrix of $(\underset{\sim}{Z}(x), Z(\underset{\sim}{x}+\Delta))$ so that it has the necessary symmetry.

As a further computational convenience the eigenvectors of $\underset{\sim}{\Sigma}_\Delta \underset{\sim}{\Sigma}_0^{-1}$ are obtained in three steps.

(i) The original data $\underset{\sim}{Z}(x)$ are linearly transformed to any $\underset{\sim}{Z}^*(x)$ where $\text{cov}\{Z^*(x)\} = I_{p \times p}$. This may be achieved by using principal components derived from the original global covariance or correlation matrix $\underset{\sim}{\Sigma}_0$.

(ii) Form two sets of differences of the orthogonalized data, viz. $[\underset{\sim}{Z}^*(x) - \underset{\sim}{Z}^*(x+\Delta')]$ and $[\underset{\sim}{Z}^*(x) - \underset{\sim}{Z}^*(x+\Delta'')]$ where Δ' is a unit horizontal shift and Δ'' is a unit vertical shift; calculate the corresponding two global covariances matrices $\underset{\sim}{\Sigma}^*_{\Delta'}$, and $\underset{\sim}{\Sigma}^*_{\Delta''}$ and pool them to form $\underset{\sim}{\Sigma}^*_\Delta$.

(iii) Obtain the principal components corresponding to the pooled covariance matrix $\underset{\sim}{\Sigma}^*$. This is the MAF solution.

Finally, a grey scale map is produced for each of the orthogonal factors obtained for further interpretation; each of these should then be scaled to have constant variance. Typically, one might expect the first or first two maps to exhibit mostly noise. The example given in the next section shows this property quite clearly. If it is desired to map the original variables with most of the noise suppressed, then one would map their projections onto that subspace which excludes the low numbered factors.

MAF AND THE PROPORTIONAL COVARIANCE MODEL

Although it seems somewhat plausible that factors with minimum spatial autocorrelation should concentrate and isolate noise, this property of MAF can be demonstrated to hold exactly in the context of a very simple class of spatial models. Suppose the signal and noise components of the observation vector $\underset{\sim}{Z}(x)$ are uncorrelated, i.e.,

$$\mathrm{cov}\{\underset{\sim}{Z}(x)\} \equiv \underset{\sim}{\Sigma} = \underset{\sim}{\Sigma}^{S} + \underset{\sim}{\Sigma}^{\varepsilon} ,$$

where $\underset{\sim}{\Sigma}^{S}$, $\underset{\sim}{\Sigma}^{\varepsilon}$ are the covariance matrices, respectively, of the signal and noise. Furthermore, suppose the cross-covariance of the signal and noise are each attenuating at different rates as a function of spatial lag Δ. Thus,

$$\mathrm{cov}\{\underset{\sim}{S}(x),\ \underset{\sim}{S}(x+\Delta)\} = b_{\Delta}\cdot\underset{\sim}{\Sigma}^{S}$$

$$\mathrm{cov}\{\underset{\sim}{\varepsilon}(x),\ \underset{\sim}{\varepsilon}(x+\Delta)\} = c_{\Delta}\cdot\underset{\sim}{\Sigma}^{\varepsilon} .$$

Without real loss of generality we may take $\underset{\sim}{\Sigma} = I_{p\times p}$. Define $\lambda_{\Delta}(\underset{\sim}{a}) = \mathrm{Cov}\{\underset{\sim}{a}'\underset{\sim}{Z}(x),\ \underset{\sim}{a}'\underset{\sim}{Z}(x+\Delta)\}$ where $\underset{\sim}{a}'\underset{\sim}{a} = 1$. Then, for the proportional covariance model of this section,

$$\mathrm{Var}\{\underset{\sim}{a}'\underset{\sim}{\varepsilon}(x)\} = [b_{\Delta} - \lambda_{\Delta}(\underset{\sim}{a})]/[b_{\Delta} - c_{\Delta}]$$

$$\mathrm{Var}\{\underset{\sim}{a}'\underset{\sim}{S}(x)\} = [\lambda_{\Delta}(\underset{\sim}{a}) - c_{\Delta}]/[b_{\Delta} - c_{\Delta}] .$$

Therefore, the signal-to-noise ratio for the projection $\underset{\sim}{a}'\underset{\sim}{Z}(x)$ is

$$[\lambda_{\Delta}(\underset{\sim}{a}) - c_{\Delta}]/[b_{\Delta} - \lambda_{\Delta}(\underset{\sim}{a})] .$$

The MAF maximal factor does indeed maximize $\lambda_{\Delta}(\underset{\sim}{a})$ subject to $\underset{\sim}{a}'\underset{\sim}{a} = 1$. So, provided $b_{\Delta} > c_{\Delta}$, i.e., signal autocorrelation attenuates more slowly than noise autocorrelation, then the maximization, over projections $\underset{\sim}{a}$, of the signal to noise ratio is equivalent to the maximal MAF. Likewise, the minimum signal-to-noise ratio is achieved for the minimal MAF.

While the proportional covariance model is hardly universal, it does motivate the MAF procedure as an optimal procedure in the class of linear factor models operating pointwise on the data. It should be noted also that the MAF, in the present context, does not depend on the spatial shift Δ, i.e., any choice of Δ gives the same set of factors, whether or not the spatial autocorrelations are isotropic. In particular, one would expect to have the same MAF using horizontal or vertical lags of any size. As a practical matter it seems that the proportional covariance model is likely to approximate the spatial structure of an image only over very short lags. Therefore, it seems prudent to use single step lags for the MAF procedure, as described in the last section and as used in the example of the next section.

Finally, a further specialization of the proportional covariance model provides insight into the occasional or frequent success of the naive principal component procedure which uses no spatial properties at all of the image. Suppose, in addition to the proportionality described above, one also has

$$\mathrm{cov}\{\underset{\sim}{\varepsilon}(x)\} = \sigma^{2}\cdot I_{p\times p} .$$

This says that all frequency bands have the same noise variance, although not necessarily the same signal variance. Using the previous notation it follows that

$$\underset{\sim}{\Sigma}_{\Delta}\underset{\sim}{\Sigma}_{0}^{-1} = b_{\Delta}\cdot I_{p\times p} - \sigma^{2}(b_{\Delta} - c_{\Delta})\ \underset{\sim}{\Sigma}_{0}^{-1} .$$

Since the MAF procedure finds the eigenvectors of $\underset{\sim}{\Sigma}_{\Delta}\ \underset{\sim}{\Sigma}_{0}^{-1}$, then in this rather special case the MAF procedure is equivalent to finding the eigenvectors of $\underset{\sim}{\Sigma}_{0}$, i.e., the naive principal components. The spatial structure plays no role, even though both signal and noise may be spatially autocorrelated. Of course, one no longer has linear invariance; rescaling of variables, in general, will not preserve the condition of constant noise variance.

EXAMPLE

The data of the example are ten-channel gridded values produced by the U-2 Thematic Mapper Simulator. This is a high altitude scanner which simulates the spatial and spectral band characteristics of the seven LANDSAT-D Thematic Mapper plus three additional intermediate frequency bands. The grid spacing or pixel dimensions are 28 meters square and the image contains 716 × 716 pixels. Each datum is an eight bit number providing a measurement of reflected energy integrated over a specific pixel for a given frequency band.

The area of the image is the vicinity of the Silver Bell Copper Mine in Arizona. This image was chosen merely as an illustration of the the general purpose MAF procedure and no interpretive processing is proposed in this paper. The salient larger features of this image are mountains on the lower left, tailings ponds on the upper left, two working pits in the center and lower right, and a road on the right.

Figure 1 shows mapped values of the ten orthogonal factors with smallest to largest spatial autocorrelation. It seems that the first two factors have provided clear-cut noise separation, something that did not occur with a naive principal components analysis of the same data.

It is evident that even in the factor maps with smallest autocorrelation there is a recurring prominent spatial feature. This suggests strongly that this image be processed as two subimages using separate global spatial characteristics for each subimage. In general one should choose regions of "stationarity" of an image, which may be done in a somewhat interactive way as suggested here. The concept of stationarity in data analysis is an arbitrary one to a large extent, reflecting merely the extent over which one wishes to compute global statistics.

REFERENCES

(1) Switzer, C., Geometrical measures of the smoothness of random functions, J. Appl. Prob. 13 (1976), 86-95

(2) Crist, E. P. and Cicone, R. C., Investigations of thematic mapper data dimensionality and features using field spectrometer data, 17th Int. Symp. on Remote Sensing of Env., Ann Arbor, 1983.

(3) Ready, P. J. and Wintz, P. A., Information extraction, SNR improvement, and data compression in multispectral imagery, IEEE Trans. on Comm. Com-21 (1973).

(4) Hannan, E. J., Multiple Time Series (John Wiley & Sons, Inc., New York, 1970).

(5) Brillinger, D. R., Time Series: Data Analysis and Theory (Holt, Rinehart, and Winston, New York, 1981).

Geometric and Set-Valued Statistics

Organizer: *William F. Eddy, Carnegie-Mellon University*

Invited Presentations:

Aspects of Random Sets, *Richard A. Vitale, Claremont Graduate School*

Ordering of Multivariate Data, *William F. Eddy, Carnegie-Mellon University*

COMPUTER SCIENCE AND STATISTICS:
The Interface, L. Billard (ed.)

ASPECTS OF RANDOM SETS

Richard A. Vitale

Department of Mathematics
Claremont Graduate School
Claremont, California 91711

Topics in the recently emerging area of random sets are discussed. Among these are limit theorems and determining conditions for sets. Some statistical models and computational considerations are covered.

1. INTRODUCTION

The combination of probability and geometry has a long history, going back at least as far as the famous needle problem of Buffon. Later work by Crofton (1868,1885) has been of profound influence. These considerations, called variously stochastic or statistical geometry, integral geometry and geometric probability are nicely surveyed in Santaló (1976) and Solomon (1978).

With antecedents in the deep work of Choquet (1953) and the observation of Robbins (1944, 1945), there has been a recent move to more general theories. Some of this comes from new fields of application such as biology, metallurgy, mineralogy, and pattern theory (Weibel (1972), Nicholson (1972), Klein and Serra (1971), Grenander (1976,1978)). Foundations for some of this recent work can be found in Kendall (1974) and Matheron (1975).

In broad terms, the shift in attitude has been two-fold. First, there has been an emphasis on geometric objects of rather more complex type than the points, lines, and circles of earlier work. Naturally there is no sharp border between the "eras" but in large part recent work attempts to focus on such general classes of sets as the compact, convex sets of $\mathbb{R}^d$ discussed below. Along with this, the second innovation is the consideration of rather general probability measures. Older work focused primarily on uniform (i.e. Haar) measures. Recent work has attempted to construct a fairly general probabilistic structure. Along with both of these new (at any rate, newly emphasized) concerns is the impetus to investigate related statistical and computational procedures.

What follows in this paper is a discursive survey of some of these topics as they have entered the author's research. Rather than a systematic coverage, there will be a attempt to give the flavor of various aspects.

2. COMPACT, CONVEX RANDOM SETS

The class $\mathbb{K}$ of compact, convex subsets of $\mathbb{R}^d$ offers an attractive context. As well as the usual set-theoretic operations of union and intersection, there are <u>Minkowski summation</u>

$$K + L = \{x+y \mid x\in K, y\in L\}$$

and <u>scalar multiplication</u>

$$\alpha K = \{\alpha x \mid x\in K\}$$

which leave $\mathbb{K}$ invariant. The apparent additive structure invites the application of linear theories. Motivated by a growth model, Artstein and Vitale (1975) displayed a law of large numbers. In rough terms, if $X_1, X_2, \ldots$ are iid elements of $\mathbb{K}$, then $\frac{1}{n}[X_1+\cdots+X_n]$ converges to EX_1 under a natural moment assumption. The expectation of a set can be approached as follows. A random vector σ is a selection of the random set X if $\sigma \in X$ a.s. Then $EX = \{E\sigma \mid \sigma$ is a selection of $X\}$. A first moment assumption is made of the type $E\|X\| < \infty$, where $\|K\| = \sup\{x \mid x \in K\}$. By now there is a substantial literature of additive limit theorems (LLN's and CLT's) for random sets. We refer the reader to Artstein (1983), Giné and Hahn, and Zinn (1983), Hansen (1983), Hiai (1983), and Weil (1982).

An important point is that these results involve the behavior of sequences of entire sets (for behavior of certain fuctionals, see Vitale (1977). Note that EX_1 is set-valued, for instance. The implications of this view point are substantial. Rather than focusing on scalar or vector measurements (such as volume, area, etc.), there is a concern with the behavior of sets as a whole. Convergence itself (as in limit theorems) is attractively formulated: the Hausdorff metric is given by $h(K,L) = \inf\{\varepsilon>0 \mid K \subseteq L + \varepsilon B, L \subseteq K + \varepsilon B\}$, where B is the closed unit ball. $\mathbb{K}$ is then a complete, separable, locally compact metric space. Naturally a convergent sequence of sets will yield convergent sequences of continuous functionals so that, at least in principle, bookkeeping with sets is strictly stronger than that with functionals alone.

3. DETERMINING CONDITIONS

For random variables, it is well-known that all probabilities are determined by the restricted class of probabilities of intervals. This can be extended to $\mathbb{R}^d$ and even infinite dimensions. Billingsley (1968) gives a nice account of such determining conditions. It is natural to ask whether such conditions can be produced for random sets. We discuss three examples of such results.

The first is of "inclusion" type and is a special case of work of Choquet (1953). If X is a random set and F is a fixed polytope, then the event $[X \subseteq F]$ is meaningful (i.e. measurable). Indeed, the probabilities of all such events completely determine the probability measure of X. It is, in a way remarkable, that inclusion probabilities determine expected number of vertices and other detailed structure of the set.

The second condition focuses on the volume functional, $\mathrm{vol}(\cdot)$. Clearly, two random sets of very different behavior may have volumes which are equal in distribution. Thus, volumes yield some, but not decisive, information about the distribution of a random set. Can this situation be strengthened? The answer is yes, by invoking more evaluations of the volume functional. In Vitale (1984b), the following is shown. Up to location in $\mathbb{R}^d$, random sets X and X' have the same distribution if and only if the two vectors, $(\mathrm{vol}(X+K),\ldots,\mathrm{vol}(X+dK)$ and $(\mathrm{vol}(X'+K),\ldots,\mathrm{vol}(X'+dK)$. have the same distributions. This is notable in that scalar functionals, and nonlinear ones to be precise, can be invoked to determine the distribution of a random set.

The third determining condition (Vitale (1984a)) concerns a very attractive species of random set, the convex hull of a point sample. The reader can profitably consult Eddy (1980) and Eddy and Gale (1981) for related work.

Let $X_1, X_2, \ldots$ be an iid sequence in $\mathbb{R}^d$ with $E\|X\| < \infty$, and let $K_n = E\,\mathrm{co}\{X_1,\ldots,X_n\}$ be the expected convex hull. Then the common distribution of the X_i's is determined by $\{K_i\}_i^\infty$ which is a nested sequence of compact, convex subsets of $\mathbb{R}^d$ (note $K_1 = \{EX_1\}$). This generalizes a result for R and also has connections with work of Cameron and Martin (1944) and Strassen (1964).

4. STATISTICAL MODELS

In line with traditional formulations, we can pose the following problem of inference. Let $M \in \mathbb{K}$ be a fixed but unknown set. Let $\varepsilon_1, \varepsilon_2, \ldots$ be iid "noise" elements of $\mathbb{K}$. Assume that we do not see M but only versions of it produced by noise corruption. Can M be recovered - at least asymptotically? The answer, of course, depends on the type of corruption.

One situation is additive noise. That is, we see $M+\varepsilon_i$ at the ith stage. We may invoke linear processing to recover M: form $S_n = \frac{1}{n} \sum_{n=1}^{n} (M+\varepsilon_i)$. Under appropriate conditions for the law of large numbers described above, there is convergence to $M+E\varepsilon$ (recall $E\varepsilon$ is the expectation of the random set ε) and this provides of a way to recover M.

In a second example, assume additive corruption again but now invoke intersection processing. We seek conditions under which the intersection of $M+\varepsilon_1, \ldots, M+\varepsilon_n$ converges to M. Jow (1983) has considered this problem in detail and has shown among other results that convergence occurs for all M if and only if $\varepsilon (\stackrel{dw}{=} \varepsilon_1)$ satisfies certain technical conditions: (i) $0 \in \varepsilon$ a.s. and is the <u>only</u> point which a.s. lies in ε and (ii) for each $K \in \mathbb{K}$ with $0 \notin K$, $P(\varepsilon \cap K = \phi) > 0$.

The third example has noise corruption of a different type: at the ith stage, we see $co(M \cup \varepsilon_i)$ so that there is always enlargement of the unknown M. Jow (1983) has shown successive intersections converge for all M iff ε avoids every proper convex cone with positive probability.

5. EMBEDDING AND APPROXIMATION

Much of what we have discussed so far depends on an attractive analytical fact that goes back to Minkowski, namely that $\mathbb{K}$ can be embedded in a Banach space. The technique is as follows: to each $K \in \mathbb{K}$, we assign a <u>support function</u> $s_K(e) = \sup\{<x,e> | x \in K\}$, $e \in S^{d-1}$. It is not hard to show that $s_K \in C(S^{d-1})$ (indeed it is Lipschitz continuous). The embedding $\mathbb{K} \to C(S^{d-1})$ has several important features such as isometry, ordering, and preservation of algebraic operations:

$$\|s_K - s_L\| = h(K,L)$$

$$s_{K+L} = s_K + s_L$$

$$s_{\alpha K} = \alpha s_K \qquad \alpha \geq 0$$

$$K \subseteq L \Leftrightarrow s_K \leq s_L$$

As a consequence of these facts, a random compact, convex set may be realized as a random element of $C(S^{d-1})$ and standard operations invoked. This is in fact the program in Artstein and Vitale (1975) and Weil (1982).

Apart from any dominating stochastic features, the embedding allows exploration of interesting features of sets, such as approximation. As indicated above, the Hausdorff metric is equivalent to the uniform norm of the difference the associated support functions. Other metrics are constructed using L_p norms. McClure and Vitale (1975) study a number of approximation problems in this context for polygons.

In Davis, Vitale, and Ben-Sabar (1977) the problem of approximating a triangle by a disc is taken up. If the measure of discrepancy is taken to be the Hausdorff metric, then the problem reduces to an equi-oscillation condition well-known in (functional) approximation theory.

Finally, there is in Vitale (1979) an attempt to supplement known results on set-valued functions with an approximation theory. Using the support function embedding, a theorem of Bohmann-Korovki type is shown.

6. COMPUTATIONAL CONSIDERATIONS

We conclude with some brief remarks on related computation.

Some of the work discussed above has been implemented in a library of APL routines (Vitale and Tarr (1975)). This collection has recently been updated and supplemented.

In computing with convex sets, the interesting question of mechine representation arises. To be concrete, consider sets in the plane. One can invoke descretization immediately and thus deal with polygons. These may be saved as collections of vertices or they may be saved in a support function representation: let the jth face be at a distance s_j from the origin and have (outward) normal e_j. Then it is enough to save pairs (s_j, e_j). The full polygon is then the intersection of the half-planes $\{(x,y) | <(x,y),e_j> \leq s_j\}$.

On the other hand, the support function embedding is sufficiently attractive for certain applications that a very different kind of discretization may be in order, namely, expanding each support function in a fixed basis of functions. This seems to be an unexplored area which may yield practical benefits.

REFERENCES:

[1] Artstein, Z. (1983). Convexification in limit laws of random sets in Banach spaces. Technical Report, Weizmann Institute of Science.

[2] Artstein, Z. And Vitale, R. A. (1975). A strong law of large numbers. Ann. Probab. 3, 879-882.

[3] Bilingsley, P. (1968). Convergence of Probability Measures. Wiley, New York.

[4] Cameron, R. H. and Martin, W. T. (1944). Transformations of Wiener integrals under translations. Ann. Math. 45, 386-396.

[5] Choquet, G. (1953). Theory of capacities. Ann. Inst. Fourier V, 131-295.

[6] Crofton, M. W. (1868). On the theory of local probability. Phil. Trans. Roy. Soc. London 158, 181-199

[7] Crofton, M. W. (1885). Probability Encyclopaedia Brittanica, 9th ed. 19, 768-788.

[8] Davis, P. J., Vitale, R. A. and Ben-Sabar, E. (1977). On the deterministic and stochastic approximation of regions. J. Approx. Th. 21, 60-88.

[9] Eddy, W. F. (1980). The distribution of the convex hull of a Gaussian sample. J. Appl. Probab. 17, 686-695.

[10] Eddy, W. F. and Gale, J. D. (1981). The convex hull of a spherically symmetric sample. Adv. in Appl. Probab. 13, 751-763.

[11] Giné, E., Hahn, M. G., and Zinn, J. (1983). Limit theorems for random sets: an application of probability in Banach space results. Springer-Verlag, Berlin, 112-135.

[12] Grenander, U. (1976). Pattern Synthesis-Lectures in Pattern Theory I. Springer-Verlag, New York.

[13] Grenander, U. (1978). Pattern Analysis-Lectures in Pattern Theory II. Springer-Verlag, New York.

[14] Hansen, J. C. (1983). A strong law of large numbers for random compact sets in Banach space., Technical report, University of Minnesota.

[15] Hiai, F. (1983). Multivalued conditional expectations, multivalued Radon-Nikodym theorems, integral representations of additive operators, and multivalued strong laws of large numbers. Technical report, Science University of Tokyo.

[16] Jow, R. L. (1983). Some contributions to the theory of random sets. Ph.D. dissertation, Claremont Graduate School.

[17] Kendall, D. G. (1974). Foundations of a theory of random sets. In Stochastic Geometry (E. F. Harding and D. G. Kendall, Eds.). Wiley, New York.

[18] Klein, J. C. and Serra, J. (1971). The texture analyzer. J. Microsc. 95, 349-356.

[19] Matheron, G. (1975). Random Sets and Integral Geometry. Wiley, New York.

[20] McClure, D. E. and Vitale, R. A. (1975). Polygonal approximation of plane convex bodies. J. Math. Anal. Appl. 51, 326-358.

[21] Nicholson, W. L. (ed.) (1972). Proceedings of the Symposium on Statistical and Probabilistic Problems in Metallurgy. Spec. Suppl. to Adv. Appl. Probab.

[22] Robbins, H. E. (1944). On the measure of a random set, I. Ann. Math. Statist. 15, 70-74.

[23] Robbins, H. E. (1945). On the measure of a random set, II. Ann. Math. Statist. 16,

342-247.

[24] Santalo, L. A. (1976). Integral Geometry and Geometric Probability. Encyclopedia of Mathematics and its Applications (G.-C. Rota, ed.) Addison-Wesley, Reading, Mass.

[25] Solomon, H. (1978). Geometric Probability. SIAM, Philadelphia.

[26] Strassen, V. (1964). An invariance principle for the law of the iterated logarithm. Z. Wahrsch. Verw. Gebiete 3, 211-226.

[27] Vitale, R. A. and Tarr, A. (1975). An APL package for convex geometry. APL-75, Pisa.

[28] Vitale, R. A. (1977). Asymptotic area and perimeter of sums of random plane convex sets. Math. Research Center (Madison). TSM # 1770.

[29] Vitale, R. A. (1979). Approximation of convex set-valued functions. J. Approx. Th. 26, 301-315.

[30] Vitale, R. A. (1984a). Expected convex hulls, in preparation.

[31] Vitale, R. A. (1984b). Determination of random set distributions by volume evaluations, in preparation.

[32] Weibel, E. R. (1972). The value of stereology in analyzing structure and function of cells and organisms. J. Microsc. 95, 3-13.

[33] Weil, W. (1982). An application of the central limit theorem for Banach-space-valued random variables to the theory of random sets. Z. Wahrsch. Verw. Gebiete 60, 203-208.

COMPUTER SCIENCE AND STATISTICS:
The Interface, L. Billard (ed.)

ORDERING OF MULTIVARIATE DATA

William F. Eddy

Carnegie-Mellon University

1. INTRODUCTION

The properties of order statistics in one dimension have been extensively studied and are well-known (see, e.g., David, 1981). According to Kendall (1966): "Order properties ... exist in only one dimension;" according to Barnett (1976) "No reasonable basis exists for fully ordering a set of multivariate observations." Because these beliefs are pervasive and almost persuasive there has not been any satisfactory generalization of order statistic methodology to dimensions higher than one. However, there have been studies of the joint marginal distributions of the order statistics that arise from multivariate observations (see, e. g., Weiss, 1964; Galambos, 1975; and Pickands, 1981).

In one dimension Wilks (1942) has shown that order statistics determine distribution-free tolerance intervals and Robbins (1944) has shown that only order statistics determine distribution-free tolerance intervals. Consequently, in one dimension there is a direct correspondence between order statistics and tolerance intervals. In dimensions higher than one the properties of tolerance regions and, in particular, their probability content, have been extensively studied beginning with a series of papers by Scheffe and Tukey (1945), and Tukey (1947,1948).

Here we will choose a particular form of these multivariate nonparametric tolerance regions, namely nested convex polygons, and will demonstrate that, by their order and distributional properties, these sets deserve to be called multivariate order statistics. The particular definition of these convex sets is the outgrowth of a study of the convex hulls of random samples (Eddy, 1980 and Eddy and Gale, 1981). Earlier results have been reported in Eddy (1982) and Eddy (1983). The same idea was suggested, along with several other similar ideas, by Tukey (1975) but no properties of the resulting sets were given.

There have recently been at least two other methods suggested for inducing orderings on multivariate point sets. The first of these, Terrell (1983), defines the "ordering" by means of the function which transforms a certain uniform distribution into the multivariate distribution of the observations. The resulting "order statistics" are partially ordered vectors. The second of these, Goodman and Pollack (1984), defines the "ordering" by the cardinality of the set of points on one side of every d-1 dimensional hyperplane through d points; these cardinalities for all ${}_nC_d$ possible "directed" hyperplanes determine the *order type* of the n points. At this point there is no distribution theory for these order types but there is a notion of *canonical ordering.* There is very possibly a close connection between the concepts introduced by Goodman and Pollack and the methods in this paper but these connections have not yet been explored.

The remainder of the paper is organized as follows. In Section 2 I will give the formal definition of the multivariate order statistics in the two dimensional case. I am going to only discuss the two dimensional case here for notational simplicity. Also for theoretical simplicity I am going to focus on spherically symmetric distributions; the construction and the finite sample distribution theory will hold in any case. In Section 3 I will review some of the properties of convex sets which are essential to the calculations that follow. In particular, I will describe the notion of support function of a convex set which provides a nice tool for deriving the distribution theory of the convex sets. In Section 4 I will give the finite sample distribution theory. This theory closely parallels the one dimensional theory of order statistics; it depends on the multivariate binomial distributions as generalizations of the one dimensional binomial argument. In Section 5 I will briefly describe the asymptotic distribution theory for intermediate order statistics again through the parallel with the one dimensional theory. In Section 6 I will describe the asymptotic distribution theory for extreme values. Here the method relies on the properties of an underlying Poisson point process. In the final section I will discuss computational methods and some potential applications.

2. DEFINITION OF MULTIVARIATE ORDER STATISTICS

Let (R_1,θ_1), ..., (R_n,θ_n) be n independent bivariate random variables with common distribution P. The polar form is being used to represent the random variables because some of the later notation will be simpler. Let H be the collection of half-planes defined by

$$H_{\gamma,p} = \{(r,\theta) \mid r\cos(\gamma-\theta) \le p,\ 0 \le \theta < 2\pi,\ 0 \le r < \infty\}$$

for $0 \le \gamma < 2\pi$ and $-\infty < p < \infty$. Suppose that under P

$$\Pr\{(R,\theta) \in H_{\gamma,p}\} = G(\gamma,p). \tag{2.1}$$

Since the collection of half-planes H are a determining class for the Borel sets, the function $G(\gamma,p)$ determines the probability measure P in exactly the way the more usual distribution function $F(x,y)$ does. It is convenient therefore to refer to the function $G(\gamma,p)$ as the distribution function of (R,θ). For fixed γ, $G(\gamma,p)$ regarded as a function of p, is exactly the usual distribution function of the random variable $R\cos(\gamma-\theta)$. The empirical distribution function of $\{R_i,\theta_i\}$ is given by

$$G_n(\gamma,p) = n^{-1} \Sigma_{i=1}^n I\{(R_i,\theta_i) \in H_{\gamma,p}\}$$

where $I\{\cdot\}$ is the indicator of its argument. For each integer k define the collection of half-planes

$$H_k = \{H_{\gamma,p} \mid G_n(\gamma,p) \ge k/n\}$$

and then define

$$Q_k = \bigcap_{H \in H_k} H, \qquad k=1,...,n.$$

It is immediate from the construction that the $\{Q_k\}$ are convex sets and that $Q_n \supseteq Q_{n-1} \supseteq \ldots$ Obviously Q_n is the convex hull of $\{R_i,\Theta_i\}$. It is also clear that if $k < \lceil n/2 \rceil$ then Q_k is empty; it is less clear but can also be shown that if $k \ge \lceil (2n)/3 \rceil$ then Q_k is nonempty. For $\lceil n/2 \rceil \le k < \lceil (2n)/3 \rceil$ whether Q_k is empty or not depends on the particular configuration of the sample points.

The $\{Q_k\}$ are nonparametric tolerance regions or statistically equivalent blocks. The sets $\{Q_k\}$ will be referred to as multivariate order statistics; the ordering is by set-inclusion. Obviously, since $\{(R_i,\theta_i)\}$ are random variables the $\{Q_k\}$ are random convex sets.

3. CONVEX SETS

Let C be the collection of nonempty compact convex subsets of the plane. Define the Minkowski sum of two elements of C by

$$C_1+C_2 = \{c_1+c_2 \mid c_1 \in C_1,\ c_2 \in C_2\}$$

and define a positive homothetic image in C by

$$\lambda C = \{\lambda c \mid c \in C,\ \lambda > 0\}$$

Let B be the unit ball and define the Hausdorff distance between two elements of C by

$$H(C_1,C_2) = \inf\{\lambda \mid C_1 \subseteq C_2+\lambda B, C_2 \subseteq C_1+\lambda B\}$$

The support function of $C \in C$ is

$$b_c(u) = \sup_{c \in C} \{c \cdot u \mid u \cdot u = 1\}$$

where $\cdot$ is the usual inner product. Since $\mathbf{u} = (\cos\gamma, \sin\gamma)$, $0 \le \gamma < 2\pi$ and $c = (c_1,c_2)$

$$b_c(u) = b_c(\gamma) = \sup_{c \in C} \{c_1 \cos\gamma + c_2 \sin\gamma\}.$$

For each $C \in C$, the support function is a continuous function on the unit circle. The mapping $C \to b_c$, from C onto its range S in the space of continuous functions on the unit circle is isometric and isomorphic. Precisely,

$$H(C_1,C_2) = \sup_u |b_{C_1}(u) - b_{C_2}(u)|,$$

and

$$b_{C_1+C_2}(u) = b_{C_1}(u) + b_{C_2}(u),$$

$$b_{\lambda C}(u) = \lambda b_C(u).$$

Also $C_1 \subseteq C_2$ if and only if

$$\inf_\gamma \{b_2(\gamma) - b_1(\gamma)\} \ge 0.$$

The set S is closed with respect to the operation of pointwise maximum. Let $b_i = b_{C_i} \in S$ when $C_i \in C$. If b_1, $b_2 \in S$ and

$b_3(\gamma) = \max(b_1(\gamma), b_2(\gamma))$ then $b_3 \in S$ and

$$C_3 = CH(C_1, C_2)$$

where $CH(\cdot,\cdot)$ is the convex hull of its arguments. The set S is not closed with respect to the operation of pointwise minimum. If C_1, $C_2 \in C$ and $C_3 = C_1 \cap C_2$ then

$$b_3 = \sup_S \{S \mid S \le \min(b_1,b_2)\};$$

if $C_1 \cup C_2 \in C$ then $b_3 = \min(b_1,b_2)$.

A single point is trivially a convex set and, letting $c = (c_1,c_2)$,

$$b_c(u) = c_1\cos\gamma + c_2\sin\gamma = b_c(\gamma).$$

In polar coordinates

$$r = (c_1^2+c_2^2)^{1/2}$$

$$\theta = \tan^{-1}(c_2/c_1),$$

and

$$b_c(\gamma) = r \cos\theta \cos\gamma + r \sin\theta \sin\gamma = r\cos(\theta-\gamma).$$

These and other properties of convex sets can be found in, e.g., Valentine (1967).

4. FINITE SAMPLE DISTRIBUTION THEORY

The n observations $\{(R_i,\theta_i)\}$ have support functions $\{B_i\}$ where $B_i(\gamma) = R_i \cos(\gamma-\theta_i)$. For fixed γ, the order statistics of $\{B_i(\gamma)\}$ are denoted by

$$D_n(\gamma) \geq D_{n-1}(\gamma) \geq \ldots$$

The event $\{D_k(\gamma) \leq x\}$ is equivalent to the event $\{nG_n(\gamma,x) \geq k\}$. Since $nG_n(\gamma,x)$ is a binomial random variable with parameters n and $G(\gamma,x)$ we find

$$\Pr\{D_k(\gamma) \leq x\} = \Pr\{nG_n(\gamma,x) \geq k\}$$

$$= \Sigma^n_{i=k} \binom{n}{i} [G(\gamma,x)]^i \, [1 - G(\gamma,x)]^{n-i}$$

This is just the distribution of the kth order statistic of a sample of size n from the (one-dimensional) distribution given by $G(\gamma,x)$ for γ fixed. As mentioned above $G(\gamma,x)$ is the distribution function of $R\cos(\gamma-\theta)$ for γ fixed. Thinking of $D_k(\gamma)$ as a continuous-time stochastic process (with γ in the role of the time parameter) we naturally wish to know the joint distribution of $\{D_k(\gamma_1),\ldots,D_k(\gamma_t)\}$ for every finite set $\{\gamma_1,\ldots,\gamma_t\}$.

Generalizing (2.1) let

$$\Pr\{(R,\theta) \in H_{\gamma_1,p_1} \cap H_{\gamma_2,p_2}\} = G(\gamma_1,\, p_1,\, \gamma_2,\, p_2).$$

The event $\{D_k(\gamma_1) \leq x_1$ *and* $D_k(\gamma_2) \leq x_2\}$ is equivalent to the event

$$\{A\} = \{nG_n(\gamma_1,x_1) \geq k \text{ and } nG_n(\gamma_2,x_2) \geq k\}.$$

Consider the following two-way table.

	x_1		
x_2	i−m	n−i−j+m	n−j
	m	j−m	j
	i	n−i	n

Because we are thinking of the event described by this table as a bivariate binomial, the probability of the event

$$\{i \geq k_1 \text{ and } j \geq k_2\}$$

is given by

$$\Sigma^n_{i=k_1} \Sigma^n_{j=k_2} \Sigma^t_{m=s} C(i,j,m)\, p_1^m\, p_2^{i-m}\, p_3^{j-m}\, p_4^{n-i-j+m}$$

where

$$s = \max(0,\ i+j-n)$$
$$t = \min(i,j)$$

$$C(i,j,m) = \frac{n!}{m!(i-m)!(j-m)!(n-i-j+m)!}$$

$$p_1 = G(\gamma_1,x_1,\gamma_2,x_2)$$

$$p_2 = G(\gamma_1,x_1) - G(\gamma_1,x_1,\gamma_2,x_2)$$

$$p_3 = G(\gamma_2,x_2) - G(\gamma_1,x_1,\gamma_2,x_2)$$

and

$$p_4 = 1 - p_1 - p_2 - p_3$$

(see, e.g., David, 1981, Problem 2.2.2). This formula can be rewritten as

$$\Sigma^n_{m=0} \Sigma^n_{i=a} \Sigma^t_{j=b} C(i,j,m)\, p_1^m\, p_2^{i-m}\, p_3^{j-m}\, p_4^{n-i-j+m}$$

where

$$a = \max\,(m,k_1)$$

and

$$b = \max\,(m,k_2).$$

The event $\{A\}$ above is just the event $\{i \geq k$ *and* $j \geq k\}$. Similar but more complicated multinomial sums result from considering three or more angles simultaneously.

5. ASYMPTOTIC DISTRIBUTIONS OF INTERMEDIATE VALUES

In Section 2 Q_k was defined as a certain convex set. Let S_k be the support function of Q_k. It is apparent from the construction that

$$S_k(\gamma) \leq D_k(\gamma)$$

with equality only for those γ which are normal to the faces of Q_k. This is directly related to the fact that S is not closed with respect to the operation of pointwise minimum. It can be shown that

$$D_k(\gamma) - S_k(\gamma) = O_p(n^{-1})$$

Consequently the asymptotic distribution theory for S_k is identical to that for D_k.

There are two well-known general procedures for proving asymptotic normality of one-dimensional order statistics. The first is to perform a Taylor series expansion of the density and show that the density is locally Gaussian (Mosteller, 1946). We eschew this approach because of the complexity of the density (See the Appendix). The second approach is by way of the

Bahadur (1966) representation of order statistics; this approach, due to Ghosh (1971) (see David, 1981, p. 254ff), is unavailable because the strong representation has not yet been developed in the multivariate case.

Since the D_k, and equivalently the S_k, are, for fixed γ, ordinary one-dimensional order statistics, the one-dimensional marginal distributions are asymptotically normal. It is fairly straightforward to show that

$$\mathrm{Cov}[nG_n(\gamma_1, x_1), nG_n(\gamma_2, x_2)] =$$

$$G(\gamma_1, x_1, \gamma_2, x_2) - G(\gamma_1, x_1)\, G(\gamma_2, x_2).$$

It follows that if $(\partial G)/(\partial x) = g(x)$ is independent of γ and $G(\gamma, x_\lambda) = \lambda$ for all γ then

$$n^{1/2}\, g(x)\, [S_{n\lambda}] - x_\lambda] \overset{W}{\to} Z$$

where Z is a mean-zero Gaussian process with covariance function $G(\gamma_1, x_\lambda, \gamma_2, x_\lambda) - G(\gamma_1, x_\lambda) G(\gamma_2, x_\lambda)$. The proof depends on a result of Weiss (1964) showing that the asymptotic joint distribution of marginal order statistics from multivariate observations is the appropriate Gaussian distribution.

6. ASYMPTOTIC DISTRIBUTIONS OF EXTREME VALUES

When $k = n$, $S_n = D_n$ and the asymptotic distribution is related to the extreme-value distributions. This theory has been developed in Eddy (1980) and Eddy and Gale (1981). For fixed k the asymptotic distribution of S_{n-k} has been indicated in Eddy (1982).

Define a new sequence of processes by

$$L_{n-k,i}(t) = a_n [D_{n-k}(\gamma_0 + c_n t) - b_n]$$

where γ_0 is fixed and $\{a_n\}, \{b_n\}, \{c_n\}$ are sequences of constants to be chosen in a manner specified below. It is possible to show that

$$\sup_i L_{n-k,i} \overset{W}{\to} M_{jk}.$$

where M_{jk} is an extreme-value process. The index j is used to denote one of the three families which are familiar in the one dimensional case and which correspond to the tail behavior of the radial distribution in the plane. We refer to them by the nature of their tail decrease as (1) algebraic, (2) exponential, and (3) truncated.

The proof of convergence to the M_{jk} depends on a proof that an underlying sequence of point processes converges to a Poisson point process. The limits M_{jk} are derived as simply the kth largest function of the corresponding point process.

For the algebraic tails, assume that

$$\Pr\{R > r\} = r^{-\alpha}.$$

Then the constants are given by

$$a_n = (nc)^{-1/\alpha}$$

$$b_n = 0$$

$$c_n = 1$$

$$\gamma_0 = 0.$$

where

$$c = (2\pi)^{-1} B[1/2, (\alpha+1)/2]$$

and B is the complete beta integral.

For the exponential tails, assume that

$$\Pr\{R > r\} = r^{\alpha} \exp(-r^{\beta}).$$

Then the constants are given by

$$a_n = \beta b_n^{\beta-1}$$

b_n is the solution of $1 - F(b_n) = n^{-1}$

$$c_n = (\beta \log n)^{-1/2}$$

γ_0 is any fixed constant.

For the truncated tails assume that

$$\Pr\{R > 1 - r\} = r^{\alpha - 1/2}.$$

Then the constants are given by

$$a_n = (nc)^{1/\alpha}$$

$$b_n = 1$$

$$c_n = (nc)^{-1/2\alpha}$$

where

$$c = \pi^{-1} 2^{1/2} B(\alpha + 1/2, 1/2)$$

γ_0 is a fixed constant.

7. DISCUSSION

Computation of all the nested convex polyhedra could potentially be quite expensive. In fact, in d dimensions there are ${}_nC_d \sim n^d$ possible hyperplanes determined by d points. All that is necessary is that for each of these hyperplanes, the number of points in the sample that are on each side be determined. This requires $O(n^{d+1})$ time and if all the hyperplanes were stored it would require

$O(n^d)$ space. Fortunately, all the hyperplanes do not need to be stored because the intersections that correspond to each of the nested convex polygons can be partially determined as each hyperplane is assigned to one of the sets. This could have a dramatic effect on the amount of storage required but in practice it doesn't seem to.

Since the only requirement which the construction of these sets had to satisfy was that they be nonparametric tolerance regions, it is interesting to speculate about what other possibilities might exist. For example, if one were to use a different determining class than halfplanes, what would the resulting sets look like? It is natural to consider the "lower-left" orthants as one such class. The resulting ordered sets have boundaries which look like multidimensional staircases. Unfortunately, there is not, to my knowledge, a nice representation of such sets as the support function represents the convex sets. Consequently further theory will be difficult to derive. One strong argument against other determining classes is that "half-planes" is the *only* class for which the resulting sets are invariant, or more accurately equivariant, under linear transformations.

APPENDIX

There are several ways to derive the bivariate density of multivariate order statistics. The simplest and most tedious way is to differentiate the outer (upper) tail of the distribution function given in Section 4 above. Another more interesting method is to generalize the argument outlined in David (1981, p.9) as follows.

In order that there be k_1-1 X's less than x, one X between x and $x+\delta x$, and $n-k_1$ X's greater than $x+\delta x$ and, simultaneously, that there be k_2-1 Y's less than y, one Y between y and $y+\delta y$, and $n-k_2$ Y's greater than $y+\delta y$ the n bivariate observations must be distributed according to the following diagram.

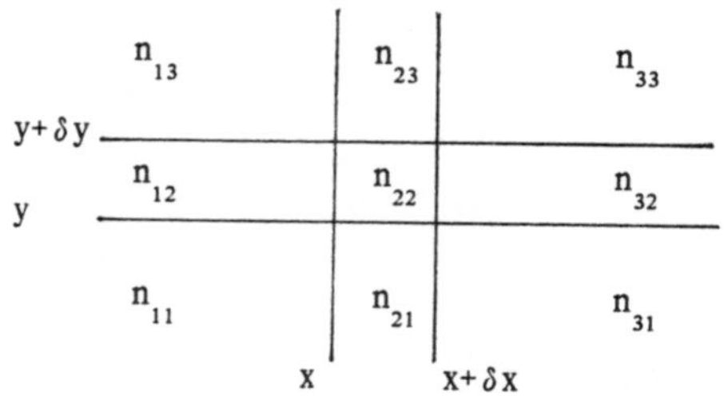

where the margins of the table are given by

$$n_{1.} = k_1-1$$

$$n_{2.} = 1$$

$$n_{3.} = n-k_1$$

$$n_{.1} = k_2-1$$

$$n_{.2} = 1$$

$$n_{.3} = n-k_2$$

Now given n_{11} there are five possible ways that the observations can be distributed in the cells and achieve these marginal totals. They are given in the table below.

The bivariate density is just the sum over the five entries in the table of the density conditional on a particular row. This latter density is given by

$$\Sigma^{v}_{n_{11}=u} C(n_{11},n_{13},n_{31},n_{33})\ \Pi^{3}_{i=1}\ \Pi^{3}_{j=1}\ p_{ij}^{\,n_{ij}}$$

where

$$C(n_{11},n_{13},n_{31},n_{33}) = \frac{n!}{n_{11}!\ n_{13}!\ n_{31}!\ n_{33}!},$$

$$u = \max(0,\ n_{11}-n_{33}),$$

and

$$v = \min(k_1-1,\ k_2-1).$$

	n_{12}	n_{13}	n_{21}	n_{22}	n_{23}	n_{31}	n_{32}	n_{33}
I	1	$k_1-n_{11}-2$	1	0	0	$k_2-n_{11}-2$	0	$n-k_1-k_2+n_{11}+2$
II	1	$k_1-n_{11}-2$	0	0	1	$k_2-n_{11}-1$	0	$n-k_1-k_2+n_{11}+1$
III	0	$k_1-n_{11}-1$	1	0	0	$k_2-n_{11}-2$	1	$n-k_1-k_2+n_{11}+1$
IV	0	$k_1-n_{11}-1$	0	0	1	$k_2-n_{11}-1$	1	$n-k_1-k_2+n_{11}$
V	0	$k_1-n_{11}-1$	0	1	0	$k_2-n_{11}-1$	0	$n-k_1-k_2+n_{11}+1$

The cell probabilities are given by

$$p_{11} = F(x,y)$$
$$p_{12} = F_x(x,y)$$
$$p_{13} = F(\infty,y) - F(x,y)$$
$$p_{21} = F_y(x,y)$$
$$p_{22} = F_{xy}(x,y)$$
$$p_{23} = F_y(\infty,y) - F_y(x,y)$$
$$p_{31} = F(x,\infty) - F(x,y)$$
$$p_{32} = F_x(x,\infty) - F_x(x,y)$$
$$p_{33} = 1 - F(x,\infty) - F(\infty,y) + F(x,y)$$

where F_x, F_y, and F_{xy} denote the partial derivatives of F.

REFERENCES

[1] Bahadur, R.R. (1966). A note on quantiles in large samples. *Ann. Math. Statist.*, **37**, 577–580.

[2] Barnett, V. (1976). The ordering of multivariate data (with discussion). *J.R. Statist. Soc. A*, **139** 318–354.

[3] David, H.A. (1981). *Order Statistics* (2nd edition). Wiley, New York.

[4] Donaho, D.L. (1982). Breakdown properties of multivariate location estimators. Technical Report, Department of Statistics, Harvard University.

[5] Eddy, W.F. (1980). The distribution of the convex hull of a Gaussian sample. *J. Appl. Prob.*, **17**, 686–695.

[6] Eddy, W.F. (1982). Convex hull peeling. *COMPSTAT 1982 - Part I: Proceedings in Computational Statistics*, 42–47. Physica-Verlag, Vienna.

[7] Eddy, W.F. (1983). Set-valued orderings for bivariate data. To appear in *Stochastic Geometry, Geometric Statistics, and Stereology*. Tuebner, Leipzig.

[8] Eddy, W.F. and J.G. Gale (1981). The convex hull of a spherically symmetric sample. *Adv. Appl. Prob.*, **13**, 751–763.

[9] Galambos, J. (1975). Order statistics of samples from multivariate distributions. *J. Amer. Statist. Assoc.*, **70**, 674–680.

[10] Ghosh, J.K. (1971). A new proof of the Bahadur representation of quantiles and an application. *Ann. Math. Statist.*, **42**, 1951–1961.

[11] Goodman, J.E. and R. Pollack (1984). Multidimensional sorting. Invited lecture. Computer Science and Statistics: Sixteenth Symposium on the Interface.

[12] Kendall, M.G. (1966). Discrimination and classification. *Multivariate Analysis I*. P.R. Krishnaiah (ed.). Academic Press, New York.

[13] Mosteller, F. (1946). On some useful "inefficient" statistics. *Ann. Math. Statist.*, **17**, 377–408.

[14] Pickands, J. (1981). Multivariate Extreme Value Distributions (with discussion). Bull. Inter. Statist. Inst. **49**, 859–878.

[15] Robbins, H. (1944). On distribution-free tolerance limits in random sampling. *Ann. Math. Statist.* **15**, 214–216.

[16] Scheffe, H. and J.W. Tukey (1945). Nonparametric estimation I: Validation of order statistics. *Ann. Math. Statist.*, **16**, 187–192.

[17] Terrell, G.R. (1983). Multivariate Quantile Functions. Techincal Report, Department of Mathematical Sciences, Rice University.

[18] Tukey, J.W. (1947). Nonparametric estimation II: Statistically equivalent blocks and tolerance regions – The continuous case. *Ann. Math. Statist.*, **18**, 529–539.

[19] Tukey, J.W. (1948). Nonparametric estimation III: Statistically equivalent blocks and multivariate tolerance regions – The discontinuous case. *Ann. Math. Statist.*, **19**, 30–39.

[20] Tukey, J.W. (1975). Mathematics and the picturing of data. *Proc. Int. Cong. Math. Vancouver 1974*, 523–531.

[21] Valentine, F.A. (1967). *Convex Sets*. McGraw-Hill, New York.

[22] Weiss, L. (1964). On the asymptotic joint normality of quantiles from a multivariate distribution. *J. Res. Nat. Bur. Stds.*, **68B**, 65–66.

[23] Wilks, S.S. (1942). Statistical prediction with special reference to the problem of tolerance limits. *Ann. Math. Statist.*, **13**, 400–409.

Developing Statistical Workstations

Organizer: *L. Billard, University of Georgia*

Invited Presentations:

Statistical Software: Progress and Prospects, *J. A. Nelder and R. J. Baker, Rothamsted Experimental Station*

Responsibilities, Problems and Some Solutions for the Profession's Input into Microcomputer Software, *Brian P. Murphy, University of Western Australia*

COMPUTER SCIENCE AND STATISTICS:
The Interface, L. Billard (ed.)

STATISTICAL SOFTWARE: PROGRESS AND PROSPECTS

by

J.A.Nelder and R.J.Baker

Statistics Department, Rothamsted Experimental Station, Harpenden, Herts., AL5 2JQ., England.

A categorization of current statistical software will be given; implications for the future will be discussed under the headings of hardware, languages, operating systems, user interface management systems and the growth of artificial-intelligence techniques.

1. INTRODUCTION

Statistical software has proliferated to the extent that a catalogue of software for survey analysis alone now runs to hundreds of entries. This proliferation has involved a prodigious amount of reinventing of wheels, and leaves the intending user with a most complex matching problem in trying to discover what package best suits his needs for a particular form of analysis. We attempt here a categorization of current software and then look at likely future developments in several areas of importance.

2. CATEGORIES OF CURRENT STATISTICAL SOFTWARE

We look first at four types of package, and the implications for the user. We distinguish between a general-purpose language (GPL) such as Fortran, Pascal, etc. and a problem-oriented language (POL) such as that of GLIM (Baker and Nelder, 1978) and other packages.

2.1. Types of package

Type 1. Package driven by user-supplied main program

These packages consist of pre-compiled sets of sub-programs for which the user supplies a driving program usually (but not necessarily) written in the same GPL as the package. Some software for micros follows this route, to save space, and APL packages are usually driven in this way, though the mechanism of runnning is here slightly different. For packages written in a GPL, three job steps are required for each job:

compile driver, link, run

For this type we have

Pro :- Full flexibility of GPL available to user
- Efficient execution

Anti:- User needs detailed knowledge of internal structure at the GPL level
- Each job needs three job steps
- User needs ability to write in GPL

Type 2. Package with translator

For this type the user writes his instructions in a POL which is then translated by the translator into GPL source code. The subsequent steps are as for Type 1. Each job now has four steps:

translate, compile, link, run

For type 2 we have

Pro :- User can write (more simply) in a POL
- Extensions can be added at the GPL level
- Efficient execution when run

Anti:- Each job needs four job steps

Type 3. Sets of programs with interpretive language

BMDP is perhaps the best known example of this type of package. Each form of analysis is the subject of a separate program, though some uniformity may be achieved for data input and the form of the interpreted instructions needed to drive the analysis. There is here only one job step:

run

and we can list

Pro :- User can write in POL
- No knowledge of internal structure needed
- One job step

Anti:- No easy access to the underlying GPL
- Less efficient execution (though loss may be small) due to interpretation
- Difficult to link steps of a complex analysis needing more than one program

Type 4. Integrated system with interpretive language

Such systems include (in alphabetical order) Genstat, GLIM, Minitab, P-Stat, S, S.A.S., S.P.S.S., and many others. They include different algorithms for various analyses, together with facilities for data manipulation. They offer the user an interpretive POL. They have the same advantages and disadvantages as type 3, except that the last disadvantage is lessened or removed entirely. The extent of its removal depends upon the data structures supported by the system, which we now discuss.

2.2. Categories of data structure

A surprising number of systems have used only a single data structure, namely the data matrix. Many data sets can be presented in this way, including multi-way tables, which can be explicitly indexed to give the data-matrix form. A mathematical matrix can also be presented as a data matrix. The data matrix thus serves well systems mainly concerned with activities of the form

Read - Calculate - Print - Stop

i.e. one-step analysis.

Multi-stage analysis requires that the components of output from an algorithm can be stored in memory as instances of data structures acceptable to the system. Here the limitations of the data matrix become apparent. Examples are its inability to deal compactly and efficiently with multi-way tables, or with symmetric matrices stored in triangular form etc. The most general form of a data structure in a statistical system is probably that of S, which allows a tree with arbitrary arrays at the nodes; access is by compound names with field selectors as components. Genstat was a system to adopt early on the multi-way table as a basic data structure supported throughout the system, and to provide a table arithmetic for operating on them. In general, though, statistical systems support a very limited subset of the data structures available in modern GPLs.

2.3. Mode of use

Three modes are discernible

1. Batch
2. Interactive
3. Conversational

Originally all systems ran in batch mode, reflecting the operating systems they ran under. Once it became possible to make a terminal both the input and output channel of, say, a Fortran program, the construction of interactive programs became straightforward, and the difference between batch and interactive modes rather small. Not all users feel that they can think fast enough to justify the interactive mode, and for these 'instant' batch may be an adequate method of working, particularly if the system being used can be dumped and restored easily (e.g. via the DUMP and RESTORE directives of GLIM). Conversational programs use menus, of varying and variable complexity, to prompt the user. User satisfaction depends critically on the design of the menu system and on the possibility of collapsing it as knowledge grows. We enter here the area of man-machine interface, which is further discussed in section 3.4.

3. THE FUTURE

3.1. Hardware

Components that are important to the statistician include

- micros with enough memory to run existing systems
- networks allowing access to programs and data elsewhere
- vector and array processors
- terminals with good graphics

The appearance of micros with 1 Mb or more of memory and a hard disc makes many existing systems directly available to the individual user. Small systems, such as GLIM, can go on to machines with 256kb. A problem to date has been the lack of software dealing with segmentation of large programs. This is about to be removed by the appearance of chips with hardware for paging. Another problem with smaller 16-bit macros has been the use of software originally designed for 8-bit machines, and inadequately upgraded. This problem should also disappear shortly.

Networks are with us, but still relatively unstandardized. Many exist, but many are one-off constructions. The establishment of standardized network protocols could have a profound effect on the way we do statistics on computers. Neither programs nor data need live on our own machine, so long as they can be accessed through the network. Existing large systems could be segmented, with parts stored on nodes where they are most used. Segmented systems will eventually be run by operating systems that will farm out different parts of the same job to different machines without the user being aware of it. The possibility of segmented systems raises new questions of design, which will need further work.

Vector and array processors may well increase the size of problems that can be tackled in reasonable time (e.g. model fitting to large data sets) by two orders of magnitude. Taking full advantage of their potentialities, however, will not be painless. Straight-forward transport of programs to such machines is not enough. The code may need modification to make the vector-processing clear to the compiler, or more importantly, algorithms may have to be redesigned to take best advantage of the new facilities.

The arrival of relatively cheap graphics terminals has exposed the need for good transportable software as part of a statistician's tool-kit. The appearance of GKS as the de facto international standard for two-dimensional graphics is a big step forward, and its availability at the hardware level is already promised. The size of graphics software packages, to say nothing of the problems of providing back ends for many mutually incompatible peripherals, is hindering the provision of easily-usable graphics for statisticians.

3.2. Languages

With languages standardization has failed; the Babel is as great as it was 20 years ago. The dominance of Fortran for scientific computing continues, though even in its 77 form it remains a low-level language looking its age. Perhaps the most remarkable, and somewhat depressing, fact is that vast amounts of programming continue to be done with tools which do not include fundamental facilities such as user-defined structures (operands) and operators. The failure of Algol 68 to take-off must be counted as a major setback, and it remains to be seen whether the Baroque complexities of Ada will fare better in the statistical community. The failure to use modern programming languages leads to programs expensive to maintain and extend, and to inefficient implementation.

We need to distinguish between languages for implementation and languages for use. Most implementation languages are GPLs with large compilers and link editors; as such they are ill-adapted to interactive use, hence the almost universal provision of interpreted languages for statistical systems. (APL-based systems are unusual in having the same user and implementation language; this works because APL is itself an interpretive language). Curiously, and in our view unfortunately, the user languages for statistical software have usually been designed by statisticians. This reflects the fact that remarkably little work seems to have been done on interpretive languages by computer scientists. Clearly there would be great gains to be made by the use of standard tools, in the form of interpretive languages, by statistical-package developers. Not only would moving between packages be made much easier for users, but the construction of special-purpose packages would be much easier. For the full exploitation of the new graphics hardware there is similarly a need for a portable picture-description language.

3.3. Operating systems

In the past operating systems have not been the most helpful of programs, and one of the reasons for the growth of large statistical packages has undoubtedly been to insulate the user from the operating system by providing him with a more friendly environment for doing his work. Because packages push the user towards using a single program, their appearance has had the undesirable effect that each package tries to do everything; commercial pressures have made this effect worse. A good operating system should make it easy to move from one tool to another, using each for what it is best at. The arrival of Unix is a revolutionary event, because it does exactly that. For example, it allows the user to make one program call another to do a particular analysis; in this way the facilities of GLIM were made available to the user of S without his having to know anything about the language of GLIM. Such activities imply the existence of standardized external representation of data structures, sufficiently general data structures supported in each program, and the ability of each program to construct a program in the other's language. The last condition would be greatly simplified, of course, if a common interactive language existed. Unix is constructed on the assumption that the user will use the operating system to join tools together, and to that extent is hostile to large self-contained packages. An interesting battle could develop here.

3.4. The new user interface

It is impossible to predict the future of user software without taking into consideration the enormous impact that the design concepts of the Smalltalk system (Goldberg and Robson, 1983) and its derivatives (e.g. the Apple Lisa, Concurrent CP/M etc.) will have on the user's image of the computer and its software. Their user-oriented approach to the user-computer interface is radically different from the previous computer-centered approach, and statistical software, if it is to be properly embedded in such systems, will need to adapt in at least two ways.

We must first recognize that such systems take an integrated approach to application software, in the sense that several application programs can be active simultaneously and that the interfacing and transfer of data between them is handled by the system. Non-integrated systems offer poor interfacing between application programs, usually at the level of a text-file. Typically, a user of such a system will retrieve information from a data-base via its query program and place it in a file for access by a statistical analysis program, which in turn will place its output in another file for access by a graphics program; the user is running exactly one program at a time and it is impossible to recall either of the other programs from the statistical program. In contrast, the integrated system views applications programs as sub-processes that can be run concurrently and, moreover, that delegate all their input and output to the system. Thus, for example, it becomes possible, while running a statistics package, to ask the system to run the DBMS query program to extract and pass new information to the statistics program and then to pass the output to the graphics program, without ever leaving the statistics program. Currently, statistics packages attempt to provide a complete environment for the user, (i.e. statistics, plus data-base manipulation, editing, graphics, etc.), within the one program. Integrated systems, however, will enable such packages to concentrate on the statistical aspects, leaving other applications to other programs.

Secondly, interactive statistical programs will have to change from their current dependence on "command-line" input and "line-file" output to a less restrictive mode of operating. Consider the analogous mutation in text-editing from the "command-line" based editors to the current "full-screen" editors. (As with batch-mode editors, so batch-mode statistical programs have their uses, but we do not consider them here.) With the former, the user operates at a distance from his text-file, giving "commands" to the editor and having to visualize in his/her own mind the effect of these commands. By contrast, the full-screen editor allows the user to operate directly on the text-file (the distinction between the screen image and the actual file being deliberately blurred) without a command interpreter interposing itself between the user and the object to be manipulated. Current statistical software has the same design concept as a line-editor; the user operates on the data at a distance, via an interposing (and often clumsy) command interpreter. The new generation of statistical software will allow direct manipulation both of the data and of the results of an analysis, the objects being presented to the user either as arrays of values (as in text-editing) or, better still, as graphical icons; for example, in the analysis of a response surface it would be desirable to present the output as a contour plot but even better if changes to data values were dynamically reflected in changes to the contour plot, thus for example, providing immediate information on the influence of potential outliers.

Such design changes have indeed already been incorporated into existing data manipulation software - in particular the very popular spreadsheet programs, such as Visicalc, and more recently Visi-On. It is ironic that though such programs have the equivalent of the statistical data matrix as their basic data structure, no similar approach has been taken by conventional statistical packages.

3.5. The influence of expert systems

The rise of artificial-intelligence (AI) ideas and techniques, particularly their role in the design of fifth-generation computers, has inevitably affected the way we look at statistical software.

There is space here to make only a few general points. First, tools: the arrival of logic programming languages, like Prolog, will have a profound effect on how we define and organize the knowledge base of statistical expert systems. Prolog uses as its basic statement a conditional assertion of the form

$$S \text{ if } C_1 \text{ and if } C_2 \text{ .... and if } C_k$$

(This is called a Horn clause; if k=0 we have a simple assertion). The distinction between specification and implementation, so characteristic of procedural languages, is here much less, tending even to disappear. Thus a statement of a sort in the form

$\underset{\sim}{y}$ is $\underset{\sim}{x}$ sorted if $\underset{\sim}{y}$ is a permutation of $\underset{\sim}{x}$ and $\underset{\sim}{y}$ is ordered

can be converted immediately into a Prolog statement of the form

x sorts_to y if x permutes_to y
and y is_ordered

Further additions defining when $\underset{\sim}{Y}$ is a permutation of $\underset{\sim}{X}$ and what an ordered set is complete both the specification <u>and</u> the program. With a logic programming language we can define a knowledge base and its accessing functions simultaneously. The effects of this will be profound.

Secondly, statistics is in a unique position as a subject for expert systems, since we are concerned not to make, e.g. diagnoses of disease for a new patient, but with the processes of diagnosis and inference (not in our view the same) themselves. To define such processes, involving as it does a formalization of the processes of a statistician doing statistical analysis, will be a formidable task. Presumably we shall see different systems built on different philosophies of inference; will their use then provide a real test of the relative value of such philosophies? It is an interesting possibility.

Thirdly, what does 'expert' refer to? Presumably, an expert system is designed <u>by</u> experts, rather that <u>for</u> experts; however, in the medical field, programs such as Mycin have undoubtedly been designed <u>for</u> experts as well as being <u>by</u> experts. You have to know what an obligate anaerobe is to use the program. In statistics it is widely assumed that the user will be non-expert and hence needs basic teaching (what is a parameter ? etc.). We suggest that the two processes, of providing an intelligent front end to a program, and instructing the user in the meaning of statistical terms, are orthogonal activities that can and should be developed quite separately. A good modern operating system (see Section 3.3.) will, of course, allow the user to switch at will between the processes.

4. CONCLUSION

We believe that recent developments in computing have great implications for statisticians generally, and for the implementors of statistical software in particular. We cannot afford to let those ignorant of statistics (however skilled they may be in computing) dominate the way in which the processes of statistical analysis and inference are presented to the user.

[1] Baker,R.J. and Nelder,J.A., The GLIM System, Release 3. (Numerical Algorithms Group, Oxford, 1978)

[2] Chambers,J.M. and Schilling,J.M., S and GLIM: an experiment in interfacing statistical systems. GLIM Newsletter 6, (1983) 43-50.

[3] Goldberg,A. and Robson,D., Smalltalk-80: the language and its implementation. (Addison-Wesley: Mass., 1983)

COMPUTER SCIENCE AND STATISTICS:
The Interface, L. Billard (ed.)

RESPONSIBILITIES, PROBLEMS AND SOME SOLUTIONS IN THE STATISTICAL PROFESSION'S INPUT INTO MICROCOMPUTER SOFTWARE

Brian P. Murphy, Faculty of Medicine, University of Western Australia

The currently emerging microcomputing machinery displays powers quite new to the statistician (1). Firstly, computing costs need rarely be considered. Secondly, the newer users will be of wider interests and computing skills. These two facts alone determine the need for new statistical software, for most of today's users will not be prepared to accept micro versions of many of our respected mainframe packages, of antique style though professionally competent, where their use requires even moderately sophisticated knowledge of either statistical theory or computing technique. New statistical packages are being provided mainly by commercial computing interests, often with appalling consequences. The statistical profession's input is urgently required, but it seems to demand a level of computer technology that statisticians rarely command, or seek. While the broader problems are being recognised and attacked in some places, we discuss some immediate considerations arising from the involvement of my group of colleagues attempting to determine and produce what is needed in their own microcomputer statistical programs.

1. INTRODUCTION

Though statisticians were amongst the first to make use of the new technology of computing in the early 1960's, it was not until well into the 1970's that respectable software became widely available. Some popular packages of today had a shaky statistical base and were oblivious of numerical problems for many years, as became clear at the 1978 COMPSTAT conference. We now are faced with an even less promising situation in that in this newer era of microcomputers, the most popular microcomputer statistical software seems to have little professional input, and again an ignorance of standard numerical methods (2). This is doubly unfortunate in that the new users are more numerous, engaged in types of work not previously associated with statistics or computing, and correspondingly statistically naive. They are however demanding in terms of ease of use of all computing products, nurtured as they have been by the word-processing and database software of today's micros. In spite of their very recent entry into computing statistics, they soon want, rightly or not, full-screen editors, menu-driven packages and on-screen help; sophisticated colour graphics is also demanded.

Few of the current mainframe packages can offer anything approaching these demands, and downloading these to micros is unlikely to improve the current situation markedly, if the transition is even feasible. But the demands are real, and can be filled at least superficially, as the marketplace shows. The statistical profession's input so far has been largely restricted to the 'super-micro' class, while waiting for the micros to grow sufficiently to emulate mainframes. This has not been very satisfactory, since few academic and research groups we meet can fund such machinery, and has led to the disastrous situation above indicated where amateurs supply the profession.

One reason is clear. Few statisticians have had much training in modern computing theory or technique, and most have treated formal computer study, and its exponents, with barely concealed disdain. Thus the computing expertise and more importantly the courage required to overhaul or replace an expensive and painful old work is not at hand, and the user interface in particular remains rooted in the early '70 mould. Most interface syntaxes are impressively convoluted while the best are stilted by business micro standards. While it has long been recognised that it is necessary to fit the computer to the user, not the reverse, the performance of the statistical software writers has not matched the theory. (I am not being unfairly severe on the concept of ease of use displayed by the mainframe packages, but I am merely echoing the words of most of my consultee colleagues).

2. CLASSES OF MODERN MICROCOMPUTERS

In such a rapidly changing field the act of attempting to classify the existing machinery and directions renders it obsolete, but it is still worthwhile to help indicate problems peculiar to microcomputing statistics. The table below gives some representative hardware and associated software. The costs are relevant, for this is the major factor in most machine purchases, and the Australian figures seem at least internally comparable with costs elsewhere. It is also reasonable to consider the hardware even if functionally obsolete since this is what is actually sold and supported.

New hardware is continually promised, but execution seems always behind schedule (I've been waiting for the IBM/370 micro for five years). The future will see micros of mainframe proportions, but interest in the machines of minimal configuration will always remain, and this is ultimately the base level at which statisticians must provide statistical software.

The software indicated in table 1 below is only part of that available, further limited to the better known or more promising. Cable and Rowe (3) give a list of some 50 programs and packages claiming microcomputer implementation with a brief statement of their facilities, as defined by the authors. Few have been reviewed; most will not be.

The processor basically defines an era or area in the stages of microcomputer development, and thus a price and facility range. Though extensions are possible at hardware level to most systems named and implied, the accompanying facilities list indicates a commonly available configuration.

At this stage, the 6502 class machines are probably the most numerous, but some millions of Z80 class machines are used in more professional circumstances. New users will however now look at the 8088 class for both home and office, as in my University. While it is obvious that this class of machine should and will receive the most attention from software producers in the immediate future, my team concentrated on the Z80 class, being then our own need. We are not clear that we would advocate further work for the Z80 - the limitations are severe as we shall see below, and no longer to be accepted.

On the other hand, we do not advocate the continued heavy accent on the more powerful processors. Not only does this not help the current situation, but it is not clear that these more sophisticated systems [James,(1)], such as the M68000 processor under the Unix Operating System, represent real solutions. The trade and trade literature also is not convinced.

Processor Type	Typical Product	Standard Facilities	Statistical Software Available
6502	Apple ($2000)	48K RAM 2x100K floppies	ASTAT, AIDA, various small
8080/Z80	Cromemco C10 ($3000)	64K RAM 2x400K floppies	ABSTAT, GLIM, MICROSTAT, MASS, MATHSTAT, STATPAK, STAN
8088,8086 8086+8087 8088+8087	NEC-APC ($4500) IBM-PC ($4500)	256K RAM 2x1200K floppies 256K RAM 2x320K floppies	ABSTAT, GLIM, MICROSTAT, MASS, MATHSTAT, STATPAK, STAN, SCSS, MINITAB, ...
M68000	NCR-Tower Wicat ($15-25000)	768K RAM 20M hard disk, multiusers.	PSTAT, SPSS, ... (i.e. most mainframe packages)
MINIS	VAX 730 HP, WANG ($40000+)	Virtual memory Virtual disks	All mainframe packages

Table 1. Current Microcomputers and Facilities

However, we are interested in 'super micros' to the point of working with M68000 and VAX, but only within the constraints of program portability. The associated compilers do provide (unnecessary) problems, and strengthen prejudices.

3. SOME PROBLEMS

Obviously, some problems of the small machines are generated by their size. They have:

1) Small random access (RAM) memory - 30K RAM for 6502, 64K for Z80 and typically 256K for 8088/6/7. Though many methods are used to increase these by certain manufacturers, this is often useless as compiler writers rarely accomodate such special features.

2) Limited disk storage - though this is more easily solved than the other limitations, and 2Megabytes is common for Z80 and 8088s. The speed of access is however often a visible limitation.

3) Poor arithmetic accuracy as supplied by compilers - by scientific standards, 32-bit real arithmetic is dangerous in statistical work. If 64-bit computation is available through software, it is very slow. However there is an increasing interest in production of 'arithmetic co-processor' chips, e.g. the AMD9511 for Z80 and the 8087 for the 8088-6 processors. These give speed factors of 10 to 1000, depending on the skills and care of the programmers and compiler writers. Again, the compiler writers do not often take advantage of these features. For instance, the 8086/8087 combination can do arithmetic at 1000 times the speed of a Z80 (which in turn is about 1/2000 of the speed of a mainframe), putting the combination in the mainframe area. We have found only a 20-fold factor using our Pascal compiler.

But the major faults lie in ourselves - as statisticians, even after 20 years programming, we do not have all the technical computing expertise to handle the interactions amongst these limitations with ease. But with good support from computing colleagues, some solutions were found.

4. SOME SOLUTIONS

The mechanical limitations noted above have a profound effect on the way all packages, and particularly statistical, are constructed. We have adopted one strategy now to be described; there may be others.

1) Overlaying of modules is necessary. For instance, the Regression code uses the same physical area within the machine memory (RAM) as the AOV code, since they can never be wanted simultaneously. The technique is old, and its days are not yet numbered (virtual memory may exist, but costs will always force a limit below the desirable in most purchases).

   Overlaying and modular compilation are non-standard in the definition of the Pascal language. But they were necessary for our work, and their implementation in Pascal MT+ was the major reason for our choice (4). In particular, it was reasonably easy to separate out the overlaying code from the essential (standard) Pascal source, as will be illustrated further below.

2) Data will not be stored in RAM. At best, some will be buffered in to a small area at a given time, but the programmer considers that he must reread the data for each statistical task. Again, this is an old technique which we hope to dispose of some day. In practice it means that our statistics package has much in common with a compiler in its programming techniques, while the user realises that he must order as much computation per data pass as possible, for minimum time-wasting.

3) Compact code is essential; efficient code is further desirable, though mandatory only at certain points, as for example at the nub of highly iterated arithmetic loops. This implies very professional programming, and we have found computing graduates more useful in our work than the best young statistics graduates. (This situation is slowly improving as more mathematics-statistics graduates are being pursuaded, often not by their teachers, to take substantial Computer Science options).

The summation of these strands is seen in our programs MASS (Microcomputer Applied Statistics System) and LOLITA (LOg-LInear Table Analysis). Designed by statisticians, with considerable input on computing matters (and much hack work) by computer experts, using the Pascal programming language in general, and the Pascal MT+ system for the overlaying and arithmetic coprocessor access on microcomputers. We have after three man years over 30000 lines of working code, of mostly professional quality; portable over Z80, 8088-6 processors and their various operating systems, and some mini - and mainframes. We do find the system highly supportable - most of any contributor's code is easily read and understood by all others (except when written as pseudo FORTRAN).

It should be pointed out that our success has had its chance elements. Though the use of a structured language was always favoured, C and UCSD-Pascal were original languages investigated, and the overlaying difficulties were then felt limiting. Thus the Pascal MT+ choice, which we found somewhat confusing at first (and still find tedious), was virtually forced on us since it was always clear that it would do what was wanted. Now it will be possible to increase the program MASS by a factor of four (if we have the stamina) in MT+ before a new system becomes necessary. But if we were starting again, Modula-2 and ADA would be our leading interests for the programming language,

5. SOME STRUCTURAL DETAILS

We will describe some of the above points more fully by referring to details of the construction of our MASS package (5). This package allows basic statistical computation (descriptive and summary statistics, elementary graphical representations, simple hypotheses testing, probabilities, etc.) with a few feature for more sophisticated analysis (eg. multi-dimensional table formulation, log-linear modelling, missing value AOVs). We are currently working on more extensive modules reflecting our own needs as consultant statisticians in mostly medical and agricultural areas (eg. survival modelling, non-linear modelling, best linear and non-linear subset identification, general AOV). Thus the program is already large (24000 lines) and growing, and overlaying is a necessity even on many mainframes.

The overlay structure is indicated in Table 2 below. The procedures are grouped into four main groups.

1) Machine dependent and other non-standard Pascal procedures. These procedures handle file, bit and string manipulations, and double precision arithmetic. The former procedures are only 40 lines in total, and are the only code to be modified as we move across machine ranges. The double precision procedures are (painful) assembly language, required only for the Z80 version (we could have done these more easily in Fortran, but copyright problems were at the time threatening).

   None of these dependent routines are directly called in the body of the code, but via a dummy in the library. This double call is considered a small overhead for the advantages of portability gained. The double precision routines are called from only two procedures, and all of this disappears for the larger machines.

2) The root module routines, held permanently in RAM. These include most of the user interface, and the accesses to the applications procedures.

3) The library routines, which are separately compiled and called in many applications procedures. It was not practical to put all these in the root module, but their frequent use meant that many copies were needed over the various applications. Since they are compiled only once, and linked often, they do not multiply in the source code. Of course there is no confusion in calls to the various copies of a procedure - each is effectively internal to the current calling module.

4) The modules for the various applications. Each module consists of a number of standard Pascal procedures, and is bound together by the non-standard overlay linker interface. Some are sketched in the Table. It is seen that the standard and non-standard code are never actually mixed on the source files, but that the overlay module code calls in, by the $INCLUDE macro, each standard procedure wanted in that overlay. The scheme is really quite simple and logical, and our only complaint is the need to specify the overlay area number at compile time. Overlay changes then require recompilation and relinking, a major waste of time in the early stages of putting the system together.

The result is however quite satisfactory and we can link in new complete procedures, even with further nested overlaying in a matter of hours in the first instance. We await contributions!

As we progress to minis and mainframes, the overlay code falls away, leaving for example, the VAX module which consists only of $INCLUDE statements.

6) CONCLUSIONS

We have argued that statisticians should be more concerned with supplying statistical software for small machines. A scheme by which some of the limitations can be satisfactorily circumvented is indicated. We could also argue directly for the use of structured computing languages in all future statistical work, but will leave that topic to unfolding events. Suffice it to say that we have been most helped by the use of recursion at several points - it produced compact and understandable code and is efficient if properly done, contrary to often stated objections. It also facilitates new statistical searching procedures, as in LOLITA (6).

7) ACKNOWLEDGEMENTS

It is a pleasure to acknowledge the help, work and influence of my colleagues in the MASS project - Jens Poulsen, Kim Wearne, John Henstridge (UWA) and Tony Greenfield (Queen's Uni. Belfast). Very special thanks must go to our wives and families, putting up with our absences secreted for hundreds of hours with our machines. There are also many contributions from statisticians and computer scientists from many institutions worldwide. Even our unfriendly critics have helped much. Further particular acknowledgement must be made to Caspar Boon, our MASS organising programmer, whose influence and work has united the many strands of the package. He and his computing mentors have clearly shown the statisticians how many things must be done.

Procedure Group	Examples
Compiler/System Dependent	open-file set-a-bit length-string
Library procedures (Wanted in many modules)	t-proby ascii-to-real prompt-integer normal-deviate logit-p
Root module (Procedures wanted at all times)	parse-line prompt-file-name process-data-case menu-help
Application drivers (1st overlay level code and data store)	aov-drive xtab-drive correln-drive ttest-drive
Applications (i) AOV (level 2 procedures)	aov-1-read aov-2-calc aov-print
(ii) REGN/ CORRLN (level 2 & 3 procedures)	correln-mx-form invert-mx find-residuals
(iii) XTAB (level 2 & 3 procedures)	get-table-indexes variable-names calc-sizes print-with-margins

Module Sketches

```
module main
external [16] ttest-drive
external [17]   aov-drive

..

$I parse-line
$I prompt-integer

..

module-end.
```

```
module aov-drive
external [37] aov1-read
external [40] aov2-calc

..

$I aov-tables-allocate
$I aov-print-2

..

module-end.
```

```
module correln-mx-form
external [21] helmert

..

$I cross-products-calc
$I print-incidences

..

module-end.
```

Table 2. Structure of the MASS package overlays

8) REFERENCES

[1] James, E.B., Microcomputers: the coming revolution in Statistics. Proc. 44 ISI Conference, Madrid, 213-225 (1983).

[2] Lachenbruch, P.A., Statistical Programs for Microcomputers, Byte, 260-270 (November, 1983).

[3] Cable, D. and Rowe, B., Software for Statistical and Survey Analysis. Report for the Study Group on Computers in Survey Analysis, Central Statistical Office, London (1983).

[4] Pascal MT+ (Vers. 5.5) Manual. Digital Research Institute, California (1981).

[5] Hentridge, J.D., Murphy, B.P., Poulsen, J.C., Wearne, K.L. Mass User Manual. Western Australian Regional Computing Centre, Nedlands, W.A. (1984).

[6] Murphy, B.P., LOLITA User Manual. Raine Medical Statistics Unit, University of Western Australia (1982).

Z80 is a trade mark of Zilog Inc.

8086, 8087, 8088 are trademarks of Intel Corp.

MT+ and CP/M are trademarks of Digital Research Institute.

VAX is a trademark of Digital Equipment Corp.

MASS is a copyright product of Westat Associates W.A.

LOLITA is a copyright product of University of Western Australia and B.P. Murphy.

M68000 is a trademark of Motorola Semiconductor Corporation.

Unix is a trademark of Bell Laboratories.

Reliability of Computer Software and Computing Networks

Organizer: *Nozer D. Singpurwalla, The George Washington University*

Invited Presentations:

A Bayes Empirical Bayes Approach for (Software) Reliability Growth, *Michio Horigome, Tokyo University of Mercantile Marine, Nozer D. Singpurwalla, The George Washington University, and Refik Soyer, Tokyo University of Mercantile Marine*

Bayesian Inference for the Weibull Process with Applications to Assessing Software Reliability Growth and Predicting Software Failures, *Jerzy Kyparisis, Florida International University, and Nozer D. Singpurwalla, The George Washington University*

COMPUTER SCIENCE AND STATISTICS:
The Interface, L. Billard (ed.)

A BAYES EMPIRICAL BAYES APPROACH FOR (SOFTWARE) RELIABILITY GROWTH

Michio Horigome, Nozer D. Singpurwalla[1] and Refik Soyer[2]

Tokyo University of Mercantile Marine, Tokyo, Japan;
The George Washington University, Washington, D.C., U.S.A.

In this paper we introduce a simple type of model for describing reliability growth or decay, and show that an appropriate transformation reduces our model to a random coefficient autoregressive process of order 1. Our model thus fits into the general framework of Empirical Bayes problems; however, we take a proper Bayesian approach for inference by viewing the situation as a Bayes Empirical Bayes problem. We illustrate the usefulness of our approach by applying it to some real life data on software reliability testing, and argue that our model and its analysis provide us with useful information about software reliability.

1. INTRODUCTION, BACKGROUND, AND OVERVIEW

A complex newly developed system such as a piece of software, undergoes several stages of testing before it is put into operation. After each stage of testing, corrections and modifications are made to the system, with the hope of increasing its reliability (failure free performance). This procedure is termed *reliability growth*, and is important enough to be codified as MIL-HBK-189 by the U.S. Department of Defense. It is important to recognize that the term reliability growth is a misnomer, and that it may not be an appropriate description of what may actually be happening to the system. It is possible that a particular modification, or series of modifications, could lead to a deterioration in performance of the system. However, the intent of the modifications is to improve performance, and thus the term in question continues to be used. Irrespective of the terminology used, the important statistical issue is how to model and how to describe the changes in the performance of the system as a result of the modifications. The final goal is to be able to predict the behavior of the system after the last modification, so that a decision maker can either continue the test-modify cycle, or terminate it, and put the system into final operation.

To introduce some notation, let $1,2,\ldots,t$ denote the various stages of testing, where the testing at a particular stage follows a modification to the system at that stage. At each stage we may test a single copy of the system, or several copies, depending on the situation at hand. Let X_t denote the life length of the system at the t-th stage of testing. Having observed X_t, we would like to be able to:

(a) determine whether the latest modification, i.e., the one at stage t, has been beneficial;

(b) determine whether our policy of deciding upon the nature of the modifications and implementing them has been such that there is an overall growth (or decay) in reliability; and

(c) make uncertainty statements about X_{t+1}, the life length of the system after the next modification (i.e., obtain the predictive distribution of X_{t+1}).

In addressing the above issues it seems reasonable that we take into consideration all the knowledge that we have about the system, both due to the physical nature of the modifications and the results of all the previous tests. Furthermore, given the nature of the reliability growth process, it is also reasonable to assume that the reliability at the t-th stage is related to the reliability at the previous stages.

In view of the above, the reliability growth process can therefore be viewed as a time series, with the various stages of testing serving as the indices of time. A Box-Jenkins (1970) method for analyzing reliability growth data has been proposed by Singpurwalla (1978), in recognition of the above notion. Other approaches for modelling reliability growth involve the use of nonhomogeneous Poisson processes, and these are referenced in Kyparisis and Singpurwalla (1984). A Bayesian scheme involving notions of isotonic regression has been proposed by Singpurwalla (1982) for estimating reliability growth under exponentially distributed lifetimes.

In this paper, we propose a simple *power law*, which relates the lifetimes from one stage to the next, as a model for describing the reliability growth process. Our model is simple and intuitively believable, yet realistic, and recognizes the time series nature of the reliability growth process. Furthermore, it performs reasonably well when applied to some real life data on software reliability. A logarithmic transformation reduces our model to an autoregressive process of order 1. The special feature here is our allowance of the autoregressive coefficient to change from stage to stage, and our assumption that the coefficients over all stages constitute a sample from a distribution in the sense of what is known as an "empirical Bayes" setup [see, for example, Morris (1983)]. Our analysis of the model is of course fully Bayesian in the sense of Deely and Lindley's (1981) "Bayes empirical Bayes." Since the autoregressive coefficient at stage t is also the power coefficient in the power law, we are able to give a motivation for the need of an empirical Bayes setup, in the context of describing the reliability growth process. To facilitate our analysis we have to make some distributional assumptions. For this, we find it most convenient, and also reasonable, to assume that the life lengths X_t, t = 1,2,..., are lognormally distributed.

First order autoregressive models with random coefficients have been considered before in the economics and statistics literatures, by Swamy (1971), Anderson (1978), and Liu and Tiao (1980). However, the statistical paradigm, and/or the method of analysis considered by the above, is different from that considered here. The motivation for reliability growth modelling is of course new.

In Section 2 we present our model and give a motivation for it in the context of describing reliability growth. In Section 3 we present some key results on inference for our model which are of interest to us from the point of view of our intended application. In a later paper by Horigome, Singpurwalla, and Soyer (1984), we shall present details on the development of our results, an interpretation of our results, their relationships to results from similar models, and their use in forecasting and updating forecasts. There we shall also show the relationship between our model and the Kalman filter model [see, for example, Meinhold and Singpurwalla (1983)], and argue that the latter is a special case of the former. In Section 4 we show how our model performs when applied to some real life data on software failures and comment on its potential use for monitoring software reliability.

2. A POWER LAW MODEL FOR RELIABILITY GROWTH

We recall from the notation of Section 1 that X_t denotes the time to failure of the system at stage t, *after* the t-th modification to it is made. Let X_0 denote the time to failure of the system when it is tested for the very first time, that is, before we attempt to make any modification to it. Also, we have assumed that X_t is lognormal for all t, t = 0,1,2,....

Since modifications to the system typically involve minor but important changes to its design and configuration, it is reasonable to assume that X_t will be related to X_{t-1}, and it is hoped it will be larger than X_{t-1}. Of course, it is also possible that the design changes could be poorly conceived so that X_t is equal to X_{t-1}, or even smaller than X_{t-1}. To reflect these features, we may write

$$X_t = X_{t-1}^{\theta_t}, \text{ for } t = 1,2,..., \tag{2.1}$$

where θ_t is a coefficient. Relationship (2.1) is the familiar power law, which has proved to be useful in reliability and biometry. Without loss of generality we shall assume that $X_t \geqslant 1$, for all t, a requirement easily achieved by introducing a known threshold parameter for the lognormal distribution of the X_t's. Then, values of θ_t greater than 1 would describe growth in reliability, and those less than 1 its decay. To introduce some uncertainty to our specification of the power law as a model for reliability growth, or to account for the possibility of some slight deviation from it, either systematic or sudden, we introduce a multiplicative error term δ_t, and generalize (2.1) by writing

$$X_t = X_{t-1}^{\theta_t} \delta_t . \tag{2.2}$$

Technical convenience demands that we also assume δ_t to be lognormal with known parameters, say 0 and σ_1^2.

The special feature of our model arises because of the fact that we allow the power coefficient θ_t to change from stage to stage. We are able to offer several arguments to justify the changing nature of the power coefficient, the most plausible one being that initial modifications to the system are typically due to errors in workmanship and tend to show more improvement in reliability than the later ones. Thus the sequence $\{\theta_t\}$ should be stochastically decreasing in t, with values of θ_t greater than 1 for small t, and closer to 1 for large t. However, this description of θ_t may not always be realistic, because design alterations, typically dictated by changes in the system requirements or changes in the political and economic climate, occur at any stage, and could make the system worse. Thus in practice, it is often not possible to assign a time pattern to the θ_t's. In the context of software reliability, for example, the process of correcting an error at any stage could introduce new errors, making the software worse than before. In view of this, it seems most reasonable to regard the θ_t's as a sample from some distribution, say G, and with density function g. That is, each θ_t has density $g(\theta_t)$, t = 1,2,....

If we take the natural logarithms on both sides of (2.2), and let $\varepsilon_t = \log\delta_t$, t = 1,2,..., then our power law model for reliability growth becomes

$$Y_t = \theta_t Y_{t-1} + \varepsilon_t , \tag{2.3}$$

where $Y_t \overset{\text{def}}{=} \log X_t$ and ε_t are both normally distributed, the latter with mean 0 and variance σ_1^2. It is clear from the above that the sequence $\{Y_t\}$, $t = 1,2,\ldots$, is described by a *first order autoregressive process with a random coefficient* θ_t. In what follows, we shall focus attention on the variables Y_t.

2.1 The Bayes Empirical Bayes Setup

Having observed $Y_1 = y_1, Y_2 = y_2, \ldots, Y_t = y_t$, the empirical Bayes approach would call for the empirical estimation of g by, say, $\hat{g}$, and then using $\hat{g}$, make an inference about θ_t using the Bayes formula [Deely and Lindley (1981)].

A fully Bayesian attitude would be to describe g probabilistically, by indexing it by a vector of hyperparameters, say $\underset{\sim}{\lambda}$, by specifying $g(\theta|\underset{\sim}{\lambda})$ the density of θ given $\underset{\sim}{\lambda}$, and by specifying $\pi(\underset{\sim}{\lambda})$ the prior density of $\underset{\sim}{\lambda}$. This is the attitude that we wish to take here. Accordingly, our first task is to specify $g(\theta|\underset{\sim}{\lambda})$, and in what follows we motivate our choice of $g(\theta|\underset{\sim}{\lambda})$.

From (2.2) we note that all values of $\theta_t > 1$ imply growth, that $\theta_t = 1$ implies neither growth nor decay, and that all values of $\theta_t < 1$ imply decay. When $\theta_t < 0$, the decay in reliability is drastic and is likely to happen when the modification is a major design change. The case of $\theta_t = 0$ is interesting, because from (2.3) we see that $Y_t = \varepsilon_t$ implies that Y_t does not depend on Y_{t-1}, and that it is best described by ε_t, where ε_t is normal with mean 0 and variance σ_1^2. When $\theta_t = 0$ for all t, (2.3) implies that the sequence $\{Y_t\}$ is a "band limited white noise process" in the sense of Jenkins and Watts (1968, p. 149). If this were to happen, none of the previous models for describing reliability growth would be applicable. It would be interesting to see if any reliability growth data could be described by such a process.

It is clear from the above that the coefficients θ_t can take any value in the range $(-\infty,+\infty)$. In light of our previous distributional assumptions, it is reasonable to assume that the density of θ is normal with a mean, say λ, and a variance, say σ_2^2. When σ_2^2 is small, values of λ close to 0 would tend to emphasize a decay in reliability, whereas those in the vicinity of 1 and above 1 would tend to emphasize reliability growth. The value of σ_2^2 would reflect our views about the consistency of our policies regarding modifications and design changes. For example, some design changes could be much more elaborate and involved than others. When this happens σ_2^2 would tend to be large. If the magnitudes of the design changes are more or less of the same order, say all of them are minor, then σ_2^2 would tend to be small. To simplify matters, we shall treat σ_2^2 as being fixed but known, and complete our specification of the model by assuming λ to be normal with a known mean μ and a known variance σ_3^2. In our subsequent paper we shall treat λ as fixed but known, and assume a prior distribution for σ_2^2. Because of our discussion about the influence of the possible values of λ on the growth or decay of reliability, an innocuous choice for μ is .5. The value σ_3^2 should reflect the strength of our belief about our choice of μ.

Thus, to summarize, our model for the growth or decay of reliability, for $Y_t = \log X_t$, $t = 1,2,\ldots$, is of the form:

$$Y_t = \theta_t Y_{t-1} + \varepsilon_t\ , \text{ with}$$

$$\varepsilon_t \sim N(0,\sigma_1^2)\ , \qquad \sigma_1^2 \text{ known,}$$

$$\theta_t \sim N(\lambda,\sigma_2^2)\ , \qquad \sigma_2^2 \text{ known, and}$$

$$\lambda \sim N(\mu,\sigma_3^2)\ , \qquad \mu \text{ and } \sigma_3^2 \text{ known.} \tag{2.4}$$

In what follows, we shall let $y^{(t)} = (y_1,\ldots,y_t)$, and given $y^{(T)}$ our objective is to make inference about θ_T, λ, Y_{T+1}, and if necessary $Y_T^* \overset{def}{=} \log X_T^*$, where X_T^* is the time to failure of another copy of the system.

3. THE KEY RESULTS ON INFERENCE

The emphasis of this paper is a motivation for our model for reliability growth, and its application to some data on software reliability. Thus the details for developing the necessary formulae for inference, and an interpretation of results, have been delegated to our subsequent paper. What we present here is merely a statement of our final results.

For inference about λ and θ_T, given $y^{(T)}$, we use the *law of the extension of the conversation*, Bayes' theorem, and the first order Markov property of our model to obtain the following:

- $$p(\lambda|y^{(T)}) = \frac{1}{\sqrt{2\pi}\,\sigma_T} \exp\left\{-\frac{1}{2}\frac{(\lambda-\mu_T)^2}{\sigma_T^2}\right\}, \tag{3.1}$$

where

$$\mu_T = \left(\frac{\mu}{\sigma_3^2} + \sum_{t=1}^{T} \frac{y_t y_{t-1}}{\omega_{t-1}}\right)\sigma_T^2\ ,$$

$$\sigma_T^2 = \left(\frac{1}{\sigma_3^2} + \sum_{t=1}^{T} \frac{y_{t-1}^2}{\omega_{t-1}}\right)^{-1}, \text{ and}$$

$$\omega_{t-1} = \sigma_2^2 y_{t-1}^2 + \sigma_1^2 .$$

$$\bullet\ p\left(\theta_T | y^{(T)}\right) = \frac{\omega_{T-1}}{\sqrt{2\pi\sigma_1^2\left(\omega_{T-1}\sigma_2^2+\sigma_1^2\sigma_T^2\right)}}$$

$$\times \exp\left\{-\frac{1}{2}\frac{\left(\theta_T - \dfrac{\sigma_1^2\mu_T+\sigma_2^2 y_T y_{T-1}}{\omega_{T-1}}\right)^2}{\sigma_1^2\left(\omega_{T-1}\sigma_2^2+\sigma_1^2\sigma_T^2\right)/\omega_{T-1}^2}\right\}. \quad (3.2)$$

The predictive distribution of Y_{T+1} given $y^{(T)}$ is a normal with mean $\mu_T y_T$ and variance $\sigma_T^2 y_T^2 + \omega_T$. That is,

$$\bullet\ p\left(y_{T+1} | y^{(T)}\right) = \frac{1}{\sqrt{2\pi\left(\sigma_T^2 y_T^2+\omega_T\right)}}$$

$$\times \exp\left\{-\frac{1}{2}\frac{\left(y_{T+1}-\mu_T y_T\right)^2}{\sigma_T^2 y_T^2+\omega_T}\right\}. \quad (3.3)$$

A $(1-\alpha)100\%$ credibility interval for y_{T+1} is therefore given by

$$\mu_T y_T \pm z_{\alpha/2} \sqrt{\sigma_T^2 y_T^2+\omega_T}\ , \quad (3.4)$$

where $z_{\alpha/2}$ is the $(1-\alpha/2)$-th percentile point of a standard normal distribution. Under a squared error loss, $\hat{y}_{T+1} = \mu_T y_T$, the mean of the above predictive distribution, is our point estimator of the next time to failure.

The posterior distribution of θ_{T+1} given $y^{(T)}$ is also a normal:

$$\bullet\ p\left(\theta_{T+1} | y^{(T)}\right) = \frac{1}{\sqrt{2\pi}\sqrt{\sigma_2^2+\sigma_T^2}}$$

$$\times \exp\left\{-\frac{1}{2}\frac{\left(\theta_{T+1}-\mu_T\right)^2}{\sigma_2^2+\sigma_T^2}\right\}. \quad (3.5)$$

The above results can also be used for obtaining the predictive distribution of Y_{T+j} for $j = 1, 2, \ldots$. These results are not given here since they are not used in Section 4.

4. APPLICATION OF THE POWER LAW MODEL TO MUSA'S DATA ON COMPUTER SOFTWARE FAILURES

Musa (1979) has published several sets of data on the failure times (actually execution times) of computer software which undergoes a debugging process. We shall apply the model and the inference procedures of this paper to see how our model performs on some of these data, and to see what insights about reliability growth we can obtain from our analysis.

In Table 1, column 2, we present values of $Y_t = \log_e X_t$, $t = 0,1,\ldots,100$, where X_t are the execution times given by Musa in his data set labelled as "System 40 data." In column 3 we present the values of $\hat{Y}_t$, the means of our predictive distributions of Y_t [see Equation (3.3)], for $t = 2,3,\ldots,100$. In column 4 we present the 95% credibility intervals for Y_t, $t = 2,\ldots,100$. A comparison of the entries in columns 2 and 3 shows that our model performs quite well for predicting the (logarithms of) the next execution times. A visual perspective of the predicted and actual times gives a better feel for the performance of our model -- this is given in Figure 1. In undertaking the computations which lead us to the above results, the values of μ, σ_1, σ_2, and σ_3 that we choose are .5, 1.0, .16, and 1.0, respectively. Given the large amount of data that we have, our final conclusions are not too sensitive to the choice of these values.

In Table 2, we show $E\left(\theta_t | y^{(t)}\right)$, the means of the posterior distributions of θ_t given $y^{(t)}$, $t = 1,\ldots,100$, and $E\left(\lambda | y^{(t)}\right)$, the mean of the posterior distribution of λ given $y^{(t)}$, $t = 1, \ldots,100$, for the data of Table 1 and the analysis described above; see Equations (3.2) and (3.1), respectively. As stated in Section 2, the value $E\left(\theta_t | y^{(t)}\right)$ gives us information about the reliability growth or decay from stage $(t-1)$ to stage t. An overall impression for the growth or decay of reliability can be obtained by plotting $E\left(\theta_t | y^{(t)}\right)$ vs. t, and this is shown in Figure 2. A more formal impression about growth or decay can be obtained by looking at $E\left(\lambda | y^{(t)}\right)$ for $t = 1,2,\ldots,100$. If $E\left(\lambda | y^{(t)}\right)$ tends to be greater than 1, for most of the values of t, especially the larger values, then we may conclude that there is an overall growth in reliability. For the data of Table 1, this appears to be the case. A plot of $E\left(\lambda | y^{(t)}\right)$, for $t = 1,\ldots,100$, is given in Figure 3 -- also shown for perspective is the value $\lambda = 1$. We

Table 1:
Data on Software Failures taken from Musa (1979)
(System 40 Data)

t	Y(t)	Predicted Value of Y(t)	95% Probability Intervals for Y(t)
0	5.7683		
1	9.5743		
2	9.1050	14.11	(3.33,24.91)
3	7.9655	11.12	(2.11,20.13)
4	8.6482	8.83	(1.32,16.34)
5	9.9887	9.54	(1.67,17.42)
6	10.1962	11.12	(2.28,19.96)
7	11.6399	11.21	(2.31,20.08)
8	11.6275	12.85	(2.87,22.84)
9	6.4922	12.68	(2.79,22.58)
10	7.9010	6.71	(0.97,12.42)
11	10.2679	8.29	(1.48,15.09)
12	7.6839	10.99	(2.34,19.65)
13	8.8905	8.03	(1.43,14.60)
14	9.2933	9.35	(1.84,16.86)
15	8.3499	9.77	(1.96,17.58)
16	9.0431	8.70	(1.64,15.75)
17	9.6027	9.44	(1.86,17.02)
18	9.3736	10.03	(2.03,18.04)
19	8.5869	9.75	(1.94,17.57)
20	8.7877	8.88	(1.69,16.07)
21	8.7794	9.08	(1.75,16.42)
22	8.0469	9.06	(1.74,16.39)
23	10.8459	8.27	(1.51,15.02)
24	9.7416	11.28	(2.37,20.02)
25	7.5443	10.07	(2.07,18.13)
26	8.5941	7.73	(1.38,14.08)
27	11.0399	8.84	(1.69,15.99)
28	10.1196	11.45	(2.42,20.50)
29	10.1786	10.46	(2.14,18.78)
30	5.8944	10.51	(2.15,18.87)
31	9.5460	6.02	(0.90,11.09)
32	9.6197	9.88	(2.01,17.74)
33	10.3852	9.96	(2.03,17.86)
34	10.6301	10.76	(2.25,19.26)
35	8.3333	11.01	(2.31,19.69)
36	11.3150	8.57	(1.65,15.48)
37	9.4871	11.73	(2.51,20.94)
38	8.1391	9.78	(1.99,17.58)
39	8.6713	8.37	(1.60,15.11)
40	6.4615	8.91	(1.75,16.07)
41	6.4615	6.60	(1.10,12.09)
42	7.6955	6.59	(1.10,12.08)
43	4.7005	8.16	(1.54,14.79)
44	10.0024	4.78	(0.56, 8.98)
45	11.0129	10.36	(2.19,18.54)
46	10.8621	11.43	(2.48,20.38)
47	9.4372	11.26	(2.42,20.10)
48	6.6644	9.75	(2.01,17.48)
49	9.2294	6.85	(1.20,12.47)
50	8.9671	9.53	(1.96,17.12)
51	10.3534	9.25	(1.88,16.62)
52	10.0998	10.70	(2.27,19.14)
53	12.6078	10.43	(2.19,18.67)
54	7.1546	13.08	(2.90,23.25)
55	10.0033	7.36	(1.36,13.35)
56	9.8601	10.35	(2.19,18.50)
57	7.8675	10.20	(2.15,18.24)

Table 1: *continued*

t	Y(t)	Predicted Value of Y(t)	95% Probability Intervals for Y(t)
58	10.5757	8.20	(1.57,14.63)
59	10.9294	10.94	(2.35,19.54)
60	10.6604	11.31	(2.44,20.18)
61	12.4972	11.02	(2.36,19.68)
62	11.3745	12.95	(2.87,23.02)
63	11.9158	11.76	(2.55,20.96)
64	9.5750	12.32	(2.70,21.95)
65	10.4504	9.87	(2.04,17.69)
66	10.5866	10.78	(2.29,19.27)
67	12.7201	10.92	(2.32,19.51)
68	12.5982	13.15	(2.91,23.39)
69	12.0859	13.02	(2.87,23.16)
70	12.2766	12.47	(2.72,22.22)
71	11.9602	12.66	(2.77,22.56)
72	12.0246	12.33	(2.68,21.90)
73	9.2873	12.39	(2.69,22.10)
74	12.4950	9.54	(1.94,17.13)
75	14.5569	12.88	(2.83,22.95)
76	13.3279	15.04	(3.38,26.70)
77	8.9464	13.74	(3.05,24.45)
78	14.7824	9.19	(1.85,16.51)
79	14.8969	15.29	(3.46,27.13)
80	12.1399	15.40	(3.48,27.33)
81	9.7981	12.52	(2.74,22.30)
82	12.0907	10.07	(2.10,18.05)
83	13.0977	12.48	(2.72,22.21)
84	13.3680	13.52	(2.99,24.03)
85	12.7206	13.79	(3.06,24.52)
86	14.1920	13.12	(2.88,23.33)
87	11.3704	14.64	(3.27,26.01)
88	12.2021	11.69	(2.51,20.88)
89	12.2793	12.56	(2.74,22.38)
90	11.3667	12.64	(2.76,22.52)
91	11.3923	11.68	(2.50,20.86)
92	14.4113	11.70	(2.51,20.90)
93	8.3333	14.85	(3.32,26.38)
94	8.0709	8.54	(1.68,15.40)
95	12.2021	8.27	(1.61,14.93)
96	12.7831	12.56	(2.75,22.38)
97	13.1585	13.17	(2.89,23.43)
98	12.7530	13.55	(2.99,24.10)
99	10.3533	13.13	(2.88,23.27)
100	12.4897	10.64	(2.24,10.03)

observe that $E(\lambda|y^{(t)})$, for $t = 1,\ldots,100$, tends to be over 1, although not by much, implying the tendency for an overall growth in reliability. Furthermore, $E(\lambda|y^{(t)})$ appears to settle down soon at the value 1.03 for $t \geqslant 19$, implying some type of consistency in the policy which influences the growth in reliability.

The situation with Musa's data set labelled "System 3 Data" is quite different. In Table 3 we show the values of $E(\theta_t|y^{(t)})$, for $t = 1, \ldots,37$, and $E(\lambda|y^{(t)})$, for $t = 1,\ldots,37$. The

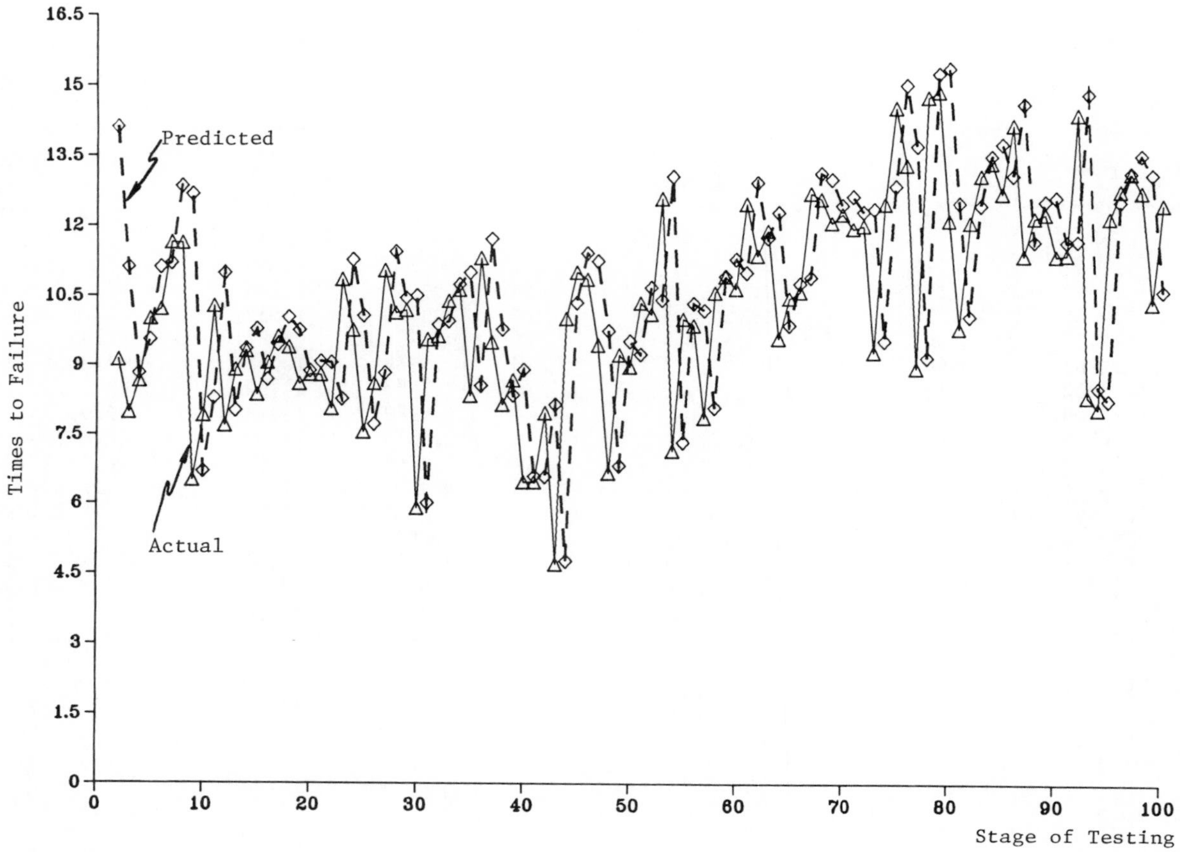

Figure 1: A comparison of the actual and predicted values of times to software failure

Table 2: Posterior Means of θ_t and λ for System 40 Data

t	$E(\theta_t \mid y^{(t)})$	$E(\lambda \mid y^{(t)})$
1	1.631	1.475
2	0.968	1.222
3	0.891	1.109
4	1.087	1.104
5	1.152	1.114
6	1.025	1.098
7	1.140	1.104
8	1.003	1.091
9	0.579	1.031
10	1.195	1.048
11	1.279	1.071
12	0.765	1.044
13	1.147	1.052
14	1.046	1.051
15	0.908	1.041
16	1.080	1.044
17	1.061	1.045
18	0.980	1.041
19	0.924	1.034
20	1.024	1.034

Table 2: *continued*

t	$E(\theta_t \mid y^{(t)})$	$E(\lambda \mid y^{(t)})$
21	1.002	1.032
22	0.925	1.027
23	1.321	1.041
24	0.905	1.035
25	0.790	1.024
26	1.128	1.029
27	1.265	1.038
28	0.922	1.033
29	1.007	1.033
30	0.604	1.017
31	1.530	1.035
32	1.009	1.034
33	1.077	1.035
34	1.024	1.035
35	0.797	1.028
36	1.331	1.037
37	0.847	1.031
38	0.869	1.027
39	1.062	1.028
40	0.766	1.021
41	1.003	1.020
42	1.206	1.025

Table 2: *continued*

t	$E(\theta_t \| y^{(t)})$	$E(\lambda \| y^{(t)})$
43	0.628	1.015
44	1.887	1.036
45	1.097	1.038
46	0.989	1.037
47	0.877	1.033
48	0.727	1.026
49	1.342	1.033
50	0.976	1.032
51	1.146	1.034
52	0.979	1.033
53	1.236	1.037
54	0.585	1.028
55	1.359	1.035
56	0.989	1.034
57	0.812	1.030
58	1.316	1.035
59	1.034	1.035
60	0.978	1.034
61	1.165	1.036
62	0.915	1.034
63	1.047	1.034

Table 2: *continued*

t	$E(\theta_t \| y^{(t)})$	$E(\lambda \| y^{(t)})$
64	0.813	1.031
65	1.088	1.032
66	1.014	1.031
67	1.193	1.034
68	0.992	1.033
69	0.962	1.032
70	1.016	1.032
71	0.977	1.031
72	1.006	1.031
73	0.783	1.027
74	1.324	1.031
75	1.160	1.033
76	0.919	1.032
77	0.683	1.027
78	1.608	1.035
79	1.009	1.034
80	0.821	1.032
81	0.816	1.029
82	1.222	1.031
83	1.081	1.032
84	1.021	1.032

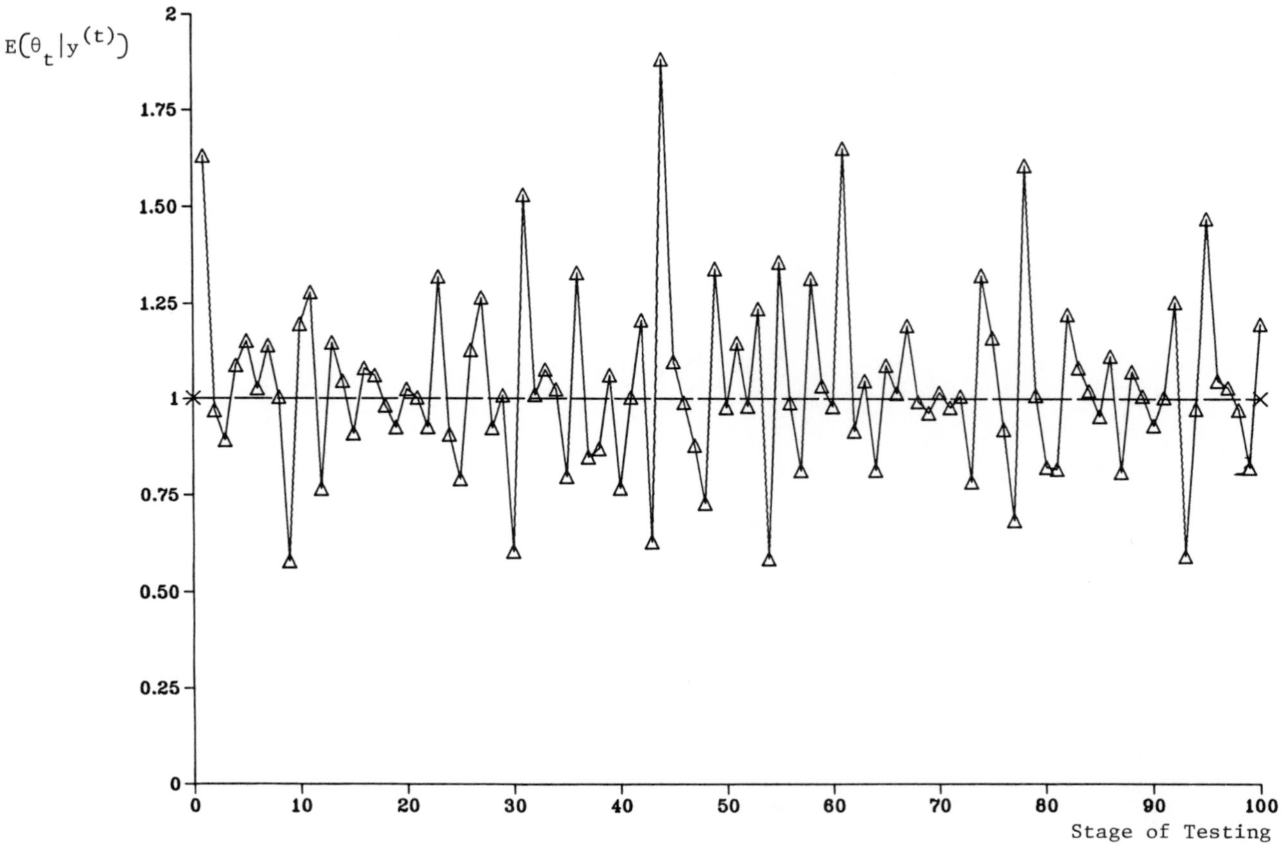

Figure 2: Posterior mean of θ_t

Table 2: *continued*

t	$E(\theta_t \| y^{(t)})$	$E(\lambda \| y^{(t)})$
85	0.954	1.031
86	1.113	1.032
87	0.808	1.029
88	1.071	1.029
89	1.007	1.029
90	0.930	1.028
91	1.003	1.028
92	1.254	1.030

Table 2: *continued*

t	$E(\theta_t \| y^{(t)})$	$E(\lambda \| y^{(t)})$
93	0.591	1.025
94	0.973	1.025
95	1.470	1.030
96	1.047	1.030
97	1.029	1.030
98	0.971	1.029
99	0.820	1.027
100	1.197	1.029

values of μ, σ_1^2, σ_2^2 and σ_3^2 that are chosen are 0.5, 1.0, 1.0, and 0.16, respectively. We first remark that $E(\theta_t|y^{(t)})$ fluctuates quite a bit between values greater than and smaller than 1. For t = 28, the value of $E(\theta_t|y^{(t)})$ is as large as 3.825 -- the smallest value of $E(\theta_t|y^{(t)})$ is .018. The value $E(\lambda|y^{(t)})$ also fluctuates quite a bit for quite some time and settles down to a value close to 1 only after $t > 28$. In addition to the above, $\hat{Y}_t$, the means of the predictive distribution of Y_t, do not do quite as well either -- these are not shown. Thus it appears that this data set cannot be described by our model.

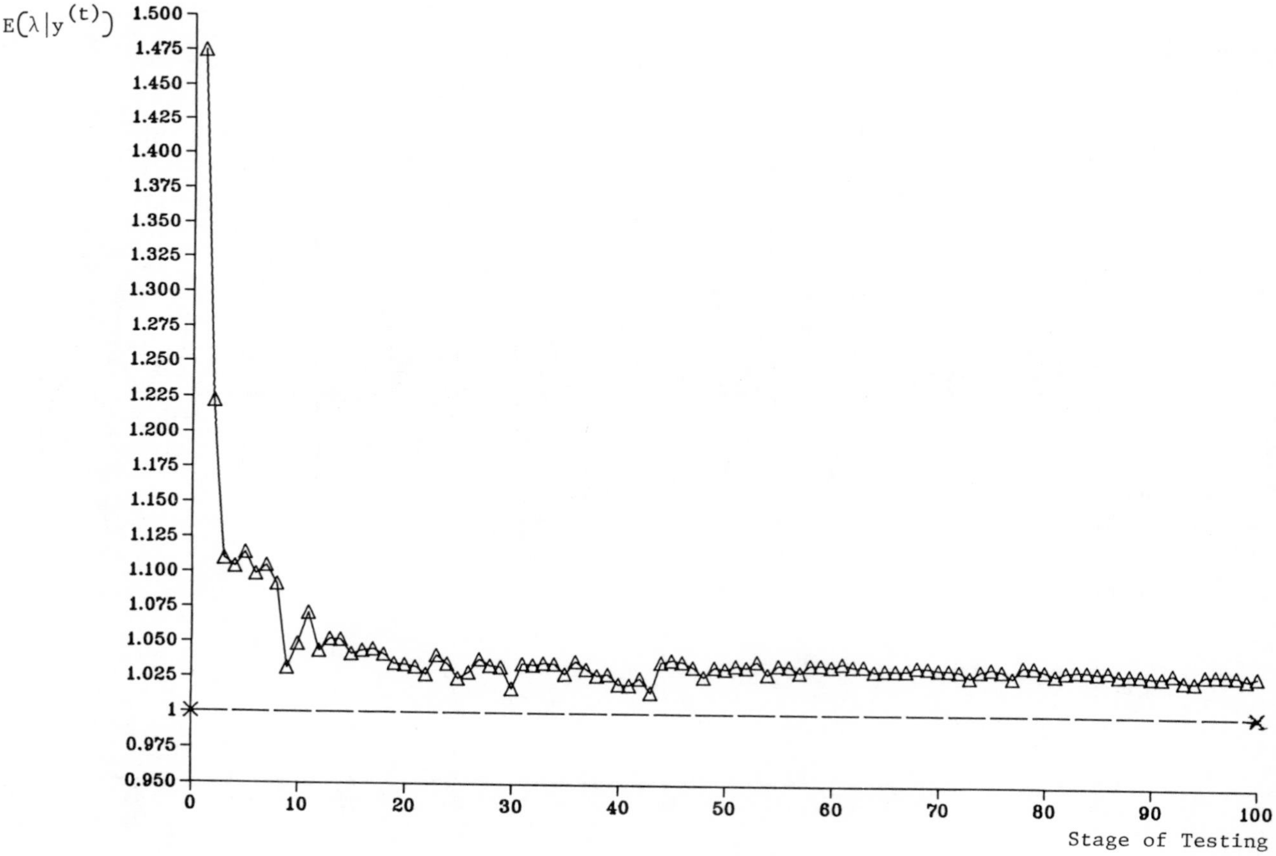

Figure 3: Posterior mean of λ

Table 3:
Posterior Means of θ_t and λ for Musa's System 3 Data

t	$E(\theta_t \mid y^{(t)})$	$E(\lambda \mid y^{(t)})$
1	0.018	0.434
2	0.434	0.434
3	1.410	0.520
4	1.001	0.572
5	0.921	0.607
6	1.392	0.678
7	0.392	0.654
8	0.961	0.678
9	1.558	0.741
10	0.860	0.749
11	1.070	0.769
12	1.477	0.811
13	1.099	0.827
14	0.527	0.811
15	1.743	0.859
16	0.811	0.857
17	0.794	0.854
18	1.469	0.881
19	0.991	0.886
20	0.435	0.867
21	2.048	0.914
22	1.253	0.927
23	0.956	0.928
24	1.164	0.936
25	0.801	0.932
26	1.203	0.941
27	0.231	0.918
28	3.825	1.008
29	0.958	1.007
30	1.145	1.011
31	0.688	1.002
32	1.246	1.008
33	0.820	1.003
34	1.324	1.012
35	1.084	1.014
36	0.942	1.012
37	0.891	1.009

FOOTNOTES

[1] and [2] The work of these authors was supported by the Office of Naval Research under Contract N00014-77-C-0263, Project NR 042-372, and by the Army Research Office under Grant DAAG 29-83-K-0013, with the George Washington University.

ACKNOWLEDGMENT

Conversations with Dr. Richard J. Meinhold are gratefully acknowledged.

REFERENCES

[1] Anderson, T.W., Repeated measurements on autoregressive processes, J. Amer. Statist. Assoc. 73 (1978) 371-378.

[2] Box, G.E.P., Time Series Analysis: forecasting and control (Holden-Day, San Francisco, 1970).

[3] Deely, J.J. and Lindley, D.V., Bayes empirical Bayes, J. Amer. Statist. Assoc. 76 (1981) 833-841.

[4] Horigome, M., Singpurwalla, N.D., and Soyer, R., Bayes empirical Bayes approach to random coefficient autoregressive processes, Dept. of Oper. Res., George Washington Univ., paper in progress (1984).

[5] Jenkins, G.W. and Watts, D.G., Spectral Analysis and Its Applications (Holden-Day, San Francisco, 1968).

[6] Kyparisis, J. and Singpurwalla, N.D., Bayesian inference for the Weibull process with applications to assessing software reliability growth and predicting software failures, in Computer Science and Statistics: Proceedings of the 16th Symposium on the Interface (L. Billard, Ed.) (Atlanta, Georgia, March 14-16, 1984).

[7] Liu, L.M. and Tiao, G.C., Random coefficient first-order autoregressive models, J. Econometrics 13 (1980) 305-325.

[8] Meinhold, R.J. and Singpurwalla, N.D., Understanding the Kalman filter, Amer. Statistician 37 (1983) 123-127.

[9] Morris, C.N., Parametric empirical Bayes inference: theory and applications, J. Amer. Statist. Assoc. 78 (1983) 47-65.

[10] Musa, J.D., Software reliability data, deposited in IEEE Computer Society repository (1979).

[11] Singpurwalla, N.D., Estimating reliability growth (or deterioration) using time series analysis, Naval Res. Logist. Quart. 25 (1978) 1-14.

[12] Singpurwalla, N.D., A Bayesian scheme for estimating reliability growth under exponential failures, TIMS Studies in the Management Sciences 19 (1982) 281-296.

[13] Swamy, P.A.V.B., Statistical Inference in Random Coefficient Regression Models (Springer-Verlag, New York, 1971).

COMPUTER SCIENCE AND STATISTICS:
The Interface, L. Billard (ed.)

BAYESIAN INFERENCE FOR THE WEIBULL PROCESS WITH APPLICATIONS TO ASSESSING SOFTWARE RELIABILITY GROWTH AND PREDICTING SOFTWARE FAILURES

Jerzy Kyparisis[1], Florida International University, Miami, Florida
and
Nozer D. Singpurwalla[2], The George Washington University, Washington, D.C.

We present here a Bayesian approach for making inferences about the number of future failures, and the time to next failure, when the process generating failures is assumed to be nonhomogeneous Poisson process with a special type of an intensity function. Two types of scenarios under which the process is observed are considered. We illustrate our approach by considering some real life data on software failures, and point out its usefulness.

1. INTRODUCTION AND OVERVIEW

Over the years, several authors have suggested the use of Poisson processes to assess the reliability growth of complex repairable systems and to predict their failure behavior. See for example Crow (1975), Lee (1978, 1980 a, b), Goel and Okumoto (1979), and Thompson (1981). Inference procedures considered by the above have been sample theoretic, and have predominantly involved a use of the method of maximum likelihood. Even though such approaches may have, in the past, produced reasonable answers, they are from Bayesian point of view deficient, since prior information about the situation being modelled is not considered. Bayesian approaches to inference for nonhomogeneous Poisson processes are to the best of the authors knowledge nonexistant, and this is what is considered here -albeit in a limited manner.

As an illustration of the usefulness of our approach, we address here the question of assessing the reliability growth of software undergoing the debugging process, predicting the number of software failures in a specified interval of time, and specifying the distribution function of the time to the next software failure. In undertaking the above, we consider some real life software failure data.

In a subsequent paper [Kyparisis and Singpurwalla (1984)] we describe an application of our approach to a problem in railroad engineering, where our goal is to predict the number of defects per mile of railroad as a function of the load carried by it (in million gross tons). A novel feature of this application is the use of an engineering model based on some deterministic theories of fatigue and fracture, to specify the required prior distributions.

With either application, the desirability of an individual work station for the analyst and the role of computer graphics to undertake the analysis proposed by us, become evident.

1.1 THE UNDERLYING MODEL

The model considered here is a nonhomogeneous Poisson process with intensity function r(t), where

$$r(t) = (\beta/\alpha)(t/\alpha)^{\beta-1}, \quad t \geq 0 \qquad (1.1)$$

where α and β are (unknown) parameters.

Since r(t) behaves like the failure rate function of a Weibull distribution [Mann, Schafer, and Singpurwalla (1974), p. 184], it is common to refer to this process as a <u>Weibull process</u>.

In many applications of the nonhomogeneous Poisson process, the index t generally denotes time. However, this need not be so. For example, in our railroad engineering example t would denote the million gross tonnage of the load carried by a specified length of the rail. In what follows, we shall, for convenience, always refer to t as the time.

Let N(t) denote the number of occurences of an event (failure in our case) in time (0,t], and let $M(t) \stackrel{def}{=} EN(t)$ be the expectation of N(t). Then, it is well known [Parzen (1962), p.125], that for the above process

$$M(t) \doteq \int_0^t r(u)du = (t/\alpha)^\beta. \quad (1.2)$$

Furthermore, if $N(t_1, t_2)$ denotes the number of failures in time interval $(t_1, t_2]$, $t_2 > t_1$, then $N(t_1, t_2)$ has a Poisson distribution with mean $M(t_1, t_2)$, where

$$M(t_1, t_2) \doteq E[N(t_2)-N(t_1)],$$
$$= (t_2/\alpha)^{\beta}-(t_1/\alpha)^{\beta}. \qquad (1.3)$$

Thus, for any k=0, 1, 2, ...,

$$P(N(t_1, t_2)=k)= e^{-M(t_1, t_2)} (M(t_1, t_2))^k/k!. \qquad (1.4)$$

Having observed the process for some interval of time, say (0,T], our goal is to make uncertainty (probability) statements about: i) N(T, T+h), for some h>0, and ii) the time to the occurrence of the next failure, given the time of occurence of the last failure. This is best achieved by first making some probability statements about α and β; that is, obtaining their posterior distributions.

Recall that N(T, T+h) denotes the number of failures in a future interval of length h. Also, ii) above is often referred to as the predictive distribution of the time to the next failure.

In practice, observation on the process during an interval (0, T] can be undertaken in several ways. We have considered two such ways. In Section 2 we focus attention on the case in which the actual times to failure are not known, but what are observed are the number of failures in several sub-intervals of (0, T]. All the subintervals are assumed disjoint, and they need not be of equal lengths; furthermore, the union of all these subintervals need not be (0, T]. The observation scheme described above is usually necessitated by the physical impracticability of our obtaining the exact t at which failure occurs, as is true in our railroad engineering example.

In Section 3 we consider the case in which the actual times to occurences of the consecutive failures are known, as is true in the case of software failures. The times in question here, are the execution times of the software.

2. ANALYSIS FOR THE CASE OF INTERVAL DATA

Assume that failures occur according to a Weibull process, and let N_i denote the number of failures in a time interval $(t_{i1}, t_{i2}]$, where $t_{i2} > t_{i1}$, and i=1, 2, ..., m. Let n_i be the realization of N_i. Then, from (1.1)-(1.4), it follows that

$$P\{N_i=n_i|\alpha,\beta\}=e^{-\mu_i} (\mu_i)^{n_i}/n_i!, \; n_i=0,1,2,\ldots, \qquad (2.1)$$

where $\mu_i=(t_{i2}/\alpha)^{\beta}-(t_{i1}/\alpha)^{\beta}$, i=1,...,m.

Given $\underline{n}=(n_1,\ldots,n_m)$, the likelihood function of α and β, is

$$L_1(\alpha,\beta;\underline{n}) = \prod_{i=1}^{m} \frac{e^{-\mu_i}\mu_i^{n_i}}{n_i!}$$

$$\alpha \prod_{i=1}^{m} \left[\left(\frac{t_{i2}}{\alpha}\right)^{\beta} - \left(\frac{t_{i1}}{\alpha}\right)^{\beta}\right]^{n_i} \cdot$$

$$\cdot \exp\left[-\left(\frac{t_{i2}}{\alpha}\right)^{\beta} + \left(\frac{t_{i1}}{\alpha}\right)^{\beta}\right]. \qquad (2.2)$$

2.1 PRIOR DISTRIBUTIONS FOR α AND β

The assignment of prior distributions for α and β is by no means a trivial matter. Engineers and scientists do not think in terms of α and β, fictitious constants introduced by the statistician to describe a mechanism which generates the N_i's. It is more reasonable to expect a scientific opinion on M(t) or possibly even $M(t_1, t_2)$, in the form of a personal probability distribution of an expert or a group of experts. This probability distribution is necessarily subjective, but could be based on previous data which the experts may possess. In our railroad engineering example, an engineering fracture mechanics model is used to generate expert opinion, and this is in terms of an empirical distribution for M(t). Recall that t here denotes the million gross tonnage carried by a mile of railroad. Given a probability distribution for M(t), it is possible to deduce a probability distribution for α and β. Methods for eliciting expert opinions, incorporating one's judgement about the quality of the expert opinion, and for combining the opinions of several experts are given by Lindley (1983). An adaptation of such methods for problems in reliability and fault tree analysis, including the situation considered here, is currently under progress. In the meantime, we shall propose the following as suitable prior distributions for α and β, recognizing fully well that these choices are still arbitrary.

Since α is a scale parameter, and since we do not have any specific knowledge about the process generating our failures, it would not be too unreasonable if we assume that α is uniform on $(0,\alpha_0]$, where α_0 is a specified constant. Thus, the probability density function of α is

$$g_0(\alpha)= \frac{1}{\alpha_0}, \quad 0<\alpha \le \alpha_0. \qquad (2.3)$$

The β in (1.1) is a shape parameter whose values determine the growth or the decay of reliability. For example, values of β greater than 1 imply an increase in the frequency of failures with time, and this is characteristic of decay in reliability. When $\beta=1$, the underlying process is a homogeneous Poisson process-this is characteristic of neither a growth nor a decay in reliability. When $\beta<1$, there is reliability growth.

In view of the above, a suitable choice for the prior probability density function of β is a beta density with support on (β_1, β_2), where $\beta_1 \geq 0$. Thus we propose

$$g_o(\beta) = \frac{\Gamma(k_1+k_2)}{\Gamma(k_1)\Gamma(k_2)} \quad \frac{(\beta-\beta_1)^{k_1-1}(\beta_2-\beta)^{k_2-1}}{(\beta_2-\beta_1)^{k_1+k_2-1}}, \tag{2.4}$$

for $0 \leq \beta_1 < \beta < \beta_2$, where $\Gamma(z) = \int_o^\infty e^{-u} u^{z-1} du$, and k_1, $k_2 > 0$ are specified constants.

For convenience, we shall also assume for now, that the prior distributions for α and β are independent. We recognize that this assumption too, may not be realistic.

In our railroad engineering example, the fracture mechanics model can be used, not only to generate the empirical distributions for α and β, should we so desire, but also to pin down the constants α_0, β_1, β_2, k_1 and k_2 in the prior distributions (2.3) and (2.4) given above.

2.2 THE POSTERIOR DISTRIBUTIONS OF α AND β AND THEIR USE

Let $g_1(\alpha,\beta|\underset{\sim}{n})$ denote the joint posterior density function of α and β. Then, from Bayes' Theorem, we have

$$g_1(\alpha,\beta|\underset{\sim}{n}) \alpha (\beta-\beta_1)^{k_1-1}(\beta_2-\beta)^{k_2-1} \prod_{i=1}^{m} [(\frac{t_{i2}}{\alpha})^\beta - (\frac{t_{i1}}{\alpha})^\beta] \cdot$$

$$\cdot \exp[-(\frac{t_{i2}}{\alpha})^\beta + (\frac{t_{i1}}{\alpha})^\beta]. \tag{2.5}$$

The marginal posterior density of α, say $g_1(\alpha|\underset{\sim}{n}) = \int_{\beta_1}^{\beta_2} g_1(\alpha,\beta|\underset{\sim}{n}) d\alpha$ cannot be obtained in closed form. However, the marginal posterior distribution of β, say $g_1(\beta|\underset{\sim}{n})$ which is of greater practical interest can be obtained in closed form, but as an approximation, as

$$g_1(\beta|\underset{\sim}{n}) \alpha (\beta-\beta_1)^{k_1-1}(\beta_2-\beta)^{k_2-1} \cdot \frac{S(\beta)^{1/\beta}}{\beta} \cdot$$

$$\cdot \Gamma(n_o - \frac{1}{\beta}) \prod_{i=1}^{m} \frac{(t_{i2}^\beta - t_{i1}^\beta)^{n_i}}{S(\beta)}, \tag{2.6}$$

where $S(\beta) = \sum_{i=1}^{m} (t_{i2}^\beta - t_{i1}^\beta)$ and $n_o = \sum_{i=1}^{m} n_i$.

In obtaining (2.6) we use the approximation

$$\int_o^{\alpha_o} (\frac{1}{\alpha^\beta})^{n_o} \exp(-\frac{S(\beta)}{\alpha}) d\alpha \doteq \frac{\Gamma(n_o - 1/\beta)}{\beta \cdot S(\beta)^{n_o - 1/\beta}}, \tag{2.7}$$

which works very well if $\alpha_o \geq s(\beta)^{1/\beta}$.

The posterior distribution $g_1(\beta|\underset{\sim}{n})$ enables us to assess if there is indeed reliability growth or not, and if so, its extent. For example, if most of the mass of the posterior density $g_1(\beta|\underset{\sim}{n})$ is concentrated on the interval $(0,1)$, then there is a strong evidence of reliability growth.

Besides assessing reliability growth, we often wish to make probability statements about N_o, the number of failures in some future interval of time $(t_{o1}, t_{o2}]$.

This is most conveniently done by evaluating

$$P(N_o=k|\underset{\sim}{n}) = \int_o^{\alpha_o}\int_{\beta_1}^{\beta_2} P(N_o=k|\alpha,\beta) g_1(\alpha,\beta|\underset{\sim}{n}) d\alpha d\beta$$

$$= \int_o^{\alpha_o}\int_{\beta_1}^{\beta_2} [(\frac{t_{o2}}{\alpha})^\beta - (\frac{t_{o1}}{\alpha})^\beta] \exp[-(\frac{t_{o2}}{\alpha})^\beta + (\frac{t_{o1}}{\alpha})^\beta](k!)^{-1} \cdot$$

$$\cdot g_1(\alpha,\beta|\underset{\sim}{n}) d\alpha d\beta, \tag{2.8}$$

for $k=0, 1, \ldots$; $g_1(\alpha,\beta|\underset{\sim}{n})$ is given by (2.5).

The final computations to obtain $P(N_o = k|\underset{\sim}{n})$ have to be done numerically via a computer code described in Kyparisis, Soyer and Daryanani (1984). An application of the above results in predicting future railroad defects is given in Kyparisis and Singpurwalla (1984).

3. ANALYSIS FOR THE CASE OF ACTUAL TIMES TO FAILURE DATA

Let $t_1 \leq t_2 \leq \ldots \leq t_m$ be the observed times to failure, when the Weibull process is observed over a time interval $(O, T]$, where $t_m \leq T$. Then, the likelihood function for α and β, given $\underset{\sim}{t} = (t_1, \ldots, t_m)$ is

$$L_2(\alpha,\beta;\underset{\sim}{t}) = \prod_{i=1}^{m} r(t_i) \exp(-M(t_m)) \tag{3.0}$$

$$= (\beta/\alpha)^m \prod_{i=1}^{m} (t_i/\alpha)^{\beta-1} \exp(-(t_m/\alpha)^\beta).$$

Here again, we assume the priors (2.3) and (2.4) for α and β, respectively, and arrive at the following as their joint posterior distribution:

$$g_2(\alpha,\beta|\underset{\sim}{t}) \alpha (\beta-\beta_1)^{k_1-1}(\beta_2-\beta)^{k_2-1}(\beta/\alpha)^m \cdot$$

$$\cdot \prod_{i=1}^{m} (t_i/\alpha)^{\beta-1} \exp(-(t_m/\alpha)^\beta). \tag{3.1}$$

As before, the marginal posterior distribution of α, say

$$g_2(\alpha|\underset{\sim}{t}) = \int_{\beta_1}^{\beta_2} g_2(\alpha, \beta|\underset{\sim}{t})d\beta$$

could not be obtained by us in closed form. However, the marginal posterior distribution of β, $g_2(\beta|\underset{\sim}{t})$ can be reasonably well approximated as

$$g_2(\beta|\underset{\sim}{t}) \propto (\beta-\beta_1)^{k_1-1}(\beta_2-\beta)^{k_2-1}\beta^{m-1} \cdot \Gamma(m - \frac{1}{\beta}) \cdot (\prod_{i=1}^{m} t_i)^{\beta-1}(t_m)^{1-m\beta}. \quad (3.2)$$

In obtaining the above, we use the approximation (3.3)

$$\int_0^{\alpha_0} (\frac{1}{\alpha^\beta})^m \exp(-(t_m/\alpha)^\beta)d\alpha \doteq \frac{\Gamma(m - 1/\beta)}{\beta(t_m^\beta)^{m-1/\beta}},$$

which works well when $\alpha_0 \geq t_m$.

For the case of this section, there are two quantities of interest for which uncertainty statements are desired; these are:

i) N_0 the number of failures in $(t_{01}, t_{02}]$, and

ii) $Z_k \overset{def}{=} T_{m+k}-T_m$, the time to the (m+k)-th failure from T_m, the time to the m-th failure.

3.1 THE POSTERIOR DISTRIBUTION OF N_0

The posterior distribution of N_0 can be obtained in a manner analogous to (2.8) except that now we must use $g_2(\alpha,\beta|\underset{\sim}{t})$ in place of $g_1(\alpha,\beta|\underset{\sim}{n})$. Thus we have

$$P(N_0=k|\underset{\sim}{t}) = \int_0^{\alpha_0}\int_{\beta_1}^{\beta_2} P(N_0 = k|\alpha,\beta) \cdot g_2(\alpha,\beta|\underset{\sim}{t})\, d\alpha d\beta$$

$$= \int_0^{\alpha_0}\int_{\beta_1}^{\beta_2} [(\frac{t_{02}}{\alpha})^\beta - (\frac{t_{01}}{\alpha})^\beta]^k \cdot \exp[-(\frac{t_{02}}{\alpha})^\beta + (\frac{t_{01}}{\alpha})^\beta] \cdot (k!)^{-1} g_2(\alpha,\beta|\underset{\sim}{t})\, d\alpha d\beta. \quad (3.4)$$

A simplification of (3.4) via the approximation (3.3) does not seem possible. The final computations necessary to obtain $P(N_0=k|\underset{\sim}{t})$ have to be undertaken numerically; these are described in the computer code by Kyparisis, Soyer, and Daryanani (1984). The computer code can also plot $P(N_0=k|\underset{\sim}{t})$, for k=0, 1,....

3.2 PREDICTIVE DISTRIBUTION OF THE TIME TO NEXT FAILURE

To obtain the distribution of Z_k given that $T_m=t_m$, we use the well known result (see Parzen (1962), p. 126) which states that if $T_1, T_2, \ldots$, are the times to failure in a Weibull process, then $(T_1/\alpha)^\beta, (T_2/\alpha)^\beta, \ldots$, can be viewed as the times to failure in a homogeneous Poisson process with intensity function r(t)=1. Thus, given α and β, the quantity $V_k = \left(\frac{T_m+k}{\alpha}\right)^\beta - \left(\frac{T_m}{\alpha}\right)^\beta$ has a gamma distribution with a shape parameter k and a scale parameter 1. The probability density function of V_k is therefore

$$f(v)=v^{k-1}e^{-v}/(k-1)!\ , \quad v \geq 0. \quad (3.5)$$

It now follows that the distribution function of Z_k, given α, β, and $T_m=t_m$ is

$$P(Z_k \leq z|\alpha,\beta, t_m) = \int_0^{v(t_m,z)} \frac{v^{k-1}e^{-v}}{(k-1)!} dv,$$

$$\text{where } v(t_m,z) = (\frac{t_m + z}{\alpha})^\beta - (\frac{t_m}{\alpha})^\beta \quad (3.6)$$

For the special case of k=1, (3.6) reduces to

$$P(Z_1 \leq z|\alpha,\beta,t_m) = 1 - \exp[-(\frac{t_m + z}{\alpha})^\beta + (\frac{t_m}{\alpha})^\beta]. \quad (3.7)$$

Note that (3.7) is the distribution function of a Weibull density function which is truncated to the left at the point t_m, and which has a scale parameter of α and a shape parameter of β.

The distribution function of Z_k conditional on all the observed times to failure $\underset{\sim}{t}$ is therefore

$$P(Z_k \leq z|\underset{\sim}{t}) = \int_0^{\alpha_0}\int_{\beta_1}^{\beta_2} P(Z_k \leq z|\alpha,\beta, t_m) \cdot g_2(\alpha,\beta|\underset{\sim}{t})\, d\alpha d\beta$$

$$= \int_0^{\alpha_0}\int_{\beta_1}^{\beta_2} (\int_0^{v(t_m,z)} \frac{v^{k-1}e^{-v}}{(k-1)!} dv)\ g_2(\alpha,\beta|\underset{\sim}{t})\, d\alpha d\beta. \quad (3.8)$$

Expression (3.8) above involves three integrals which can be numerically evaluated without much difficulty using an efficient algorithm for evaluating incomplete gamma functions. The form of $g_2(\alpha,\beta|\underset{\sim}{t})$ is relatively simple. The computer code by Kyparisis, Soyer and Daryanani (1984) can be used to evaluate (3.8).

When k=1, (3.8) is the predictive distribution of the time to next failure. It would be the truncated Weibull distribution (3.7) with its parameters α and β averaged out with respect to their posterior distribution $g_2(\alpha,\beta|\underset{\sim}{t})$. For practical applications this distribution has much value, since it enables a user to specify the odds for the next time to failure. The complement of (3.8) would be $P(Z_k \geq z \mid \underset{\sim}{t})$; this is our current estimate of the reliability of the system being studied.

3.3 APPLICATIONS TO SOFTWARE FAILURE DATA

We illustrate the methodology developed in this section by applying it to some software failure data reported by Musa (1979), and reproduced below in Table 1. The recorded times are actually execution times, not the actual running times, and are in seconds. Musa gives the times between failures Δt_i, $i=1,\ldots,38$; we need to convert these to the consecutive times to failure $0=t_0<t_1\leq t_2\leq\ldots\leq t_{38}$, and these are also given in Table 1.

Table 1

DATA ON SOFTWARE FAILURES TAKEN FROM MUSA (1979)

Δt_i	115	0	83	178	194	136	
t_i	115	115	198	376	570	706	
Δt_i	1077	15	15	92	50	71	
t_i	1783	1798	1813	1905	1955	2026	
Δt_i	606	1189	40	788	222	72	
t_i	2632	3821	2861	4649	4871	4943	
Δt_i	615	589	15	390	1863	1337	
t_i	5558	6147	6162	6552	8415	9752	
Δt_i	4508	834	3400	6	4561	3168	10571
t_i	14260	15094	18494	18500	23061	26229	36800
Δt_i	563	2770	652	5593	11696	6724	2546
t_i	37363	40133	40785	46378	58074	64798	67344

The prior distributions used are those given by (2.3) and (2.4), with $\alpha_0 = 500$, $\beta_1 = .1$, and $\beta_2=2$. The values of k_1 and k_2 which specify the shape of the beta density for the shape parameter β, are taken to be $k_1=k_2=1$ (in this case β has a uniform density), $k_1=k_2=2$, and $k_1=2$, $k_2=3$, respectively. In Figures 3.1a, b, c, we show the prior density functions of α (which is always a uniform) and $g_2(\alpha \mid \underset{\sim}{t})$, resultant posterior density functions for α, for the above 3 pairs of choices for k_1 and k_2. In all the 3 cases, we see that the posterior distributions of α are relatively similar, with a modal value of about 10. In Figures 3.2a, b, and c, we show the various prior densities for β and the resultant posterior densities $g_2(\beta \mid \underset{\sim}{t})$-equation (3.2). The prior density for α is always uniform. In all the 3 cases the posterior density is concentrated heavily around $\beta=.5$, clearly indicating an overall growth in software reliability. The similarity of the 3 posterior densities for β, despite the distinct differences in the priors, is noteworthy.

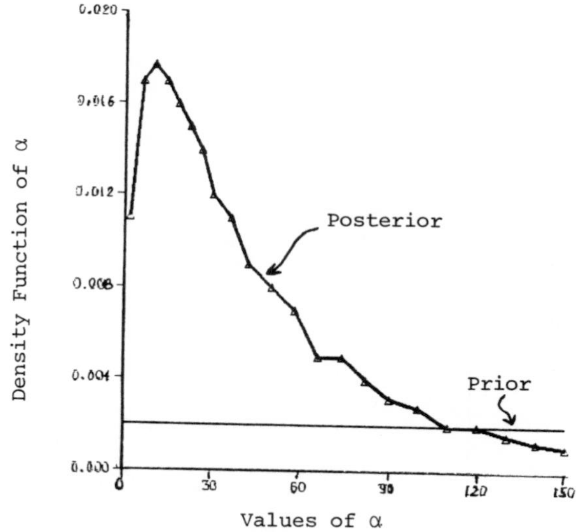

Figure 3.1a: Plots of the prior and the posterior densities of the scale parameter α when the prior on the shape parameter β is uniform.

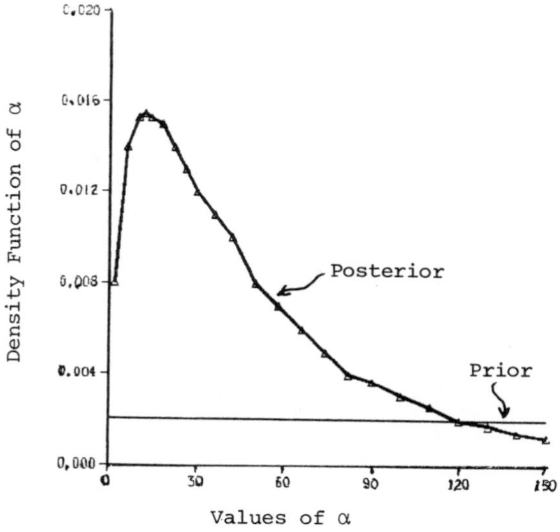

Figure 3.1b: Plots of the prior and the posterior densities of the scale parameter α when the prior on the shape parameter β is a beta density with $k_1=k_2=2$.

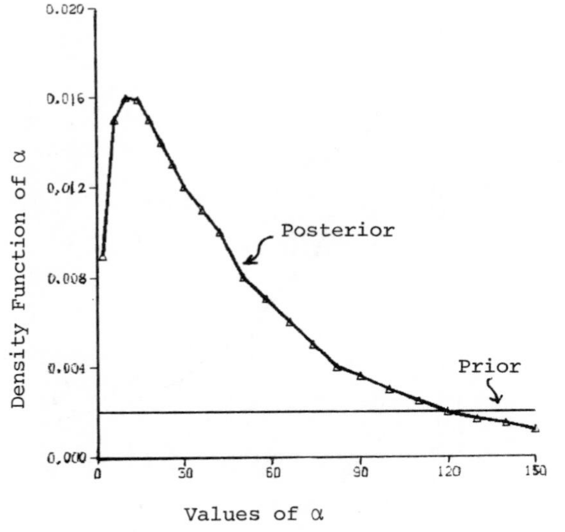

Figure 3.1c: Plots of the prior and the posterior densities of the scale parameter α when the prior on the shape parameter β is a beta density with $k_1=2$ and $k_2=3$.

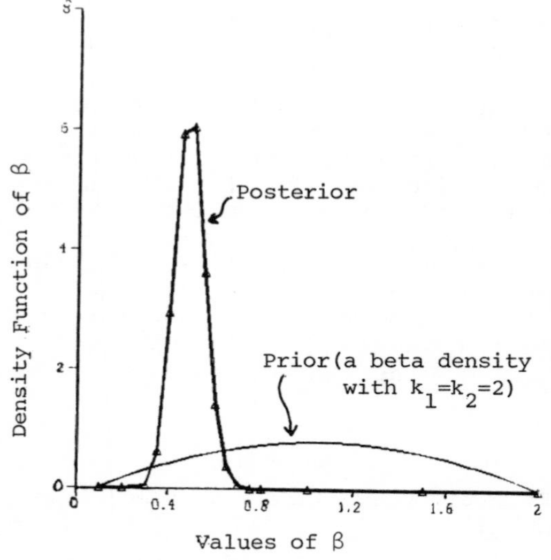

Figure 3.2b: Plots of the prior and the posterior densities of the shape parameter β when the prior on the scale parameter is uniform.

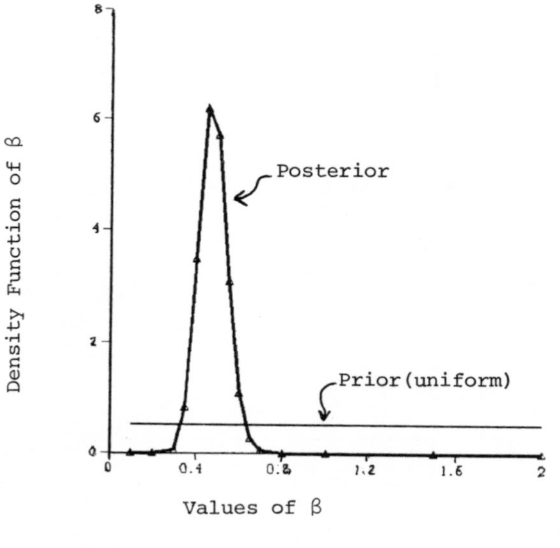

Figure 3.2a: Plots of the prior and the posterior densities of the shape paramter β, when the prior on the scale parameter is uniform.

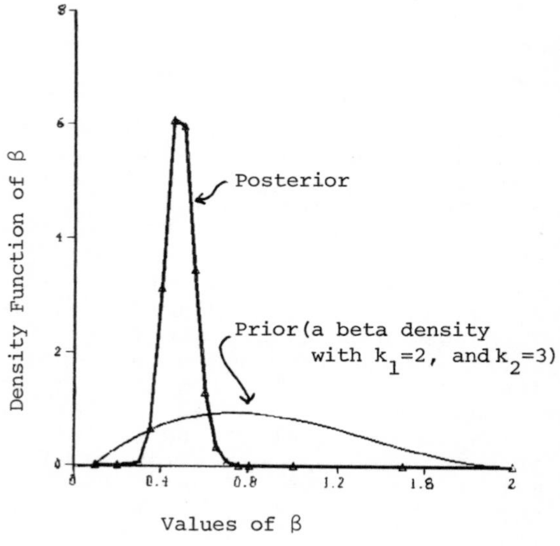

Figure 3.2c: Plots of the prior and the posterior densities of the shape parameter β, when the prior on the scale parameter is uniform.

In Table 1, the last observed failure is at 67344. The posterior mass function of the number of failures in the interval (67344, 80000] is computed using (3.4). A plot of this posterior mass function for k=0,..., 9, when the prior density of β is a beta, with $k_1=2$, and $k_2=3$, is shown in Figure 3.3. The posterior mass functions for other forms of the prior densities on β are similar to this one and are thus not shown.

Finally, the posterior distribution of the time to the next software failure, given that the last failure occurs at 67344, the predictive distribution, is computed using (3.8). This for the case of a beta prior density on β with $k_1=2$ and $k_2=3$ is shown in Figure 3.4. Plots of the predictive distribution for the other prior distributions of β are almost identical and are thus omitted. The complement of the curve in Figure 3.4 describes our current software reliability after 67344 seconds of testing.

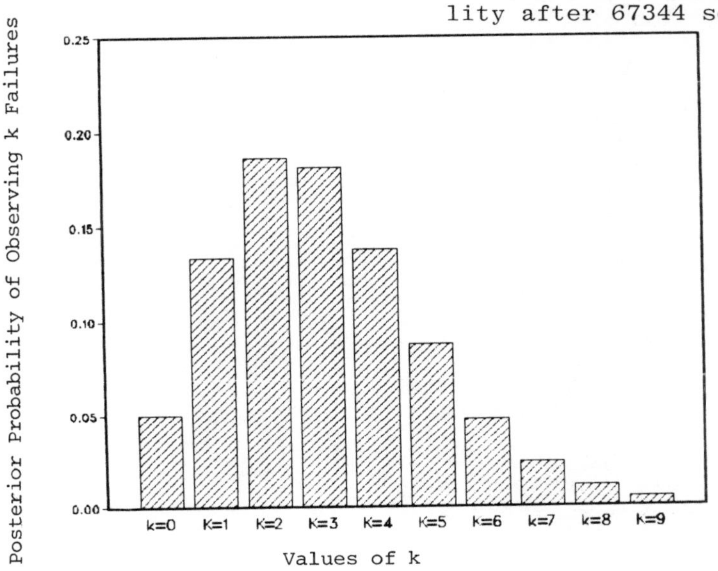

Figure 3.3: Posterior probability of observing k failures in the interval (67344, 80000] when the prior on β is a beta density with $k_1=2$, $k_2=3$.

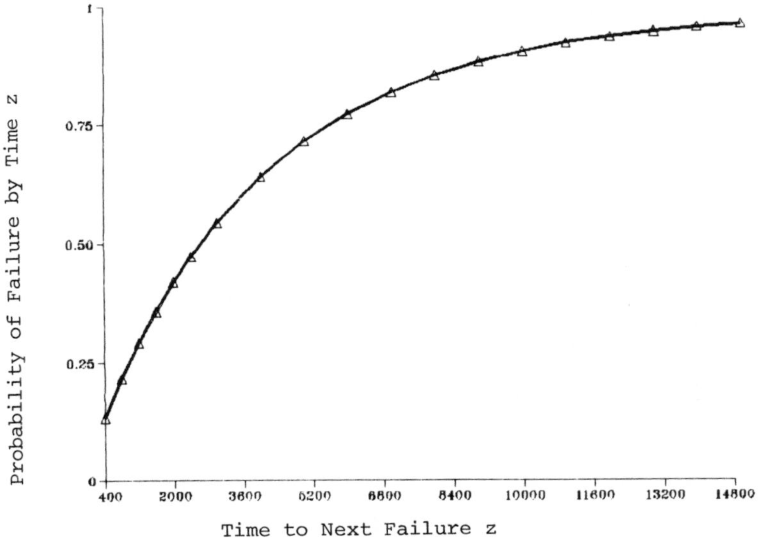

Figure 3.4: A plot of the predictive distribution of the time to the next failure.

REFERENCES

CROW, L.H. (1974). "Reliability Analysis for Complex Repairable Systems". Reliability and Biometry, ed. by F. Proshan and R.J. Serfling, SIAM, Philadelphia, 379-410.

CROW, L.H. (1975). "Tracking Reliability Growth". Proceedings of the Twentieth Conference on the Design of Experiments, ARO Report 75-2, 741-754.

GOEL, A.L., K. OKUMOTO (1979). "Time-Dependent Error-Detection Rate Model for Software Reliability and Other Performance Measures". IEEE Trans. Reliability, Vol. R-28, No. 3, 206-211.

KYPARISIS, J., N.D. SINGPURWALLA (1984). "Bayesian Inferences for the Weibull Process with Applications to Predicting Rail Fatigue", in preparation.

KYPARISIS, J., R. SOYER, and S. DARYANANI (1984). "Computer Programs for Bayesian Inference for the Weibull Process".

LEE, L., S.K. LEE (1978). "Some Results on Inference for the Weibull Process". Technometrics, Vol. 20, No. 1, 41-45.

LEE, L. (1980a). "Testing Adequacy of the Weibull and Log Linear Rate Models for a Poisson Process". Technometrics, Vol. 22, No. 2, 195-199.

LEE, L. (1980b). "Comparing Rates of Several Independent Weibull Processes". Technometrics, Vol. 22, No. 3, 427-430.

LINDLEY, D. (1983). "Reconciliation of Probability Distributions". Operations Research, Vol. 31, No. 5, 866-880.

MUSA, J.D. (1979). "Software Reliability Data". Deposited in IEEE Computer Society Repository.

PARZEN, E. (1962). "Stochastic Processes", Holden-Day, San Francisco.

THOMPSON, W.A. Jr. (1981). "On the Foundations of Reliability". Technometrics, Vol. 23, No. 1, 1-13.

---

[1] Supported in part by the Research and Test Department of the Association of American Railroads, Washington D.C.

[2] Supported by the Army Research Office under Grant DAAG29-83-K-0013 and the Naval Air Systems Command under Contract N00019-83-C-0358 with the George Washington University.

NUMERICAL METHODS

Organizer: *Douglas M. Bates, Queen's University and University of Wisconsin*

Invited Presentations:

Computational Methods for Generalized Cross-Validation, *Douglas M. Bates, University of Wisconsin and Queen's University*

Secondary Storage Methods for Statistical Computational Operations, *Setrag N. Khoshafian, Douglas M. Bates and David J. DeWitt, University of Wisconsin*

COMPUTER SCIENCE AND STATISTICS:
The Interface, L. Billard (ed.)

COMPUTATIONAL METHODS FOR GENERALIZED CROSS-VALIDATION

Douglas M. Bates

Dept. of Statistics, U. of Wisconsin, Madison
and
Dept. of Math. and Statistics, Queen's University, Kingston

Generalized cross-validation, a method for the choice of regularization parameters such as the ridge parameter in ridge regression, has proven to be a valuable statistical tool. Unfortunately, its use with large data sets is complicated by the computational cost of some of the intermediate steps in the method. We present some methods based on non-iterative matrix decompositions such as the QR decomposition and the Cholesky decomposition to reduce the computational burden of the calculations. In particular, we show a truncated singular value decomposition (TSVD) which reduces the time taken in the main step of the computation. The gain from the TSVD, however, may be because of a minor coding error in the original Linpack singular value decomposition code. These methods can be applied to ridge regression, spline smoothing, deconvolution with missing data, and many other problems. Examples with deconvolution are shown.

1. Introduction

Generalized Cross-Validation (GCV), a method of determining the amount of smoothing to apply in data-smoothing problems and other regularization problems, has been made popular mostly through the work of Professor Grace Wahba and her co-authors. See, for example, Craven and Wahba [1979], Golub, Heath, and Wahba [1979], Wahba [1980a], Wahba [1980b], Wahba and Wendelberger [1980], Wahba [1983], and Nychka, Wahba, Goldfarb, and Pugh [1983].

In data smoothing problems the objective may be to create a smooth function of one or more variables which passes "close to" the observed data. A basic trade-off that exists in such situations is to balance the smoothness of the estimated function with fidelity to the data. Since many of the examples of GCV use, as the approximating function, one with as many parameters as there are data points, it is possible to create an interpolating function which passes through all the data points. This, while numerically rather simple, usually provides a function that is too bumpy when the data is noisy. At the other extreme, a constant function with height equal to the average data value provides an extremely smooth function but usually does not provide the desired fidelity to the data.

The cases where the approximating function has as many parameters as there are data points result in a computational procedure which is $O(n^3)$ where n is the number of data points. Such a procedure is not well suited to use on large data sets. One way to avoid this unfortunately rapid increase in computational costs is to create a set of basis functions whose number does not increase with n and to express the smoothing function in terms of this basis. This will usually make the cost of the computing something like $O(np^2)$ where p is the number of basis functions. We will describe this type of application of GCV.

The calculations for GCV with basis functions are relatively quick and straightforward once the singular value decomposition (SVD) of an n by p matrix Z has been computed. The computational problems and delays are usually encountered in taking this decomposition. We found that, in one example cited below, the Linpack (Dongarra et al. [1979]) SVD routine required that the maximum number of iterations for each singular value be reset from 30 to 90 before convergence to the singular values could be achieved. For large matrices such slow convergence can be very expensive. Furthermore, we discovered that the convergence difficulties were with the small singular values which had virtually no contribution in the ensuing calculations. To speed up this part of the calculations we developed a truncated singular value decomposition (TSVD) which determines the larger singular values of a matrix while providing better conditioning for the iterative algorithm.

Recently, though, we have been informed that there is a minor coding error in the original Linpack code for the SVD routine which is the code we were using. We have not been able yet to run series of tests with the coding error corrected so that we can see if the poor performance which we had previously encountered was due to the coding error or was inherent in the SVD algorithm. We do, however, describe here the example which gave us trouble so that others can try the SVD code on it. We would encourage this so that the behavior on a variety of machines can be determined.

In section 2 we describe the GCV algorithm with basis functions. Section 3 contains a description of the example which gave us trouble and section 4 contains the description of the TSVD method.

2. GCV with Basis Functions

The GCV calculations with basis functions closely resemble ridge-regression calculations. In fact, Golub, Heath, and Wahba [1979] describes the use of GCV for choosing a ridge parameter and the computational methods described in there are the basis for the following description. A data-smoothing problem for one-dimensional data on the unit interval would involve a data vector $\underline{y}=(y_1,\ldots,y_n)^T$ assumed to be generated as

$$y_i = \int_0^1 K(t_i,s)f(s)ds + \varepsilon_i \qquad (2.1)$$

For example, a simple case could have K as an impulse function at t=s so the data would have the classical regression form of

$$y_i = f(t_i) + \varepsilon_i \qquad i=1,\ldots,n\ . \qquad (2.2)$$

For a given value of the regularization parameter λ, the regularized estimate f_λ is the minimizer of

$$\frac{1}{n}\sum_{i=1}^{n}[(Kf)(t_i)-y_i]^2 + \lambda \int_0^1 (f^{(m)}(s))^2 ds \qquad (2.3)$$

In (2.3) the first term measures the fidelity to the data in the least squares sense while the second part measures the smoothness of the function using the integral of the square of the m'th derivative. In almost all cases, m is set equal to 2, the value we will assume in the following.

When f is represented as a linear combination of some basis functions $\{b_1,\ldots,b_p\}$,

$$f(s) = \sum_{j=1}^{p} \theta_j b_j(s) \qquad (2.4)$$

the regularized estimate of the function is given by $\underline{\theta}_\lambda$ which minimizes

$$\frac{1}{n}||X\underline{\theta}-\underline{y}|| + \lambda^2\underline{\theta}^T\Sigma\underline{\theta} \qquad (2.5)$$

where

$$x_{i,j} = \int_0^1 K(t_i,s)b_j(s)ds \qquad (2.6)$$

and

$$\sigma_{i,j} = \int_0^1 b_i^{(m)}(s)b_j^{(m)}(s)ds\ . \qquad (2.7)$$

In the simple case mentioned above, $x_{i,j}$ would be the value of the j'th basis function at the i'th value of t.

The minimizer of (2.5) could be written as

$$\underline{\theta}_\lambda = (X^TX + n\lambda\Sigma)^{-1}X^T\underline{y} \qquad (2.8)$$

although it would generally not be computed in

this way. The GCV estimate of the regularization parameter λ is chosen to minimize the GCV function

$$V(\lambda) = \frac{||[I-A(\lambda)]\underline{y}||^2/n}{[\frac{1}{n}\operatorname{tr}(I-A(\lambda))]^2} \qquad (2.9)$$

where $A(\lambda)$ is the equivalent of the "hat" matrix. That is,

$$A(\lambda) = X(X^TX + n\lambda\Sigma)^{-1} X^T \quad . \qquad (2.10)$$

If Σ is positive definite, it has a Cholesky decomposition

$$\Sigma = R^TR \qquad (2.11)$$

with R upper triangular so we can form

$$Z = XR^{-1} \qquad (2.12)$$

and change the optimization problem (2.5) to

$$\frac{1}{n}||y-Z(R\underline{\theta})||^2 + \lambda(R\underline{\theta})^T(R\underline{\theta}) \quad . \qquad (2.13)$$

The expression of $V(\lambda)$ can be changed to a simple rational function of λ in this case by taking a singular value decomposition of Z as

$$Z = UBV^T \qquad (2.14)$$

and forming the p-dimensional vector

$$\underline{z} = U^T\underline{y} \; . \qquad (2.15)$$

Then

$$V(\lambda) = E_1(\lambda)/E_2(\lambda) \qquad (2.16)$$

where

$$E_1(\lambda) = n\{||y||^2-||z||^2 \qquad (2.17)$$

$$+ \sum_{j=1}^{p} z_j^2[n\lambda/(b_j^2+n\lambda)]^2\}$$

and

$$E_2(\lambda) = [n - p + \sum_{j=1}^{p} n\lambda/(b_j^2 +n\lambda)]^2 . \qquad (2.18)$$

The crux of the calculations is the evaluation of the singular values and the first p left singular vectors of Z.

When Σ is not positive definite, as would be the case, for example, when using a basis of B-splines, it is possible to re-cast the calculations in this form by using a pivoted Cholesky decomposition of Σ and a bit of other pre-processing as described in Bates and Wahba [1983].

It is interesting to note that the singular values of Z only enter into the generalized cross-validation function of (2.16) as expressions of the form

$$b_j^2 + n\lambda$$

so any singular values whose squares are negligible compared to $n\lambda$, and the singular vectors associated with such values, do not need to be determined.

3. A Numerically Difficult Example

The example which motivated our consideration of modifications of the singular value decomposition was the deconvolution of irregularly spaced, noisy data. The data is of the form

$$y_i = \int_0^1 f(s)h(t_i-s)ds + \varepsilon_i \qquad (3.1)$$

where h(s), the kernel function, is known. The integral in (3.1) is defined by extending both f and h periodically with period 1. In our example, the kernel was chosen to be a normal density function with mean zero and standard deviation 0.05. For p, an even number of basis functions, both f and h are represented by their fourier series representations

$$f(t) = \alpha_0 + 2\sum_{j=1}^{m} [\alpha_j \cos(2\pi jt) + \beta_j \sin(2\pi jt)] + \alpha_{m+1}\cos(p\pi t) \qquad (3.2)$$

and

$$h(t) = \xi_0 + 2\sum_{j=1}^{m} \xi_j \cos(2\pi jt) + \xi_{m+1}\cos(p\pi t) \qquad (3.3)$$

The Fourier series for h has no sine terms since h is an even function.

The p-dimensional parameter of interest is

$$\underline{\theta}^T = (\underline{\alpha}^T, \underline{\beta}^T) \ . \qquad (3.4)$$

Since h is assumed known, we can calculate

$$\xi_j = [\sum_{k=1}^{p} \cos(2\pi jk/p) h(k/p)]/p \qquad (3.5)$$

for $j=0,\ldots,m+1$. For p on the order of 50 or more, the Fourier expansion is virtually indistinguishable from the normal density. If we set

$$g(t,\underline{\theta}) = \int_0^1 f(s)h(t-s)ds \qquad (3.6)$$

and evaluate it through the series, we obtain

$$g(t) = \xi_0\alpha_0 + 2\sum_{j=1}^{m} [\alpha_j\xi_j \cos(2\pi jt) + \beta_j\xi_j \sin(2\pi jt)] + [\alpha_{m+1}\xi_{m+1}\cos(p\pi t)] \qquad (3.7)$$

and the minimization problem becomes

$$\min_{\underline{\theta}} ||X\underline{\theta} - \underline{y}||^2 + n\lambda \underline{\theta}'\Sigma\underline{\theta} \qquad (3.8)$$

where

$$x_{i,j} = \begin{cases} \xi_0 & j=1 \\ 2\xi_{j-1}\cos[2\pi(j-1)t_i] & j=2,\ldots,m+1 \\ \frac{1}{2}\xi_{m+1}\cos(p\pi t_i) & j=m+2 \\ 2\xi_{j-m-2}\sin[2\pi(j-m-2)t_i] & j=m+3,\ldots,p \end{cases} \qquad (3.9)$$

and

$$\Sigma = \mathrm{diag}(0,\delta_1,\ldots,\delta_m,\tfrac{1}{2}\delta_{m+1},\delta_1,\ldots,\delta_m) \qquad (3.10)$$

with

$$\delta_j = (2\pi j)^4 .$$

This puts a heavy penalty on the high frequency components if λ is large. Noise in the data will introduce a high frequency component which λ will tend to damp out.

The matrix Σ is not positive definite in this case but the calculations described in Bates and Wahba [1983] for using a positive semi-definite smoothing term effectively amount in this case to producing Z from X by deleting the first column of X and centering each of the other columns (subtracting column means), then scaling each column by the reciprocal of the square root of the corresponding diagonal element of Σ.

This, then, is the way of producing the matrix Z on which the Linpack (Dongarra et al. [1979]) SVD code converged slowly. The t_i's were chosen as uniformly distributed over [0,1] and n was chosen on the order of 200 while p was on the order of 100. As can be imagined, the resulting singular values spanned many orders of magnitude and Z would often be judged computationally singular. It was almost always the case that only the first 30 or so singular values would have any effect on the calculation of $V(\lambda)$ for values of λ in the range of the GCV estimate of λ. The others would be far too small to make any difference in expressions of the form $b_j^2 + n\lambda$.

The test runs with poor performance of the SVD code were performed on a VAX using double precision arithmetic. Thus 64 bit floating point values with an 8 bit exponent were being used. This combination is reputed to cause some problems with the SVD code.

The poor performance of the SVD code does not depend on the data $\underline{y}$ but only on the t_i's which are used. To give some idea of the effect of the smoothing parameter λ on the resulting function estimates, though, we show the function which was used to simulate the observations and the resulting estimates for a large value of λ, an intermediate value and a small value in Figure 1. Notice that, as λ increases, the function becomes smoother but begins to miss the peaks. As λ decreases the function follows the peaks more closely but also has too much high frequency noise.

4. A Truncated Singular Value Decomposition

If the convergence of the SVD code is being hampered by the ill-conditioning of the Z matrix but the smaller singular values and their associated singular vectors are not needed, it should be possible to speed the convergence of the SVD by replacing the matrix Z with a better conditioned matrix whose singular values and vectors are close to those of Z. In particular, we wish to have the larger singular values and vectors very close to those of Z.

It can be shown (see Sun [1983]) that if X and Y are two n by p matrices with ordered singular values d_i and s_i, i=1,...,p respectively then

$$\sum_{i=1}^{p}(d_i-s_i)^2 \leq ||X-Y||^2 = tr(X-Y)^T(X-Y) \quad . \quad (4.1)$$

Thus the sum of the squares of the deviations in the singular values is bounded by the square of the Frobenius norm of the difference. If this norm of the difference can be made quite small while still producing better conditioning, the larger singular values, in particular, can still be expected to be well determined.

The truncated singular value decomposition procedes by taking a pivoted QR decomposition of Z where

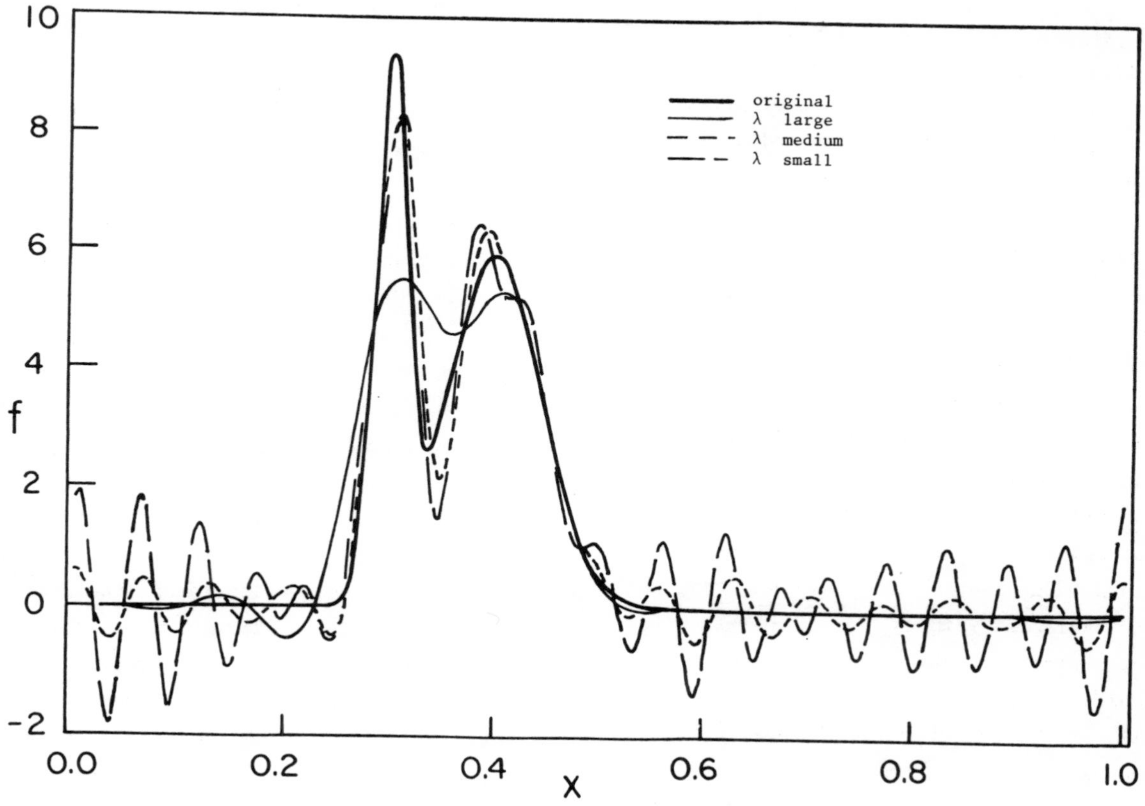

$$ZE = QR \qquad (4.2)$$

with Q orthogonal, R zero below the main diagonal, and E a permutation matrix. Furthermore, R has the property that

$$r_{k,k}^2 \geq \sum_{i=k}^{j} r_{i,j}^2 \qquad j=k,\ldots,p \qquad (4.3)$$

A singular value decomposition of R provides the singular values of Z and the left singular vectors of Z are obtained from the left singular vectors of R and the first p columns of the matrix Q.

To provide better conditioning, though, we truncate R after the k'th row where k is chosen so that

$$\left(\sum_{i=k+1}^{p} \sum_{j=i}^{p} r_{i,j}^2\right)/||Z|| < \varepsilon \qquad (4.4)$$

where ε is chosen to be some suitably small value. The double sum in (4.4) can be evaluated a row at a time starting at the p'th row until the condition is violated and k is determined. At this point, the singular values of R_k, the truncated version of R, are evaluated as are the left singular vectors. These are used in combination with the first k columns of Q to provide the approximation to the left singular vectors of Z and the λ which optimizes $V(\lambda)$ is obtained.

A check can be made on the effect of the error introduced in the truncation by comparing the value of $n\lambda$ with the square of the norm of the discarded part of R. If the discarded part of R is small in comparison then all of the important singular values (those which make a non-trivial contribution to the calculation of $V(\lambda)$) are well determined.

In practice, it has not been necessary to re-calculate an SVD with a different k if the original k is chosen with ε small, say 10^{-8}. We have also been able to compute the SVD of R_k without having to allow more than 30 iterations per singular value so the method has saved considerable amounts of computing time. It is still not known, though, if similar savings could be obtained by simply correcting the coding error in the Linpack SVD code.

That error, by the way, is in the calculation of the shift during the "chasing" part of the algorithm. In the routine SSVDC (and DSVDC, etc.) the line following statement 550 should read

```
F = (SL + SM)*(SL - SM) + SHIFT
```

The original code has "-" instead of "+" before SHIFT.

REFERENCES:

[1] Bates, D.M. and Wahba, G., A Truncated Singular Value Decomposition and Other Methods for Generalized Cross-Validation, TR#715, Dept. of Statistics, U. of Wisconsin, Madison (1983)

[2] Craven, P. and Wahba, G., Smoothing Noisy Data with Spline Functions: Estimating the Correct Degree of Smoothing by the Method of Generalized Cross-Validation, Numer. Math. 31 (1979) 377-403.

[3] Dongarra, J.J., Bunch, J.R., Moler, C.B., and Stewart, G.W., Linpack User's Guide (S.I.A.M., Philadelphia, 1979).

[4] Golub, G.H., Heath, M., and Wahba, G., Generalized Cross-Validation as a Method for Choosing a Good Ridge Parameter, Technometrics 21 (1979) 215-224.

[5] Nychka, D., Wahba, G., Goldfarb, D., and Pugh, T., Cross-Validated Spline Methods for the Estimation of Three Dimensional Tumor Size Distribution from Observations on Two-Dimensional Cross Sections, TR#711, Dept. of Statistics, U. of Wisconsin, Madison (1983).

[6] Sun, J-G., Perturbation Analysis for the Generalized Singular Value Problem, SIAM J. Numer. Anal. 20 (1983) 611-625.

[7] Wahba, G., Ill-Posed Problems: Numerical and Statistical Methods for Mildly, Moderately, and Severely Ill-Posed Problems with Noisy Data, TR#595, Dept. of Statistics, U. of Wisconsin (1980a)

[8] Wahba, G., Spline Bases, Regularization, and Generalized Cross-Validation for Solving Approximation Problems with Large Quantities of Noisy Data, in W. Cheney (ed.), Approximation Theory III (Academic Press, New York, 1980b) 905-912.

[9] Wahba, G., Surface Fitting with Scattered, Noisy Data on Euclidean d-Spaces and the Sphere, Rocky Mountain J. of Math. (1983)

[10] Wahba, G. and Wendelberger, J., Some New Mathematical Methods for Variational Objective Analysis Using Splines and Cross-Validation, Monthly Weather Rev. 108 (1980) 36-57.

COMPUTER SCIENCE AND STATISTICS:
The Interface, L. Billard (ed.)

SECONDARY STORAGE METHODS FOR STATISTICAL COMPUTATIONAL OPERATIONS

by
Setrag N. Khoshafian
Douglas M. Bates
David J. DeWitt

University of Wisconsin - Madison

Research work in SDBM's has generally ignored the data management issues of the computational methods. This paper concentrated on the I/O problems and analyzes the performance of three important operations: X'X, QR and SVF. Vector Building Block, Vector-Matrix and Direct Implementations of these computational methods are introduced. The performance evaluation also compares the relational and transposed secondary storage organizations.

1. Introduction

Research work in statistical database management systems has primarily concentrated on the data management of SDB's guided through the general characteristics of of statistical databases. Several interesting solutions to the special problems of large SDB's have emerged. The proposed solutions have mostly been in the areas of data storage, data compression, semantic modeling, generation and management of views and management of metadata. Surprisingly there have been few attempts to characterize the data management features of the statistical computational techniques.

In statistical computing, on the other hand, the time required to perform a specific statistical analysis is usually measured by the time to perform the calculations involved. In fact, early comparisons of algorithms only considered the number of floating point multiplications involved as this time was assumed to be the predominant part of the execution time [GENT73]. Later, as the relative speeds of different floating point operations has changed, it has become customary to measure the computational cost of an algorithm by the number of floating point operations where a floating point operation includes a floating point multiplication, a floating point addition, and associated indexing operations. This still assumes, though, that the cost of moving the data within an algorithm is negligible compared to calculation times. When working with large data sets, however, it is frequently the case that the time for data movement can be comparable with the calculation time. As the size of the database extends to tens of thousands of observations on hundreds of variables or more, the time for input/output operations can, in fact, dominate calculation time. It could be argued that sampling and subsetting will reduce the data size and, hence, eliminate the data retrieval and update problems of the complex computations. Although this could be true for the exploratory phase of the analysis, the purpose of the confirmatory phase is to apply the hypothesis testing to the original database.

This paper analyzes the secondary storage problems of three important computational methods: X'X, QR Decomposition and the Singular Value Factorization. The comparative performance evaluation is with respect to three alternative types of implementations (Vector Building Block, Vector-Matrix, and Direct) and two secondary storage organizations:: transposed and relational. Section 2 introduces the building blocks approach. In Section 3 we describe the alternative transposed and relational secondary storage organizations. Section 4 presents the system and data models. In Section 5 we analyze the performance of alternative algorithms for X'X, QR and SVF. Section 6 summarizes the conclusions.

2. Building Blocks for Computational Methods

For statistical analysis, there is a large and growing number of techniques that a statistician can choose from when analyzing a data matrix X. This set of tools includes a variety of regression techniques (linear, stepwise, robust, ridge, iterative reweighted, non-linear), analysis of variance and covariance, canonical correlation, principal component analysis, discriminant analysis, etc. The difficulty with statistical database systems is caused by the dynamic and evolutionary nature of analytical methods. Better and alternative analytical techniques are continually developing. Therefore it is very difficult, if not impossible, to cover all the possible computational tools of statistical analysis.

Faced with this formidable problem, we tried to discover the most commonly used analytical method and came to the conclusion that we should concentrate on fitting linear statistical models. This is also called multiple linear regression analysis. While fitting linear models is the main-stay of statistical analysis, it may seem an oversight to neglect other methods that have been or may yet be developed. However, most other statistical models utilize linear models as a basic step in iterative fitting procedures. The Generalized Linear Models of Nelder and Wedderburn [McCU83], logistic regression models, and nonlinear regression models all utilize the linear models calculations as a basic iterative step. It should also be noticed that the statistical area called analysis of variance (and analysis of covariance) is also part of linear regression analysis.

There are a number of alternative computational techniques for multiple linear regression. However one or the other of the following two approaches is generally used: either the symmetric matrix X'.X is formed [SEBER77, KENN80] and the analysis proceeds with this matrix, or the matrix X is decomposed and the analysis proceeds with the factors of X. The most common decompositions of a data matrix X are the upper triangularization of X (through Givens rotations or the QR decomposition [GOLU73, SEBER77, KENN80, DONG79]) and the Singular Value Decomposition [STEW73, DONG79, WILL71 , KENN80, CUPP81, MAND82]. This research concentrates on the secondary storage problems of these three operations.

We have tried to analyze the performance of the operations with respect to three abstraction levels. The first level attempts to implement the computational methods through vector operations only. The argument here is that it is possible to express these matrix operations as a set of vector operations, and, once these vector operations are identified, efficient implementations of the vector building blocks will correspondingly yield efficient implementations of the computational methods. The advantage of this approach is that a relative small set of vector operations will enable us to implement all the matrix computations. The disadvantage is that the set of vector operations which implements a matrix operation is completely unaware of the special reference patterns of the operations. In some cases the performance degradation will become intolerable.

The approach of the second level is intermediate between the approaches for levels one and three, and here an attempt is made to identify vector-matrix operations and express the matrix operations in terms of a set of these vector-matrix operations. For example the matrix product of an n by p matrix with a p by q matrix can be implemented as n vector-times-matrix operations. We should note, however, that vector operations still need to be implemented since some applications might use one vector or two vector operations. The advantage of this approach is similar to the first, however there is room for more enhancements since a vector-matrix operation references larger sets of the data. Although the degradation should be less serious, it is very feasibly that a more direct implementation will perform much better than an implementation through vector-matrix building blocks.

Finally the approach of the third level is to discover the most efficient direct implementations of the matrix operations. Here there will be one implementation per matrix operation, which will take into consideration, the secondary storage layout, the main storage size, the CPU speed etc., of the underlying system. The goal is to come up with an optimal algorithm: optimal in secondary storage reference and also in overall total execution time.

3. File Organization

One of the primary goals of this research was to compare the performance of the operations with respect to two secondary storage organizations: the relational row-wise and the transposed column-wise. Statisticians usually view their data sets as "flat files", and, therefore, the relational row-wise secondary storage organization is a natural implementation of this view. However, there are at least two reasons why such a secondary storage organization might not be an attractive alternative for a large statistical database.

The first deals with data compression. In statistical analysis it is common to analyze "qualitative" data. That is, data with a very small range of values (for example SEX, MARITAL STATUS, etc.). For qualitative attributes only a small number of bits are needed to code all possible data values. In general a data set might have several qualitative (each with a different number of code-bits) and quantitative attributes. If the data is stored attribute-wise it is easy to implement "run length" [EGGE81] compression techniques. Achieving the same degree of compression will be more difficult in record oriented secondary storage organizations.

A second reason why a relational row-wise storage organization might not be a suitable organization for statistical databases, is that statistical operations usually encompass most (or all) of the observations (rows) and few of the variables (columns). That is most of the time only a fraction of the columns are referenced. For example if all the rows and only 10% of the columns are accessed, all the relation must be retrieved. This implies an unnecessary retrieval of potentially 90% of the relation. For large databases this can have serious performance implications.

These objections, suggest using an alternative storage organization known as the ***transposed*** [TURN79, BATO80] file organization for storing statistical data sets. The two types of transposed file organizations are: (1) partially transposed and (2) fully transposed. In the partially transposed organization the set of attributes is decomposed into a mutually exclusive collection of subsets of attributes and the attributes in each subset are stored together. Hopefully the attributes that are stored together are those which are also accessed together. If each subset contains exactly one attribute we get the fully transposed organization. The problem of pre-determining the partitioning of the attributes for a particular query mix turns out to be very hard [BATO80, HOFF76]. Therefore in this paper we have only considered the fully transposed secondary storage organization.

As indicated, it is common in statistical analysis to process only a fraction of the columns (henceforth called the "active" columns). Some of the operations (such as the QR decomposition and the SVF) iteratively update the active columns. For these operations the updated active columns are copied into temporary files and the matrix transformations are subsequently applied to the copies. The original data matrix X is kept intact.

4. System Parameters

In this section the parameters used in the cost equations of the computational methods are introduced. Besides the disk and CPU parameters, several model parameters are also introduced. These parameters include the size of the relation, the size of the transposed files, the number of attributes, the number of active columns and the buffer size. For each parameter the value or range of values of the parameter are indicated.

4.1. Disk Parameters

The mass storage device is assumed to be a disk. The parameters for a disk are: (1) the track size (BSIZE); (2) the number of tracks per cylinder (DCYL); (3) the average time to read/write a page (Tio); (4) the average random seek time (Tdac); and (5) the cylinder-to-cylinder seek time (Tsk). The values of the disk parameters are those of the IBM 3350 disk drive [IBM77]. All the values are in milliseconds (ms.). A page (the unit of transfer between the disk and main store) will be the same size as a disk track throughout.

BSIZE	page size	19069	bytes
DCYL	number of pages per cylinder	30	pages
Tio	page read/write time	25	ms.
Tdac	average access time	25	ms.
Tsk	time to seek 1 track	10	ms.

4.2. CPU Parameters

The arithmetical computations of the computational methods either use the basic step of an "Inner Product" or the basic step of an "AXPY" operation:

Inner Product: $a = a + x_j \cdot x_i$

AXPY: $y_i = a \cdot x_i + y_i$

Here the unit of execution is a "floating point operation" (a "flop") [DONG79], which involves the execution time of a double precision floating point multiplication, a double precision floating point addition, some indexing operations and storage references. Our own experiments and the timing indicated in [DONG83], suggest that, 0.5 to 25 μ seconds (micro seconds) per flop is a reasonable range of processing speeds.

4.3. Model Parameters

Since the relational and the transposed organizations are being compared it is imperative to define the parameters of each. In relational form, the data set is assumed to have 100 attributes and 230,000 tuples. All the attributes are eight byte numbers. With the above disk parameter values, this implies that there are 23 tuples per page (that is nt = 23). In the transposed organization, each page will contain 2383 elements. To simplify the subsequent analysis it is assumed 2300 elements are stored in each page of a transposed file. Hence each attribute will occupy 100 pages. Thus in both the row-wise organization and the transposed organization the relation will occupy 10,000 pages. These parameters are as follows:

R number of pages occupied by the data set X 10,000

N number of pages for a column(transposed) 100

w number of attributes 100

n number of tuples 230,000

q number of elements per page 2,300

p number of active columns
for the matrix operations the values considered are 10 to 100 active columns

M the size of the main storage
the values considered are 10 to 200 pages

5. Performance Evaluation for X'X, QR and SVF

In this section we present some of the results of a comparative performance evaluation for a number of algorithms for X'X, QR and SVF.

5.1. X'X

The special matrix product X'X can be implemented through:

(a) $\frac{p \cdot (p-1)}{2}$ inner products (VBB)

(b) p-1 vector-times-matrix operations (VM)

(c) a stripe wise implementation (DIR)

For (c), the approach is to reference a "stripe" consisting of the corresponding pages of the active columns, and accumulate all the $\frac{p \cdot (p-1)}{2}$ partial inner products.

If we were to measure the effectiveness of an algorithm by the number of pages transfers, the stripe wise algorithms are obviously optimal since they require all the active columns of the data matrix to be read exactly once. Comparing the horizontal stripes algorithm with the vector building block and the vector times matrix algorithms, we make the following observations:

(1) with a completely transposed secondary storage organization, this algorithm requires at least p (p being the number of active columns) pages of primary storage

(2) since the algorithm requires corresponding pages of the active columns to be accessed simultaneously, with a given memory size, the algorithm processes the matrix columns in smaller blocks than either the vector building block or the vector times matrix algorithms. This could imply more disk seeks.

(3) the amount of computation within the overlap region is substantially greater than either the vector times matrix or the vector building block algorithms.

Here is an example of a direct implementational stripe wise algorithm:

-Divide the main storage into p+1 equal subdivisions

-If there is a free M/(p+1) page block, read the next block while concurrently accumulating inner products of resident block pairs

-If all the partial inner products for a column are accumulated free the block occupied by the column.

First note that any algorithm under the fully transposed secondary storage organization which processes the data matrix X stripe wise will involve only $p \cdot N$ page transfers. On the other hand the vector building block and the vector-matrix implementations will involve, respectively, $p^2 \cdot N$ and $\frac{p^2}{2} N$ page transfers. The algorithms with respect to the relational secondary storage organization will involve at least $w \cdot N$ page transfers. Since $p \leq w$, the stripe wise algorithms (direct implementation) will always involve a smaller amount of page transfers for any p. However, in Figure 1 we have the curves for the total I/O times of the above stripe wise algorithm (with a fully transposed organization) and the total I/O of accessing the data matrix once, when X is stored relational. Note that the stripe wise algorithm performs better than a stripe wise algorithm for the relational secondary storage organization only if the number of active columns is less or equal to 50. This shows the effect of the random and track-to-track seeks on the total I/O for these types of algorithms.

Let us note that, if the main storage size is held at 75 pages, the vector building block algorithms under the transposed secondary storage organization perform better than the stripe wise algorithm for the relational secondary storage organization if p (th number of active columns) is less or equal to 10. The corresponding value of p for the vector-matrix approach is 13.

In Figure 2 we have the curves for the total execution times as functions of the processing speed (time per flop). The underlying secondary storage organization for these curves is the fully transposed organization. One important observation here is that the stripe wise (direct) algorithm becomes CPU bound much faster than the other algorithms. This is a desirable property, since rendering the execution of an algorithm CPU bound basically solves the problem of I/O overhead.

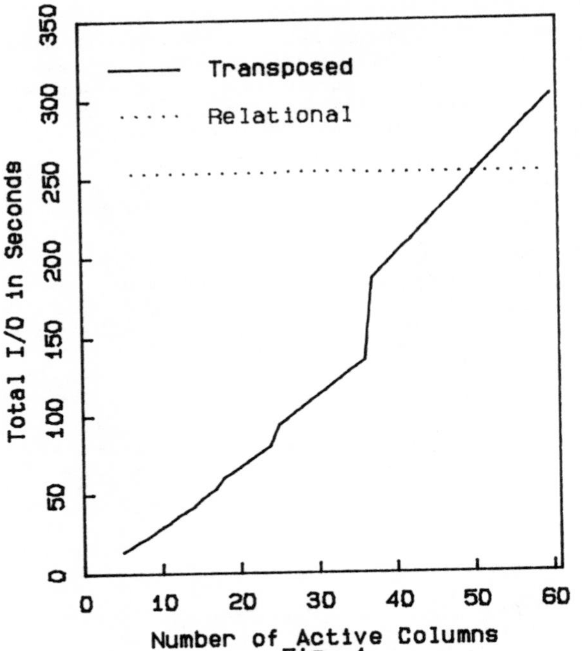

Fig. 1

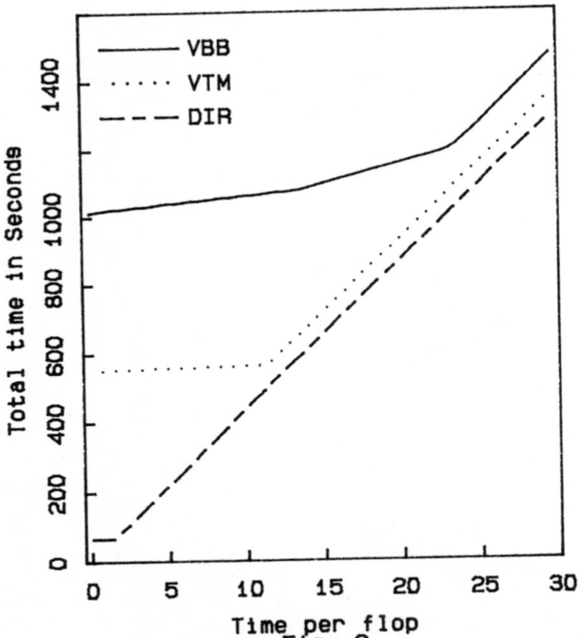

Fig. 2

5.2. QR Decomposition

For the QR decomposition of X, we apply p Householder transformations on X to reduce it to upper triangular form. The kth Householder transformation zeroes the subdiagonal elements of the kth column. Let H1, H2, ..., Hp be the p Householder transformations applied (on the left) to X. Then

$$Hp \cdots H2 \cdot H1 \cdot X = R$$

where R is an n x p upper triangular matrix. Let $Q = H1 \cdot H2 \cdots Hp$. Note that $Q' \cdot Q = Q \cdot Q' = I$ (that is Q is an orthogonal matrix). Therefore:

$$Q' \cdot X = R \text{ or } X = Q \cdot R$$

Since $n \gg p$, the last (n - p) rows of R are zeros. So for R, the storage requirement is of order $O(p^2)$. Q (or Q') can be recovered through the u's and c's of the Householder transformations (see for example [STEW73]). Therefore, rather than storing Q (which is of order $O(n^2)$) explicitly, we can store the u's in the zeroed lower triangular part of X. Whenever Q is needed, the Householder transformations can be applied to the nxn identity matrix. In most applications only the first p columns of Q are needed. In this case the Householder transformations are applyed to the first p columns of the nxn identity matrix. This is one scheme for accumulating Q or a submatrix of Q. In the next Section we shall introduce a more efficient way for accumulating the transformations and constructing Q (or the first p columns of Q). As we shall see, our method will imply a substantial saving in the I/O overhead.

Note that we need the 2-norm of the pivot in order to define the transformation. There will be a substantial savings in I/O and computation if the 2-norms of the non-pivotal columns are updated (vs. recalculated). The formula for the update is:

$$||X_j^{k+1}|| = \left[||X_j^k||^2 - |r_{kj}|^2\right]^{1/2} \tag{5.2.1}$$

where $||X_j^k||$ is the 2-norm of the jth column before the kth iteration, $||X_j^{k+1}||$ is the 2-norm of the same column after the jth transformation, and r_{kj} is the element in the kth row and j^{th} column of R. It is given by:

$$r_{kj} = X_{kj} - u'_k \cdot X_j \tag{5.2.2}$$

Therefore if the inner products of the kth pivot with the remaining columns and the kth row of the current X are available, by (5.2.2) and (5.2.1), it is possible to determine the 2-norms before actually applying the transformation.

For a vector building block implementation of the QR decomposition, all we need are the "Inner Product" and "AXPY" vector operations. For a vector matrix implementation of the QR decomposition, we the "Vector-Times-Matrix" and Householder transformations as building blocks. For a direct implementation we introduce the following "look-ahead" approach. Our technique is simply this: retain in primary storage corresponding pages of the current pivot and the next pivot, and accumulate the dot products for the next transformation while applying the current transformation. In the usual stripe-wise implementation of the QR decomposition (with the columns stored in a transposed organization), the current pivot is accessed in blocks and the corresponding blocks of the remaining columns are read, processed and written back. This goes on until all the blocks of the current pivot apply the transformation on all the corresponding blocks of the remaining columns. For the next iteration, a pass is made on the next pivot and the remaining columns to accumulate the inner products. Once the inner products are evaluated, the application of the transformation proceeds as before. With our scheme, we retain not only the current block of the pivot, but also the current block of the next pivot. Then processing the corresponding blocks of the remaining columns involves first applying the current transformation and second accumulating the inner product of the transformed block with the transformed block of the next pivot. To make this scheme work, we need to know the index of the next pivot before applying the current transformation. If the the ith pivot is the ith column, this is trivial. If the algorithm is to pick the next pivot as, say, the column with the largest norm, we must first determine the column which will have the largest norm after the current transformation is applyed, before actually applying the transformation. This is possible by (5.2.1).

For the QR decomposition we have assumed two concurrent I/O subsystem. One subsystem is dedicated to reading the pages of the current X and the other subsystem is dedicated to writing the updated pages of X. The "read", "process" and "write" operations can be performed in parallel. For the relational secondary storage organization, we have assumed an initial pass is made to project the matrix X unto the space of the active columns and then apply the QR decomposition to the (partially transposed) file of the active columns.

The "Vector Building Block", "Vector-Matrix" and "Look Ahead" schemes of the transposed secondary storage organization, involve, respectively, $N \cdot 2.5 \cdot p^2$, $N \cdot 1.5p^2$, and $N \cdot p^2$ page transfers. For the relational secondary storage organization, the minimum number of page transfers is $R + N \cdot 2 \cdot p^2$. However, in comparing the total execution times, in Figure 3 we have the total execution time in seconds as a function of the number of active columns. Here the VBB, VM and LA algorithms are all with a fully transposed secondary storage organization. The time per floating point operation is assumed to be 0.5 microseconds and the main storage size is held at 100 pages. Note that the LA scheme is always a lower bound. The VBB approach performs better than the algorithm for the relational organization if the number of active columns is less or equal to approximately 10. The corresponding value of p for VM is approximately 50. One general observation for the QR decomposition is that there is an iterative decrease in the number of currently active columns. Therefore the fully transposed secondary storage organization has better performance.

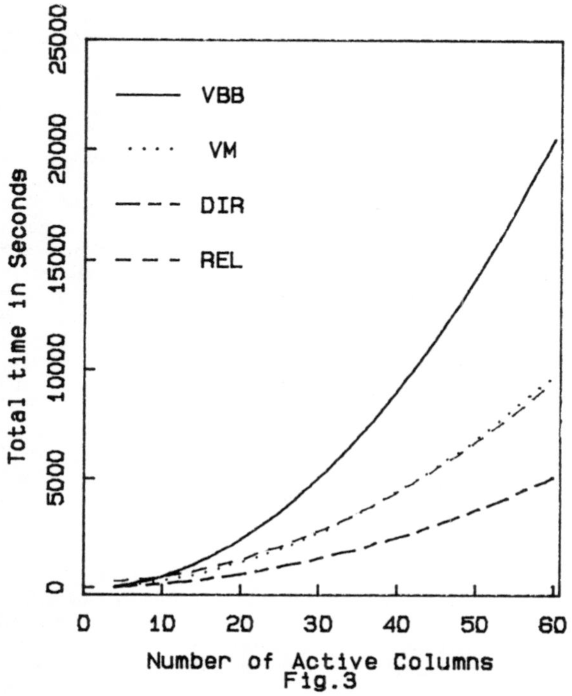

Fig.3

5.3. SVF

This matrix building blocks attempts to compute an n by p matrix W, a pxp orthogonal matrix V, and a pxp diagonal matrix D such that

$$X = W \cdot D \cdot V'$$

The p columns of W are the eigenvectors associated with the p largest eigenvalues of X.X'. The columns of V are the orthonormalized eigenvectors of X'.X . The non-ascending ($s_1 \geq s_2 \geq s_3 \geq .. \geq s_p$) diagonal elements of D are the non-negative square roots of the eigenvalues of X'.X (also called the "singular values" of X). Both D and V are of order $O(p^2)$, and therefore are stored in primary memory. W, however, is of order O(n.p), and should be stored on disk. With the Golub-Reinsch algorithm [WILK71], the decomposition precedes in two main steps:

Step 1- Reduction to Bidiagonal Form: This is accomplished by premultiplying X with p Householder transformations and postmultiplying it with p-2 Householder transformations.

Step 2 - Decomposition of the Bidiagonal Matrix: This is done through the implicitly shifted QR algorithm [WILL71, STEW73]. The details of this algorithm will not be discussed here. It is an infinitely iterative algorithm which tries to render the superdiagonal elements of the bidiagonal matrix negligible. Each iteration consists in pre and post multiplication of the bidiagonal matrix with Givens rotations. At the end of each iteration the resulting matrix remains bidiagonal. If B is the bidiagonal pxp matrix, this algorithms results in orthogonal matrices J and T (both pxp) such that

$$J \cdot B \cdot T' = D \quad (\text{or } B = J' \cdot D \cdot T)$$

Let the n by p matrix S be given by:

$$S = \begin{bmatrix} J' \\ 0 \end{bmatrix}$$

where O is the (n-p)xp zero matrix. Then W is:

$$W = L_1 \cdot L_2 \ldots L_p \cdot S$$

where the L_i's are the left Householder transformations. V' is:

$$V' = T \cdot R_{p-2} \cdots R_1$$

where the R_i's are the right transformations.

A direct implementation of the Golub-Reinsch algorithm is not economical in secondary storage references. We saw in the previous chapters that a vector building block implementation of a matrix operation always yields the worst performance (for transposed files). To minimize the secondary storage overhead we shall propose a looping and lookahead scheme, similar to those used for X'X and the QR decomposition.

An approach, due to Chan [CHAN82], is to first triangularize the matrix X using Householder transformations and then, subsequently, apply the Golub-Reinsch algorithm to the n by n upper triangular matrix. Therefore if:

$$Q' \cdot X = \begin{bmatrix} R \\ 0 \end{bmatrix}$$

$$R = L \cdot D \cdot V'$$

then

$$W = Q \cdot \begin{bmatrix} L \\ O \end{bmatrix}$$

Although Chan's motivation is primarily optimizing the computation, this approach also results in minimizing the I/O overhead, especially since the rotations are not applied to the current n by p matrix W. W can be obtained through either applying the left transformations to the first p columns of the identity n by n matrix and then performing a matrix multiplication with L. This involves accessing an n x p matrix O(p) times. However, it can be shown that through just one sweep we can obtain W, provided the first p elements of each u and the inner product of the u's are available. The inner product of the u's can be accumulated while applying the transformations (for example if the matrix is stored relational or if a horizontal-stripes scheme is used with the completely transposed organization). On the other hand, we saw in the previous chapter that the most efficient algorithm of the QR decomposition is the "Lookahead" scheme. It is not possible to accumulate all the inner products of the u's through this buffer management algorithm. Therefore there needs to be another pass over the transposed columns which store the u's to accumulate the inner products. This means that X'X can also be used as a building block to SVF.

Next let us show that if the inner product of the u's and the first p elements of each u is available, it is possible to accumulate the left Householder transformations and W. Suppose we want to evaluate:

$$Q = (I - \rho_1 u_1 \cdot u_1').(I - \rho_2 u_2 \cdot u_2') \cdots (I - \rho_p u_p \cdot u_p')$$

It can easily be shown that:

$$Q = I + \sum_{i=1}^{p} \sum_{j=i}^{p} c_{i,j} u_i \cdot u_j'$$

where the $c_{i,j}$'s are in terms of the ρ_i's and the inner products of the u's. The first p elements of the kth row of $u_i \cdot u_j'$ is given by:

$$u_{i,k} \cdot [\, u_{j,1},\ u_{j,2},\ \cdots,\ u_{j,p}\,]$$

where the first (j-1) elements of u_j are zero. Let U be the matrix of the u's and Q_p the first p columns of P. The rows k through m of P_p can be obtained by accessing the rows k through m of U, and performing a matrix multiplication of the (m-k)+1 by p submatrix of U with the upper triangular matrix T where:

$$T_{i,j} = \sum_{k=i}^{j} c_{i,k} \cdot u_{k,j} \ ; \quad 1 \le i \le j \le p$$

If $k \le p$ we need to add 1 to the diagonal elements to this matrix product. Therefore,

$$W = Q_p \cdot L = (I_p + U \cdot T) \cdot L = I_p \cdot L + U \cdot (T \cdot L)$$

and W could be obtained basically through the product of the n by p matrix U with the p by p matrix matrix T.L.

For the performance evaluation we did not specify any particular scheme for the diagonalization step. However we used Chan's approach in first performing a QR decomposition of X, and applying the GR algorithm (or a modification) to the upper triangular matrix.

It is important to analyze the contribution of the QR and U'U steps to the cost functions. For the percentage of page transfers as a function of the number of active columns, with the VBB strategy the QR decomposition step involved about 35% percent of the total number of page transfers and the U'U step about 15%. The corresponding percentages for the VM strategy were, respectively, approximately 47% and 16%. However, for the direct implementations, the percentage of the QR decomposition step went up from about 61% to 95% when we varied the number of active columns from 4 to about 60. The percentage of the U'U step went down from about 0.12% to 0.015%. Table I, gives the percentages of the total I/O as a function of the number of active columns. Here again, p varies from 4 to 60.

Strategy	QR	U'U
VBB	35%	15%
VM	40%	15%
DIR	61% to 93%	12% to 1%

Table I

Therefore, the QR step constitutes a substantial percentage of the total I/O, for the algorithms with the transposed organization. For the direct implementations it is at least 60% of the total I/O.

For the percentages of the total execution times, Table I is more or less representative of the I/O bound cases. However, for the CPU bound cases all three strategies showed similar behavior, with the QR step constituting approximately 40% of the total execution time and the U'U approximately 20%. This was to be expected since the total number of floating point operations for U'U is approximately $0.5 \cdot p^2 \cdot N \cdot q$, and for the QR and matrix product steps approximately $p^2 \cdot N \cdot q$ for each.

To compare the algorithms of the transposed organization with the special algorithm for the relational organization, for an I/O bound execution the VBB performs better than the relational organization only if the number of active columns is less or equal to 5. The VM strategy performs better only if the number of active columns is less or equal to 7. These results show the cumulative effect of the VBB and VM approaches on the cost functions. The direct implementations perform better than the relational for all values of p. Note, however, that with a CPU bound execution the VBB, VM and direct implementations perform better than the relational organization if the number of active columns are less than 6 and 15 respectively. The reason is that with slower CPU's (hence computation bound execution), the fixed "start-up" I/O overheads for the relational organization (in other words the step forming the partially transposed file) offsets the gains in I/O access times.

6. Conclusions

This research work concentrated on the secondary storage problems of three important operations: X'X, QR Decomposition and the Singular Value Factorization. The underlying data set was assumed to be much larger than the primary storage size. This study is a first step in the identification of the data access and retrieval problems of statistical computations. We introduced implementations of these important computational methods at three abstraction levels: Vector Building Block, Vector-Matrix and Direct Implementations. For the direct implementations, the algorithms were extensively analyzed to determine look-ahead and buffering schemes which reduce the I/O overhead. For X'X, the optimal strategy was to process the data matrix X stripe wise. The number of page transfers with this approach is linear in p (the number of active columns). For the QR decomposition the strategy was to accumulate the inner products for the next transformation while applying the current transformation. This basically eliminated the I/O overhead for the accumulation of the inner products. For the Singular Value Factorization, a substantial savings in I/O was obtained for the construction of W, by using a "matrix product" approach to the accumulation of the transformations.

Another important contribution was the comparative analysis of the transposed and relational secondary storage organizations. The general conclusion here is that we really need the direct implementations for the transposed secondary storage organizations in order to obtain substantial enhancements in the performance.

Our work also proposes a methodology for analyzing the performance and the secondary storage problems of other important computational methods

References

[BATO79] Batory, D. S., "On Searching Transposed Files," ACM TODS Vol. 4, No. 4, pp. 531-544, December, 1979.

[CHAN82] Chan, T. F. "An Improved Algorithm for Computing the Singular Value Decomposition," ACM Transactions on Mathematical Software 8, 1, pp. 72-83.

[CUPP81] Cuppen, J.J.M., "The Singular Value Decomposition in Product Form," Mathematisch Instituut, Amesterdam, pp. 81-106, April, 1981.

[DONG79] Dongarra, J., Moler, C., Bunch, J., and G. Stewart, "Linpack Users' Guide," SIAM, 1979.

[DONG83] Dongerra, J. "Redesigning Linear Algenra Algorithms," Bulletin De La Direction Des Etudes Et Des Rescherches Serie C, No 1, pp. 51-59, 1983.

[EGGE81] Eggers, S.J., Olken, F., and A. Shoshani, "A Compression Technique for Large Statistical Databases," Proceedings of the 7th International Conference on Very Large Data Bases, France, 1981, pp. 424-434.

[GOLU73] Golub, G. and G. Styan, "Numerical Computations for Univariate Linear Models," Journal Statistical Computing, Vol. 2, pp. 253-274, 1973.

[IBM 77] IBM, "Reference Manual for IBM 3350 Direct Access Storage," GA26-1638-2, File No. S370-07, IBM General Products Division, San Jose, California, April, 1977.

[KENN80] Kennedy, W. and J. Gentle, *Statistical Computing*, Marcel Dekker, Inc., 1980.

[McCu83] McCullagh, P., and, Nelder, J. A. Generalized Linear Models, New York. Chapman and Hall, 1983.

[MAND82] Mandel, John, "Use of Singular Value Decomposition In Regression Analysis," The American Statistician Vol. 36, No. 1, February, 1982.

[SEBER77] Seber, G., *Linear Regression Analysis*, John Wiley & Sons, 1977.

[STEW73] Stewart, G., *Introduction to Matrix Computations*, Academic Press, 1973.

[TURN79] Turner, M.J., Hammond, R., and Cotton, P., "A DMBS for LArge Statistical Databases," Proceedings of the 5th International Conference on VLDB, pp. 319-327, 1979.

[WILL71] Wilkinson, J.H. and Reinsch, C., *Linear Algebra*, Springer-Verlag, 1971.

Computational Geometry and Statistical Applications

Organizer: *Robert J. Serfling, The Johns Hopkins University*

Invited Presentations:

A Class of Problems in Statistical Computation: Generalized L- and Related Statistics, *Robert J. Serfling, The Johns Hopkins University*

Algorithms for Selection in Sets, with Applications to Statistics, *Greg N. Frederickson, Purdue University, and Donald B. Johnson, The Pennsylvania State University*

The Application of Voronoi Diagrams to Nonparametric Decision Rules, *Godfried T. Toussaint, McGill University, Binay K. Bhattacharya, Simon Frazer University, and Ronald S. Poulsen, McGill University*

Multidimensional Sorting -- An Overview, *Jacob E. Goodman, City College CUNY, and Richard Pollack, Courant Institute NYU*

COMPUTER SCIENCE AND STATISTICS:
The Interface, L. Billard (ed.)

A CLASS OF PROBLEMS IN STATISTICAL COMPUTATION: GENERALIZED L- AND RELATED STATISTICS

Robert J. Serfling

Department of Mathematical Sciences
The Johns Hopkins University
Baltimore, Maryland, U.S.A.

Let $X_1,\ldots,X_n$ be an i.i.d. sample and $h(x_1,\ldots,x_m)$ a "kernel". Consider the evaluations $h(X_{i_1},\ldots,X_{i_m})$ with $i_1,\ldots,i_m$ distinct and denote their ordered values by $W_{n1} \leq \ldots \leq W_{n,\binom{n}{m}}$. The class of statistics of form

$$\Sigma_i c_{ni} W_{ni},$$

with c_{ni} arbitrary constants, generalizes two well-known classes (U-statistics and L-statistics) and contains important new varieties such as median $\{m^{-1}(X_{i_1}+\ldots+X_{i_m})\}$, which generalizes the well-known Hodges-Lehmann location estimator (corresponding to $m = 2$). The asymptotic distribution theory of such statistics has recently been worked out in reasonable generality. This paper presents issues regarding their efficient computation.

1. INTRODUCTION

A recent accomplishment of the interface between computer science and statistics is the development of efficient algorithms for computation of the Hodges-Lehmann location estimator, given by

$$\text{(1.1)} \quad HL = \text{median}\{\tfrac{1}{2}(X_i+X_j)\},$$

based on a sample $X_1,\ldots,X_n$ from a probability distribution function F. Earlier, by analogy with the problem of computing the sample median, it was thought that $O(n^2 \log n)$ or $O(n^2)$ steps are necessary. However, the work of Shamos (1976) showed how to compute HL in only $O(n\log n)$ steps, by an algorithm first ordering $X_1,\ldots,X_n$ in $O(n \log n)$ steps and then reducing the problem in $O(\log n)$ iterations until the median is found.

In this sense, HL has been an anomaly in statistical computation, most other statistics typically used in practice falling into natural classes for which efficient computation has not been so subtle a problem. However, recently, some new and more complicated statistics have been formulated by Bickel and Lehmann (1976, 1979) to achieve properties in accord with certain criteria for nonparametric estimation of dispersion and spread. Also, some important new general classes of statistics have been formulated and investigated by Serfling (1984) and Janssen, Serfling and Veraverbeke (1983). These developments have brought to the fore a new class of problems in statistical computation similar in subtlety to the problem of computing HL.

Following general background in Section 2, new varieties of statistics will be presented in Section 3. Available knowledge and open issues regarding their efficient computation will be reviewed in Sections 4 and 5.

2. BACKGROUND

Let $X_1,\ldots,X_n$ be a sample of independent observations having distribution F and $h(x_1,\ldots,x_m)$ a given "kernel". The corresponding "U-statistic (introduced by Hoeffding (1948)) is given by

$$\text{(2.1)} \quad U_n = \binom{n}{m}^{-1} \Sigma h(X_{i_1},\ldots,X_{i_m}),$$

where the sum is taken over all $\binom{n}{m}$ combinations $\{i_1,\ldots,i_m\}$ distinct integers from $\{1,\ldots,n\}$. The class of U-statistics includes, for example, the sample mean (corresponding to m=1 and $h(x)=x$) and the sample variance $(n-1)^{-1}\Sigma_{i=1}^n (X_i-\bar{X})^2$ (corresponding to m=2 and $h(x_1,x_2) = \tfrac{1}{2}(x_1-x_2)^2$). Basically, the class of such statistics may be viewed as a generalization of the idea of forming the sample mean. However, for the purposes of "nonparametric" or "robust" estimation, a somewhat different principle is appropriate, in order to achieve a reduction in the impact of "outliers" on the value of the estimator. In this regard, "trimmed means" (average of the middle 90% of the observations, for example) become of interest. More generally, the class of "L-statistics," which are of the form

$$\text{(2.2)} \quad \Sigma_{i=1}^n c_{ni} X_{ni},$$

with c_{ni} arbitrary constants and $X_{ni} \le \ldots \le X_{nn}$ the ordered X_i's, has received much study. Other important classes are "M-statistics" (whose members are given by minimizing some function) and "R-statistics" (whose members are functions only of the ranks of the X_i's). Comprehensive discussion of these four classes of statistics may be found in Serfling (1980), Chapters 5, 7, 8 and 9 respectively. None of these classes generate special issues in statistical computation; however, the above discussion is necessary to the formulation and understanding of the class of statistics in the next section. For this purpose, it will be convenient to utilize a representation of L-statistics as "statistical functionals", following von Mises (1947)(or see Serfling (1980), Chapter 6). We introduce the usual sample distribution function,

$$F_n(x) = n^{-1}\Sigma_{i=1}^n 1(X_i \le x), \ -\infty < x < \infty,$$

and consider the particular functional $T(\cdot)$, defined on distribution functions G, given by

$$(2.3) \quad T(G)=\int_0^1 G^{-1}(t)J(t)dt + \Sigma_{j=1}^d a_j G^{-1}(p_j),$$

where $G^{-1}(t) = \inf\{x: G(x)\ge t\}$, the quantile function associated with G. Such a functional weights the quantiles $G^{-1}(t)$, $0<t<1$, of G according to a specified function $J(\cdot)$ for smooth weighting and/or specified weights $a_1,\ldots,a_d$ for discrete weighting. A particular "L-functional" is thus determined by specifying $J(\cdot)$, d, $p_1,\ldots,p_d$ and $a_1,\ldots,a_d$. The corresponding L-statistic is then simply $T(F_n)$. Noting that $T(F_n)$ may be written in the form

$$(2.4) \quad T(F_n)=\Sigma_{i=1}^n [\int_{(i-1)/n}^{i/n} J(t)dt]F_n^{-1}(i/n) + \Sigma_{j=1}^d a_j F_n^{-1}(p_j),$$

and that $F_n^{-1}(i/n)=X_{ni}$, we see that statistics of the form (2.3) form a wide subclass of those of the form (2.2).

3. GENERALIZED L-STATISTICS

Continuing with the preceding notation, we denote for any fixed kernel $h(x_1,\ldots,x_m)$ the ordered values of $h(X_{i_1},\ldots,X_{i_m})$ by

$$W_{n,1} \le \ldots \le W_{n,\binom{n}{m}},$$

and we consider the class of statistics of form

$$(3.1) \qquad \Sigma_{i=1}^{\binom{n}{m}} c_{ni} W_{ni}$$

with c_{ni} arbitrary constants. The form (3.1) is quite general. It includes the U-statistic with kernel h, given by (3.1) with $c_{ni} = 1/\binom{n}{m}$, all i. It includes the class (2.2) of L-statistics, given by (3.1) for the particular kernel $h(x)=x$. Moreover, it includes statistics such as HL (see (1.1)), which is neither a U-statistic nor an L-statistic. In this way (3.1) provides a unifying framework within which to view various familiar statistics; but also (3.1) embraces important new statistics, such as "trimmed U-statistics" or a generalization of HL, namely

$$(3.2) \qquad HL_{(m)} = \text{median}\{m^{-1}(X_{i_1}+\ldots+X_{i_m})\}.$$

As an example of a trimmed U-statistic, we mention the "trimmed variance", given by

$$(3.3) \quad T(H_n)=(1-\alpha-\beta)^{-1} \sum_{i=[\binom{n}{m}\alpha]}^{[\binom{n}{m}(1-\beta)]} [\tfrac{1}{2}(X_{i_1}-X_{i_2})]^2,$$

which serves as a nonparametric dispersion measure (here the kernel is $h(x_1,x_2) = (x_1-x_2)^2$.). Both (3.2) and (3.3) offer novel challenges in computational statistics.

In order to employ a functional representation as with L-statistics, we introduce an associated empirical distribution function

$$H_n(y)=\binom{n}{m}^{-1}\Sigma 1(h(X_{i_1},\ldots,X_{i_m})\le y), \ -\infty<y<\infty,$$

which reduces to F_n in the case of $h(x)=x$ but in general has more complicated structure due to statistical dependence among summands. (In particular, for each fixed y, $H_n(y)$ is of the form (2.1) and hence a U-statistic.) It follows by analogy with (2.4) that a large subclass of statistics of form (3.1) are given by

$$(3.4) \quad T(H_n)=\Sigma_{i=1}^{\binom{n}{m}} [\int_{(i-1)/\binom{n}{m}}^{i/\binom{n}{m}} J(t)dt]H_n^{-1}(i/\tbinom{n}{m}) + \Sigma_{j=1}^d a_j H_n^{-1}(p_j),$$

where $T(\cdot)$ is the same (L-) functional given by (2.3). The parameter estimated by this "generalized L-statistic" (GL-statistic) may be expressed as $T(H_F)$, where H_F is the distribution function estimated by H_n, i.e.,

$$H_F(y) = P_F\{h(X_1,\ldots,X_m)\le y\}, \ -\infty<y<\infty,$$

the distribution function of the random variable $h(X_1,\ldots,X_m)$. Under broad assumptions, statistics of the form (3.4) are asymptotically normal in distribution (see Serfling (1984)), which makes them suitable for use in practice as test statistics and estimators, provided that computational ease is not sacrificed unduly.

A further development in generalizing the class of L-statistics was introduced by Janssen, Serfling and Veraverbeke (1984), who considered a functional somewhat more general that (2.3), namely

$$(3.5) \qquad \tilde{T}(G) = \int_0^1 q(T_t(G))dK(t),$$

where G is again a df, q is a real-valued function of a real variable, K denotes a df on [0,1], and for each t in the support S of K, $T_t(\cdot)$ denotes a functional of form (2.3). They then considered parameters of the form given by $\tilde{T}(H_F)$ and established asymptotic normality of estimators of the form $\tilde{T}(H_n)$ under broad conditions. Examples: (i) With h(x)=x, so that $H_F=F$, and with q(x)=x and $T_t(\cdot)=T(\cdot)$ (independent of t), the form (3.5) reduces to the simple L-functional (2.3). (ii) With these same substitutions but allowing arbitrary kernel h, we obtain the GL-functional $T(H_F)$ considered above. (iii) With h(x)=x, take $q(x)=|x|^\gamma$ and define $T_t(G)=|G^{-1}(1-t)-G^{-1}(t)|$, $0<t<1$. Then (3.5) becomes

$$\tilde{T}(F) = \int_0^1 |F^{-1}(t)-F^{-1}(1-t)|^\gamma dK(t),$$

a form of functional proposed by Bickel and Lehmann (1979) as a nonparametric measure of spread of a (not necessarily symmetric) df F. In particular, they suggest the case $\gamma=2$ and K(·) uniform on $(\beta,1-\beta)$, where $0<\beta<\frac{1}{2}$, giving

$$\tilde{T}_\beta(F)=(\tfrac{1}{2}-\beta)^{-1}\int_{\frac{1}{2}}^{1-\beta}[F^{-1}(t)-F^{-1}(1-t)]^2dt.$$

The corresponding estimator $\tilde{T}_\beta(F_n)$ presents no computational subtleties. However, a little more interesting is another nonparametric spread measure, also introduced by Bickel and Lehmann (1979), given by $\tilde{T}(H_n)$, for estimation of $\tilde{T}(H_F)$, with $\tilde{T}(\cdot)$ the functional

$$(3.6) \qquad \tilde{T}(G) = (1-\alpha-\beta)^{-1}\int_\alpha^{1-\beta}[G^{-1}(\tfrac{t+1}{2})]^2dt,$$

and with H_F defined by the kernel $h(x_1,x_2) = x_1-x_2$. (Thus H_F is the symmetric df of X-X', where X and X' denote independent random variables with df F. In the case that F is already assumed to be symmetric with known median 0, a more direct nonparametric spread, or "dispersion", measure is simply $\tilde{T}(F_n)$, with $\tilde{T}(\cdot)$ given by (3.6). Such a statistic was introduced by Bickel and Lehmann (1976).) Computation of (3.6) involves ordering the differences X_i-X_j. (See Section 5 for further discussion.)

4. COMPUTATION OF $HL_{(m)}$

Continuing the discussion of $HL_{(2)}$ in Section 1, we note that various authors have worked further on this problem. In particular, see Johnson and Kashdan (1978), Johnson and Mizoguchi (1978), and Frederickson and Johnson (1982). Various algorithms and results are presented, making it now clear that $HL_{(2)}$ can be computed in O(n log n) steps and that this rate is optimal. (Also, it is not necessary to sort the X_i's first.)

Regarding $HL_{(m)}$ for m > 2, this also is treated by Johnson and Mizoguchi (1978), who establish the rate $O(n^{\lceil m/2\rceil}\log n)$, where $\lceil x\rceil$ denotes the smallest integer $\geq$ x. Their method is to reduce the case of order n to cases of lower order, using relations such as

$$\text{median}\{X_{i_1}+\ldots+X_{i_4}\} = \text{med}\{Y_i + Y_j\},$$

for example, where Y denotes the multiset of pairwise sums x_i+x_j taken from $\{x_1,\ldots,x_n\}$. The above rate thus follows immediately, using the rate O(n log n) known for selecting median $\{x_i+y_j\}$, given sets $\{x_1,\ldots,x_n\}$ and $\{y_1,\ldots,y_n\}$. However, they do not consider the question of optimality of this rate (although they do consider such questions with respect to certain other problems studied in the paper).

5. KERNELS OTHER THAN X_i+X_j

The rate O(n log n) for median $\{X_i+X_j\}$ extends readily to median$\{\alpha X_i+\beta X_j\}$, as discussed by Johnson and Kashdan (1978). They consider also the case of an <u>arbitrary</u> kernel $h(x_i,x_j)$, but only for the case m=2 arguments, and they address only the question of <u>lower</u> bounds. In particular, they establish the rate Ω(n log n) on the complexity of finding median$\{h(X_i,X_j)\}$. The notation $\Omega(f(n))$ denotes a function greater than cf(n) for some positive c and all but finitely many n.) It would be of interest to know whether for all kernels the complexity of finding median$\{h(X_{i_1},\ldots,X_{i_m})\}$ is $\Omega(n^{\lceil m/2\rceil}\log n)$. Another kernel of special interest is $h(x_1,x_2) = |x_1-x_2|$, in connection with statistics such as median$\{\frac{1}{2}(X_i-X_j)^2\}$, a simple measure of dispersion. Finally, in connection with the statistics mentioned in Section 3, an interesting general problem is that of computing

$$\int_\alpha^{1-\beta} q(H_n^{-1}(t))dt$$

for general classes of kernels h and functions q. Essentially, this means efficiently <u>ordering</u> the middle $1-\alpha-\beta$ proportion of values $h(X_{i_1},\ldots,X_{i_m})$. These and related questions represent timely pursuits in the interface of computer science and statistics.

6. ACKNOWLEDGEMENT

This research was supported by the U.S. Department of Navy under Office of Naval Research Contract No. N00014-79-C-0801. Reproduction in whole or in part is permitted for any purpose of the United States Government.

REFERENCES

Bickel, P.J. and Lehmann, E.L. (1976), "Descriptive statistics for nonparametric models. III. Dispersion", *Ann. Statist.* 4, 1139-1158.

Bickel, P.J. and Lehmann, E.L. (1979), "Descriptive statistics for nonparametric models. IV. Spread", in *Contributions to Statistics. Hájek Memorial Volume* (ed. by Jurečková), Academia, Prague, 33-40.

Frederickson, Greg N. and Johnson, Donald B. (1982), "The complexity of selection and ranking in X + Y and matrices with sorted columns", *J. Comp. and Syst. Sc.*, 24, 197-208.

Hoeffding, W. (1948 "A class of statistics with asymptotically normal distribution", *Ann. Math. Statist.*, 19, 293-325.

Janssen, Paul, Serfling, Robert and Veraverbeke, Noël (1984), "Asymptotic normality for a general class of statistical functions and applications to measures of spread", *Ann. Statist.*, 12, to appear.

Johnson, Donald B. and Kashdan, Samuel D. (1978), "Lower bounds for selection in X + Y and other multisets", *J. ACM*, 25, 556-570.

Johnson, Donald B. and Mizoguchi, Tetsuo (1978), "Selecting the k-th element in X + Y and $X_1+X_2+...+X_m$", *SIAM J. Comput.*, 7, 147-153.

Serfling, R.J. (1980), *Approximation Theorems of Mathematical Statistics*, Wiley, New York.

Serfling, Robert J. (1984), "Generalized L-, M- and R-statistics", *Ann. Statist.*, 12, to appear.

Shamos, M.J. (1976), "Geometry and Statistics: problems at the interface", in *New Directions and Recent Results in Algorithms and Complexity* (ed. by J.F. Traub), Academic Press, New York, 251-280.

von Mises, R. (1947), "On the asymptotic distribution of differentiable statistical functions", *Ann. Math. Statist.*, 18, 309-348.

COMPUTER SCIENCE AND STATISTICS:
The Interface, L. Billard (ed.)

ALGORITHMS FOR SELECTION IN SETS, WITH APPLICATIONS TO STATISTICS

Greg N. Frederickson*
Department of Computer Sciences
Purdue University

Donald B. Johnson†
Computer Science Department
The Pennsylvania State University

Recently, the computational complexity has been established for the problem of finding an element of given rank, such as the median, in multisets of the form $X + Y = \{x + y \mid x \in X, y \in Y\}$. Selection procedures for this problem are directly applicable to finding the Hodges-Lehmann estimator. We survey efficient methods for determining an element of given rank in sets of this form, where the input sets X and Y are either in sorted or unsorted order. We also discuss a number of generalizations of this structure, and give optimal algorithms for selecting in sets with these structures.

1. Introduction

Consider a multiset $\mathbf{X}$ of elements drawn from a universe with a total order. The problem of *selection* in $\mathbf{X}$ is to determine, for a given rank k, an element that is k-th in some total ordering of $\mathbf{X}$. The problem of selecting an element of given rank has received considerable attention [FG, H, Ki, PY, SPP, Yp] since its complexity was first demonstrated to be proportional to the cardinality of the set [B]. A more general version of this problem, which we study here, is one in which the set $\mathbf{X}$ is constrained to possess a certain structure. The structures we consider are simple and mathematically interesting, such as for example, the Cartesian set $X + Y = \{x + y \mid x \in X, y \in Y\}$, where X and Y are two input sets. We present a number of variations of this structure, and survey efficient methods for determining an element of given rank in sets organized according to these structures. Our algorithms for these problems are asymptotically optimal.

Selection in $X + Y$ can be used to compute the Hodges-Lehmann estimator in statistics [HL, MR, JR, S]. It is desired to estimate the difference in the means of the two populations from which sets of observations X and Y, respectively, have been drawn. The Hodges-Lehmann estimator for this difference is the median of $X + (-Y)$. In the case that the sets X and Y are unsorted, algorithms for finding the median in $X + Y$ have been presented in [JM] and [S] which require $O(n \log n)$ time, where $|X| = n > |Y| = m > 1$. This is improved somewhat in [FJ1], where the time required is shown to be $\Theta(n \log m)$. All three methods take advantage of the ability to represent the set $X + Y$ in a matrix form, called a *Cartesian matrix*, and in fact manipulate a succinct representation of this matrix.

In the case that the sets X and Y are sorted, it is possible to do better. We show that the time complexity for selecting the median in the sorted Cartesian matrix $X + Y$ is $\Theta(m \log(2n/m))$, assuming that the sorted sets X and Y have already been read into memory. That X and Y are already sorted can reflect the situation that there are many sets of observations, and estimates are to be obtained between many pairs of them. Then the cost of sorting the sets would be a preprocessing cost that would be overwhelmed by the many median-finding computations.

Our methods can handle more general problems than computing the Hodges-Lehmann estimator. We discuss these in the hope that statistical applications might be forthcoming for them. Note that the elements in any row or column of a sorted Cartesian matrix are in sorted order. In fact, our algorithms work just as well on *sorted matrices*, which have such a property, as long as individual elements can be computed as needed, or the cost of inputting the sorted matrix is not born by the selection procedure. We can handle sets which are collections of sorted matrices, *i.e.*, $\mathbf{X} = \{\mathbf{X}_j\}_{j=1}^{N}$, where each $\mathbf{X}_j$ is a sorted matrix of dimensions $n_j \times m_j$. We can select an element of given rank in $\Theta(\sum_{j=1}^{N} m_j \log(2n_j/m_j))$ time, assuming $m_j \le n_i$. This version is fairly general, since it includes as special cases: 1) a single sorted matrix (*i.e.*, $N = 1$),

---

*Work of this author partially supported by the National Science Foundation under grant MCS-7909259.

† Work of this author partially supported by the National Science Foundation under grants MCS 77-21092 and MCS 80-002684.

2) a set of thin matrices ($N > 1$ and $m_i = 1$ for $i = 1, \cdots, N$), and 3) a set of elements ($N > 1$ and $n_i = 1$ for all i). In all cases but the latter, the complexity of selection is asymptotically less than the cardinality of the set: $\sum_{j=1}^{N} m_j n_j$. The Cartesian matrices can be succinctly presented. For other sorted matrices, sublinear algorithms are possible when the cost of inputting can be distributed over several computations.

An example of an application of selection in such a set is the following graph problem. A *p-center* of a nonnegatively- weighted network is a set of p "supply" vertices chosen so as to minimize the maximum distance from any vertex to a supply point. An efficient method to locate *p-centers* in networks with tree topologies uses repeated selection of intervertex path lengths [CT1, CT2, KH, MTZC, FJ2]. As we show in [FJ2], the set of all path lengths may be represented as a collection of Cartesian matrices $X_i + Y_i$ where X_i and Y_i are sorted. The selection algorithms in this paper may be used to select optimally in such a collection.

In addition to selecting for the median, our methods can handle selecting an element of any rank k. In fact, the complexity of selecting in such constrained sets depends not only on the matrix dimensions, but also on the rank k. For instance, selection in an $n \times m$ sorted matrix may require anywhere from constant time up to time that is $\Theta(m \log(2n/m))$, depending on the rank k. This dependence on k in our constrained problems is in marked contrast to the situation of the unconstrained problem, in which the value of k affects only the constant factor.

An example of an application in which k is much smaller than the rank of the median is the problem of optimum discrete distribution of effort for m concave functions $\{f_j\}$ [Ko, GM, FJ1]. It is desired to distribute discretely n units of "effort" among the $\{f_j\}$ so as to maximize the sum of the function values, i.e., maximize $\sum_{j=1}^{m} f_j(a_j)$ subject to $\sum_{j=1}^{m} a_j = n$ for nonnegative integers $\{a_j\}$. The problem is solved by selecting the n-th largest element in $\mathbf{X} = \{f_j(i+1) - f_j(i) \mid j = 1, \cdots, m, \ i = 0, \cdots, n-1\}$, where the concavity of the functions yields one sorted $n \times 1$ matrix in $\mathbf{X}$ for each j.

To present the inherent complexity of our problems in in a form involving k, we factor out of our discussion certain simple problem reductions. It is reasonable to expect that any selection problem on N sorted matrices of dimension $n_j \times m_j$ will be presented in what we call *reduced* from where $m_j \le n_j \le k$, for all j, and $k \le \lceil \frac{1}{2} \sum_{j=1}^{N} m_j n_j \rceil$. Details of how to transform a problem into reduced form can be found in [FJ3].

In section 2, we give a basic algorithm for selection in a sorted matrix or, more generally, in a set of sorted matrices all of the same size. In section 3, we show how to aggregate sorted matrices of different sizes into a form that may be handled by the basic algorithm. the algorithms in these sections are asymptotically optimal for selecting medians.

Methods for selecting optimally for any k are presented in section 4. We outline algorithms which are optimal over the whole range of k for selecting optimally in a single sorted matrix, in a set of thin sorted matrices, and in collections of sorted matrices. A more complete version of these results, along with a treatment of the complementary problem of ranking, can be found in [FJ3].

2. Basic Algorithm for Selection in a Sorted Matrix

In this section we give our basic algorithm for selection and apply it to a single sorted matrix of dimensions $n \times m$ where $1 < m \le n$. (When $m = 1$ a solution can be found in constant time.) The running time of the basic algorithm is independent of k and will later be shown to be optimal on reduced problems where $k = \Theta(nm)$. (As described in the introduction any problem where n exceeds k can immediately be reduced in dimensions so that $m \le n \le k$.) The basic algorithm may also be applied to a set of equal-sized matrices or to an input with the essential properties of such a set.

Our basic algorithm performs a sequence of selections on elements representing submatrices of the given problem. (See Figure 1.) The selections are performed in pairs, yielding upper and lower bounds on the k-th element and identifying submatrices that need no longer be considered. At each iteration the remaining submatrices are subdivided to allow refined bounds to be gotten by the next pair of selections. These iterations finally reduce the submatrices to single elements from among which a solution is found directly by selection.

A submatrix of a given matrix is termed a *cell*. Associated with each cell C is a smallest element $min(C)$, chosen as the element with smallest row and column indices, and a largest element $max(C)$, chosen as the element with largest row and column indices. Initially there is a single cell, the matrix $\mathbf{X}$, of dimensions $n \times m$ and number of elements $S = nm$. An iteration begins by splitting all remaining cells into four parts. If both dimensions of a cell are greater than one, then the cell is called *thick*, and each dimension is split in half. If one dimension is equal to one, then the cell is called *thin*, and the other dimension is split into quarters. For ease of exposition it is assumed that S is a power of 4. Hence, every cell will be of size a power of 4 and each dimension greater than 1 will be divisible by 2. It is sufficiently easy to realize this restriction by means of implicit padding of matrices so that the restriction is of little practical consequence.

Algorithm SELECT ($CELLS$, k)

(1) $k' \leftarrow k$

(2) **for** $p \leftarrow 1$ **to** $\log_4 S$ **do**

(2.1) Split each cell in $CELLS$.

(2.2) Let $q \leftarrow \lceil k'/(S/4^p) \rceil + B_p$. If $q \leq |CELLS|$, select a q-th element x_u in the multiset $\{\min(C) | C \in CELLS\}$. Discard $|CELLS| - q + 1$ cells from $CELLS$, retaining every cell C with $min(C) < x_u$ and no cell C with $min(C) > x_u$.

(2.3) Let $r \leftarrow \lfloor k'/(S/4^p) \rfloor - B_p$. If $r \geq 1$, select an r-th element x_l in the multiset $\{max(C) | C \in CELLS\}$. Discard r cells from $CELLS$, retaining every cell C with $max(C) > x_l$ and no cell C with $max(C) < x_l$. Set $k' \leftarrow k' - r(S/4^p)$.

(3) Select the k'-th element in $CELLS$.

Figure 1. The basic selection algorithm.

The structure of the matrix induces a partition of the set of remaining cells into subsets called *chains*. If the cells are thick, then two cells belong to the same chain if and only if they are in the same diagonal of the matrix of submatrices obtainable from the original matrix by partitioning it into submatrices of the same dimensions as the cells. If the cells are thin, then two cells are in the same chain if and only if they come from the same column in the original matrix. In either case, it is easily seen that if two cells C' and C'' are in the same chain, then either $max(C') \leq min(C'')$ or $max(C'') \leq min(C')$. Let B_p be the maximum possible number of chains after splitting cells on the p-th iteration. If cells are thick, then the maximum possible number of chains is $2^{p+1}-1$; otherwise it is m. Since $2^{p+1}-1 < m$ if and only if cells are thick, $B_p = \min\{m, 2^{p+1}-1\}$.

After the remaining cells have been split, two selection computations are performed. In the first, the smallest elements of the remaining cells are selected among to find a q-th element x_u, where $q = \lceil k'4^p/S \rceil + B_p$ and k' is the rank to be selected for in the set of elements in the remaining cells. The value x_u is an upper bound for more than k' remaining elements. Thus all but $q-1$ cells may be discarded, such that each cell C with $min(C) = x_u$. Similarly, the largest elements of remaining cells are selected among to find an r-th element x_l, where $r = \lfloor k'4^p/S \rfloor - B_p$. The value x_l is a lower bound for all but fewer than k' elements, and thus r cells may be discarded following a discarding rule similar to the above.

After $\log_4 S$ iterations, all remaining cells will be single elements, and there will be at most $O(m)$ of them. A linear-time selection algorithm is employed to select the appropriate element.

Lemma 1. The basic algorithm SELECT correctly computes a k-th element in a collection of cells of equal size, a power of 4.

Proof. We first establish that, after every iteration, a k'-th element in the multiset union of the set of cells is a k-th element in matrix **X**. This is shown by induction on the number of iterations. The above claim is certainly true after zero iterations. Consider the p-th iteration, $p > 0$. Each cell is of size $S/4^p$. Hence there are fewer than $\lceil k'/(S/4^p) \rceil$ cells with all values less than the k'-th element. Since there are no more than B_p chains, there are no more than B_p cells with some values less than the k'-th element and some values greater than or equal to the k'-th element in the same cell. Thus x_u is the minimum of a cell in which there are no values smaller than the k'-th element. Therefore discarding according to the rule presented will retain k' elements no larger than the k'-th element and discard no element that is smaller.

By a similar argument it can be shown that the second selection retains an element that is k'-th before the second selection and discards no element greater than this element. Therefore k' is adjusted correctly. So, by induction, at every iteration there is a k'-th element which is k-th in the original matrix. Hence the final selection in the set of singleton submatrices yields and element that is k-th in the original matrix as required. □

Theorem 1. A selection problem on a sorted matrix of dimensions $n \times m$, $1 < m \leq n$, is solved by the basic algorithm in $O(m \log(2n/m))$ time.

Proof. Correctness follows from Lemma 1. At most $q-1-r \leq 2B_p$ cells remain at the end of the p-th iteration of step 2. Since remaining cells are split into quarters, at most $4(2B_p)$ elements are selected among in the $(p+1)$-th iteration. If a linear-time selection algorithm [B] is used, then the time per iteration is proportional to the number of cells. Thus the complexity of step 2 is at most proportional to

$$\sum_{p=1}^{\log_4 S} B_p \leq \sum_{p=1}^{\log_4 S} \min\{2^{p+1}, m\}$$
$$= \sum_{p=1}^{\log_2 m-1} 2^{p+1} + \sum_{p=\log_4 m^2}^{\log_4 nm} m$$
$$< 2m + 2m \log_4(n/m) = O(m \log(2n/m))$$

At the completion of step 2, there will be no more than $2m$ single elements, so that step 3 will run in time $O(m)$. □

Since the dimensions m and n which parameterize the bound in Theorem 1 can always be made to satisfy $m \leq n \leq k$ in constant time, they may be taken to be $\min\{m, k\}$ and $\min\{n, k\}$, respectively. The bound in Theorem 1 can be improved significantly when $k = o(nm)$. We deal with this case in section 4.

3. Selection in a Collection of Sorted Matrices

We consider selection in a collection of $N > 1$ sorted matrices $\{\mathbf{X}_j\}, j=1, \cdots, N$, of dimensions $n_j \times m_j$, where $n_j \geq m_j$ for each j. The basic algorithm in section 2 can solve this selection problem if the input matrices are first combined into a single matrix-like aggregate with all of the essential properties of the cells on which the basic algorithm operates. The aggregate is generated by repeatedly combining four smaller structures of the same size into a larger structure, until a single structure results. The aggregate and smaller structures will be split and selected among in a fashion analogous to that presented in section 2. As before, it is assumed in the presentation of the algorithm that $n_j m_j$ is a power of 4, for all j.

In order to combine all matrices, it may be necessary to create additional matrices, with all elements of value ∞, called *dummy matrices*. Structures created by combining are called synthetic cells. A *synthetic cell C* of size S is a collection of four structures $\{C_1, C_2, C_3, C_4\}$ of size $S/4$, where a structure is an original matrix of any shape, a dummy matrix, or a synthetic cell. It is not hard to combine matrices so as to minimize the total number of dummy matrices. If this is done, there will be no more than three dummy matrices of each size less than the size of the aggregate. It follows that the number of original and dummy matrices is one more than three times the total number of synthetic cells. The number of synthetic cells is thus less than the number of cell sizes used plus one third the number of original matrices.

Synthetic cells are handled in a fashion similar to cells representing submatrices. When split, a synthetic cell is replaced by its four components. Any dummy matrices so generated are discarded immediately. Associated with a synthetic cell C are two values, $min(C)$ and $max(C)$, upon which selections are performed. The value $min(C)$ is $\min\{min(C') \mid C' \in C\}$, and $max(C)$ is similarly defined. Each synthetic cell is defined to be in a chain by itself.

With these conventions established it may be seen from the proof of Lemma 1 that the basic algorithm selects correctly in any synthetic cell. Let S be the number of elements in the largest synthetic cell, and let B_p be, as before, the maximum possible number of chains after splitting cells on the p-th iteration. The value of B_p may be described as follows. For $j=1, \cdots, N$, let B_p^j be the maximum possible number of chains in $\mathbf{X}_j$ on the p-th iteration, if the current cell size is not larger than the size of $\mathbf{X}_j$, and zero otherwise. Let B_p^0 be the maximum number of synthetic cells active on the p-th iteration. Then

$$B_p = B_p^0 + \sum_{j=1}^{N} B_p^j$$

Let S_j be the size of $\mathbf{X}_j$. Then it can be seen that $B_p^j = \min\{m_j, \lceil 2^{p+1}\sqrt{S_j/S}\,\rceil - 1\}$.

Theorem 2. A selection problem in a collection of sorted matrices $\{\mathbf{X}_1, \cdots, \mathbf{X}_N\}$ in which $\mathbf{X}_j$ has dimension $n_j \times m_j$, $n_j \geq m_j$, can be solved in $O(\sum_{j=1}^{N} m_j \log(2n_j/m_j))$ time.

Proof. The method, aggregation into a single synthetic cell followed by application of the basic algorithm, has been described in the preceding paragraphs. Correctness of this method follows from Lemma 1. If the objects to be aggregated are bucket sorted according to size, aggregation can be performed in time proportional to $N + \log S$. By construction, $S < 4\sum_{j=1}^{N} S_j$. Thus $\log_4 S < \sum_{j=1}^{N} \log_4(4n_j m_j) \leq \sum_{j=1}^{N} m_j \log_4(4n_j/m_j)$. It follows that aggregation is $O(\sum_{j=1}^{N} m_j \log(2n_j/m_j))$.

In a fashion similar to that in Theorem 1, the complexity of step 2 of the basic algorithm is found to be at most proportional to $\sum_{p=1}^{\log_4 S} B_p = \sum_{p=1}^{\log_4 S} \sum_{j=0}^{N} B_p^j = \sum_{j=1}^{N} \sum_{p=1}^{\log_4 S} B_p^j + \sum_{p=1}^{\log_4 S} B_p^0$. The second sum is the total number of synthetic cells which, by previous remarks is less than $\log_4 S + N/3$. For any $j=1, \cdots, N$, we have

$$\sum_{p=1}^{\log_4 S} B_p^j = \sum_{p=1}^{\log_4 S} \min\{\lceil 2^{p+1}\sqrt{S_j/S}\ \rceil -1, m_j\}$$
$$\leq \sum_{p=1}^{\log_4 S_j} \min\{2^{p+1}, m_j\} = O(m_j \log(2n_j/m_j)).$$

Using the bound just obtained for $\log_4 S$, it follows that the complexity of step 2 is $O(\sum_{j=1}^{N} m_j \log_2(2n_j/m_j))$ At the completion of step 2, there are $O(\sum_{j=1}^{N} m_j)$ single elements remaining, in which to select. □

We note that it is not necessary to combine all matrices into a single synthetic cell. The combining process need only be continued to the first point at which all structures to be combined are the same size. The basic algorithm may then be applied to this set, with the value of S set to this size. It may be verified that the time complexity of this variant is no greater, and that correctness follows from the correctness of the algorithm presented. We also note that the bound of Theorem 2 does not depend on reduced inputs though, as later results show, the bound is optimal for selecting medians in reduced inputs, i.e. when $m_j \leq n_j \leq k$ for all j and $k = \Theta(\sum_{j=1}^{N} m_j n_j)$. the bound of Theorem 2 can be improved when $k = o(\sum_{j=1}^{N} m_j n_j)$.

4. Selection When k is Small

Our basic algorithm for selection in a sorted matrix is correct for any value of k, but its running time is suboptimal if $k = o(nm)$. To realize and optimal running time as a function of k, m, and n, it suffices to extract from the given matrix a certain set of submatrices guaranteed to contain all elements less than the k-th and at least k elements no larger. Although these submatrices are of different shapes, they are of equal size and thus the basic algorithm may be applied directly without the combining presented in section 3. We continue our assumption that nm is a power of 4.

The submatrices are identified as follows. Let K be the smallest power of 4 no smaller than k, and let $H = \min\{\sqrt{K}, m\}$. Let $\mathbf{X}_0$ be a submatrix with dimension $K/H \times H$ in the upper left corner of $\mathbf{X}$. Extending downward (in the direction of increasing row number) is a series of submatrices $\mathbf{X}_1, \cdots, \mathbf{X}_{\log_2 H}$ of dimensions $n_j \times m_j = (2^{j-1}K/H) \times (H/2^{j-1})$ for $j=1, \cdots, \log_2 H$. Thus $\mathbf{X}_j$ is the submatrix of $\mathbf{X}$ with index range $[\,2^{j-1}K/H, 2^j K/H\,] \times [\,1, H/2^{j-1}\,]$. If $n < K$, then $\mathbf{X}$ is assumed to be padded implicitly with elements of value ∞. If $H = \sqrt{K}$, then there is an analogous sequence $\mathbf{X}'_1, \cdots, \mathbf{X}'_{\log_2 H}$ to the right of $\mathbf{X}_0$, of dimensions $(H/2^{j-1}) \times (2^{j-1}K/H)$ for $j=1, \cdots, \log_2 H$. As before, implicit padding is used as necessary.

It is sufficient to confine the search for a k-th element to the union of these submatrices. Since the rows and columns of $\mathbf{X}$ are sorted, it follows that every element discarded is no smaller than k elements that are retained. Thus a k-th element in the elements retained is k-th in the original matrix.

Theorem 3. Selection of a k-th element in a sorted matrix of dimensions $n \times m$, $n \geq m > 1$, can be performed in $O(h \log(2k/h^2))$ time where $h = \min\{\sqrt{k}, m\}$. □

While we have shown how to take advantage of a small value of k to yield a faster algorithm for selection in a single sorted matrix, the running time of our algorithm for selection in a collection of sorted matrices is insensitive to k. We next give an algorithm for selection in a collection of sorted matrices restricted to the form $\{\mathbf{X}_j\}$, $j=1, \cdots, N$, where each matrix $\mathbf{X}_j$ is of dimension $n_j \times 1$. We call such matrices *thin matrices*. The matrices are preprocessed, yielding a problem which is solved by the basic algorithm. The preprocessing is in two steps. First the matrices are truncated to satisfy requirements on matrix sizes that reflect the value of k. Then the matrices are combined as in section 3.

Truncation is done according to the following generalization of the truncation given in [FJ1]. Let $i^* = \lceil (k+1)/(\lfloor N/2 \rfloor +1) \rceil$. The matrices $\mathbf{X}_1, \cdots, \mathbf{X}_N$ are reordered so that for $a \leq \lfloor N/2 \rfloor \leq b$, the i^*-th value in $\mathbf{X}_a$ is not greater than the i^*-th value in $\mathbf{X}_b$. If $i^* > n_j$, assume the i^*-th value of $\mathbf{X}_j$ to be ∞. Truncate matrices $\mathbf{X}_j$, $j=\lfloor N/2 \rfloor +1, \cdots, N$, by resetting $n_j = \min\{n_j, i^*-1\}$. Repeat the process recursively with the first $\lfloor N/2 \rfloor$ matrices, until $i^* > n_j$ for all $\mathbf{X}_j$.

When the discarding is completed, at least k elements remain and any element that is k-th among them is a k-th element in the original problem. This follows since whenever a (noninfinite) element is discarded there must be at least $(\lfloor N/2 \rfloor +1)i^* -1 \geq k$ elements retained that are no larger than it.

A linear-time selection algorithm may be used among the i^*-th elements to determine the reordering of the matrices. The time for the first reordering is $O(N)$, and thus the total time for the truncation is proportional to at most $N + \lfloor N/2 \rfloor + \cdots + 1$, which is $O(N)$. The resulting set of truncated matrices has an order that satisfies $n_j \leq \lceil (k+1)/(N/2) \rceil \, 2^{\lfloor \log(N/j) \rfloor} - 1 < 4k/j - 1$ for all j.

The truncated matrices are aggregated as in section 3 and the basic algorithm is then applied. To describe the time required for completing the problem, we introduce the following definition. We call $K = \{k_j\}$ an *N-partition* (or simply a *partition*) of k when K consists of N nonnegative integers that sum to k. Let $\bar{K} = \{\bar{k}_j\}$ be a partition of k where $\bar{k}_j \leq n_j$ for all j. $\bar{K}$ is called a *maximizing partition of k* if $\sum_{\bar{k}_j > 0} \log \bar{k}_j$ is maximized. As the following theorem states, the running time of the thin matrix algorithm is bounded by a quantity proportional to $\sum_{j=1}^{N} \log(\bar{k}_j + 1)$. The theorem states this bound in a form compatible with later results.

Theorem 4. Selection of a k-th element in a set of $N > 1$ sorted matrices $\{\mathbf{X}_j\}$, $j = 1, \cdots, N$, of dimensions $n_j \times 1$ can be solved in time $O(N + \sum_{\bar{k}_j > 0} \log \bar{k}_j)$, where $\bar{K} = \{\bar{k}_j\}$ is a maximizing partition of k. □

We now bring together the previous ideas in this section to give an asymptotically optimal algorithm for selecting a k-th element in any set of sorted matrices $\{\mathbf{X}_j\}$, $j = 1, \cdots, N$, of dimensions $n_j \times m_j$. As before, we assume that $N > 1$ and $m_j \leq n_j$. The algorithm follows the same pattern as previous algorithms: preprocessing of the matrices, aggregation, and application of the basic algorithm to the aggregated problem. The preprocessing is done in three stages. First the matrices are cut down to dimensions $n_j' \times m_j'$, where $\sum_{j=1}^{N} (n_j' + m_j') \leq 2k$, by applying the thin matrix algorithm to the set of all first rows and first columns of the given matrices. Next, consider a partition $\{k_j\}$ of k, for which a k-th element in $\bigcup_i \mathbf{X}_i$ has (virtual) rank k_j in $\mathbf{X}_j$, for each j. We find upper bounds $\{\hat{k}_j\}$ for the $\{k_j\}$. The upper bounds $\{\hat{k}_j\}$, obtained by weighted selection in the matrices of dimensions $n_j' \times m_j'$, have the property $\sum_{j=1}^{N} \hat{k}_j = O(k)$ and therefore serve as estimates of $\{k_j\}$. The upper bounds can thus be used in the final stage of preprocessing to identify sets of submatrices in each $\mathbf{X}_j$, as in section 4, to which the search for a k-th element may be confined. It is this entire collection of submatrices from each given matrix that is aggregated for submission to the basic algorithm.

We now extend the definition of a maximizing partition of k to a general set of sorted matrices. Call $\bar{K} = \{\bar{k}_j\}$ a maximizing partition of k if $\bar{K}$ maximizes the expression $\sum_{h_j > 0} (h_j \log(2\bar{k}_j / h_j^2))$, where $h_j = \min\{\sqrt{\bar{k}_j}, m_j\}$ for $j = 1, \cdots, N$.

Theorem 5. Selection of a k-th element in a collection of sorted matrices $\{\mathbf{X}_j\}$, $j = 1, \cdots, N$, in which X_j has dimensions $n_j \times m_j$, $n_j \geq m_j$, can be solved in $O(N + \sum_{h_j > 0} h_j \log(2\bar{k}_j / h_j^2))$ time where $\bar{K} = \{\bar{k}_j\}$ is a maximizing partition of k, and $h_j = \min\{\sqrt{\bar{k}_j}, m_j\}$, $j = 1, \cdots, N$. □

The bound in Theorem 5 reduces to the bound for medians in single matrices (Theorem 1) when $N = 1$, $k = \Theta(nm)$, and $m > 1$, and the bound for medians in collections (Theorem 2) when $k = \Theta(\sum_j n_j m_j)$; it reduces to the bound for small k in a single matrix (Theorem 3) when $N = 1$ and $m > 1$; it reduces to the bound for collections of thin matrices (Theorem 4) when $m_j = 1$ for all j. The bound of Theorem 5 can be shown to be optimal on reduced inputs.

5. Optimality

The lower bounds are based on counting arguments in decision trees, extending the results of [FJ1] to the problems addressed here. We consider two varieties of decision trees. If algorithms are restricted to making comparisons between single input values, as is the case with every algorithm in this paper, then the lower bounds hold for any input domain with a total order. If comparisons are allowed between linear functions over the input values then our lower bounds hold for nay dense domain on which a total order is defined on the set of all linear functions of values in the domain. Bounds on other problems have been obtained in a similar manner by [PY, Yo, JK, FG, FW].

Any finitely presented algorithm which solves a problem by means of the comparisons which we allow may be represented by a family of decision trees, one tree for all inputs of a given problem size and a given set of constraints on the total orders allowed for the inputs. (Certain algorithms which are not finitely presented may have this representation also.) Each tree contains interior nodes, representing comparisons, which have three children, one for each of the outcomes $<$, $=$, and $>$. Leaves of trees for selection are labeled with a single answer of the form "the k-th element has value t." A selection tree is uniform for a given k, and at each leaf t is given by index in the input. A leaf that is reached over a path from the root on which only $<$ and $>$ branches are taken is called *strict*, as is also the path to a strict leaf.

For any input $\mathbf{X} = \{x_i\}$ regardless of its structure, a *configuration* of $\mathbf{X}$ with respect to t drawn from the same domain is a set $I_{\mathbf{X}}$ for which $\{i \mid x_i < t\} \subset I_{\mathbf{X}} \subset \{i \mid x_i \le t\}$. When all members of $\mathbf{X}$ are distinct, as we may assume in arguments for lower bounds, then $I_{\mathbf{X}}$ is uniquely specified by $\mathbf{X}$ and t. We call an input with distinct members a *simple* input.

We need two results which we present together in the following lemma.

Lemma 3. Any algorithm that can determine that value t is k-th in inputs where all values are distinct

(a) using only elementary comparisons and over any input domain with a total order, or

(b) using only comparisons between linear forms of the input and over any dense input domain with a total order defined on the comparands

must expend $\Omega(\log P)$ comparisons, where P is the number of distinct input configurations allowed by the parameters and constraints of the problem. □

The following lemmas characterize selection in thin matrices and in a sorted matrix. Proofs can be found in [FJ3].

Lemma 4. Selection of a k-th element in a collection of thin sorted matrices $\{X_1, \cdots, X_N\}$, of dimensions $n_j \times 1$, requires time $\Omega(N + \sum_{\bar{k}_j > 0, j \ne i_L} \log \bar{k}_j)$ where $\bar{K} = \{\bar{k}_j\}$ is a maximizing partition of k. □

Lemma 5. Selection of a k-th element in a sorted matrix $\mathbf{X}$ of dimension $n \times m$, $1 < m \le n$, requires time $\Omega(h \log(2k/h^2))$, where $h = \min\{\sqrt{k}, m\}$ and $k \le \lceil nm/2 \rceil$. □

Theorem 6. Selection of a k-th element in a collection of sorted matrices $\{\mathbf{X}_1, \cdots, \mathbf{X}_N\}$ in which matrix $\mathbf{X}_j$ has dimensions $n_j \times m_j$, $m_j \le n \le k$, is of complexity $\Theta(N + \sum_{h_j > 0} h_j \log(\bar{k}_j / h_j^2))$ where $\bar{K} = \{\bar{k}_j\}$ is a maximizing partition of $k \le \lceil \sum_{j=1}^{N} m_j n_j / 2 \rceil$, and $h_j = \min\{\sqrt{\bar{k}_j}, m_j\}$ for $j = 1, \cdots, N$. □

References

[BY] Bentley, J.L. and A.C. Yao, An almost optimal algorithm for unbounded searching, *Inf. Proc. Letters* 5 (1976) 82-87.

[B] Blum, M., R.W. Floyd, V.R. Pratt, R.L. Rivest, and R.E. Tarjan, Time bounds for selection, *J. Comput. Sys. Sci. 7* (1972) 448-461.

[CT1] Chandrasekaran, R. and A. Tamir, Polynomially bounded algorithms for locating P-centers on a tree, *Math Prog. 22* (1982) 304-315.

[CT2] Chandrasekaran, R. and A. Tamir, An $O((n \log P)^2)$ algorithm for the continuous P-center problem on a tree, *SIAM J. Alg. Disc. Math. 1* (1980) 370-375.

[FJ1] Frederickson, G.N. and D.B. Johnson, The complexity of selection and ranking in $X + Y$ and matrices with sorted columns, *J. Comput. Sys. Sci. 24* (1982) 197-208.

[FJ2] Frederickson, G.N. and D.B. Johnson, Finding kth paths and p-centers by generating and searching good data structures, *J. Algorithms 4* (1983) 61-80.

[FJ3] Frederickson, G.N. and D.B. Johnson, Generalized selection and ranking: sorted matrices, *SIAM J. Comput. 13* (1984) 14-30.

[FW] Fredman, M.L. and B. Weide, On the complexity of computing the measure of $\bigcup [a_i, b_i]$, *C. ACM 21* (1979) 540-543.

[FG] Fussenegger, F. and H.N. Gabow, A counting approach to lower bounds for selection problems, *J. ACM 26* (1979) 227-238.

[GM] Galil, Z. and N. Megiddo, A fast selection algorithm and the problem of optimum distribution of effort, *J. ACM 26* (1979) 58-64.

[HL] Hodges, J.L. and E.L. Lehmann, Estimates of location based on rank tests, *Ann. Math. Stat. 34* (1963) 598-611.

[H] Hyafil, L., Bounds for selection, *SIAM J. Comput. 5*, 1 (March 1976) 109-114.

[JK] Johnson, D.B. and S.D. Kashdan, Lower bounds for selection in $X + Y$ and other multisets, *J. ACM 25* (Oct. 1978) 556-570.

[JM] Johnson, D.B. and T. Mizoguchi, Selecting the k-th element in $X+Y$ and $X_1+X_2+\cdots+X_m$, *SIAM J. Comput.* *7* (1978) 147-153.

[JR] Johnson, D.B. and T.A. Ryan, Jr., Fast computation of the Hodges Lehmann estimator - Theory and practice, *Proc. Ann. Statistical Assoc. 138th Ann. Meeting,* San Diego (1978) 1-2.

[KH] Kariv, O. and S.L. Hakimi, An algorithmic approach to network location problems I: The p-centers, *SIAM J. Appl. math. 37,* (Dec. 1979) 513-538.

[Ki] Kirkpatrick, D.G., A unified lower bound for selection and set partitioning problems, *J. ACM 28,* 1 (January 1981) 150-165.

[Ko] Koopman, B.O., The optimum distribution of effort, *J. ORSA 1,* (1953) 52-63.

[MR] McKean, J.W., and T.A. Ryan, Jr., ALGORITHM 516 An algorithm for obtaining confidence intervals and point estimates based on ranks in a two-sample location problem, *ACM Trans. Math. Software 3,* 2 (June 1977) 183-185.

[MTZC] Megiddo, N., A. Tamir, E. Zemel, and R.Chandrasekaran, An $O(n\log^2 n)$ algorithm for the k-th longest path in a tree with applications to location problems, *SIAM J. Comput. 10,* 2 (May 1981) 328-337.

[PY] Pratt, V.R. and F.F. Yao, On lower bounds for computing the i-th largest element, *Proc. 14th Annual Symp. Switching and Automata Theory,* Iowa City, Iowa, 1973, 70-81.

[R] Rabin, M.O., Proving simultaneous positivity of linear forms, *J. Comptr. Syst. Sci. 6,* (Dec. 1972) 639-650.

[SPP] Schönhage, A., M. Paterson, and N. Pippenger, Finding the median, *J. Comput. Syst. Sci 13,* (1976) 184-199.

[S] Shamos, M.I., Geometry and Statistics: problems at the interface, in *Algorithms and Complexity: New Directions and Recent Results,* J.F. Traub, ed. (1976) 251-280.

[Yo] Yao, A. C.-C., On the complexity of comparison problems using linear functions, *Proc. 16th Annual Symp. Foundations of Computer Science,* Berkeley, CA, 1975, 85-89.

[Yp] Yap, C.K., New upper bounds for selection, *comm. ACM 19,* 9 (Sept. 1976) 501-508.

COMPUTER SCIENCE AND STATISTICS:
The Interface, L. Billard (ed.)

THE APPLICATION OF VORONOI DIAGRAMS TO NONPARAMETRIC DECISION RULES

Godfried T. Toussaint, Binay K. Bhattacharya, Ronald S. Poulsen

School of Computer Science, 805 Sherbrooke Street West, McGill University, Montreal, Quebec, Canada

Dept. of Computer Science, Simon Frazer University, Burnaby, B.C., Canada

Macdonald Stewart Biomedical Image Processing Laboratory, McGill University, Montreal, Quebec, Canada

Nonparametric decision rules, such as the nearest neighbor (NN) rule, are very powerful from the point of view that no a priori knowledge is required concerning the underlying distributions of the data. A drawback of the NN-rule is the large amounts of storage and computation involved due to the apparent necessity to store all the sample data. Thus there has been considerable interest in "editing" or "thinning" the sample data in an attempt to store only a fraction of it. In this paper several geometric methods are proposed for editing data in the NN-rule. The methods are all derived from the Voronoi diagram of the sample data. The methods are compared empirically through experiments on synthetic data and "real world" data, and algorithms for the efficient implementation of these techniques are discussed.

I. INTRODUCTION

In the nonparametric classifiication problem we have available a set of n objects denoted by $\{X,\theta\} \equiv \{(X_1,\theta_1), (X_2,\theta_2), \ldots, (X_n,\theta_n)\}$, where X_i and θ_i denote, respectively, the vector of measurements made on the ith object and the classification of the ith object. The labels $\theta_i \in \{1,2,\ldots,M\}$ and the $X_i \in R^d$. Let $X_n' \in \{X_1,X_2,\ldots,X_n\}$ be the observation nearest to X, a new object to be classified, and let θ_n' be the classification associated with X_n'. The nearest-neighbour decision rule (NN-rule) classifies the unknown object X as belonging to class θ_n'. Let $P_e^{(n)}(NN) = Pr\{\theta \neq \theta_n'\}$ denote the resulting probability of error and let $P_e(NN) = \lim_{n\to\infty} P_e^{(n)}(NN)$. It has been shown by Cover and Hart [1] that as $n \to \infty$ the asymptotic nearest neighbour error rate is bounded in terms of the Bayes error P_e by:

$$P_e \leq P_e\,(NN) \leq P_e\,[2 - M\,P_e/(M-1)].$$

Cover and Hart [1] had some restrictions on the underlying distributions but more recently Devroye [2] and Stone [3] proved the above results for all distributions.

These bounds, together with the transparent simplicity of the rule, make the rule very attractive. However, the apparent necessity to store all the data $\{X,\theta\}$ and the resulting excessive computational requirements, have discouraged many researchers from using the rule in practice.

In order to combat the storage problem, and resulting computation, many researchers, starting with Hart [4], proposed schemes for "editing" (also "thinning" and "condensing") the original data $\{X,\theta\}$ so that fewer feature vectors could be stored. Denote the edited subset of $\{X,\theta\}$ by $\{X,\theta\}_E$. Other examples of editing methods can be found in [5] - [15]. All these techniques have several properties in common. For one, they are sequential in nature and the resulting $\{X,\theta\}_E$ is a function of the order in which $\{X,\theta\}$ is processed. Secondly they all attempt to obtain an edited set that will implement only approximately the same decision boundary in R^d as the original data set. To this end they use heuristics which complicate the algorithms, in some cases requiring a great deal of computation, and generally result in rather clumsy and involved procedures. While some of the schemes [4] result in an edited set that is *training-set consistent* (i.e., $\{X,\theta\}_E$ classifies all objects in $\{X,\theta\}$ correctly), none of them yield an edited set which is *decision-boundary consistent* (i.e., $\{X,\theta\}_E$ defines precisely the same decision boundary in R^d as $\{X,\theta\}$). Thus with the existing editing schemes we have not only the disconcerting fact that $\{X,\theta\}_E$ does not implement the originally intended decision boundary, but we do not even know the relationship that exists, if any, between the resulting $\{X,\theta\}_E$ and one that is decision-boundary consistent.

In this paper we propose several new methods for editing the data in the NN-rule and compare them experimentally, with respect to error rate and storage requirements, to the exhaustive (full training set) rule. The proposed approaches are based on well-known graph structures that are first computed on $\{X,\theta\}$. The graph structures are all based on the Voronoi diagram of $\{X,\theta\}$. The methods are exact and yield edited sets independent of the order in which the data are processed. Furthermore, one method yields edited sets which are both *training-set* and *decision-boundary* consistent. Finally algorithms are given for obtaining the edited sets efficiently.

II. THE VORONOI DIAGRAM APPROACH

2.1 A Geometric Look at the Nearest Neighbour Rule

We shall explain most concepts in the plane. The arguments extend to higher dimensions. Let $\{X,\theta\}$ consist of 20 planar points which are correctly classified as either Class 1 or Class 2 points [Fig. 1]. The points denoted

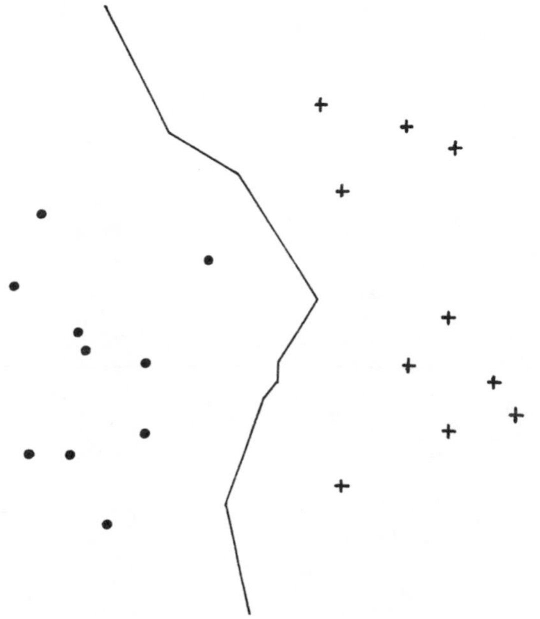

Fig.1: This decision boundary results when the NN-rule is applied to two-class data points denoted by '.' and '+'.

by '.' belong to Class 1 and the points denoted by '+' belong to Class 2. The nearest-neighbor decision boundary (NN-boundary) is defined as the boundary which separates the points of $\{X,\theta\}$ in such a way that any point on the NN-boundary is nearest to at least two data points of $\{X,\theta\}$ belonging to different classes. Fig.1 also shows the NN-boundary defined by the data points. The plane is thus partitioned, for the data points shown in Fig.1, into two disjoint regions such that all the samples in one region belong to the same class. An unknown point in the Class 1 region will have a sample point of $\{X,\theta\}$ belonging to Class 1 as its nearest neighbor. Therefore, by the NN-rule, the unknown point is classified as a Class 1 point. Similarly, any unknown point, lying in the Class 2 region, is classified as a Class 2 point. Thus, the problem of classifying an unknown sample, using the NN-rule, reduces to the problem of determining the region, generated by the NN-boundary, in which the given unknown sample lies [16].

The algorithm of Dasarathy and White [16] is the only known algorithm which generates the NN-boundary directly from the reference set using the fact that any arbitrary point on the NN-boundary is nearest to at least two data points of the reference set belonging to different classes. They consider generating the NN-boundary as an application of the maxmin problem [16]. The worst-case complexity of their algorithm, to find the NN-boundary determined by a reference set containing n data points in d-space, is $O(dn^{d+2})$. Even for a moderate size problem the computation time is phenomenal. The authors also conclude that the average complexity of their algorithm in 3-space is $O(n^{3.85})$.

The algorithm described by Toussaint and Poulsen [17] is the only algorithm which reduces the reference set in such a way that the NN-boundaries, defined by the reduced set and the reference set, are exactly the same, i.e., the reduced set is decision boundary consistent and therefore, also reference set consistent.

2.2 The Voronoi Thinning Algorithm

The Voronoi thinning algorithm [17] finds a reduced reference set by using the Voronoi diagram of the reference set.

Let us consider the same reference set as shown in Fig. 1. The Voronoi diagram of the reference set is shown in Fig. 2. The early

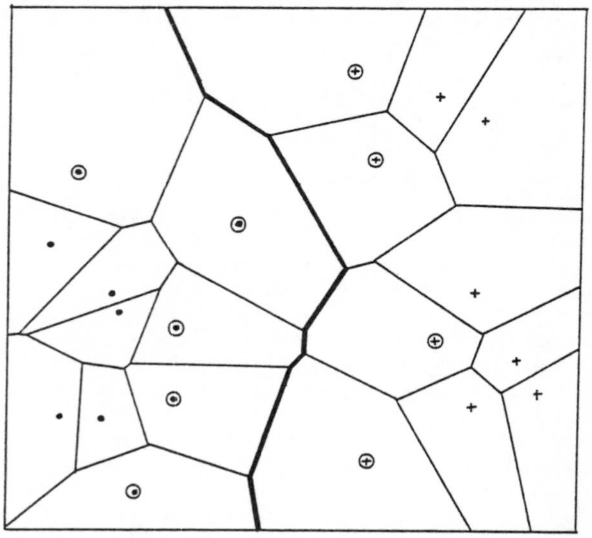

Fig.2: The Voronoi diagram of the data set shown in Fig.1 contains the NN-boundary. Each marked point indicates that at least one of its Voronoi neighbors belongs to a different class. The thick lines form the exact NN-boundary.

work on the Voronoi diagram, its construction, and other associated properties are discussed in detail in [18] - [31]. From Fig. 2 it is noticed that the NN-boundary (shown in thick lines) is contained in the Voronoi diagram. This is due to the fact that the Voronoi diagram contains all the necessary proximity information defined by a given set of data points [27].

Algorithm-Voronoi Thinning

Begin
Step 1: Construct the Voronoi diagram of $\{X,\theta\}$.
Step 2: Visit each data point of $\{X,\theta\}$ and find all its Voronoi neighbors. Mark the data point just visited if all its Voronoi neighbors are not from the same class as the visited point.
Step 3: Discard all points that are not marked. Marked points form the Voronoi thinned set.
End

The marked (circled) points in Fig. 2 are shown in Fig. 3 and constitute the Voronoi thinned set of the data points of Fig. 1.

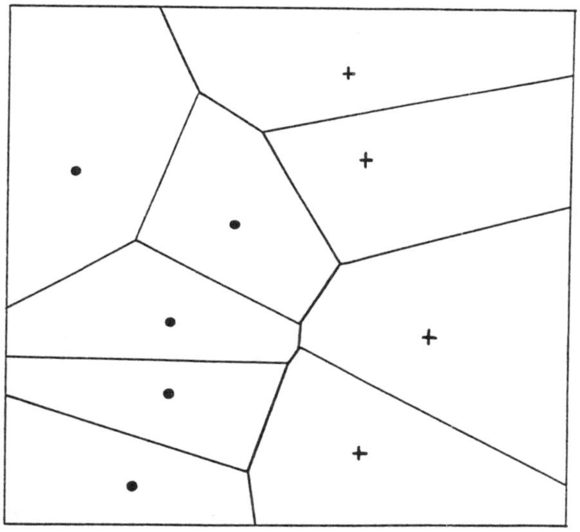

Fig. 3: The Voronoi diagram of the Voronoi thinned set shown in Fig. 1. The exact NN-boundary as shown in Fig. 1 is still maintained.

It is clear from the construction and definition of the Voronoi diagram that the Voronoi thinned set, which is a subset of the reference set, maintains the original NN-boundary exactly [Fig. 3]. For the sake of brevity, a rigorous proof of this statement is omitted here. Hence, the Voronoi thinned set is *decision boundary consistent* and therefore, is also *reference set consistent*. It is also independent of the order in which the reference set is processed. Furthermore, notice that it is an *implicit* way of generating the NN-boundary, as opposed to the *explicit* generation in [16]. The worst-case complexity of the algorithm to obtain the Voronoi thinned set from the reference set containing n data points in d-space is $O(n^{[d/2]+1}) + O(d^3 n^{[d/2]} \log n)$ where $[d/2] = k$ when $d=2k$ or $2k-1$ using the algorithm of Avis and Bhattacharya [31]. This compares very well with the algorithm of Dasarathy and White [16] whose worst-case complexity to generate the NN-boundary is $O(dn^{d+2})$. However, the Voronoi thinned set is not minimal as is illustrated in Fig. 4. Let the points denoted by '.' belong to Class 1 and the points denoted by '+' belong to Class 2. The Voronoi diagram of this set is also shown in Fig. 4 It is easy to see that the Voronoi thinned set keeps all the points but no more than two points are sufficient to implement the same decision boundary.

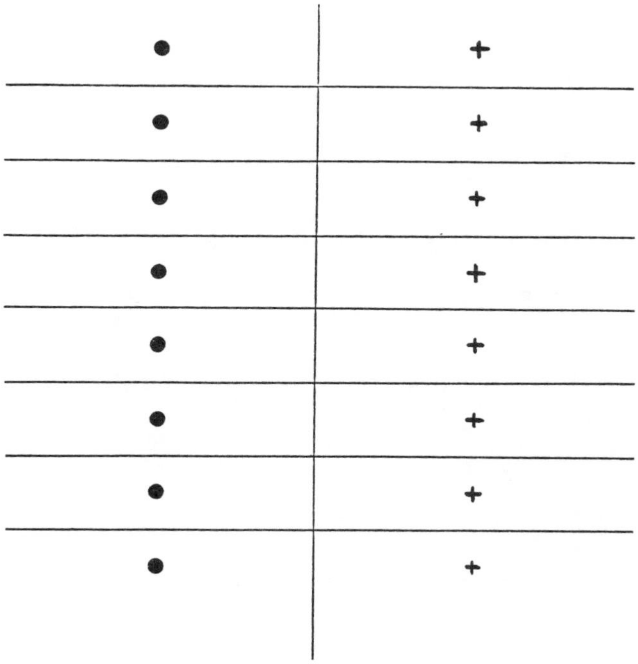

Fig. 4: A pathological example showing that the Voronoi thinned set need not be minimal.

2.3 Drawbacks of the Voronoi Thinning Algorithm

If we look at Fig. 2 it is observed that the two top-most marked data points, one from each class, are kept in the Voronoi thinned set, even though they are well separated. This case is more clearly illustrated in Fig. 5, where 30 data points were uniformly distributed in [0,1] between the circles

$$(x-1/2)^2 + y^2 = 0.4^2$$

and

$$(x-1/2)^2 + (y-1)^2 = 0.4^2.$$

After the application of the Voronoi thinning algorithm, the marked data points were kept in the Voronoi thinned set. Note that the Voronoi thinned set also maintains the NN-boundary outside the region of interest which, for practical purposes, is not necessary. Thus, the Voronoi thinning algorithm treats all regions of the feature space with equal importance. If the unknown data point to be classified comes from the same distribution as the sample points of the reference set, the NN-boundary outside the region of interest is of very little importance. Therefore, all those data points in the Voronoi thinned set, which only maintain the NN-boundary outside the "region of interest", could be neglected.

Furthermore, the construction of the Voronoi diagram in high dimensions is still a time consuming process [31]. These drawbacks of Voronoi thinning from the practical point of view led us to consider two alternative methods to which we now turn.

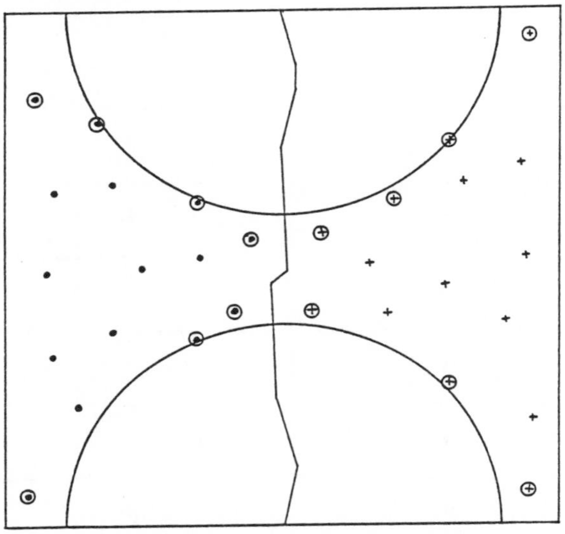

Fig. 5: The marked points constitute the Voronoi thinned set. The points were generated uniformly in (0,1) between the two circles. Each point whose x-coordinate was less than 0.5 was assigned as class 1, denoted by '.', otherwise it was assigned as a class 2 point, denoted by '+'.

III. GABRIEL THINNING

3.1 The Gabriel Thinning Algorithm

The Gabriel thinning algorithm is similar in spirit to the Voronoi thinning algorithm except for the fact that the Gabriel thinning algorithm, as the name suggests, uses the Gabriel graph of the reference set instead of the Voronoi diagram. The Gabriel graph is defined as follows. For each pair of points (p_i, p_j) in the reference set, construct the diametrical sphere $S(p_i, p_j)$, i.e., the sphere such that (p_i, p_j) forms the diameter of $S(p_i, p_j)$. Two points (p_i, p_j) are Gabriel neighbors if $S(p_i, p_j)$ is empty, i.e., if no points of the reference set other than p_i and p_j lie in S. The Gabriel graph is obtained by joining a pair of points with an edge if they are Gabriel neighbors. For the properties and algorithms for computing the Gabriel graph the reader is referred to [32] - [33].

Algorithm-Gabriel Thinning

Begin

Step 1: Construct the Gabriel graph of the reference set.

Step 2: Visit each data point of the reference set and determine all its Gabriel neighbors. Mark the visited point if all its Gabriel neighbors are not from the same class as the visited point.

Step 3: Discard all points that are not marked. Marked data points of the reference set form the Gabriel thinned set.

End

Figures 6 and 7 illustrate the results obtained with this algorithm. Fig. 7 also shows the NN-boundary determined by the Gabriel thinned set. This boundary, when compared with the NN-boundary defined by the original reference set, differs in the region (near the convex hull of the reference set) which is usually of not much interest to the classification problem. The Gabriel thinning algorithm is also applied to the reference set given in Fig. 5. The Gabriel thinned set and the corresponding NN-boundary are shown in Fig. 8. It is observed that the Gabriel thinning algorithm has completely ignored those points of the reference set which maintain the NN-boundary outside the region of interest.

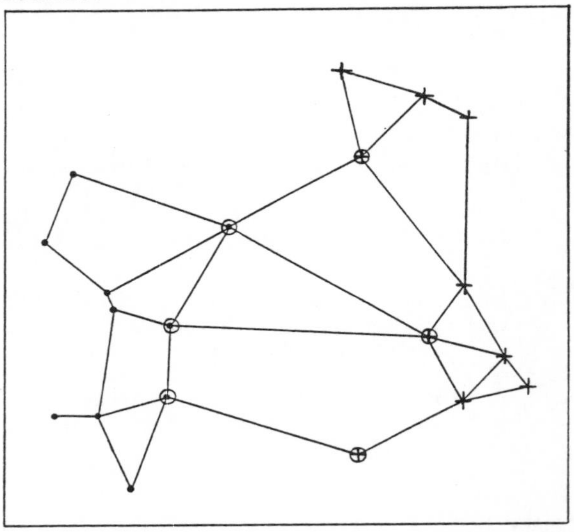

Fig.6: The Gabriel graph of the data set shown in Fig.1. Each marked point indicates that at least one of its Gabriel neighbors is from a class different than itself.

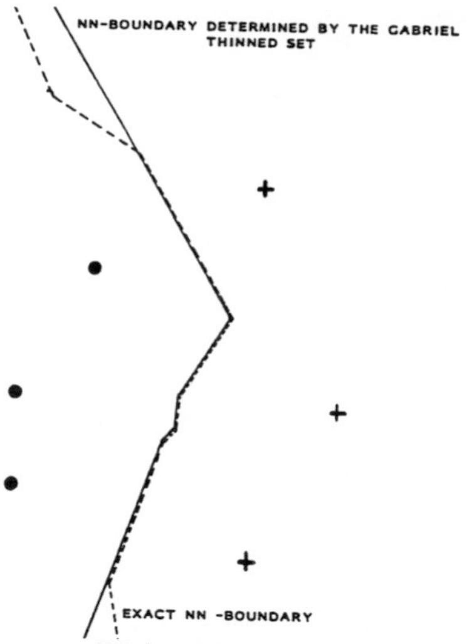

Fig. 7: The exact NN-boundary and the NN-boundary determined by the Gabriel thinned set (marked points of Fig. 6) differ only near the convex hull boundary of the union of the two sets.

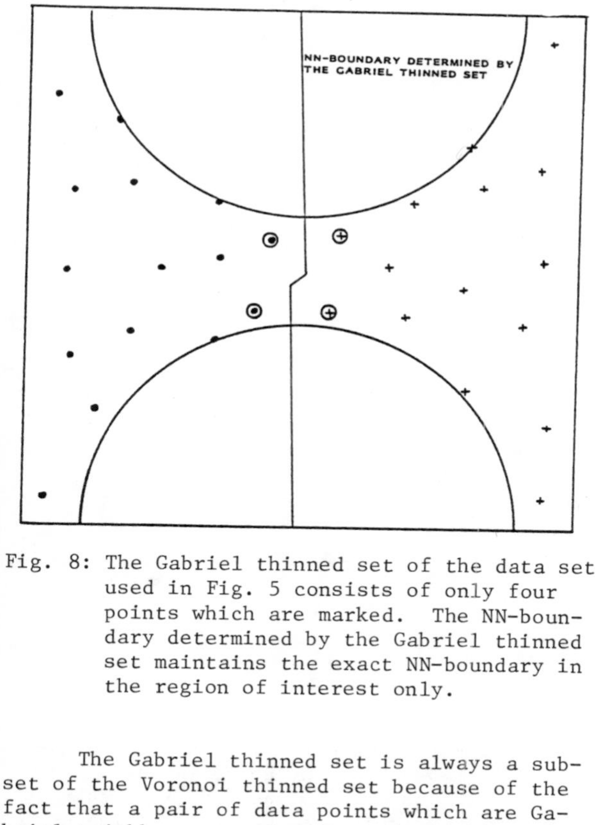

Fig. 8: The Gabriel thinned set of the data set used in Fig. 5 consists of only four points which are marked. The NN-boundary determined by the Gabriel thinned set maintains the exact NN-boundary in the region of interest only.

The Gabriel thinned set is always a subset of the Voronoi thinned set because of the fact that a pair of data points which are Gabriel neighbors are also Voronoi neighbors [32]. Therefore, it can be said that the Gabriel thinning algorithm reduces the Voronoi thinned set further.

It is clear that the Gabriel thinned set is not decision boundary consistent. From Fig. 9, it is seen that the Gabriel thinned set is also not reference set consistent. However, as we will see later, this phenomenon does not appear to degrade the performance of the Gabriel thinned set in practice.

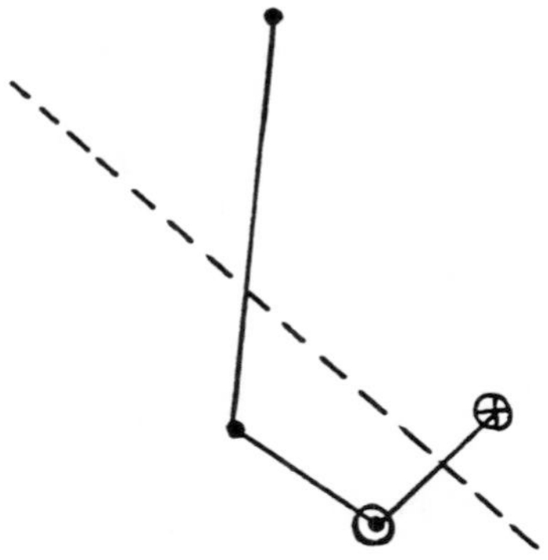

Fig. 9: An instance when the Gabriel thinned set is not reference set consistent. The reference set consists of 4 points where points denoted by '.' belong to class 1 and points denoted by '+' belong to class 2. Two marked poits constitute the Gabriel thinned set.

3.2 Construction of the Gabriel Graph in d-Space

3.2.1 The brute force method

The construction of the Gabriel graph of a planar set of points has been described in [32]. This method uses the Voronoi diagram construct as the preprocessing step. Since our main intention is to construct the Gabriel graph efficiently in higher dimensions, the use of the Voronoi diagram construct is not desirable. Therefore, we present an algorithm to construct the Gabriel graph in d-space which does not require computing the Voronoi diagram.

By definition, two data points of a set are Gabriel neighbors if and only if their circle of influence is empty. We can always construct the Gabriel graph once all the Gabriel neighbors of the set are known. The Gabriel neighbors of a set can be determined exhaustively by using the brute-force method. Let our given set be $\{X\}=\{X_1,X_2,\ldots,X_n\}$. Then the steps of the brute-force method are:

Step 1: Consider all the pairs of points (X_i,X_j), for $i,j=1,2,\ldots,n$; $i<j$.

Step 2: For each such pair (X_i,X_j) test whether there exists a point X_k belonging to $\{X\}$ such that

$$d^2(X_i,X_j) > d^2(X_i,X_k) + d^2(X_j,X_k), X_k \neq X_i, X_j.$$

If such a point does not exist, X_i and X_j are Gabriel neighbors.

Step 1 of the algorithm requires $O(n^2)$ operations to yield $O(n^2)$ pairs. For each such pair of points (X_i,X_j), Step 2 requires $O(nd)$ operations. Hence the overall complexity of the algorithm is $O(dn^3)$.

Thus the complexity of the brute-force method is primarily dependent on the number of data points of the set. This is not the case when the Voronoi diagram is used to compute the Gabriel graph because in that case the worst-case complexity is $O(dn^{[d/2]+1})+O(d^3n^{[d/2]}\log n)$. Thus, for $d > 4$, the brute force method with a complexity of $O(dn^3)$ is much faster than the method that uses the Voronoi diagram.

3.2.2 A heuristic method

The number of pairs of Gabriel neighbors in a set of n points is, in general, very much less than the total number of pairs $n(n-1)/2$ considered in the brute-force method. For example, in Fig. 5 there are 31 pairs of Gabriel neighbors out of 190 possible pairs. Thus if by some means we can reduce the number of pairs to be tested for Gabriel neighbors, then the brute-force method will be even more efficient. A heuristic approach to achieve this goal is described below.

Here, we consider the two dimensional case. Generalization to higher dimensions is straightforward. Let us consider the set of points shown in Fig. 10. Let p be a data point of the set whose Gabriel neighbors we are interested in. Consider a point q belonging to $\{X\}$. Draw a line $B(p,q)$ through q, which is perpendicular to the line joining p to q. Let $LH(B,p)$ be the half-space, determined by $B(p,q)$, which contains the point p. Let $RH(B,p)$ be the half-space which does not contain the point p. We then have the following theorem.

Theorem 1

No point of the set in $RH(B,p)$ can be a Gabriel neighbor of p.

Proof: Straightforward.

Using the above heuristic, the brute-force method can then be modified as follows.

Algorithm-Gabriel

Begin

Step 1: Consider each point of the given set separately.

Step 2: Start with $N_i=\{p_1,p_2,\ldots,p_{i-1},p_{i+1},\ldots,p_n\}$ as the set of potential Gabriel neighbors of the point p_i.

Step 3: For each potential Gabriel neighbor p_r belonging to N_i do the following:
For every point p_k of S, $p_k \neq p_i, p_r$:

- i) Test whether p_k lies inside the circle of influence determined by p_i and p_r. If so, remove p_r from the set N_i and start Step 3 with a new potential Gabriel neighbor.
- ii) If $p_k \in N_i$, then test whether p_r lies inside the circle of influence determined by p_i and p_k. If so, remove p_k from the set N_i.

Step 4: Accept the remaining points of the set N_i as the Gabriel neighbors of p_i.

End

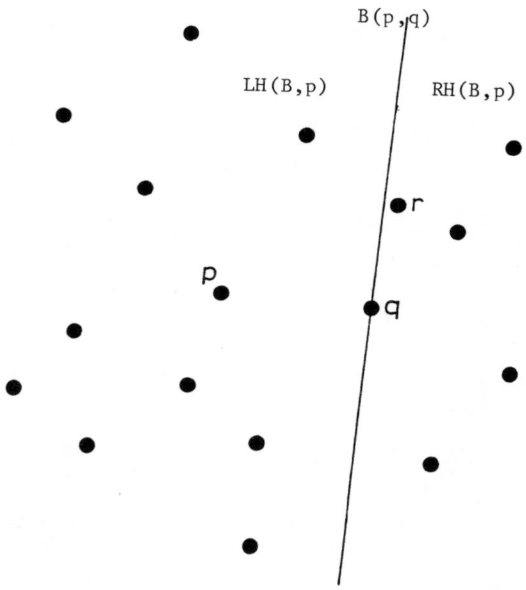

Fig. 10: When testing q for the Gabriel neighborhood of p, any point in $RH(B,p)$ determined by the line $B(p,q)$ which is perpendicular to the line joining p and q, could be rejected as it can't be a Gabriel neighbor of p.

3.2.3 Monte Carlo simulation

A Monte Carlo simulation was carried out to determine the extent to which the heuristic method rejects pairs of data points. The experiment was performed by generating sets of data points of sizes 100, 300, 500, 700 and 1000 uniformly distributed in a unit of d-cube, d=2, 3 or 4. Each case was repeated 20 times and the average value is shown in Table 1. The percent of pairs rejected, in a set of n points, was calculated as follows:

$$\% \text{ of pairs rejected} = \frac{\text{Tot.\# pairs rejected}}{0.5 * n(n-1)} \times 100$$

From Table 1, it is observed that most of the pairs can be rejected before they are tested. For example, when n=500 and d=3, on an average 119,120 number of pairs (out of 124,750) need not be considered at all for the Gabriel

Number of points	percent of pairs rejected		
	d=2	d=3	d=4
100	91.37	86.01	80.51
300	96.23	93.45	90.41
500	97.46	95.49	93.30
700	98.04	96.49	94.67
1000	98.43	97.31	95.92

Table 1: Monte Carlo simulation result to determine the percent of pairs not considered for the Gabriel neighborhood test.

neighborhood test. For a particular dimension, the percent of pairs rejected increases as n increases, while for a particular number of points, the percent of pairs rejected decreases as the dimension of the points increases.

Thus it can be concluded that the brute-force method of computing the Gabriel neighbors when modified heuristically, saves a lot of computation over the method via the Voronoi diagram for high dimensions.

IV. RELATIVE NEIGHBORHOOD GRAPH THINNING

4.1 Introduction

We have seen that the Gabriel thinning algorithm reduces the Voronoi thinned set. It is thus logical to extend this concept further, i.e., to further reduce the Gabriel thinned set. One way of accomplishing this is to use the same idea on a subgraph of the Gabriel graph. The thinning algorithm discussed in this section is based on the geometrical construct known as the relative neighborhood graph (RNG) [34]. The RNG of a planar set has also been discussed in detail in [35] - [41]. The formal definition of the RNG and its properties, relevant to our problem, which are discussed here, are based on [34].

4.2 The Relative Neighborhood Graph

Let $\{X\}$ be a set of n points in d-space: $\{X\}=\{X_1,X_2,\ldots,X_n\}$. Two points X_i and X_j are defined as being "relatively close" if

$$d(X_i,X_j) \le \max\,[d(X_i,X_k),\ d(X_j,X_k)]$$

$$\text{for } k=1,2,\ldots,n;\ k\neq i,j.$$

The relative neighborhood graph is obtained by constructing an edge between points X_i and X_j for all $i,j = 1,2,\ldots,n$; $i \neq j$, if X_i and X_j are relatively close. Fig. 11 shows the RNG of the set of points given in Fig. 1.

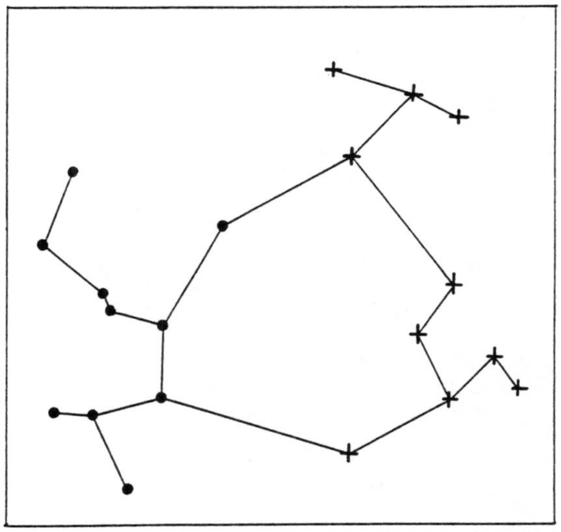

Fig. 11: The RNG of the data set given in Fig.1.

<u>Theorem 2</u>
The RNG of a set is a subgraph of the Gabriel graph of the set.

<u>Proof</u>: Straightforward.

4.3 The RNG Thinning Algorithm

THE RNG thinning algorithm is similar to the Gabriel algorithm and thus we leave out the details.

When the RNG thinning algorithm is applied to the reference set, given in Fig. 1, the reduced reference set obtained is shown in Fig. 12.

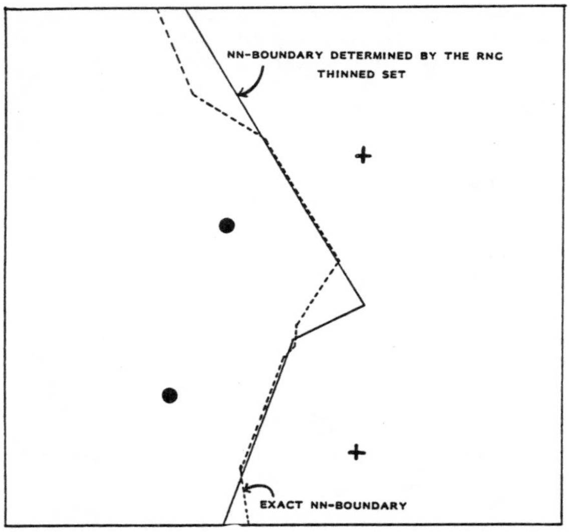

Fig. 12: Four points costitute the RNG thinned set of the reference set given in Fig. 1. The NN-boundary determined by the RNG thinned set differs considerably from the exact NN-boundary.

This reduced set, called the RNG thinned set, is a subset of the Gabriel set [Figs. 7 and 12]. Therefore, we notice that

RNG thinned set $\subseteq$ Gabriel thinned set $\subseteq$ Voronoi thinned set $\subseteq$ Reference set.

The NN-boundary generated by the RNG thinned set, when compared with the NN-boundary, determined by the Voronoi thinned set (and hence by the original reference set) [Fig. 12], differs considerably. Since the RNG thinned set is contained in the Gabriel thinned set, the RNG thinned set is neither decision boundary consistent nor reference set consistent.

The RNG of a set can be constructed by first computing the set of all relative neighbors exhaustively. The brute-force method similar to the one for the Gabriel graph can be used. The brute-force method can also be modified using the same heuristic described earlier.

V. EXPERIMENTAL RESULTS

5.1 Introduction

The three thinning algorithms were compared experimentally to determine the number of points deleted and the resulting error rate in each case. Several Monte Carlo simulations were performed with different distributions and varying dimensions for both synthetic and "real world" data sets. We report here only two experiments with "real world" data in the interest of brevity. The conclusions for synthetic data are very strong and identical to those reported here. For details the reader is referred to [42].

5.2 Iris Data

The so called Iris data consists of four measurements made on each of 150 flowers. There are three pattern classes, Virginica, Setosa, and Versicolor corresponding to three different types of Iris. Therefore, in this case the reference set consists of 150 feature vectors in 4-space each of which is assigned to one of the three above mentioned classes. This data was first collected by R.A. Fisher [43] in 1936 and since then has become somewhat of a classic "text book" example on which to try out ideas and algorithms. Obtaining an estimate of the performance or error rate of a decision rule is a field unto itself [44]. In these experiments, the NN-error rate was estimated using Effron's [45] bootstrap method with a uniform window.

Table 2 shows the results when the thinning algorithms are applied to the Iris data. As expected the NN-error rate using the Voronoi thinned set is the same as the exact NN-error rate. 109 sample data points were selected to maintain the NN-boundary exactly. The size of the Gabriel thinned set is only 39, almost one third of the Voronoi thinned set. But the number of misclassifications of the NN-rule on the unknown bootstrapped data [45] using the Voronoi thinned set (and hence the original reference set) and the Gabriel thinned set are the same. On the other hand the RNG thinned set increases the NN-error rate by almost 100%. Thus by removing 70 additional sample points from the Voronoi thinned set, the performance of the NN-classifier remains the same, but if we remove only 18 sample points on top of that from the Gabriel thinned set the NN-error rate doubles. Therefore, the Gabriel thinned set appears to contain sufficient information for discrimination of the Iris data with the NN-rule.

REFERENCE SET			VORONOI THINNED SET			GABRIEL THINNED SET			RNG THINNED SET		
Size	NN error	Variance	Size	NN error	Variance	Size	NN error	Variance	Size	NN error	Variance
150	.013	.31E-4	109	.013	.31E-4	39	.013	.31E-4	21	.021	.81E-4

Table 2: 150 Iris data in 4-space is thinned using the three thinning algorithms. The table summarizes their performance.

REFERENCE SET			VORONOI THINNED SET			GABRIEL THINNED SET			RNG THINNED SET		
Size	NN error	Variance	Size	NN error	Variance	Size	NN error	Variance	Size	NN error	Variance
1999	.059	.71E-4	1313	.059	.71E-4	820	.060	.67E-4	452	.097	.45E-4

Table 3: 1999 cervical cell data in 4-space was thinned using the three thinning algorithms. The table summarizes their performance.

5.3 Cervical Cell Data

The Biomedical Image Processing Laboratory at McGill University has a data base of about 2000 cervical cell images which are assigned to one of 13 cell types (subclasses). Eight of the types are considered to be subclasses of the normal cell class and the other five types are subclasses of the abnormal cell class [46]-[49].

The images were subjected to the preprocessing and feature extraction methods described in [47]-[48]. Each cell is represented by a four-dimensional feature vector using the features

(1) log (cytoplasm diameter/nucleus diameter),

(2) log (nucleus area),

(3) average cytoplasm density, and

(4) average nucleus density.

We have only considered the two-class problem - normal and abnormal classes. Thus our reference set contains 1999 samples in 4-space labelled either as normal or abnormal. The results of the thinning algorithms are shown in Table 3.

As in the previous cases, the Gabriel thinned set contains fewer sample points than the Voronoi thinned set even though the corresponding NN-error rates are not significantly different. The RNG thinned set increases the NN-error rate considerably.

VI. CONCLUDING REMARKS

We have shown in this paper that by sacrificing the properties of *reference set* and *decision boundary* consistency we can obtain editing schemes, such as Gabriel-graph-thinning, that in practice keep far fewer data points with no deterioration in performance. It is tempting to be greedy here and the RNG thinning is certainly an unsatisfactory outcome of this greediness. However there may exist other graphs sparser than the Gabriel graph that will discard additional points without deterioration in performance. Such graphs have recently been explored in other contexts [50], [51] and may well be very fruitful for the editing problem in nonparametric decision rules.

REFERENCES

[1] Cover, T.M. and Hart, P.E., "Nearest neighbor pattern classification," IEEE Transactions on Information Theory, Vol. IT-13 No.1, 1967, pp.21-27.

[2] Devroye, L.P., "On the inequality of Cover and Hart in nearest neighbor discrimination," IEEE transactions on Pattern analysis and Machine Intelligence, Vol. PAMI-3, January 1981, pp.75-78.

[3] Stone, C.J.,"Consistent nonparametric regression," Annals of Statistics, Vol.5, 1977 pp.595-645.

[4] Hart, P.E., "The condensed nearest-neighbor rule," IEEE Transactions on Information Theory, Vol. IT-4, May 1968, pp.515-516.

[5] Ritter, G.L., et al. "An algorithm for a selective nearest neighbor decision rule," IEEE Trans. Inf. Th., Vol. IT-21, Nov. 1975, pp.665-669.

[6] Tomek, I., "Two modifications of CNN," IEEE Trans Systems, Man and Cybernetics, Vol. SMC-6, Nov. 1976, pp.769-772.

[7] Tomek, I., "An experiment with the edited nearest neighbor rule," IEEE Transactions on Systems, Man and Cybernetics, Vol. SMC-6, June 1976, pp.448-452.

[8] Swonger, C.W., "Sample set condensation for a condensed nearest neighbor decision rule for pattern recognition," in Frontiers in Pattern Recognition, Ed. S. Watanabe, Academic Press, 1972, pp.511-526.

[9] Gowda, K.C. and Krishna, G., "The condensed nearest-neighbor rule using the concept of mutual nearest neighborhood," IEEE Transactions on Information Theory, Vol. IT-25, No.4, 1979, pp.488-490.

[10] Fisher, F.P. and Patrick, E.A., "A preprocessing algorithm for nearest neighbor decision rules," Proc. National Electronics Conf., Dec. 1970, pp.481-485.

[11] Ullmann, V.R., "Automatic selection of reference data for use in a nearest-neighbor method of pattern classification," IEEE Trans. Information Theory, Vol. IT-20, July 1974, pp.541-544.

[12] Gates, G.W., "The reduced nearest neighbor rule," IEEE Trans. Information Theory, Vol. IT-18, May 1972, pp.431-433.

[13] Chang, C.-L., "Finding prototypes for nearest neighbor classifiers, IEEE Trans. Computers, Vol. C-23, November 1974, pp.1179-1184.

[14] Fukunaga, K. and Mantock, J.M., "Nonparametric data reduction," IEEE Trans. Pattern Analysis and Machine Intelligence, Vol. PAMI-6, January 1984, pp.115-118.

[15] Oliver, L.H., Automatic image processing and pattern recognition for biomedical research, Ph.D. Thesis, School of Computer Science, McGill University, 1979.

[16] Dasarathy, B. and White, L.J., "A characterization of nearest neighbor rule decision surfaces and a new approach to generate them," Pattern Recognition, Vol. 10, 1978, pp.41-46.

[17] Toussaint, G.T. and Poulsen, R.S., "Some new algorithms and software implementation methods for pattern recognition research," Proc. Third International COMPSAC, Chicago, Illinois, November 1979, pp.55-63.

[18] Voronoi, G., "Nouvelles applications des parameters continues a la theorie des formes quadratiques," Deuxieme Mamoire, Recherches sur les paralleloedres primitifs, Journal Reine Angew. Math., Vol. 134, 1908, 198-287.

[19] Horspool, R.N., "Constructing the Voronoi diagram in the plane," Technical Report SOCS - 79.12, School of Computer Science, McGill University, July 1979.

[20] Howe, S.E., Estimating regions and clustering spatial data: analysis and implementation of method using the Voronoi diagram, Ph.D. Thesis, Brown University, 1978.

[21] Bowyer, A., "Computing Dirichlet tessellations," The Computer Journal, Vol.24, No.2, 1981, pp.162-166.

[22] Brassel, K.E. and Rief, D., "A procedure to generate Thiessen polygons," Geographical Analysis, Vol.11, No.3, 1979, pp.289-303.

[23] Brown, K.Q., Geometric transforms for fast geometric algorithms, Ph.D. Thesis, Carnegie-Mellon University, Department of Computer Science, 1979.

[24] Brown, K.Q., "Voronoi diagrams from convex hulls," Information Processing Letters, Vol.9, No.5, 1979, pp.223-228.

[25] Brostow, W., Dussault, J.P. and Fox, B.L., "Construction of Voronoi polyhedra," Journal of Computational Physics, Vol.29, 1978, pp.81-92.

[26] Green, P.J. and Sibson, R., "Computing Dirichlet tessellations in the plane," The Computer Journal, Vol.21, No.2, 1978, pp. 168-173.

[27] Shamos, M.I., Computational geometry, Ph.D. Thesis, Department of Computer Science, Yale University, May 1978.

[28] Klee, V., "On the complexity of d-dimensional Voronoi diagrams," Arch. Math., Vol. 34, 1980, pp.75-80.

[29] Rhynsburger, D., "Analytic delineation of Thiessen polygons," Geographical Analysis, Vol.5, No.2, 1973, pp.133-144.

[30] Watson, D.F., "Computing the n-dimensional Delaunay tessellation with application to Voronoi polytopes," The Computer Journal, Vol.24, No.2, 1981, pp.167-172.

[31] Avis,D. and Bhattacharya, B.K., "Algorithms for computing d-dimensional Voronoi diagrams and their duals," in Computational Geometry, Ed., F.P. Preparata, JAI Press, 1983, pp.159-180.

[32] Matula, D.W. and Sokal, R.R., "Properties of Gabriel graphs relevant to geographic variation research and the clustering of points in the plane," Geographical Analysis Vol.12, 1980, pp.205-222.

[33] Urquhart, R.B., "Some new techniques for pattern recognition research and lung sound signal analysis," Ph.D. Thesis, University of Glasgow, 1983.

[34] Toussaint, G.T., "The relative neighbourhood graph of a finite planar set," Patterm Recognition, Vol.12, No.4, 1980.

[35] Urquhart, R.B., "Algorithms for computation of relative neighborhood graph," Electronics Letters, Vol.16, 1980, pp.556-557.

[36] Toussaint, G.T. and Menard, R., "Fast algorithms for computing the planar relative neighborhood graph," in Methods of Operations Research, Koln, August 1980, pp. 425-428.

[37] O'Rourke, J., "Computing the relative neighborhood graph in the L_1 and L_∞ metrics," Pattern Recognition, Vol.15, No.3, 1982, pp.189-192.

[38] Supowit, K.J., "The relative neighborhood graph with an application to minimum spanning trees," Tech. Rept., Dept. of Computer Science, University of Illinois, Urbana-Champaign, Aug. 1980.

[39] Supowit, K., Topics in computational geometry, Ph.D. Thesis, Department of Computer Science, University of Illinois at Urbana-Champaign, 1981.

[40] Toussaint, G.T., "Pattern recognition and geometrical complexity," Proceedings Fifth International Conference on Pattern Recognition, Miami Beach, December 1980.

[41] Toussaint, G.T., "Computational geometric problems in pattern recognition", in Pattern Recognition Theory and Applications, Ed. Kittler, J., NATO Advanced Study Institute, Oxford University, April 1981.

[42] Bhattacharya, B.K., "The application of computational geometry to pattern recognition problems," Ph.D. Thesis, McGill University, November 1981.

[43] Fisher, R.A., "The use of multiple measurements in taxonomic problems," Annals of Eugenics, Vol.7, Part2, 1936, pp.179-188.

[44] Toussaint, G.T., "Bibliography on estimation of misclassification," IEEE Transactions on Information Theory, Vol.IT-20, No.4, 1974, pp.472-479.

[45] Effron, B., "Bootstrap methods: another look at the jackknife," The Annals of Statistics, Vol.7, No.1, 1979, pp.1-26.

[46] Cahn, R.L., Poulsen, R.S. and Toussaint, G.T., "Segmentation of cervical cell images", Journal of Histochemistry and Cytochemistry, Vol.25, 1977, pp.681-688.

[47] Poulsen, R.S., Oliver, L.H. Cahn, R.L., Louis, C. and Toussaint, G.T., "High resolution analysis of cervical cells - a progress report", Journal of Histochemistry and Cytochemistry, Vol.25, 1977, pp.689 - 695.

[48] Oliver, L.H., Poulsen, R.S., Toussaint, G.T. and Louis, C., "Classification of atypical cells in the automatic cytoscreening for cervical cancer," Pattern Recognition, Vol.11, 1979, pp.205-212.

[49] Oliver, L.H., Poulsen, R.S. and Toussaint, G.T., "Estimating false positive and false negative error rates in cervical cell classification", Journal of Histochemistry and Cytochemistry, Vol.25, 1977, pp.696-701.

[50] Urquhart, R., "Graph theoretical clustering based on limited neighborhood sets," Pattern Recognition, Vol.15, No.3, 1982, pp.173-187.

[51] Kirkpatrick, D.G. and Radke, J.D., "Tools for computational morphology," in *Computational Geometry*, Ed. G.T. Toussaint, North Holland, to appear in 1984.

COMPUTER SCIENCE AND STATISTICS:
The Interface, L. Billard (ed.)

MULTIDIMENSIONAL SORTING - AN OVERVIEW[1]

Jacob E. Goodman[2] Richard Pollack[3]

City College (CUNY) Courant Institute (NYU)

If $C = \{P_1,\ldots,P_n\}$ is a configuration of points in the euclidean plane, not all collinear, and for each i,j we know the cardinality of the set $\Lambda(i,j)$ of points to the left of the directed line P_iP_j , then we can determine the set $\Lambda(i,j)$ itself. This result extends to higher dimensions, and permits us to generalize, both theoretically and algorithmically, the notion of sorting points on a line to a theory of sorting a configuration of points in d-dimensional space.

Suppose the points $P_1,\ldots,P_n$ are arranged on a straight line, and we are told -- for each index i -- the cardinality $\lambda(i)$ of the set $\Lambda(i)$ of points which lie to the left of P_i:

$$\lambda(i) = |\Lambda(i)| = |\{j \mid P_j < P_i\}| .$$

In Figure 1a, for example, we have $\lambda(1) = 3$, $\lambda(2) = 0$, etc. Then of course we can immediately deduce what the sets $\Lambda(i)$ themselves are: just take all the points P_j for which $\lambda(j) < \lambda(i)$.

Now suppose $P_1,\ldots,P_n$ do not lie on a line any more, but in a plane, and suppose -- for each pair i,j now -- we know how many points $\lambda(i,j)$ lie to the left of the directed line P_iP_j , and we would like to know which ones $(\Lambda(i,j))$ do. For the configuration in Figure 1b, for example, the value of $\lambda(i,j)$ is indicated as the i,j-th entry of the matrix

$$(\lambda(i,j)) = \begin{pmatrix} 5 & 0 & 3 & 1 & 2 \\ 3 & 5 & 1 & 2 & 0 \\ 0 & 2 & 5 & 1 & 3 \\ 2 & 1 & 2 & 5 & 1 \\ 1 & 3 & 0 & 2 & 5 \end{pmatrix} ;$$

here the "undefined" values of λ are listed as "n" (in this case n = 5) on the diagonal of the λ-matrix. Now it is not so simple to deduce $\Lambda(i,j)$. But surprisingly enough, it turns out that one can again determine the sets $\lambda(i,j)$ just from knowing their cardinalities. And in

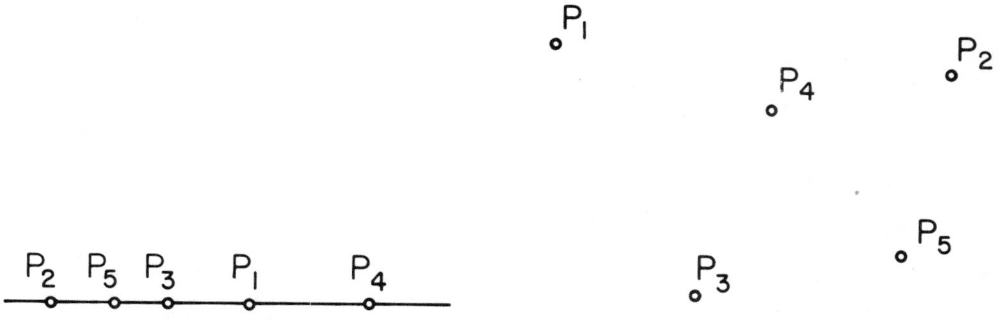

(a) (b)

Figure 1

---

1 This paper is an update of the authors' paper Geometric Sorting Theory, see References.
2 Supported in part by NSF Grant MCS 82-01831.
3 Supported in part by NSF Grant MCS 82-01342.

fact one can do this in any dimension d: If we know -- for each d-tuple $i_1,\ldots,i_d$ -- the number of points on the positive side of the oriented hyperplane spanned by $P_{i_1},\ldots,P_{i_d}$, then we can determine the points themselves. This works even if the configuration $\{P_1,\ldots,P_n\}$ is not simple -- in other words if more than two points are sometimes collinear, or more than three sometimes coplanar, and so on; and in fact even if the points $P_1,\ldots,P_n$ are not all distinct.

Basic Theorem of Geometric Sorting. If $\{P_1,\ldots,P_n\}$ is a configuration in R^d and, for every ordered d-tuple $(i_1,\ldots,i_d)$, we have

$$\Lambda(i_1,\ldots,i_d) = \{j \mid P_j \text{ is on the positive side of the oriented hyperplane } \langle P_{i_1},\ldots,P_{i_d}\rangle\}$$

and

$$\lambda(i_1,\ldots,i_d) = |\Lambda(i_1,\ldots,i_d)|,$$

then λ determines Λ.

A proof appears in [9], and -- in a generalization of the 2-dimensional case to "generalized configurations" or oriented matroids of rank 3 -- in [10]. Moreover, R. Cordovil has extended the Basic Theorem of Geometric Sorting to oriented matroids of arbitrary rank [3]. Here we present the proof for a planar configuration, where the argument is fairly straightforward, at least if we restrict ourselves to the simple case (no collinear triples).

Suppose then that $P_1,\ldots,P_n$ are distinct points, no three collinear, in the plane, and suppose for each i,j we know the number $\lambda(i,j)$ of points to the left of the directed line P_iP_j. The first step is to realize that we can immediately tell which points P_i are extreme points of the convex hull of the set $\{P_1,\ldots,P_n\}$: they are precisely the ones for which $\lambda(i,j) = n-2$ for some j.

Now if P_n, say, is an extreme point, and if we swing a ray counterclockwise around P_n, we can tell the order in which it passes through the points $P_1,\ldots,P_{n-1}$ by listing them in the order in which $\lambda(n,i)$ decreases. This means we can tell just which points P_j lie to the left of P_nP_i, and this means we can tell whether P_n is to the right or left of P_iP_j (see Figure 2). That, in turn, means that if we let λ_n be the coresponding λ-function for the set $\{P_1,\ldots,P_{n-1}\}$, we can determined λ_n from λ:

$$\lambda_n(i,j) = \begin{cases} \lambda(i,j)-1 & \text{if } P_n \text{ is to the left of } P_iP_j, \\ \lambda(i,j) & \text{otherwise.} \end{cases}$$

This suggests using induction on n, the theorem being trivial if n = 3 (there are only two

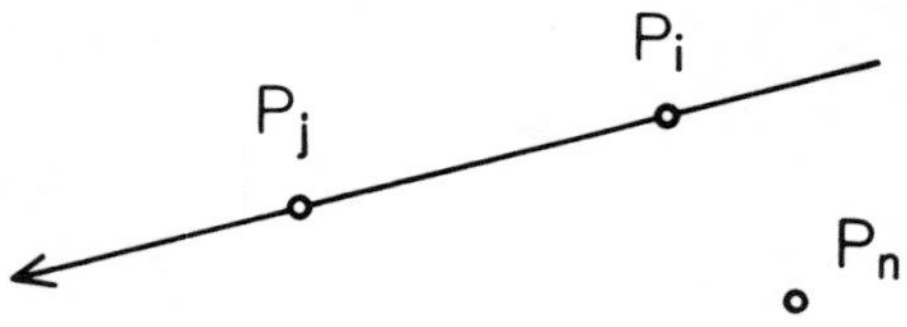

Figure 2

possible configuration types), so by induction hypothesis we can determine Λ_n, the Λ-function for $\{P_1,\ldots,P_{n-1}\}$. But since we know where P_n itself lies with respect to each P_iP_j, we can reconstruct the Λ-function for the full configuration:

$$\Lambda(i,j) = \begin{cases} \Lambda_n(i,j) \quad \{n\} & \text{if } P_n \text{ is to the left of } P_iP_j, \\ \Lambda_n(i,j) & \text{otherwise,} \end{cases}$$

and that finishes the proof.

Notice, by the way, that if we do not distinguish left from right, the theorem becomes false: Figure 3 shows two sets of points, S and S′, such that each line P_iP_j cuts S into two subsets of the same pair of cardinalities as $P_i'P_j'$ cuts S′, but not into corresponding pairs of sets.

Now let us see what this theorem has to do with sorting.

Suppose we have two numbered sets of distinct points on the line: $\{P_1,\ldots,P_n\}$ and $\{Q_1,\ldots,Q_n\}$. When are they in the same order? Clearly when -- for every i and j --

$$P_i < P_j \iff Q_i < Q_j.$$

This takes n^2 comparisons to verify, or actually just $n(n-1)/2$; but of course we can do it in much less time by "sorting" the two sets first, i.e., finding the permutations π and π' for which

$$P_{\pi(1)} < P_{\pi(2)} < \ldots < P_{\pi(n)} \text{ and}$$

$$Q_{\pi'(1)} < Q_{\pi'(2)} < \ldots < Q_{\pi'(n)},$$

and then just checking whether $\pi(i) = \pi'(i)$ for every i. Once the numbers are sorted, which can be done in time $O(n \log n)$ [13], to see whether they are in the same order then just takes n comparisons instead of n^2. The moral is that

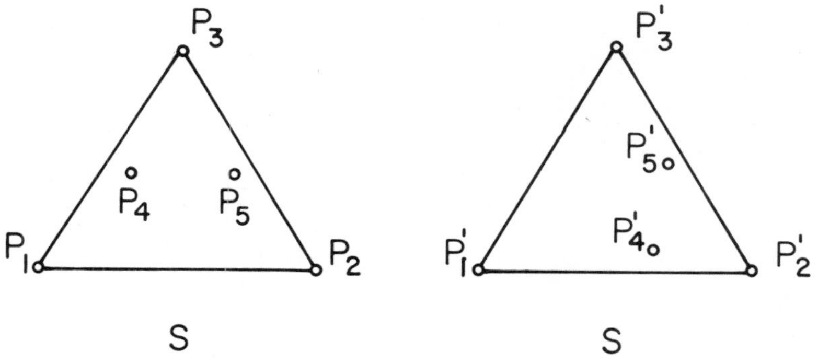

Figure 3

sorting a set of numbers encodes all the n^2 pieces of information "for every i,j, $P_i < P_j$ or > " into a more compact form, of size n, which carries all the information within it.

Now suppose we have two numbered sets of distinct points in the <u>plane</u>, $\{P_1,\ldots,P_n\}$ and $\{Q_1,\ldots,Q_n\}$, as in Figure 4, and let us assume for simplicity that no three points are collinear in either set. When are <u>they</u> in the same order, in some sense? The question is, of course, what do we mean by that? Well, just as the basic unit of order on the line is a pair, P_iP_j , which can be oriented either positively or negatively, let us use as our basic unit of order in the plane a <u>triple</u>, $P_iP_jP_k$, which -- likewise -- can be oriented either positively or negatively; here, of course, that would mean either counterclockwise or clockwise. Then for the two sets to have the same "order type" means that for each triple i,j,k,

$P_iP_jP_k$ is counterclockwise

<=> $Q_iQ_jQ_k$ is counterclockwise.

Now this would take n^3 (or actually n(n-1)(n-2)/6) comparisons to verify; but it follow immediately from the theorem above that it can be done in just n^2 comparisons, as soon as the points are "sorted" in the sense that -- for each i,j -- we determine just how many lie to the left of the directed line P_iP_j , i.e. determine the λ-matrix, since that in turn determines <u>which</u> ones do, i.e. determines the orientation of every triple $P_iP_jP_k$. So this process of <u>sorting geometrically</u>, which is the name we give to calculating the λ-matrix, once again compresses all the n^3 pieces of information "$P_iP_jP_k > 0$" or " < 0 " into size n^2 (namely the λ-matrix, which occupies that storage, carries all the n^3 pieces of information within it, by the theorem above). So just as in the linear case, we can save

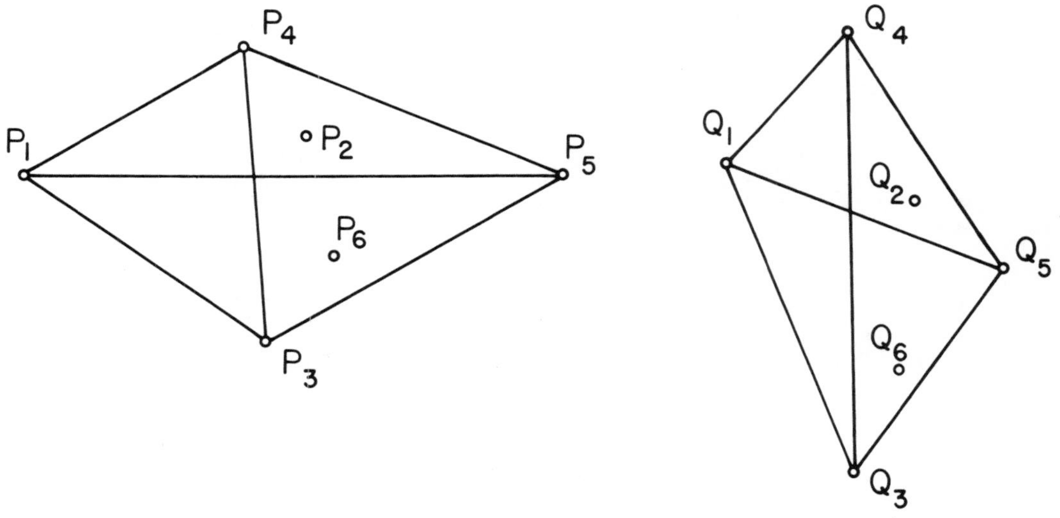

Figure 4

essentially an order of magnitude by sorting first. And the sorting procedure itself -- which on the line takes time $O(n \log n)$ -- can be accomplished in the plane in time $O(n^2 \log n)$ [9]. More recently, Edelsbrunner, O'Rourke, and Seidel [6] have found an algorithm to do it in time $O(n^2)$. In fact, their algorithm works in R^d in time $O(n^d)$, which is clearly optimal. Their method exploits a fast algorithm which they have found [6] to construct arrangements of hyperplanes in R^d, and the well-known duality between arrangements of hyperplanes and configurations of points [2,8].

Notice, by the way, that if we just wanted the vertices of the convex hull of the set, in counterclockwise order, say, we could find them -- by various algorithms [16] -- in time $O(n \log n)$; but when we sort the points geometrically, we determine not only the convex hull (which can be read off immediately from the λ-matrix, as in the proof before), but the relative positions of <u>all</u> the points in relation to each other. So it is not surprising that it should take an order of magnitude more time. Notice also that just as the problem of finding the minimum and maximum of a set S of points on a line becomes, in higher dimensions, the problem of finding the convex hull of a configuration C, so the problem of sorting <u>all</u> the points of S becomes the problem of sorting C geometrically, i.e., finding its λ-matrix.

Thus the result is that in the plane we can sort and compare, together, in time $O(n^2)$; in higher dimensions the exponent of n goes up, just as it does in the convex hull algorithms.

But suppose, now, that we are given two configurations to compare which are <u>un</u>-numbered, or only <u>randomly</u> numbered, and that we want to decide whether there is some renumbering in which their order types match. (This problem is more likely to come up in "real life" than the problem of matching numbered configurations, for example if we are looking at an application to pattern recognition or classification -- see below.) On the face of it, it looks like we would have to try all the n! different renumberings of one of them, and change the λ-function correspondingly in order to find a renumbering in which their order types might agree. But it turns out that we can do much better than this -- in fact we can get away with at most k renumberings, where k is the number of extreme points; so certainly with at most n renumberings. Here is an example:

Figure 5 shows two configurations, S and S′, which obviously have the same order type, but not with the numbering shown. Sorting each gives the λ-matrices

$$\lambda = \begin{pmatrix} 6 & 4 & 1 & 0 & 3 & 2 \\ 0 & 6 & 4 & 2 & 1 & 3 \\ 3 & 0 & 6 & 4 & 2 & 1 \\ 4 & 2 & 0 & 6 & 3 & 1 \\ 1 & 3 & 2 & 1 & 6 & 3 \\ 2 & 1 & 3 & 3 & 1 & 6 \end{pmatrix}, \quad \lambda' = \begin{pmatrix} 6 & 3 & 1 & 1 & 3 & 2 \\ 1 & 6 & 2 & 0 & 4 & 3 \\ 3 & 2 & 6 & 3 & 1 & 1 \\ 3 & 4 & 1 & 6 & 2 & 0 \\ 1 & 0 & 3 & 2 & 6 & 4 \\ 2 & 1 & 3 & 4 & 0 & 6 \end{pmatrix}.$$

Choose an extreme point i of S, by finding an entry $\lambda(i,j) = 0$; say $i = 1$. Similarly, find <u>all</u> the extreme points of S′ from λ': they are $\overline{2,5}$,6,4. (Notice that if our configurations are not simple, this method of locating extreme

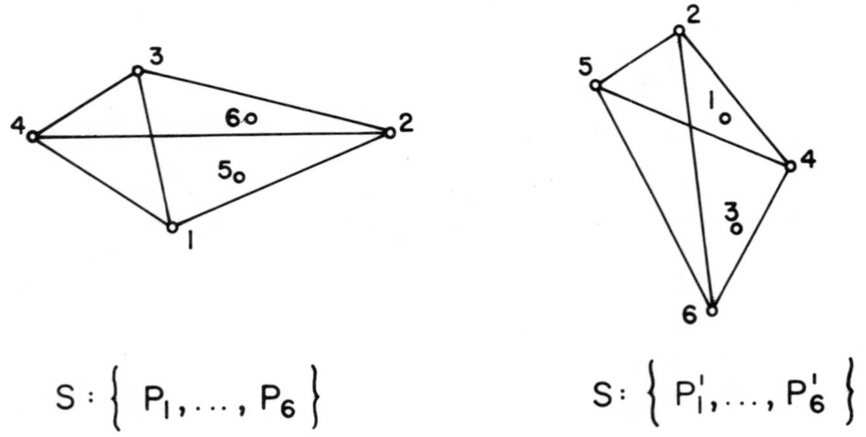

Figure 5

points must be modified; see [9].) Next, read off the 1-sequence from λ, by reading the indices j such that $\lambda(1,j)$ is in decrasing order: 125634. Do the same for each extreme point of S':

256314, 563412, 643125, 421536.

Then we have only to try renumbering S according to each permutation

$$\binom{125634}{256314}, \binom{125634}{563412}, \binom{125634}{643125}, \binom{125634}{421536},$$

and -- if there is <u>any</u> renumbering which will make the λ'-matrix agree with the λ-matrix, it must be one of these, since the extreme points must agree, in cyclic order, and the sequences for the corresponding extreme points must also agree. We see that only the third of these, call it π, satisfies

$$\lambda(i,j) = \lambda'(\pi(i),\pi(j))$$

for every i,j, which means that if S is renumbered according to π it will have the same order type as S'.

This matrix of $\leq$ n renumberings that must be checked means that the time for comparing two unnumbered (or randomly numbered) configurations is $O(n^3)$, which is considerably better than the $O(n! \cdot n^2)$ we would need if we had to try all the possible renumberings!

(Notice also that we can get all the orientation-preserving symmetries (up to order type) in this way -- just take $S' = S$.)

In higher dimensions this renumbering procedure generalizes in an interesting way: it turns out to be necessary to consider all the flags of faces of the convex hull of the configuration; each one gives rise to an ordering of the points in a canonical way, and we have to try all of these "canonical orderings" when we renumber. There are roughly $n^{[d/2]}$ in all, in dimension d; for details, see [9].

Now all of this leads to a number of possible applications. For one thing, we now have a powerful tool that we can use in pattern recognition problems, which can easily be implemented on a computer in order to compare and identify point patterns (and therefore many other images, since these can be reduced to point patterns by various techniques). And in fact one does not necessarily have to insist that the λ-matrices in question be <u>identical</u>, but only that they <u>correlate</u> highly, in order to have two point patterns that resemble each other. This might be useful in machine recognition of hand-printed characters, for example, where one would not expect to get a perfect match. J. O'Rourke, in fact, has recently extended the idea of the λ-matrix of a configuration to the "signature" of a curve, which is essentially the proportion of the curve to the left of the directed tangent at each point, and has discussed the applicability of this notion to handwritten character analysis [14,15].

Another application is to what is called stereochemistry, which deals with the structure of molecules in three-dimensional space; it turns out that the right-handedness or left-handedness of certain configurations of atoms within a molecule plays a role in determining the chemical properties of the molecule, and the sorting procedure we have been discussing gives a compact way of encoding all this information. In fact a chemist, A. Dreiding, together with a mathematician, K. Wirth, came up with a scheme for encoding precisely the same information in an article published not long ago [4]: their idea was to list all the ordered quadruples of points in a 3-dimensional configuration in lexicographic order, and write a "1" for a right-handed one and a "0" for a left-handed one, thereby getting the binary representation of an integer. The result, which they call the "signature" of the configuration, has $\Omega(n^4)$ bits, hence requires calculation time of $\Omega(n^4)$, while geometric sorting in 3-space takes only $O(n^3)$, and carries the same information, as a result of the theorem discussed earlier, so it constitutes an improvement by a factor of n.

One more application we can mention is to cluster analysis, a branch of statistics which concerns itself with identifying "clusters" of points in d-dimensional space. There are many ways of getting hold of these clusters, but one technique [7,12] consists of repeatedly splitting off what are called semispaces, that is, subconfigurations which are separated from the remaining points by hyperplanes. It turns out [10] that two numbered configurations have the same semispaces if and only if they have precisely the same order type in our sense; this means that our sorting methods give an efficient way of classifying point sets from the point of view of cluster analysis. In fact we can easily read off all the semispaces of a configuration during the process of sorting it; see [9] for further remarks.

An interesting problem that comes up in relation to this work has to do with the question of the optimality of our sorting procedure. The problem is: how many distinct configurations of n points are there in R^d ? Here, "distinct" means having distinct order types, in other words distinct λ-functions. This problem is unsolved already in the plane. An upper bound of $\exp(c\, n^2 \log n)$ follows immediately from our sorting theory for what are called information-theoretic reasons -- and in fact, as a result of the algorithm in [6], this can be improved to $O(n^2)$. On the other hand, H. Edelsbrunner [5] has shown that there are at least exp(cn log n) unnumbered configurations of n points in R^2, as well as $2^{cn^{2-\epsilon}}$ in R^3, for every $\epsilon > 0$. We can show, however, that there are at least exp(c n^2) generalized configurations in the plane [9], a generalized configuration being a configuration in which each pair of points is joined not by a straight line, but by a "pseudoline", or topological line, any two of which meet just once and cross there. (Generalized configurations in the plane are essentially eqiuvalent to oriented matroids of rank 3.) This therefore narrows the gap between the lower and upper bounds in the case of generalized configurations, since λ-matrices also encode the order type of the latter, but the gap remains wide open for ordinary configurations.

Finally, there is the question of which integer matrices can be λ-matrices of configurations. A solution would give a new characterization of coordinatizable oriented matroids. D. Avis [1] has observed that Tarski's decision procedure [17] would give a super-exponential algorithm to test whether a given matrix is the λ-matrix of a configuration.

References

[1] Avis, D., private communcation.

[2] Brown, K.Q., Geometric Transforms for Fast Geometric Algorithms, Ph.D. Thesis, Dept. of Computer Science, Carnegie-Mellon Univ. (1980).

[3] Cordovil, R., Oriented matroids and geometric sorting, Canad. Math. Bull. 26 (1983) 351-354.

[4] Dreiding, A.S. and Wirth, K., The multiplex - a classcification of finite ordered point sets in oriented d-dimensional spaces, Match 8 (1980) 341-352.

[5] Edelsbrunner, H., private communication.

[6] Edelsbrunner, H., O'Rourke, J., and Seidel, R., Constructing arrangements of lines and hyperplanes with applications, in Twenty-fourth Annual FOCS Symposium (1983) 83-91.

[7] Edwards, A.W.F. and Cavalli-Sforza, L.L., A method for cluster analysis, Biometrics 21 (1965) 362-375.

[8] Goodman, J.E. and Pollack, R., A theorem of ordered duality, Geometriae Dedicata 12 (1982) 63-74.

[9] Goodman, J.E. and Pollack, R., Multidimensinal sorting, SIAM Jrnl. on Comput. 12 (1983) 484-507.

[10] Goodman, J.E. and Pollack, R., Semispaces of configurations, cell complexes of arrangements, Jrnl. of Combinatorial Theory, Ser. A, to appear.

[11] Goodman, J.E. and Pollack, R., Geometric sorting theory, in Discrete Geometry and Convexity (New York Acad. of Sci., 1984), to appear.

[12] Harding, E.F., The number of partitions of a set of N points in k dimensions induced by hyperplanes, Proc. Edinb. Math. Soc. 15 (1967) 285-289.

[13] Knuth, D.E., the Art of Computer Programming, Vol. 3, Sorting and Searching (Addison-Wesley, Reading, 1973).

[14] O'Rourke, J., The signature of a plane curve, SIAM Jrnl. on Comput., to appear.

[15] O'Rourke, J. and Washington, R., The signature of a curve: a new tool for pattern recognition, in Computational Geometry (G.T. Toussaint, ed., North-Holland, 1984), to appear.

[16] Shamos, M.I., Computational Geometry, Ph.D. Thesis, Dept. of Computer Science, Yale Univ. (1978).

[17] Tarski, A., A Decision Method for Elementry Algebra and Geometry, 2nd ed., rev. (Univ. of California Press, Berkeley, 1951).

Computer-Supported Instruction: Prospects and Pitfalls

Organizer: *Lucio Chiaraviglio, Georgia Institute of Technology*

Panel Discussion:

Panelists - *James L. Carmon, University of Georgia, James Doyle, Atlanta University, John Goda, Georgia Institute of Technology, and Brian Schott, Georgia State University*

Moderator - *Lucio Chiaraviglio, Georgia Institute of Technology*

COMPUTER SCIENCE AND STATISTICS:
The Interface, L. Billard (ed.)
© Elsevier Science Publishers B.V. (North-Holland), 1985

COMPUTER SUPPORTED INSTRUCTION: PROSPECTS AND PITFALLS

Lucio Chiaraviglio

SCHOOL OF INFORMATION AND COMPUTER SCIENCE
GEORGIA INSTITUTE OF TECHNOLOGY
ATLANTA, GEORGIA 30332

The prospects as well as some of the pitfalls of computer supported instruction were discussed by the following panelists: Dr. James L. Carmon, Vice Chancellor for Computing, The University of Georgia; Dr. James Doyle, Atlanta University; Professor John Goda, Georgia Institute of Technology; Dr. Brian Schott, Georgia State University; Dr. L. Chiaraviglio was the moderator.

Dr. Carmon described the increasingly distributed hierarchical environment being deployed in support of instruction at the University of Georgia. The trend is towards a network of computing-information processing facilities that begin with personal work-stations at the student or faculty desk. These personal resources may be hosted by megaminis and these in turn serve as gateways to main-frames and supercomputers. Similar trends were present at all the institutions represented. Not surprisingly the networking heterogenous systems is one of the major organizational and technical challenges facing these institutions. An even greater number of non-traditional users are being recruited. These new users, both faculty and students, (e.g. in the Humanities) have information processing requirements that are not within the competence of the traditional computer center staff nor are the users by themselves capable of acquiring the necessary knowledge and skills. All of this translates into major training effort which the University of Georgia is accomplishing by offering a large number of short courses for student and faculty. A similar large re-orientation of the technical support staff must occur to enable appropriate servicing of the new users.

Dr. Doyle noted the large personal investment needed from the part of the faculty to incorporate effectively computers into the instructional processes. These efforts include self training, extensive development of instructional software and the tailoring of still relatively unfriendly systems to the requirements of instruction. All of these tasks are time consuming and institutions generally do not make adequate provisions for faculty release time. Technology is providing the basic means for better support of instruction. However, these means are not usable without value added and this value is too often unpaid faculty time.

Professor Goda described the Computer Supported Project within the School of Information and Computer Science. This project services some instructional needs in Computer Science as well as some of these needs in Mathematics, Social Sciences and English. Classroom-laboratories with terminals or personal computers networked to megaminis are being used to schedule instructors and students in computer supported instructional sessions. Immediate feedback between presented concepts and illustrative laboratory exercises is thereby facilitated. Technical staff under the direction of the faculty is progessively tailoring the system to support all the time consuming housekeeping tasks associated with instruction (e.g. on-line submission of exercises, student records, grading aids, etc.). Faculty aided by graduate teaching assistants are producing courseware which often consists of exercise harnesses to which the student has to add code modules in order to complete the total design. Very little tutorial type courseware is being developed. General faculty feeling is that CAI type materials that exist are not appropriate for higher education and often of low quality. There is considerable faculty interest in automatic grading and analysis, intelligent testing systems and the elimination of all paper. The general consensus is that efforts along these lines will be more productive than conventional CAI.

Dr. Schott described the increase in use by faculty and students of computing resources especially microcomputers. Access to micros is becoming increasingly common both on and off campus. Undergraduate access to microcomputers ranged from a low of 16% of the students at the Sophomore level to a high of 28% for Freshmen while 45% of the graduates reported regular access to micros. Fifty nine percent of these respondents had access to micros at work. Fifty seven percent favored the integration of computers in courses and forty three did not.

The presentation of the panelists was followed by open discussion and questions from the audience. This selected audience had positive attitudes towards computer support of instruction. However, many had met with the problems discussed by the panel. Acquisition of equipment still seems to be a major difficulty even though vendors are materially aiding this process in several ways. The training of faculty, students and required staff seemed to be the second largest problem area. Poor quality and/or unavailability of appropriate instructional software appears to be a close third. Surprisingly few comments were made about possible student or faculty resistance to expanded use of computers in instruction.

Optimal Transformations in Regression

Organizer: *John P. Sall, SAS Institute*

Invited Presentations:

Quantitative Analysis of Qualitative Data, *Forrest W. Young, University of North Carolina*

A Comparison of the ACE and MORALS Algorithms in an Application to Engine Exhaust Emissions Modeling, *Robert N. Rodriguez, SAS Institute*

COMPUTER SCIENCE AND STATISTICS:
The Interface, L. Billard (ed.)

ESTIMATING OPTIMAL TRANSFORMATIONS FOR MULTIPLE REGRESSION*

Leo Breiman
Department of Statistics
University of California
Berkeley, California 94720

and

Jerome H. Friedman
Stanford Linear Accelerator Center
and
Department of Statistics
Stanford University
Stanford, California 94305

In regression analysis, the response variable Y and the predictor variables $X_1, \ldots, X_p$ are often replaced by functions $\theta(Y)$ and $\phi_1(X_1), \ldots, \phi_p(X_p)$. We discuss a procedure for estimating those functions θ^* and $\phi_1^*, \ldots, \phi_p^*$ that minimize

$$e^2 = \frac{E\{[\theta(Y) - \sum_{j=1}^{p} \phi_j(X_j)]^2\}}{Var[\theta(Y)]}$$

given only a sample $\{(y_k, x_{k1}, \ldots, x_{kp}), 1 \leq k \leq N\}$ and making minimal assumptions concerning the data distribution or the form of the solution functions.

1. Introduction

Nonlinear transformation of variables is a commonly used practice in regression problems. Two common goals are stabilization of error variance and symmetrization/normalization of error distribution. A more comprehensive goal, and the one we adopt, is to find those transformations that produce the best fitting additive model. Knowledge of such transformations aid in the interpretation and understanding of the relationship between the response and predictors.

Let $Y, X_1, \ldots, X_p$ be random variables with Y the response and $X_1, \ldots, X_p$ the predictors. Let $\theta(Y), \phi_1(X_1), \ldots, \phi_p(X_p)$ be arbitrary measurable mean-zero functions of the corresponding random variables. The fraction of variance not explained (e^2) by a regression of $\theta(Y)$ on $\sum_{i=1}^{p} \phi_i(X_i)$ is

$$e^2(\theta, \phi_1, \ldots, \phi_p) = \frac{E\{[\theta(Y) - \sum_{i=1}^{p} \phi_i(X_i)]^2\}}{E\theta^2(Y)}. \tag{1.1}$$

Then define *optimal transformations* as functions $\theta^*, \phi_1^*, \ldots, \phi_p^*$ that minimize (1.1): i.e.

$$e^2(\theta^*, \phi_1^*, \ldots, \phi_p^*) = \min_{\theta, \phi_1, \ldots, \phi_p} e^2(\theta, \phi_1, \ldots, \phi_p). \tag{1.2}$$

It can be shown (Breiman and Friedman, 1985) that optimal transformations exist and satisfy a complex system of integral equations. The heart of our approach is that there is a simple iterative algorithm using only bivariate conditional expectations which converges to an optimal solution. When the conditional expectations are estimated from a finite data set, then use of the algorithm results in estimates of the optimal transformations.

This method has some powerful characteristics. It can be applied in situations where the response and/or the predictors involve arbitrary mixtures of continuous ordered variables and categorical variables (ordered or unordered). The functions $\theta, \phi_1, \ldots, \phi_p$ are real valued. If the original variable is categorical, the application of θ or ϕ_i assigns a real valued score to each of its categorical values.

The procedure is nonparametric. The optimal transformation estimates are based solely on the data sample

* Work supported by Office of Naval Research under contracts N00014-82-K-0054 and N00014-81-K-0340. This is a condensed version of a paper to appear in the Journal of the American Statistical Association, March 1985.

$\{(y_k, x_{k1}, \ldots, x_{kp}), 1 \leq k \leq N\}$ with minimal assumptions concerning the data distribution and the form of the optimal transformations. In particular, we do not require the transformation functions to be from a particular parameterized family or even monotone. (We illustrate below situations where the optimal transformations are not monotone.)

It is applicable to at least three situations

random designs in regression
autoregressive schemes in stationary ergodic times series
controlled designs in regression

In the first of these, we assume the data $(y_k, \underline{x}_k)$, $k = 1, \ldots, N$ are independent samples from the distribution of $Y, X_1, \ldots, X_p$. In the second, a stationary mean-zero ergodic time series $X_1, X_2, \ldots$ is assumed, the optimal transformations are defined to be the functions that minimize

$$e^2 = \frac{E\{[\theta(X_{p+1}) - \sum_{j=1}^{p} \phi_j(X_j)]^2\}}{E\theta^2(X_{p+1})}$$

and the data consists of $N + p$ consecutive observations $x_1, \ldots, x_{N+p}$. This is put in a standard data form by defining

$$y_k = x_{k+p}, \underline{x}_k = (x_{k+p-1}, \ldots, x_k), \quad k = 1, \ldots, N.$$

In the controlled design situation, a distribution $p(dy|\underline{x})$ for the response variable Y is specified for every point $\underline{x} = (x_1, \ldots, x_p)$ in the design space. The $N^t h$ order design consists of a specification of N points $x_1, \ldots, \underline{x}_N$ in the design space and the data consists of these points together with measurements on the response variables $y_1, \ldots, y_N$. The $\{y_k\}$ are assumed independent with y_k drawn from the distribution $P(dy|\underline{x}_k)$.

Denote by $\hat{P}_N(d\underline{x})$ the empirical distribution that gives mass $1/N$ to each of the points $\underline{x}_1, \ldots, \underline{x}_N$. Assume further that

$$\hat{P}_N \overset{w}{\to} P$$

where $P(dx)$ is a probability measure on the design space. Then $P(dy|\underline{x})$ and $P(d\underline{x})$ determine the distribution of random variables $Y, X_1, \ldots, X_p$ and the optimal transformations are defined as in (1.2).

For the bivariate case, $p = 1$, the optimal transformations $\theta^*(Y), \phi^*(X)$ satisfy

$$\rho^*(X,Y) = \rho(\theta^*, \phi^*) = \max_{\theta,\phi} \rho[\theta(Y), \phi(X)]$$

where ρ is the product moment correlation coefficient. The quantity $\rho^*(X, Y)$ is known as the *maximal correlation* between X and Y, and is used as a general measure of dependence [Gebelein (1947); see also Renyi (1959) and Samanov (1958A,B) and Lancaster (1958)]. The maximal correlation has the following properties [Renyi (1959)]:

(a) $0 \leq \rho^*(X, Y) \leq 1$

(b) $\rho^*(X, Y) = 0$ if and only if X and Y are independent

(c) If there exists a relation of the form $u(X) = v(Y)$ where u and v are Borel-measurable functions with $var[u(X)] > 0$, then $\rho^*(X, Y) = 1$.

Therefore in the bivariate case, our procedure can also be regarded as a method for estimating the maximal correlation between two variables, providing as a by-product estimates of the functions θ^*, ϕ^* that achieve the maximum.

In the next section, we describe our procedure for finding optimal transformations using algorithmic notation, deferring mathematical justifications to Breiman and Friedman (1985). We next illustrate the procedure in Section 3 by applying it to a simulated data set where the optimal transformations are known. The estimates are surprisingly good. Our algorithm is also applied to the Boston housing data of Harrison and Rubinfeld (1978), as listed in Belsey, Kuh and Welsch (1980). The transformations found by the algorithm generally differ from those applied in the original analysis. Finally, we apply the procedure to a multiple time series arising from an air pollution study. A FORTRAN implementation of our algorithm is available from either author. Section 4 presents a general discussion and relates this procedure to other empirical methods for finding transformations.

There is relevant previous work. Closest in spirit to the ACE algorithm we developed is the MORALS algorithm due to Young et.al. (1976) [see also deLeeuw et.al. (1976)]. It uses a similar alternating least squares fit, but restricts transformations on discrete ordered variables to be monotonic and transformations on continuous variables to be linear or polynomial. No theoretical framework for MORALS is given.

Renyi [1959] gives a proof of the existence of optimal transformations in the bivariate case under conditions similar to ours in the general case. He also derived integral equations satisfied by θ^* and φ^* with kernels depending on the bivariate density of X and Y, and concentrated on finding solutions assuming this density known. The equations seem generally intractable with only a few known solutions. He did not consider the problem of estimating θ^*, φ^* from data.

Kolmogorov (see Sarmanov and Zaharov [1960], Lancaster [1969]) proved that if $Y_1, \ldots, Y_q, X_1, \ldots, X_p$ have a joint normal distribution, then the functions $\theta(Y_1, \ldots, Y_q)$, $\phi(X_1, \ldots, X_p)$ having maximum correlation are linear. It follows from this that in the regression model

$$\theta(Y) = \sum_{i=1}^{p} \phi_i(X_i) + Z \tag{1.4}$$

if the $\phi_i(X_i), i = 1, \ldots, p$ have a joint normal distribution and Z is an independent $N(0, \sigma^2)$, then the optimal transformations as defined in (1.2) are $\theta, \phi_1, \ldots, \phi_p$. Generally, for a model of the form (1.4) with Z independent of $(X_1, \ldots, X_p)$, the optimal transformations are not equal to $\theta, \phi_1, \ldots, \phi_p$. But in examples with simulated data generated from models of the form (1.4), with non-normal $\{\phi_i(X_i)\}$, the estimated optimal transformations were always close to $\theta, \phi_1, \ldots, \phi_p$.

Finally, we note the work in a different direction by Kimeldord, May, and Sampson [1982], who construct a linear programming type algorithm to find the monotone transformations $\theta(Y), \phi(X)$ that maximize the sample correlation coefficient in the bivariate case $p = 1$.

2. The Algorithm

Our procedure for finding $\theta^*, \phi_1^*, \ldots, \phi_p^*$ is iterative. Assume a known distribution for the variables $Y, X_1, \ldots, X_p$. Without loss of generality, let $E\theta^2(Y) = 1$, and assume that all functions have expectation zero.

To illustrate, we first look at the bivariate case:

$$e^2(\theta, \phi) = E[\theta(Y) - \phi(X)]^2 \tag{2.1}$$

Consider the minimization of (2.1) with respect to $\theta(Y)$ for a given function $\phi(X)$ keeping $E\theta^2 = 1$. The solution is

$$\theta_1(Y) = E[\phi(X)|Y] / \| E[\phi(X)|Y] \| \tag{2.2}$$

with $\| \cdot \| \equiv [E(\cdot)^2]^{1/2}$. Next, consider the unrestricted minimization of (2.1) with respect to $\phi(X)$ for a given $\theta(Y)$. The solution is

$$\phi_1(X) = E[\theta(Y)|X]. \tag{2.3}$$

Equations (2.2) and (2.3) form the basis of an iterative optimization procedure involving <u>alternating conditional expectations</u> (ACE):

```
BASIC ACE ALGORITHM
    set θ(Y) = Y/ || Y ||;
    ITERATE UNTIL e²(θ, φ) fails to decrease:
        φ₁(Y) = E[θ(Y)|X];
        replace φ(X) with φ₁(X);
        θ₁(Y) = E[φ(X)|Y]/ || E[φ(X)|Y] ||;
        replace θ(Y) with θ₁(Y);
    END ITERATION LOOP;
    θ and φ are the solutions θ* and φ*;
END ALGORITHM;
```

This algorithm decreases (2.1) at each step by alternatingly minimizing with respect to one function holding the other fixed at its previous evaluation. Each iteration (execution of the iteration loop) performs one pair of these single function minimizations. The process begins with an initial guess for one of the functions ($\theta = Y / \| Y \|$ above) and ends when a complete iteration pass fails to decrease e^2. In Breiman and Friedman [1985], we prove that the algorithm converges to optimal transformations θ^*, ϕ^*.

Now consider the more general case of multiple predictors $X_1, \ldots, X_p$. We proceed in direct analogy with the basic ACE algorithm; we minimize

$$e^2(\theta, \phi_1, \ldots, \phi_p) = E\left[\theta(Y) - \sum_{j=1}^{p} \phi_j(X_j)\right]^2, \tag{2.4}$$

holding $E\theta^2 = 1$, $E\theta = E\phi_1 = \ldots = E\phi_p = 0$, through a series of single function minimizations involving bivariate conditional expectations. For a given set of functions $\phi_1(X_1), \ldots, \phi_p(X_p)$, minimization of (2.4) with respect to $\theta(Y)$ yields

$$\theta_1(Y) = E[\sum_{i=1}^{p} \phi_i(X_i)|Y] / \| E[\sum_{i=1}^{p} \phi_i(X_i)|Y] \| . \tag{2.5}$$

The next step is to minimize (2.4) with respect to $\phi_1(X_1), \ldots, \phi_p(X_p)$ given $\theta(Y)$. This is obtained through another iterative algorithm. Consider the minimization of (2.4) with respect to a single function $\phi_k(X_k)$ for given $\theta(Y)$ and a given set $\phi_1, \ldots, \phi_{k-1}, \phi_{k+1}, \ldots, \phi_p$. The solution is

$$\phi_{k,1}(X_k) = E[\theta(Y) - \sum_{i \neq k} \phi_i(X_i)|X_k]. \tag{2.6}$$

The corresponding iterative algorithm is then:

```
set φ₁(X₁), ..., φₚ(Xₚ) = 0;
ITERATE UNTIL e²(θ, φ₁, ..., φₚ) fails to decrease;
    FOR k = 1 TO p DO:
        φₖ,₁(Xₖ) = E[θ(Y) − Σ_{i≠k} φᵢ(Xᵢ)|Xₖ];
        replace φₖ(Xₖ) with φₖ,₁(Xₖ);
    END FOR LOOP;
END ITERATION LOOP;
φ₁, ..., φₚ are the solution functions;
```

Each iteration of the inner FOR loop minimizes e^2 (2.4) with respect to the function $\phi_k(X_k)$, $k = 1, \ldots, p$ with all other functions fixed at their previous evaluations (execution of the FOR loop). The outer loop is iterated until one complete pass over the predictor variables (inner FOR loop) fails to decrease e^2 (2.4).

Substituting this procedure for the corresponding single function optimization in the bivariate ACE algorithm gives rise to the full ACE algorithm for minimizing the (2.4) e^2.

ACE ALGORITHM:
set $\theta(Y) = Y / \| Y \|$ and $\phi_1(X_1), \ldots, \phi_p(X_p) = 0$;
ITERATE UNTIL $e^2(\theta, \phi_1, \ldots, \phi_p)$ fails to decrease;
ITERATE UNTIL $e^2(\theta, \phi_1, \ldots, \phi_p)$ fails to decrease;
FOR $k = 1$ TO p DO:

$$\phi_{k,1}(X_k) = E[\theta(Y) - \sum_{i \neq k} \phi_i(X_i) | X_k];$$

replace $\phi_k(X_k)$ with $\phi_{k,1}(X_k)$;
END FOR LOOP;
END INNER ITERATION LOOP;

$$\theta_1(Y) = E[\sum_{i=1}^{p} \phi_i(X_i)|Y] / \| E\left[\sum_{i=1}^{p} \phi_i(X_i)|Y\right] \|$$

replace $\theta(Y)$ with $\theta_1(Y)$;
END OUTER ITERATION LOOP;
$\theta, \phi_1, \ldots, \phi_p$ are the solutions $\theta^*, \phi_1^*, \ldots, \phi_p^*$;
END ACE ALGORITHM;

In Breiman and Friedman[1985], we prove that the ACE algorithm converges to optimal transformations.

3. Applications

In the previous section, the ACE algorithm was developed in the context of known distributions. In practice, data distributions are seldom known. Instead, one has a data set $\{(y_k, x_{k1}, \ldots, x_{kp}),\ 1 \leq k \leq N\}$ that is presumed to be a sample from $Y, X_1, \ldots, X_p$. The goal is to estimate the optimal transformation functions $\theta(Y), \phi_1(X_1), \ldots, \phi_p(X_p)$ from the data. This can be accomplished by applying the ACE algorithm to the data with the quantity $e^2, \| \ \|$, and the conditional expectations replaced by suitable estimates. The resulting functions $\hat{\theta}^*, \hat{\phi}_1^*, \ldots, \hat{\phi}_p^*$ are then taken as estimates of the corresponding optimal transformations.

The estimate for e^2 is the usual mean squared error for regression,

$$e^2(\theta, \phi_1, \ldots, \phi_p) = \frac{1}{N} \sum_{k=1}^{N} \left[\theta(y_k) - \sum_{j=1}^{p} \phi_j(x_{kj})\right]^2 .$$

If $g(y, x_1, \ldots, x_p)$ is a function defined for all data values, then $\| g \|^2$ is replaced by

$$\| g \|_N^2 = \frac{1}{N} \sum_{k=1}^{N} g^2(y_k, x_{k1}, \ldots, x_{kp}).$$

For the case of categorical variables, the conditional expectation estimates are straightforward:

$$\hat{E}[A|Z = z] = \sum_{z_j = z} A_j / \sum_{z_j = z} 1$$

where A is a real valued quantity and the sums are over the subset of observations having (categorical) value $Z = z$. For variables that can assume many ordered values, the estimation is based on smoothing techniques. Such procedures have been the subject of considerable study (see, for example, Gasser and Rosenblatt [1979], Cleveland [1979], Craven and Wahba [1979]). Since the smoother is repeatedly applied in the algorithm, high speed is desirable as well as adaptability to local curvature. We use a smoother employing local linear fits with varying window width determined by local cross-validation ("super smoother", Friedman [1984]).

The algorithm evaluates $\hat{\theta}^*, \hat{\phi}_1^*, \ldots, \hat{\phi}_p^*$ at all corresponding data values, i.e., $\hat{\theta}^*(y)$ is evaluated at the set of data values $\{y_k\}, k = 1, \ldots, N$. The simplest way to understand the shape of the transformations is by means of a plot of the function versus the corresponding data values, that is, through the plots of $\hat{\theta}^*(y_k)$ versus y_k and $\hat{\phi}_1^*, \ldots, \hat{\phi}_p^*$ versus the data values of $x_1, \ldots, x_p$ respectively.

In this section, we illustrate the ACE procedure by applying it to various data sets. In order to evaluate performance on finite samples, the procedure is first applied to simulated data for which the optimal transformations are known. We next apply it to the Boston housing data of Harrison and Rubinfeld [1978], as listed in Belsey, Kuh and Welsch [1980], contrasting the ACE transformations with those used in the original analysis. For our last example, we apply the ACE procedure to a multiple time series to study the relation between air pollution (ozone) and various meteorological quantities.

Our first example consists of 200 bivariate observations $\{(y_k, x_k), 1 \leq k \leq 200\}$ generated from the model

$$y_k = \exp[x_k^3 + \epsilon_k]$$

with the x_k^3 and the ϵ_k drawn independently from a standard normal distribution $N(0,1)$. Figure 1a shows a scatterplot of these data. Figures 1b-1d show the results of applying the ACE algorithm to the data. The estimated optimal transformation $\hat{\theta}^*(y)$ is shown in the plot, Figure 1b, of $\hat{\theta}^*(y_k)$ versus $y_k, 1 \leq k \leq 200$. Figure 1c is a plot of $\hat{\phi}^*(x_k)$ versus x_k. These plots suggest the transformations $\theta(y) = \log(y)$ and $\phi(x) = x^3$ which are optimal for the parent distribution. Figure 1d is a plot of $\hat{\theta}^*(y_k)$ versus $\hat{\phi}^*(x_k)$. This plot indicates a more linear relation between the transformed variables than that between the untransformed ones.

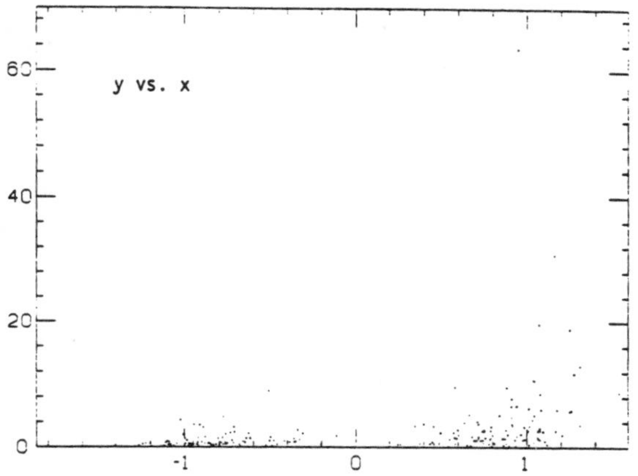

Figure 1a

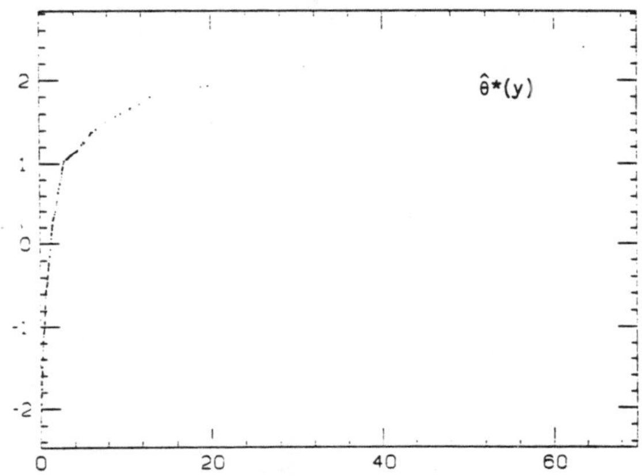

Figure 1b

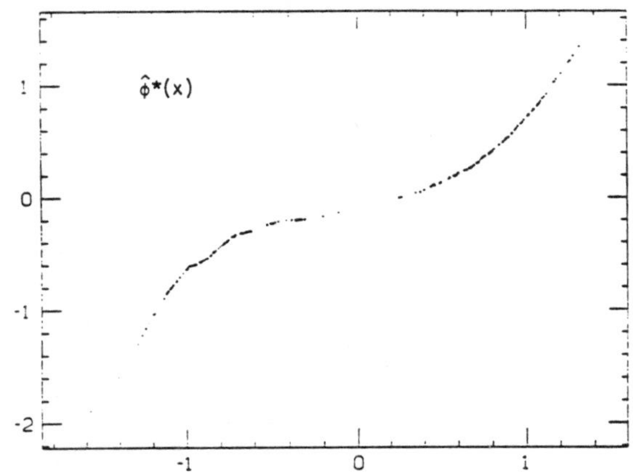

Figure 1c

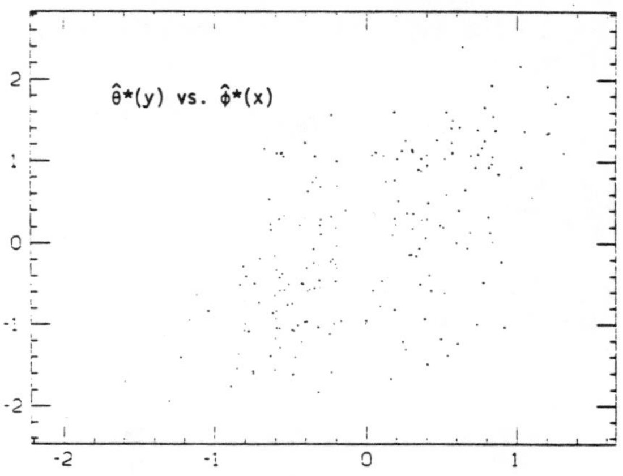

Figure 1d

The next issue we address is how much the algorithm overfits the data due to the repeated smoothings, resulting in inflated estimates of the maximal correlation ρ^* and of $R^{*^2} = 1 - e^{*^2}$. The answer, on the simulated data sets we have generated, is surprisingly little.

To illustrate this, we contrast two estimates of ρ^* and R^{*^2} using the above model. The known optimal transformations are $\theta(Y) = \log Y, \phi(X) = X^3$. Therefore, we define the *direct* estimate for ρ^* given any data set generated as above by

$$\hat{\rho}^* = \frac{1}{N}\sum_{k=1}^{N} (\log y_k - \overline{\log y})(x_k^3 - \overline{x^3})$$

and $\hat{R}^{*^2} = \hat{\rho}^{*^2}$. The ACE algorithm produces the estimates

$$\hat{\rho}^* = \frac{1}{N}\sum_{k=1}^{N} \hat{\theta}^*(y_k)\hat{\phi}^*(x_k)$$

and $\hat{R}^{*^2} = 1 - \hat{e}^{*^2} = \hat{\rho}^{*^2}$. In this model $\rho^* = 0.707$ and $R^{*^2} = 0.5$.

For 100 data sets, each of size 200, generated from the above model, the means and standard deviations of the ρ^* estimates are

	means	s.d.
ρ^* direct	.700	.034
ACE	.709	.036

The means and standard deviations of the R^{*^2} estimates are

	means	s.d.
R^{*^2} direct	.492	.047
ACE	.503	.050

We also computed the differences $\hat{\rho}^* - \hat{\rho}^*$ and $\hat{R}^{*^2} - \hat{R}^{*^2}$ for the 100 data sets. The means and standard deviations are

	means	s.d.
$\hat{\rho}^* - \hat{\rho}^*$	.001	.015
$\hat{R}^{*^2} - \hat{R}^{*^2}$	.012	.022

The above experiment was duplicated for smaller sample size N = 100. In this case, we obtain

	means	s.d.
$\hat{\rho}^* - \hat{\rho}^*$	.029	.034
$\hat{R}^{*^2} - \hat{R}^{*^2}$	.042	.051

We next show an application of the procedure to simulated data generated from the model

$$y_k = \exp[\sin(x_k) + \epsilon_k/2] \quad (1 \le k \le 200)$$

with the x_k sampled from a uniform distribution $U(0, 2\pi)$ and the ϵ_k drawn independently of the x_k from a standard normal distribution $N(0,1)$. Figure 2a shows a scatterplot of these data. Figures 2b and 2c show the optimal transformation estimates $\hat{\theta}^*(y)$ and $\hat{\phi}^*(x)$. Although $\log(y)$ and $\sin(x)$ are not the optimal transformations for this model (owing to the non-normal distribution of $\sin(x)$), these transformations are still clearly suggested by the resulting estimates.

Our next example consists of a sample of 200 triples $\{(y_k, x_{k1}, x_{k2}), 1 \le k \le 200\}$ drawn from the model $Y = X_1 X_2$ with X_1 and X_2 generated independently from a uniform distribution $U(-1,1)$. Note that $\theta(Y) = \log(Y)$ and $\phi_j(X_j) = \log X_j$ $(j = 1,2)$ cannot be solutions here since Y, X_1 and X_2 all assume negative values. Figure 3a shows a plot of $\hat{\theta}^*(y_k)$ versus y_k, while Figures 3b and 3c show corresponding plots of $\hat{\phi}_1^*(x_{k1})$ and $\hat{\phi}_2^*(x_{k2})$ $(1 \le k \le 200)$. All three solution transformation functions are seen to be double valued. The optimal transformations for this problem are $\theta^*(Y) = \log|Y|$ and $\phi_j^*(X_j) = \log|X_j|$ $(j = 1,2)$. The estimates clearly reflect this structure except near the origin where the smoother cannot reproduce the infinite discontinuity in the derivative.

This example illustrates that the ACE algorithm is able to produce non-monotonic estimates for both response as well as predictor transformations.

Figure 2a

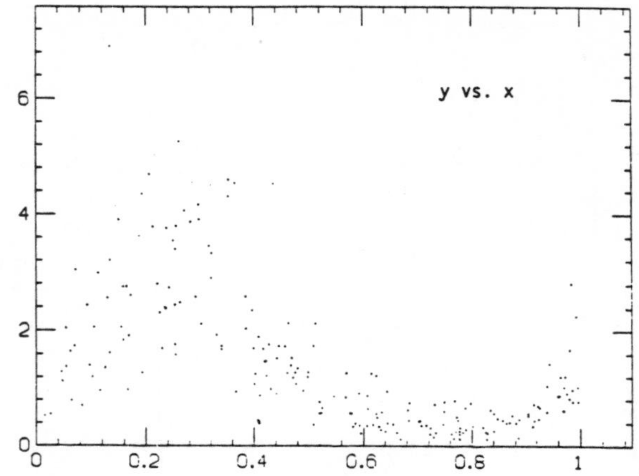

Figure 2b

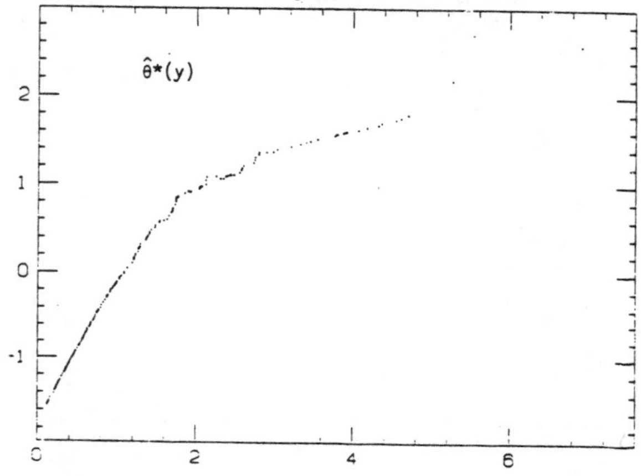

Figure 2c

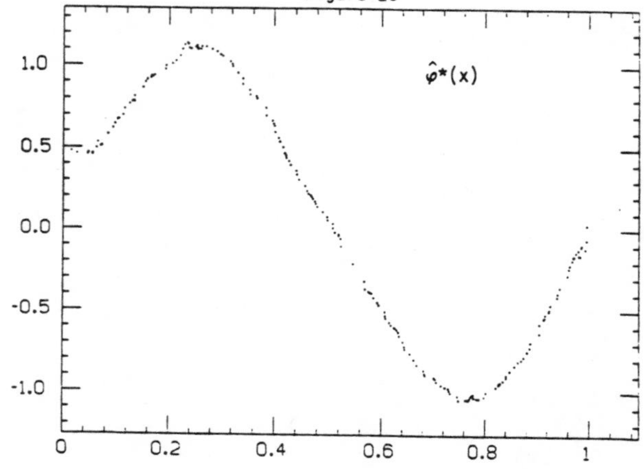

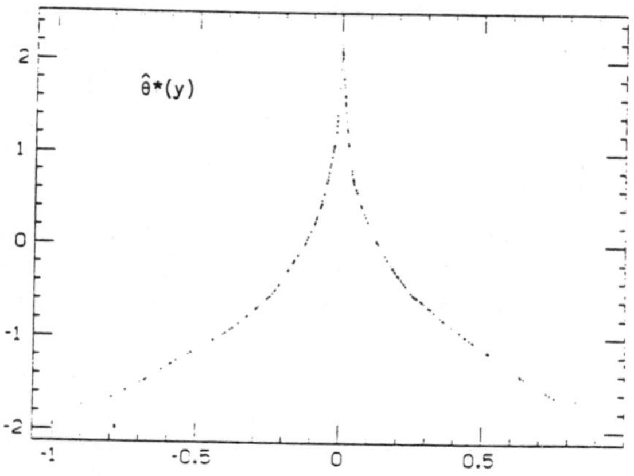

Figure 3a

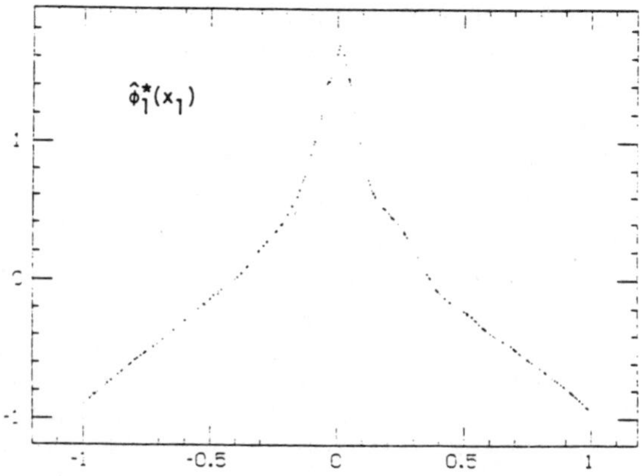

Figure 3b

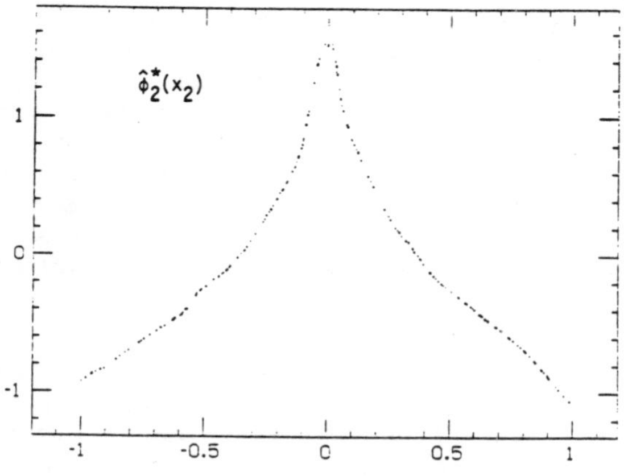

Figure 3c

For our next example, we apply the ACE algorithm to the Boston housing market data of Harrison and Rubinfeld [1978]. A complete listing of these data appear in Belsey, Kuh and Welsch [1980]. Harrison and Rubinfeld used these data to estimate marginal air pollution damages as revealed in the housing market. Central to their analysis was a housing value equation which relates the median value of owner-occupied homes in each of the 506 census tracts in the Boston Standard Metropolitan Statistical Area, to air pollution (as reflected in concentration of nitrogen oxides) and to 12 other variables that are thought to effect housing prices. This equation was estimated by trying to determine the best fitting functional form of housing price on these variables. By experimenting with a number of possible transformations of the 14 variables (response and 13 predictors), Harrison and Rubinfeld settled on an equation of the form

$$\begin{aligned}\log(MV) =& \alpha_1 + \alpha_2(RM)^2 + \alpha_3 \text{ AGE}\\ &+\alpha_4 \log(DIS) + \alpha_5 \log(RAD) + \alpha_6 \text{ TAX}\\ &+\alpha_7 PTRATIO + \alpha_8(B - 0.63)^2\\ &+\alpha_9 \log(LSTAT) + \alpha_{10} CRIM + \alpha_{11} ZN\\ &+\alpha_{12} INDUS + \alpha_{13} CHAS + \alpha_{14}(NOX)^p + \epsilon.\end{aligned}$$

A brief description of each variable is given in Table 1. (For a more complete description, see Harrison and Rubinfeld [1978], Table IV.) The coefficients $\alpha_1, \ldots, \alpha_{14}$ were determined by a least squares fit to measurements of the 14 variables for the 506 census tracts. The best value for the exponent p was found to be 2.0 by a numerical optimization (grid search). This "basic equation" was used to generate estimates for the willingness to pay for, and the marginal benefits of, clean air.

TABLE 1

Variables Used in the Housing Value Equation of Harrison and Rubinfeld (1978)

VARIABLE	DEFINITION
MV	Median value of owner-occupied homes
RM	Average number of rooms in owner units
AGE	Proportion of owner units built prior to 1940
DIS	Weighted distances to five employment centers in the Boston region
RAD	Index of accessibility to radial highways
TAX	Full property tax rate ($/$10,000)
PTRATIO	Pupil-teacher ratio by town school district
B	Black proportion of population
LSTAT	Proportion of population that is lower status
CRIM	Crime rate by town
ZN	Proportion of town's residential land zoned for lots greater than 25,000 square feet
INDUS	Proportion of nonretail business acres per town
CHAS	Charles River dummy: = 1 if tract bounds the Charles River; = 0 if otherwise
NOX	Nitrogen oxide concentration in pphm

Harrison and Rubinfeld note that the results are highly sensitive to the particular specification of the form of the housing price equation.

We applied the ACE algorithm to the transformed measurements $(y', x' \dots x'_{13})$ (using $p = 2$ for NOX) appearing in the basic equation. To the extent that these transformations are close to the optimal ones, the algorithm will produce almost linear functions. Departures from linearity indicate transformations that can improve the quality of the fit.

In this (and the following) example, we apply the procedure in a forward stepwise manner. For the first pass we consider the 13 bivariate problems ($p = 1$) involving the response y' with each of the predictor variables $x'_k (1 \leq k \leq 13)$ in turn. The predictor k_1 that maximizes $\hat{R}^2[\hat{\theta}_1(y'), \hat{\phi}_{1,k}(x'_k)]$ is included in the model. The second pass (over the remaining 12 predictors) includes the 12 trivariate problems ($p = 2$) involving y', x'_{k_1}, x'_k $(k \neq k_1)$. The predictor that maximizes $\hat{R}^2[\hat{\theta}_2(y'), \hat{\phi}_{2,k_1}(x'_{k_1}), \hat{\phi}_{2,k}(x'_k)]$ is included in the model. This forward selection procedure is continued until the best predictor of the next pass increases the $\hat{R}^2$ of the previous pass by less than 0.01.

The resulting final model involved four predictors and had an $\hat{R}^2$ of 0.89. Applying ACE simultaneously to all 13 predictors results in an increased $\hat{R}^2$ of only 0.02.

Figure 4a shows a plot of the solution response transformation $\hat{\theta}(y')$. This function is seen to have a positive curvature for central values of y', connecting two straight line segments of different slope in either side. This suggests that the logarithmic transformation may be too severe. Figure 4b shows the transformation $\hat{\theta}(y)$ resulting when the (forward stepwise) ACE algorithm is applied to the original *untransformed* census measurements. (The same predictor variable set appears in this model.) This analysis indicates that, if anything, a mild transformation involving *positive* curvature is most appropriate for the response variable.

Figures 4c-4f show the ACE transformations $\hat{\phi}_{k_1}(x'_{k_1} \dots \hat{\phi}_{k_4}(x'_{k_4})$ for the (transformed) predictor variables x' appearing in the final model. The standard deviation $\sigma(\hat{\phi}^*_j)$ is indicated in each graph. This provides a measure of how strongly each $\hat{\phi}^*_j(x_j)$ enters into the model for $\hat{\theta}^*(y')$. The two terms that enter most strongly involve the number of rooms squared (Figure 4c) and the logarithm of the fraction of population that is of lower status (Figure 4d). The nearly linear shape of the latter transformation suggests that the original logarithmic transformation was appropriate for this variable. The transformation on the number of rooms squared variable is far from linear, however, indicating that a simple quadratic does not adequately capture its relationship to housing value. For less than six rooms, housing value is roughly independent of room number, while for larger values there is a strong increasing linear dependence. The remaining two variables that enter into this model are pupil-teacher ratio and property tax rate. The solution transformation for the former, Figure 4e, is seen to be approximately linear while that for the latter, Figure 4f, has considerable nonlinear structure. For tax rates up to $320, housing price seems to fall rapidly with increasing tax, while for larger rates the association is roughly constant.

Although the variable $(NOX)^2$ was not selected by our stepwise procedure we can try to estimate its marginal effect on median home value by including it with the four selected variables and running ACE with the resulting five predictor variables. The increase in $\hat{R}^2$ over the four predictor model was .006. The solution transformations on the response and original four predictors changed very little. The solution transformation for $(NOX)^2$ is shown in Figure 4g. This curve is a non-monotonic function of NOX^2 not well approximated by a linear (or monotone) function. This makes it difficult to formulate a simple interpretation of the willingness to pay for clean air from these data. For low concentration values, housing prices seem to *increase* with increasing $(NOX)^2$, whereas for higher values this trend is substantially reversed.

Figure 4h shows a scatterplot of $\hat{\theta}^*(y_k)$ versus $\sum_{j=1}^{4} \hat{\phi}_j^*(x_{kj})$ for the four predictor model. This plot shows no evidence of additional structure not captured in the model

$$\hat{\theta}^*(y) = \sum_{j=1}^{4} \hat{\phi}_j^*(x_j) + \epsilon.$$

The $\hat{e}^{*2}$ resulting from the use of the ACE transformations was 0.11 as compared to the e^2 value of 0.20 produced by the Harrison and Rubinfeld [1978] transformations involving all 14 variables.

For our final example, we use the ACE algorithm to study the relationship between atmospheric ozone concentration and meteorology in the Los Angeles basin. The data consist of daily measurements of ozone concentration (maximum one hour average) and eight meteorological quantities for 330 days of 1976. Table 2 lists the variables used in the study. The ACE algorithm was applied here in the same forward stepwise manner as in the previous (housing data) example. Four variables were selected. These are the first four listed in Table 2. The resulting $\hat{R}^2$ was 0.78. Running the ACE algorithm with all eight predictor variables produces an $\hat{R}^2$ of 0.79.

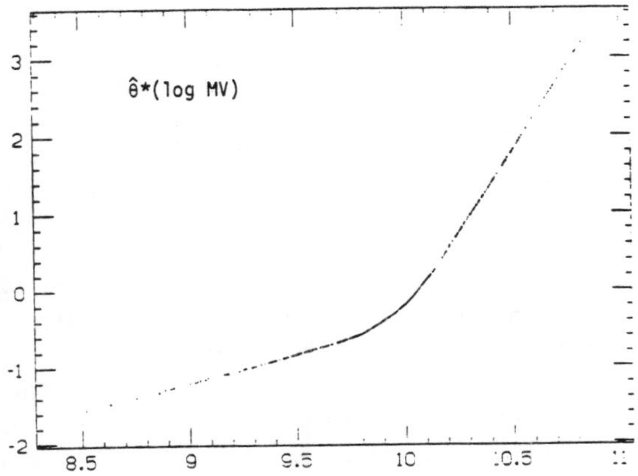

Figure 4a

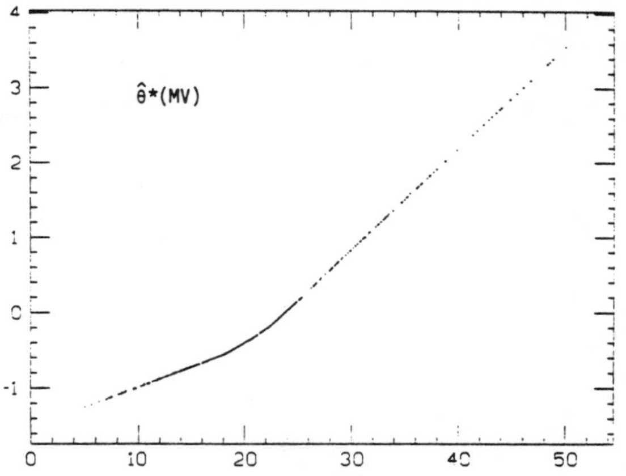

Figure 4b

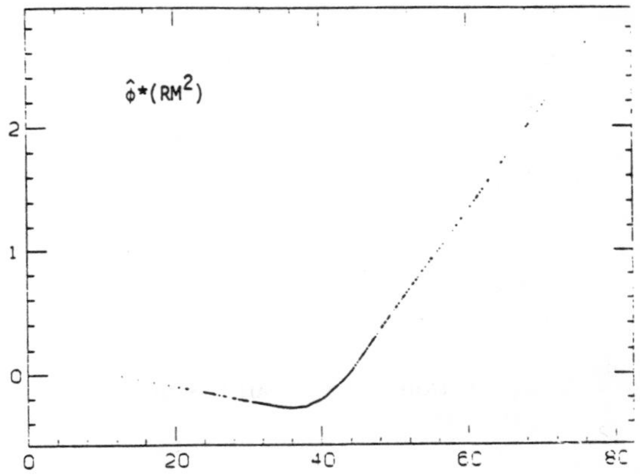

σ = 0.492 Figure 4c

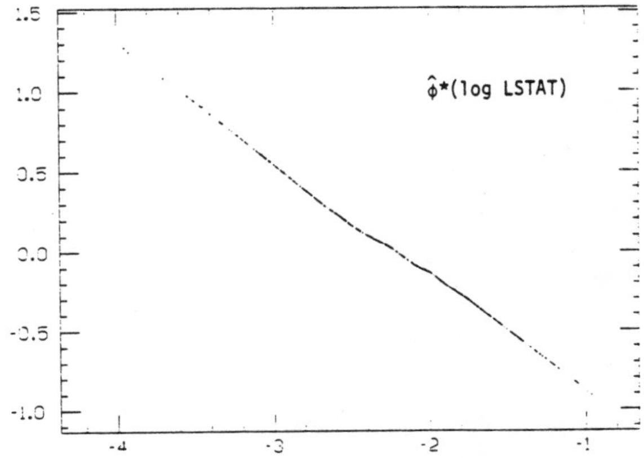

σ = 0.417 Figure 4d

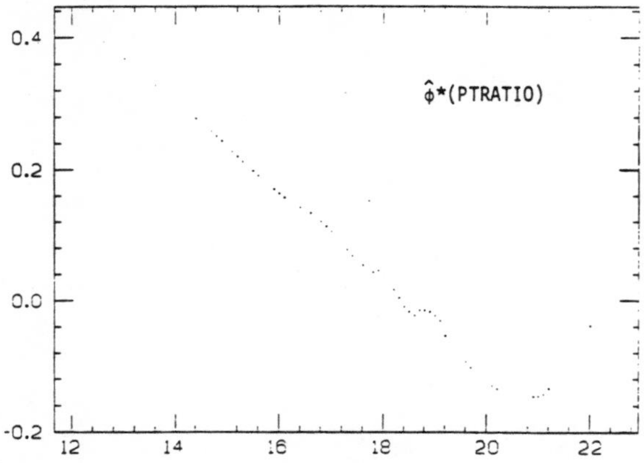

σ = 0.147 Figure 4e

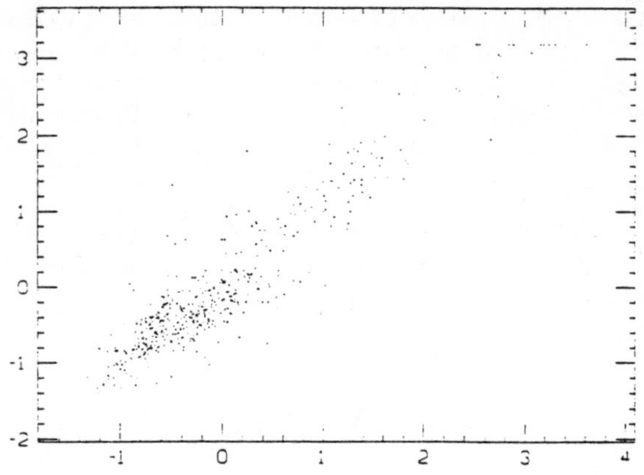

Figure 4h

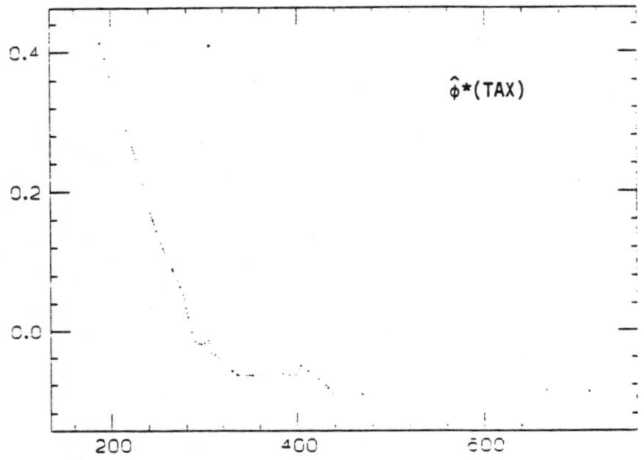

σ = 0.122 Figure 4f

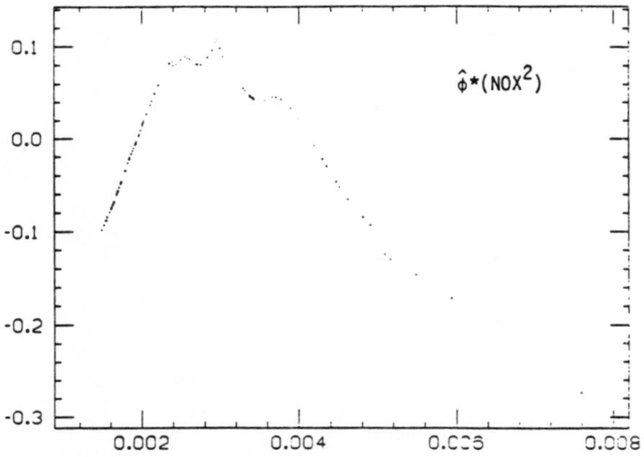

σ = 0.09 Figure 4g

TABLE 2

Variables Used in the Ozone Pollution Example

SBTP:	**Sandburg Air Force Base temperature ($C°$)**
IBHT:	**Inversion base height (ft.)**
DGPG:	**Daggett pressure gradient (mmhg)**
VSTY:	**Visibility (miles)**
VDHT:	**Vandenburg 500 millibar height (m)**
HMDT:	**Humidity (percent)**
IBTP:	**Inversion base temperature ($F°$)**
WDSP:	**Wind speed (mph)**
	Dependent Variable
UP03:	**Upland ozone concentration (ppm)**

In order to assess the extent to which these meteorological variables capture the daily variation of the ozone level, the variable day-of-the-year was added and the ACE algorithm was run with it and the four selected meteorological variables. This can detect possible seasonal effects not captured by the meteorological variables. The resulting $\hat{R}^2$ was 0.82. Figures 5a-5f shows the optimal transformation estimates.

The solution for the response transformation, Figure 5a, shows that, at most, a very mild transformation with negative curvature is indicated. Similarly, Figure 5b indicates that there is no compelling necessity to consider a transformation on the most influential predictor variable, Sandburg Air Force Base temperature. However, the solution transformation estimates for the remaining variables are all highly nonlinear (and nonmonotonic). For example, Figure 5d suggests that the ozone concentration is much more influenced by the magnitude than the sign of the pressure gradient.

The solution for the day-of-the-year variable, Figure 5f, indicates a substantial seasonal effect after accounting for the meteorological variables. This effect is minimum at the year boundaries and has a broad maximum peaking at about May 1. This can be compared with the dependence of ozone pollution on day-of-the-year alone without taking into account the meteorological variables. Figure 5g shows a smooth of ozone concentration on day-of-the-year. This smooth has an $\hat{R}^2$ of 0.38 and is seen to peak about three months later (August 3).

The fact that the day-of-the-year transformation peaked at the beginning of May was initially puzzling to us since the highest pollution days occur during July to September. This latter fact is confirmed by the day-of-the-year transformation with the meteorological variables removed. Our current belief is that with the meteorological variables entered, day-of-the-year becomes a partial surrogate for hours of daylight before and during the morning commmuter rush. The decline past May 1 may then be explained by the fact that daylight savings time goes into effect in Los Angeles on the last Sunday in April.

This data illustrates that ACE is useful in uncovering interesting and suggestive relationships. The form of the dependence on the Daggett pressure gradient and on the day-of-the-year would be extremely difficult to find by any previous methodology.

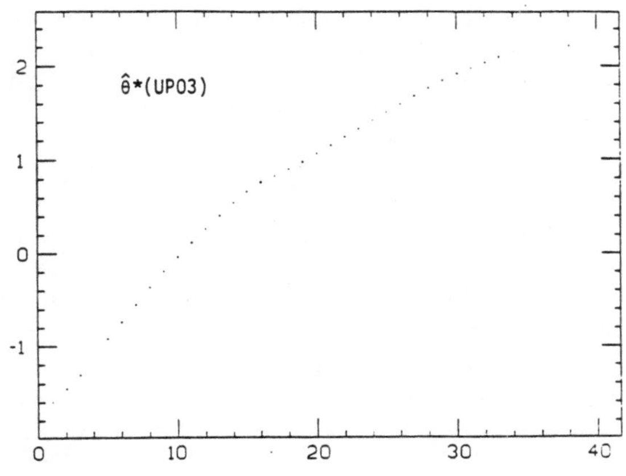

σ = 1.0

Figure 5a

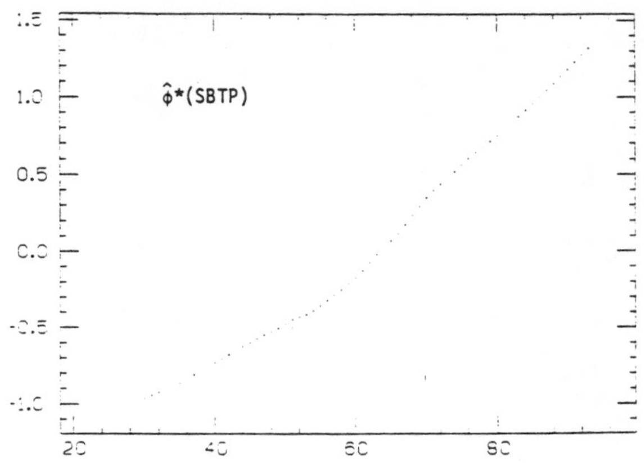

σ = 0.56

Figure 5b

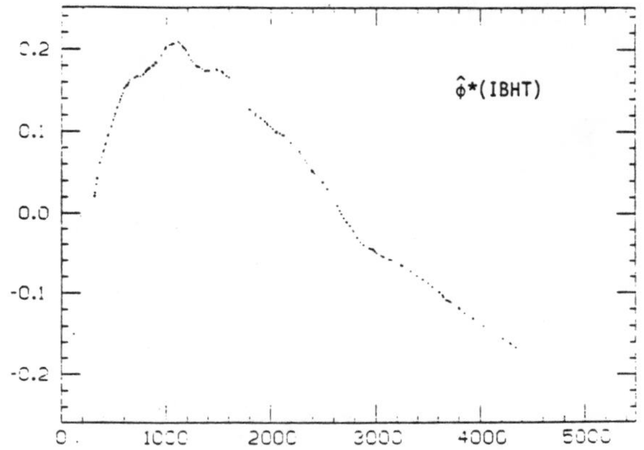

Inversion Base Height, σ = 0.16

Figure 5c

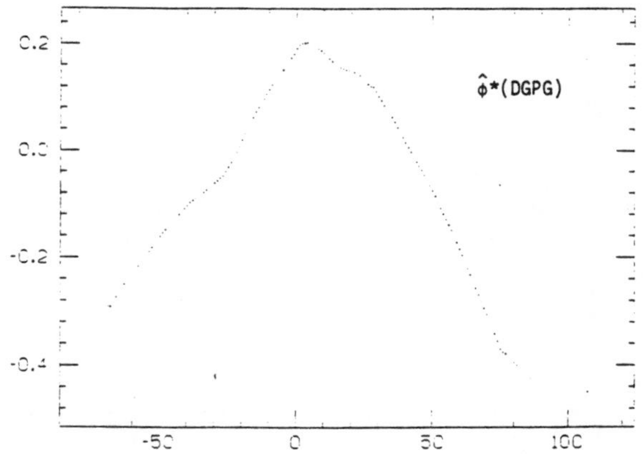

σ = 0.16

Figure 5d

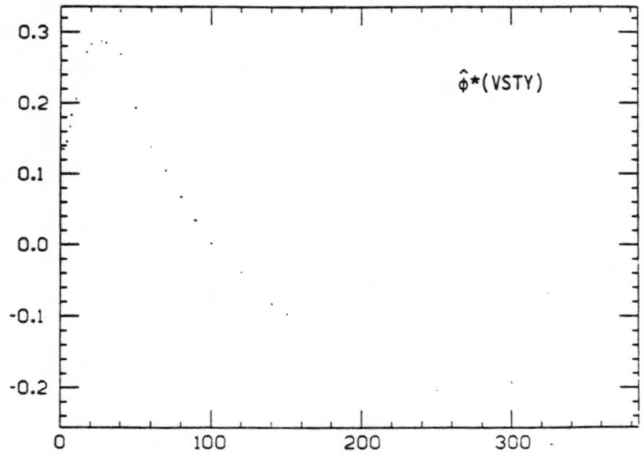

σ = 0.16

Figure 5e

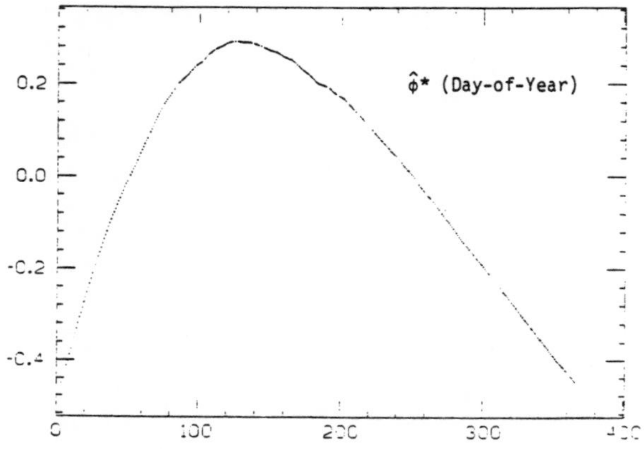

σ = 0.23

Figure 5f

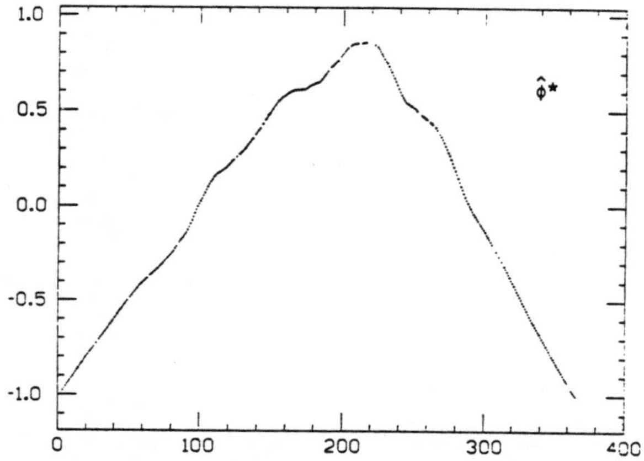

Day-of-the-Year as Single Independent Variable, $\hat{R}^2 = 0.38$

Figure 5g

4. Discussion

The ACE algorithm provides a fully automated method for estimating optimal transformations in multiple regression. It also provides a method for estimating maximal correlation between random variables. It differs from other empirical methods for finding transformations (Box and Tidwell [1962]; Anscombe and Tukey [1963]; Box and Cox [1964]; Kruskal [1964], [1965]; Fraser [1967]; Linsey [1972]; Box and Hill [1974]; Linsey [1972], [1974]; Wood [1974]; Mosteller and Tukey [1977]; and Tukey [1982]) in that the "best" transformations of the response and predictor variables are unambiguously defined and estimated without use of ad hoc heuristics, restrictive distributional assumptions, or restriction of the transformation to a particular parametric family.

The algorithm is reasonably computer efficient. On the Boston housing data set comprising 506 data points with 14 variables each, the run took 12 seconds of CPU time on an IBM 3081. Our guess is that this translates into 2.5 minutes on a VAX 11/750 with FP. To extrapolate to other problems, use the estimate that running time is proportional to (number of variables) x (sample size).

A strong advantage of the ACE procedure is the ability to incorporate variables of quite different type in terms of the set of values they can assume. The transformation functions $\theta(y), \phi_1(x_1), \ldots, \phi_p(x_p)$ assume values on the real line. Their arguments can, however, assume values on any set. For example, ordered real, periodic (circularly valued) real, ordered and unordered categorical variables can be incorporated in the same regression equation. For periodic variables, the smoother window need only wrap around the boundaries. For categorical variables, the procedure can be regarded as estimating optimal scores for each of their values. (The special case of a categorical response and a single categorical predictor variable is known as canonical analysis –see Kendall and Stuart [1967], p.568– and the optimal scores can, in this case, also be obtained by solution of a matrix eigenvector problem.)

The ACE procedure can also handle variables of mixed type. For example, a variable indicating present marital status might take on an integer value (numer of years married) or one of several categorical values (N=never, D=divorced, W=widowed, etc.). This presents no additional complication in estimating conditional expectations. This ability provides a straightforward way to handle missing data values (Young et al. [1976]). In addition to the regular sets of values realized by a variable, it can also take on the value "missing."

In some situations the analyst, after running ACE, may want to estimate values of y rather than $\theta^*(y)$, given a specific value of $\underline{x}$. One method for doing this is to attempt to compute $\hat{\theta}^{*^{-1}}(\sum_{j=1}^{p} \hat{\phi}_j^*(x_j))$. However, letting

$$Z = \sum_{j=1}^{p} \phi_j^*(X_j),$$

we know that the best least squares predictor of Y of the form $\chi(Z)$ is given by $E(Y|Z)$. This is implemented in the current ACE program by depicting y as the function of $\sum_{j=1}^{p} \hat{\phi}_j^*(x_j)$ gotten by smoothing the data values of y on the data values of $\sum_{j=1}^{p} \hat{\phi}_j^*(x_j)$. We are grateful to Arthur Owen for suggesting this simple and elegant prediction procedure.

The solution functions $\hat{\theta}^*(y)$ and $\hat{\phi}_1^*(x_1), \ldots, \hat{\phi}_p^*(x_p)$ can be stored as a set of values associated with each observation $(y_k, x_{k1}, \ldots, x_{kp})$ $1 \le k \le N$. However, since $\theta(y)$ and $\phi(x)$ are usually smooth (for continuous y, x), they can be easily approximated and stored as cubic spline functions (deBoor [1978]) with a few knots.

As a tool for data analysis, the ACE procedure provides graphical output to indicate a need for transformations, as well as to guide in their choice. If a particular plot suggests a familiar functional form for a transformation, it can be substituted for the empirical transformation estimate and the ACE algorithm can be rerun using an option which alters only the scale and origin of that particular transformation. The resulting e^2 can be compared to the original value. We have found that the plots themselves often give surprising new insights into the relationship between the response and predictor variables.

As with any regression procedure, a high degree of association between predictor variables can sometimes cause the individual transformation estimates to be highly variable even though the complete model is reasonably stable. When this is suspected, running the algorithm on randomly selected subsets of the data, or on bootstrap samples (Efron [1979]) can assist in assessing the variability.

The ACE method has generality beyond that exploited here. An immediate generalization would involve multiple response variables $Y_1, \ldots, Y_q$. The generalized algorithm would estimate optimal transformations $\theta_1^*, \ldots, \theta_q^*$, $\theta_1^*, \ldots, \phi_p^*$ that minimize

$$E\left[\sum_{\ell=1}^{q} \theta_\ell(Y_\ell) - \sum_{j=1}^{p} \phi_j(X_j)\right]^2$$

subject to $E\theta_\ell = 0, \ell = 1, \ldots, q$, $E\phi_j = 0, j = 1, \ldots, p$ and $\| \sum_{\ell=1}^{q} \theta_\ell(Y_\ell) \|^2 = 1$.

This extension generalizes the ACE procedure in a sense similar to that in which canonical correlation generalized linear regression.

The ACE algorithm (Section 2) is easily modified to incorporate this extension. An inner loop over the response variables, analogous to that for the predictor variables, replaces the single function minimization.

REFERENCES

Anscombe, F.J. and Tukey, J.W. (1963). The examination and analysis of residuals. *Technometrics* 5, 141-160.

Belsey, D.A., Kuh, E. and Welsch. R.E. (1980). *Regression Diagnostics*, John Wiley and Sons.

Box, C.E.P. and Tidwell, P.W. (1962). Transformations of the independent variables. *Technometrics* 4, 531-550.

Box, G.E.P. and Cox, D.R. (1964). An analysis of transformations. *J.R. Statist. Soc.* B26, 211-252.

Box, G.E.P. and Hill, W.J. (1974). Correcting inhomogeneity of variance with power transformation weighting. *Technometrics* 16, 385-389.

Breiman, L. and Friedman, J. (1985). Estimating optimal transformations for multiple regression and correlation. *J. Ammer. Statis. Assn.*, March 1985 (with discussion)

Cleveland, W.S. (1979). Robust locally weighted regression and smoothing scatterplots. *J. Amer. Statist. Assn.* 74, 828-836.

Craven, P. and Wahba, G. (1970). Smoothing noisy data with spline functions. Estimating the correct degree of smoothing by the method of generalized cross-validation. *Numerische Mathematik* 31, 317-403.

deBoor, C. (1978). *A Practical Guide to Splines*, Springer-Verlag.

deLeeuw, J., Young, F.W., Takane, Y. (1976). Additive structure in qualitative data: An alternating least squares method with optimal scaling features. *Psychometrika*, 1976, 471-503.

Efron, B. (1979). Bootstrap methods: another look at the jackknife. *Ann. Statist.* 7, 1-26.

Fraser, D.A.S. (1967). Data transformations and the linear model. *Ann. Math. Statist.* 38, 1456-1465.

Friedman, J.H. (1984). A variable span smoother, Dept. of Statistics, Stanford University, Tech. Report LCS005.

Gasser, T. and Rosenblatt, M. (eds.) (1979). *Smoothing Techniques for Curve Estimation*, in Lecture Notes in Mathematics 757, New York: Springer-Verlag.

Gebelein, H. (1947). Das statitistiche problem der korrelation als variations und eigenwert problem und sein Zusammenhang mit der Ausgleichung-srechnung. *Z. Angew. Math. Mech.* 21, 364-379.

Harrison, D. and Rubinfeld, D.L. (1978). Hedonic housing process and the demand for clean air. *J. Environ. Econ. Mngmnt* 5, 81-102.

Kendall, M.A. and Stuart, A. (1967). *The advanced Theory of Statistics*, Volume 2, Hafner.

Kimeldorf, G. May, J.H., and Sampson, A.R. (1982). Concordant and discordant monotone correlations and their evaluations by nonlinear optimization. In *Studies in the Management Sciences* 19, Optimization in Statistics, S.H. Zanakis and J.S. Rustagi, Eds., North-Holland, pp 117-130.

Kruskal, J.B. (1964). Nonmetric multidimensional scaling: a numerical method. *Psychometrika* 29, 115-129.

Kruskal. J.B. (1965). Analysis of factorial experiments by estimating monotone transformations of the data. *J.R. Statist. Soc.* B27, 251-263.

Lancaster, H.O. (1958). The structure of bivariate distributions. *Ann. Math. Statist.* 29, 719-736.

Lancaster, H.O. (1969). *The Chi-Squared Distribution*, John Wiley and Sons.

Linsey, J.K. (1972). Fitting response surfaces with poor transformations. *J.R. Statist. Soc.* C21, 234-237.

Linsey, J.K. (1974). Construction and comparison of statistical models. *J.R. Statist. Soc.* B36, 418-425.

Mosteller, F. and Tukey, J.W. (1977). *Data Analysis and Regression*, Addison-Wesley.

Renyi, A. (1959). On measures of dependence. *Acta. Math. Acad. Sci. Hungar.* 10, 441-451.

Sarmanov, O.V. (1958a). The maximal correlation coefficient (symmetric case). *Dokl. Acad. Nauk. SSSR* 120, 715-718.

Sarmanov. O.V. (1958b). The maximal correlation coefficient (nonsymmetric case). *Dokl. Acad. Nauk. SSSR* 121, 52-55.

Sarmanov. O.V. and Zaharov. V.K. (1960). Maximum coefficients of multiple correlation. *Dokl. Adad. Nauk SSSR* 130, 269-271.

Stone, C.J. (1977). Consistent nonparametric regression. *Ann. Statist.* 7, 139-149.

Tukey, J.W. (1982). The use of smelting in guiding re-expression, in *Modern Data Analysis*, Laurner and Siegel (eds.), Academic Press.

Wood. J.T. (1974). An extension of the analysis of transformations of Box and Cox. *Appl. Statist. (J.R. Statist. Soc.)* C23.

Young, F.W., deLeeuw, J., Takane, Y. (1976). Regression with qualitative and quantitative variables: an alternating least squares method with optimal scaling features. *Psychometrika*, 1976, 505-529.

COMPUTER SCIENCE AND STATISTICS:
The Interface, L. Billard (ed.)

QUANTITATIVE ANALYSIS OF QUALITATIVE DATA[1]

Forrest W. Young

L. L. Thurstone Psychometric Laboratory
University of North Carolina at Chapel Hill

This paper presents an overview of an approach to the quantitative analysis of qualitative data with theoretical and methodological explanations of the two cornerstones of the approach, Alternating Least Squares and Optimal Scaling. Using these two principles, my colleagues and I have extended a variety of analysis procedures originally proposed for quantitative (interval or ratio) data to qualitative (nominal or ordinal) data, including additivity analysis and analysis of variance; multiple and canonical regression; principal components; common factor and three mode factor analysis; and multidimensional scaling. The approach has two advantages: (a) If a least squares procedure is known for analyzing quantitative data, it can be extended to qualitative data; and (b) the resulting algorithm will be convergent. Three completely worked through examples of the additivity analysis procedure and the steps involved in the regression procedures are presented.

Perhaps one of the main impediments to rapid progress in the development of the social, behavioral and biological sciences is the omnipresence of qualitative data. All too often it is simply impossible to obtain numerical data; the researcher has the choice of qualitative data or no data at all. Many times it is only possible to determine the category in which a particular datum falls. The sociologist, for example, obtains categorical information about the religious affiliation of her respondents; the botanist obtains categorical information about the family to which his plants belong; and the psychologist obtains categorical information about the psychosis of her patient. Even in the best of circumstances it is often impossible to obtain anything beyond the order in which the data categories fall. When our sociologist observes the amount of education of the respondents in her sample she knows that the observational categories are ordered, but she is unable to assign precise numerical values to the categories. When the psychologist obtains rating scale judgments, the judgments may reasonably be viewed as ordinal, but not always as numerical.

Given the ubiquity of qualitative data, one can understand the long and persistent interest in its quantification. If one could somehow develop a method for assigning "good" numerical values to the data categories, then the data would be quantified and would be susceptible to more meaningful analysis. Curiosity about the topic is nascent in the classical work by Yule [1910], and methods for quantification first began to appear around 1940. Probably the first widely disseminated procedure was Fisher's "appropriate scoring" technique [Fisher, 1938, pp. 285-298] which was introduced at about the same time as a method proposed by Guttman [1941]. Several authors worked on the problem in the early 50's [Burt, 1950, 1953; Hayashi, 1950; Guttman, 1953] with this work being summarized by Torgerson [1958, pp. 338-345]. Much work has occurred recently [Benzecri, 1973, 1977; de Leeuw, 1973; Mardia, Kent & Bibby, 1979; Nishisato, 1980; Saito, 1973; Saporta, 1975; Tenenhaus, Note 1 & Note 2].

In this paper we refer to the process of quantifying qualitative data as "optimal scaling," a term first introduced by Bock [1960]. This is our definition:

> Optimal scaling is a data analysis technique which assigns numerical values to observation categories in a way that maximizes the relation between the observations and the data analysis model while respecting the measurement character of the data.

Note that this is a very general definition: There is no precise specification of the nature of the model, nor is there precise specification of the measurement character of the data. Working with this definition of optimal scaling, we have developed a group of programs for quantifying qualitative data (see Table 1). The programs permit the data to have a variety of measurement characteristics, and permit data analysis with a variety of models. We refer to these programs as ALSOS programs since they use the Alternating Least Squares (ALS) approach to Optimal Scaling (OS).

The ALSOS programs describe qualitative data by quantitative models falling into three general classes: (a) the General Linear Model; (b) the Component (Factor) Model; and (c) the General Euclidean Model. As you can see in Table 1, the GLM programs are specifically oriented towards analysis of variance (MANOVALS, ADDALS and WADDALS), regression analysis (MORALS, CORALS,

Table 1

ALSOS Programs

Program	Analysis	Data	Source	Primary Reference
ADDALS	Additivity analysis (analysis of variance)	Two or three way tables. Nonorthogonal and incomplete designs permitted.	UNC	de Leeuw, Young & Takane (1976)
WADDALS	Weighted additivity analysis	Same as ADDALS	UNC	Takane, Young & de Leeuw (1980)
MANOVALS	Multivariate analysis of variance	Multi-way tables	RUL	Gifi (1981)
MORALS CORALS & CANALS	Multiple and canonical analysis	Mixed measurement level multivariate data	UNC or RUL	Young, de Leeuw & Takane (1976)
OVERALS	Canonical analysis	Multiple set mixed measurement level multivariate data	RUL	Gifi (1981)
CRIMINALS	Multiple group discriminant analysis	Mixed measurement level predictors	RUL	Gifi (1981)
PATHALS	Path analysis	Mixed measurement level multivariate data	RUL	Gifi (1981)
PRINCALS & PRINCIPALS	Principal components analysis	Mixed measurement level multivariate data	UNC or RUL	Young, Takane & de Leeuw (1978)
HOMALS	Principal components analysis	Multivariate nominal data	RUL	de Leeuw & van Rijkevorsel (1976)
ALSCOMP & TUCKALS	Three-mode factor analysis	Mixed measurement level multivariate data	UNC or RUL	Sands & Young (1978) de Leeuw & van Rijkevorsel (1976)
FACTALS	Common-factor analysis	Mixed measurement level multivariate data	UNC	Takane, Young & de Leeuw (1978)
ALSCAL	Two or three-way multidimensional scaling	Similarity data	UNC	Takane, Young & de Leeuw (1977)
GEMSCAL	Two or three-way multidimensional scaling	Similarity data	UNC	Young, Null & De Soete (Note 5)

Note: The column headed "Source" in Table 1 indicates the address from which the program is available, as follows: UNC: Forrest W. Young, Psychometric Laboratory, Davie Hall 013A, University of North Carolina, Chapel Hill, NC 27514, USA; and RUL: Jan de Leeuw, Data Theory, Rijksuniversiteit te Leiden, Breestraat 70, 2311 CS Leiden, The Netherlands.

CANALS, OVERALS), discriminant analysis (CRIMINALS) and path analysis (PATHALS). The component programs perform principal components analysis (ALSCOMP and TUCKALS); and common-factor analysis (FACTALS). The General Euclidean Model is fit by ALSCAL and GEMSCAL.

For most of the ALSOS programs the data may be defined at the binary, nominal, ordinal or interval levels of measurement (and the ratio level with the General Euclidean Model programs), and may be thought of as having been generated by either a discrete or continuous underlying process. All of these programs also permit arbitrary patterns of missing data. Some permit boundary or range restrictions on the values assigned to the observation categories, and some permit the use of partial orders with ordinal data. Information on obtaining these programs may be obtained as indicated on Table 1.

As we will show in this paper, the ALSOS approach to algorithm construction has one very important implication for data analysis:

> If a procedure is known for obtaining a least squares description of numerical (interval or ratio measurement level) data, then an ALSOS algorithm can be constructed to obtain a least squares description of qualitative data (having a variety of measurement characteristics).

1. OVERVIEW

Each of the ALSOS programs optimizes an objective loss function by using an algorithm based on the alternating least squares (ALS) and

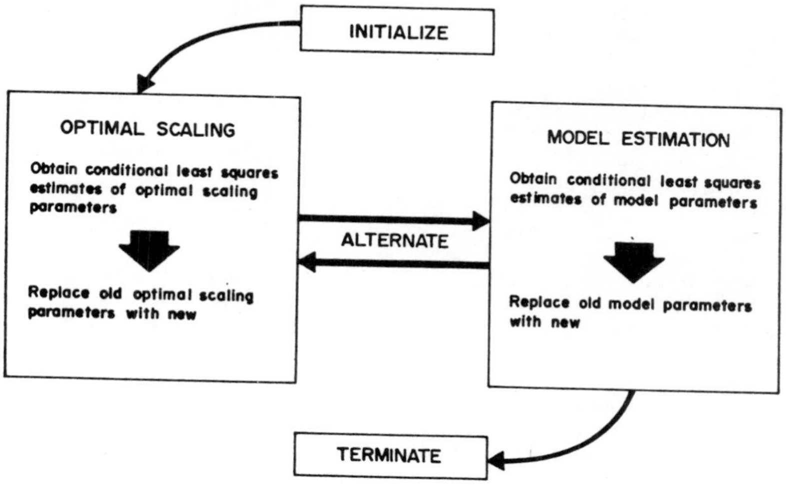

Figure 1
Flow of the ALSOS algorithms

optimal scaling (OS) principles.

The OS principle involves viewing observations as categorical, and then representing each observation category by a parameter. This parameter is subject to constraints implied by the measurement characteristics of the variable (e.g., order constraints for ordinal variables).

The ALS principle involves dividing all of the parameters into two mutually exclusive and exhaustive subsets: (a) the parameters of the model; and (b) the parameters of the data (called optimal scaling parameters). We then proceed to optimize a loss function by alternately optimizing with respect to one subset, then the other (see Figure 1). Note that each subset may itself consist of several subsets which are mutually exclusive and exhaustive. For example, in ALSCAL the model has several parameter subsets, and in the multivariate programs there is a subset of data parameters for each variable.

The optimization proceeds by obtaining the least squares estimates of the parameters in one subset while assuming that the parameters in all other subsets are constants. We call this a conditional least squares estimate, since the least squares nature is conditional on the values of the parameters in the other subsets. Once we have obtained conditional least squares estimates, we immidiately replace the old estimates of these parameters by the new estimates. We then switch to another subset of parameters and obtain their conditional least squares estimates. We alternately obtain conditional least squares estimates of the parameters in the model subsets, then in the data subsets, until convergence (which is assured under certain conditions discussed in later portions of this paper) is closely approached. The flow of an ALSOS procedure is diagrammed in Figure 1.

Certain strong correspondences exist between an ALSOS procedure and the NILES approach to algorithm construction developed by Wold and Lyttkens [1969], and the class of numerical analysis algorithms known as successive block algorithms [Hageman & Porsching, 1975]. The main difference between these metric algorithms and the nonmetric ALSOS algorithms is the optimal scaling features of the ALSOS algorithm. The scaling feature permits the analysis of qualitative data, whereas the previous procedures can only analyze quantitative data.

There are also strong connections between the nonmetric algorithms developed by Kruskal [1964, 1965], Roskam [1968], Young [1972], and others. The main difference between these gradient (non-ALS) procedures and ALSOS algorithms is the least squares feature of the model estimation phase.

One of the main advantages of combining the ALS and OS principles is that the OS phase of an ALSOS algorithm does not need to know the type of model involved in the analysis. A parallel and equally important advantage is that the model estimation phase does not need to know anything about the measurement characteristics of the data.

The practical effect of these aspects of ALSOS procedures is enormous: If a least squares procedure exists for fitting a particular model to numerical (i.e., interval or ratio) data, then we can use that procedure in combination with the OS procedures to be discussed to develop an ALSOS algorithm for fitting the model to qualitative data. All we have to do is alternate the numerical least squares procedure with the OS procedure which is suited to the measurement characteristics of the data being analyzed.

There is one hooker: The ALSOS procedure does not guarantee convergence on the globally least squares solution, rather it guarantees convergence on a particular type of local least squares solution. The particular local optimum upon which an ALSOS procedure converges is determined by only one thing, the initialization process. It is possible that two different types of initialization procedures will lead an ALSOS procedure into two different local optima, perhaps giving radically different results. For this reason, and since each phase in an ALSOS procedure is a conditional least squares solution (conditional on the current values of the parameters in the other subset), we refer to the convergence point of an ALSOS procedure as the "conditional global optimum," a somewhat grandiose way of emphasizing that the convergence point is more than simply a local optimum, but may not be the overall global optimum. [The convergence properties of an ALSOS algorithm have been discussed by de Leeuw, Young and Takane (1976) and de Leeuw (Note 3) who prove that such a procedure is indeed convergent if (a) the function being optimized is continuous; and (b) if each phase or subphase of the algorithm optimizes the function.]

Since the initialization procedure is of such importance in the overall process, it is important to employ the best initialization that is available. In all ALSOS programs we define best initialization to mean that we should optimize the fit of the model to the raw data. Thus, each ALSOS program is initiated by applying a least squares procedure to the raw data under the assumption that the raw data are quantitative, as the user has coded them. (Note that a different coding of the data, while still consistent with the data's measurement characteristics, may provide a better start. The start is not "best" in this sense. There is evidence that for ALSCAL, this procedure reduces the frequency of local minimum solutions [Young & Null, 1978].

Once the process is initiated, the procedure for obtaining the conditional least squares estimates of the model parameters is the procedure used to obtain ordinary least squares estimates when the data are numerical. The only difference is that the procedure is applied to the optimally scaled data (which is numerical, after all) instead of to the raw data. Since we are applying the model estimation procedure to the optimally scaled data, we are not violating the measurement assumptions of the raw data, whatever they might be. We are not even using the raw data in the model estimation phase, thus we do not need to know its measurement characteristics. Equally important, we do not have to think up a new way of trying to fit the model to qualitative data, we simply use existing procedures for fitting it to quantitative data.

2. OPTIMAL SCALING

Since the ALS aspects of our work are by now fairly traditional [Wold & Lyttkens, 1969], we do not spend any effort to explicate them. Rather, we fully discuss the OS aspects in the remainder of this paper.

These unique OS aspects of our work permit our ALSOS algorithms to be very flexible in the assumptions the user can make concerning the measurement characteristics of his/her data, as reviewed above.

2.1 Measurement Theory

To appreciate fully the OS aspect of our work, we must first discuss the theoretical foundations of our project, our view of measurement theory.

We begin by emphasizing a concept which is crucial to our work: It is our view that all observations are categorical. That is, we view an observation variable as consisting of observations which fall into a variety of categories, such that all observations in a particular category are empirically equivalent. Furthermore, we take this "categorical" view regardless of the variable's measurement characteristics.

Put more simply, it is our view that the observational process delivers observations which are categorical because of the finite precision of the measurement and observation process, if for no other reason. For example, if one is measuring temperature with an ordinary thermometer (which is likely to generate interval level observations reasonably assumed to reflect a continuous process) it is doubtful whether the degrees are reported with any more precision than whole degrees. Thus, the observation is categorical; there are a very large (indeed infinite) number of different temperatures which would all be reported as, say, 40°. Therefore, we say that the observation of 40° is categorical.

At this point we need to define a column vector of n raw observations. We denote this observation vector as $\underline{o}$, with general element o_i. (Underlined lower case letters refer to column vectors.) We also define the model estimates $\underline{\hat{z}}$, with general element $\hat{z}_i$, and the optimally scaled observations $\underline{z}^*$, with general element z_i^*. The elements of $\underline{o}$ are organized so that all observations in a particular category are contiguous. The elements of $\underline{\hat{z}}$ and $\underline{z}^*$ are organized in a fashion having a one to one correspondence with the elements of $\underline{o}$. The element z_i^* is the parameter representing the observation o_i. The vector $\hat{z}$ is called the "model estimates" because it is the model's estimates, in a least squares sense, of the optimally scaled data $\underline{z}^*$.

With these definitions we can formally represent the OS problem as a transformation problem, as follows. We wish to obtain a transformation $\mathcal{t}$ (script letters indicate transformations) of the raw observations which generates the optimally scaled observations,

$$\mathcal{t}[\underline{o}] = [\underline{z}^*], \qquad (1)$$

where the precise definition of $\mathcal{t}$ is a function

of the measurement characteristics of the observations, and is such that a least squares relationship will exist between the model's estimates of the scaled data ($\hat{z}$) and the actual scaled data ($\underline{z}^*$), given that the measurement characteristics of $\underline{o}$ are strictly maintained. The numerical value assigned to z_i^*, then, is the optimal parameter value for the observation o_i.

Various types of restrictions are placed on the transformation t, with the type of restriction depending on the measurement characteristics of the data. We distinguish three types of measurement restrictions, termed measurement level, measurement process, and measurement conditionality. As we shall see, these three types concert three different aspects of the observation categories. Measurement process concerns the relationships among all of the observations within a single category; measurement level concerns the relationships among all of the observations between different categories; and measurement conditionality concerns the relationships within sets of categories. Each of the several types of processes, levels and conditionalities implies a different set of restraints placed on the transformation t (1).

In Tables 2, 3, and 4 we summarize the six types of measurement resulting from combining three levels with two processes. A verbal description is given in Table 2, the mathematical restrictions on t are given in Table 3, and the optimal scaling methods are given in Table 4. Measurement conditionality is discussed at the end of this section.

Measurement process. There are two types of measurement process restrictions, one invoked when we assume that the generating process is discrete, and the other when we assume that it is continuous. One or the other assumption must always be made. If we believe that the process is discrete (sex is an example of a discrete underlying process) then all observations in a particular category (female or male) should be represented by the same real number after the transformation t^d (the superscript indicates discreteness) has been made. On the other hand, if we adopt the continuous assumption (as we probably should for a weight variable), then each of the observations within a particular category (97.2 Kg., for example) should be represented by a real number selected from a closed interval of real numbers. In the former case the discrete nature of the process is reflected by the fact that we choose a single (discrete) number to represent all observations in the category; whereas in the latter case the continuity of the process is reflected by the fact that we choose real numbers from a closed (continuous) interval of real numbers. Formally, we define the two restrictions as follows: The discrete restriction is

$$t^d: (o_i \sim o_m) \rightarrow (z_i^* = z_m^*) \qquad (2)$$

where $\sim$ indicates empirical equivalence (i.e., membership in the same catetory). The continuous restriction is represented as

$$t^c: (o_i \sim o_m) \rightarrow (z_i^- = z_m^-) \leq \begin{Bmatrix} z_i^* \\ z_m^* \end{Bmatrix} \leq (z_i^+ = z_m^+) \qquad (3)$$

where z_i^- and z_i^+ are the lower and upper bounds of the interval of real numbers. Note that one of the implications of empirical (categorical) equivalence is that the upper and lower boundaries of all observations in a particular category are the same for all the observations. Thus, the boundaries are more correctly thought of as applying to the categories rather than the observations, but to denote this would involve a somewhat more complicated notational system. Note also that for all observations in a particular category the corresponding optimally scaled observations are required to fall in the interval but need not be equal.

Measurement level. We now turn to the second set of restraints on the several measurement transformations, the level restraints. With these restraints we determine the nature of the allowable transformations t so that they correspond to the assumed level of measurement of the observation variables. There are, of course, a variety of different restraints which might be of interest, but we only mention three here. With these three we can satisfy the characteristics of Stevens' four measurement levels, as well as the measurement level characteristics of missing data, and of binary data.

For the nominal level of measurement, and for data that is either missing or are binary, we introduce no measurement-level restraints. The characteristics of these three types of measurement are completely specified by the measurement process restraints. The reason that we need no additional restraints is that for these levels we only know the category of an observation. We know nothing about the relationships of observations in different categories. Thus, these levels are completely specified by restrictions imposed within observation categories, there being no restrictions on the relationships which may exist among observations in different categories.

The difference between nominal, binary and missing data is in the number of observation categories. For nominal data there must be at least three observation categories. When there are only two observation categories the data are binary. (Binary data are somewhat anomolous since they may be thought of as being at any level of measurement. Since the higher levels of measurement all involve additional between-category restrictions, it is most parsimonious to describe binary data as being at the nominal level.)

Missing data, on the other hand, can be viewed as a particular type of data about which we know only one thing: It is missing. Thus, we may view missing data as nominal but having only one

Table 2

Measurement Characteristics
for Six Types of Measurement

Level	Process	
	Discrete	Continuous
Nominal	Observation categories represented by a single real number	Observation categories represented by a closed interval of real numbers
Ordinal	Observation categories are ordered and tied observations remain tied	Observation categories are ordered but tied observations become untied
Numerical	Observation categories are functionally related and all observations are precise	Observation categories are functionally related but all observations are imprecise

Table 3

Measurement Restrictions
for Six Types of Measurement

Level	Process	
	Discrete	Continuous
Nominal	t^{d}: $(o_i \sim o_m) \rightarrow (z_i^* = z_m^*)$	t^{c}: $(o_i \sim o_m) \rightarrow (z_i^- = z_m^-) \leq \begin{Bmatrix} z_i^* \\ z_m^* \end{Bmatrix} \leq (z_i^+ = z_m^+)$
Ordinal	t^{do}: $(o_i \sim o_m) \rightarrow (z_i^* = z_m^*)$ $(o_i \prec o_m) \rightarrow (z_i^* \leq z_m^*)$	t^{co}: $(o_i \sim o_m) \rightarrow (z_i^- = z_m^-) \leq \begin{Bmatrix} z_i^* \\ z_m^* \end{Bmatrix} \leq (z_i^+ = z_m^+)$ $(o_i \prec o_m) \rightarrow (z_i^* \leq z_m^*)$
Numerical	t^{dp}: $(o_i \sim o_m) \rightarrow (z_i^* = z_m^*)$ $z_i^* = \sum_{q=0}^{p} \delta_q o_i^q$	t^{cp}: $(o_i \sim o_m) \rightarrow (z_i^- = z_m^-) \leq \begin{Bmatrix} z_i^* \\ z_m^* \end{Bmatrix} \leq (z_i^+ = z_m^+)$ $z_i^* = \sum_{q=0}^{p} \delta_q o_i^q$

Table 4

Optimal Scaling Methods
for Six Types of Measurement

Level	Process	
	Discrete	Continuous
Nominal	Means of model elements	Means of model estimates, followed by primary monotonic transformations
Ordinal	Kruskal's secondary monotonic transformations	Kruskal's primary monotonic transformations
Numerical	Simple linear (or non-linear) regression	Simple linear (or non-linear) regression followed by boundary estimation

category of (non) observation, the "missing" category. It would appear that we could simply call "missing" data an additional category of our nominal data. However, this does not suffice when we have data missing from a set of observations defined at some level of measurement other than nominal. When we introduce the notion of measurement conditionality at the end of this section, we will be able to completely clarify the manner in which we view missing data. Until then, we must be satisfied by simply viewing missing data as being defined at the nominal level, and as having only one "observation category.

It should be mentioned that data consisting entirely of only one observation category are, logically, equivalent to missing data in their measurement level characteristics. That is, they have no measurement level at all. This is true regardless of the supposed measurement level of the data. Thus, to define the measurement level of a set of observations, the absolute minimum number of observation categories is two, and there must be at least three for any level of measurement above the nominal level.

For the nominal measurement level, and for binary and missing data, there are no level restraints: The characteristics of these data are completely specified by the process restraints. Since there are two types of processes, there are two types of nominal, binary and missing observations. This discrete-nominal level is quite common, with the sex of a person being such a variable. It is clear that this is a nominal (binary) variable, and it is reasonable to assume that the two observation categories (male and female) are generated by a discrete underlying process. An example of a continuous-nominal measurement variable is that of color words. The various observation categories may be blue, red, yellow, green, etc., which, while nominal, actually represent a continuous underlying process (wave length). Even missing data comes in two varieties: Discrete-missing data implies that the observer believes all the observations would have been identical had they been observed; whereas continuous-missing data implies that they wouldn't have been identical. More will be said on this at the end of this section.

For ordinal variables, we require, in addition to the process restraints, that the real numbers assigned to observations in different categories represent the order of the empirical observations:

$$\mathcal{t}^{o}: (o_i \prec o_m) \rightarrow (z^*_i < z^*_m) \qquad (4)$$

where the superscript on $\mathcal{t}^{o}$ indicates the order restriction, and where $\prec$ indicates empirical order. The problem of what to do about ties has already been handled by the process notion. If the variable is discrete-ordinal ($\mathcal{t}^{do}$), then tied observations remain tied after transformation, whereas, for continuous-ordinal ($\mathcal{t}^{co}$) variables, tied observations may be untied after transformation. The discrete-ordinal case is well exemplified by data obtained from subjects who order n-1 kinship terms according to their similarity to the n'th term. A continuous-ordinal variable might be the income level of one's father, as it is usually obtained in survey data. The observation categories might be "less than \$5,000," "\$5,000-10,000," "\$10,000-20,000," and "more than \$20,000," and one can imagine the continuous process by which such ordered categories are produced.

For numerical (interval or ratio) variables we require that the real numbers assigned to the observations be functionally related to the observations. For example (other examples are easily constructed), we might require that the optimally scaled and raw observations be related by some polynomial rule:

$$\mathcal{t}^{p}: z^*_i = \sum_{q=0}^{p} \delta_q o_i^q \qquad (5)$$

If p=2, for example, we have a quadratic relationship between the optimally scaled and raw observations. When p=1 we obtain the familiar linear relationships used with interval level variables (and with ratio level variables when δ_o=0).

It is important to note that with numerical variables the role played by the discrete-continuous distinction is that of measurement precision. If we think that our observations are perfectly precise, then we wish that all observations should be related to the optimally scaled observations by exactly the function specified by (5). However, if we think that there is some lack of precision in the measurement situation, then we may wish to let the optimally scaled observations "wobble" around the function specified by (5) just a bit. The former case corresponds to the discrete-interval or discrete-ratio case in which we allow no within observation category variation, and the latter case corresponds to the continuous-interval or continuous-ratio case in which we do permit some within category variation. Note that this notion is sensible even when there is only one observation in a particular observation category, as is usually the case.

Let us re-emphasize that even though the data are viewed as categorical, it is just as possible to obtain a categorical datum which is measured at the interval level of measurement but which was generated by a discrete process, as it is possible to obtain a categorical datum which is measured at the nominal level of measurement but which was generated by a continuous process. There is no necessary relationship between the presumed underlying generating process and the level of measurement, and in any case the datum is categorical.

Measurement conditionality. The final type of restraints placed on the measurement transformations $\mathcal{t}$ are referred to as conditi nality restraints. These restraints operate on the relationships which may exist among observations within sets of observation categories. As has been emphasized by Coombs [1964], it may be, for a particular set of data, that the measurement characteristics of the observations are conditional on some aspect of the empirical situation. When this is the case it follows that some of the observations cannot be meaningfully compared with other observations. Thus, we should subdivide all of the observations into groups such that those observations within a group are those which can be meaningfully compared to each other. Then we must restrict the measurement level and process transformations so that they only apply to observations within a group, not between groups. We call such groups partitions, since they partition the data into subsets, and we redefine the restrictions given by (2) through (5) so that they only enforce the desired relationships to exist among the observations within a partition. There are no restrictions enforced on the relationships which may exist among observations which are in different partitions.

There are several types of conditionality which can be distinguished, some of which are relevant to certain kinds of data analysis, others to other kinds. We do not go into them in detail here, but choose to mention only two.

One type, matrix conditional, is found in the following example. If we have asked several subjects to judge the similarity of all pairs of a set of stimuli, then we usually are unwilling to compare one subject's responses with another. That is, one subject's response of 7 (on, say, a similarity scale of 1 through 9) cannot be said to represent more similarity than another subject's response of 6. Furthermore, we can't say that one subject's response category of 6 means the same as another subject's category of 6. We just are not sure that the several subjects are using the response scale in identical ways. In fact, we are pretty sure that they do not use the scale identically. Thus, we say that the "meaning" of the measurements are conditional on which subject (matrix) is responding. Thus, we call this type of data matrix-conditional. Furthermore, for matrix-conditional data each matrix is a partition of the data.

Another common type of conditionality, column conditional, is exemplified by multivariate data. In multivariate data each column of data represents a measurement variable (such as the sex of a person, the person's socio-economic level, the person's height and weight, her IQ score, etc.). The important notion is that multivariate data are (essentially always) column conditional.

This example is a nice example of the fact that the measurement characteristics of one partition do not have to correspond to those of another partition. One of the variables is sex, which is binary; another is socio-economic level, which is probably continuous-ordinal; a third is height and a fourth weight, which are both ratio and may be reasonably thought of as discrete; and a fifth was IQ score, which may be either ordinal or interval.

Formally, we state that the domain of the measurement transformation t is dependent on the type of conditionality. For matrix-conditional data the domain is a single matrix of data and the transformation is denoted t_k to indicate that there is a separate transformation for each matrix k. For column-conditional data the domain is a single column of a single matrix, and the transformation is denoted t_{jk}. The previous discussion of measurement level and process was implicitly in terms of unconditional data. While all of the definitions of level and process must be modified appropriately, we do not explicate these modifications as they are both lengthy and obvious.

Missing data. We can now fully explicate our missing data notion. We have already stated that missing data can be viewed as being defined at the nominal level, and as having only one "observation" category (that of nonobservation). We noted, however, that we needed one more concept, that of conditionality, to fully explain our missing data notion. Thus, the full idea of just what missing data is can now be stated. We view missing data as observations cells which form their own separate partitions, called, naturally enough, the missing data partitions. All of the missing "observations" in a particular missing data partition fall in one observation category, the "missing" category.

Since the missing data partition has only one category of observation, and since the notion of measurement level refers to restraints between categories, none of the measurement level restraints [Eqs. (4) and (5)] apply. Thus, there is no measurement level for missing data. However, since the notion of measurement process refers to restraints within observation categories, the notion of the measurement process does apply to missing data. While this may sound a bit strange, it in fact corresponds to a common concern that a researcher has when faced with what to do about several missing observations. He wonders what it is that caused the missing observations. One of the possibilities is to assume that every missing observations was caused by a common underlying process, whereas another possibility is to assume that the missing observations were caused by a variety of processes. The former view, which says that a single thing caused the data to be missing, implies that all of the missing observations should be assigned a single number by the optimal scaling. Thus, this view corresponds with what we call discrete missing data. The latter view, that a variety of things contributed to the missing observations, implies that a continuum of numbers ought to be assigned. Thus, this view is what we think of as continuous missing data.

Finally, as implied above when we said that there can be several missing data partitions, we wish to point out that missing data can be conditional. For example, if we have multivariate data and there are data missing on two different variables, we would probably assign the missing observations to two separate partitions, one for each variable.

2.2 Indicator Matrices

In the previous section we discussed our measurement theory from the perspective of restraints imposed on data transformations. In this section we discuss our theory from a different perspective, that provided by conceiving of the data as being represented by parameters whose values we wish to estimate.

Now it may sound a bit unusual to discuss data parameters. After all, we always associate parameters with models. However, with qualitative data it is useful to think of each observation category as being represented by a parameter whose value we wish to estimate in some optimal way. (Gifi, 1981, explores the possibility of several parameters per category.) The value assigned to each observation category parameter is the "quantification" of that category. After determining the best parameter values we have "optimally scaled" the data.

To restate the goal of optimal scaling in this new light: We wish to estimate values for the data (observation category) parameters so that two characteristics are met: First, the estimation must perfectly satisfy the stated measurement restrictions; and second, it must yield a least squares relationship to the model, given that the measurement restrictions are perfectly satisfied, and given certain normalization considerations.

To discuss optimal scaling from the viewpoint of estimating data parameters we must introduce one new notion, called the indicator matrix. This matrix represents the data of a specified partition in a way which indicates the category in which each observation resides. There is an indicator matrix for each partition.

For now we define the indicator matrix $\underline{U}_p$ (underlined capital letters refer to matrices) as an $(n \times n_c)$ binary matrix with a row for each of the n observations in partition p, and a column for each of the n_c categories. (This definition will be generalized below.) The elements of $\underline{U}_p$ indicate category membership:

$$u_{pic} = \begin{cases} 1 \text{ iff } o_i \in \text{category } c \\ 0 \text{ otherwise} \end{cases}$$

In the remainder of this section we drop the p from $\underline{U}_p$, but it is to be understood that we are discussing only the data for a specific partition, and that the discussion applies to any and all partitions with no loss of generality.

Nominal data. With the definition of $\underline{U}$ given above we can look at the t^{dn} (discrete-nominal) transformation as a very simple parameter estimation process. In fact, it is Fisher's optimal scoring technique [Fisher, 1938, pp. 285-298] which consists of estimating the value of the optimally scaled datum z_i^* as the mean of all the model estimates $\hat{z}_j$ which correspond to those observations o_j that are in the same category as o_i. Since the z_i^* are the mean of the appropriate $\hat{z}_j$, we minimize the residuals $||\hat{z}-z^*||$ under the t^{dn} measurement restrictions. However, the index we wish to minimize is a normalized residuals index, Kruskal's [1964] Stress index:

$$S = \left[\frac{||\hat{z}-z^*||}{||z^*||} \right]^{1/2} . \tag{6}$$

Because z* appears in both the denominator and numerator, S is not minimized by the values which minimize its numerator. A normalization must be made of the z* to minimize (6), as discussed in section 2.4. To emphasize this aspect, we introduct the unnormalized scaled data, denoted z^u, which minimize the unnormalized residuals $||\hat{z}-z^u||$, and we reserve z* for the normalized scaled data which minimize (6). Formally, z^u is defined as

$$t^{dn}: z^u = \underline{U}(\underline{U}'\underline{U})^{-1}\underline{U}'z. \tag{7}$$

where $\underline{U}$ is defined above. Note that $\underline{U}'\underline{U}$ is a diagonal $(n_c \times n_c)$ matrix with a row and column for each observation category, and with the number of observations in each category on the diagonal. Also $\underline{U}'\hat{z}$ is an n_c element vector with the sum of the $\hat{z}_j$'s as its elements. Finally, $(\underline{U}'\underline{U})^{-1}\underline{U}'\hat{z}$ is an n_c element column vector with the mean of the appropriate $\hat{z}_j$'s as its elements. These are the unnormalized least squares estimates of the n_c data parameters for the partition under consideration.

The continuous-nominal situation is more complex than the discrete-nominal situations. The added complexity is introduced because the continuous-nominal situation, as discussed to this point, involves no measurement restrictions. For t^{cn} we impose the continuous process restrictions $[t^n, (3)]$ that each optimally scaled observation should reside in some interval, and we have placed no restrictions on the formation of the intervals. Thus, we could select arbitrarily large upper and lower boundaries which would permit all optimally scaled observations to be set equal to all raw observations, thus minimizing the squared differences trivially and totally.

Naturally, such a process is meaningless. Therefore, we propose an alternative process which yields nonoverlapping contiguous intervals, thus disallowing the trivial possibilities outlined above.

The estimation procedure for the continuous-nominal transformation t^{cn} involves the following two-phase process: In the first phase we treat the data as though they are discrete-nominal and perform a complete ALSOS analysis based on this assumption. When this process has terminated we enter the second phase in which we treat the data as though they are continuous-ordinal (see below) and perform a second complete ALSOS analysis. Note that in neither phase do we actually assume that the data are continuous-nominal.

However, the assumptions that are used do not violate the continuous-nominal nature of the data. In the first phase we use the categorical information to obtain the least squares quantification of each category. In the second phase the quantification from the first phase is used to define an order for the observation categories, which is then used to define interval boundaries.

Three things should be noted about this two-phase procedure. First, it yields a least squares quantification which is consistent with, but stricter than, the continuous-nominal restrictions discussed above. Specifically, the procedure yields nonoverlapping intervals, whereas the restrictions discussed above would permit overlapping intervals. Second, the procedure outlined here is not the same as the pseudo-ordinal procedure discussed by de Leeuw, Young and Takane [1976], but is a newer procedure which avoids the divergence problems mentioned in that paper. Third, the procedure is convergent but not strictly least squares because it may converge on a nonoptimal interval order. The only way to avoid this problem is to try all possible interval orders, a prohibitively expensive process.

Ordinal data. The estimation procedures for the ordinal transformations $\mathcal{t}^{do}$ and $\mathcal{t}^{co}$ necessitate extending the indicator matrix definition given above. We still define $\underline{U}$ as a binary matrix, but it is now an n x n_b matrix, where n_b is the number of blocks required to impose the ordinal restriction. An element of $\underline{U}$ indicates block membership in a fashion parallel to the indication of category membership for nominal level.

For the discrete ordinal situation n_b is never greater than n_c (the number of categories) and $\underline{U}$ represents a merging of observation categories. Given the proper $\underline{U}$, Young [1975a] has shown that

$$\mathcal{t}^{do}: \underline{z}^u = \underline{U}(\underline{U}'\underline{U})^{-1}\underline{U}'\hat{\underline{z}}. \tag{8}$$

Here $\underline{U}$ is constructed by Kruskal's [1964] secondary least squares monotonic transformation, which he proved to be least squares. $\underline{U}$ indicates which categories must be merged (blocked) to satisfy the ordinal restrictions. Note that $\underline{U}'\underline{U}$ is a diagonal (n_b x n_b) matrix containing the number of observations in each block on its diagonal. Also $(\underline{U}'\underline{U})^{-1}\underline{U}'\hat{\underline{z}}$ is the n_b element vector of the unnormalized optimal scale values that are the least squares parameter values which preserve the data's discrete-ordinal measurement characteristics. An example is given in section 3.1.

For the continuous-ordinal situation, n_b may or may not be greater than n_c. $\underline{U}$ indicates which observations (not categories) must be merged (blocked) in order to preserve the ordinal restrictions. Given the proper $\underline{U}$, Young [1975a] has shown that

$$\mathcal{t}^{co}: \underline{z}^u = \underline{U}(\underline{U}'\underline{U})^{-1}\underline{U}'P\hat{\underline{z}}, \tag{9}$$

where $\underline{U}$ and $\underline{P}$ are constructed by Kruskal's primary least squares monotonic transformation [see de Leeuw, 1975, for a least squares proof, and de Leeuw, 1977a, for an additional ordinal transformation]. The matrix P is a binary (n x n) block-diagonal permutation matrix. It has n_b blocks, each of which has an order equal to the corresponding element of $\underline{U}'\underline{U}$. Each block is a permutation matrix having a single one in each row and column. $\underline{P}$ has only zeros outside of the blocks. The matrix $\underline{U}'\underline{U}$ id interpreted as before (number of observations in each block), and $(\underline{U}'\underline{U})^{-1}\underline{U}'\underline{P}\hat{\underline{z}}$ contains the unnormalized least squares observation category parameter estimates.

In section 3.1 we present detailed examples of $\underline{U}$ for $\mathcal{t}^{dn}$ and for $\mathcal{t}^{do}$, as well as $\underline{U}$ and $\underline{P}$ for $\mathcal{t}^{co}$ The examples also present the process by which $\underline{U}$ (and $\underline{P}$) are constructed for the ordinal situations. It is very important to note that only for $\mathcal{t}^{dn}$ do we know $\underline{U}$ before the analysis takes place: It is simply the category structure of the data. For the ordinal situations we must determine $\underline{U}$ (and $\underline{P}$) so that the ordinal properties of the data are maintained. In these cases $\underline{U}$ (and $\underline{P}$) are not known prior to the analysis, but must be solved for! They are variables to be solved for, whereas $\underline{U}$ is a constant when the data are discrete-nominal.

This is a crucial difference with several implications. One implication is that the solution for $\underline{z}^u$ is much slower and more complex for ordinal data. Another implication is that the ability to determine degrees-of-freedom is lost with ordinal data. The latter implication implies in turn that inferential procedures are more difficult to determine for ordinal data, as is well known.

Missing data. When we have missing data the empty observation cells are removed from whatever partition they were in and placed in one or more separate partitions called missing data partitions. There is one missing data partition for unconditional missing data and more than one for conditional missing data.

For discrete-missing data all of the missing observations in a partition are thought of as residing in one category. Thus $\underline{U}$ is a column vector of n one's, where n is the number of missing observations in the partition. Equation (7) is applied to calculate $\underline{z}^u$ (the optimally scaled missing data) which, due to the nature of $\underline{U}$, is a vector whose elements are all the mean of $\hat{\underline{z}}$, the model estimates of the missing data.

For continuous-missing data the missing data are coded, in $\underline{U}$, as though they are each in a separate category. Thus, the number of categories equals the number of missing observations, and $\underline{U}$ is an (n x n) identity matrix. Therefore, (7) simplifies to $\underline{z}^u = \hat{\underline{z}}$, and each missing datum is optimally scaled by setting it equal to its model estimate. Note that this way of treating continuous-missing data is not in keeping with the discussion at the end of section 2.1. However, it is mathematically equivalent and simpler to use the present definition of $\underline{U}$.

Quantitative data. While the focus of this paper is on qualitative data, it is worthwhile to spend a moment on the estimation process for quantitative data. With the proper definition of $\underline{U}$ the t^p transformation can be written, in matrix notation, as

$$t^p: \underline{z}^u = \underline{U}\delta. \tag{10}$$

Here $\underline{U}$ is a matrix with a row for each observation and with p + 1 columns, each column being an integer power of the vector $\underline{o}$ of observations. The first column is the zero'th power (i.e., all ones), the second column is the first power (i.e., is $\underline{o}$ itself), the third column is the squares $\underline{o}^2$, etc. The unnormalized least squares estimates of $\underline{z}^u$ is

$$t^p: \underline{z}^u = \underline{U}(\underline{U}'\underline{U})^{-1}\underline{U}'\hat{\underline{z}}. \tag{11}$$

Note that in this case $\underline{U}$ is, once again, known before the analysis takes place. It is, then, only for the ordinal cases that $\underline{U}$ is unknown prior to the analysis.

2.3 Conic Projection

It is important to note that for all of the types of measurement characteristics discussed here, the corresponding transformation t may be viewed, for each partition, as though we are regressing the model estimates $\hat{\underline{z}}$ onto the row observation $\underline{o}$ in an unnormalized least squares sense and under the appropriate measurement restrictions. In particular, each t can be represented by a projection operator of the form

$$E = \underline{U}(\underline{U}'\underline{U})^{-1}\underline{U}' \tag{12}$$

where the particular definition of U depends on the measurement characteristics, as noted above. This means that we can make the important point that

$$\underline{z}^u = E\hat{\underline{z}} \tag{13}$$

When we formally note that the least squares notion is defined as

$$\phi^2 = ||\underline{z}^u-\hat{\underline{z}}|| = (\underline{z}^u-\hat{\underline{z}})'(\underline{z}^u-\hat{\underline{z}}) \tag{14}$$

and when we define F = 1-E, then we see that

$$\phi^2 = \hat{\underline{z}}'F\hat{\underline{z}} \tag{15}$$

emphasizing the fact that each of the transformations can be viewed as optimizing the vector product of the model estimates and some linear combination of the very same model estimates, where the linear combination is determined by the measurement restrictions. This point has been emphasized in a more restricted situation by Young [1975a], and was first noted in the present context by Young, de Leeuw, and Takane [1976].

Geometrically, the projection operator E projects the model estimates $\hat{\underline{z}}$ onto the nearest surface of a data cone $\underline{o}$. The projection is the unnormalized optimally scaled data $\underline{z}^u$.

Speaking geometrically, the model's estimates, the optimally scaled data, and the raw data can each be seen as subspaces of a space whose dimensionality is very high. We can also picture the model's parameters as existing in a parameter space.

Figure 2 presents the geometric relations among the model, data and optimal scaling subspaces, as well as the parameter space. Note that the model, data and optimal scaling subspaces are subspaces of a single "problem" space of dimensionality n, with each observation represented by a dimension of the space. We refer to this space as the "problem" space because it is in this space that we characterize and solve the data analysis problem under consideration. Note that the problem space is a space of real numbers, and that the space has a dimension for all observations in all partitions including missing data partitions (if there are any).

We emphasize that the parameter space is not a subspace of the problem space. The parameter space is of dimensionality p, one dimension for each of the p parameters. Usually p is much less than n, the reduction in dimensionality representing the parsimony of the model's description of the data. We also emphasize that the model, scaling and data subspaces have fewer than n dimensions, but are subspaces of the problem space. Furthermore, each partition is represented by its own unique model, scaling, and data subspace, so when there are m partitions the problem space contains m model subspaces, m optimal scaling subspaces, and m data subspaces. In Figure 2 we only display the geometry for one partition for simplicity and without loss of generality.

In the problem space we have, geometrically, represented the model estimates and the optimally scaled data subspaces as vectors and the raw data subspace as a cone. Furthermore, the two vectors and cone all intersect at the origin of the problem space. We have chosen the type of representation for each of the three subspaces for specific reasons. We represent the optimal scaling subspace as a geometric vector running through the origin to emphasize the fact that the elements of the algebraic vector $\underline{z}^u$ define a point in the problem space, and that, if we form the geometric vector which connects that point to the origin of the problem space, then all of the other points on the geometric vector are equivalent to $\underline{z}^u$ at the ratio level of measurement. In terms of the restrictions discussed above, any point in the optimal scaling subspace in Figure 2 is equivalent to any other point. (The normalization restrictions will select a specific point $\underline{z}^*$ on the optimal scaling vector, as discussed in section 2.4.) We represent the model subspace as a geometric vector for the same type of reasons.

On the other hand, we represent the data subspace as a geometric cone, not a geometric vector. Although the representation is different,

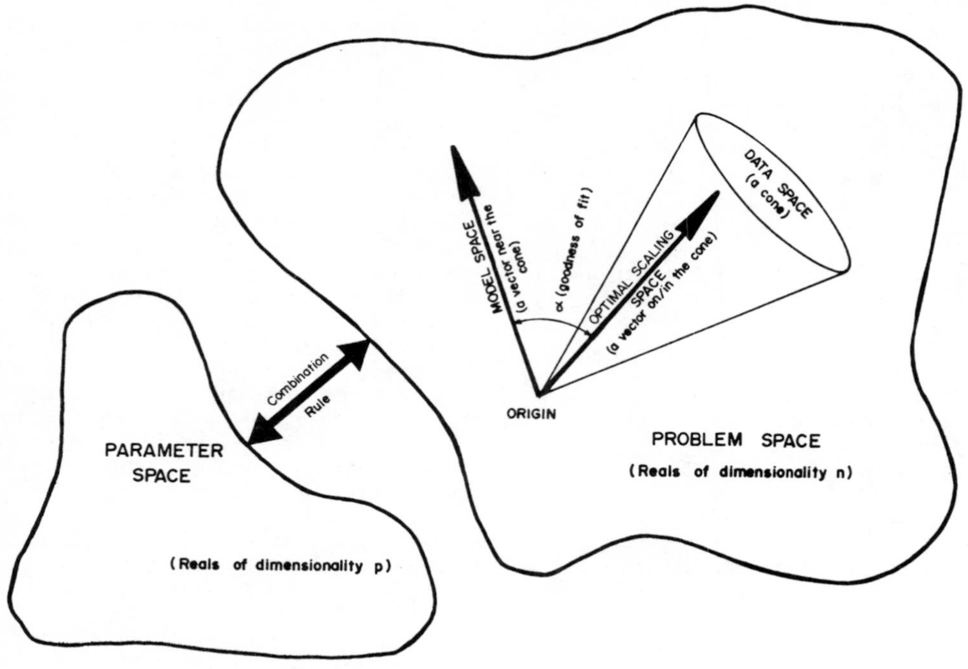

Figure 2
Geometrical foundations of the ALSOS algorithms with emphasis on conic projection

the reasoning underlying the representation is the same: For the data subspace a cone properly represents the measurement characteristics, whereas for the model and optimal scaling subspace a geometric vector is the proper representation. If you reflect on the restrictions given in (2) through (5), you will see they can all be represented geometrically as cones (some restrictions imply certain degenerate cones, for example vectors). This point has been discussed by de Leeuw, Young and Takane [1976] and by de Leeuw [1975; Note 3].

You will note that the optimal scaling vector is represented as being on the surface of the cone. Since the optimal scaling and data subspaces are completely equivalent in terms of the measurement characteristics of the data, the optimal scaling vector must be contained in the data cone. Since the model and optimal scaling subspaces are as nearly alike as possible in a least squares sense, the optimal scaling vector must be "near" the model vector. Thus it is usually the case that the optimal scaling vector is on the surface of the cone, since the surface is the part of the cone which is generally closest to the model subspace. (The only time that the optimal scaling vector is inside the cone is when the model subspace also happens to be in the cone, which only happens when the model perfectly fits the data.)

Finally, note the angle α between the model and optimal scaling vectors. The angle α represents the goodness-of-fit between the two vectors, the fit being measured by (14). The smaller the angle the better the fit. When the angle is zero the fit is perfect (this usually means that the model and optimal scaling vectors are inside the data cone, but it may mean that the two are on the surfact of the cone). Note that there is a difficulty associated with a model subspace consisting entirely of zeros. In this case, (14), the fit between the model and optimal scaling vectors, is perfect, and the angle α in Figure 2 is zero. However, the fit is perfect only in a trivial and uninteresting sense. Thus we must ensure that whatever procedures we adopt will not yield a solution at the origin of the problem space. Such solutions are avoided by normalizing the length of the model and optimal scaling vectors to some arbitrary nonzero length.

2.4 Normalization

As we just mentioned, a trivial and undesirable way of minimizing (14) is to set the model subspace $\underline{\hat{z}}$ equal to zero. Then $\underline{z}^u$ is also zero for all transformations, and hence ϕ^2 is zero for each partition. It is for this reason that the remarks about normalization conditions were made just prior to (6). In this section we discuss the normalization.

Several different normalizations are used in the ALSOS programs. All of the normalizations are introduced to avoid solutions represented by the origin of the problem space (see Figure 2) or other types of trivial solutions. The several normalization conditions have been discussed by Kruskal and Carroll [1969], Sands and Young [1980], Young [1972]; and de Leeuw [Note 3].

Two of these conditions are equivalent to defining either

$$\phi_a^2 = \frac{(\underline{z}_a^* - \hat{\underline{z}})'(\underline{z}_a^* - \hat{\underline{z}})}{\hat{\underline{z}}'\hat{\underline{z}}} \tag{16}$$

or

$$\phi_b^2 = \frac{(\underline{z}_b^* - \hat{\underline{z}})'(\underline{z}_b^* - \hat{\underline{z}})}{\underline{z}_b^{*\prime}\underline{z}_b^*} \tag{17}$$

where $\underline{z}_a^*$ and $\underline{z}_b^*$ are the "normalized" versions of $\underline{z}^u$ which optimize ϕ_a^2 and ϕ_b^2, respectively.

Now it should be clear that $\underline{z}^u$ minimizes (16) since we know from section 2.3 that it minimizes the numerator of (16), and since $\underline{z}^u$ is not involved in the denominator of (16). Thus,

$$\underline{z}_a^* = \underline{z}^u \tag{18}$$

Also, by the measurement characteristics of $\underline{z}^u$, and as pictured in Figure 2,

$$\underline{z}_b^* = b\underline{z}^u = \underline{z}^* \tag{19}$$

where b is a "normalization value" which is to be determined. Notice that we are specifically using $\underline{z}^*$ to refer to the normalization of $\underline{z}^u$ which minimizes (17).

By looking at Figure 3 we may understand the relationships between ϕ^2 and ϕ_b^2, and the relationships between $\underline{z}^u$ and $\underline{z}^*$. This figure presents, in more detail, a portion of the problem space shown in Figure 2. Specifically, we are looking down at a portion of the <u>surface</u> of the data cone, with the surface represented by the irregularly shaped area. Above the cone's surface is shown the model vector $\hat{\underline{z}}$. Note that it emanates from the origin of the problem space and data cone, the origin denoted o.o. The orthogonal projection of the model vector onto the surface of the cone gives $\underline{z}^u$, the <u>unnormalized</u> optimally scaled data. As we saw in section 2.3, this projection is represented by the operator E (12) which minimizes ϕ^2 (14), the <u>unnormalized</u> index of fit. Geometrically, the projection minimizes the angle α between $\hat{\underline{z}}$ and $\underline{z}^u$, and thus the length of the vector of residuals $\underline{r}^u$, and thus (14) which is simply the square of the length of the residuals vector.

However, $\underline{z}^u$ does <u>not</u> minimize ϕ_b^2, even though it minimizes ϕ^2, as we shall now demonstrate. Recall that α, the angle between $\hat{\underline{z}}$ and $\underline{z}^u$, has been minimized by orthogonally projecting $\hat{\underline{z}}$ onto the cone's surface. It is simple to see that the projection defines a right triangle such that

$$\sin^2\alpha = \frac{\underline{r}^u}{\hat{\underline{z}}^2} = \frac{\underline{r}^{u\prime}\underline{r}^u}{\hat{\underline{z}}'\hat{\underline{z}}} = \phi_a^2, \tag{20}$$

since the orthogonal projection of $\hat{\underline{z}}$ <u>onto</u> the cone's surface requires a right angle at the surface of the cone (indicated by the lower 90° angle). However, if we project orthogonally <u>from</u> $\hat{\underline{z}}$ (indicated by the upper 90° angle) onto the surface of the cone in the plane defined by $\hat{\underline{z}}$ and $\underline{z}^u$, we obtain a projection $\underline{z}^*$ and a <u>new</u> right triangle such that

$$\sin^2\alpha = \frac{\underline{r}^2}{\underline{z}^{*2}} = \frac{\underline{r}'\underline{r}}{\underline{z}^{*\prime}\underline{z}^*} = \phi_b^2, \tag{21}$$

and since

$$\underline{r} = \underline{z}^* - \hat{\underline{z}}, \tag{22}$$

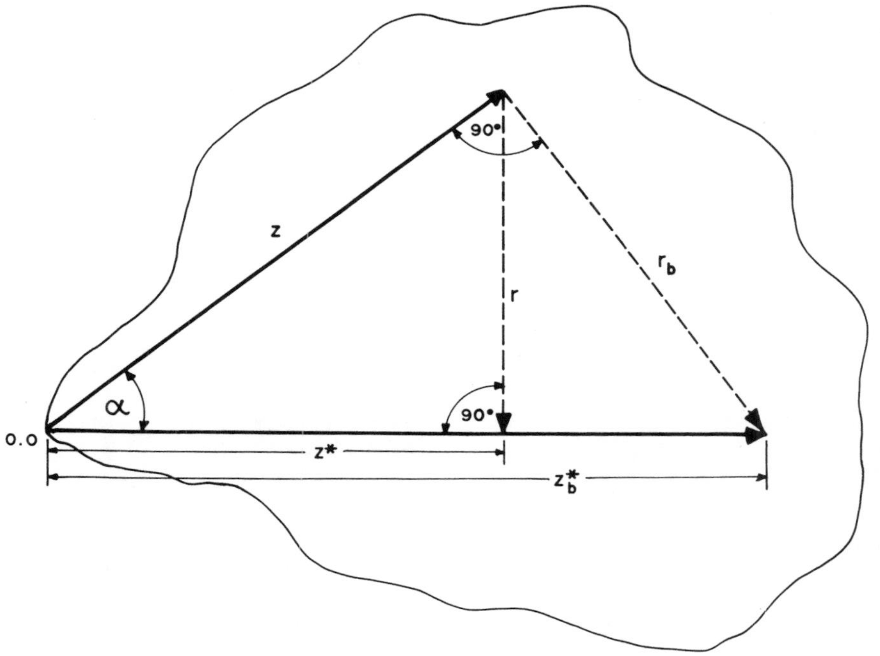

Geometrical representation of the normalization aspect of ALSOS algorithms
Figure 3

we see that

$$\sin^2 \alpha = \frac{(\underline{z}^*-\hat{\underline{z}})'(\underline{z}^*-\hat{\underline{z}})}{\underline{z}^{*\prime}\underline{z}^*}. \tag{23}$$

Thus the vector $\underline{z}^*$ minimizes ϕ_b^2 (17). Furthermore, when $\underline{z}^u$ is used in ϕ_a^2 and $\underline{a}^*$ in ϕ_b^2, it is the case [from (20) and (23) that

$$\phi_a^2 = \phi_b^2. \tag{24}$$

Thus, these two apparently different formulas are in fact equal, and it makes no difference which normalization is chosen.

We have not, however, discovered how to obtain $\underline{z}^*$ from $\underline{z}^u$; that is, we still need to determine the value of b in (19). The value of b is obtained by noting that

$$\cos^2 \alpha = \frac{\underline{z}^{u\prime}\underline{z}^u}{\hat{\underline{z}}'\hat{\underline{z}}} \tag{25}$$

and that

$$\cos^2 \alpha = \frac{\hat{\underline{z}}'\hat{\underline{z}}}{\underline{z}^{*\prime}\underline{z}^*} \tag{26}$$

Thus

$$\frac{\hat{\underline{z}}'\hat{\underline{z}}}{\underline{z}^{*\prime}\underline{z}^*} = \frac{\underline{z}^{u\prime}\underline{z}^u}{\hat{\underline{z}}'\hat{\underline{z}}} \tag{27}$$

and

$$\underline{z}^{*\prime}\underline{z}^* = \frac{(\hat{\underline{z}}'\hat{\underline{z}})(\hat{\underline{z}}'\hat{\underline{z}})}{(\underline{z}^{u\prime}\underline{z}^u)} \tag{28}$$

Noting that the values within parentheses are scalars, we see that

$$\underline{z}^{*\prime}\underline{z}^* = \frac{(\hat{\underline{z}}'\hat{\underline{z}})(\underline{z}^{u\prime}\underline{z}^u)(\hat{\underline{z}}'\hat{\underline{z}})}{(\underline{z}^{u\prime}\underline{z}^u)(\underline{z}^{u\prime}\underline{z}^u)}$$

$$= \left[\frac{(\hat{\underline{z}}'\hat{\underline{z}})}{(\underline{z}^{u\prime}\underline{z}^u)}\,\underline{z}^{u\prime}\right]\left[\underline{z}^u\frac{(\hat{\underline{z}}'\hat{\underline{z}})}{(\underline{z}^{u\prime}\underline{z}^u)}\right]. \tag{29}$$

Thus is follows that

$$\underline{z}^* = \left[\underline{z}^u\,\frac{(\hat{\underline{z}}'\hat{\underline{z}})}{(\underline{z}^{u\prime}\underline{z}^u)}\right] \tag{30}$$

Therefore, in (19) we see that

$$b = \frac{(\hat{\underline{z}}'\hat{\underline{z}})}{(\underline{z}^{u\prime}\underline{z}^u)}. \tag{31}$$

A little study of Figure 3 or (25) will reveal that

$$b = \frac{1}{\cos^2 \alpha}$$

$$= \frac{1}{1-\phi_b^2} \tag{32}$$

Thus we also note that

$$\phi_a^2 = \phi_b^2 = 1 - \frac{1}{b}. \tag{33}$$

Finally, the orthogonality of $\underline{z}^u$ and $\underline{r}^u$ allows us to also show that

$$b = \frac{(\hat{\underline{z}}'\hat{\underline{z}})}{(\hat{\underline{z}}'\underline{z}^u)}. \tag{34}$$

These relationships among the various expressions for b were first noted by Sands and Young [1980]. The fact that optimizing the unnormalized loss function by a projection operator is simply related to the more difficult problem of optimizing a normalized loss function was first discussed by de Leeuw [1975] and de Leeuw, Young and Takane [1976] and proved by de Leeuw [Note 3].

Both Sands and Young [1980] and de Leeuw [Note 3] also discuss relations between two versions of Kruskal's [1965] second stress formula

$$\phi_c^2 = \frac{(\underline{z}_c^*-\hat{\underline{z}})'(\underline{z}_c^*-\hat{\underline{z}})}{(\hat{\underline{z}}-\bar{\hat{\underline{z}}})'(\hat{\underline{z}}-\bar{\hat{\underline{z}}})}, \tag{35}$$

and

$$\phi_d^2 = \frac{(\underline{z}_d^*-\hat{\underline{z}})'(\underline{z}_d^*-\hat{\underline{z}})}{(\underline{z}_d^*-\bar{\underline{z}}_d^*)'(\underline{z}_d^*-\bar{\underline{z}}_d^*)}, \tag{36}$$

where the bar over a symbol indicates a constant vector of means of the indicated vector. reasoning like that presented above leads to the conclusion that

$$\underline{z}_c^* = \underline{z}^u \tag{37}$$

and that

$$\underline{z}^* = (\underline{z}^u-\hat{\underline{z}})\,\frac{(\hat{\underline{z}}-\bar{\hat{\underline{z}}})'(\hat{\underline{z}}-\bar{\hat{\underline{z}}})}{(\underline{z}^u-\bar{\underline{z}}^u)'(\underline{z}^u-\bar{\underline{z}}^u)} + \hat{\underline{z}}. \tag{38}$$

2.5 Partitions

The final point to be made in this section concerns what we term "measurement partitions." In some sets of data all of the observations are thought of as having arisen from a single measurement source. Furthermore, with some of these sets of data the measurement source generates data in such a way that all of the observations are reasonably assumed to have the same measurement characteristics. For example, when a subject makes similarity judgments concerning pairs of stimuli, then all of the judgments can reasonably be thought of as having been generated by a single source (the subject) and as all having the same measurement characteristics (discrete ordering of the similarity judgments). However, for other types of data it is clearly the case that the data arise from several measurement sources, or on several scales.

For example, when we obtain multivariate survey data with variables such as sex, age, hair color, income, educational background and political preference from a set of people, we would probably think of each variable as a unique measurement source having its own separate measurement characteristics: Sex is binary; age is ratio; hair color is nominal; income may be interval, educational background may be ordinal; and preference is ordinal. In this case we would wish to partition the data space into a set of mutually exclusive and exhaustive subspaces (one for each variable).

While the notion of partitions most clearly relates to multivariate data, the notion is also useful for other types of data. For example, Coombs' [1964] notion of conditional similarities data (for which a subject rank orders the similarity of n-1 "comparison" stimuli with respect to the n'th "standard" stimulus, and then does this n times, each time with a different stimulus as the "standard") is a situation in which a single measurement source (the subject) generates n different measurement scales (the rank orders). For this type of data measurement partitions are also of great use.

When the data are partitioned, the OS phase of an ALSOS procedure is slightly more complicated than when they are not partitioned, but only slightly. The difference is that we must perform the OS and normalization for each partition separately, one partition at a time. Since the partitions are mutually exclusive, and since the OS is performed for each partition separately, the measurement characteristics of one partition need bear no special relationship to those of another partition. This means, for example, that many of the procedures oriented towards multivariate data (see Table 1) can analyze data with mixtures of measurement characteristics. These data, which we call mixed measurement level data, can have one set of measurement characteristics for one variable, and a completely different set for another variable. A multivariate procedure (MORALS) is discussed in Section 3.2.

Note that for partitioned data the overall loss function is defined as the root-mean-square of the loss functions for each partition. Thus, if ϕ_i^2 denotes the normalized loss function for the i'th of p partitions, we define the overall loss as

$$\phi = \left[\frac{1}{p} \sum_i^p \phi_i \right]^{1/2} \tag{39}$$

There is a very important consideration here, however, which must not be overlooked. It is usually imperative that right after performing the optimal scaling for a particular partition we immediately replace the old optimal scaling with the new optimal scaling. As will become clear from the next portion of this paper, the immediate replacement is imperative when the partitions are dependent. (Partitions are "dependent" if the optimal scale values for at least one partition, assuming the others are fixed, are a function of the optimal scale values for at least one partition, assuming the others are fixed, are a function of the optimal scale values for at least one other partition.) Since dependence is generally a characteristic of multivariate data, the programs which analyze such data involve immediate replacement. This point has been emphasized in Young, de Leeuw, & Takane [1976].

If, in fact, the partitions are dependent, then there is one additional consideration. Let's say, for the multivariate data case, that we have completed a cycle of optimal scaling and replacement for each variable. Now let's say that we repeat the optimal scaling of one of the variables. If we do this, then the second optimal scaling of the variable does not yield the same quantification as the first optimal scaling. Why is this? Because the variables are dependent. The quantification obtained by optimally scaling one variable depends on the quantification of each of the other variables.

While this all sounds somewhat bothersome, it can be shown [de Leeuw, Young & Takane, 1976] that were we to perform "inner" iterations ("inner" with respect to the scheme in Figure 1) of the cycle of optimal scaling and replacement, then this process would converge to a point where the quantifications would no longer change upon repeated optimal scaling. In our work we do not perform such inner optimal scaling iterations, however, only performing the process once for each variable (or partition) before switching to the model estimation phase (see Figure 1). Our experience has been that such inner iteration only serves to decrease the overall efficiency of the procedure, and de Leeuw [Note 3] has proven that the number of inner iterations has no effect on the eventual convergence point.

3. ALSOS ALGORITHMS

In this section we discuss two ALSOS algorithms in detail, the ADDALS and MORALS algorithms. In conjunction with the ADDALS discussion we present the discrete-nominal, discrete-ordinal and continuous-ordinal transformation processes (in terms of indicator matrices) in detail.

3.1 ADDALS Algorithm

In this section we discuss the overall ADDALS algorithm [de Leeuw, Young & Takane, 1976] for additivity (conjoint) analysis. The steps of the algorithm are presented in Figure 4. We discuss the ADDALS algorithm first because it is the simplest.

The ADDALS algorithm describes tabular data by using the simple additive model. This is the "main effects" analysis of variance model, the analysis of variance model which has no interaction term:

$$\underline{z}_{ij}^* \underline{\sim} \alpha_i + \beta_j + \mu. \tag{40}$$

Note that we have reorganized the vector $\underline{z}^*$ with element $\underline{z}_i^*$ into a two-way table Z* with element $\underline{z}_{ij}^*$.

The initialization of ADDALS is very simple (see step START of Figure 4). We simply call the raw data the initial "optimally scaled" data (Z*=0). These initial "scaled" data serve as the input to the model estimation step that is next.

The model estimation phase of ADDALS (step MODEL in Figure 4) begins by estimating the parameters α_i, β_j and μ of (40). The estimation method is well known: We use the grand mean of Z* to estimate μ, and the mean of the i'th row's (or j'th column's) deviation from μ to estimate α_i

ADDALS ALGORITHM

START:	READ O AND ITS MEASUREMENT CHARACTERISTICS. NORMALIZE O AND SET $Z^* = O$.	INITIALIZATION
MODEL:	CALCULATE α_I, β_J, AND μ AS THE ROW, COLUMN AND GRAND MEANS OF Z^*.	MODEL PARAMETERS
	$\hat{z}_{IJ} = \alpha_I + \beta_J + \mu$	MODEL ESTIMATES
FIT:	$\phi = \left[\|\|\hat{Z}-Z^*\|\|/\|\|Z^*\|\|\right]^{1/2}$	FIT
	IF ϕ IS SMALL, OR IF THE CHANGES IN ϕ, α_I, β_J AND μ ARE SMALL, GO TO QUIT, OTHERWISE GO TO SCALE.	TERMINATION
SCALE:	$z^U = U(U'U)^{-1}U'\hat{z}$	SCALING
	$z^* = z^U \left[\frac{\|\|\hat{Z}\|\|}{\|\|Z^U\|\|}\right]$	NORMALIZATION
	GO TO MODEL	
QUIT:	OUTPUT RESULTS AND STOP.	

Figure 4
The major steps in the ADDALS algorithm

(or to estimate β_j). This is the same as with regular analysis of variance, except we use the optimally scaled data Z* in place of the raw data O.

Following the parameter estimation step we calculate the model estimates $\hat{z}_{ij}$ by applying the model in (40). These $\hat{Z}$ are the values that minimize ϕ for the particular Z* we have on the current iteration.

The goodness of fit ϕ is calculated in step FIT. If ϕ is small (good fit) or if ϕ, α_i, β_j and μ all haven't changed much from the previous iteration (convergence), we quit. Otherwise we proceed to rescale the data.

The model estimates $\underline{\hat{z}}$ from step MODEL serve as input to the optimal scaling (step SCALE). (Note that we have just reshaped the p by q matrix $\hat{Z}$ into a vector $\underline{\hat{z}}$ which has p times q elements. This simplifies the notation.) The projection operator $U(U'U)^{-1}U'$ is applied to the estimates $\underline{\hat{z}}$ to obtain the unnormalized scaled data $\underline{z}^u$, which in turn are normalized to obtain the optimally scaled data $\underline{z}^*$. These $\underline{z}^*$ are the values that minimize ϕ for the particular $\underline{\hat{z}}$ we have on the current iteration. The indicator matrix U, of course, is defined by whatever process corresponds to the measurement characteristics of the data O, as discussed in section 2.2. We now reshape $\underline{z}^*$ into Z* and return to step MODEL to obtain new model estimates based on the newly scaled data Z*.

In the remainder of this section we present three detailed and completely worked out artificial examples of the ADDALS algorithm. The three examples all involve analyzing the same 3 x 3 table of data, but under three different sets of measurement assumptions: discrete-nominal, discrete-ordinal, and continuous-ordinal. The table of data is (arbitrarily):

A	C	B
A	B	B
C	A	B

These data could have been obtained, for example, in a 3 x 3 experiment in which the two experimental variables are wind-speed (none, slow, fast) and temperature (-10°C, 0°C, and 10°C), and in which we ask people to judge the relative perceived temperatures as being cold (C); colder (B); and coldest (A).

Discrete-nominal. In Figure 5 we present the first two iterations of ADDALS when the data are presumed to be discrete-nominal. Each iteration is divided into four sections called Model Estimation, Optimal Scaling, Normalization, and Fit. Note that the data on the first iteration ($\underline{Z}^*$, the left-most matrix in the Model Estimation section of the top panel) use different symbols to code the categories than the A, B, and C given above. We must use numbers, not letters, because the initialization requires them. Thus, we have chosen to set A = 2, B = 5, and C = 7. This initial $\underline{Z}^*$, then, is arbitrary, and any other initial assignment of numbers to the categories A, B, and C would suffice. The initial assignment may cause the algorithm to obtain a local minimum as a solution, instead of the global minimum [Young & Null, 1978]. Thus, we should be careful at this point. In fact, it is desirable to try several different assignments and to observe their effect on the results, particularly when the categories are truly unordered. For the example given (perceived temperature), the categories are potentially ordered, and we have chosen numbers which are in that potentially "correct" order. However, the analysis is nominal, thus the initial order need not be preserved.

To the right of $\underline{Z}^*$ are the values of the model parameters α_i, β_j, and μ. The mean of $\underline{Z}^*$ is μ, and the deviation of the row and column means from μ are the α_i and β_j, respectively. To the right of the parameters is the matrix of estimates $\hat{Z}$ and the measure of fit (called stress since this is Kruskal's Stress index). The parameters yield estimates $\hat{Z}$ which are a least stress fit to $\underline{Z}^*$, conditional on the arbitrary initial coding of the three observation categories. Note that what has been done to this point is a classical ANOVA of the $\underline{Z}^*$ using the main effects model.

ADDALS now proceeds to the optimal scaling on the first iteration. Figure 5 presents the raw data vector $\underline{o}$, with the observations coded as A, B and C, and with all observations in a given category being adjacent to each other. (The order of the observations in this vector is irrelevant. The order shown simplifies the presentation.) Directly below $\underline{o}$ is $\underline{U}$, the indicator matrix (note that the transpose of $\underline{U}$ is shown). $\underline{U}$ has three columns, one for each category, and nine rows, one for each observation. Finally, note that the vector of nine model estimates, $\underline{\hat{z}}$, appears directly below $\underline{U}$. The order of the elements of $\underline{\hat{z}}$ is not arbitrary, but is in the order dictated by the order of the elements in the vector $\underline{o}$. The first element in the vector $\underline{\hat{z}}$ (3.90) corresponds to the first observation in the vector $\underline{o}$ (an A) because the value 3.90 comes from a cell in the matrix $\underline{\hat{Z}}$ which corresponds to an A observation in the $\underline{O}$ matrix. The correspondence between the elements of the vectors $\underline{\hat{z}}$ and $\underline{o}$ is the same throughout: Each value in the vector $\underline{\hat{z}}$ is the model's least squares estimate of the current numerical coding (quantification) of the category given in the vector $\underline{o}$ above.

The input to the optimal scaling step is the indicator matrix $\underline{U}$ and the model estimates $\underline{\hat{z}}$. The outpur is the unnormalized scaled data $\underline{z}^u$. You will recall that $\underline{z}^u = U(U'U)^{-1}U'\underline{\hat{z}}$, according to (7). We note that the diagonal of U'U is [3,4,2], which is the number of observations in each category. Of course $DIAG[(U'U)^{-1}] = [1/3,1/4,1/2]$. Furthermore, the projection operator $E = U(U'U)^{-1}U'$ is a block diagonal matrix with three blocks, one for each category. The order of a block equals the number of observations in the corresponding category, and all elements in a block equal the reciprocal of the category frequency. Finally, the transpose of $(U'U)^{-1}U'\underline{\hat{z}}$ is [4.01,4.81,4.40]. These three values are the unnormalized scale values for the three observation categories, also called the unnormalized observation category parameter values. Note that these three values are not in the anticipated order: Category B, which had the middle initial value (5), now has the largest value.

ADDALS now proceeds to the normalization step in Figure 5. As discussed in section 2.4 and illustrated in Figure 3, the vector $\underline{z}^u$ which was just computed minimizes the unnormalized fit to $(||\underline{z}^u-\underline{\hat{z}}||)$, but not the normalized Stress index $(||\underline{Z}^*-\underline{\hat{Z}}||/||Z^*||)^{1/2}$ at the top of Figure 5. As we showed in section 2.4, to minimize the normalized Stress index we must compute the normalization constant b given by (31). For the first iteration b = 1.015, as is shown on the bottom left portion of Figure 5. This yields the matrix of (normalized) optimally scaled data $\underline{Z}^*$ (given next in the Figure) and a (normalized) Stress value of .1209. We see that the optimal scaling has improved the fit from .3681 to .1209, a big improvement.

Note that we can also calculate the Stress using the unnormalized $\underline{Z}^u$ if we make sure to use the model estimates in the denominator [(16) above]. The value for this formula, which is shown at the bottom of the left panel of Figure 5, must also be .1209. The question might be asked, then, why normalize if we can use the unnormalized $\underline{Z}^u$ to calculate Stress just by using a slightly different Stress formula? The answer is that while it is true that we can use $\underline{Z}^u$ to calculate Stress, we must have $\underline{Z}^*$ in order to start the next iteration properly.

The second iteration is shown in the bottom panel of Figure 5. We are only going to comment on the values of Stress on this iteration. We see that Stress is .0460 after the second model estimation, and goes down further to .0295 after the second optimal scaling. These values of fit will always improve (decrease) until ADDALS converges on a point of no further change. This is the convergent nature of all ALSOS algorithms: The fit never worsens and eventually stabilizes. Note that if we had used different initial values for the observation categories the algorithm would still remain convergent, but would perhaps have converged on a different Stress value. If so, the larger Stress value would ba a local minimum [Young & Null, 1978].

ADDALS would take a few more iterations to reach a point where Stress ceases to improve by very much, and would then stop. We do not report the rest of these iterations. Note that we stop after the model estimation because at that point the data are scaled in a fashion which yields the parameters and Stress just calculated.

Discrete-ordinal. We now discuss the discrete-ordinal analysis of these same data. The first two iterations are shown in Figure 6. The discrete-ordinal ADDALS algorithm is exactly the same as the discrete-nominal ADDALS algorithm, with but a single exception: An order constraint is imposed on the observation categories during the optimal scaling. The constraint is introduced via the U matrix.

One implication of this relationship between the discrete-nominal and discrete-ordinal algorithms is that the model estimation step on iteration one is precisely the same (compare Figures 5 and 6). In fact, the optimal scaling step starts out in the same way for both levels of measurement. Specifically, for the discrete-ordinal case the indicator matrix U starts out to be the same as the indicator matrix used for the discrete-nominal case: It simply indicates the category structure. Thus, the FIRST TRY (top panel of Figure 6) computes the same Z^u as is computed for the discrete-nominal case (top panel of Figure 5). However, when the Z^u values are inspected we see that they are not in the required order: The middle raw observation category (5) has been assigned the largest Z^u (4.81), and the largest category (7) a smaller Z^u (4.40).

To cope with this order violation we modify U and have a SECOND TRY. The new U still has nine rows, one for each observation, but it has only two columns, one for the smallest observation category and one for the two order violating categories. Thus, we have merged the two violating categories into one "block." We now repeat the calculation of Z^u using this new U and check to see if its values are properly ordered. They are, so we proceed to the normalization step. Of course, if the Z^u entries were still disordered we would have tried again with the order violating columns of U merged.

Note that we have just looked in detail at the critical difference between the nominal and ordinal levels. For nominal, U is known before ana-

FIRST ITERATION

• MODEL ESTIMATION

Data Z^*; Model Parameters α, β, μ; Model Estimates $\hat{z}_{IJ} = \alpha_I + \beta_J + \mu$; Stress $\sqrt{\frac{||Z^* - \hat{Z}||}{||Z^*||}}$

$$\begin{bmatrix} 2 & 7 & 5 \\ 2 & 5 & 5 \\ 7 & 2 & 5 \end{bmatrix} \quad \begin{bmatrix} .22 \\ -.44 \\ .22 \end{bmatrix} \quad \begin{bmatrix} -.77 \\ .22 \\ .55 \end{bmatrix} \quad 4.44 \quad \begin{bmatrix} 3.90 & 4.90 & 5.23 \\ 3.23 & 4.23 & 4.56 \\ 3.90 & 4.90 & 5.23 \end{bmatrix} \quad .3681 = \sqrt{\frac{28.45}{210}}$$

• OPTIMAL SCALING

Raw Data $O' = \begin{bmatrix} A & A & A & B & B & B & B & C & C \end{bmatrix}$

Indicator Matrix $U' = \begin{bmatrix} 1 & 1 & 1 & 0 & 0 & 0 & 0 & 0 & 0 \\ 0 & 0 & 0 & 1 & 1 & 1 & 1 & 0 & 0 \\ 0 & 0 & 0 & 0 & 0 & 0 & 0 & 1 & 1 \end{bmatrix}$

Model Estimates $\hat{Z}' = \begin{bmatrix} 3.90 & 3.23 & 4.90 & 5.23 & 4.23 & 4.56 & 5.23 & 4.90 & 3.90 \end{bmatrix}$

Unnormalized Scaled Data $Z^{U'} = \begin{bmatrix} 4.01 & 4.01 & 4.01 & 4.81 & 4.81 & 4.81 & 4.81 & 4.40 & 4.40 \end{bmatrix}$

• NORMALIZATION

$$B = \frac{182.17}{179.50} = 1.015 \quad \text{AND} \quad Z^* = \begin{bmatrix} 4.07 & 4.47 & 4.88 \\ 4.07 & 4.88 & 4.88 \\ 4.47 & 4.07 & 4.88 \end{bmatrix}$$

• FIT

$$\sqrt{\frac{||Z^* - \hat{Z}||}{||Z^*||}} = \sqrt{\frac{2.7031}{184.91}} = .1209 \qquad \sqrt{\frac{||Z^U - \hat{Z}||}{||\hat{Z}||}} = \sqrt{\frac{2.6643}{182.27}} = .1209$$

SECOND ITERATION

• MODEL ESTIMATION

Data Z^*; Model Parameters α, β, μ; Model Estimates $\hat{z}_{IJ} = \alpha_I + \beta_J + \mu$; Stress $\sqrt{\frac{||Z^* - \hat{Z}||}{||Z^*||}}$

$$\begin{bmatrix} 4.07 & 4.47 & 4.88 \\ 4.07 & 4.88 & 4.88 \\ 4.47 & 4.07 & 4.88 \end{bmatrix} \quad \begin{bmatrix} -.047 \\ .095 \\ -.047 \end{bmatrix} \quad \begin{bmatrix} -.319 \\ -.049 \\ .367 \end{bmatrix} \quad 4.52 \quad \begin{bmatrix} 4.15 & 4.42 & 4.84 \\ 4.29 & 4.57 & 4.98 \\ 4.15 & 4.42 & 4.84 \end{bmatrix} \quad .0460 = \sqrt{\frac{.3915}{184.91}}$$

• OPTIMAL SCALING

Raw Data $O' = \begin{bmatrix} A & A & A & B & B & B & B & C & C \end{bmatrix}$

Indicator Matrix $U' = \begin{bmatrix} 1 & 1 & 1 & 0 & 0 & 0 & 0 & 0 & 0 \\ 0 & 0 & 0 & 1 & 1 & 1 & 1 & 0 & 0 \\ 0 & 0 & 0 & 0 & 0 & 0 & 0 & 1 & 1 \end{bmatrix}$

Model Estimates $\hat{Z}' = \begin{bmatrix} 4.15 & 4.29 & 4.42 & 4.84 & 4.57 & 4.98 & 4.84 & 4.42 & 4.15 \end{bmatrix}$

Unnormalized Scaled Data $Z^{U'} = \begin{bmatrix} 4.29 & 4.29 & 4.29 & 4.81 & 4.81 & 4.81 & 4.81 & 4.29 & 4.29 \end{bmatrix}$

• NORMALIZATION

$$B = \frac{||\hat{Z}||}{||Z^U||} = \frac{184.46}{184.30} = 1.001 \qquad Z^* = \begin{bmatrix} 4.29 & 4.29 & 4.81 \\ 4.29 & 4.81 & 4.81 \\ 4.29 & 4.29 & 4.81 \end{bmatrix}$$

• FIT

$$\sqrt{\frac{||Z^* - \hat{Z}||}{||Z^*||}} = \sqrt{\frac{.1613}{184.91}} = .0295 \qquad \sqrt{\frac{||Z^U - \hat{Z}||}{||\hat{Z}||}} = \sqrt{\frac{.1613}{184.46}} = .0295$$

Figure 5
Discrete-Nominal ADDALS example

lysis, remains constant, and simply indicates the observation category structure. For ordinal (discrete or continuous), U is not known but must be determined. It is not constant, but is variable. And for discrete-ordinal U does not indicate category structure, but does indicate blocks of categories which must be merged to maintain order.

We will not discuss the remainder of Figure 6 in

detail; rather, we let you peruse it at your leisure. Note that the normalization procedures are the same as with any other measurement characteristics, although the numbers are different than in Figure 5 because of the ordinal constraint in the optimal scaling. Note also that the Stress values are all larger than with the discrete-nominal assumptions, because we have had to impose order constraints.

FIRST ITERATION

• MODEL ESTIMATION

DATA Z^*; MODEL PARAMETERS α, β, μ; MODEL ESTIMATES $\hat{Z}_{IJ} = \alpha_I + \beta_J + \mu$; STRESS $\sqrt{\frac{||Z^* - \hat{Z}||}{||Z^*||}}$

$$\begin{bmatrix} 2 & 7 & 5 \\ 2 & 5 & 5 \\ 7 & 2 & 5 \end{bmatrix} \quad \begin{bmatrix} .22 \\ -.44 \\ .22 \end{bmatrix} \quad \begin{bmatrix} -.77 \\ .22 \\ .55 \end{bmatrix} \quad 4.44 \quad \begin{bmatrix} 3.90 & 4.90 & 5.23 \\ 3.23 & 4.23 & 4.56 \\ 3.90 & 4.90 & 5.23 \end{bmatrix} \quad 0.3681 = \sqrt{\frac{28.45}{210}}$$

• OPTIMAL SCALING

RAW DATA $$O' = \begin{bmatrix} 2 & 2 & 2 & 5 & 5 & 5 & 5 & 7 & 7 \end{bmatrix}$$

MODEL ESTIMATES $$\hat{Z}' = \begin{bmatrix} 3.90 & 3.23 & 4.90 & 5.23 & 4.23 & 4.56 & 5.23 & 4.90 & 3.90 \end{bmatrix}$$

FIRST TRY

INDICATOR MATRIX $$U_0' = \begin{bmatrix} 1 & 1 & 1 & 0 & 0 & 0 & 0 & 0 & 0 \\ 0 & 0 & 0 & 1 & 1 & 1 & 1 & 0 & 0 \\ 0 & 0 & 0 & 0 & 0 & 0 & 0 & 1 & 1 \end{bmatrix}$$

UNNORMALIZED SCALED DATA $$Z^{U'}_0 = \begin{bmatrix} 4.01 & 4.01 & 4.01 & 4.81 & 4.81 & 4.81 & 4.81 & 4.40 & 4.40 \end{bmatrix}$$

SECOND TRY

INDICATOR MATRIX $$U_1' = \begin{bmatrix} 1 & 1 & 1 & 0 & 0 & 0 & 0 & 0 & 0 \\ 0 & 0 & 0 & 1 & 1 & 1 & 1 & 1 & 1 \end{bmatrix}$$

UNNORMALIZED SCALED DATA $$Z^{U'}_1 = \begin{bmatrix} 4.01 & 4.01 & 4.01 & 4.67 & 4.67 & 4.67 & 4.67 & 4.67 & 4.67 \end{bmatrix}$$

• NORMALIZATION AND FIT

STRESS $\sqrt{\frac{||Z^* - \hat{Z}||}{||Z^*||}} = \sqrt{\frac{||Z^U - \hat{Z}||}{||\hat{Z}||}}$

$$B = ||\hat{Z}|| / ||Z^U|| \qquad 1.018 = \frac{182.27}{179.09} \qquad Z^* = \begin{bmatrix} 4.08 & 4.75 & 4.75 \\ 4.08 & 4.75 & 4.75 \\ 4.75 & 4.08 & 4.75 \end{bmatrix} \qquad .1260 = \sqrt{\frac{2.94}{185.31}} = \sqrt{\frac{2.89}{182.27}}$$

SECOND ITERATION

• MODEL ESTIMATION

DATA Z^*; MODEL PARAMETERS α, β, μ; MODEL ESTIMATES $\hat{Z}_{IJ} = \alpha_I + \beta_J + \mu$; STRESS $\sqrt{\frac{||Z^* - \hat{Z}||}{||Z^*||}}$

$$\begin{bmatrix} 4.08 & 4.75 & 4.75 \\ 4.08 & 4.75 & 4.75 \\ 4.75 & 4.08 & 4.75 \end{bmatrix} \quad \begin{bmatrix} 0.0 \\ 0.0 \\ 0.0 \end{bmatrix} \quad \begin{bmatrix} -.22 \\ 0.00 \\ .22 \end{bmatrix} \quad 4.53 \quad \begin{bmatrix} 4.30 & 4.53 & 4.75 \\ 4.30 & 4.53 & 4.75 \\ 4.30 & 4.53 & 4.75 \end{bmatrix} \quad .0568 = \sqrt{\frac{.5986}{185.31}}$$

• OPTIMAL SCALING

RAW DATA $$O' = \begin{bmatrix} 2 & 2 & 2 & 5 & 5 & 5 & 5 & 7 & 7 \end{bmatrix}$$

MODEL ESTIMATES $$\hat{Z}' = \begin{bmatrix} 4.30 & 4.30 & 4.53 & 4.75 & 4.53 & 4.75 & 4.75 & 4.53 & 4.30 \end{bmatrix}$$

FIRST TRY

INDICATOR MATRIX $$U_0' = \begin{bmatrix} 1 & 1 & 1 & 0 & 0 & 0 & 0 & 0 & 0 \\ 0 & 0 & 0 & 1 & 1 & 1 & 1 & 0 & 0 \\ 0 & 0 & 0 & 0 & 0 & 0 & 0 & 1 & 1 \end{bmatrix}$$

SCALED DATA $$Z^{U'}_0 \quad \begin{bmatrix} 4.38 & 4.38 & 4.38 & 4.69 & 4.69 & 4.69 & 4.69 & 4.42 & 4.42 \end{bmatrix}$$

SECOND TRY

INDICATOR MATRIX $$U_1' = \begin{bmatrix} 1 & 1 & 1 & 0 & 0 & 0 & 0 & 0 & 0 \\ 0 & 0 & 0 & 1 & 1 & 1 & 1 & 1 & 1 \end{bmatrix}$$

SCALED DATA $$Z^{U'}_1 = \begin{bmatrix} 4.38 & 4.38 & 4.38 & 4.60 & 4.60 & 4.60 & 4.60 & 4.60 & 4.60 \end{bmatrix}$$

• NORMALIZATION AND FIT

STRESS $\sqrt{\frac{||Z^* - \hat{Z}||}{||Z^*||}} = \sqrt{\frac{||Z^U - \hat{Z}||}{||\hat{Z}||}}$

$$B = ||\hat{Z}|| / ||Z^U|| \qquad 1.001 = \frac{184.7202}{184.5132} \qquad Z^* = \begin{bmatrix} 4.38 & 4.61 & 4.61 \\ 4.38 & 4.61 & 4.61 \\ 4.61 & 4.38 & 4.61 \end{bmatrix} \qquad .0331 = \sqrt{\frac{.2030}{185.07}} = \sqrt{\frac{.2026}{184.72}}$$

Figure 6
Discrete-Ordinal ADDALS example

Continuous-ordinal. The algorithm for continuous-ordinal is precisely the same as the previous two measurement cases except for two differences, both in the optimal scaling step.

The first difference is that a permutation matrix P is used. The order of P equals the number of observations. Furthermore, P is block diagonal, with the number of blocks equaling the number of categories, and the order of each block equaling the number of observations in each category. The permutation matrix permutes (sorts) the model estimates $\hat{Z}$ into order within each observation category.

For the example we've been discussing (Figure 7) the permutation matrix on the first iteration is

$$\begin{bmatrix} 0 & 1 & 0 & & & & & & \\ 1 & 0 & 0 & & & & & & \\ 0 & 0 & 1 & & & & & & \\ & & & 0 & 1 & 0 & 0 & & \\ & & & 0 & 0 & 1 & 0 & & \\ & & & 1 & 0 & 0 & 0 & & \\ & & & 0 & 0 & 0 & 1 & & \\ & & & & & & & 0 & 1 \\ & & & & & & & 1 & 0 \end{bmatrix}$$

This matrix, when applied to the model estimates, yields the permuted $\hat{Z}$ shown in Figure 7. Note that P is a variable, varying between iterations, just as does U.

The second difference between continuous-ordinal and the previous two measurement cases is that U starts out being the identity matrix whose order equals the number of observations (not the number of categories). Note that U does not start out reflecting the category structure. Because of this U does not end up reflecting the category structure nor the structure of categories which must be blocked to preserve order. Rather, U ends up indicating which observations (not categories) must be blocked to preserve order. We are not going to review Figure 7 in detail.

3.2 The MORALS Algorithm

In this section we briefly review the overall MORALS algorithm [Young, de Leeuw, & Takane, 1976] for multiple regression with multivariate data whose variables each have their own independent measurement characteristics. We discuss only the algorithm. We present no detailed examples like those in the previous section, as we deem them unnecessary.

The important aspect of MORALS is that it permits the multivariate data to have any mix of measurement types: Some variables can be nominal, others ordinal, and yet others interval. Similarly, any variable can be discrete or continuous. This flexibility applies to the dependent variable as well as the independent variables. In fact, the algorithm has been extended to the case where there are multiple dependent variables with mixed measurement characteristics [CORALS and CANALS by Young, de Leeuw & Takane, 1976] and to the case where there are multiple sets of variables

FIRST ITERATION

• MODEL ESTIMATION

Raw Data	Model Parameters			Model Estimates	Stress
Z^*	α	β	μ	$\hat{z}_{IJ} = \alpha_I + \beta_J + \mu$	$\sqrt{\frac{\|\|Z^*-\hat{Z}\|\|}{\|\|Z^*\|\|}}$
$\begin{bmatrix} 2 & 7 & 5 \\ 2 & 5 & 5 \\ 7 & 2 & 5 \end{bmatrix}$	$\begin{bmatrix} .22 \\ -.44 \\ .22 \end{bmatrix}$	$\begin{bmatrix} -.77 \\ .22 \\ .55 \end{bmatrix}$	4.44	$\begin{bmatrix} 3.90 & 4.90 & 5.23 \\ 3.23 & 4.23 & 4.56 \\ 3.90 & 4.90 & 5.23 \end{bmatrix}$	$.3681 = \sqrt{\frac{28.45}{210}}$

• OPTIMAL SCALING

Raw Data $O' = [2\ 2\ 2\ 5\ 5\ 5\ 5\ 7\ 7]$

Model Estimates $\hat{Z}' = [3.90\ 3.23\ 4.90\ 5.23\ 4.23\ 4.56\ 5.23\ 4.90\ 3.90]$

Permuted M.E. $\hat{Z}' = [3.23\ 3.90\ 4.90\ 4.23\ 4.56\ 5.23\ 5.23\ 3.90\ 4.90]$

FIRST TRY $U = I$, $Z^U = \hat{Z}$

SECOND TRY

$$U' = \begin{bmatrix} 1&0&0&0&0&0&0&0&0 \\ 0&1&0&0&0&0&0&0&0 \\ 0&0&1&1&0&0&0&0&0 \\ 0&0&0&0&1&0&0&0&0 \\ 0&0&0&0&0&1&0&0&0 \\ 0&0&0&0&0&0&1&1&0 \\ 0&0&0&0&0&0&0&0&1 \end{bmatrix}$$

$Z^{U'} = [3.23\ 3.90\ 4.57\ 4.57\ 4.56\ 5.23\ 4.57\ 4.57\ 4.90]$

THIRD TRY

$$U' = \begin{bmatrix} 1&0&0&0&0&0&0&0&0 \\ 0&1&0&0&0&0&0&0&0 \\ 0&0&1&1&1&0&0&0&0 \\ 0&0&0&0&0&1&1&1&0 \\ 0&0&0&0&0&0&0&0&1 \end{bmatrix}$$

$Z^{U'} = [3.23\ 3.90\ 4.56\ 4.56\ 4.56\ 4.79\ 4.79\ 4.79\ 4.90]$

• NORMALIZATION AND FIT

$B = \|\|\hat{Z}\|\|/\|\|Z^U\|\|$	Z^*	Stress
$1.008 = \frac{182.27}{180.87}$	$\begin{bmatrix} 3.93 & 4.94 & 4.83 \\ 3.25 & 4.60 & 4.60 \\ 4.83 & 4.60 & 4.83 \end{bmatrix}$	$.088 = \sqrt{\frac{1.41}{183.88}} = \sqrt{\frac{1.40}{182.27}}$

SECOND ITERATION

• MODEL ESTIMATION

Data	Model Parameters			Model Estimates	Stress
Z^*	α	β	μ	$\hat{z}_{IJ} = \alpha_I + \beta_J + \mu$	$\sqrt{\frac{\|\|Z^*-\hat{Z}\|\|}{\|\|Z^*\|\|}}$
$\begin{bmatrix} 3.93 & 4.94 & 4.83 \\ 3.25 & 4.60 & 4.60 \\ 4.83 & 4.60 & 4.83 \end{bmatrix}$	$\begin{bmatrix} .08 \\ -.34 \\ .26 \end{bmatrix}$	$\begin{bmatrix} -.48 \\ .22 \\ .26 \end{bmatrix}$	4.49	$\begin{bmatrix} 4.09 & 4.79 & 4.83 \\ 3.67 & 4.37 & 4.41 \\ 4.27 & 4.97 & 5.02 \end{bmatrix}$	$.066 = \sqrt{\frac{.7964}{183.88}}$

• OPTIMAL SCALING

Raw Data $O' = [2\ 2\ 2\ 5\ 5\ 5\ 5\ 7\ 7]$

Model Estimates $\hat{Z}' = [4.09\ 3.67\ 4.97\ 4.37\ 4.83\ 4.41\ 5.01\ 4.27\ 4.79]$

Permuted M.E. $\hat{Z}' = [3.67\ 4.09\ 4.97\ 4.37\ 4.41\ 4.83\ 5.01\ 4.27\ 4.79]$

First Try $U' = I$ and $Z^U = \hat{Z}$

Second Try

$$U' = \begin{bmatrix} 1&0&0&0&0&0&0&0&0 \\ 0&1&0&0&0&0&0&0&0 \\ 0&0&1&1&0&0&0&0&0 \\ 0&0&0&0&1&0&0&0&0 \\ 0&0&0&0&0&1&0&0&0 \\ 0&0&0&0&0&0&1&1&0 \\ 0&0&0&0&0&0&0&0&1 \end{bmatrix}$$

$Z^{U'} = [3.67\ 4.09\ 4.67\ 4.67\ 4.41\ 4.83\ 4.64\ 4.64\ 4.79]$

Third Try

$$U' = \begin{bmatrix} 1&0&0&0&0&0&0&0&0 \\ 0&1&0&0&0&0&0&0&0 \\ 0&0&1&1&1&0&0&0&0 \\ 0&0&0&0&0&1&1&1&0 \\ 0&0&0&0&0&0&0&0&1 \end{bmatrix}$$

$Z^{U'} = [3.67\ 4.09\ 4.58\ 4.58\ 4.58\ 4.70\ 4.70\ 4.70\ 4.79]$

• NORMALIZATION AND FIT

$B = \frac{\|\|\hat{Z}\|\|}{\|\|Z^U\|\|}$	Z^*	Stress
$1.004 = \frac{183.05}{182.34}$	$\begin{bmatrix} 4.10 & 4.79 & 4.72 \\ 3.68 & 4.60 & 4.60 \\ 4.72 & 4.60 & 4.72 \end{bmatrix}$	$.053 = \sqrt{\frac{.525}{183.61}} = \sqrt{\frac{.523}{183.05}}$

Figure 7
Continuous-Ordinal ADDALS example

MORALS ALGORITHM

START:	Read Y and X and their measurement characteristics.	
	Set $Y^* = Y$ and $X^* = X$.	Initialization
MODEL:	$\beta = (X^{*\prime}X^*)^{-1}X^*Y^*$	Model Parameters
FIT:	Calculate multiple R^2. If it hasn't improved "enough" from last iteration, quit.	Termination
SCALE:	$\hat{Y} = X^*\beta$	Model Estimates
	$Y^U = U_Y(U_Y'U_Y)^{-1}U_Y'\hat{Y}$	Optimal Scaling
	$Y^* = Y^U\left(\frac{\|\|\hat{Y}\|\|}{\|\|Y^U\|\|}\right)$	Normalization
LOOP:	For J=1,M variables	
	$\hat{X}_J = \frac{1}{\beta_J}(Y^* - \sum_{I \neq J}\beta_I X_I^*)$	Model Estimates
	$X_J^U = U_J(U_J'U_J)^{-1}U_J'\hat{X}$	Optimal Scaling
LOOPEND:	$X_J^* = X_J^U\left(\frac{\|\|\hat{X}_J\|\|}{\|\|X_J^U\|\|}\right)$	Normalization
	GO TO MODEL	

Figure 8
The major steps in the MORALS algorithm

instead of two sets, each set having mixed measurement variables [OVERALS, by Gifi, 1981]. Closely related is the PATHALS algorithm for path analysis with mixed measurement level data [Gifi, 1981], and the CRIMINALS algorithm for discriminant analysis with mixed measurement level predictors [Gifi, 1981].

The reason we choose to discuss the MORALS algorithm is because it is the simplest algorithm that involves the concept of measurement partitions, a concept not illustrated by the ADDALS algorithm. The partitions notion, discussed in section 2.5, is very appropriate to multivariate data, since it is usually the case that the observations on one variable are not directly comparable to those on another variable.

The structure of the MORALS algorithm is presented in Figure 8. In this figure $\underline{y}$ is a vector of K raw observations on one dependent variable, and $\underline{X}$ is a matrix of K raw observations on M independent variables. Each of the M+1 variables has its own measurement characteristics and has its own partition. Thus, there are M+1 partitions, M+1 indicator matrices, and M+1 optimal scaling steps.

The START step is similar to that used in the ADDALS algorithm: The initial "optimally scaled" data are simply the raw data. The MODEL step is simply a multiple regression analysis of the optimally scaled variables y* and X*. The FIT step is similar to the ADALS FIT step.

The new aspect is the SCALE step. Notice that it is divided into two major sections, the first for the single dependent variable (at step SCALE), and the second for the M independent variables (at step LOOP). For each variable we calculate the model's estimate of that variable ($\hat{\underline{y}}$ or $\hat{\underline{x}}_j$), then use the estimate with the appropriate indicator matrix ($\underline{U}_y$ or $\underline{U}_j$) to calculate the unnormalized optimally scaled data ($\underline{y}^u$ or $\underline{x}_j^u$), and then perform the normalization to obtain $\underline{y}^*$ or $\underline{x}_j^*$. Notice that the newly computed $\underline{y}^*$ or $\underline{x}_j^*$ replace their previous values. The model estimate equation for the dependent variable is straightforward, and the one for the independent variable has been explained by Young, de Leeuw and Takane [1976]. The scaling and normalization steps are the same as with the other algorithms.

The difference, then, is that we have several partitions and that we do the model estimation, scaling, and normalization for each one. It is important to point out that the partitions are <u>not independent</u>, that is, the values being calculated for one partition are dependent on the values calculated for all other partitions. To assure convergence and to maintain the ALS aspect of an algorithm with nonindependent partitions we must immediately replace the previous scaled data with the newly computed (normalized) scaled data.

The nonindependence of the partitions also brings up another important point. If, after the LOOPEND in Figure 8 we return to step SCALE instead of step MODEL, and if we repeated the scaling of each variable, we would obtain a new and different scaling which would fit better than before. Thus, to make the scaling of all variables least squares (in an overall sense) we would have to perform "inner" iterations on the scaling of the variables until convergence is reached on their scaling. However, we have found this to be inefficient, and instead return to the MODEL step to obtain improved values for the model parameters.

3.3 The ALSCAL Algorithm

Most of the procedures that have been developed on the ALSOS principle are simple in the model estimation phase. For example the PRINCIPALS and PRINCIP procedures apply the principal components model to mixed measurement level multivariate data [Young, Takane, & de Leeuw, 1978; de Leeuw & van Rijkevorsel, Note 4]. For these algorithms the model estimation phase is nothing more than a standard eigenvalue decomposition of the optimally scaled data.

The only procedure that involves a fairly complicated model estimation phase is the ALSCAL algorithm [Young, Takane, & Lewyckyj, 1978, 1980; Young & Lewyckyj, 1979, 1980] for performing individual differences multidimensional scaling [Takane, Young, & de Leeuw, 1977]. However, the complexity of the model estimation phase lies in the very nature of the model: There are several sets of parameters that are not mutually independent (as, for example, are the several sets of parameters of the additive model) and that are not all linearly related to the loss function (as is also the case in the additive model). These characteristics of the model can be seen from the equation defining the model:

$$\hat{z}_{ijk} = \sum_{a=1}^{t} v_{ia} w_{ka} (x_{ia} - y_{ja})^2 \qquad (41)$$

where $\hat{z}_{ijk}$ is a tabular reorganization of the model estimates $\hat{\underline{z}}$, with subscripts i and j referring to objects or events about which we have some sort of similarity information, and subscript k referring to situations (subjects, experimental conditions, etc.) under which the similarity information is observed. The parameters v_{ia} are "stimulus weights" of the asymmetric Euclidean model [Young, 1975b], w_{ka} are subject weights of the individual differences model discussed by Carroll and Chang [1970] and Horan [1969], x_{ia} are stimulus object points in a Euclidean space, and y_{ja} are ideal points for Coombs' unfolding model [1964] or attribute points for preference data.

When we say that the several sets of parameters are not mutually independent we mean that estimating the values of at least one set of parameters involves estimates already obtained for at least one of the other sets of parameters. When parameters are not independent, the values of the parameters in one set affect the values estimated for the parameters in the other set. This way of looking at the difficulty immediately suggests a solution to the problem, however. All we have to do is to define an ALS "inner" iteration that estimates parameters, one set at a time. Thus, for ALSCAL, which is based on the model in (41), the inner iteration has four phases each using the values of the parameters in three of the sets (and the optimally scaled data) to obtain conditional least squares estimates for the parameters in the fourth set. Once the parameters in a set are estimated, they are immediately used to replace their old values, and the procedure moves on to another one of the four model parameter sets. This four phase ALS procedure could be iterated until convergence is obtained (there would be inner iterations).

Actually, ALSCAL does not use the inner iteration procedure outlined in the previous paragraph. It would be very slow to require the inner iterations of the model estimation phase to converge before going on to the optimal scaling phase. Experience shows that we should only cycle through the four phases of the inner iteration once, defining that to be a complete model estimation phase. Note that the considerations about nonindependent data partitions apply in precisely the same fashion to nonindependent model parameter sets.

The second source of complexity in the ALSCAL algorithm is the nonlinear relationship between the stimulus-object points x_{ia} and y_{ja} and the model estimates $\hat{z}_{ijk}$. We do not go into this problem here except to say that the solution we use is to apply the ALS principle yet a third time (defining what might be called "innermost" iterations) to estimate the conditional least squares value for a single point's coordinates, one coordinate at a time, under the assumption that all of the other coordinates are constant. This innermost iteration involves n*t phases, one for each of the n points on each of the t dimensions.

The ALSCAL algorithm involves a concept that does not arise in the other algorithms: The parameters of the model are not mututally independent. The algorithm, then, serves to illustrate on method for coping with parameter dependence, namely the use of inner iterations to reapply the ALS principle. The algorithm also serves to illustrate that we do not have to iterate the inner iterations until convergence is reached (one "iteration can suffice).

As mentioned above, the notion of inner iteration is involved in the ALSOS system in one other critical place: the method for optimally scaling data that are partitioned into dependent partitions. When we view the observation categories as parameters and the optimal scale values assigned to each category as parameter values, then we see that we need knowledge of some parameter values in estimating other parameter values. This is precisely the definition of dependence given above, except that the problem occurs in the optimal scaling phase of the algorithm instead of in the model estimation phase. Note that data partitions are not always dependent [for example, the data partitions discussed by de Leeuw, Young, & Takane, 1976, for ADDALS, and by Takane, Young, & de Leeuw, 1977, for ALSCAL are independent] just as parameters are not always dependent. However, when dependence exists the ALS inner iteration approach is a viable approach to deal with the problem.

4. CONCLUSIONS

The combination of alternating least squares and optimal scaling, which forms the foundation of the ALSOS approach to algorithm construction, has two primary advantages: (a) If a least squares procedure is known for analyzing numerical data, then it can be used to analyze qualitative data simply by alternating the procedure with the optimal scaling procedure appropriate to the qualitative data; and (b) under certain fairly general circumstances the resulting ALSOS algorithm is convergent and has no difficulties associated with estimating step size. It is the opinion of the author that the second advantage implies that ALSOS algorithms have fewer local minimum problems than gradient procedures which require step-size estimation.

We do not mean to imply that an ALSOS algorithm is the be-all and end-all of algorithms. It is not. It is simply a relatively straightforward approach to algorithm construction which has certain nice convergence properties. The resulting algorithm may not be very simple. With ALSCAL, for example, even though each step is not very complicated, the overall structure is rather complex due to the necessity of inner and innermost iterations. Furthermore, in some circumstances there are some indeterminacies of construction that may have great effect on the overall speed of the algorithm (such as the number of inner iterations performed on each outer iteration). Finally, perhaps the biggest drawback is that the ALSOS approach does not guarantee convergence on the global optimum, but on a potentially local optimum. Since the convergence point is conditional on the initialization point, it is sometimes the case that the initialization procedure can become very complicated, and may be very crucial. We conclude, however, that the ALSOS approach to algorithm construction provides flexible and well-behaved methods for quantitative analysis of qualitative data.

REFERENCE NOTES

1. Tenenhaus, M. Principal components analysis of qualitative variables. Report No. 175/1981. Jouy-en-Josas, France, Centre d'Enseignement Superieur des Affaires, 1981.
2. Tenenhaus, M. Principal components analysis of qualitative variables. Les Cahiers de Recherche No. 175/1981. Jouy-en-Josas, France, CESA, 1981.
3. de Leeuw, J. A normalized cone regression approach to alternating least squares algorithms. Unpublished note, University of Leiden, 1977b.
4. de Leeuw, J., & van Rijkevorsel, J. How to use HOMALS 3. A program for principal components analysis of mixed data which uses the alternating least squares method. Unpublished mimeo, Leiden University, 1976.
5. Young, F.W., Null, C.H., & De Soete, G. The general Euclidean Model. (in preparation).

REFERENCES

Benzecri, J.P., L'analyse des donnees - Tome II: Correspondances Dunod, Paris, 1973.

Benzecri, J.P., Histoire et Prehistoire de l'analyse des donnees; l'analyse des correspondence. Les Cahiers de l'Analyse des Donnees (Volume II), Paris, 1977.

Bock, R.D., Methods and applications of optimal scaling. Psychometric Laboratory Report #25, University of North Carolina, 1960.

Burt, C., Scale analysis and factor analysis. British Journal of Statistical Psychology, Statistical Section, 1950, 3, 166-185.

Burt, C., Scale analysis and factor analysis. British Journal of Statistical Psychology, 1953, 6, 5-24.

Carroll, J.D. & Chang, J.J., Analysis of individual differences in multi-dimensional scaling via an n-way generalization of "Eckart-Young" decomposition. Psychometrika, 1970, 35, 283-319.

Coombs, C.H., A Theory of Data. New York: Wiley, 1964.

de Leeuw, J., Canonical analysis of categorical data. University of Leiden, The Netherlands, 1973.

de Leeuw, J. Normalized cone regression. Leiden, The Netherlands: University of Leiden, Data Theory, mimeographed paper, 1975.

de Leeuw, J., Correctness of Kruskal's algorithms for monotone regression with ties. Psychometrika, 1977a, 42, 141-144.

de Leeuw, J., Young, F.W. & Takane, Y., Additive structure in qualitative data: An alternating least squares method with optimal scaling features. Psychometrika, 1976, 41, 471-503.

Fisher, R. Statistical methods for research workers. (10th ed.) Edinburgh: Oliver and Boyd, 1938.

Gifi, A., Nonlinear multivariate analysis (preliminary version). University of Leiden, Data Theory Department, 1981.

Guttman, L., The quantification of a class of attributes: A theory and method of scale construction. In P. Horst (Ed.), The prediction of personal adjustment. New York: Social Science Research Council, 1941.

Gutmann, L., A note on Sir Cyril Burt's "Factorial Analysis of Qualitative Data," The British Journal of Statistical Psychology, 1953, 7, 1-4.

Hageman, L.A., & Porsching, T.A., Aspects of nonlinear block successive over-relaxation. SIAM Journal of Numerical Analysis, 1975, 12, 316-335.

Hayashi, C., On the quantification of qualitative data from the mathematico-statistical point of view. Annals of the Institute of Statistical Mathematics, 1950, 2, 35-47.

Horan, C.B., Multidimensional scaling: Combining observations when individuals have different perceptual structures. Psychometrika, 1969, 34, 139-165.

Kruskal, J.B., Nonmetric multidimensional scaling. Psychometrika, 1964, 29, 1-27, 115-129.

Kruskal, J.B., Analysis of factorial experiments by estimating monotone transformations of the data. Journal of the Royal Statistical Society, Series B, 1965, 27, 251-263.

Kruskal, J.B. & Carroll, J.D., Geometric models and badness-of-fit functions. In P.R. Krishnaiah (Ed.), Multivariate analysis (Vol. 2).

Mardia, K.V., Kent, J.T., & Bibby, J.M., Multivariate analysis. London: Academic Press, 1979.

Nishisato, S., Analysis of categorical data: Dual scaling and its applications. University of Toronto Press, 1980.

Roskam, E.E., Metric analysis of ordinal data in psychology. Voorschoten, Holland: VAM, 1968.

Saito, T., Quantification of categorical data by using the generalized variance. Soken Kiyo, Nippon UNIVAC Sogo Kenkyn-Sho, 61-80, 1973.

Sands, R. & Young, F.W., Component models for three-way data: An alternating least squares algorithm with optimal scaling features. Psychometrika, 1980, 45, 39-67.

Saporta, G., Liasons entre plusieurs ensembles de variables et codages de donnes qualitatives. These de Doctorat de 3eme cycle, Paris, 1975.

Takane, Y., Young, F.W. & de Leeuw, J., Nonmetric individual differences multidimensional scaling: An alternating least squares method with optimal scaling features. Psychometrika, 1977, 42, 7-67.

Takane, Y., Young, F.W. & de Leeuw, J., An individual differences additive model: An alternating least squares method with optimal scaling features. Psychometrika, 1980, 45, 183-209.

Torgerson, W.S., Theory and methods of scaling. New York: Wiley, 1958.

Wold, H. & Lyttkens, E., Nonlinear iterative partial least squares (NIPALS) estimation procedures. Bulletin ISI, 1969, 43, 29-47.

Young, F.W., A model for polynomial conjoint analysis algorithms. In R.N. Shepard, A.K. Romney & S. Nerlove (Eds.), Multidimensional scaling: Theory and applications in the behavioral sciences. New York: Academic Press, 1972.

Young, F.W., Methods for describing ordinal data with cardinal models. Journal of Mathematical Psychology, 1975a, 12, 416-436.

Young, F.W., An asymmetric Euclidian model for multi-process asymmetric data. U.S.-Japan Seminar on Multidimensional Scaling, 1975b.

Young, F.W., de Leeuw, J. & Takane, Y., Multiple (and canonical) regression with a mix of qualitative and quantitative variables: An alternating least squares method with optimal scaling features. Psychometrika, 1976, 41, 505-529.

Young, F.W. & Lewyckyj, R., ALSCAL Users Guide. Carrboro, NC: Data Analysis and Theory, 1979.

Young, F.W. & Lewyckyj, R., The ALSCAL procedure. In SAS Supplemental Library User's Guide, Reinhardt, P. (Ed.). SAS Institute, Raleigh, NC, 1980.

Young, F.W. & Null, C.H., Multidimensional scaling of nominal data: The recovery of metric information with ALSCAL. Psychometrika, 1978, 43, 367-379.

Young, F.W., Takane, Y. & de Leeuw, J., The principal components of mixed measurement level data: An alternating least squares method with optimal scaling features. Psychometrika, 1978, 43, 279-282.

Young, F.W., Takane, Y., & Lewyckyj, R., ALSCAL: A nonmetric multidimensional scaling program with several individual differences options. Behavioral Research Methods and Instrumentation, 1978, 10, 451-453.

Young, F.W., Takane, Y., & Lewyckyj, R., ALSCAL: A multidimensional scaling package with several individual differences options. American Statistician, 1980, 34, 117-118.

Yule, F.U., An introduction to the theory of statistics. London: Griffin, 1910.

[1]Reprinted with permission from Psychometrika, 1981, 46, 357-388. Presented as the Presidential Address to the Psychometric Society, May, 1981. I wish to express my deep appreciation to Jan de Leeuw and Yoshio Takane. Our "team effort" was essential for the developments reported in this paper. Portions of this paper appear in Lantermann, E.D. & Feger, H. (Eds.) Similarity and Choice, Hans Huber, Vienna, 1980. The present paper benefits greatly from a set of detailed comments made by Joseph Kruskal on the earlier paper.

COMPUTER SCIENCE AND STATISTICS:
The Interface, L. Billard (ed.)
© Elsevier Science Publishers B.V. (North-Holland), 1985

A COMPARISON OF THE ACE AND MORALS ALGORITHMS IN AN APPLICATION TO ENGINE EXHAUST EMISSIONS MODELING

Robert N. Rodriguez
SAS Institute

Abstract

This is the text of the prepared discussion for the session on "Optimal Transformations in Regression". The ACE and MORALS algorithms are applied to an analysis of engine emissions data, and similarities and differences between the algorithms are summarized.

1. Introduction

The interface between statistics and computer technology is clearly evident in the presentations by Jerome Friedman and Forrest Young:

1. The problem of determining suitable transformations for regression variables is encountered in many areas of statistical application, and it is increasingly the subject of theoretical research.

2. The solutions described by Friedman and Young are computer algorithms whose output is most easily understood graphically.

In practice, the algorithms have been applied to a variety of problems, and, as Young has shown, the methods extend beyond a regression setting. In a different direction, considerable theoretical work--much of it by Leo Breiman in connection with ACE--has been done to prove that the algorithms perform optimally.

While this breadth is one of the most intriguing aspects of the methods described by Friedman and Young, it precludes a thorough discussion in the space available here. Instead, I will simply compare the methods in the context of a specific application.

In what follows, I will use the acronym ACE to refer to the preliminary version of the "alternating conditional expectations" algorithm introduced by Breiman and Friedman (1). A newer version of ACE, which implements an improved smoother, is under development at Stanford, but was not available at the time this discussion was written.

There is also more than one version of the MORALS ("Multiple Optimal Regression by Alternating Least Squares") algorithm introduced by Young et al. (4). Here, I will refer to the version that is outlined in Figure 8 of the paper by Young in this Proceedings volume. (This is also Figure 8 in Young (3).)

2. Ethanol Engine Data: Some Background

The problem that I will consider arises from an experiment carried out by Brinkman (2) to measure the efficiency and exhaust emissions of a single-cylinder engine running on ethanol.

Ethanol has gained support as an important alternative automotive fuel, and in Brazil, vehicles which operate entirely on ethanol are being manufactured. In order to design any engine, it is necessary to know how engine efficiency and exhaust emissions vary with engine and fuel parameters. But unlike experiments performed with gasoline engines, there have been few studies of ethanol engines.

Brinkman's tests were conducted to provide previously unavailable data for quantifying the effects of two specific engine parameters, air-fuel equivalence ratio and compression ratio, on efficiency and emissions. In addition to tests in which the fuel was pure ethanol, Brinkman included tests in which the fuel was clear Indolene, the gasoline used in the United States to certify compliance to emission standards. Consequently, the gasoline-to-ethanol effect of fuel on emissions can be estimated.

Brinkman analyzed his data by building regression models for five separate response variables: engine efficiency and four different emissions. The models subsequently formed the basis for conclusions about the tradeoffs between efficiency and emissions. Here, we will focus on one of the emissions, nitrogen oxide (NOx measured in $\mu g/J$).

Appendix B of Brinkman's paper summarizes two regression models for NOx, one for ethanol and one for gasoline. The independent variables are compression ratio (CR) and equivalence ratio (ϕ). (Equivalence ratio is defined as the ratio of stoichiometric air-fuel ratio to actual air-fuel ratio.)

From the start, Brinkman realized the need for transforming these variables in order to obtain close-fitting models. He identified his transformations with stepwise regression, selecting terms from mixed polynomials involving powers--up to and including the fourth power--of compression ratio and equivalence ratio. The log transformation of NOx was taken to further improve the fit.

In the ethanol model for log(NOx), the "significant" terms are the intercept, ϕ, CR, ϕ^2, ϕCR, ϕ^3, ϕ^2CR, ϕ^4, and ϕ^3CR. In the gasoline model for log(NOx), the "significant" terms are the intercept, ϕ^2, ϕ^3, and ϕ^4. (Mixed terms do not appear in the gasoline model, since the Indolene tests were conducted at a single compression ratio.) For both models, the value of r^2 is 0.99.

Brinkman was mainly interested in "passing curves through the data", but the complexity (and hence the stability and interpretability) of the fitted models was also a concern. When he later brought this problem to my attention, he raised the following question: What methods other than stepwise regression might be used to identify simpler transformations, even at the expense of a decrease in r^2?

3. Application of Nonparametric Regression

The ACE and MORALS algorithms are practical alternatives to stepwise regression in this problem, provided that one assumes an **additive** model for the data. In response to Brinkman's question, I applied ACE and MORALS to the combined data (110 observations in all) which he obtained from tests with ethanol and Indolene. Rather than analyzing the ethanol and gasoline data separately, I took fuel as the third independent variable in a single model, in order to be able to estimate the fuel effect.

The data are listed below in the Appendix, since they are not provided in Brinkman's paper (2). Note that the variables have different measurement characteristics: Equivalence ratio and NOx are both continuous and numerical. Compression ratio is a continuous, numerical quantity but was set at discrete values in the experiment. Fuel is a nominal variable with two discrete values.

4. Transformation Types

Before applying ACE and MORALS, one must decide whether the transformation for each variable is to be general (possibly not monotone), monotone, or linear (equivalent to not making a transformation).

Since it is known from combustion theory that the dependence of NOx on equivalence ratio is not monotone, equivalence ratio is a natural candidate for a general transformation. However, when this transformation is computed, a major difference between ACE and MORALS becomes apparent: whereas general ACE transformations can be determined directly for continuous numerical variables, general MORALS transformations cannot be determined unless the values of such variables are first grouped (treated as discrete).

In our applications of MORALS (but not ACE), we grouped the values of equivalence ratio into the eight equally spaced intervals (0.5,0.6), (0.6,0.7), ..., (1.2,1.3), including the left endpoint in each interval, and taking the midpoint of each interval as the grouped value.

Grouping was not necessary in order to obtain general MORALS transformations for compression ratio, since these values were assigned discretely in the experiment.

We tried three combinations of transformation types for NOx: In our first run, we used a general ACE and a monotone MORALS transformation for NOx. In a second run, we tried a monotone ACE and a monotone MORALS transformation for NOx (to allow direct comparison). Finally, in a third run, we specified a linear ACE and a linear MORALS transformation for NOx.

5. R^2 Values

The values of r^2 for each run are given in Table 1. For ACE, r^2 corresponds to $1-e^2$ in Friedman's notation. For MORALS, r^2 is the "multiple R^2" obtained from the final regression step in the algorithm.

Table 1

	NOX TRANSFORMATION			
RUN	ACE	MORALS	R^2 (ACE)	R^2 (MORALS)
1	General	Monotone	0.94	0.85
2	Monotone	Monotone	0.95	0.85
3	Linear	Linear	0.93	0.88

On the whole, there is little variation among the r^2 values for each method. All of the r^2 values are substantially higher than the r^2 of 0.23 obtained with a standard multiple regression model for NOx involving no transformations. The r^2 values for MORALS are consistently slightly lower than the values for ACE, because the equivalence ratios were grouped.

Other measures of fit can be quoted. For instance, one might report Kruskal's Stress index, which is analogous to the square root of $1-r^2$. Moreover, as pointed out by a member of the session audience, r^2 and e^2 can have very different interpretations!

6. Transformation Plots

The transformations obtained for NOx, equivalence ratio, and compression ratio are plotted in Figures 1, 2, and 3, which correspond to Runs 1, 2, and 3.

An obvious difference between the ACE and MORALS transformations is that the ACE transformations are smooth, whereas the MORALS transformations are discrete. (Of course, the ACE curves in the Figures should not be interpreted as smooth fits to the MORALS points.) Smoothing is important in this application, since it allows the fitted response to be interpolated for compression ratios and equivalence ratios not observed in the experiment.

In Figure 1a, the general ACE transformation of NOx is essentially monotone and nearly linear. The MORALS transformation of NOx is monotone by construction, and seems to exhibit more bending, depending on how one perceives the "steps". Both of the transformations for equivalence ratio shown in Figure 1b are non-monotonic, and they are shaped similarly except for slight shifts in peaks (possibly due to grouping). In Figure 1c, the ACE transformation for compression ratio is nearly linear, whereas there is a pronounced bend in the corresponding MORALS transformation.

These results are nearly duplicated in Figures 2a, 2b, and 2c for the second run, in which monotone ACE and MORALS transformations are specified for NOx. This is not surprising, since the general ACE transformation for NOx in Figure 1a turned out to be monotone.

The discrepancy between the ACE and MORALS transformations for compression ratio in Figures 1c and 2c is harder to explain. There are 44 observations at the lowest compression ratio, but the distribution of compression ratios is otherwise balanced, and there is no reason to suspect that the NOx values at high compression ratios are outliers. The linearity of the ACE transformations may be due to excessive smoothing. (The values set for the smoother parameters were ALPHA=0.1, RESPAN=0.25, and IBIN=1, and modifying them made little difference in the transformation for compression ratio.) It will be interesting to regenerate these transformations using the newer version of ACE.

The linear ACE and linear MORALS transformations for NOx in Figure 3a are identical. The transformations for equivalence ratio in Figure 3b have the same shape as those in Figures 1b and 2b. However, the bend in the MORALS transformations of compression ratio in Figures 1c and 2c is not evident in Figure 3c.

7. Uses of the Nonparametric Models

Since the transformations of NOx are approximately linear in all three runs, the transformation plots for the independent variables can be interpreted as their marginal effects on NOx. For instance, Figure 3B tells us that for any fixed combination of fuel and compression ratio, NOx peaks at an equivalence ratio of $\phi_0=0.90$.

The standard deviations given in the Figure captions are a measure of how strongly the transformed independent variables enter into the model for the transformation of NOx. In the case of FUEL, the standard deviations are around 0.31 (ACE) and 0.34 (MORALS) for the three runs. Therefore, equivalence ratio enters most strongly, followed by fuel and compression ratio.

The transformed values of FUEL (not plotted) provide estimates of the marginal fuel effect. In Run 3, ACE yielded transformed values of 0.627 for Indolene and -0.157 for ethanol, while MORALS yielded transformed values of 0.676 for Indolene and -0.169 for ethanol. (Similar results were obtained for the other runs.) We can use these quantities to estimate the additive effect of FUEL on NOx as follows: The linear transformation of NOx in Figure 3a has the equation

$$\hat{\theta}^*(\mathrm{NOx}) = 0.730(\mathrm{NOx}) - 1.661 \ .$$

Applying the inverse of this transformation to the **difference** of the transformed ACE values for ethanol and Indolene, we find that the impact of replacing Indolene with ethanol is a 1.07 µg/J **decrease** in NOx. Using the transformed MORALS values, the impact is a 1.16 µg/J decrease.

Unfortunately, this approach does not give us confidence intervals for the Indolene-to-ethanol effect. However, the computer run times in this example were fast enough (around 0.46 seconds for ACE on an IBM 3081) that one could bootstrap the algorithms, as pointed out by Friedman, in order to obtain pseudo-confidence intervals.

One additional limitation should be mentioned. Although it seems natural to invert the ACE and MORALS transformations for NOx in order to predict NOx for unobserved combinations of equivalence ratio and compression ratio, ACE and MORALS are optimal for regression rather than prediction. Friedman briefly described PACE, a "predictive ACE" algorithm recently developed at Stanford which would provide the best **predictive** model for NOx. (I suspect that the differences

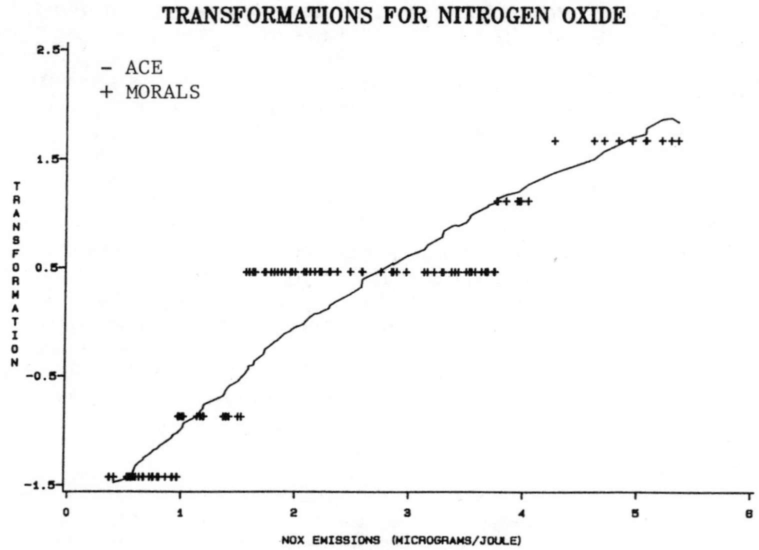

Figure 1a.
General ACE and monotone MORALS transformations for NOx.

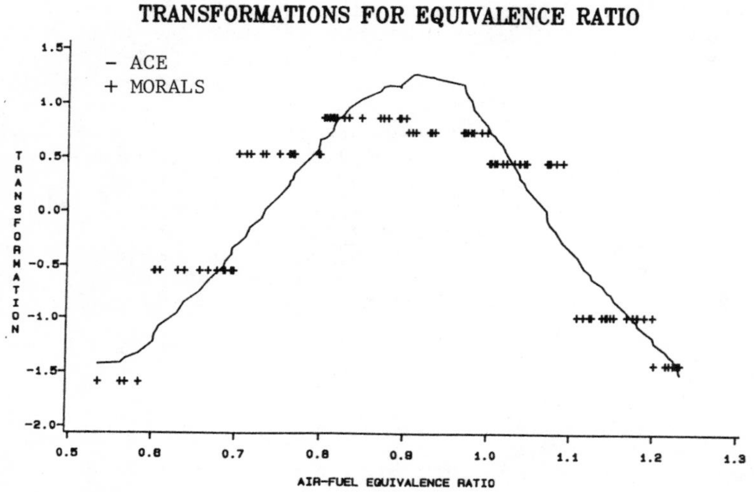

Figure 1b.
Transformations for equivalence ratio. The standard deviations of the transformed values are 0.87 (ACE) and 0.84 (MORALS). General ACE and monotone MORALS transformations are assumed for NOx.

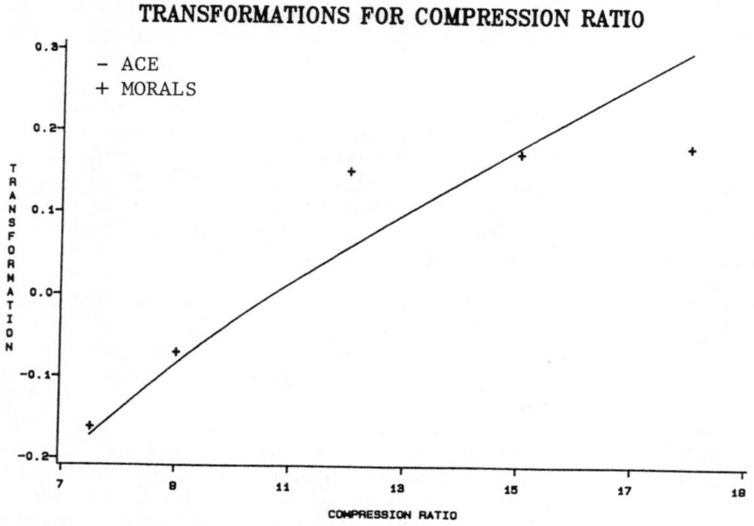

Figure 1c.
Transformations for compression ratio. The standard deviations of the transformed values are 0.18 (ACE) and 0.15 (MORALS). General ACE and monotone MORALS transformations are assumed for NOx.

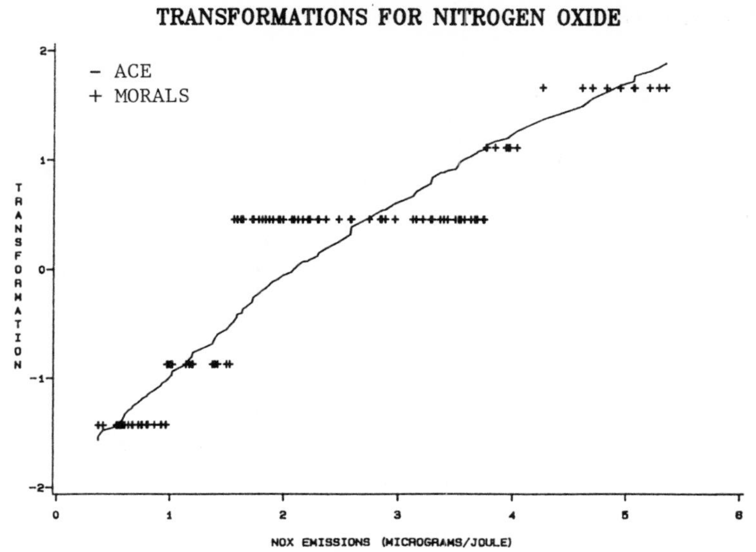

Figure 2a.
Monotone ACE and monotone MORALS transformations for NOx.

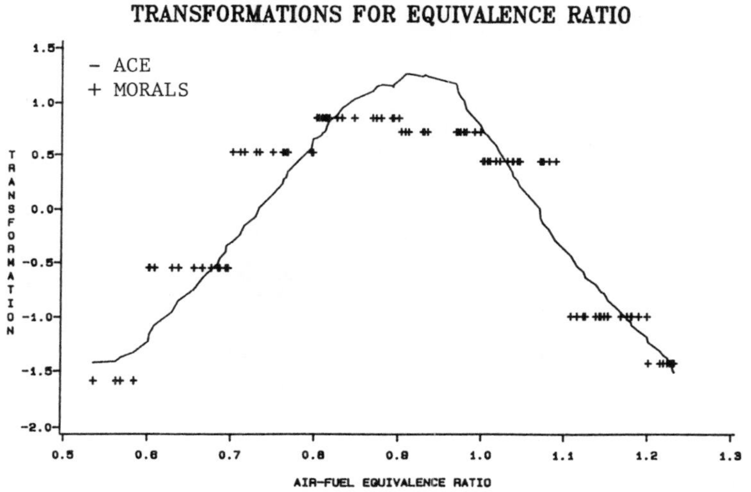

Figure 2b.
Transformations for equivalence ratio. The standard deviations of the transformed values are 0.88 (ACE) and 0.84 (MORALS). Monotone ACE and monotone MORALS transformations are assumed for NOx.

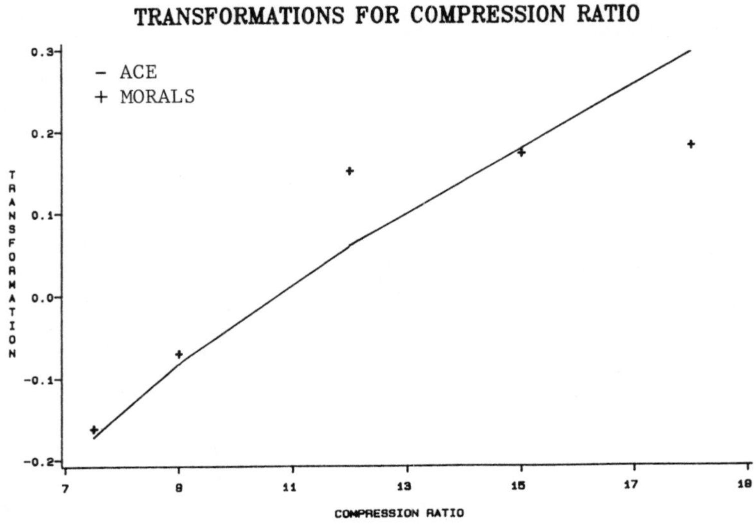

Figure 2c.
Transformations for compression ratio. The standard deviations of the transformed values are 0.18 (ACE) and 0.15 (MORALS). Monotone ACE and monotone MORALS transformations are assumed for NOx.

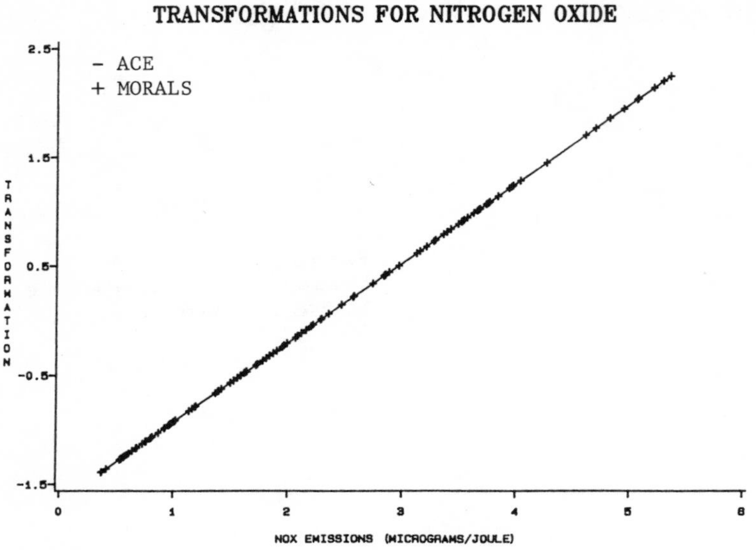

Figure 3a.
Linear ACE and linear MORALS transformations for NOx.

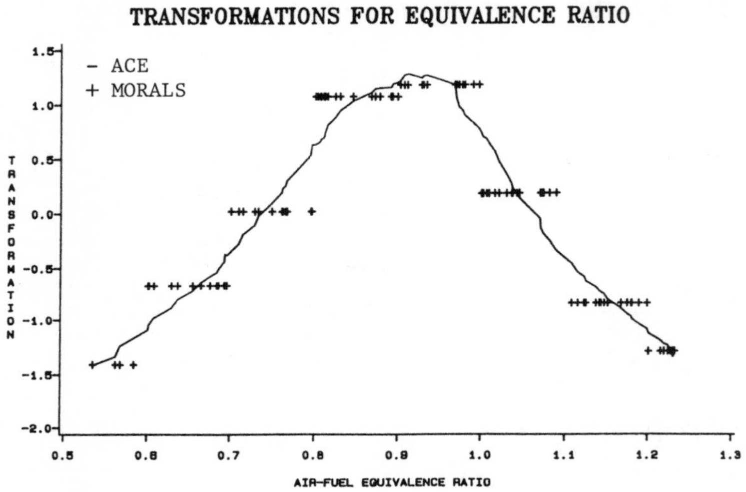

Figure 3b.
Transformations for equivalence ratio. The standard deviations of the transformed values are 0.83 (ACE) and 0.86 (MORALS). Linear ACE and linear MORALS transformations are assumed for NOx.

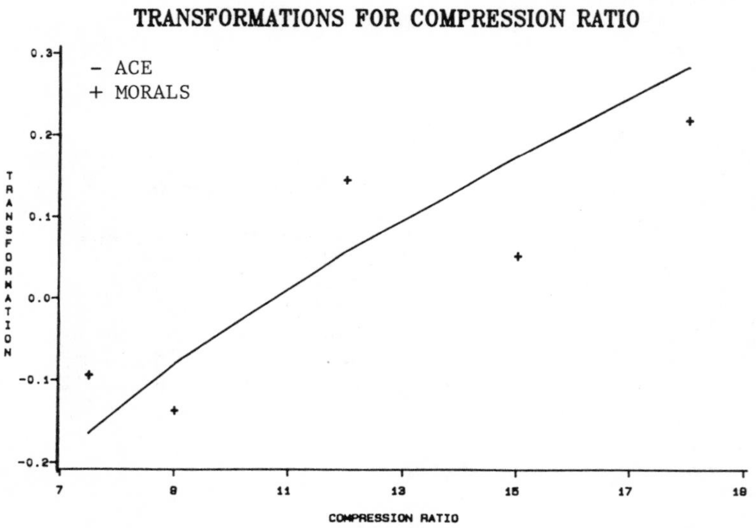

Figure 3c.
Transformations for compression ratio. The standard deviations of the transformed values are 0.17 (ACE) and 0.13 (MORALS). Linear ACE and linear MORALS transformations are assumed for NOx.

between the ACE and PACE transformations for the ethanol data would be minor, since the general ACE transformation for NOx is approximately linear.)

8. Identification of Parametric Models

The plots suggest familiar functional transformations that lead to simplified parametric models for NOx.

A linear transformation for NOx is indicated by the ACE plots in Figures 1a and 2a. One might also consider a log transformation, since there is a mild curvature in the ACE plots, but the log function slightly "over-transforms" NOx. (If Run 3 is redone with log(NOx) as the response, the r^2 value for ACE drops to 0.87.) Using the MORALS plots in Figures 1a and 2a, it is more difficult to decide whether a linear or a log transformation is appropriate for NOx.

In Figures 1c and 2c, ACE suggests a linear transformation for compression ratio, while MORALS suggests a log transformation. Both methods suggest a quadratic transformation for equivalence ratio.

The r^2 values for parametric models using various combinations of these functional transformations are given in Table 2. As a further aid to model selection, Kolmogorov-Smirnov P-values for tests of normality on the residuals are also shown. Residual normality is not the objective of either ACE or MORALS, but it should be checked if, for example, confidence limits are to be computed subsequently.

Table 2

PARAMETRIC TRANSFORMATIONS

NOx	Compression Ratio	Equivalence Ratio	R^2	K-S P-value For Residuals
Linear	Linear	Quadratic	0.82	>0.15
Linear	Log	Quadratic	0.82	0.10
Log	Linear	Quadratic	0.92	0.08
Log	Log	Quadratic	0.92	>0.11

The first and fourth models in Table 2 fit the data closely without sacrificing normality or functional simplicity:

$$NOx = \alpha_0+\alpha_1 CR+\alpha_2(\phi-\phi_0)^2+\alpha_3 FUEL$$

$$\log(NOx)=\beta_0+\beta_1\log(CR)+\beta_2(\phi-\phi_0)^2+\beta_3 FUEL$$

The least squares estimate of ϕ_0, the "peak" equivalence ratio, is 0.90 under both models.

If we assign the value of 1 to ethanol and the value of 0 to Indolene, the least squares estimate of α_3, the gasoline-to-ethanol impact on NOx, is -1.28 μg/J. (The corresponding 95% confidence limits are -1.60 μg/J and -0.964 μg/J.) The least squares estimate of β_3 is -0.437, which translates to a 35.4% decrease in NOx associated with ethanol. (The corresponding 95% confidence limits translate to decreases of 28.0% and 42.1%.)

Since the purpose of Brinkman's experiment was to quantify NOx rather than log(NOx), the model for log(NOx) is more conveniently expressed as

$$NOx = \beta_0(CR)^{\beta_1}\exp\{\beta_2(\phi-\phi_0)^2+\beta_3 FUEL\}.$$

Strictly speaking, nonlinear least squares estimation should then be applied to the parameters.

Additional work needs to be done to decide which, if any, of the NOx models we have considered is "best". However, the points to be made here about the ethanol application are that:

1. ACE and MORALS enabled us to identify simplified **parametric** models in a direct fashion.

2. The **nonparametric** models obtained with ACE and MORALS can be used for many of the same purposes as the parametric models.

9. Summary

To conclude, I would like to summarize various aspects of the methods themselves:

Algorithms. ACE and MORALS share some basic properties: For discrete variables, both algorithms compute conditional expectations (conditioning over variables taken one at a time) to minimize the same least squares criterion. For discrete and continuous numerical variables, both algorithms optionally compute Kruskal's monotonic transformation. A fundamental difference in the methods is that ACE incorporates a data smoother, which allows general transformations to be obtained directly for continuous variables. To obtain general transformations of continuous variables with MORALS (as in the case of equivalence ratio), the variable values must first be grouped.

Theory. Convergence of the MORALS and basic ACE algorithms follows from minimization of least squares. For the general ACE algorithm, existence, convergence, and consistency results are obtained with Hilbert space methods.

Transformation plots. Since the two algorithms minimize the same objective function, ACE and MORALS transformation plots have similar shapes--especially for discrete data. The smoothness of ACE plots facilitates interpolation and functional identification, but the smoother itself can influence the shape of the transformation.

Practical advantages. By comparison with methods such as stepwise regression, it is relatively easy for researchers with limited statistical backgrounds to grasp the graphical output from ACE and MORALS. Both ACE and MORALS transform variables with different levels of measurement. Neither algorithm requires distributional assumptions. Both algorithms are useful for parametric model building, and, moreover, the nonparametric models obtained can be applied directly. Run times for both algorithms are reasonable, and convergence problems are seldom encountered in practice.

Practical disadvantages. Additive models are not always adequate; for example, neither MORALS nor ACE may be appropriate in situations where none of the main effects variables require transformation but strong interaction effects are present. To some extent, interaction can be accounted for by transforming functions of two or more main effects; however, these functions must be specified parametrically, and typically their forms will not be known in advance. Neither method provides tests of significance, confidence bands, or confidence limits for parameters (such as the fuel effect on NOx). Neither method is optimal for prediction.

Extensions of the methods. Young emphasized that multiple regression is just one of many types of analysis in which alternating least squares and optimal scaling can be combined; other examples include canonical analysis and analysis of variance. Friedman described two recently developed algorithms which are optimal for prediction and for multiple response problems such as classification.

Interpretation. There are various ways to interpret transformations in a regression analysis. MORALS was originally developed for social and behavioral science applications where transformations are often used to quantify (rescale) qualitative data; there, the user expresses conclusions in the transformed units of measurement. In the applications of ACE that we have seen (including the ethanol data analysis), transformations serve as a tool for building a model which the user interprets or predicts with in the original units of measurement.

The ACE and MORALS algorithms are powerful tools for transforming variables in many kinds of situations, but the question "What do the transformations mean?" must inevitably be answered by the user.

Acknowledgement

I would like to thank Norman D. Brinkman of the Fuels and Lubricants Department, General Motors Research Laboratories, for providing the data listed in the Appendix.

References

1. Breiman, L. and Friedman, J. H., Estimating Optimal Transformations for Multiple Regression and Correlation, ORION 010, Department of Statistics, Stanford University (July 1982).

2. Brinkman, N. D., Ethanol fuel--A single-cylinder engine study of efficiency and exhaust emissions, SAE Transactions 90 (1981) 1410-1424. (SAE Paper Number 810345).

3. Young, F. W., Quantitative analysis of qualitative data, Psychometrika 46 (1981) 357-388.

4. Young, F. W., de Leeuw, J., and Takane, Y., Regression with qualitative and quantitative variables: an alternating least squares method with optimal scaling features, Psychometrika 41 (1976) 505-529.

Appendix: Ethanol and Indolene Data

NITROGEN OXIDE (μg/J)	FUEL	COMPRESSION RATIO	EQUIVALENCE RATIO
3.741	ETHANOL	12.0	0.907
2.295	ETHANOL	12.0	0.761
1.498	ETHANOL	12.0	1.108
2.881	ETHANOL	12.0	1.016
0.760	ETHANOL	12.0	1.189
3.120	ETHANOL	9.0	1.001
0.638	ETHANOL	9.0	1.231
1.170	ETHANOL	9.0	1.123
2.358	ETHANOL	12.0	1.042
0.606	ETHANOL	12.0	1.215
3.669	ETHANOL	12.0	0.930
1.000	ETHANOL	12.0	1.152
0.981	ETHANOL	15.0	1.138
1.192	ETHANOL	18.0	0.601
0.926	ETHANOL	7.5	0.696
1.590	ETHANOL	12.0	0.686
1.806	ETHANOL	12.0	1.072
1.962	ETHANOL	15.0	1.074
4.028	ETHANOL	15.0	0.934
3.148	ETHANOL	9.0	0.808
1.836	ETHANOL	9.0	1.071
2.845	ETHANOL	7.5	1.009
1.013	ETHANOL	7.5	1.142
0.414	ETHANOL	18.0	1.229
0.812	ETHANOL	18.0	1.175

NITROGEN OXIDE (μg/J)	FUEL	COMPRESSION RATIO	EQUIVALENCE RATIO
0.374	ETHANOL	15.0	0.568
3.623	ETHANOL	15.0	0.977
1.869	ETHANOL	7.5	0.767
2.836	ETHANOL	7.5	1.006
3.567	ETHANOL	9.0	0.893
0.866	ETHANOL	15.0	1.152
1.369	ETHANOL	15.0	0.693
0.542	ETHANOL	15.0	1.232
2.739	ETHANOL	15.0	1.036
1.200	ETHANOL	15.0	1.125
1.719	ETHANOL	9.0	1.081
3.423	ETHANOL	9.0	0.868
1.634	ETHANOL	7.5	0.762
1.021	ETHANOL	7.5	1.144
2.157	ETHANOL	7.5	1.045
3.361	ETHANOL	18.0	0.797
1.390	ETHANOL	18.0	1.115
1.947	ETHANOL	18.0	1.070
0.962	ETHANOL	18.0	1.219
0.571	ETHANOL	9.0	0.637
2.219	ETHANOL	9.0	0.733
1.419	ETHANOL	9.0	0.715
3.519	ETHANOL	9.0	0.872
1.732	ETHANOL	7.5	0.765
3.206	ETHANOL	7.5	0.878
2.471	ETHANOL	7.5	0.811
1.777	ETHANOL	15.0	0.676
2.571	ETHANOL	18.0	1.045
3.952	ETHANOL	18.0	0.968
3.931	ETHANOL	15.0	0.846
1.587	ETHANOL	15.0	0.684
1.397	ETHANOL	7.5	0.729
3.536	ETHANOL	7.5	0.911
2.202	ETHANOL	7.5	0.808
0.756	ETHANOL	7.5	1.168
1.620	ETHANOL	7.5	0.749
3.656	ETHANOL	7.5	0.892
2.964	ETHANOL	7.5	1.002
3.760	ETHANOL	18.0	0.812
0.672	ETHANOL	18.0	1.230
3.677	ETHANOL	18.0	0.804
3.517	ETHANOL	12.0	0.813
3.290	ETHANOL	12.0	1.002
1.139	ETHANOL	9.0	0.696
0.727	ETHANOL	9.0	1.199
2.581	ETHANOL	9.0	1.030
0.923	ETHANOL	15.0	0.602
1.527	ETHANOL	15.0	0.694
3.388	ETHANOL	15.0	0.816
2.085	ETHANOL	15.0	1.037
0.966	ETHANOL	15.0	1.181
3.488	ETHANOL	7.5	0.899
0.754	ETHANOL	7.5	1.227
0.797	ETHANOL	9.0	1.180
2.064	ETHANOL	7.5	0.795
3.732	ETHANOL	18.0	0.990
0.586	ETHANOL	18.0	1.201
0.561	ETHANOL	7.5	0.629
0.563	ETHANOL	9.0	0.608
0.678	ETHANOL	12.0	0.584
0.370	ETHANOL	15.0	0.562
0.530	ETHANOL	18.0	0.535
1.900	ETHANOL	18.0	0.655
4.818	INDOLENE	7.5	0.831
2.849	INDOLENE	7.5	1.045
3.275	INDOLENE	7.5	1.021
4.691	INDOLENE	7.5	0.970
4.255	INDOLENE	7.5	0.825
5.064	INDOLENE	7.5	0.891
2.118	INDOLENE	7.5	0.710
4.602	INDOLENE	7.5	0.801
2.286	INDOLENE	7.5	1.074
0.970	INDOLENE	7.5	1.148
3.965	INDOLENE	7.5	1.000
5.344	INDOLENE	7.5	0.928
3.834	INDOLENE	7.5	0.767
1.990	INDOLENE	7.5	0.701
5.199	INDOLENE	7.5	0.807
5.283	INDOLENE	7.5	0.902
3.752	INDOLENE	7.5	0.997
0.537	INDOLENE	7.5	1.224
1.640	INDOLENE	7.5	1.089
5.055	INDOLENE	7.5	0.973
4.937	INDOLENE	7.5	0.980
1.561	INDOLENE	7.5	0.665

Time Series

Organizer: *G. C. Tiao, University of Chicago*

Invited Presentations:

Computer Investigation of Some Non-linear Time Series Models, *Clive Granger, Frank Huynh, Alvaro Escribano and Chowdhury Mustafa, University of California at San Diego*

Model-Based Treatment of a Manic-Depressive Series, *Agustin Maravall, Bank of Spain*

Seasonality and Seasonal Adjustment of Time Series, *Steven Hillmer, University of Kansas*

COMPUTER SCIENCE AND STATISTICS:
The Interface, L. Billard (ed.)

COMPUTER INVESTIGATION OF SOME NON-LINEAR TIME SERIES MODELS

Clive Granger, Frank Huynh, Alvaro Escribano and Chowdhury Mustafa

Department of Economics
University of California, San Diego
La Jolla, CA 92093

Time series modelling has expanded from the classical univariate ARIMA forms to multivariate, time-varying parameter and non-linear models. A new attempt to combine non-theoretical time-series ideas with economic theories results in the error-correction models. An application of some of these methods to forecasting electricity demand is presented at the end of the paper.

1. INTRODUCTION

There is no particular reason to believe that the time series observed in the real world are generated linearly, in fact a non-linear generation process is more likely. One problem with this statement is that the theory for some fields of research, particularly in the social sciences, is not sufficiently advanced that it can suggest the correct functional forms to be used in a non-linear modelling process. This paper will discuss practical techniques for analysis of some simple univariate non-linear models. Although most series are almost certainly generated by a multivariate, causal non-linear mechanism there will always be a sub-optimal, associated univariate model. Experience with linear models suggest that consideration of the univariate model is a useful stepping stone towards building a causal model, as information about the presence of trends, seasonality and the level of integratedness is obtained. A univariate model also provides a useful device against which more complicated models can be compared, in terms of their goodness of fit or forecasting abilities. Any model will be an approximation to the truth and univariate models are a convenient place to start a sequence of models which hopefully provide an increasingly better level of approximation. As they are approximations, not all features of a model have implications about the truth and, in particular, although the approximation is generally adequate, there may be occasions when it is much less than adequate. As an example, consider a series that is generated by a random walk with reflecting barriers, these barriers being far apart and thus only rarely in operation. A linear model, the pure random walk, will be an excellent approximation except near the barriers, when it will be quite inadequate.

This paper will concentrate on non-linear autoregressive (NLAR) models of the form

$$x_{t+1} = f(x_t) + \epsilon_{t+1} \qquad (1.1)$$

where ϵ_t is a zero-mean white noise, that is models that are Markov in the observation time interval for which data is available. Extensions to models with more lags will be considered on some other occasion. Methods whereby the function $f(x)$ can be estimated are considered and the resulting forecasts compared to those from linear and bilinear models. Two particular models of this class will be given special attention, the rational autoregressive models (RAR), one example of which is

$$x_{t+1} = \frac{(a_1 + b_1 x_t + c_1 x_t^2)\, x_t}{a_2 + b_2 x_t + c_2 x_t^2} + \epsilon_{t+1} \qquad (1.2)$$

and series that are almost integrated (AINT) of order 1, generated for example by

$$x_{t+1} = x_t \exp(-x_t^2) + \epsilon_{t+1} \ . \qquad (1.3)$$

RAR models have been considered earlier by Granger and Weiss (1982) and although not necessarily of practical importance, they are useful for generation of non-linear data and to illustrate problems with NLAR models. AINT models are potentially of considerable practical importance and will be discussed separately. The paper should be viewed as just a pilot study on an interesting but complicated topic. More detailed results will be presented elsewhere.

In recent years a number of papers have considered non-linear time series models, a good starting point being Priestley (1980). He reviews several particular models and then places them within a comprehensive, non-linear state-space format. The final state-space representation is too general for practical use in its present state of development. The particular models include threshold autoregressive (Tong and Lin (1980)), an example of which is

$$x_t = a_t x_{t-1} + \epsilon_t$$

where
$$a_t = 1 \quad \text{if} \quad x_{t-1} < 0$$
$$\quad = 2 \quad \text{if} \quad x_{t-1} > 0$$

so that the parameter values of the AR model change in a step-wise fashion as past x's go through thresholds, exponential autoregressive models (Haggan and Ozaki (1980)), an example of which is

$$x_t = (a + b\exp(-\gamma^2 x_{t-1}^2))\,x_{t-1} + \epsilon_t ,$$

and bilinear models, an example of which is

$$x_t = a\,x_{t-1} + b\,x_{t-1}\epsilon_{t-1} + \epsilon_t$$

where ϵ_t is white noise in each example.

If

$$\underline{z}_t = (\epsilon_{t-\ell+1}, \ldots, \epsilon_{t-1}, \epsilon_t, x_{t-k+1}, \ldots, x_{t-1}, x_t)$$

is a vector representing the "state" of the process at time t, Priestley considers non-linear models of the form:

$$x_t + \sum_{j=0}^{k} \phi_j(\underline{z}_{t-1})\,x_{t-j} = \mu(\underline{z}_{t-1}) + \sum_{j=1}^{\ell} \psi_j(\underline{z}_{t-1})\,\epsilon_{t-j} + \epsilon_t$$

that is an ARMA model with coefficients, and mean, varying through time and non-linear functions of the contents of $\underline{z}_{t-1}$. He calls this a 'state-dependent model (SDM) of order (k, ℓ),' and discusses how it can be written in the single lag, state-space vector form

$$\underline{z}_{t+1} = f(z_t) + \epsilon_{t+1}\, g(z_t)$$
$$x_t = h(z_t) \quad .$$

The bilinear models, in which the generating process can be ARMA plus cross-products of lagged x_t and the white noise input have been discussed by Granger and Andersen (1978) and Subba Rao (1979) and applied by Maravall (1983). According to Priestley (1980) they have the "outstanding property . . . that although they involve only a finite number of parameters they can, over a finite time interval, approximate with arbitrary accuracy any 'reasonable' general non-linear relationship between (the sequences x_t and ϵ_t." The practical implementation of this theoretical result has yet to be demonstrated.

R. H. Jones (1965) briefly considered the RAR model (1.2), derived from meteorological theory and D. A. Jones (1978) discussed the general NLAR model (1.1), concentrating on the questions of stability and the form of the marginal distribution for x_t when stationary. A number of other authors have considered similar questions for particular forms of (1.1) starting with deterministic chaotic generators. These papers generally consider theoretical aspects of the models, whereas it is the objective of this paper to concentrate on practical aspects of detecting and using non-linearity in data.

2. ANALYSIS OF NON-LINEAR AUTO-REGRESSIVE DATA

Suppose that it is assumed, correctly, that a set of data has been generated by the model

$$x_{t+1} = f(x_t) + \epsilon_{t+1} \tag{2.1}$$

where ϵ_{t+1} is zero-mean white noise, but that the form of the function $f(x)$ is unknown. One possible method of attack is to consider a particular mathematical function, and to fit it to the data. The rational functions, such as (1.2), using ratios of polynomials in x give good approximation to virtually any smooth function as well-known results in numerical analysis testify. However, simulations by Granger and Weiss (1982) suggest that when using data generated by RAR and using the correct specification, parameter estimates achieved are often unsatisfactory. It thus seems that RAR models are not particularly promising for practical empirical analysis. To use more restricted parametric models might not give a good approximation to the true function.

An alternative is to use a non-parametric curve fitting procedure. Doukhan and Ghindes (1980) use the equivalent of a histogram estimate for a density function, whereas a great deal of work by statisticians recently has considered the equivalent of smoothed histograms. These latter methods, using spline functions, have been proposed and analyzed by Wahba (1975), Rice and Rosenblatt (1983) and others. To outline this method, consider a sample from a bivariate random variable (X, Y), the data being (x_i, y_i), $i = 1, \ldots, n$, and the assumed generating mechanism is

$$y_i = f(x_i) + e_i \tag{2.2}$$

where $E(e_i) = 0$, $\mathrm{var}(e_i^2) = \sigma^2$ and $E[e_i e_j] = 0$, $i \neq j$, all i.

Suppose that there are k distinct observed values of the x variable in the data, where $k \leq n$. In practice, some grouping of values may be necessary. For ease of exposition, assume that these x values are equally spaced - in practice this assumption is easily removed - and order these k distinct values from the smallest to the largest, with $x_{(j)}$ denoting the jth value and denote

$$\beta_j = f(x_{(j)}), \qquad j = 1, \ldots, k$$

(2.2) may then be written as

$$\underline{y} = \underline{X}\underline{\beta} + \underline{\varepsilon} \tag{2.3}$$

where $\underline{y}'$ is the vector of observed y values, β the $k \times 1$ vector of β_j's and $\underline{X}$ is an $n \times k$ data matrix which indicates the value of x corresponding to each observation on y.

If $\underline{\beta}$ were estimated directly from (2.3), by least squares say, it would not incorporate a belief that f(x) is a smooth function of x. This smoothness could be incorporated by preferring any three adjacent β's to be nearly on a straight line, so that $\beta_{j-1} + \beta_{j+1} - 2\beta_j$ should be small. This preference can be used by choosing the β's to minimize the quantity

$$\underline{e}'\underline{e} + \lambda \beta' \underline{U}\,\underline{U}'\underline{\beta} \tag{2.4}$$

where $$\underline{e} = \underline{y} - \underline{X}\beta$$

and $\underline{U}$ is a matrix incorporating the smoothness requirements and has on its jth row ($j \neq 1$ or k) -2 on the diagonal and 1 on each side of the diagonal and zero elsewhere. The first and last rows will be all zeros. λ is a parameter that can be used to penalize unsmoothness and is at our choice. The solution to this optimization problem is shown by standard analysis to be

$$\hat{\underline{\beta}} = (\underline{X}'\underline{X} + \lambda \underline{U}'\underline{U})^{-1}\underline{X}'\underline{y} \tag{2.5}$$

There are a number of criteria that can be used to choose λ but a particularly appealing one is known as cross-validation. The method drops one data point, estimates the model, evaluates how well the model forecasts the missing data by forming actual minus estimated, repeats this for all individual data points and then chooses λ to minimize the resulting sum of squares of errors. The technique is computationally expensive but efficient algorithms are available or an apparently equivalent criteria known as "generalized cross-validation" can be used. Details of the procedure and an application investigating the very non-linear relationship between temperature and electricity demand for a region may be found in Engle, Granger, Rice and Weiss (1984). Taking $Y = x_t$ and $X = x_{t-1}$ in the above procedure will give an estimate of f(x) in (2.1) provided this function is smooth. Engle et al. (1984) also add other explanatory variables, linearly, and allow the residual to be AR(1). Thus, in our context the model considered is

$$x_{t+1} = f(x_t) + \sum_j \beta_j z_{jt} + e_{t+1}$$

where z_{jt} could be further lagged x's and e_t can be AR(1). The addition of further separable non-linear terms in the other lags of x_t is feasible but quickly becomes computationally very expensive.

The pilot simulation experiment discussed in that paper will use data generated by a rational autoregressive model of the form

$$x_{t+1} = \frac{(\alpha_0 + \alpha_1 x_t + \alpha_2 x_t^2)\, x_t}{1 + \beta_2 x_t^2} + \epsilon_{t+1}$$

where ϵ_t is zero-mean white noise with variance V. Granger and Weiss (1982) found that an interesting variety of non-linear shapes for f(x) could be approximated by such a model and that data generation is easy. One thing that was noted is that for certain combinations of parameters in this model and V, only part of f(x) was operative, that is, the data only utilized part of the function. For example, if $x = 0$ is an unstable equilibrium, so that any x near zero is driven away from this value by the function, and if V is small, then if x_0 is positive all other x's will be inclined to be positive, and the series has trouble "breaking through" the origin. If V is increased somewhat, then breakthroughs will occur occasionally, so that a long run of positive x's will be followed by a long run of negative values. Thus, certain parameter values will either give series that have an obviously different appearance to series generally found in practice. When only parts of the function are operative it is obvious that estimation of the complete function becomes impossible and that constraints placed on the function to achieve stability may be irrelevant.

The analysis then proceeds as follows:

(i) 550 terms are generated by an RAR model, the first 50 are dropped to reduce start-up problems, the next 400 are used to estimate $f(x)$ using the non-parametric procedure outlined above. The terms $x_t - \hat{f}(x_{t-1}) \equiv e_t$ are tested for autocorrelation and, if necessary, a simple linear AR is fitted. The resulting estimated model is then used to provide one-step forecasts for the last 100 terms of the generated sample, and the forecast errors analyzed. The last 100 terms may be called the "post-sample" and the previous 400 terms the "sample."

(ii) A linear ARIMA model will be fitted to the sample using standard Box-Jenkins techniques and one-step forecasts made over the post-sample.

(iii) The various sets of forecasts will be compared in terms of mean-squared errors. Combinations of forecasts can also be considered.

The results of a simple pilot study are reported below.

3. ALMOST INTEGRATED MODELS

A series is said to be integrated of order zero, denoted $x_t \sim I(0)$, if its spectrum $f(\omega)$ has the property $0 < f(0) < \infty$. If a series needs to be differenced d times to achieve this property it is called integrated of order d, denoted $x_t \sim I(d)$. Empirical studies using economic data often find that series are $I(1)$, examples being stock market prices, commodity prices, some interest rates and various production series. This evidence runs from some early work on typical spectral shapes to recent specific tests by Nelson and Plosser (1982). Although the evidence is clear, there remains a dis-belief amongst some economists that this can be the correct model, as $I(1)$ series can drift very widely whereas some economic series, such as interest rates and real balance of trade are thought to be inherently bounded. The almost integrated (AINT) models are designed to model both the empirical evidence and also the economist's belief. If x_t is given by

$$x_{t+1} = f(x_t) + z_{t+1}$$

where $z_t \sim I(0)$ and $f(x)$ approximates x for those values of x that mostly occur, but $|f(x)| < |x|$ as $|x|$ becomes large, then when $\text{var}(z_t)$ is small, the series generated by this model will appear to be $I(1)$ as only rarely will terms occur in the region where $|f(x) - x|$ is appreciable in size. Thus, the non-linear part of $f(x)$ will only occasionally be operative giving an $I(1)$ approximation, but the existence of the non-linearity will ensure that var x_t is finite and that x_t cannot wander too far from its 'typical' values. An example of such a model is the particular exponential AR given by

$$y_{t+1} = y_t \exp(-y_t^2/m^2) + \eta_{t+1} \qquad (3.1)$$

where η_t is white noise. It should be noted that the transformation $x_t = y_{t/m}$ gives the model

$$x_{t+1} = x_t \exp(-x_t^2) + \epsilon_{t+1} \qquad (3.2)$$

and so the only parameter remaining in the model is the variance of ϵ_t, denoted by V.

The computer analysis being undertaken on this model is to generate data using (3.2) and various values for V, and thus to determine the relationship between the variance and autocorrelations of x_t to the size of this parameter. The effectiveness of the non-parametric curve fitting procedure discussed in the previous section will then be determined using both this generated data and also some real interest rate series.

Some initial calculations with model (3.2) showed that if $V = \text{var}\ \epsilon_t$ takes the value 0.05 then the correlogram is virtually that of a random walk, but the plot of x_t against x_{t-1} showed some curvature for large values of x_{t-1}. If $V = 0.01$ the series appeared to be a random walk but $V = 0.1$ or greater gave a series that identified as stationary AR(1). Investigation of some interest rate data gave plots that are similar to these models, but are limited to positive values. Further investigation is now under way.

4. EXPERIENCES WITH NON-PARAMETRIC CURVE FITTING

Data were generated by the model

$$x_{t+1} = f(x_t) + \varepsilon_{t+1}$$

where

$$f(x) = \frac{(\alpha_0 + \alpha_1 x + \alpha_2 x^2)x}{1 + \beta_2 x^2}$$

and ε_t is white noise, N(0, V). In Model A, the values used were

$$\alpha_0 = 10, \ \alpha_1 = 1, \ \alpha_2 = 1.5, \ \beta_2 = 2$$

and V varied from 0.25 to 10.0. For this model, x_{t+1} and x_t are positively related and the non-linearity is rather subtle. In Model B, the values used were

$$\alpha_0 = 10, \ \alpha_1 = 0, \ \alpha_2 = -1.5, \ \beta_2 = 2$$

and V again varying from 0.25 to 10.0. This function is very non-linear, with a positive slope at zero, peaks near ± 1 and then there is a negative relationship between x_{t+1} and x_t beyond the peaks. Some values for f(x) from Model B are

x	0	0.5	1.0	1.5	2	2.5	3.0
f(x)	0	3.21	2.43	1.20	0.44	0.04	-0.28

The linear properties of the various samples are shown in table 1, that is the mean, range, variance and first 10 autocorrelations. The samples used had 400 terms after the initial 50 terms were dropped. For Model A, with low V values the series stays on one side of zero, which side will depend on the start-up process. At V = 3, the series will occasionally switch sides but remains on one side for long periods, giving the high autocorrelations. As V increases to 10.0, the switches through zero become more frequent and autocorrelations drop in magnitude. For these larger V values, the series has a different appearance than a series generated by a linear ARMA model.

For Model B, the series takes both negative and positive values for all V values and have no distinctive non-linear appearance. The autocorrelations are generally small, with r_1 becoming increasingly negative as more extreme parts of f(x) become operative.

Table 2 shows the in-sample ARIMA models identified and estimated by standard Box-Jenkins procedures for the generated data. A distinct difference is seen between the two parts of the table. For Model A, the residuals of the AR models have variances near the V-values, indicating that the linear model will produce forecasts very near to the optimal models. On the other hand, for Model B, the residual variances are much larger than the corresponding V-values, suggesting that the linear models fit, and will forecast, much less well than a non-linear model.

Some attempt was also made to identify and estimate bilinear models, but it was generally found that either no simple model would explain the autocorrelations or that the model estimated was non-invertible and so could not be used for forecasting. Because of time constraints, further investigation was not possible.

The non-parametric curve fitting procedure outlined in section 2 was applied to a number of these samples. As expected from the linear model results, when applied to Model A data, the curve-fitting procedure did not produce a convincing non-linear curve. On the other hand, when applied to data from Model B, very distinct non-linear curves resulted. For example, the curve using Model B data with V = 0.5, well approximates the actual underlying generating curve. The analysis initially used equal sized intervals over the range of the data, but once the rough shape was determined, closer intervals were used around the apparent turning points.

As evidence of the usefulness of the non-parametric curve fitting procedure, the post-sample forecasting ability of the linear, AR models were compared to the non-linear AR model using the estimated curve. For Model B, V = 0.5, over the next 100 out-of-sample terms, the one-step forecast error mean squared errors were 4.91 for the AR model and 1.19 for the non-linear AR model. Experience with other models is planned.

Table 1A. Linear Properties of Samples, Non-Linear Models

Model A	V =							
	.25	.50	1.00	2.0	3.0	4.0	5.0	10.0
mean	4.25	-4.29	4.20	-4.59	-1.49	.76	1.78	.45
variance	0.34	0.72	1.11	2.22	25.2	24.0	28.9	42.4
max	5.87	-1.27	8.03	-0.16	15.4	10.8	12.6	14.0
min	2.81	-6.52	0.50	-8.80	-10.2	-10.6	-13.7	-14.5
Autocorr. k =								
1	.48	.53	.40	.44	.91	.89	.88	.86
2	.20	.25	.15	.15	.86	.83	.81	.74
3	.07	.13	.02	.03	.82	.79	.76	.68
4	-.004	.07	.05	.01	.79	.79	.73	.63
5	-.03	.05	.05	.13	.78	.74	.69	.58
6	.00	-.00	.08	.17	.76	.72	.65	.51
7	-.01	.03	.07	.14	.74	.70	.61	.44
8	.05	.01	-.02	.06	.73	.69	.59	.41
9	.07	-.07	.01	.02	.70	.66	.56	.40
10	-.02	-.10	.09	.04	.69	.64	.53	.32

Model B	V =							
	.25	.50	1.0	2.0	3.0	4.0	5.0	10.0
mean	-.09	-.23	.03	.05	.13	-.04	.07	.16
variance	4.15	4.35	5.02	6.44	7.64	7.06	11.21	17.00
max	3.95	4.62	6.40	6.84	6.38	8.83	8.47	11.18
min	-4.45	-5.53	-6.40	-7.21	-7.41	-6.34	-8.17	-12.32
Autocorr. k =								
1	.17	.12	.03	-.16	-.24	-.16	-.38	-.45
2	-.10	-.07	-.10	.04	.07	-.06	.17	.15
3	-.01	-.03	.02	.09	-.06	-.04	-.04	-.08
4	.12	.01	-.03	-.08	-.02	.07	.07	-.00
5	.01	-.05	-.08	.15	.08	-.02	-.08	.09
6	-.01	-.02	.08	.05	.00	.01	.05	-.02
7	-.05	.09	-.01	-.01	-.03	-.07	-.08	-.07
8	.03	-.01	-.05	-.02	.00	.10	.05	.09
9	.05	-.08	-.01	-.00	-.05	-.00	.05	-.10
10	-.04	-.08	-.03	.02	.04	.00	-.06	.06

Table 2. ARIMA Models Fitted to Non-Linear Data

Model A

V value	Model	Residual variance
0.25	$x_t = 2.2 + 0.48\, x_{t-1}$	0.26
0.50	$x_t = -2.04 + 0.53\, x_{t-1}$	0.52
1.00	$x_t = 2.52 + 0.4\, x_{t-1}$	0.93
2.00	$x_t = -2.54 + 0.45\, x_{t-1}$	1.79
3.00	$x_t = -0.10 + 0.71\, x_{t-1} + 0.22\, x_{t-2}$	4.18
4.00	$x_t = 0.05 + 0.69\, x_{t-1} + 0.05\, x_{t-2} + 0.024\, x_{t-3} + 0.17\, x_{t-4}$	4.34
5.00	$x_t = 0.15 + .76\, x_{t-1} + 0.04\, x_{t-2} + .11\, x_{t-3}$	5.98
10.00	$x_t = 0.06 + .84\, x_{t-1} - .16\, x_{t-2} + .6\, x_{t-3}$	11.02

Model B

V value	Model	Residual variance
0.25	$x_t = -.07 + .19\, x_{t-1} - .12\, x_{t-2}$	3.86
0.50	$x_t = -.21 + .12\, x_{t-1}$	4.28
1.00	$x_t = .04 + .03\, x_{t-1} - .103\, x_{t-2}$	4.96
2.00	$x_t = .06 - .165\, x_{t-1}$	6.26
3.00	$x_t = .16 - .24\, x_{t-1}$	7.16
4.00	$x_t = -.05 - .16\, x_{t-1}$	6.85
5.00	$x_t = .09 - .38\, x_{t-1}$	9.58
10.00	$x_t = .23 - .46\, x_{t-1}$	13.48

REFERENCES

[1] Doukhan, P. and Ghindes, M., Estimations dans le processeni $x_{n+1} = f(x_n) + \epsilon_n$, Comptes Rendus, Acad. Sci. Paris, 291A (1980) 61-64.

[2] Engle, R. F., Granger, C.W.J., Rice, I., and Weiss, A. A., Non-parametric estimates of the relation between weather and electricity demand, to appear (1984).

[3] Granger, C.W.J. and Andersen, A.P., An introduction to bilinear time series models (Vandenhoeck and Ruprecht, Göttinger, 1978).

[4] Granger, C.W.J. and Weiss, A. A., Rational autoregressive models, Working paper 82-27, Dept. of Economics, UCSD (1982).

[5] Haggan, V. and Ozaki, T., Modelling non-linear vibrations using an amplitude-dependent autoregressive time series model, Biometrika 68 (1981) 189-196.

[6] Jones, D. R., Non-linear autoregressive processes, Proc. Roy. Soc., London, A360 (1978) 71-95.

[7] Jones, R. H., An experiment in non-linear prediction, J. Appl. Meteorology, 4 (1965) 701-705.

[8] Maravall, A., An application of non-linear time series forecasting, J. Bus. & Econ. Stat., 1 (1983) 66-74.

[9] Nelson, C. R. and Plosser, C. I., Trends and random walks in macro-economic time series, some evidence and implications, J. Monetary Econ. 10 (1982) 139-162.

[10] Priestley, M. B., State-dependent models; a general approach to non-linear time series analsyis, J. Time Series Anal. 1 (1980) 47-72.

[11] Rice, J. and Rosenblatt, M., Smoothing splines: regression, derivatives and deconvolution, Annals of Statistics 11 (1983) 141-156.

[12] Subba Rao, On the theory of bilinear time series models, J. Roy. Stat. Soc. (B) 43 (1984) 244-255.

[13] Tong, H. and Lim, K. S., Threshold autoregression, limit cycles and cyclical data, J. Roy. Stat. Soc. (B), 42 (1980) 252-292.

[14] Wabba, G., Smoothing noisy data with spline functions, Num. Math. 24 (1975) 309-317.

COMPUTER SCIENCE AND STATISTICS:
The Interface, L. Billard (ed.)

MODEL-BASED TREATMENT OF A MANIC-DEPRESSIVE SERIES

Agustín Maravall

Bank of Spain

By means of a "real world" application we use an ARIMA model-based method to estimate signals used in monitoring the evolution of a key economic variable. We conclude that the seasonally adjusted series is of little use and focus instead on trend estimation.
The sensitivity of the series decomposition to changes in the ARIMA specification is analysed. It is seen that the ambiguity always present in the ARIMA selection provides a relative ample margin to improve the quality of the signal. Thus when an ARIMA model is to be used for signal extraction, the selection of the model should consider the characteristics of the implied components.

1. THE PROBLEM

The Spanish economy is widely believed to be crucially dependent on foreign trade, and exports to play a key role in determining GNP. The monthly release of the export series is closely watched by policy makers as well as the media. However, the monthly export series misbehaves. The first column in Table 1 displays the monthly rate of growth, expressed (as is standard procedure for many economic series) in annualized percent points, for 1979. In November the series grew at an annual rate of more than 2000%, while in September it decreased to less than 1/12 (on an annual basis) of its previous level.

Table 1

Monthly Rates of Growth (1979)

	Original	S.A. X11 Concurrent	S.A. X11 Final
Jan.	-79.5	9.1	374.1
Feb.	302.9	73.9	-30.8
Mar.	-41.0	30.4	-17.4
Abr.	-44.0	24.1	17.7
May.	133.7	-11.2	5.2
Jun.	45.4	205.9	115.6
Jul.	-13.6	-22.7	7.7
Aug.	-59.0	81.0	160.0
Sep.	-92.3	-81.8	-86.6
Oct.	730.8	33.0	51.4
Nov.	2223.1	687.6	549.8
Dic.	475.0	11.0	-30.6

Inevitably, it induces a manic-depressive mood in its followers, swinging from spectacular highs to gloomy downs. Indeed, it is difficult to know what is happening.

The way the series was treated at the Bank of Spain was to, once a year, run X11 on it and to seasonally adjust the series with the forecasted factors. (This is standard treatment for many hundred other series.) There was, however, an unhappy feeling. So, there came the (typically ambiguous) policy maker request: "can we do something about it?"

2. SEASONAL ADJUSTMENT WITH X11 ARIMA

For reasons given in [9], the period selected was January 74-December 83 (T=120). We used the multiplicative version of X11 ARIMA, which shall be abbreviated to X11A, with an ARIMA specification that shall be given later. (Although the results that follow were practically unaffected when, for example, the Automatic option was used.) Adjustment was done concurrently, instead of once-a-year, since it reduced revisions by approximately 40%.

The original and seasonally adjusted series and the estimated factors are given in Figures 1, 2 and 3. Seasonality seems to evolve somewhat rapidly, still no residual seasonality could be detected in the adjusted series. However, from an applied point of view, these present two important problems:

a) Although somewhat damped, the seasonally adjusted series behaves quite erratically. The second column in Table 1 displays the annualized rate of growth of the concurrently adjusted series. The manic-depressive behavior is still present.

b) The adjusted series is subject to very large revisions. Since -assuming that we are using adequate filters- the best estimate is the final estimate, if revisions are large, the concurrent measure will be a poor estimate. The third column of Table 1 displays the annualized rates of growth of the

Figure 1

Original Series

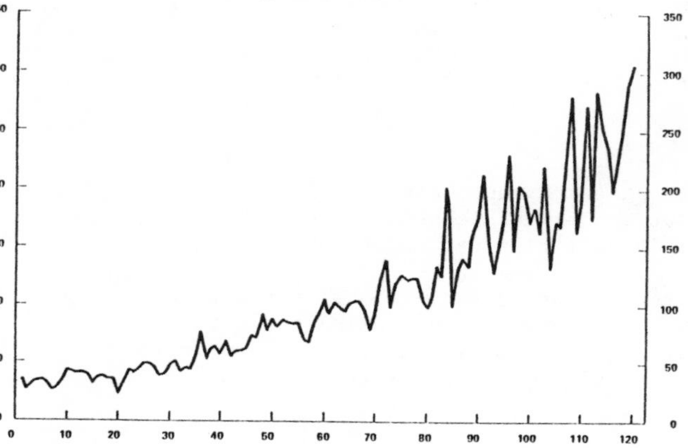

Figure 2

Seasonally Adjusted Series

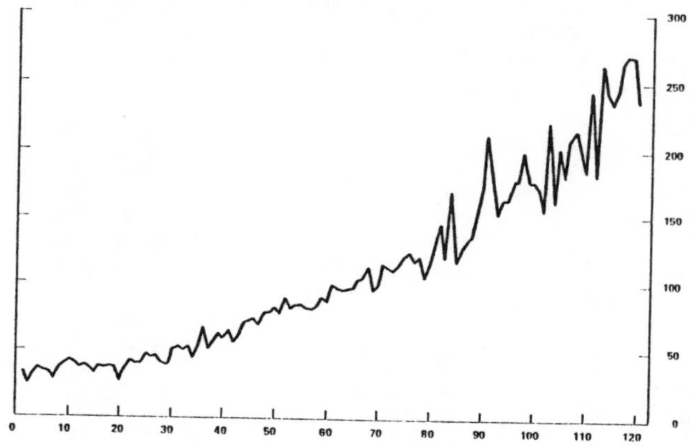

Figure 3

Seasonal Factor

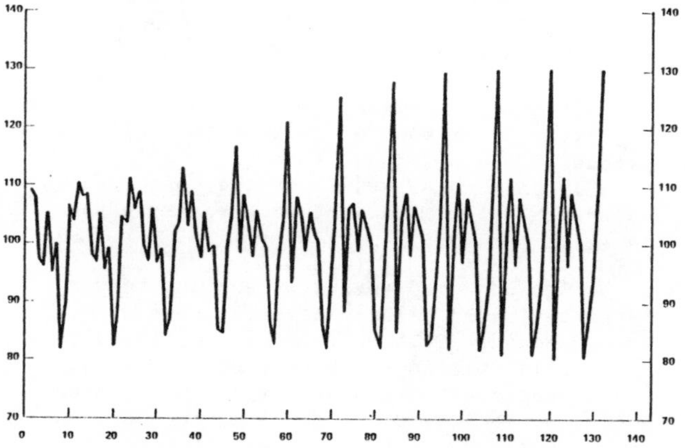

seasonally adjusted series for 1979 after 4 additional years of data have become available. (In fact, the revision induced by the fourth year is negligible.) What was thought in January 79 a very small growth (well below the average) turned out to be very large. In February, a preliminary increase of 74% was finally changed to a 37% decrease. The rest of the months also present important differences between the concurrent and final measures. Obviously, the concurrent estimate is close to worthless.

Perhaps it could be possible to obtain a more satisfactory seasonally adjusted series using a different method. It is well-known (see [5]) that X11 is appropriate for series with a certain Autocorrelation Function (ACF). That ACF is associated (broadly) with an ARIMA structure of the type:

$$\nabla\nabla_{12} \log x_t = \theta(B)\, a_t \quad , \qquad (1)$$

where a_t is white-noise (w.n.), $\theta(B)$ is a relatively long polynomial (which implies $\theta_{12} \simeq .4$). Perhaps the export series does not fit into that type.

3. STRUCTURE OF THE SERIES

The need for a ∇_{12} is obvious. The ACF of $z_t = \nabla_{12} \log x_t$ (Figure 4) shows no indication of nonstationarity and the variance of z_t is smaller than that of any other differencing. (For example, Var z_t = .0286, while Var $(\nabla\nabla_{12} \log x_t)$ = .0413.) Aside from a lag-12 autocorrelation which can be captured with the MA factor $(1-\theta_{12} B^{12})$, the only non-zero autocorrelation of z_t is $\rho_1 = .23$, a relatively small value. This small low-order autocorrelation can be captured with an AR(1) factor, an MA(1) factor or with an ARMA(1,1) for which $(\phi-\theta)$ is small. Thus, letting

$$z_t = \nabla_{12} \log x_t$$

$$b_t = (1-\theta_{12} B^{12}) a_t \quad ,$$

where a_t is w.n., the following specifications provided similar fits, all of them acceptable:

(A) $(1-\phi B) z_t = b_t + c$

(B) $z_t = (1-\theta B) b_t + c$

(C) $(1-\phi B) z_t = (1-\theta) b_t + c$

If a regular AR(2) was used, $\phi_2 \simeq 0$; if the fitted model was simply $z_t = b_t + c$, the residuals displayed significant first-order autocorrelation. Finally, the model:

(D) $\nabla z_t = (1-\theta B) b_t \quad ,$

Figure 4

ACF of $\nabla_{12} \log x_t$

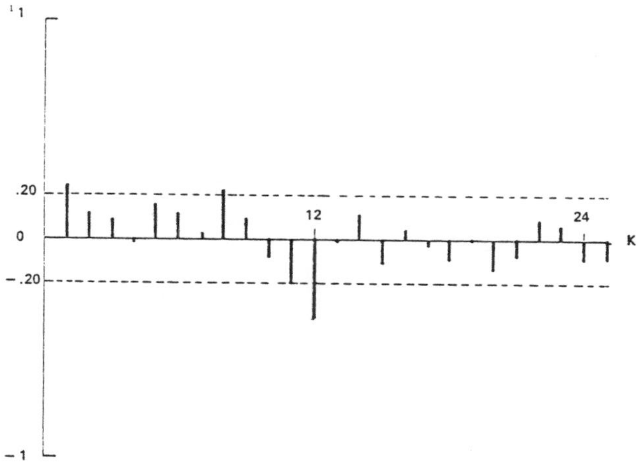

the so-called "Airline model" (see [3]) gave results rather close to those of (A), (B) and (C). This is not surprising, since the likelihood function is very flat in the direction $\phi = \theta + .2$ (see Figure 5). The estimation results are summarized in Table 2. The residuals for the four models can be taken as white-noise. The standard error of the residuals vary from .1417 (model C) to .1433 (model D). However, the correlation between the estimated parameters ϕ and θ in (C) is .95. Thus (C) represents a non-parsimonious model, and a reasonable starting choice seems to be model (A), that is:

$$(1-.182B)\nabla_{12} \log x_t = (1-.635\, B^{12})a_t + .175 \quad . \quad (2)$$

This was the model used to extend the series when running X11 ARIMA.

Table 2

Estimation Results

Model	ϕ	θ	θ_{12}	SE(a_t)	Q_{24}
A	.182 (.094)	–	.635 (.077)	.1421	20.2
B	–	-.159 (.094)	.626 (.076)	.1424	21.6
C	.824 (.167)	.688 (.217)	.625 (.078)	.1417	20.1
D	–	.843 (.052)	.641 (.075)	.1433	20.1

In parenthesis: SE of estimates.
Q_{24}: Ljung-Box statistics.

Figure 5

Likelihood Function

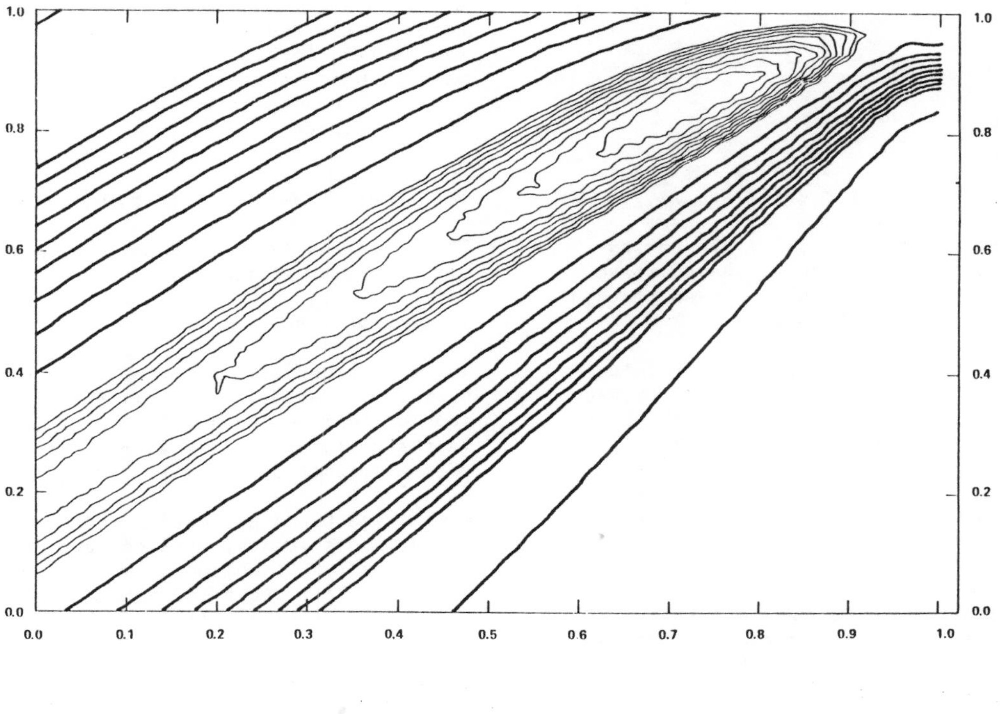

4. MODEL BASED-SEASONAL ADJUSTMENT

Since (1) is not quite like (2), perhaps a model-based approach using (2) would provide more reasonable seasonally adjusted series. ARIMA model-based seasonal adjustment methods have been developed recently (key references are [2], [4] and [6].) Burman has made available a very efficient program which, briefly, adjusts the series in the following manner:

Let $h_z(x)$ denote the spectrum of the ARIMA model, where $x = \cos \omega$, and unit roots are allowed in the AR polynomial (see [1].) Then $h_z(x) = U(x)/V(x)$, where $U(x)$ and $V(x)$ are associated with the MA and AR parts of the model, respectively. The function $h_z(x)$ can be expressed as the partial fractions decomposition:

$$h_z(x) = M_p(x)/V_p(x)+M_s(x)/V_s(x)+Q(x),$$

where $V_p(x)$ and $V_s(x)$ are associated with the trend and seasonal roots of the AR polynomial, respectively, and $Q(x)$ is a constant (for "bottom heavy" or "balanced" models) or a low order polynomial (for "top heavy" models, see [4].) The first and second fraction provide the trend and seasonal spectrums, $h_p(x)$ and $h_s(x)$, and $Q(x)$ will be assigned to the irregular. The decomposition is made unique by setting min. $[h_p(x)+h_s(x)] = 0$. Finally, the seasonal component is estimated with the filter $h_s(x)/h_z(x)$.

For the case of model (A), it can be seen that the corresponding models for the components have to be of the type:

$$(1-\phi B) \quad \nabla \log p_t = \alpha_p(B)\ c_t + k$$

$$U(B) \log s_t = \alpha_s(B)\ b_t$$

$$\log u_t \sim \text{w.n.}$$

where $U(B) = 1 + B + \ldots + B^{11}$, $\alpha_p(B)$ and $\alpha_s(B)$ are polynomials of order 2 and 11, respectively, and c_t, b_t and u_t are independent white-noises. (Since the series has a multiplicative structure, the additive decomposition in the model based method applies to the logs of the series.)

We adjusted the export series with Burman's program using model (2). The results were very similar to those obtained with X11A. The first two columns in Table 3 display the ACF of $y_t = \nabla \log x_t^A$ (where x_t^A denotes the adjusted series) for X11 and the model-based approach which uses model A. Aside from the negative ρ_1 -partly induced by the fact that the same month enters with opposite signs in two consecutive values of y_t- nothing much seems to remain; they both behave quite erratically. In fact, the variance of the one obtained with Burman's program is slightly larger than the X11A one. As for the precision of the concurrent estimate, the standard deviation of the revision error of y_t (multiplied by 12 and expressed in percent points) is 68.3 for the model-based adjustment and 70.0 for X11A.

Table 3

ACF of $\nabla \log x_t^A$

Lag	X11A	A	C	D
1	-.46	-.45	-.44	-.44
2	-.02	-.02	-.03	-.03
3	-.04	-.03	-.02	-.03
4	-.09	-.07	-.07	-.06
5	.12	.09	.09	.09
6	.04	.07	.06	.06
7	-.17	-.22	-.22	-.22
8	.19	.22	.22	.22
9	-.03	-.01	-.01	-.01
10	.02	.00	.00	.00
11	-.06	-.03	-.03	-.03
12	-.15	-.20	-.20	-.19
13	.08	.12	.13	.12

Thus the model-based method does not improve the behavior of the seasonally adjusted series. After all, if the irregular component is large, it should be contained in the seasonally adjusted series, making them highly erratic. Also, if seasonality changes fast, the concurrent estimate will be unreliable. Hence the two problems associated with the seasonally adjusted series do not seem to be due to insufficiencies of the seasonal adjustment methods, but to characteristics of the series. Perhaps we should try tc find a measure which does not behave so erratically and which can be estimated concurrently with more precision.

5. TREND ESTIMATION: PRELIMINARY RESULTS

If the series is the sum of a trend, seasonal and irregular components:

$$z_t = p_t + s_t + u_t \quad ,$$

let's consider estimation of the trend. If u_t is white-noise, the erratic behavior should decrease. We shall also be interested in the revisions as a measure of the stability of the concurrent estimate.

A standard trend estimation procedure is to use moving averages, derived from LS local approximation to polynomials in time (see, for example, [8].) The trend estimate provided by X11 implies such a procedure: a sequence of two filters is passed twice. The first filter is a symmetric [2x12] moving average and the second a Henderson moving-average (see [10].) Since we are looking for a measure which has to be estimated routinely and often, it is of interest to consider the trend estimate of X11A, say p_t^X.

Figure 6 displays p_t^X; the first column of Table 4 the ACF of its monthly rate of growth. For the second half of the period, p_t^X appears to be somewhat bumpy. Also the large negative value of ρ_{12} would be associated with a small 2-year period effect, whose presence is undesirable in a trend. Finally, the standard deviation of the revision error in the (annualized) monthly trend's rate of growth is equal to 8.6 percent points.

Similarly to X11A, Burman's program provides an estimate of the trend, computed through the filter $h_p(x)/h_z(x)$, where the h-functions were described in Section 4. Using model A (i.e. equation (2)), the estimated trend, p_t^A is displayed in Figure 6. The ACF of its monthly rate of growth appears in the 2nd column of Table 4. The trend behaves rather erratically with too much short-term variation. Also the standard deviation of the revision error in its monthly rate of growth equals 13.6 percent points.

Table 4

ACF of $\nabla \log p_t$

Lag	X11A	A	C	D
1	.83	.31	.82	.94
2	.44	-.45	.48	.82
3	.01	-.35	.24	.70
4	-.27	-.04	.14	.60
5	-.31	.11	.13	.51
6	-.18	.00	.13	.42
7	-.01	.03	.12	.33
8	.06	.20	.07	.24
9	-.03	.23	-.05	.12
10	-.22	-.08	-.24	.00
11	-.39	-.39	-.38	-.10
12	-.42	-.29	-.36	-.15
13	-.30	.14	-.22	-.17

Figure 6

Trends

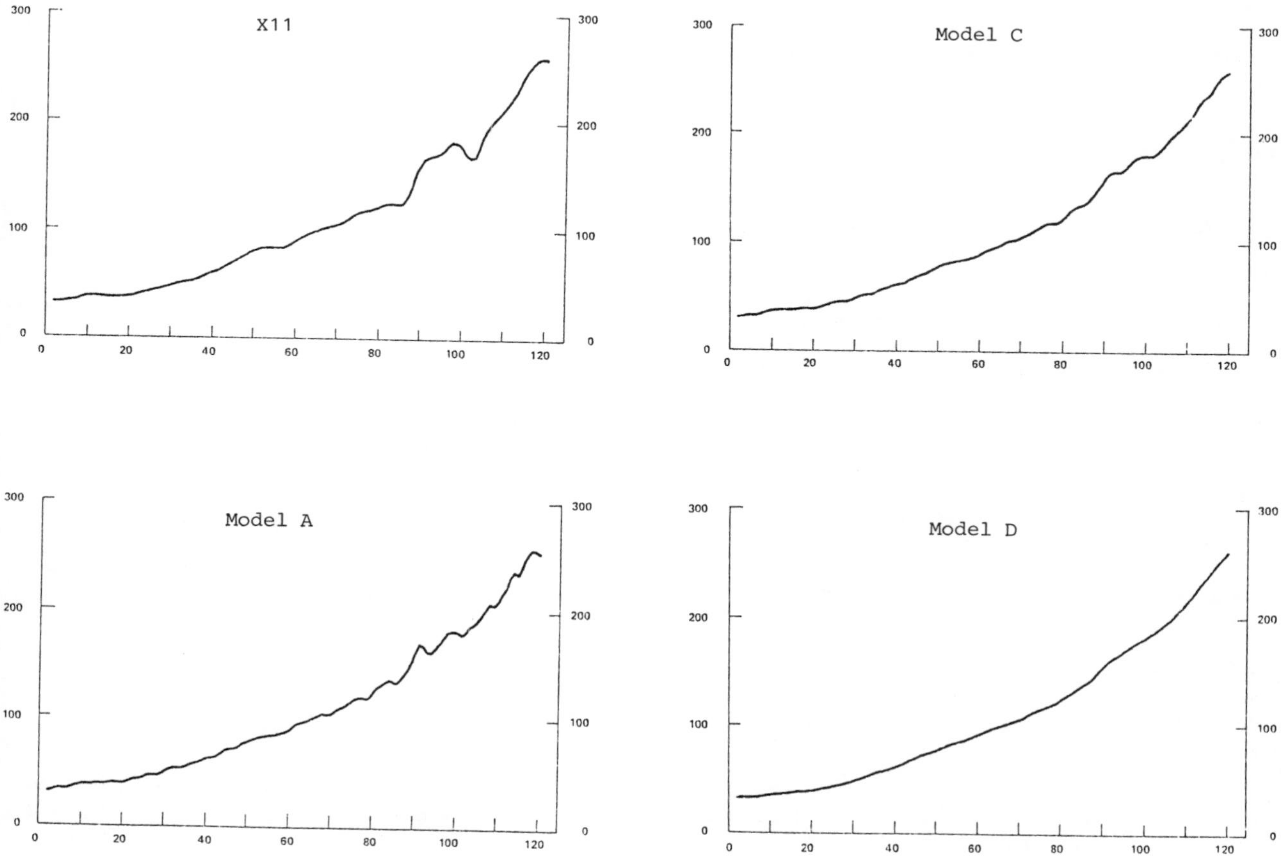

Comparing p_t^X and p_t^A, the former seems preferable. In both cases the difference between the seasonally adjusted series and the trend (i.e., the irregular component) could be accepted as white noise. The Q-statistic for the first 12 autocorrelations were 14.58 (X11A) and 21.86 (model-based). The difference is mostly due to a relatively large negative value of ρ_{12} for the model-based irregular (ρ_{12} = -.20). Also, the variance of the X11A irregular is larger.

6. SERIES COMPATIBLE MODELS

For the case of the seasonally adjusted series, both approaches yielded similar results. We concluded that the problems were related to the properties of the series. However, when estimating the trend, the two methods difer substantially. This suggests that the poor performance of the model-based approach could be due to inadequacies in the method. One possibility that comes to mind is that the chosen ARIMA model is inappropriate. Thus we are interested in determining how sensitive the estimated components are to relatively small changes in the ARIMA model.

Of course, it would not make sense to use an ARIMA model not in agreement with the time series in question (in fact, one of the advantages of the model-based approach is that forecasts and components estimation is done with the same model.) But, as we saw in Section 3, there are several ARIMA specifications that are approximately equally compatible with the series. This is a standard fact in applied ARIMA estimation: In most cases, the limitations of the sample do not permit to assert that one and only one specification is acceptable. We shall refer to this (loosely defined) group of models which are compatible with a given series as the group of "series - compatible" models. Naturally, this group may include slightly non-parsimonious models, with very large autocorrelation between parameter estimates, or with some parameter whose estimate is not quite significant. The models in this group will basically satisfy three conditions:

a) they provide clean residual ACF,
b) the residual variances are of a similar (approximately minimum) size, and
c) they provide similar forecasts.

7. SENSITIVITY OF THE DECOMPOSITION TO CHANGES IN ARIMA SPECIFICATION.

Back to our application, in section 3 we discussed the estimation results of several models. A, B, C and D produced white-noise residuals. The residual variance for D was slightly larger, though the difference was in the order of only 1%. As for the forecasts, Figure 7 displays the 12-period ahead forecast function of the four models. They are

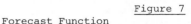

Figure 7

Forecast Function

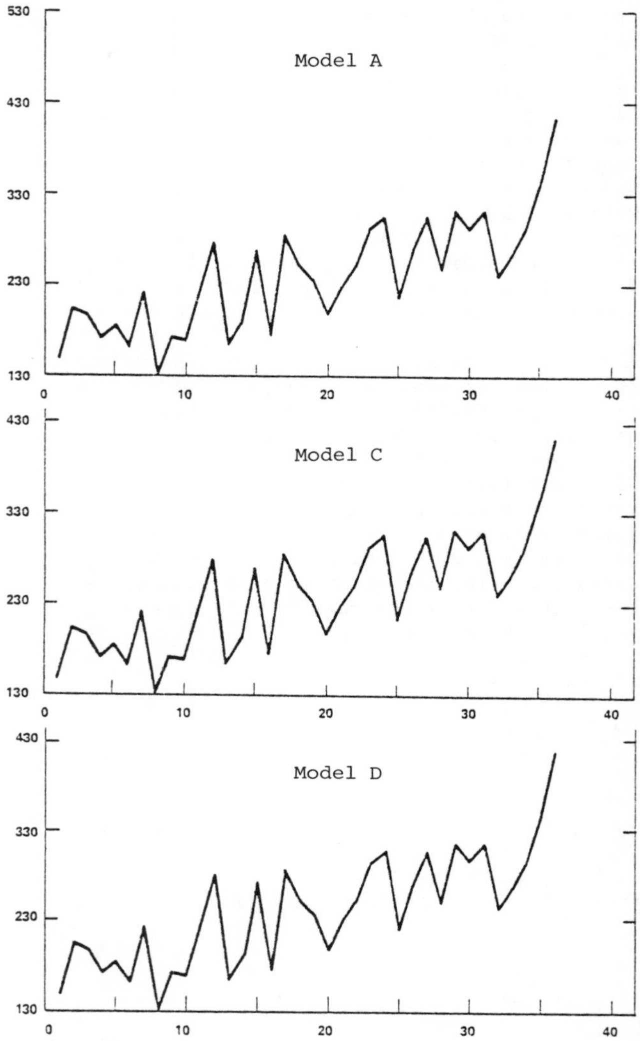

practically indistinguishable. In fact, the standard deviation of the one-period ahead forecast error for 1983 was slightly smaller for models C and D, although the difference was in all cases smaller than 2%. Since the four models provide similar fits and forecasts, they are series compatible. Does this implies that the way they decompose into trend, seasonal and irregular is also similar?

If X11 ARIMA is used, since the ARIMA model only influences the last years of the estimation period, and since the differences among the forecasts obtained with the four models are very small, the decomposition is quite insensitive.

As for the model-based decomposition, first we notice that model A is bottom-heavy, and C and D are balanced. Thus the three of them should yield white-noise irregulars. However, model B is top-heavy (the MA order is larger than the AR order), hence it should provide -using Burman's decomposition- an MA(1) irregular. In fact, ρ_1 for the estimated irregular is .20. Since our objective was to remove from the monthly series uncorrelated, white-noise, variation, we shall not consider model B. (It is interesting to notice that, if the MA parameter -which is not significant- was dropped, and the model used was:

$$\nabla_{12} \log x_t = (1-\theta_{12} B^{12})a_t + c \quad ,$$

the results were similar to the ones obtained with B. In particular, the lag 1 - autocorrelation present in the residuals showed up in the irregular, which had ρ_1 = .20.)

We compare next the model-based trend-seasonal -irregular decomposition of A, C and D.

a) Seasonally Adjusted Series

Figure 8 displays the three spectrums $h_s(\cos\omega)$ for the range $0 \leq \omega \leq \pi$, and Table 3 (last three columns) shows the ACF of $\nabla \log x_t^A$. The seasonally adjusted series are very much alike. This, after all, is not surprising, since the seasonal factors in the multiplicative ARIMA specification are in all cases approximately the same (an IMA $(1,1)_{12}$ structure, with $\theta_{12} \simeq .6$.)

b) Trend

The second, third and fourth column of Table 4 present the ACF of $\nabla \log p_t$; they differ markedly. The three estimated trends are shown in Figure 6: model A produces the most erratic one, while model D produces the most stable one. The differences in trend behavior are in agreement with the ARIMA models:

$$(1-.182B)\ \nabla \log p_t = \alpha_A(B)\ c_t + k$$

$$(1-.824B)\ \nabla \log p_t = \alpha_C(B)\ c_t + k$$

$$\nabla^2 \log p_t = \alpha_D(B)\ c_t \ ,$$

(where $\alpha_A(B)$, $\alpha_C(B)$ and $\alpha_D(B)$ are low-order polynomials) implicit in the model-based decomposition of A, C and D.

We mentioned earlier that the size of the revision in the concurrent estimate is of applied interest, since it is an indication of how reliable measures of the present evolution can be. Revisions were computed for the annualized monthly rate of growth of p_t for the years 1979 and 1980, after three years of additional data have become available. In all cases, the means could be assumed zero and the standard deviations were the following (expressed in percent points):

Table 5

Model:	A	C	D	X11A
σ	13.58	3.76	2.45	8.60

Figure 8

Spectrum of the Seasonal Component

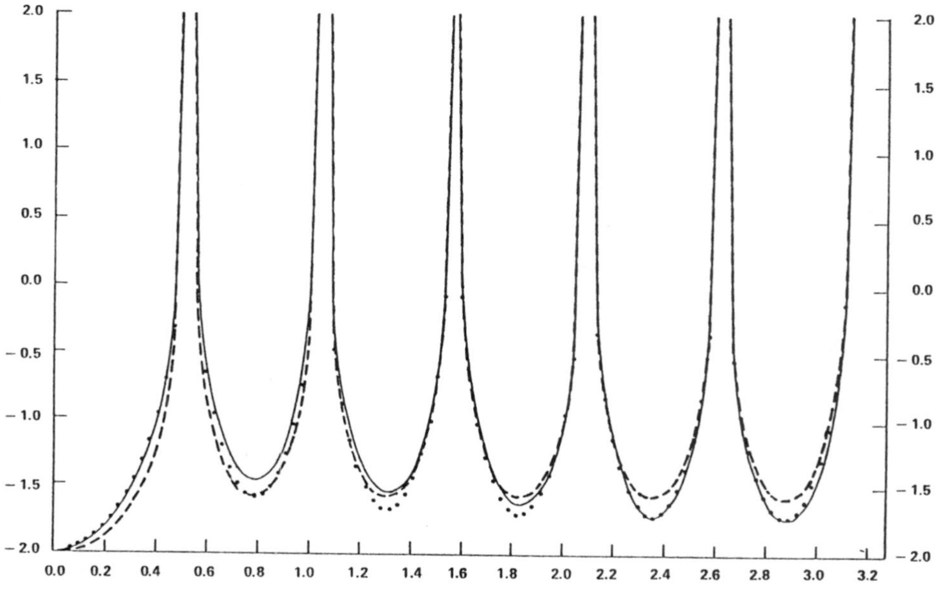

Thus the trends obtained for C and D represent a large improvement in the precision of the concurrent estimate, when compared with those obtained for A and X11A.

Comparison of $h_p(\cos\omega)$ – Figure 9 – is particularly revealing. A contains a much larger contribution of frequencies not associated with a trend than D (C stands in between). The effect of the ARIMA specification on the trend spectrum is illustrated with a 4th example:
If a second AR parameter is added to A, the estimated AR(2) polynomial is:

$$\phi(B) = 1-.180B-.079B^2 \qquad (3)$$
$$\quad (.095) \quad (.095)$$

where the numbers below are the corresponding standard errors. Thus $\phi_2 \simeq 0$. Reestimating the model setting $\phi_2 = 0$ yields, as we saw, (1-.182B). If the AR(2) specification is nevertheless used, the residuals and forecasts are practically unaffected. However $h_p(x)$ becomes the dotted line in Figure 9. It differs substantially from that of model A. The difference between them becomes apparent if (3) is factorized, which gives:

$$\phi(B) = (1-.380B)(1+.205B)$$

The first factor implies a root larger than .182, hence it accounts for the steeper decline in $h_p(x)$ for the AR(2) model. Also, the peak in the spectrum for $\omega = \pi$ is associated with the second factor.

c) ψ-weights versus AR factors

The sensitivity of the decomposition to changes in the ARIMA specification -within the set of series-compatible models- can be explained in the following manner:
Let z_t be the outcome of the ARIMA model:

$$\phi(B)z_t = \theta(B)\ a_t \ , \qquad (4)$$

which can also be expressed as:

$$z_t = \psi(B)\ a_t \ .$$

The "series-compatible" models could be taken to be the ones with similar ψ-weights. (So that, for a given series, the differences are not significant.) However, expressing $\psi(B)$ as $\theta(B)/\phi(B)$, similar $\psi(B)$'s may imply considerably different $\phi(B)$ polynomials (models A and C provide a clear illustration.) Since the AR roots of $\phi(B)$ dominate the spectrum of p_t and s_t, it follows that series compatible models may yield fairly different decompositions.

d) Irregular

Table 6 displays the ACF of the three estimated irregulars (in logs). Except for a negative seasonal autocorrelation, they are close to that of white-noise. Since the irregular is computed as the residual, after the seasonal and trend have been estimated and removed from the series, its spectrum will display dips for seasonal and low-frequencies. This could explain the negative value of ρ_{12} and the small negative value of ρ_1. The standard deviation of the three irregulars are .0719 for model A, .0837 for model C, and .0857 for model D; they are displayed in Figure 10.

Figure 9

Spectrum of the Trend

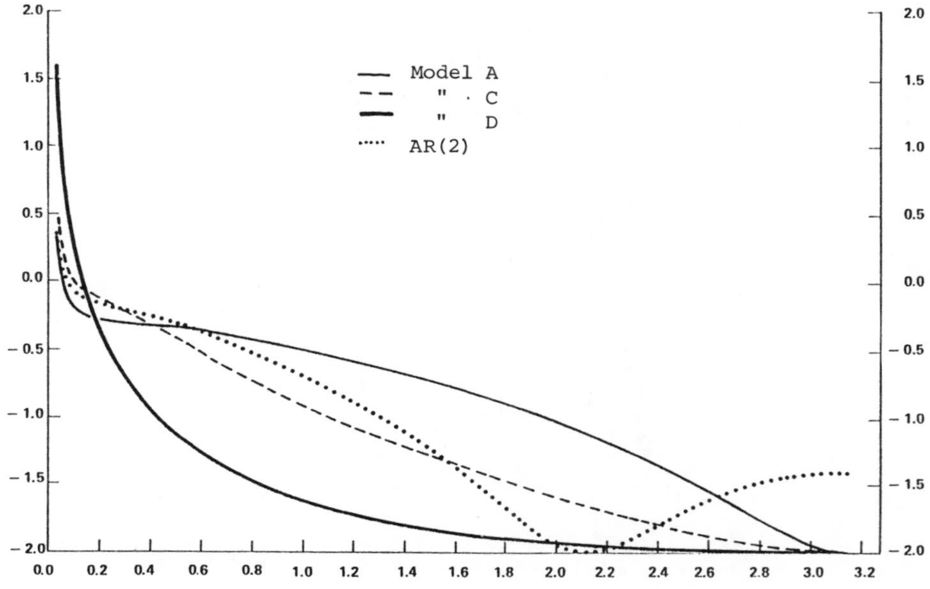

Table 6

ACF of Irregular (log u_t)

Lag	A	C	D	X11A(1)
1	-.09	-.08	-.02	-.10
2	.07	-.11	-.09	-.19
3	.03	-.11	-.11	-.22
4	.00	-.08	-.09	-.19
5	.13	.09	.07	.06
6	.10	.05	.03	.06
7	-.12	-.11	-.11	-.06
8	.23	.22	.20	.27
9	.01	.06	.03	.11
10	-.01	-.05	-.08	-.04
11	-.08	-.17	-.21	-.19
12	-.20	-.25	-.26	-.31
13	.08	.10	.07	.14
Q_{24}	36.1	40.7	37.7	43.3

e) The Preferred Decomposition

Of the three models, D removes more irregular variation and provides a smoother trend. Since the seasonality removed was pretty much the same in the three cases, D is the model which provides a more satisfactory decomposition. It seems also preferable to X11A; in particular, the trend is also smoother and has smaller revisions (see Table 5).

However, the model-based extraction consisted only of linear filters, while X11A was used under the standard option for outliers. If only the linear filters are used (and no outlier treatment is performed), the trend obtained with X11A becomes smoother. Still, it is not as smooth as p_t^D and is subject to larger revisions (σ = 4.04). Moreover, the irregular deteriorated strongly, as shown by its ACF, displayed in the last column of Table 6.

Therefore, the model-based method (using Burman's program) applied to the specification D clearly provides the best decomposition among the ones we have considered. Figure 11 shows the estimated components (in logs), and Figure 12 the rates of growth of the seasonally adjusted series and of the trend. If the latter measure is used instead of the seasonally adjusted one, besides the enormous increase in the stability of the contemporaneous measure, the manic-depressive behavior disappears. This is achieved by additionally removing from the series irregular variation, which is basically uncorrelated white-noise.

Figure 10

Irregular

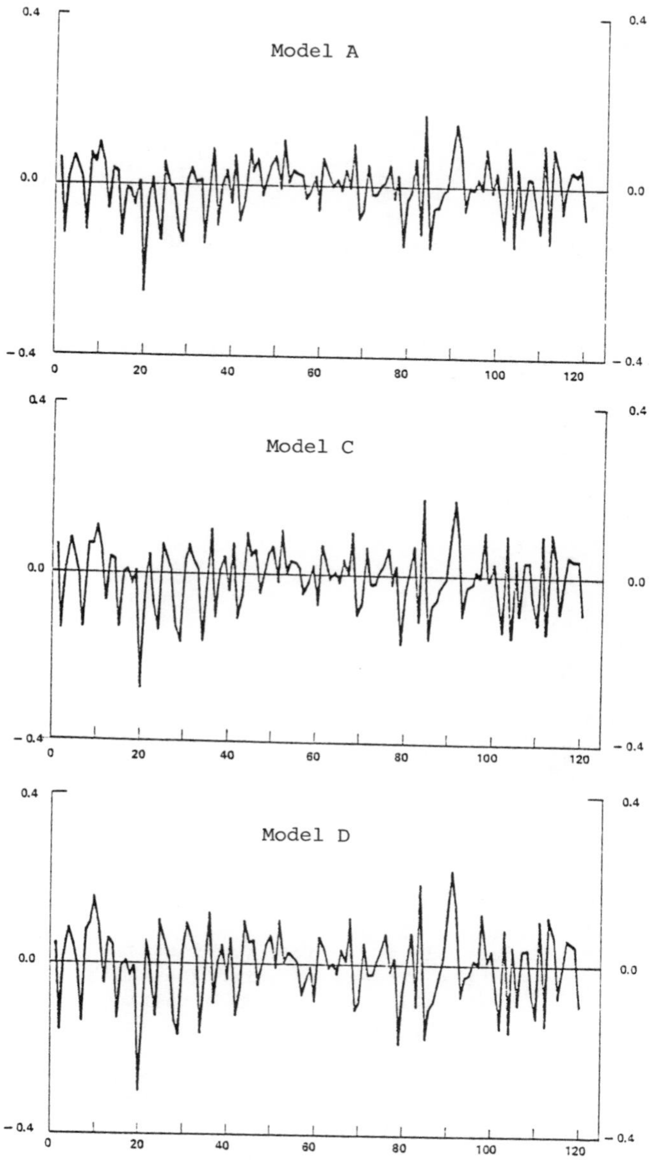

8. A COMMENT ON ARIMA SPECIFICATION

In applied analysis, whatever the method used for tentative identification, the selection of an ARIMA model depends ultimately on two factors: the quality of the pre-whitening achieved and the accuracy of forecasts. This simply reflects the fact that pre-whitening and forecasting have been the most important applications of ARIMA models.

In our discussion, we have seen that models which differ little in terms of fits or forecasts may provide remarkably different

Figure 11

Trend, Seasonal and Irregular

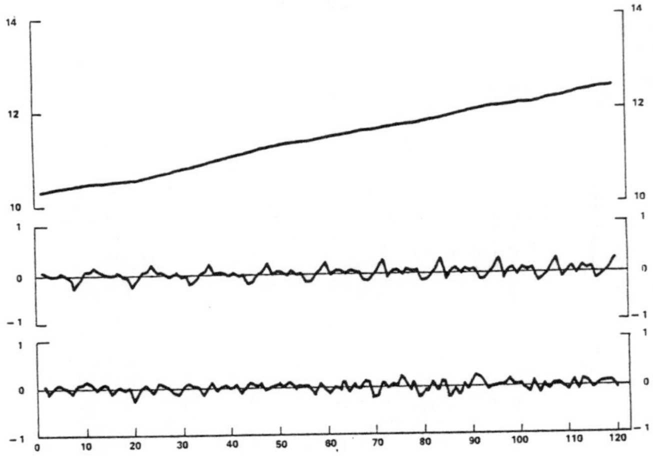

Figure 12

Rates of growth of adjusted series and of trend

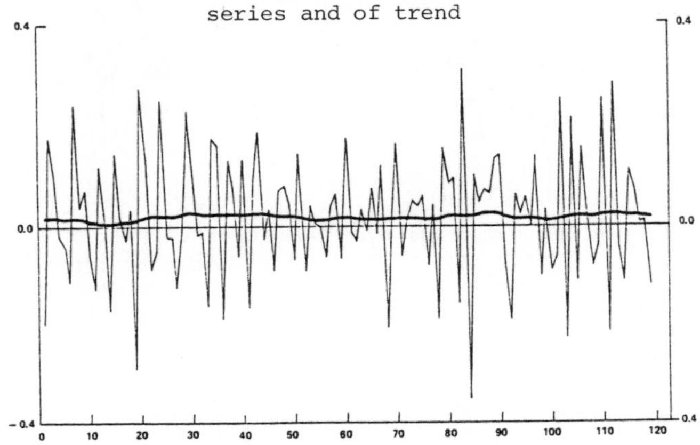

decompositions. In particular, we focussed on changes in the "regular" structure which yielded, in all cases, reasonable specifications to account for the small low-order autocorrelation present in z_t. The differences in the estimated components were particularly noticeable for the trend. Therefore, when signal extraction (likely, on top of forecasting) is to be performed, the usual criteria for ARIMA model selection may be innapropriate. Attention should be paid to the way the model "decomposes". Useful (and easy to compute) tools in this respect are the frequency domain representation of the seasonal and trend models, which are implied by the overall ARIMA, and the ACF of the estimated irregular.

A reasonable model selection strategy would, from the set of series-compatible models, pick up the one which yields the best decomposition. In our application, this led us to an "Airline model" specification, which is known to decompose nicely (see [7].)

This way of proceeding somewhat combines the two alternative approaches to signal extraction. One of them (exemplified by X11) is to use "ad hoc" filters for the signal, with desirable properties, at the risk of violating the series stochastic structure. The other approach models the series first, and from this derives the implied filters, which may present undesirable properties.

What we have seen is that the limitations imposed by the sample information, and the relatively large sensitivity of the model-based decomposition to changes in the ARIMA specification, may provide an ample room for signal improvement, within the set of series-compatible models.

REFERENCES:

[1] Bell, W.R., "Signal Extraction for Non-stationary Time Series", Annals of Statistics, 12. (forthcoming.)

[2] Box, G.E.P., Hillmer, S.C. y Tiao, G.C., "Analysis and Modeling of Seasonal Time Series" in Seasonal Analysis of Economic Time Series, ed. A. Zellner (U.S. Department of Commerce, Bureau of the Census, Washington, D.C., 1978.)

[3] Box, G.E.P. y Jenkins, G.M., Time Series Analysis, (Holden Day: San Francisco, 1970)

[4] Burman, J.P., "Seasonal Adjustment by Signal Extraction" Journal of the Royal Statistical Society, A, 143 (1980) 321-337.

[5] Cleveland, W. P. and Tiao, G. C., "Decomposition of Seasonal Time Series: A Model for the Census X11 Program", Journal of the American Statistical Association, 71 (1976) 581-587.

[6] Hillmer, S. C. y Tiao, G. C., "An ARIMA-Model-Based Approach to Seasonal Adjustment", Journal of the American Statistical Association, 77 (1982) 63-70.

[7] __________, "Time Series: Estimation, Smoothing and Seasonal Adjustment" Ph. D. Dissertation, Department of Statistics, The University of Wisconsin, 1976.

[8] Kendall, M., Time-Series (Griffin and Co. Ltd., London, 1976.)

[9] Maravall, A., "Analisis de las Series de Comercio Exterior", Documento de trabajo (Banco de España, Madrid, 1984.)

[10] Shiskin, J., Young, A.H. and Musgrave, J.C., "The X11 Variant of Census Method II Seasonal Adjustment Program", Technical Paper 15 (U.S. Department of Commerce, Bureau of the Census, Washington, D.C., 1967.)

COMPUTER SCIENCE AND STATISTICS:
The Interface, L. Billard (ed.)

Seasonality and Seasonal Adjustment of Time Series

Steven Hillmer

The University of Kansas

1. Introduction

Seasonality in a time series is characterized by the recurrence at roughly periodic intervals of values for the time series which have about the same magnitude. As an illustration of a time series which exhibits seasonality, consider the monthly U.S. total inventories of tobacco products from January 1958 to September 1979. This series is plotted in Figure 1. The regular yearly movements of this series are evident from the plot. Frequently, it is supposed that a seasonal time series, Z_t, is composed of two unobserved parts: a seasonal part, S_t, and a nonseasonal part, N_t. The process of decomposing Z_t into S_t and N_t is called seasonal adjustment. Many people believe that the seasonal component is relatively uncontrolable and thus a nuisance. To these people the main reason for seasonal adjustment is to obtain estimates of the nonseasonal component.

Seasonal adjustment has a long history which has been dominated by empirical methods. An empirical method of seasonal adjustment is a procedure which has been developed by a process of trial and error with little basis in any underlying statistical theory. The principle example of an empirical seasonal adjustment approach is the Bureau of Census's X-11 method. This was developed under the guidance of Julius Shiskin from 1954 to 1967. It is the final product of eleven trial seasonal adjustment programs.

Many empirical seasonal adjustment methods use symmetric moving averages in estimating S_t and N_t. A symmetric moving average of Z_t is $\sum_{j=-m}^{m} \alpha_j Z_{t-j}$ where $\alpha_j = \alpha_{-j}$. Young (1968) and Wallis (1974) have shown that the estimates of S_t and N_t derived from the X-11 program may be approximated by symmetric moving averages.

Because the seasonal and nonseasonal components are not observed, it is important to obtain some kind of a consensus about what people believe are the properties of these components. One way to accomplish this is to study the X-11 method because it produces answers which many people believe are appropriate. A number of conclusions result from this analysis. (1) The seasonal component is assumed to change over time. (2) There is not any specified mathematical model for the components. (3) The sum of the seasonal component over any entire year is presumed to be close to zero. (4) There is a need to somehow deal with extreme observations. (5) For some time series, there is the need to be able to adjust for known influences related to the construction of the calendar.

The trial and error approach that was used in the development of X-11 and other empirical methods of seasonal adjustment was the only realistic way to study the kind of complex seasonality present in economic time series because at the time of their development, the appropriate statistical theory was not available. However, since 1970 the statistical theory of time series and associated computer software have advanced substantially. At the same time, there has been some dissatisfaction with certain aspects of X-11 and a desire to correct these perceived defects, see Kallek (1978). At the present time it is difficult to make substantive changes in X-11 by trial and error methods because X-11 is very complex so that it is hard to know what effect changes will have on the final results. Thus, if progress is going to be made it will occur most rapidly by using a more theoretical approach. In recent years, there have been a number of attempts to study the problems of seasonal adjustment from a theoretical point of view, e.g. Grether and Nerlove (1970), Cleveland and Tiao (1976), Pierce (1978), Burman (1980), Hillmer and Tiao (1982), and Gersch and Kitagawa (1984). The methods developed from these studies will be called model-based approaches to seasonal adjustment.

Signal Extraction

The signal extraction problem is to estimate a signal, S_t, in an observed times series, $Z_t = S_t + N_t$. By identifying S_t and N_t as the seasonal and nonseasonal components, seasonal adjustment may be viewed as a problem in signal extraction. The problem of finding the best linear unbiased estimates of S_t and N_t given Z_t has been solved, see Bell (1984) and references therein. Thus, the signal extraction framework provides a theoretical foundation for the problem of seasonal adjustment. It is important that the solution of a signal extraction problem requires that the covariance structure of the S_t and N_t components is known even though these components are unobservable. Therefore, any model-based seasonal adjustment procedure must make assumptions that uniquely specify the covariance structure of the seasonal and nonseasonal components. Since the seasonal or nonseasonal components of a time series have never been observed, the assumptions leading to their definition are arbitrary to a large extent. This issue is discussed more fully in Bell and Hillmer (1984).

In the development of model-based procedures, it is assumed that $Z_t = S_t + N_t$. Sometimes it is necessary to transform the observed data so that the additive structure applies (if $Z_t = S_t \cdot N_t$ then the additive structure applies to $\ell n Z_t$). Since the Z_t series is observed, it is reasonable to assume that the model generating this series (or equivalently its covariance structure) is approximately known. For example, Box and Jenkins (1976) give procedures to build time series models for Z_t. Because of the additive relationship between the components and Z_t, the model for Z_t will impose restrictions upon the models for S_t and N_t. In the deriving unique models for S_t and N_t to be used in the theory of signal extraction, it is reasonable to restrict the choice of these models to be consistent with the model for Z_t. In this way, the component models will be consistent with any information available in the data about the seasonality. Thus, a necessary requirement of a seasonal adjustment method is that it is consistent with the information in the observed data.

Classification of Seasonal Adjustment Methods

Model-based approaches are linear methods and Young (1968) has shown that X-11 is approximately linear (Young's arguments would also apply to many other empirical methods). As a general aid in comparing methods of seasonal adjustment and assessing their consistency with observed data, they can be classified according to how they arrive at their linear filters. Methods can be divided into three groups. (1) Methods which choose the filters directly. (2) Methods which directly choose the models for the components and then use signal extraction theory to derive the filters. (3) Methods which model the observed data, deduce models for the components based upon that model, and then derive the filters from signal extraction theory.

Because of the nature of seasonal adjustment, the way in which one may judge whether or not a particular method is consistent with a given set of observed data is complex. One way to approach this problem is discussed in Bell and Hillmer (1984). However, some general comments about methods in each of the three groups can be made. For methods in group 1, one would have to be lucky in general to make a choice of filter which is consistent with an adequate model for Z_t. This is because the filters are chosen directly and frequently the same filter is applied to many different series. The methods in group 2 provide the opportunity to begin with reasonable component models and frequently provide some flexibility by estimating some parameters using the Z_t series. However, there is no reason to believe that these methods will lead to filters which are consistent with the data in general. The methods in group 3 are designed to be consistent with the information in Z_t in general. Thus, they have a theoretical advantage over the methods in the other two groups.

2. An ARIMA Model-Based Approach to Seasonal Adjustment

To satisfy the minimum requirement it will be assumed that our approach to seasonal adjustment will be consistent with the model for Z_t and the additive structure $Z_t = S_t + N_t$. However, the model for Z_t is not sufficient to uniquely specify the models for S_t and N_t; therefore we must make additional assumptions. The approach followed here is described more fully in Hillmer and Tiao (1982). They specify assumptions that when combined with a given model for Z_t lead to unique component models.

We use the seasonal ARIMA time series model (Box and Jenkins (1976)) to represent the covariance structure of Z_t,

$$\phi(B)Z_t = \theta(B)a_t \qquad (1)$$

where $\phi(B) = 1 - \phi_1 B - \cdots - \phi_p B^p$ is a polynomial in the backshift operator, B, whose zeros are on or outside the unit circle, $\theta(B) = 1 - \theta_1 B - \cdots - \theta_q B^q$ is a polynomial in B with zeros outside the unit circle, the pair $\{\phi(B), \theta(B)\}$ have no common zeros, and a_t is a white noise series with variance σ_a^2. Some of the parameters in (1) may be equal to zero or otherwise constrained. It is also assumed that

$$Z_t = S_t + N_t \qquad (2)$$

where S_t and N_t are mutually independent time series following the ARIMA models.

$$\phi_S(B)S_t = \eta_S(B)b_t$$

and (3)

$$\phi_N(B)N_t = \eta_N(B)c_t$$

where the pairs of polynomials in B, $\{\phi_S(B), \eta_S(B)\}$, $\{\phi_N(B), \eta_N(B)\}$ and $\{\phi_S(B), \phi_N(B)\}$ have no common zeros, and $\{b_t\}$ and $\{c_t\}$ are white noise series with variances σ_b^2 and σ_c^2 respectively. These assumptions serve to define the problem in its basic form.

Hillmer and Tiao (1982) show that it is necessary to make some additional assumptions. In particular, assume that for monthly data

$$\phi_S(B) = 1 + B + \cdots + B^{11} = U(B) \qquad (3)$$

and assume that

$$\eta_S(B) = 1 + \eta_1^S B + \cdots + \eta_{11}^S B^{11} \qquad (4)$$

so that the degree of the polynomical $\eta_S(B)$ is no greater than eleven. These two assumptions are arbitrary in the sense that they cannot be verified based upon the observed Z_t. However, they are derived from features of the X-11 program which in some sense define people's beliefs about the nature of a seasonal component. In particular the sum of S_t over any twelve consecutive months is $U(B)S_t$ and $E[U(B)S_t] = E[\eta_S(B)b_t] = 0$. Thus, the moving sum $U(B)S_t$ is a stationary time series which varies about zero. This is consistent with the ideas about seasonality implicit in X-11 in which the seasonal evolves over time in a way so that twelve month sums are close to zero.

Given these assumptions and the model for Z_t, Hillmer and Tiao (1982) show that the variance of b_t, σ_b^2 must lie in a known range $[\bar{\sigma}_b^2, \tilde{\sigma}_b^2]$ and that the models for S_t and N_t are uniquely determined once a choice of σ_b^2 is made. A decomposition corresponding to any σ_b^2 in $[\bar{\sigma}_b^2, \tilde{\sigma}_b^2]$ is called an admissable decomposition. To uniquely specify the component models, they take $\sigma_b^2 = \bar{\sigma}_b^2$ the smallest possible value and call the corresponding decomposition the canonical decomposition. The corresponding components are called the canonical seasonal and canonical nonseasonal. This choice of σ_b^2 is arbitrary. In order to justify this choice the properties of the canonical decomposition need to be examined in light of people's beliefs about the nature of the seasonal and nonseasonal components.

<u>Properties of the canonical decomposition</u>

By choosing σ_b^2 (the variance of the shocks driving the seasonal model) as small as possible, the seasonal component is made as close to being deterministic as possible while remaining consistent with the information in the known model for Z_t. Hillmer and Tiao (1982) show that by choosing $\sigma_b^2 = \bar{\sigma}_b^2$ results in the minimization of the $Var[U(B)S_t]$. A stable seasonal pattern would have $U(B)S_t$ exactly equal to zero. The canonical seasonal has the property that $U(B)S_t$ has expected value zero and a minimum possible variance. Thus, the canonical seasonal has a periodic pattern which is as stable as possible. Also, they show that for any other choice of σ_b^2 leading to an acceptable decomposition, the corresponding seasonal component, S_t', can be written as

$$S_t' = \bar{S}_t + e_t$$

where $\bar{S}_t$ is the canonical seasonal, e_t is white noise, and S_t is uncorrelated with e_t. Thus, any admissible seasonal may be viewed as the sum of the canonical seasonal and white noise. The canonical seasonal is as deterministic as possible and thus as predictable as possible while the white noise is unpredictable and is not have any seasonal characteristics. Therefore, the canonical seasonal component contains all the information about the seasonality in the original data and any other choice of seasonal component can be viewed as a noisy version of the canonical seasonal.

Of course, the choice of the canonical decomposition is arbitrary since some of the assumptions leading to its definition cannot be checked by using observable data. However, the implications for these assumptions upon the seasonal component seem to be reasonable and seem to correspond to what many people view as a seasonal component. It is important to remember that the choice of the canonical decomposition does satisfy the requirement that the component models are consistent with the information in the observed data. It is also noteworthy that while the principles leading to the definition of the canonical decomposition are set up prior to the analysis of observed data, the actual models for the components will be dependent upon the model for Z_t. Thus, there is a lot of flexibility in the resulting seasonal adjustment procedure.

Seasonal adjustment with the canonical decomposition

Once the component models have been uniquely defined via the canonical decomposition, the theory of signal extraction extended to cover ARIMA models can be applied to provide estimates of the seasonal and nonseasonal components. The explicit way to do this is described in Hillmer and Tiao (1982) and the theoretical details of how to derive the estimation procedures are given in Bell (1984). A computer program to derive the canonical decomposition from a given model for Z_t and to compute the component estimates based upon signal extraction theory is available from the author.

These procedures will be illustrated on the time series of monthly U.S. total inventories of tobacco products from January 1958 to September 1979. By following the approach of Box and Jenkins (1976) the model

$$(1-B)(1-B^{12})\ell n Z_t = (1-.78B^{12})a_t \qquad (5)$$

was determined to approximately describe the behavior of this series. For this example, the additive decomposition is appropriate for the logs of Z_t. Based upon the model for the data in (5), the two component models were computed and these were used to compute the moving averages from signal extraction theory associated with these models. The weights associated with estimating the components are reported in table 1. These weights were used in estimation of the components which are plotted in Figure 1. In this figure the nonseasonal is exponentiated to be in the same metric as the original data and the seasonal has been exponentiated and multiplied by 100 to be put on a percentage basis. It is apparent from this figure that the nonseasonal does a good job of capturing the underlying movements of the original data. Also, the seasonal component changes over time but the changes are made relatively slowly.

3. Extension of the model-based approach

One of the main advantages of a model-based approach to seasonal adjustment is that it provides a mechanism (statistical theory) to develop improvements in seasonal adjustment procedures. For instance, one criticism of empirical seasonal adjustment procedures is that they fail to provide an estimate of the variability associated with estimates of the components. However, in the ARIMA model-based approach to seasonal adjustment, the statistical theory of signal extraction provides a means to compute variances of the point estimates. Details of how to do this are given in Hillmer (1982). These procedures were applied in the previous example to compute standard errors of the point estimates and 95% confidence intervals for the nonseasonal component. The results for some selected times are reported in Table 2.

People who apply seasonal adjustment methods to real data have known for a long time that monthly time series can be affected by the construction of the calander. Examples are trading day variation and Easter holiday variation. Trading day variation is caused by the fact that the same months over the years are composed of a different number and different types of trading days. This characteristic will frequently affect the level of series which are influenced by the number of trading days in a month like retail sales. Easter holiday variation results in some series from the increased activity prior to Easter and the fact that Easter does not always fall in the same month each year. Thus, some years the value of the time series in March is affected and some years the value in April is affected. An approach to building models to describe these effects is described in Bell and Hillmer (1983) and Hillmer, Bell and Tiao (1983). The approach to the problems which is followed in these papers is to model the time series and let the models dictate how to adjust the series for trading day and Easter effects. This has the advantage that a model for a given set of data can be checked for its reasonableness. As an example of adjusting a time series affected by trading day variation, consider the monthly series of wholesale sales of drugs, drug proprietories and drugest' sundries from January, 1967 to November, 1979. Following the approach in Bell and Hillmer (1983), a model of the form

$$\ell n Z_t = \sum_{i=1}^{7} \beta_i T_{it} + \frac{(1-\theta_1 B)(1-\theta_{12}B^{12})}{(1-B)(1-B^{12})} a_t \qquad (6)$$

was fit to the data. In (6) β_i are parameters, T_{it} i=1,...,6 are respectively the number of Mondays in month t minus the number of Sundays in month t through the number of Saturdays in month t minus the number of Sundays in month t and T_{7t} is the total number of days in month t. The model (6) is a regression model with ARIMA errors. The parameter estimates along with their standard errors are reported in Table 3. Hillmer, Bell and Tiao (1983) describe how to use the model in (6) to adjust this time series for trading day effects and for seasonal effects. The results of applying this procedure are plotted along with the original data in Figure 2.

4. Comparison of model-based and empirical approaches

It is important to have a means to compare different methods of seasonal adjustment. However, because of the fact that the components are unobserved it is difficult to agree upon ways to compare the results of different methods. These problems are discussed more fully in Bell and Hillmer (1984). The ARIMA model-based approach does however, have some theoretical advantages over empirical methods of seasonal adjustment.

Underlying statistical assumptions

In model-based procedures, the underlying statistical assumptions are specified so that the methods can be criticized from a theoretical viewpoint. This makes it possible to understand the statistical principles implicit in model-based methods. In contrast, empirical methods are not based upon statistical theory and thus it is difficult or impossible to judge them on theoretical grounds.

Arbitrariness

Seasonal adjustment is inherently arbitrary. In the model-based approach discussed in this paper this arbitrariness comes from building a time series model to describe the observed data and from the assumptions needed to go from this model to the component models. Although modeling a times series is somewhat subjective, any model finally used will be subjected to appropriate diagnostic tests. Thus, the primary source of arbitrariness lies in the fact that even if the model for Z_t were known, arbitrary assumptions are needed to achieve a unique decomposition. In the ARIMA model-based procedure these assumptions are clearly specified.

Empirical adjustment procedures must also deal with the same kind of arbitrary choices as model-based approaches. The problem is that with empirical methods the nature of these choices is unclear and thus there is no way to judge their reasonableness.

Consistency with the data

The model-based seasonal adjustment method advocated here is constrained to be consistent with an appropriate model describing the observed data. This provides flexibility since we allow the adjustment procedure to change with different series as the model for Z_t changes. It seems reasonable to use the information about the seasonality in the data to help define the moving average filters.

Empirical methods are fairly inflexible in that they allow for a relatively few options. Furthermore, in practice many times the options are only used infrequently. In addition, choosing, options is subjective and without valid statistical tests to support one's judgement, inappropriate options may be selected. Thus, these methods will be consistent with the information in the data only by chance.

Optimality of filters

In empirical approaches, the moving average filters have been determined by trial and error and therefore do not necessarily satisfy any particular optimality criterion. In contrast, the moving averages for model-based approaches are derived from the theory of signal extraction so that given the models for S_t and N_t the estimates will have smaller mean squared error than any other linear unbiased estimates.

In conclusion, if one is to judge different methods of seasonal adjustment it should be done on theoretical grounds. Model-based approaches have an advantage over empirical methods in theory. It is also necessary to evaluate the assumptions made by model-based approaches for their reasonableness.

References

Bell, W. R. (1984), "Signal Extraction for Nonstationary Time Series," Annals of Statistics, 12, to appear.

Bell, W. R. and Hillmer, S. C. (1983), "Modeling Time Series with Calendar Variation," Journal of the American Statistical Association, 78, p526.

Bell, W. R. and Hillmer, S. C. (1984), "Issues Involved with the Seasonal Adjustment of Economic Time Series," Journal of Business and Economic Statistics, 2, to appear.

Box, G. E. P. and Jenkins, G. M. (1976), Time Series Analysis: Forecasting and Control, San Francisco, Holden Day.

Burman, J. R. (1980), "Seasonal Adjustment by Signal Extraction," Journal of the Royal Statistical Society Series A, 143, p321.

Cleveland, W. P. and Tiao, G. C. (1976), "Decomposition of Seasonal Time Series: A Model for the X-11 Program," Journal of the American Statistical Association, 71, p581.

Grether, D. M. and Nerlove, M. (1970), "Some Properties of 'Optimal' Seasonal Adjustment," Econometrica, 38, p682.

Hillmer, S. C. (1982), "Confidence Intervals for Seasonally Adjusted Data," Proceedings of the Business and Economics Statistics Section, American Statistical Association.

Hillmer, S. C., Bell, W. R., and Tiao, G. C. (1983), "Modeling Considerations in the Seasonal Adjustment of Economic Time Series," in Applied Time Series Analysis of Economic Data, Economic Research Report ER-5, Bureau of Census, ed. Arnold Zellner.

Hillmer, S. C. and Tiao, G. C. (1982), "An ARIMA Model-Based Approach to Seasonal Adjustment," Journal of the American Statistical Association, 77, p63.

Kallek, S. (1978), "An Overview of the Objective and Framework of Seasonal Adjustment" in Seasonal Analysis of Economic Time

Series, Economic Research Report ER-1, Bureau of the Census, ed. Arnold Zellner.

Kitagawa, G. and Gersch, W. (1984), "A Smoothness Priors-State Space Modeling of Time Series with Trend and Seasonality," Journal of the American Statistical Association, 79, to appear.

Pierce, D. A. (1978), "Seasonal Adjustment when both Deterministic and Stochastic Seasonality are Present" in Seasonal Analysis of Economic Time Series, Economic Research Report ER-1, Bureau of the Census, ed. Arnold Zellner.

Wallis, K. F. (1974), "Seasonal Adjustment and Relations Between Variables," Journal of the American Statistical Association, 69, p18.

Young, A. H. (1968), "Linear Approximations to the Census and BLS Seasonal Adjustment Methods," Journal of the American Statistical Association, 63, p445.

Table 1

Weights in the moving average to estimate S_t

j	1	2	3	4	5	6	7	8	9
α_j	.1042	-.0078	-.0099	-.0097	-.0095	-.0094	-.0092	-.0090	-.0088
j	10	11	12	13	14	15	16	17	18
α_j	-.0086	-.0084	-.0085	.0894	-.0081	-.0077	-.0076	-.0074	-.0073
j	19	20	21	22	23	24	25		
α_j	-.0071	-.0070	-.0069	-.0067	-.0066	-.0066	.0697		

Weights in the moving average to estimate N_t

j	1	2	3	4	5	6	7	8	9
α_j	.8958	.0078	.0099	.0097	.0095	.0094	.0092	.0090	.0088
j	10	11	12	13	14	15	16	17	18
α_j	.0086	.0084	.0085	-.0894	.0081	.0077	.0076	.0074	.0073
j	19	20	21	22	23	24	25		
α_j	.0071	.0070	.0069	.0067	.0066	.0066	-.0697		

Other α_j in both cases can be determined from the equation $\alpha_j = .78\alpha_{j-12}$ which is true if $j \geq 14$.

Table 2

Point estimates and variances for the inventory of tobacco products example

(Time t=258 corresponds to September 1979)

Point Estimates and Standard Errors

t	247	248	249	250	251	252
$\hat{N}_t$	3383	3369	3484	3522	3612	3595
Standard Error	18.9	19.1	19.9	20.2	20.8	20.7
t	253	254	255	256	257	258
$\hat{N}_t$	3599	3541	3571	3579	3594	3685
Standard Error	20.7	20.4	20.7	21.0	21.4	22.5

95% Confidence intervals

t	247	248	249	250	251	252
Upper Value	3420	3407	3523	3562	3653	3636
Lower Value	3346	3332	3445	3483	3572	3555
t	253	254	255	256	257	258
Upper Value	3640	3581	3612	3620	3636	3729
Lower Value	3559	3501	3531	3538	3552	3641

Table 3

Parameter Estimates for Model (6)

Parameter	Estimate	Standard Error
β_1	-.0018	.0037
β_2	.0200	.0037
β_3	.0022	.0037
β_4	.0088	.0037
β_5	.0126	.0037
β_6	-.0268	.0037
β_7	.0057	.0124
θ_1	.2629	.0852
θ_{12}	.5427	.0718

Figure 1

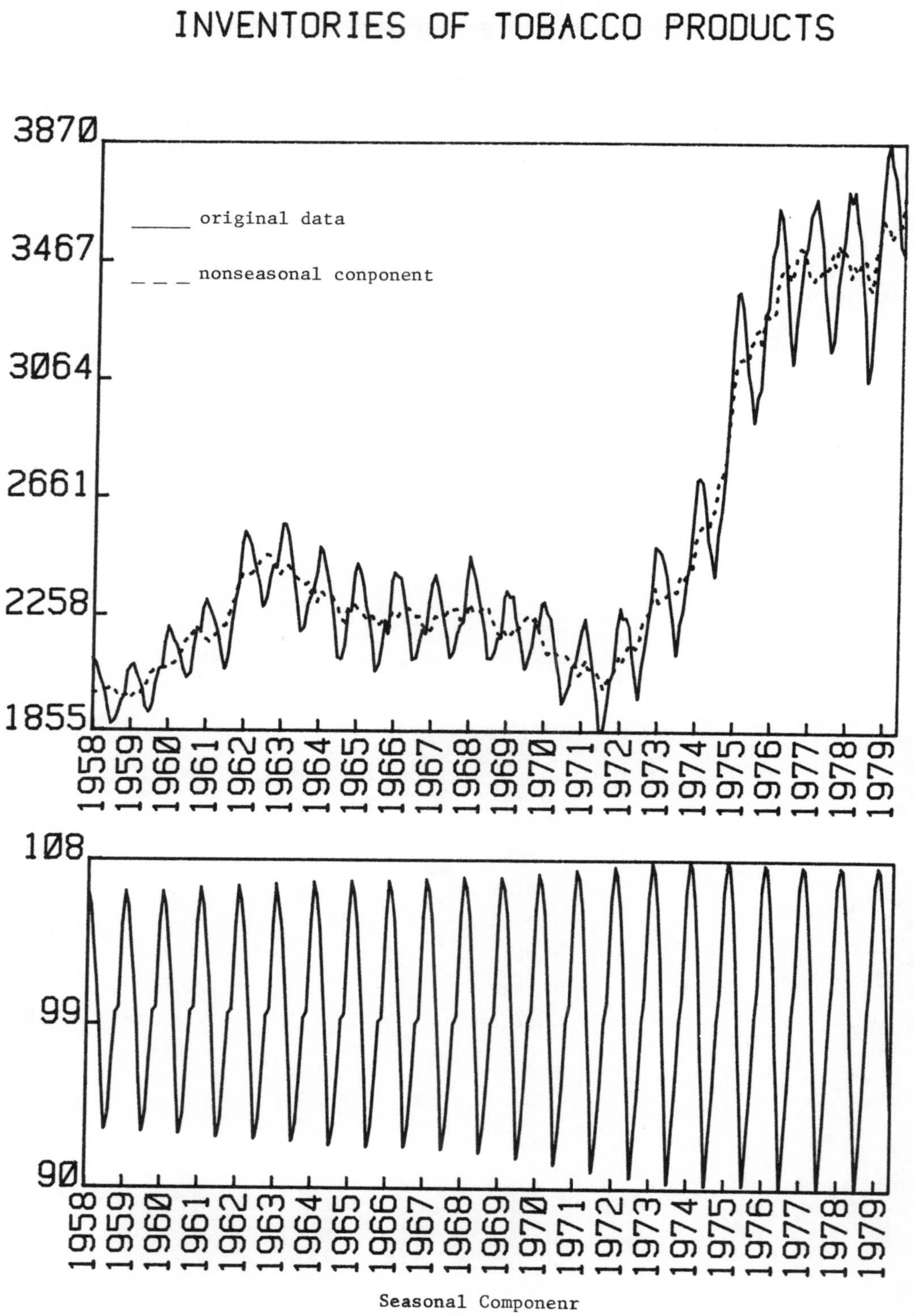

Seasonal Componenr

Figure 2

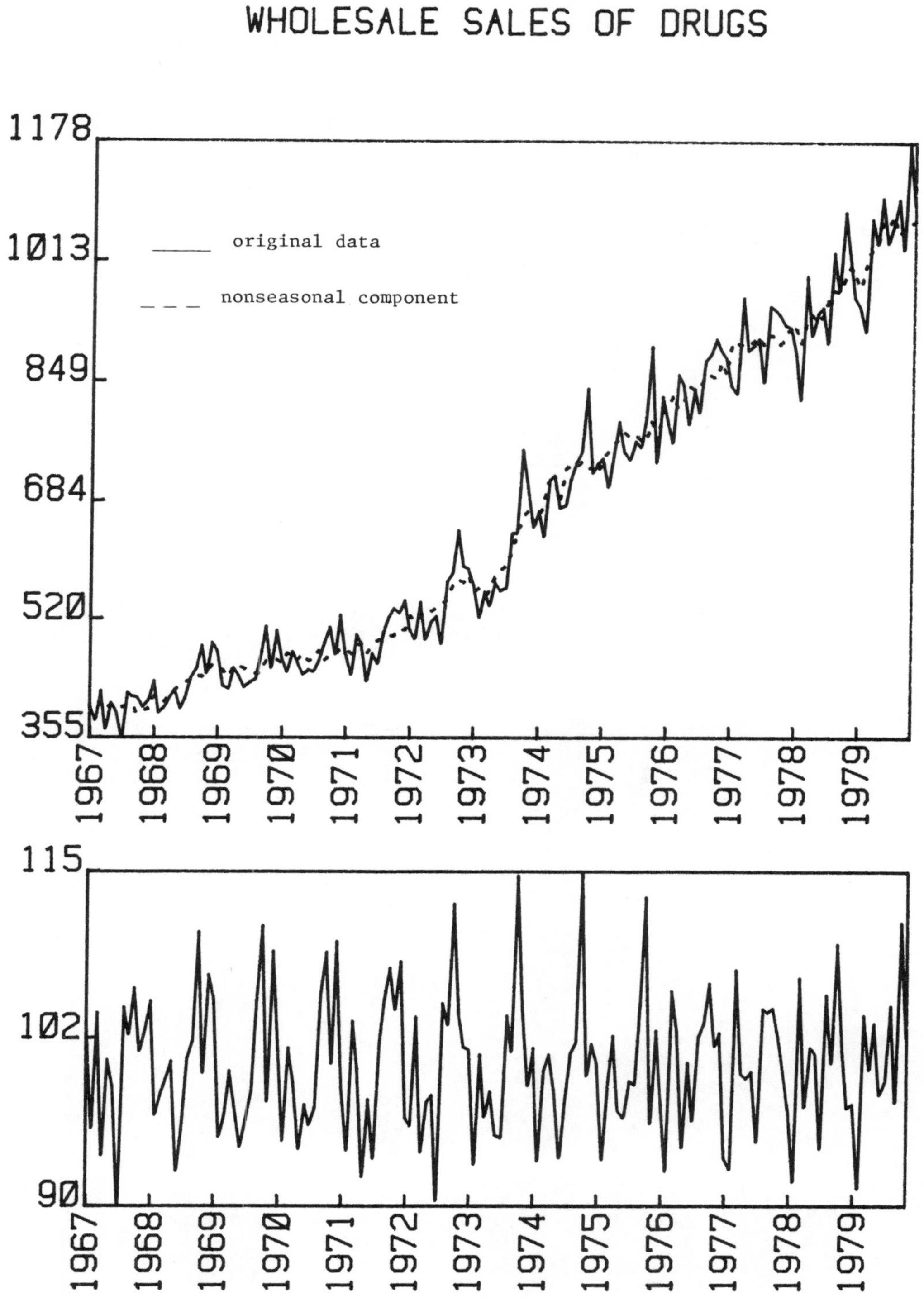

Seasonal and Trading Day Component

Figure 2 continued

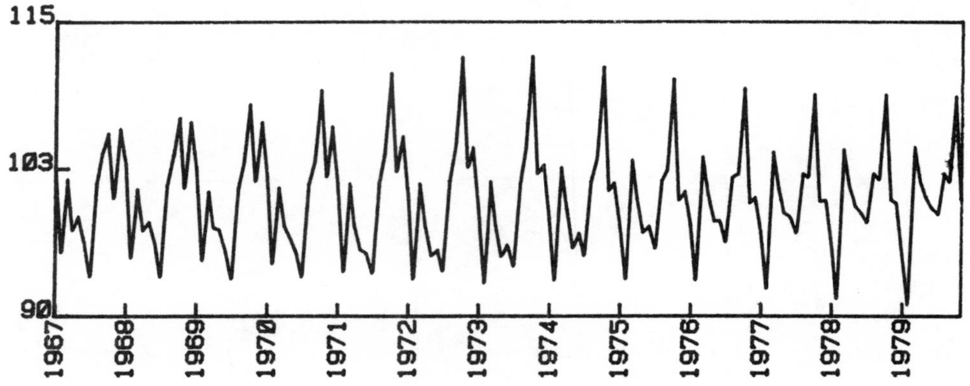

Seasonal Component

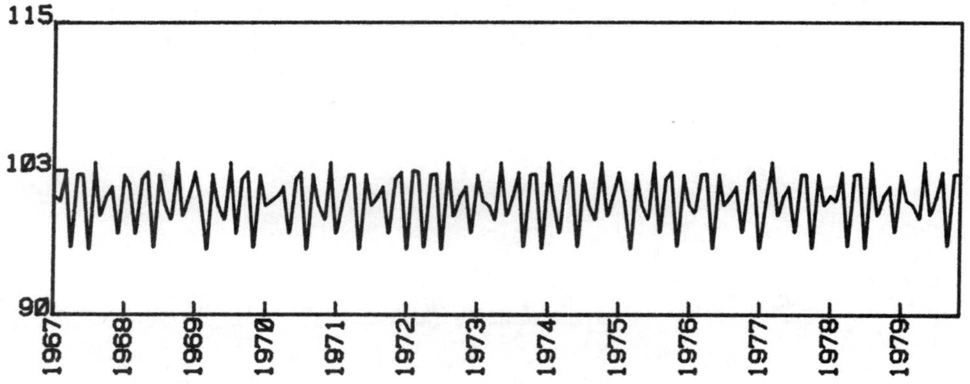

Trading Day Component

Graphical Tools for Data Analysis

Organizer: *R. McGill, Bell Laboratories*

Invited Presentations:

Looking at More Than Three Dimensions, *W. L. Nicholson and D. B. Carr, Pacific Northwest Laboratory*

COMPUTER SCIENCE AND STATISTICS:
The Interface, L. Billard (ed.)

LOOKING AT MORE THAN THREE DIMENSIONS

W. L. Nicholson[1] and D. B. Carr[1]

Pacific Northwest Laboratory
Richland, Washington 99352

Statistical graphics for data in more than three dimensions cannot be based on direct spatial representation. Three approaches have been tried with varying degrees of success. First is simultaneous presentation of two- or three-dimensional marginals with a cross-reference scheme to identify common points. Second is projection into two or three dimensions and variations on this theme. Third is a single view with higher dimensions indicated by characteristics of the plotting symbol. The first two approaches admit visualization of simple conditional relationships, but putting together pieces to understand complex relationships requires substantial intellectual effort. The third is a compromise which presents some visualization of higher dimensional relationships.
The paper emphasizes the third mode of display making use of motion, color, and geometrical characteristics of the plotting symbol as higher dimensional cues.

1. INTRODUCTION

Statistical graphics for data in more than three dimensions cannot be based on direct spatial representation. The nonspatial alternatives for representing higher dimensions are subject to variability of interpretation and require experience for effective use. Individual differences in visual perception cause many nonspatial alternatives to mean different things to different people. An informative technique for viewing higher dimensions for one analyst may be ineffective and even misleading to another. However, experience suggests that when these nonspatial alternatives work for an analyst they provide a powerful tool for understanding higher-dimension structure. In this paper we discuss some of the alternatives for looking at higher-dimensional data. While the title of the paper is "looking at more than three dimensions" the focus is on adding dimensions to routine scatterplots with nonspatial alternatives. Thus, for the analyst who routinely uses stereo 3-D scatterplots, the focus is on more than three dimensions. For the analyst who routinely uses 2-D scatterplots, the focus is on more than two dimensions.

Basically, three approaches for looking at higher-dimensional data have been used with some success by data analysts. None of the approaches are uniformly better. Each appears to be superior for specific types of applications. The first approach is juxtaposed 2-D or 3-D marginal scatterplots with a cross-reference scheme to link some or all of the data points. The second approach is projection onto a single 2-D or 3-D view based on a structure optimization metric. The third approach, also a single view, is an N-tuple scatterplot with dimensions beyond two indicated by characteristics of the plotting symbol. All approaches can be extended using sequences and/or overlays of views. All are amenable to enhancement techniques.(1,2) Further, hybrid combinations of these approaches are being used with increasing frequency. The first two approaches admit visualization of simple conditional relationships. With linked juxtaposed scatterplots a subset may be picked in one plot and the conditional bivariate relationships observed in all other plots. With projection the relationships are conditional on the projection. These approaches have been used extensively and successfully to note gross structure such as pair-wise correlations or low-dimensional, distinct clusters. Generalizing from conditional views to less obvious higher-dimensional relationships requires substantial intellectual effort. Data analysts have had varying degrees of success in accomplishing this intellectualization depending on their ability for spatial visualization and/or the complexity of the structure. The third approach is a compromise which presents some visualization of higher-dimensional relationships at the expense of not presenting all possible, or at least all the more informative, lower-dimensional views. In a few specific applications, this approach has successfully presented complex structure. We illustrate the above three approaches on real data. The literature abounds with applications of the first two, hence our emphasis is on the third approach. We consider the question of how best to "plot" nonspatially represented dimensions. Motion, color, and geometrical characteristics of the plotting symbol are all considered in our discussion of N-tuple scatterplots for displaying higher-dimensional relationships.

2. SIDE-BY-SIDE SCATTERPLOTS

Juxtaposed scatterplots are the data analysis analog of the draftsman's joint display of floor plans, sections, and exterior elevations, as 2-D views of 3-D structures. Tukey and Tukey(1) describe the organized collection of 2-D scatterplots to view all p(p - 1) ordered pairs of p dimensions. Further descriptions are found in Carr and Nicholson(3), Chambers et al.(4) and Tukey and Tukey.(5) An exotic demonstration of juxtaposed scatterplots is the Friedman et al.(6) movie of the simultaneous viewing on a graphics device of four rotation-generated, 3-D marginals of 12-D socio-economic data. Color coding cross references a select subset of data points in the four views. The information content of such a complex kinematic display is beyond quick comprehension. In fact, as a matter of course, any higher-dimensional view demands intense study in order to assimilate the information. A major problem in visualizing higher dimensions from juxtaposed marginal scatterplots is in the linking of individual data points or subsets of data points across views. Several methods have been tried to facilitate linkage. With an interactive graphics display unique cross reference can be obtained dynamically(6) by sequential identification of individual points and nearest neighbors in all views using color and shading. An alternative approach is to interactively select points in an N-dimensional parallelepiped.(7) Diaconis and Friedman(8) link two 2-D scatterplots with lines connecting nearest-neighbor subsets to create a static 4-D display. Carr and Nicholson(3) discuss interactive selection of arbitrary subsets and use color as a linkage across juxtaposed scatterplots.

Juxtaposed marginal scatterplots are an important tool for looking at higher dimensions. In fact, an exploratory data analysis could well begin with such views. Figure 1 presents a first look at precipitation chemistry data at two acid rain deposition sites, Duncan Falls, Ohio and Raleigh, North Carolina. During 1979, 69 individual rain shower epoch samples were collected at Duncan Falls and 81 at Raleigh. Depicted in Figure 1 are the results of volume (log ml), pH and three ion concentration measurements (log μmoles/cc) on each of the samples. The ten scatterplots BELOW the major diagonal are paired results for Raleigh and the ten ABOVE the major diagonal are paired results for Duncan Falls. Here juxtaposed scatterplots not only present 2-D marginals within each site but also a comparison of similarities and differences between sites. In this particular example the presentation is rather interesting. Note first that scales are calculated by combining the samples. For example, comparing the pH versus ion column at Raleigh with the pH versus ion row at Duncan Falls, pH is distributed beyond 6 at Raleigh and (excluding one value) cut off at 5 at Duncan Falls. The negative correlation of ion concentrations with pH appears much stronger at Raleigh. Likewise pair-wise ion concentrations appear stronger at Raleigh. (These last two comments need further verification. Larger-scale scatterplots with less overplotting might indicate more correlation structure at Duncan Falls.) Note, second, that when two scatterplots are compared across sites, one must be reflected through 180° about its minor diagonal for abcissa and ordinate variables to be the same. For example, the outliers for sulfate versus nitrate at the two sites are on the same side of the correlation pattern, not opposite sides as it appears at first glance.

While the side-by-side scatterplots of Figure 1 give an interesting overview of the data, detail is lost because of the large amount of overplotting. Color, aggregation and a stereo depth dimension are possible ways of reducing the effect of overplotting.(3)

3. PROJECTION INTO TWO OR THREE DIMENSIONS

Projection has long been a classic approach for the display of higher-dimensional data. Coupled with an optimization algorithm, it provides structure insight in many applications. However, even the most familiar of such techniques, principal components, demands understanding of theoretical aspects or else the results may be misleading. A classical example concerning 10 characteristic measurements on 375 grasshoppers is described by Gnanadesikan.(9) Here several arbitrary decisions on how the algorithm is to be applied produce a hodgepodge of dissimilar "optimum" 2-D and 3-D projection views. Possibly, if this analysis were being done today, insight from multidimensional graphics would allow a more meaningful and unequivocal application of principal components. A particularly rewarding use of projection is described by Friedman and Tukey.(10) They apply a projection pursuit algorithm to 7-D particle physics data. The resulting 2-D projection view consists primarily of fuzzy curves which suggests that the outcomes of most of the scattering events are strongly related in a complex nonlinear manner.

Difficulty in understanding the physical significance of the particular linear combination of variables selected as viewing axes by projection algorithms often precludes use of the results beyond the exploratory analysis stage. Also, particularly with many data points, projection algorithms tend to focus on dominant structure in the data. Patterns of outliers or even well-defined, low-dimensional structure of a small percentage of the data is only found by these algorithms through iteration based on residuals. On the other hand, a simple graphics presentation of all the data may allow quick identification of important minor structure. A challenge of statistical graphics is to combine the judgement of the analyst, based on his limited visualization of higher dimensions, with the power of computational algorithms to obtain better understanding of high-dimensional structure. We discuss one application of this idea in Section 4, below.

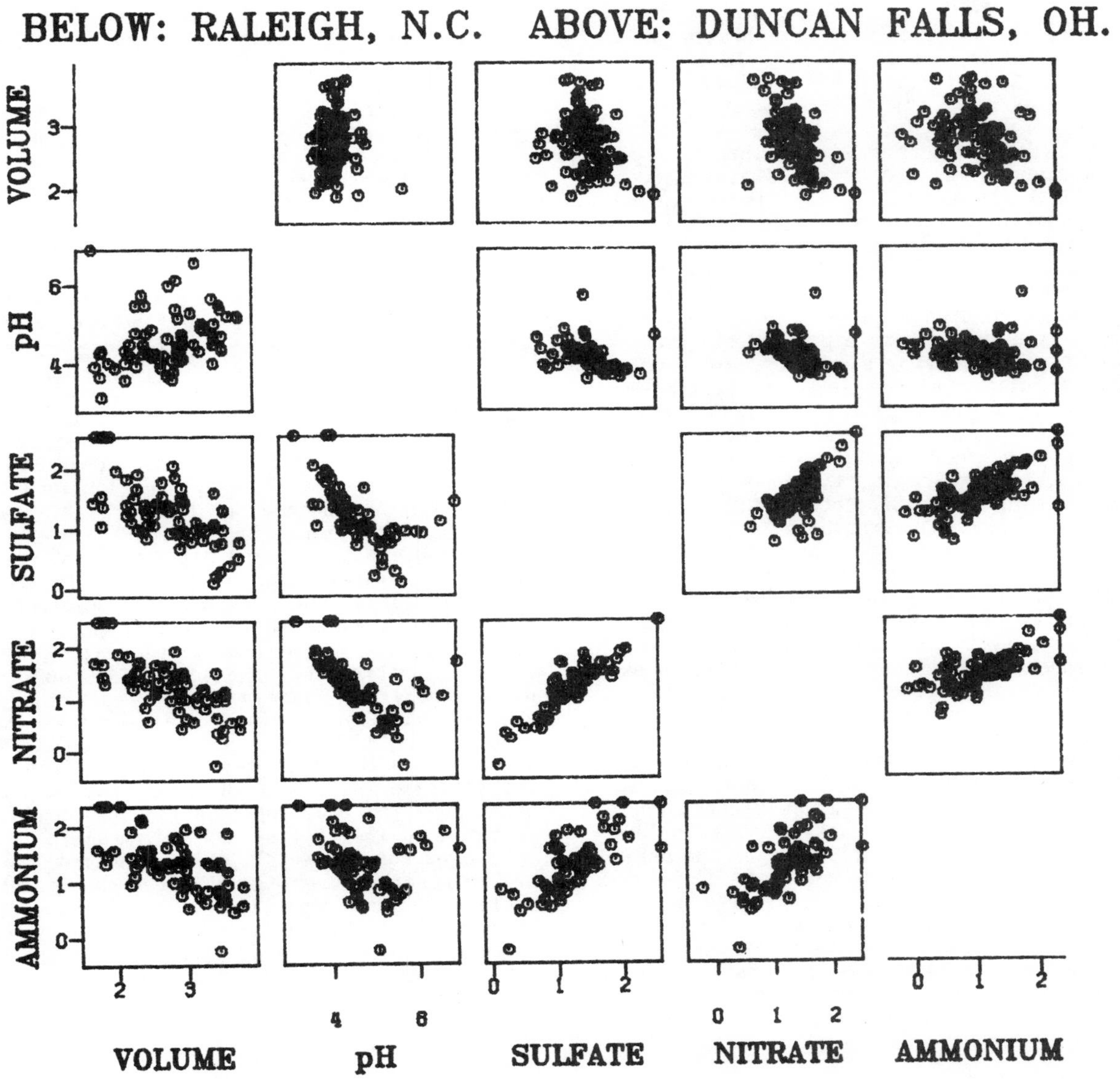

Figure 1 : Side-by-side scatterplots of precipitation chemistry data from Duncan Falls, Ohio and Raleigh, North Carolina

4. N-TUPLE SCATTERPLOTS

N-tuple scatterplots are not new. Analysts have long attempted to bind many dimensions together in a single display. As indicated above, a problem with side-by-side displays is the confusion generated by looking alternately back and forth even if there is a degree of built-in linkage. Displaying all dimensions in a single plot provides visual simultaneity. Dimensions comparison is possible--an outlier in one dimension can be checked to see if it is an outlier in other dimensions. The dimensionality of clusters shows up more readily when all dimensions are viewed simultaneously. A major problem with N-tuple scatterplots in the past has been difficulty of construction. Today, with the analysis and display power of computers, a challenge is to develop N-tuple scatterplots as a mechanism for interactive exploratory analysis of high-dimensional data. Our approach to N-tuple scatterplots builds on the work of earlier researchers. Anscombe(11) utilized mnemonic plotting symbols to represent a gross cellulation of a third dimension in scatterplots, which he aptly named "triple scatterplotting." Anscombe recognized a key point, the plotting symbol must unequivocally quantify the third dimension. He used typewriter symbols and hence the quantification was limited to several cells. The literature contains many illustrations of plotting symbols to encode quantitative information in a more-or-less continuous fashion. For example, Bickel et al.(12) use height and width of a rectangle, Bruntz et al.(13) use direction and length of a weather vane, and Nicholson and

Littlefield(14) use length and orientation of a ray, all three to display 4-D data as a "quadruple scatterplot." These displays all convey some aspect of the 4-D structure.

If N-tuple scatterplots are to be useful the plotting symbols must be selected very carefully. Cleveland and McGill(15), in an evaluation of the role of human perception on the success of simple graphics displays such as bar charts and pie charts, note that length, direction and angle generally convey more quantitative information than area, volume, curvature, shading, and color. Their experimental investigations do not suggest a strong ordering among length, direction, and angle. Interestingly enough, most of the applications of N-tuple scatterplots in the literature do utilize length and orientation. Here we do not distinguish between direction and angle, but only call it "orientation." Our experience with N-tuple scatterplots, suggests that orientation is a more useful characteristic than length (or, for that matter, size) for nonspatial representation of a dimension. Easily discernable vertical horizontal and orientations can convey the distributional aspects, central tendency and extreme, respectively. Consider the collections of ray symbols illustrated in Figure 2. Each ray orientation represents the value of an observation in a sample. Think of the ray as a pointer on a measuring instrument, such as a speedometer, increasing from left to right. A linear transformation of the sample codes the median as vertical (90°) and the minimum as left (0°) for a skewed left distribution or the maximum as right (180°) for a skewed right distribution. Thus, all the values fall between 0° and 180°. Values near the median are discernable as near vertical. Skewness in the distribution is also discernable as a single orientation for near horizontal rays. Further preventing the rays from dropping below horizontal prevents ambiguity.

Figure 2 illustrates the use of ray orientation to represent samples of 41 observations taken from uniform, negative exponential, Gaussian and

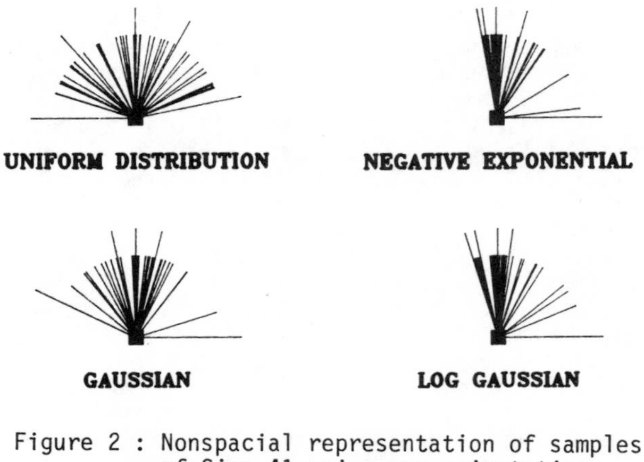

Figure 2 : Nonspacial representation of samples of Size 41 using ray orientation

log-Gaussian distributions. To help see gross features of the distributions, quartiles and median (with 41 observations ordered positions 1, 11, 21, 31, 41) are plotted with longer rays. The central peakedness of Gaussian relative to uniform is evident. The skewness of negative exponential and stronger skewness of log-Gaussian is evident.

Ray length is less quantitative than orientation but can be used for nonspatial representation of a second dimension. Length and color together do better. We have tried two approaches with varying degrees of success. Both use a linear ray length scale. For the first approach length and color are used redundantly. Since a positive length is necessary for the ray to have an orientation, the minimum length for easy visualization of orientation corresponds to the minimum of the data. If rays are too long then the scatterplot becomes cluttered. Trial and error selects minimum and maximum lengths to correspond to minimum and maximum of the data. Color can separate the ray length distribution into quantiles. For example, red and green can split lengths at the median with light and dark hues splitting at the quartiles. Variations using color ordering as described by Carr and Nicholson(3) and Nicholson and Littlefield(14) are reasonably successful at reinforcing a finer length discrimination. The second approach is a variation on the thermometer. Now all the rays are the same length. With color, the "mercury" portion of the ray, representing the quantity, is red with the rest of the thermometer closer to the background color. The thermometer approach has the advantage of a common reference scale for cross comparison of distinct rays.(15) Without color, the mercury portion can be drawn thicker. However, the additional thickness consumes space and accentuates saturation problems.

Figure 3 is a quadruple scatterplot depicting volume, pH, sulfate ion concentration and ammonium ion concentration for the Raleigh, North Carolina, acid-rain data illustrated in the BELOW triangle of Figure 1. The spatially represented variables are ammonium ion and sulfate ion concentrations, so the symbol position of Figure 3 is identical to that of the plot in Row 5, Column 3 of Figure 1. pH is coded as ray orientation, and volume is coded as ray length using the thermometer approach with mercury level represented by ray thickness. Several aspects of the four-dimensional distribution are easy to pick out.

The strong negative correlation between sulfate ion and pH is apparent as a general pattern of decreasing orientation as sulfate increases from left to right. The weaker negative correlation between ammonium ion and pH shows its gross characteristics as larger orientations in the lower left and smaller orientations in the upper right. Again, the sulfate-wise extreme symbols suggest negative correlations between both ions and volume, and positive correlation between pH and volume. The additional information, over

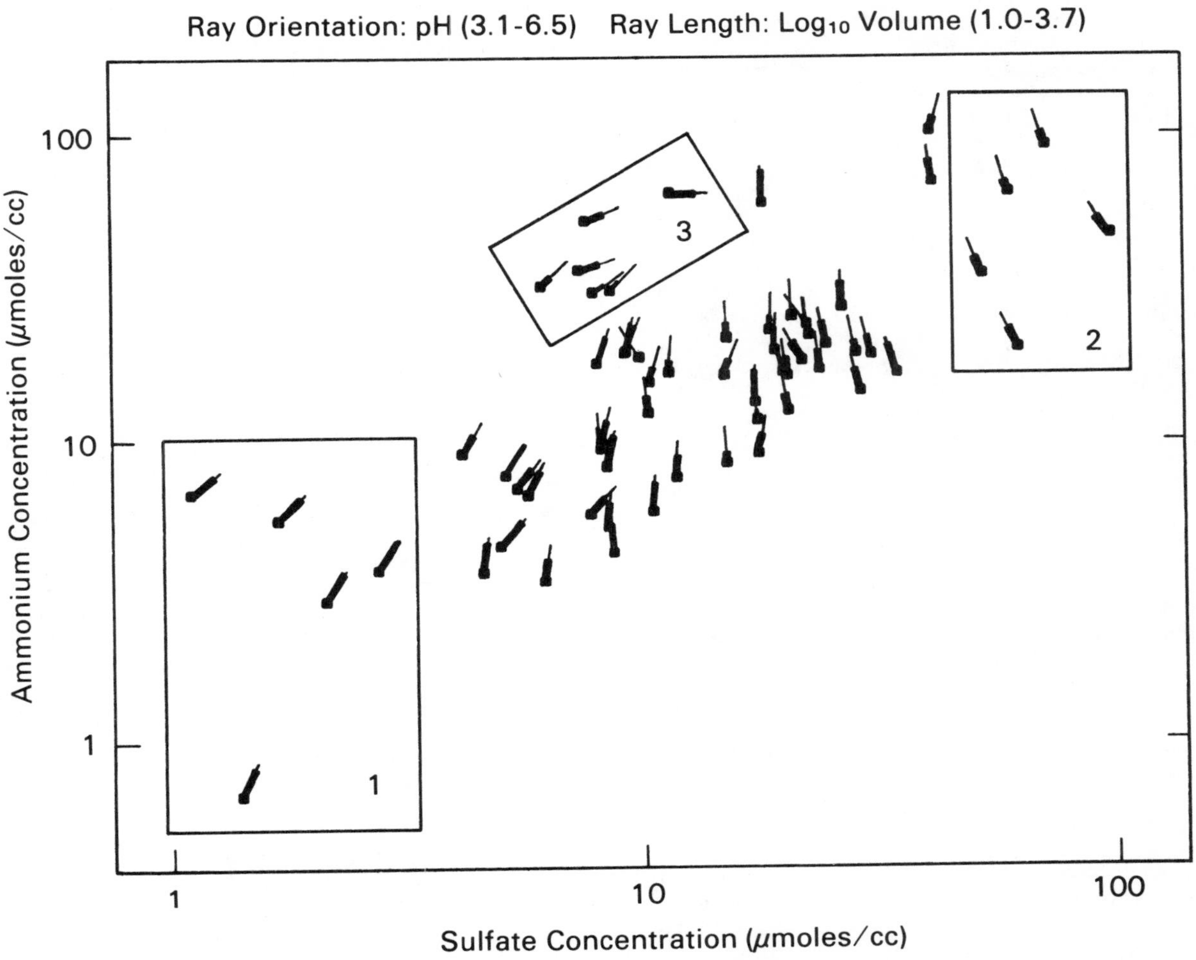

Figure 3 : Quadruple scatterplot of Raleigh, North Carolina precipitation chemistry data

that in Figure 1, relates to the definition of higher-dimensional clusters. In Figure 3, three such clusters are identified with rectangles and have the following attributes:

1. A cluster of five points with the lowest sulfate, low ammonium, high pH, and the largest volumes.

2. A cluster of five points with the highest sulfate, high ammonium, low pH, and small-to-median volume.

3. A cluster of six points with central sulfate, abnormally high ammonium (above the ammonium versus sulfate correlation structure), the highest pH in a skewed-right distribution, and small-to-median volume.

The remaining points constitute a fuzzy 4-D cluster with some systematic protrusion of small subsets of points.

4.1 3-D Scatterplots

Three-dimensional scatterplots are created with a pseudo-depth cue. Historically, perspective drawing and, with proper optical devices, stereo viewing have been used to create 3-D scatterplots. In the last 10 years computer-generated, rigid-body motion in the form of a simple rotation has been very successful at creating 3-D scatterplots. Tukey et al.(1), Donoho et al.(17) and Friedman et al.(6) describe exploratory data analysis systems for higher dimensions which utilize rotation-cued 3-D graphical display. Nicholson and Littlefield(14,18) discuss the use of a rocking motion in conjunction with anaglyph stereo and note a synergism which creates a strong 3-D cue. Analysts who have difficulty seeing stereo find that addition of the rocking permits the stereo perception; those who already see stereo still find the changing views informative. The combination of the two is particularly attractive if the analyst wishes to interact with the data in the 3-D display mode.

Such interaction is difficult when the display is moving. The stereo allows the motion to be stopped while retaining the depth cue.

N-tuple 3-D scatterplots can be created exactly like 2-D ones with the use of characteristics of the plotting symbol for nonspatial display of dimensions. Construction details necessary to create successful stereo 3-D scatterplots using color anaglyphs are described by Carr and Littlefield.(19) The 3-D cue depends upon precise matching of two colors on the display with filters in the viewing lenses. A shortcoming of 3-D scatterplots is the difficulty of producing hard copy and the expense of color.

Log nitrate ion concentration can be added to the quadruple scatterplot of Figure 3 using anaglyph stereo. The quintuple scatterplot shows that Clusters 1 and 2 and the body of the data are of one higher dimension since nitrate and sulfate are highly correlated and that the outlier characteristics of Cluster 3 can be described as atypical ammonium and pH, given sulfate, nitrate, and volume.

Anaglyph stereo 3-D depends upon color to create the depth cue. Produced with green and red, the image is yellow and produced with cyan and red, the image is white. Thus, there is still some color resolution. Similar to 2-D N-tuple scatterplots, color can distinguish above and below the median length or the mercury level in the thermometer.

4.2 Rigid Motion

To date, motion has been used almost exclusively to create a depth cue. In principle, there is no reason why the motion can not include nonspatially represented dimensions. For example, in a quadruple scatterplot with two spatial dimensions and two nonspatially represented dimensions, a simple rotation is defined by a fixed 2-D subspace, "the axis" and an orthogonal rotation subspace. If the fixed subspace is defined by the nonspatially represented dimensions, then the motion appears as a revolving of the display about a fixed point. On the other hand, if the fixed subspace is defined by the two spatial dimensions then the motion appears as a smooth change in the characteristics of each plotting symbol with the location of symbols remaining fixed. Neither of these motions is very informative in the sense of providing additional information over that in the static display. Now, suppose that the fixed subspace involves all four dimensions. For example, it might be the subspace spanned by the two vectors (1,1,1,1) and (1,-1,1,-1). The motion appears as a combination of plotting-symbol spatial movement and plotting-symbol change of characteristics. Experience suggests that rigid motion is a useful tool for discerning high-dimensional clusters and low-dimensional manifold structure. For example, distinct clusters appear as similar spatial movement/characteristic change of the plotting symbols. Low-dimensional manifolds appear as a smooth gradation of spatial position/characteristic change of the plotting symbols.

For an N-tuple scatterplot whether it is spatially 2-D or 3-D, the simplest rigid motion is defined by an origin $\underline{O}$ and an N - 2 dimensional fixed subspace spanned by linearly independent directions $\underline{D}_1, \ldots, \underline{D}_{N-2}$. Two additional orthonormal directions, $\underline{V}_1$ and $\underline{V}_2$, span the rotation subspace. Define the 2-D polar coordinate rotation matrix as

$$R(\theta) = \begin{pmatrix} \cos\theta & -\sin\theta \\ \sin\theta & \cos\theta \end{pmatrix}.$$

The position $\underline{P}(\theta)$ of the point $\underline{P}$ after rotation through angle θ is expressable as

$$\underline{P}(\theta) = \underline{O} + VV^T(\underline{P} - \underline{O})\, R(\theta) + D(DD^T)^{-1} D^T(\underline{P} - \underline{O})$$

where $V = (\underline{V}_1, \underline{V}_2)$ and $D = (\underline{D}_1, \underline{D}_2, \ldots, \underline{D}_{N-2})$.

Let $\theta(t) = \theta_o \sin(\pi t/2)$ be the relationship between the rotation angle and time t. Display of a sequence of rotated, N-tuple scatterplots for a systematic, uniformly spaced sample of t values which includes the integers, creates a rocking motion through angle $2\theta_o$ centered on the original static view. The appearance is a repetitive to-and-fro motion of plotting symbols coupled with a repetitive smooth change of plotting symbol characteristics. For $\theta_o < 10°$ the motion is quite easy to follow even with a crude sampling grid of two intermediate times between the extremes.

A more complex rigid motion is created by replacing simple 2-D polar coordinate rotation with 3-D spherical coordinate motion. The fixed subspace is N - 3 dimensional. Now motions like a figure-8 trace on the unit sphere are possible. Clearly, rigid motions of arbitrary complexity can be defined in a similar manner. Their utility is an open question. As described here, the rigid motion is a redundant cue, helping to define inter-relationships which involve nonspatially represented dimensions. In a static N-tuple display, subtle structure may be missed with the gross quantification of nonspatially represented dimensions. Adding motion can accentuate such relationships. A more ambitious use of rigid motion is to bring in additional dimensions in a fashion analogous to rotation-cued 3-D. That is, the N-tuple scatterplot is an N-dimensional projection of a M-dimensional space. With the rigid motion defined in the full space, inter-relationships among all M dimensions will begin to appear as the rocking angle increases.

The choice of the fixed subspace clearly influences the utility of rigid-motion displays. Our early investigations suggest that an algorithm such as principal components shows promise for this selection. For example, choosing the fixed subspace as the smallest principal components maximizes the movement in the display. On the other hand, if the interest is on the behavior of points that do not fit the general pattern, then the general pattern should be embedded in the fixed subspace.

To illustrate the rigid-motion concept, we use the quadruple scatterplot of Figure 3. Principal components analysis about the centroid gives the eigenvalues and eigenvectors as follows:

Eigenvalues	37.480	15.741	7.500	1.108
Eigenvectors				
Volume	0.413	0.474	0.776	0.051
pH	0.718	-0.623	0.020	-0.311
Sulfate	-0.464	-0.128	0.378	-0.791
Ammonium	-0.315	-0.609	0.505	0.525

To maximize the movement, we defined the fixed subspace with the directions whose eigenvalues are 7.500 and 1.108. Seven distinct quadruple scatterplots were then constructed by rotation about this axis of ±15° in 5-degree increments. Repetitive display of the seven views in the sequence -15, -10, -5, 0, +5, +10, +15, +10, +5, 0, -5, and -10 as a closed loop produced the rocking motion. An immediate conclusion of observing the rocking motion is the accentuation of the clusters noted in the Figure 3 display and delineation of tighter subclusters in the sense that points move and change their symbol configuration almost in unison. Outliers are also apparent as very discordant; moving, relatively speaking, fast across the display and changing their symbol characteristics in an atypical fashion. Figure 4 displays the state of the rocking motion at its extremes of -15° and +15°. Several interesting consequences of the rigid motion are noted as follows:

1. These five points are Cluster 1 in Figure 3. Excluding a slight discrepancy in length change, they move as a single symbol; i.e., they lie very close to the rotation subspace.

2. These three points maintain a very tight configuration throughout the rigid motion; i.e., they are a tight 4-D cluster.

3. These three points are half of Cluster 3 in Figure 3 where their orientation identifies them as a subcluster. Here their movement is extreme, relative to the other three points, and, in fact, the most extreme in the display, both position wise and length wise, an example of enhancement of subtle differences.

4. The decision, illustrated in Figure 3, that two points near Cluster 2 do not belong to that cluster (dotted rectangle), is corroborated by movement different from the points of Cluster 2.

The rigid-motion rocking can be misinterpreted as a 3-D rotation. For proper interpretation this illusion must be overcome.

5. CONCLUSIONS

It is too early in the evaluation of N-tuple scatterplots as an analysis tool to make any firm conclusions. However, some of our findings should be useful to others in pointing directions for further research.

First, N-tuple scatterplots can show up complexities of high-dimensional structure which are not obvious in lower-dimensional views.

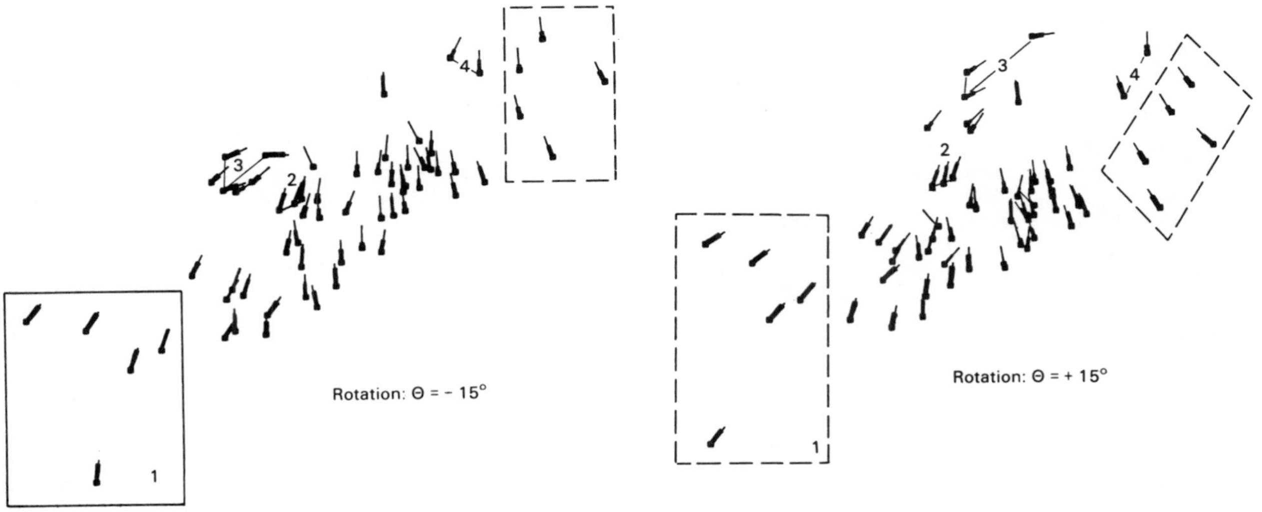

Figure 4 : Extreme quadruple scatterplot views from rigid-motion rocking of Raleigh, North Carolina precipitation data

Thus, a selected set of N-tuple presentations can improve understanding, particularly if studied in conjunction with juxtapositioned scatterplots of many 2-D views.

Second, symbol orientation is an excellent method of adding one nonspatially represented dimension. Use of easily discernable orientations like vertical and horizontal for order statistics adds to the quantification of the display. Length is also a useful method, particularly if a scale is built-in like the thermometer.

Third, more research is needed on the choice of plotting symbols, both for individual nonspatial dimension representation and in choosing sets of characteristics for several nonspatially represented dimensions. When color is available, geometry and color should be considered for redundant presentation to enhance quantification.

Fourth, investigation should continue into the use of rigid motions to help see the complexities of structure in N-tuple scatterplots. Further, the concept should be extended to viewing N dimensions as a projection of higher dimensions which is in the spirit of rotation-cued 3-D.

6. REFERENCES

[1] Tukey, P. A., and J. W. Tukey. 1981. "Graphical Display of Data Sets in Three or More Dimensions." Chapters 10, 11, and 12 in Interpreting Multivariate Data. (V. Barnett, ed.) Wiley, Chichester, United Kingdom.

[2] Cleveland, W. S., and R. McGill. 1982. The many Faces of a Scatterplot. (Submitted for publication.)

[3] Carr, D. B., and W. L. Nicholson. 1984. Graphical Interaction Tools for Multiple 2- and 3-Dimensional Scatterplots. In press.

[4] Chambers, J. M., W. S. Cleveland, B. Kleiner, and P. A. Tukey. 1983. Graphical Methods for Data Analysis. Duxbury Press, Boston, Massachusetts.

[5] Tukey, J. W., and P. A. Tukey. 1983. "Some Graphics for Studying Four-Dimensional Data." Computer Science and Statistics: Proceedings of the 14th Symposium on the Interface. Springer-Verlag, New York, New York. pp. 60-66.

[6] Friedman, J. H., J. A. McDonald and W. Stuetzle. 1982. "An Introduction to Real-Time Graphical Techniques for Analyzing Multivariate Data." In Proceedings of the Third Annual Conference and Exposition of the National Computer Graphics Association, Inc. 1:421-427.

[7] Littlefield, R. J. 1984. "Basic Geometric Algorithms for Graphic Input." In Proceedings of the National Computer Graphics Association Computer Graphics 1984 Exposition. (In press.)

[8] Diaconis, P., and J. H. Friedman. 1980. M and N Plots. Stanford Linear Accelerator Center Report PUB-2495. Stanford University, Stanford, California.

[9] Gnanadesikan, R. 1977. Methods for Statistical Data Analysis of Multivariate Observations. Wiley, New York, New York.

[10] Friedman, J. H., and J. W. Tukey. 1974. "A Projection Pursuit Algorithm for Exploratory Data Analysis." IEEE Transactions on Computer C-23:811-890.

[11] Anscombe, F. J. 1973. "Graphs in Statistical Analysis." The American Statistician 27(1):17-21.

[12] Bickel, P. J., E. A. Hammel and J. W. O'Connel. 1975. "Sex Bias in Graduate Admissions: Data from Berkeley." Science 187:398-404.

[13] Bruntz, S. M., W. S. Cleveland, B. Cleiner, and J. L. Warner. 1974. "The Dependence of Ambient Ozone on Solar Radiation, Wind, Temperature, and Mixing Height." Reprint Vol. Symp. Atmos. Diffus. Air Polut. Santa Barbara, California, American Meteorological Society, Boston, Massachusetts, p. 9-13.

[14] Nicholson, W. L., and R. J. Littlefield. 1983. "Interactive Color Graphics for Multivariate Data. Computer Science and Statistics: Proceedings of the 14th Symposium on the Interface. Springer-Verlag, New York, New York. pp. 211-219.

[15] Cleveland, W. S., and R. McGill. 1984. "Toward a Science of Graphcis Based on Human Graphical Perception." (Submitted for publication.)

[16] Tukey, J. W., J. H. Friedman and M. A. Fisherkeller. 1976. "PRIM-9, An Interactive Multidimensional Data Display and Analysis System." Proceedings of the Fourth International Congress for Stereology, September 4-9, Gaithersburg, Maryland. National Bureau of Standards Special Publication 431, U.S. Government Printing Office, Washington, D.C., 229.

[17] Donoho, D., P. J. Huber and H. M. Thoma. 1981. "The Use of Kinematic Displays to Represent High-Dimensional Data." Computer Science and Statistics: Proceedings of the 13th Symposium on the Interface. (ed. W. F. Eddy). pp. 274-278. Springer-Verlag, New York.

[18] Nicholson, W. L., and R. J. Littlefield. 1982. "The Use of Color and Motion to Display Higher-Dimensional Data." In Proceedings of the Third Annual Conference and Exposition of the National Computer Graphics Association, Inc. 1:476-485.

[19] Carr, D. B., and R. J. Littlefield. 1983. "Color Anaglyph Stereo Scatterplots--Constructions Details." Computer Science and Statistics: Proceedings of the 15th Symposium on the Interface. pp. 295-299.

---

[1] Work sponsored by the United States Department of Energy, Applied Mathematical Sciences, under Contract DE-AC06-76RLO 1930.

STATISTICAL DATABASES

Organizer: *Harry K. T. Wong, Lawrence Berkeley Laboratory*

Invited Presentation:

Anti-Sampling for Estimation, *Neil C. Rowe, Naval Postgraduate School*

COMPUTER SCIENCE AND STATISTICS:
The Interface, L. Billard (ed.)

Antisampling for estimation

Neil C. Rowe

Department of Computer Science
Code 52
Naval Postgraduate School
Monterey, CA 93943

ABSTRACT

We are developing a new way of obtaining quick estimates of simple statistics (such as count, mean, standard deviation, maximum, median, and mode frequency) on a large data set. This approach is apparently the first comprehensive attempt to base estimation on something other than sampling. Our techniques (collectively termed "antisampling") form a sort of a dual to those of sampling, and have different advantages and disadvantages. Because of this, our methods are sometimes preferable to sampling, sometimes not. While we formulate antisampling theoretically, it can only be efficient when a data is inside a computer, and thus has a close relationship to computer science and database theory in particular.

Consider some large data population P we wish to study, so big it is too much work to calculate statistics on it, even with a computer. We could create a sample S of P and calculate statistics on S, extrapolating the results to P. But we could also work from the other direction, taking some larger set known to contain P -- call it A for "antisample" -- calculating on it, then extrapolating down to P. The latter might be preferable to the former, because an antisample is bigger and can contain more information than a sample.

Antisample A must be larger than population P, and thus it would seem to be more work calculating on A than P. But cost can be amortized, or distributed across many uses, if done in advance. Just as the development cost of a good package of statistical routines can be distributed over many purchasers of that package, the effort to calculate statistics in advance on good antisamples A can be charged to many uses of those statistics. We can do this if we choose antisamples which contain interesting populations that people want to ask about, or what we call a "database abstract" for a particular database.

This talk is based on a paper which has been submitted to a journal. Contact the author for copies.

References

Rowe, N. C. Top-down statistical estimation on a database. Proceedings of the ACM-SIGMOD Annual Meeting, San Jose, California (May 1983), 135-145.

Rowe, N. C. Rule-based statistical calculations on a database abstract. Report STAN-CS-83-975, Stanford University Computer Science Department, June 1983 (Ph.D. thesis).

Rowe, N. C. Inheritance of statistical properties. Proceedings of the National Conference, American Association for Artificial Intelligence, Pittsburgh, Pennsylvania (August 1982), 221-224.

Rowe, N. C. Diophantine inferences on a statistical database. *Information Processing Letters*, **18 (1984), 25-31.**

Rowe, N. C. Absolute bounds on the mean and standard deviation of transformed data for constant-derivative transformations. Technical report, Computer Science Department, U. S. Naval Postgraduate School, April 1984.

CONTRIBUTED PAPERS

The following papers were presented as contributed papers at Poster Sessions held during the lunchtime break each day of the Symposium.

COMPUTER SCIENCE AND STATISTICS:
The Interface, L. Billard (ed.)

NONPARAMETRIC ESTIMATION OF THE MODES OF HIGH-DIMENSIONAL DENSITIES

STEVEN B. BOSWELL

School of Mathematics
Georgia Institute of Technology
Atlanta, Georgia 30332

One important distributional pattern that is easily interpreted in high dimensions is the identification of multiple modes of the parent density. Nonparametric techniques have been adapted to develop consistent estimators of local modes of a probability density function of arbitrary dimension. In addition, a simple global strategy is discussed for employing the local estimation procedures to catalog the complete set of population modes. Simulation results are presented of application of the procedures to unimodal and bimodal data in dimensions five and above.

Keywords: modes and multimodality, nonparametric density estimation, pattern recognition, clustering, optimization algorithms.

I. INTRODUCTION

The recognition of nonstandard features in low dimensional data, such as unanticipated skewness, multimodality, outliers, etc., usually relies upon some form of visual display of the data. Graphical techniques for multivariate data are developing rapidly and already see widespread use; indeed, this development is one of the recurring themes of the Symposium. Nevertheless, even for four-dimensional data, and certainly for higher dimensions, the exploration of data structure by visual means is a task of considerable algorithmic and psychological complexity. One structural characteristic that is easily interpreted in arbitrary dimension, and which requires little in the way of graphical support, is the number and location of modes (local maxima) of the parent probability density function. This paper presents a family of estimators for the local modes of a multivariate distribution. The mode estimates are supplied by iterative optimization procedures acting upon nonparametric kernel density estimators, of the type due originally to Rosenblatt [1956] and Parzen [1962]. We begin by describing some of the statistical background of the kernel density estimators and the mode-seeking algorithms. Then tests of the algorithms are discussed using simulated data in dimensions ranging from one to one hundred. Results are stated without proof. Proofs are given in Boswell [1983].

II. KERNEL ESTIMATES OF A DENSITY AND ITS DERIVATIVES

Throughout the paper $X^{(1)},\ldots,X^{(n)}$ will denote a random sample from a p-dimensional distribution with density function f, which is assumed to be bounded and continuously differentiable on its support. Additional regularity conditions on f will be assumed when necessary. Let $\underline{r} = (r_1,r_2,\ldots,r_p) \in \mathbb{R}^p$

$$|\underline{r}| = \sum_{i=1}^{p} r_i ,$$

and

$$r! = \prod_{i=1}^{p} r_i!, \quad x^{\underline{r}} = \prod_{i=1}^{p} x_i^{r_i},$$

and

$$f^{(\underline{r})}(x) = \frac{\partial^{r_1 + \ldots + r_p}}{\partial x_1^{r_1} \ldots \partial x_p^{r_p}} f(x).$$

We will employ kernel estimators for $f^{(\underline{r})}(x)$ having the form

$$\hat{f}_n^{(\underline{r})}(x;h) = \frac{1}{nh^{p+|\underline{r}|}} \sum_{i=1}^{n} K\left(\frac{X^{(i)}-x}{h}\right), \quad (1)$$

where $K: \mathbb{R}^p \to \mathbb{R}^1$ satisfies

(i) for some M, $|K(y)| \leq M$ for all $y \in \mathbb{R}^p$, (2)

(ii) $\int y^{\underline{k}} K(y)\,dy = 0$ for all $\underline{k}$ with $|\underline{k}| \leq |\underline{r}|$ but $\underline{k} \neq \underline{r}$, $\int y^{\underline{r}} K(y)\,dy = \underline{r}!$,

and

(iii) $\int \|y\|^{|\underline{r}|} K(y)\,dy < \infty$.

Kernel estimation of multivariate densities has been studied by several authors, including Cacoullos [1966], Epanechnikov [1969], Van Ryzin [1969], and Singh [1976]. For our purposes it is sufficient to observe the following result:

Theorem 1. If as $n \to \infty$, $h \to 0$ and $nh^{p+|\underline{r}|} \to \infty$, then $\hat{f}_n^{(\underline{r})}(x;h)$ is consistent in quadratic mean at all continuity points of $f^{(\underline{r})}$, and if $f^{(\underline{r})}$ is uniformly continuous over a region, the convergence of $\hat{f}_n^{(\underline{r})}$ is uniform over that region.

A related class of density estimators, originated by Loftsgaarden and Quesenberry [1965], replaces the smoothing parameter h in (1) with a function of position, $r_k(x)$, where $r_k(x)$ is the distance (typically Euclidean) from x to the kth nearest observation in the sample. These estimators, which are called nearest neighbor or variable bandwidth estimators, will be written

$$\tilde{f}_n^{(\underline{r})}(x;k) = \frac{1}{nr_k(x)^{p+|\underline{r}|}} \sum_{i=1}^{n} K\left(\frac{X^{(i)}-x}{r_k(x)}\right) \quad (3)$$

They have the same outward form as the fixed bandwidth kernel estimators, though their analytical properties are typically more elusive. However, Moore and Yackel [1977] establish that if

$$K(cu) \geq K(u) \text{ for any } 0 \leq c \leq 1 \text{ and } u \in \mathbb{R}^p \quad (4)$$

and if K has finite support, then any consistency result which is valid for $\hat{f}_n(x;h(n))$ with kernel K and smoothing sequence $\{h(n)\}$, and which remains valid if K is replaced by the uniform density over the unit ball, is also valid for the nearest neighbor estimator with kernel K and sequence of k-values $k(n) = \alpha nh(n)^p$, any $\alpha > 0$. If K has infinite support then the consistency of the nearest neighbor form may only be guaranteed over any region in which the population density function is bounded away from zero. The same result may be extended to estimators of first partial derivatives if the kernel K that is used to estimate $\partial/\partial x_m f(\cdot)$ satisfies

$$K(x) = c_1[K_1(x+we_m) - K_1(x-we_m)] - c_2K_2(x), \quad (5)$$

where c_1, c_2 and w are constants, e_m is the standard basis element for $\mathbb{R}^p$, and K_1 and K_2 are symmetric probability densities satisfying (2) for estimating f.

The simulation results we will present utilize nearest neighbor type estimators. Whether these should be preferred to fixed bandwidth estimators is debatable. The nearest neighbor calculations require a sorting operation, and the associated computational burden may be unacceptable with large sample sizes. However, there are ways to reduce the sort computations drastically without losing the nearest neighbor character, for example by using subsamples of the complete data set [Fwu, Tapia, and Thompson, 1980]. The advantage of the nearest neighbor approach is that $k(n)$, or equivalently a sample proportion, is a more convenient and apparently more robust control parameter [Breiman, et al., 1977] than the fixed bandwidth, $h(n)$.

III. CONSISTENCY OF MODE ESTIMATORS

The mode estimates are produced by iterative maximization procedures which guarantee an increase in the value of the estimated probability density function at each iteration. This monotonicity property insures the compact containment of the iterates of the mode estimation process. The following result applies to fixed bandwidth estimators, and to nearest neighbor estimators if the kernel has finite support. For any $\eta > 0$ denote by L_η the level set $L_\eta = \{x \in \mathbb{R}^p : f(x) \geq \eta\}$.

<u>Lemma 1</u>. Let f be a probability density function on $\mathbb{R}^p$, and let $f_n(\cdot)$ be an estimator of f based upon a sample of n independent observations drawn from f. Suppose that f_n is uniformly consistent in probability over $\mathbb{R}^p$. Let x_0 be a starting point, independent of n, for which $f(x_0) > 0$, and let $T = \{x_n^*, n = 1,2,\ldots\}$ be a sequence of points satisfying $f_n(x_n^*) > f_n(x_0)$. Then with probability one, there exists an integer M such that for any c, $0 < c < 1$, $\{x_n^*, n > M\} \subset L_{cf(x_0)}$.

The following version of the containment property is applicable to nearest neighbor estimators with infinite support. In this result, the nature of the algorithm generating the points $\{x_n^*\}$ is specified in order to circumvent possible problems with the nearest neighbor estimators in the tails of the parent distribution.

<u>Lemma 2</u>. All the hypotheses of Lemma 1 hold except that $f_n(\cdot)$ is uniformly consistent in probability only over L_η for any $\eta > 0$. For each n let $\{x_n^1, x_n^2, \ldots\}$ be the sequence of iterates produced by an algorithm which guarantees that $f_n(x_n^{i+1}) > f_n(x_n^i)$ for all i, unless $x_n^{i+1} = x_n^i$, and that for all $t \in (0,1)$, $f_n(x_n^i + t(x_n^{i+1} - x_n^i)) \geq f_n(x_n^i)$. Suppose that the x_n^i converge to a point x_n^*. Then, again, with probability one, there exists an integer M such that for every $c \in (0,1)$,

$$\{x_n^*, n > M\} \subset L_{cf(x_0)}.$$

Now we are able to state a general consistency result for estimators of local modes of a probability density function.

<u>Theorem 2</u>. Assume the hypotheses of Lemma 1 or Lemma 2 hold, as appropriate. Suppose in addition that for some η, $f(x_0) > \eta > 0$, and for all $x \in L_\eta$, $\nabla f_n(x) \to \nabla f(x)$ in quadratic mean as $n \to \infty$, and that $\nabla f_n(x_n^*) = \underline{0}$ for all n. Then $\nabla f(x_n^*) \to \underline{0}$ in probability as $n \to \infty$.

IV. THE WEIGHT UPDATE ALGORITHM

Theorem 2 allows considerable latitude in the construction of the algorithm which generates the estimated critical points $\{x_n^*\}$. We will concentrate on a class of update procedures which resemble the method of modified weights [Huber, 1981] for multiparameter location or regression problems. The procedures are stated in terms of the fixed bandwidth density estimator; analogous procedures for nearest neighbor estimators are obtained by replacing $\hat{f}_n(x;h)$ with $\tilde{f}_n(x;k)$ and h with $r_k(x)$.

First, we require that K be a radially symmetric probability density function satisfying the conditions (2) for estimating f. The symmetry of K implies that there exists a function $\phi(\cdot)$ defined on $[0,\infty)$ by $\phi(\|\tau\|) = K(\tau)$. Let x_c represent the current and x_+ the succeeding iterate in the update procedure. Then the algorithm for producing x_n^* is:

Algorithm 1 (Weight Update Algorithm)

$x_c = x_0$

do until (stopping criteria are satisfied)

$$x_+ = \sum_{i=1}^{n} w_i X^{(i)} / \sum_{i=1}^{n} w_i$$

$$\text{where } b_i = - \frac{\phi'\left(\frac{\|X^{(i)}-x_c\|}{h}\right)}{\left(\frac{\|X^{(i)}-x_c\|}{h}\right)}$$

$x_c = x_+$

end do

Note that the weights w_i are actually functions of the smoothing parameter h and the current location, x_c.

Lemma 3. Suppose that ϕ is decreasing and that $\phi'(t)/t$ is continuous, bounded from below, and strictly increasing on the support of ϕ. Then either $x_+ = x_c$ or $\hat{f}_n(x_+;h) > \hat{f}_n(x_c;h)$, and $\hat{f}_n(x_c + t(x_+ - x_c);h) > \hat{f}_n(x_c;h)$ for all $t \in (0,1)$. Moreover, the sequence of iterates generated by Algorithm 1 converges to a point x_n^* at which $\nabla\hat{f}_n(x_n^*;h) = 0$.

By Theorems 1 and 2, then, the weight update algorithm returns locations x_n^* which are consistent as estimators of critical points of the population density f, so long as

$$h(n) \text{ satisfies } nh(n)^{p+1} \to \infty \text{ as } n \to \infty,$$
$$\text{while } \quad h(n) \to 0 \text{ as } n \to \infty,$$

and in the nearest neighbor case, $k(n)/nh(n)^{p+1}$ has a finite positive limit as $n \to \infty$.

Examples of kernel functions which satisfy the assumptions of Lemma 3 are:

$$K_1(x) = c_1\left(1 - \frac{\|x\|^2}{2}\right) \quad \|x\| \leq 1;$$
$$\phi'(t)/t = -c_1$$

$$K_2(x) = c_2 e^{-\|x\|^2/2} \; ; \; \phi'(t)/t = -\phi(t)$$

$$K_3(x) = c_3(1 - \|x\|^2)^2, \; \|x\| \leq 1;$$
$$\phi'(t)/t = -4\phi(t)/(1-t^2). \tag{6}$$

The utility of the weight update procedure in high dimensions is indicated by Figure 1, which summarizes 25 trials of the procedure using kernel K_1 on standardized independent Gaussian data in dimensions 1, 2, 3, 4, 5, 10, 15, 20, 50, and 100. Each sample in each dimension consisted of 100 observations. A sample size of 100 will be standard for the results given here. The vertical axis records the average MSE over the 25 trials, where $MSE(x_n^*) = \|x_n^* - x^*\|^2/p$, where x_n^* is the mode estimate, x^* the true mode, p the dimension of the data, and $\|\cdot\|$ the Euclidean norm. What is significant about the figure is the rapid improvement of the mode estimation procedure as dimension increases from p = 1 or 2, and the stability of the estimates in very high dimension, even when using only 10 nearby observations to direct each update step. The ability of the procedures to negotiate erratic tail behavior is indicated in Figure 2, which reports similar statistics with Cauchy data and dimensions up to twenty.

V. MULTISTART ALGORITHM

The foremost objective in estimating the local modes of a density function is to recognize multimodal distributions. To accomplish this goal it is necessary to repeat the local maximization procedures from different vantage points in the sample space. One obvious method to consider is the multistart algorithm:

<u>Algorithm 2</u>

```
for i = 1 to n
   begin
      x_0 = x^(i);
      perform Algorithm 1 to produce
         a mode estimate m*_i:
      save m*_i in a workfile;
   end
end
Analyze the set {m*_i, i = 1,...,n},
   either by cluster analytic techniques,
   or by repeating Algorithm 2 with
   {m*_i} being treated as the input
   data set.
```

The multistart algorithm was conducted with two families of two-component Gaussian mixture densities. Both mixtures had Gaussian components with identity covariance matrices and mixing proportions of 0.3 and 0.7. For the mixture G2SKEW the separation of the means is such that the distribution remains unimodal, though on the verge of developing a secondary mode. A graph of the univariate density of G2SKEW, a typical two-dimensional scatterplot of data generated from this mixture, are given in Figure 3. For mixture G2SEP the mean separation was increased to produce two distinct local modes.

For displaying multivariate dispersion, plots were generated by taking one coordinate axis to be the line connecting the means of the component mixtures, and taking the other coordinate to represent the length of the orthogonal projection of a data point onto that line. The scatter of 100 observations from G2SKEW, dimension 5, is shown in Figure 4. The "X's" overstruck on the central bar indicate the location of the component means. The single mode of the distribution is nearly coincident with the left-hand mean. Figures 5 and 6 show the transformation of the scatter by the multistart algorithm using kernels K_1 (top panel in each block; "Mean Update") and K_2 (bottom panel; "Weighted Mean"). The sequence of plots indicate the role of the parameter in determining the degree of coalescence of the data through application of the multistart algorithm. The weighted update with Gaussian kernel performs very well here. It identifies the single mode and estimates its location with an error less than the distance to the nearest observation in the sample. It holds this estimate over a fairly broad range of values of the parameter k (for k much larger than 15, though, the mode estimate drifts to an intermediate location between the two component means).

Figure 7 gives the row scatter of a sample drawn from G2SEP, again in dimension p = 5. Figures 8 and 9 again trace the transformation of the scatter through applications of the multistart algorithm with kernels K_1 (upper panel) and K_2 (lower panel), and successive steps of the parameter k. Both kernels detect the bimodality of the distribution over this range of parameter values. The effect of oversmoothing is shown in Figure 10, where k = 30 and k = 40. With kernel K_1 the apparent position of the secondary mode has drifted well away from its true location. With kernel K_2, the secondary mode has vanished entirely. Clearly, the determination of the appropriate value of the smoothing parameter, or the number of apparent modes to accept as <u>bona fide</u>, is a central issue for future research.

ACKNOWLEDGEMENTS

The author gratefully acknowledges the direction of his dissertation advisor, Professor James R. Thompson, who suggested the first update procedure. The research was partially supported by ARO Grant DAAG-29-82-K-0014.

REFERENCES

1. Boswell, S. B. (1983). Nonparametric Mode Estimation for Higher Dimensional Densities. Doctoral dissertation, Rice University, Houston, Texas.

2. Breiman, L., Meisel, W., and Purcell, E. (1977). Variable kernel estimates of multivariate densities. Technometrics, V. 19, No. 2, p. 135-144.

3. Cacoullos, T. (1966). Estimation of a multivariate density. Ann. Math. Stat., Tokyo, V. 18, p. 179.

4. Epanechnikov, V. A. (1969). Nonparametric estimates of a multivariate probability density. Theor. Prob. Appl., V. 14, p. 153.

5. Fwu, C., Tapia, R. A., and Thompson, J. R. (1980). The nonparametric estimation of probability densities in ballistics research. Proceedings of the Twenty-Sixth Conference on the Design of Experiments in Army Research and Testing.

6. Huber, P. J. (1981). Robust Statistics. John Wiley and Sons, NY.

7. Loftsgaarden, D. O. and Quesenberry, C. P. (1965). A nonparametric estimate of a multivariate density function. Ann. Math. Statist., V. 36, p. 1049-1051.

8. Moore, D. S. and Yackel, J. W. (1977). Consistency properties of nearest neighbor density function estimates. Ann. Statist., V. 5, p. 143-154.

9. Parzen, E. (1962). On estimation of a probability density function and mode. Ann. Math. Statist., V. 33, p. 1064-1076.

10. Rosenblatt, M. (1956). Remarks on some nonparametric estimates of a density function. Ann. Math. Statist., 27, p. 832.

11. Singh, R. S. (1976). Nonparametric estimation of mixed partial derivatives of a multivariate density. J. Multivariate Analysis, V. 6, p. 111-122.

12. Van Ryzin, J. (1969). On strong consistency of densities estimates. Ann. Math. Statist., V. 40, p. 1765-1772.

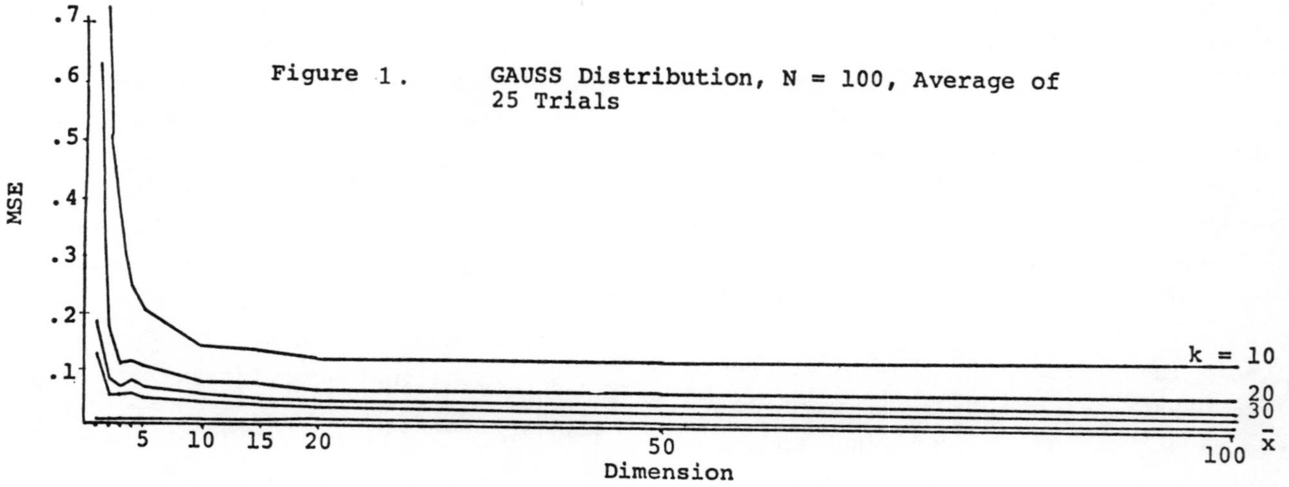

Figure 1. GAUSS Distribution, N = 100, Average of 25 Trials

Figure 7. Scatter of 100 Observations from G2SEP, p = 5

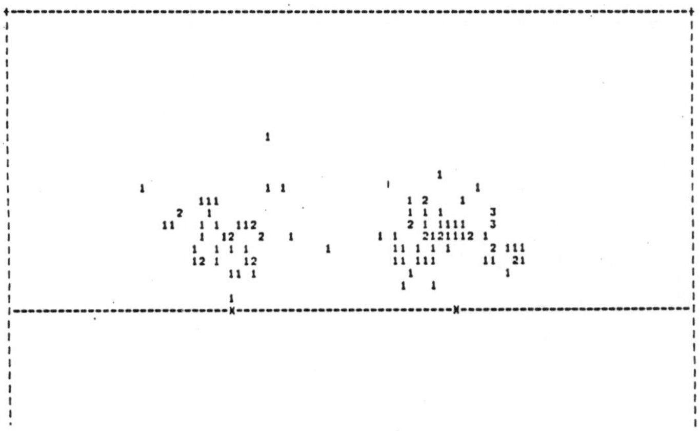

Figure 8. Transformed Scatter, G2SEP, P = 5

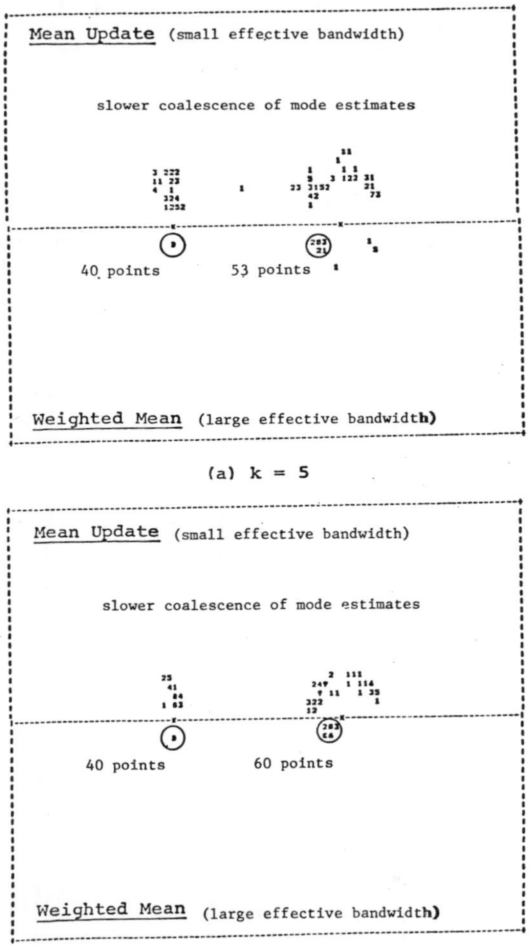

(a) k = 5

(b) k = 10

Figure 9. Transformed Scatter, G2SEP. P = 5

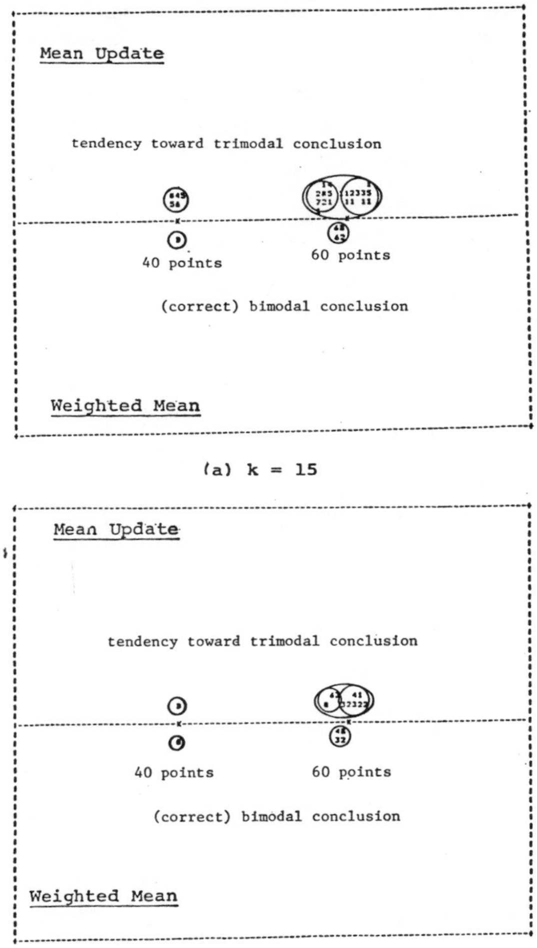

(a) k = 15

(b) k = 20

Figure 4. Scatter of 100 Observations from G2SKEW, p = 5

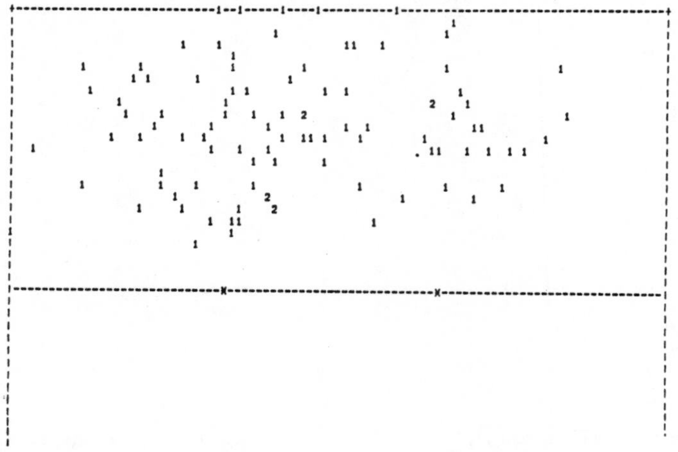

Figure 5. Transformed Scatter, G2SKEW, p = 5

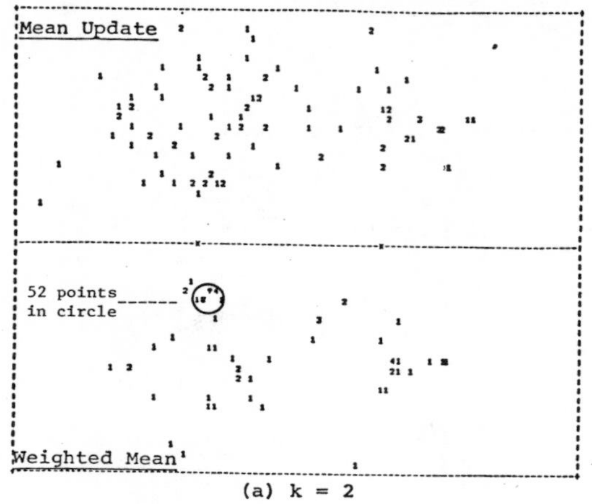

(a) k = 2

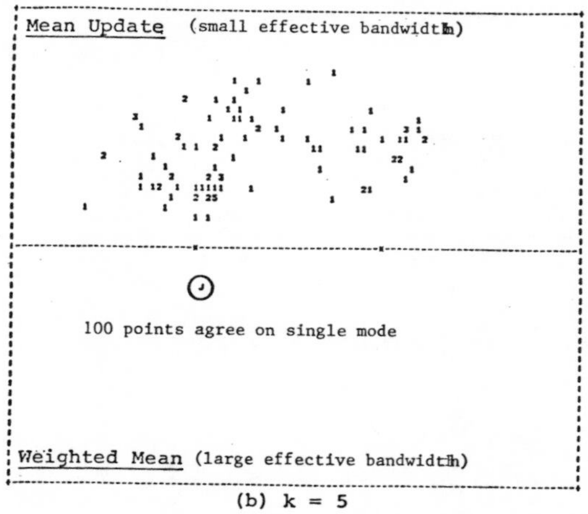

(b) k = 5

Figure 6. Transformed Scatter, G2SKEW. p = 5

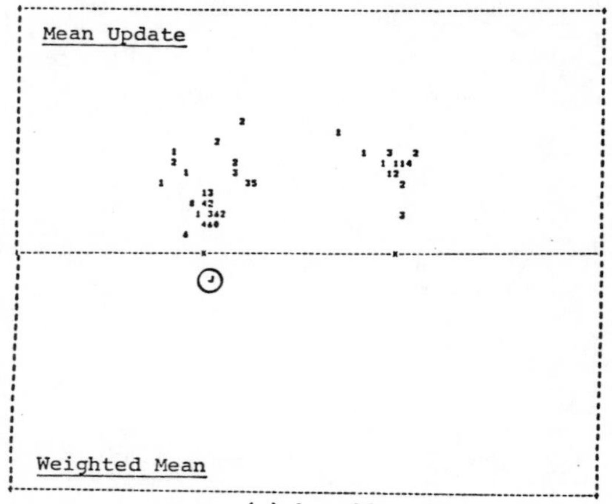

(a) k = 10

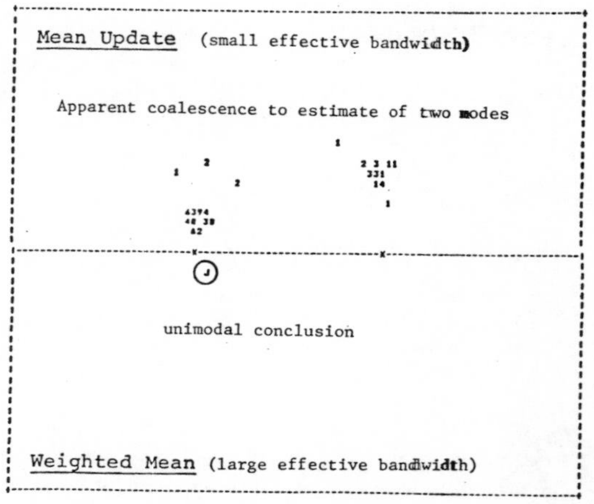

(b) k = 15

Figure 2

Cauchy Data, N=100

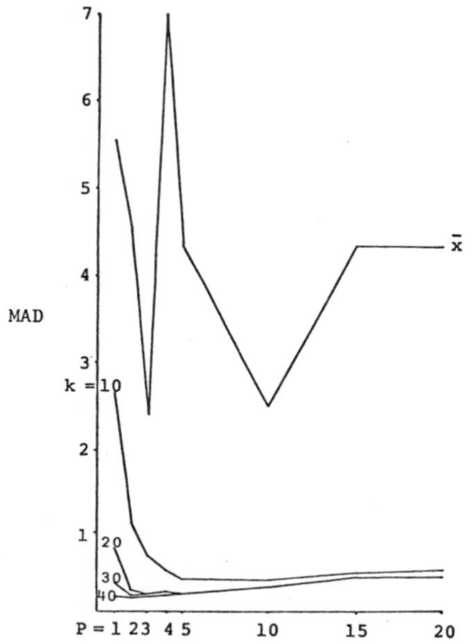

Figure 3.a Unimodal Mixture G2SKEW, Univariate Prototype

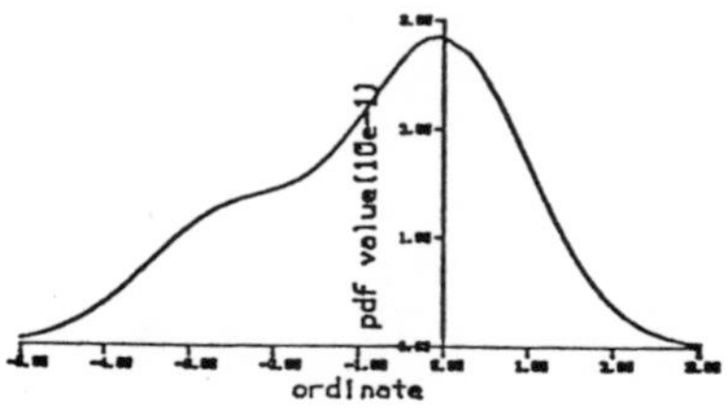

Figure 3.b Scatter Plot of G2SKEW

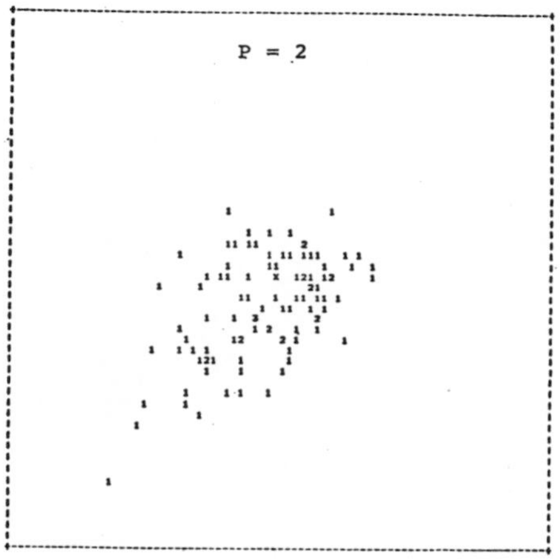

Figure 10. Transformed Scatter, G2SEP, p = 5

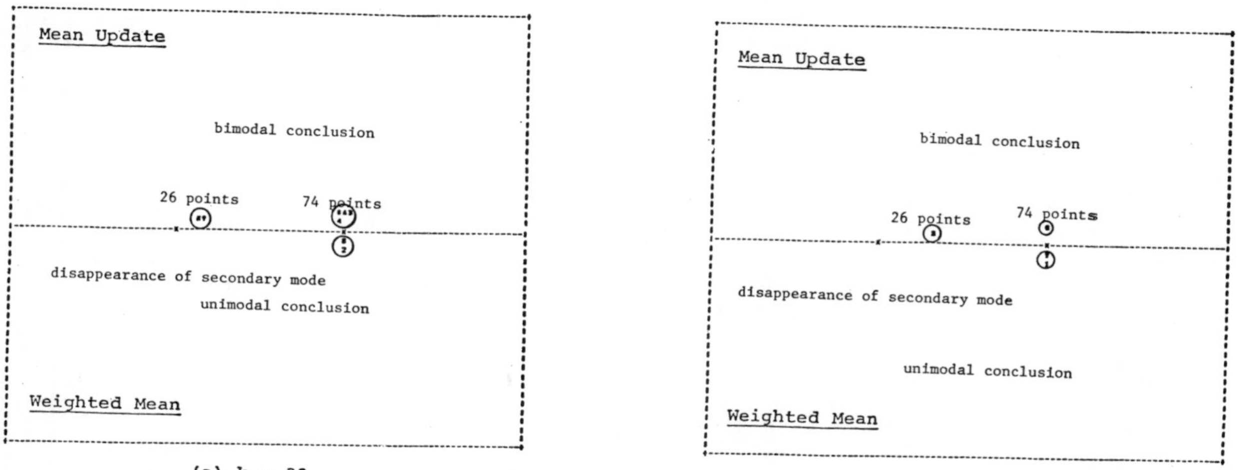

(a) k = 30

(b) k = 40

COMPUTER SCIENCE AND STATISTICS:
The Interface, L. Billard (ed.)

SPIRIT: An Intelligent Tutoring System For Tutoring Probability Theory[1]

Amos Barzilay
University of Pittsburgh and
XEROX Palo Alto Research Center

Jerrold H. May and Harry E. Pople Jr.
University of Pittsburgh

Using extensive tutoring protocols, the behavior of an expert human tutor in the probability theory domain was investigated, and tutoring strategies were identified. These strategies were used as a basis for the evolutionary design of a computerized tutor, called SPIRIT. The system uses a flexible tutoring style. As appropriate, the system may intervene only when things are going wrong, or it may manage a question and answer type of dialogue. A model of the student's aptitude governs movement between these modes. SPIRIT integrates several artificial intelligence methods that include: a theorem prover as a domain expert, a production system to represent tutoring knowledge, an object oriented system for representing knowledge about the student, and procedural knowledge embedded in LISP code.

1. INTRODUCTION

The purpose of this paper is to describe an Intelligent Tutoring System (ITS), called SPIRIT, designed to tutor a subset of probability theory, and to be used as a research tool in tutoring. SPIRIT tutors:

1. Elementary concepts of probability theory and formulation of probability problems.
2. Basic probability rules: multiplication and addition rules, conditional probability, rules of intersections and unions.
3. Special cases of probability rules: Independent events, mutually exclusive events, marginal probability.
4. Bayes' rule.

A student interacting with the system is assumed to be familiar with the basic concepts of probability theory. Word problems in probability are posed to the student, and the system follows and guides the student while he is solving the problems, focusing on the recognition of the concepts presented by the problem and on the application of probability rules in problem solving.

SPIRIT contains the three major components that should exist in Intelligent Computer Aided Instruction (ICAI) (see Clancey, 1979): a domain expert, a tutoring strategist, and a student modeling component. The domain expert in SPIRIT is a component capable of solving probability problems. The tutoring strategist or tutoring expert is capable of handling a dialogue tailored to the believed student's capability as expressed in the student model. The system maintains its beliefs about the student's strengths and weaknesses in the student model, and these beliefs are continuously revised as new evidence is collected during the dialogue.

SPIRIT integrates several Artificial Intelligence (AI) methods. It uses a production system, a theorem prover-like component, an object oriented language and procedural knowledge. Each method is used to perform the part for which it is best suited.

2. SPIRIT AS A RESEARCH TOOL

Although much progress has been achieved in the last decade as people have started to apply AI methods to the design of tutoring systems, tutoring systems today are far less competent than the experienced tutor. One of the reasons for this is the lack of a well founded theory of teaching. As Sleeman and Brown (1982, p. 3) put it:

> The tutoring strategies used by these systems are execessively ad-hoc reflecting unprincipled intuitions about how to control their behavior. Discovering consistent principles will be facilitated by constructing better theories of learning and mislearning...

A number of people have been attempting to construct theories of tutoring using empirical studies (e.g. Collins and Stevens, 1982), and suggested that their theory might be useful in the design of ITS. Such theories might be useful in the design of ITS on the conceptual level. However, on the implementation level, the theories are too general. For the purpose of designing an ITS, a theory of tutoring should exactly specify the conditions for which each tutoring action is desired. It also should precisely describe the actions the tutor should take when the appropriate conditions are satisfied. These requirements seem hard to achieve, particularly if the theory intends to be domain independent.

In SPIRIT we propose another approach. Instead

of developing a theory of tutoring to be used in the design of an ITS, we propose to develop an ITS that will be the basis for constructing a theory of tutoring. The starting point for the development of SPIRIT was the investigation of strategies used by one expert tutor. These strategies may be viewed as ad-hoc and unprincipled. Then, through a repetitive process of experimenting with and revising the system, a complete theory may evolve.

The preliminary ideas concerning tutoring strategies were derived from tutoring protocols between students and a human tutor who is an expert tutor in the subject matter. These strategies were then implemented in SPIRIT. The further development of a theory of teaching has entailed an iterative process. First, we observed how the system actually tutored. The tutoring protocols between the system and students were carefully analyzed, and we identified tutoring strategies that were missing, strategies that were used but should not have been used, and strategies that were only partially satisfactory. The system strategies were updated and the process repeated several times. We intend to carry on this process until the system reaches a steady state.

Currently, SPIRIT is not at the desired steady state, but we argue that SPIRIT, even in its present form, provides helpful tutoring, and illuminates interesting research issues in ITS.

3. SPIRIT - SYSTEM'S OVERVIEW

The major components of SPIRIT are depicted in Figure 1. In the following, we briefly describe the function of each component.

3.1 The probability expert

The probability expert can solve probability problems within the domain covered by the system. However, before the expert can solve a problem, all the events referred to in the problem must be identified, and the special cases for which probability rules are extrapolated should be explicitly described. For example, the probability expert must be told if two events are independent, because it can not deduce this information from the natural language problem text. This information is provided by the probability teacher, and is maintained in the problem model.

An example of a problem that the expert is capable of solving is the following:

> Given: $p(A/B)=0.2$, $p(A/C)=0.3$, $p(C)=0.3$, $p(B)=0.7$, $p(A/E)=0.4$, $p(E)=0.8$.
> Also it is given that C and B are exhaustive mutually exclusive events. Find $p(E/A)$.

The expert component uses backward chaining through formulas, a process that terminates when it reaches terms for which numbers given in the question can be substituted directly. In the protocols that we have collected, this was the prevailing strategy used by students.

The expert produces an AND/OR tree as shown in Figure 2. The tree means the following: "In order to find $p(E/A)$, we can apply the formula $p(E/A)=p(E \cap A)/p(A)$. In order to apply this formula, we need to find $p(E/A)$ and $p(A)$ (so we have an arc between the two links to indicate that we need to find both $p(E/A)$ and $p(A)$). In order to find $p(A)$, we need to apply the formula $p(A)=p(A/B)p(B) + p(A/C)p(C)$. In order to find $p(A/C)p(C)$ we need to find both $p(A/C)$ and $p(C)$, and in order to find $p(A/B)p(B)$ we need...etc."

The tree is built by chaining the probability rules in the backward direction. Then the tree is 'solved', which means that the numbers in the leaves of the tree are propogated up to the root, yielding the final answer. This process is based on the classic notion of a Backward Deduction System (see Nilsson, 1980). The AND/OR tree is often helpful in allowing the system to follow the student's reasoning.

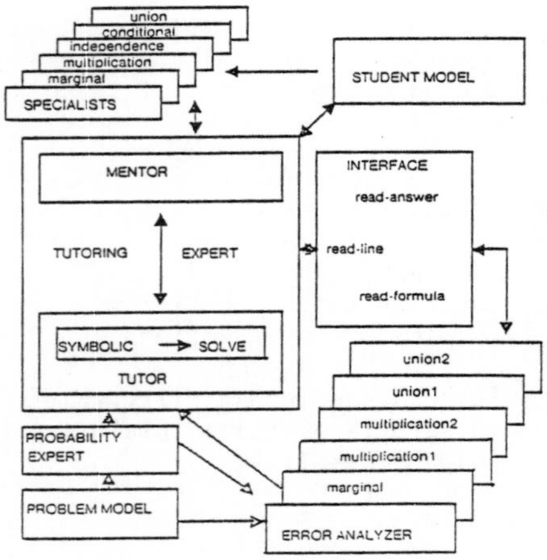

Figure 1: The main components of SPIRIT

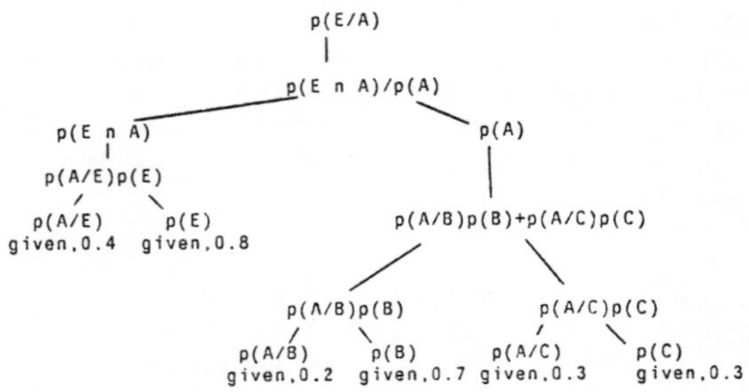

Figure 2: An example of an AND/OR tree

3.2 Problem model

Probability problems to be presented to the student in the tutoring process are represented within SPIRIT by means of a problem model. The problem model is built by the teacher. The events are described and the information needed for a problem is recorded in this model. For each probability problem in the system's database there is a problem model. The model is composed of data structures called frames, which are composed of slots that may be assigned values. With each event in the problem there is an associated frame. In addition, one frame in each problem includes some information about the problem as a whole. Each event-frame may include the following slots: event-description, event-short-name, sub-events (names of other events included in this event), super-events (names of the events that include this event), independent (list of the events that are independent of this event), mutually-exclusive (events which are mutually exclusive of this event), exhaustive, value (the probability of the event) and value-source (how this probability was derived). There may be other slots as well; some of these slots may receive default values.

3.3 Tutoring expert

The tutoring expert is implemented as a production system interfaced with LISP subroutines. The production system used is OPS5 (Forgy, 1981). Production systems have three major parts: an interpreter, a database, and a set of rules. In OPS5 a rule has the form:

```
<element 1>
<element 2>
.                           a condition part
.
<element n>                     then
->
<action 1>                    an action part
<action 2>
.
.
<action m>
```

The database is a set of elements called "working memory elements". The production system monitor selects production rules all of whose elements in the condition part match elements in the working memory. This set of productions is called the "conflict set". The OPS5 monitor selects only one production from this set and executes all the actions in its action part. The scheme a production system uses to choose a production for execution from the conflict set is called the "conflict resolution" strategy. The conflict resolution strategy used in SPIRIT is based on two important principles that seem to be suitable for an implementation of tutoring strategies. The first is called specificity and the second is recency. In a somewhat simplified way we can express this strategy as follows. The production that has the largest number of elements in the condition part and whose matched working memory elements are most recent would be executed.

The tutoring expert comprises sets of production rules. Their role is to manage the dialogue between the system and the student. The decisions made by this component are:

1. What probability problems to present to the student.
2. How to present the problem to the student.
3. At what level of detail to give a hint or an explanation.
4. When and how to provide encouragement.
5. When and how to present tutoring information, such as relating a rule that is being applied right now to another rule that has been applied before.
6. How to respond to a student's request for help.
7. What to do next in each stage of the dialogue.
8. What degree of independence to allow the student.

During an interaction with SPIRIT, with respect to each decision, there are usually several productions, arguing for different tutoring actions. These productions actively compete for the right to fire (i.e. for the right to execute their action part). The conflict resolution strategy employed provides an intuitively appealing approach for resolving these conflicts.

There are two different styles of tutoring the system uses, called the tutor and the mentor. The tutor manages a dialogue in which the student is strictly guided and is told exactly what the next move is. The tutor first goes over the natural language problem text. It poses to the student the important sentences and asks him to represent each sentence using probability notation. This process is called working in the "symbolic context". After all the important information is extracted from the problem text, the tutor guides the student along the solution process. This process uses the AND/OR tree generated by the probability expert. If the student wishes, he may jump ahead and attack any relevent intermediate problem. However, at each point along the dialogue managed by the tutor, there is an enforced "understanding" between the system and the student about what to do next.

The other style of tutoring is the mentor, which manages quite a different style of dialogue. The mentor usually does not tell the student what to do. The student uses the terminal as scratch paper. He can type whatever he wants. He may start by expressing symbolically the information given in the problem text as well as writing some formulas or algebraic expressions. The mentor analyzes each line the student types. From time to time the mentor may decide to intervene. It may correct mistakes, encourage, or transfer control to the tutor. Between the tutor and the mentor there is a smooth two way interaction. The student cannot always tell with which component he is interacting. The system behaves somewhat as a human tutor who changes his style of tutoring on the basis of the circumstances.

A summary of all that happens during the tutoring session is maintained and used by the tutor and mentor. This summary is composed of a collection of the "working memory" elements. Each element describes an elementary interaction, and indicates what the student did and how the system responded. These elements, and the subsequent student responses, are the major driving factor of the dialogue.

In addition to these driving factors, strategic decisions are made on the basis of a deeper analysis of the student, which is done in the Student Model.

3.4 Error Analysis

The purpose of the Error Analyzer is to identify students' systematic mistakes, and to find the misconceptions hidden behind the mistakes. This is the same objective underlying the development of DEBUGGY (Brown and Burton, 1978). Students' misconceptions include the following:

1. Misconceptions due to inappropriate extrapolations. This means, for example, making assumptions that events are either independent, complementary, or mutually exclusive, where in fact they are not.

2. Inability to extract information from the question.

3. Lack of familiarity with rules.

4. Misunderstanding of sample space and event operators.

The error analyzer is composed of several LISP subroutines, each subroutine corresponding to a probability rule. Each subroutine attempts to map the formula the student wrote to the correct formula. The discrepancies are identified and classified into several types corresponding to the assumed misconceptions behind the mistake. An effort is made to account for the majority of the student's mistakes. After the error analyzer identifies the type of the student's mistake, a message is sent to the tutoring expert that makes the decision whether of not to intervene immediately to correct the mistake, and if so, in what way.

3.5 Student Model

The student model analyzes the student's performance. It makes assumptions about the student's believed overall capability, and determines what skills the system should work on with this particular student. The system makes an assumption about the capability of the student, because not all students should be handled alike. A more competent student receives more complex explanations, and interacts mostly with the mentor. A weak student receives simplified explanations and interacts mostly with the tutor.

The system's beliefs are continuously revised and changed based on the circumstances. The Student Model is accessable to the tutoring expert and to the specialists, and it influences decisions made by these components.

The Student Model is implemented by structures called objects. Various system components report to these objects by sending them messages that describe how the dialogue proceeds. One object is called the capability object, and its purpose is to make assumptions about the student's overall aptitude. The capability object is more than a passive data structure. It constructs its assumptions based on measures of difficulty assigned to each step the student may take and measures of correctness assigned to each step the student may take and measures of correctness assigned to possible inaccurate student's moves. Other objects correspond to a sub-skills the student is supposed to acquire. These objects are passive data structures that accumulate knowledge in a way which facilitates the analysis of the information by other system components.

3.6 Specialists

From time to time the tutoring expert may decide to treat in more depth a student's fundamental misconception revealed in the problem solving process. This is done by transferring control to a specialist. The specialists are LISP subroutines that interact with the student. A specialist queries the student model so as to teach the student in a suitable way. The information a specialist uses includes what the student has done before and its current belief about his capabilities.

Some of the specialists currently implemented and their major objectives are the following:

(a) independent-sp: demonstrates that one must assume independence between events when a formula such as $p(A \cap B) = p(A)p(B)$ is used.

(b) marginal-sp: demonstrates the notion of marginal probability and its relationship to other important notions and rules.

(c) conditional-sp: explains and demonstrates how to identify conditional probability expressed in a natural language sentence.

(d) union-sp: explains, using a Venn diagram, how the union formula is constructed.

The specialists may present Venn diagrams, may pose questions, and may relate things done before to the current problem.

3.7 The Interface

The purpose of the interface is to analyze the student input, to parse it, and to decide what the student intends to do. Sometimes the student is asked to take a specific action. This usually happens when he interacts with the tutor. In this case, the system knows what to anticipate, and one of the subroutines "read-answer" or "read-formula" is appropriately invoked to handle the input. When the student interacts with the mentor, a line typed by the student is handled by "read-line" component that makes assumptions about the student's intentions. The various things that a student may attempt while interacting with SPIRIT are: expressing data symbolically, writing a formula, substituting numbers in a pre-written formula, writing an algebraic expression, and writing a numerical value. In addition, the student may request help, either because he is confused, or in order to solve an intermediate subproblem. He also may ask for information about either the probability values found or the formulas written until this point. In addition, the terminal can be used as a calculator at almost any point in the dialogue.

4. DISCUSSION

We presented a brief description of SPIRIT, and because of space constraints we omitted some important implementation details, such as the implementation of the Error Analyzer and the Student Model.

The system has been used by undergraduate students taking an introductory course in probability theory. Their reaction to the system is quite encouraging, and we intend to report results of experiments in the near future.

Our philosophy is that an effective system evolves through a process of experimenting and tuning. In this respect, the implementation of tutoring strategies in a production system was found to be successful, because it provided us with three important advantages.

1. Productions are relatively independent of each other, so changes in one production do not necessarily force changes in the others. As a result, we could modify the system's behavior relatively easily.

2. The principles of the conflict resolution strategy we chose were suitable for the domain.

3. The major force that drives the dialogue is the set of working memory elements. These elements are accumulated as the dialogue proceeds, and represent the elements of knowledge the human tutor acquires in a tutoring dialogue. Thus, OPS5 provides a natural way of representing the dynamic knowledge accumulated during the dialogue.

The system allows flexible dialogue style, and by that we extended the idea of mixed initiative dialogue first discussed by Carbonell (1970), and advocated by others (e.g. Clancey, 1979; Brown, Burton and Zdybel, 1972). Mixed initiative dialogue in an ITS means that the dialogue should not be driven merely by what the system wants to do, but also by the student's will. In most of the contemporary ITS, such as SCHOLAR (Carbonell, 1970), GUIDON (Clancey, 1979) and SOPHIE (Brown, Burton and Bell, 1974), this idea was implemented by a variety of options available for the student. These options often included help requests, change topic commands, or requests for explanations. In SPIRIT, in addition to these options, the student is allowed to do whatever he wishes, while the system behaves as a silent observer that intervenes only when things are really going wrong.

A system must employ extensive modeling, and needs a long tuning process in order to intelligently decide when things are really going wrong and that an intervention is required, or when it is better to let the student struggle by himself. Presently, the decisions that SPIRIT makes are not always the ones that the well experienced tutor would. We believe we have made quite a lot of progress since we started to experiment with SPIRIT. For example, the idea of achieving a flexible dialogue style by employing the tutor and the mentor came to our mind after experiments with SPIRIT in its early stages. Although this idea meant a significant change in SPIRIT's behavior, the implementation was completed in a very short time. Despite our progress, we think we have a long way to go in improving SPIRIT and getting closer to the human tutor's effectiveness.

SPIRIT needs a formal evaluation, which would enable a theory to evolve from the set of tutoring rules. Tutoring is a domain of which we have very little understanding (and this is what makes the tutoring an intelligent activity); by developing a tool for collecting tutoring strategies and testing them we believe we contributed to the study of tutoring complex domains.

The methods of production system and object oriented programming proved to be very helpful in SPIRIT in facilitating the problem of designing a system with no specifications. These methods, as well as other AI methods, have recently become available on personal machines costing about $25,000, while five years ago these methods required the computational power of a mainframe (Sheil, 1983). Thus, we would expect to see them being used, in the near future, in fields such as DSS, where AI, traditionally, has not been applied.

SPIRIT covers only a small subset of probability theory. However, in terms of complexity and size, the system is large. It employs about 120 OPS5 productions and some 100 LISP subroutines. It has been developed over a period of 18 months and it runs (with a reasonable response time) on VAX 11/780.

FOOTNOTES:

1. This research has been supported in part by the Office of Naval Research Grant No. SFRC N00014/82/k/0613

REFERENCES:

[1] Brown, J. S. and Burton, R. R., Diagnostic models for procedural bugs in basic mathematical skills, Cognitive Science 2 (1978) 155-192.

[2] Brown, J. S., Burton, R. R. and Bell, A. G., SOPHIE, a sophisticated instructional environment for teaching electronic trouble shooting (An example of AI in CAI) (Bolt, Beranek and Newman Inc., 1978).

[3] Brown, J. S., Burton, R. R., and Zdybel, A model driven questioning and answering system for mixed initiative CAI, Dept. of Information and Computer Science, University of California. (1972)

[4] Carbonell, J. R., AI in CAI: an artificial intelligence approach to computer assisted instruction, IEEE Transactions on Man-Machine Systems, Vol. MMS-11 No. 4 (1970).

[5] Clancey, W. J., Transfer of rule-based expertise through a tutorial dialogue, Dept. of Computer Science, Stanford University. (1979).

[6] Collins, A. and Stevens, A. L., Goals and strategies of inquiry teaching, in Glaser, R. (ed.), Instructional Psychology Vol. 2 (Lawrence Erlbaum, Hillsdale, NJ, 1982).

[7] Forgy, C. L., OPS manual, Dept. of Computer Science, Carnegie Mellon University. (1981).

[8] Nilsson, N. J., Principles of artifical intelligence (Tioga Pub. Co., Palo Alto, CA, 1980).

[9] Sleeman, D. and Brown, J. S., Intelligent tutoring systems (Academic Press, London, 1982).

COMPUTER SCIENCE AND STATISTICS:
The Interface, L. Billard (ed.)

INTERVAL ESTIMATION OF THE NONCENTRALITY PARAMETER OF A GAMMA DISTRIBUTION

Paul Chiou and Chien-Pai Han

East Texas State University and University of Texas at Arlington

Asymptotic confidence interval for the noncentrality parameter of a Gamma distribution (or Chi-squared distribution) is derived. An algorithm for computing the maximum likelihood estimator of the noncentrality parameter is developed. A formula for the asymptotic variance of the maximum likelihood estimator is given. From the properties of the maximum likelihood estimator an asymptotic confidence interval is obtained.

I. INTRODUCTION

Let X_i, $i = 1, 2, \ldots, \nu$, be independent normally distributed with mean μ_i and unit standard deviation, then

$$X = \sum_{i=1}^{\nu} X_i^2$$

has a noncentral chi-squared distribution with ν degrees of freedom and noncentrality parameter

$$2\lambda = \sum_{i=1}^{\nu} \mu_i^2$$

The noncentral chi-squared distribution arises in various statistical analyses. A discussion of various application of the distribution is given in Johnson and Kotz (1970, Section 28.9). The chi-squared random variable is linearly related to the gamma random variable that is if X has the chi-squared distribution with ν degrees of freedom and noncentrality parameter 2λ then $Y = X/2$ is distributed according to the gamma distribution with $p = \nu/2$ degrees of freedom and noncentrality parameter λ.

This paper deals with the computation of the maximum likelihood estimator (MLE) of the noncentrality parameter λ and the asymptotic confidence interval for the noncentrality parameter λ of a gamma distribution. An algorithm for computing the maximum likelihood estimator and the asymptotic variance of the MLE is developed. From the properties of the MLE an asymptotic confidence interval is obtained.

II. ASYMPTOTIC CONFIDENCE INTERVAL FOR λ

Let $y_1, y_2, \ldots, y_n$ denote the sample values from a gamma distribution with density function

$$f(y,\lambda) = y^{p-1} e^{-\lambda-y} \sum_{k=0}^{\infty} (\lambda y)^k/[k!\Gamma(p+k)]$$

$$= e^{-\lambda-y} (y/\lambda)^{(p-1)/2} I_{p-1} (2\sqrt{\lambda y}) ,$$

$$y > 0 \qquad (2.1)$$

where $I_p(y)$ is the modified Bessel function:

$$I_p (y) = (y/2)^p \sum_{k=0}^{\infty} (y^2/4)^k/[k!\Gamma(p+k+1)]$$

(see Abramowitz and Stegun, 1970)

After taking the logarithm of the likelihood function and then differentiating with respect to λ, the likelihood equation is found to be

$$n = \sum_{i=1}^{n} (y_i/\sqrt{\lambda y_i}) \{I_p(2\sqrt{\lambda y_i})/I_{p-1}(2\sqrt{\lambda y_i})\} \tag{2.2}$$

(see Saxena and Alam, 1982)

The maximum likelihood estimator is obtained by solving (2.2). In order to achieve this we write equation (2.2) as

$$n = \sum_{i=1}^{n} y_i \{ \sum_{k=0}^{\infty} (\lambda y_i)^k/[k!\Gamma(p+k+1)] \} / \{ \sum_{k=0}^{\infty} (\lambda y_i)^k/[k!\Gamma(p+k)] \} \tag{2.3}$$

Denoting the MLE by λ_n^*, we have that λ_n^* is uniquely given as a solution of (2.3) for $\bar{y} > p$ and $\lambda_n^* = 0$ for $\bar{y} \le p$, where $\bar{y} = \sum_{i=1}^{n} y_i/n$. Furthermore,

$$(\lambda_n^* - \lambda) \xrightarrow{L} N(0, \sigma_n^2(\lambda))$$

where

$$\sigma_n^2(\lambda) = 1/nE\{[\frac{\partial}{\partial\lambda}\log f(Y,\lambda)]^2\}$$

To find the asymptotic variance $\sigma_n^2(\lambda)$, we obtain a Taylor series expansion

$$\frac{\partial}{\partial\lambda}\log f(y,\lambda) \simeq h(\lambda;\lambda,p) + h'(\lambda;\lambda,p)(y-\lambda)$$

where

$$h(y;\lambda,p) = \frac{\partial}{\partial\lambda}\log f(y,\lambda)$$

$$= \{ y \sum_{k=0}^{\infty} (\lambda y)^k/[k!\Gamma(p+k+1)] / \sum_{k=0}^{\infty} (\lambda y)^k/[k!\Gamma(p+k)] \} - 1$$

$$h'(y;\lambda,p) = \frac{\partial^2}{\partial y\partial\lambda}\log f(y,\lambda)$$

$$= \sum_{k=0}^{\infty} (\lambda y)^k/[k!\Gamma(p+k+1)] / \sum_{k=0}^{\infty} (\lambda y)^k/[k!\Gamma(p+k)] + \lambda y \{ \sum_{k=0}^{\infty} (\lambda y)^k/[k!\Gamma(p+k+2)] / \sum_{k=0}^{\infty} (\lambda y)^k/[k!\Gamma(p+k)] - [\sum_{k=0}^{\infty} (\lambda y)^k/[k!\Gamma(p+k+1)] / \sum_{k=0}^{\infty} (\lambda y)^k/[k!\Gamma(p+k)]]^2\}$$

It follows

$$E\{[\frac{\partial}{\partial\lambda}\log f(Y,\lambda)]^2\}$$
$$\simeq h^2(\lambda;\lambda,p) + 2h(\lambda;\lambda,p)\,h'(\lambda;\lambda,p)\,E(Y-\lambda) + [h'(\lambda;\lambda,p)]^2 E[(Y-\lambda)^2]$$
$$= h^2(\lambda;\lambda,p) + 2h(\lambda;\lambda,p)\,h'(\lambda;\lambda,p)\,p + [h'(\lambda;\lambda,p)]^2(2\lambda + p + p^2) \tag{2.4}$$

When n is large, an asymptotic $100(1-\alpha)\%$ confidence interval is given as

$$\lambda_n^* \pm z_{1-\alpha/2}\,\sigma_n(\lambda_n^*)$$

where $z_{1-\alpha/2}$ is the 100 $(1 - \alpha/2)$ percentage point of the standard normal distribution and $\sigma_n(\lambda_n^*)$ is obtained by replacing λ by λ_n^* in equation (2.4).

A double precision FORTRAN program was written for computing the MLE of λ in equation (2.3). The method used to solve equation (2.3) is the bisection method. The series are truncated when the relative error is less than 10^{-12}. A program listing is available free upon request from the first author.

III. EXAMPLE

Thirty random deviates from a gamma distribution with 2.5 degrees of freedom and noncentrality parameter 8.0 were generated,

11.674 ,	16.475 ,	15.678 ,
6.037 ,	10.898 ,	8.800 ,
7.807 ,	9.269 ,	9.545 ,
4.904 ,	13.432 ,	4.710 ,
12.936 ,	14.157 ,	7.259 ,
6.563 ,	10.029 ,	7.523 ,
3.963 ,	8.706 ,	16.394 ,
9.524 ,	10.932 ,	11.003 ,
15.619 ,	7.176 ,	10.398 ,
9.188 ,	8.585 ,	8.540 .

Using the FORTRAN program we obtained $\lambda_n^* = 7.572$, $\sigma_n^2(\lambda_n^*) = 0.430$. Hence a 95% confidence interval for λ is (6.287, 8.857).

REFERENCES

[1] Abramowitz, M. and Stegun, I. A. (1970), Handbook of Mathematical Functions. Dover, New York.

[2] Johnson, N. L. and Kotz, S. (1970), Continuous Univariate Distributions-2. Houghton Mifflin, Boston.

[3] Saxena, K. M. L. and Alam, K. (1982) "Estimation of the noncentrality parameter of a chi-squared distribution," Ann. Statist. 10, pp. 1012-1016.

COMPUTER SCIENCE AND STATISTICS:
The Interface, L. Billard (ed.)

FUZZY SET THEORY USED TO PRIORITIZE GEOCHEMICAL NUCLEAR WASTE RESEARCH

Kenneth S. Czyscinski and William V. Harper

Office of Nuclear Waste Isolation
Battelle Memorial Institute
Columbus, Ohio 43201

Fuzzy set theory was used to evaluate confidence in radionuclide retention provided by a four compartment isolation system. Within each compartment (barrier), subjective estimates were made of the predictability and efficiency of each mechanism, weighting factors for each mechanism within the barriers, and each barrier in the system. Weighted sums were used to evaluate confidence in the barrier and total system performance. Fuzzy set programs were developed for sensitivity analyses, including blurring and contrast intensification techniques. Results suggest that increased understanding of radionuclide solubility relationships and water/rock reactions would enhance overall system predictability under both expected and unexpected conditions.

1. INTRODUCTION

The Office of Nuclear Waste Isolation (ONWI) is involved in the task of predicting the performance of a multibarrier radioactive waste isolation system composed of natural (a geologic repository in salt) and engineered barriers. Both systems are in turn combinations of multicomponent subsystems whose performance is controlled by many variables. Statistical techniques using objective numerical data such as kriging, stochastic hydrology and conditional simulation can be applied to components of the total system. However, performance evaluations for many aspects of the overall system and subsystems rely on subjective evaluations of predictability, data sufficiency, scenario definition, etc., which often lack well-defined boundaries. This vagueness may be handled mathematically by fuzzy set theory.

In this paper, fuzzy set theory is applied to the prediction of radionuclide retention in a four compartment (barrier) system, with respect to the geochemical mechanisms which function to retard or release radionculides in each compartment. "Fuzzy" computer algorithms are detailed which treat the "predictability" of given radionuclide's behavior, based on subjective estimates of existing knowledge (the predictability scale defined below) and estimates of retardation efficiency. Blurring and contrast intensification techniques are used to perform the sensitivity analyses in addition to the basic fuzzy set mathematics. The goal of these analyses is to prioritize the areas requiring additional research efforts to lessen the uncertainty in the total system's performance. While this paper focuses on geochemical issues, the fuzzy algorithms are general in nature and can mathematically treat imprecise subjective data not well suited for standard statistical approaches.

2. WHY USE FUZZY SETS?

The nonexistence of well-defined set boundaries is the basis of fuzzy set theory. The basic concepts of set theory underlie statistical and probabilistic techniques. A set may consist of the possible outcomes of the roll of a die (1,2,3,4,5,6), or may be so large that a listing of all possible elements is impractical, e.g., the set of all living people. In either case, the set boundaries are well defined so one can decide if a given object does or does not belong to a particular set (Freund, 1971). Many subjective assessments do not lend themselves to classical statistical treatment because well-defined boundaries for the sets do not exist (Gupta, 1983). For example, in estimating underground mine safety, no clear-cut boundary exists separating safe from unsafe mines. While there are obviously safe and unsafe mines, the transition is not well defined, and therefore mine safety often implies a subjective assessment. Fuzzy set mathematics may be used in such subjective evaluations.

For overall systems evaluations, "fuzzy" data may be of more value than other more quantitative data. In the mine safety example, "fuzzy" subjective data on overall mine safety supplied by mining experts are often more valuable than highly quantifiable data from a particular stress-strain instrument. The ability to combine and compare fuzzy data is the main purpose of fuzzy set theory.

3. FUZZY SET THEORY BASIS

In usual (or crisp) set theory, an element either does or does not belong to a given set; elements have a degree of membership in a fuzzy set. This graded membership measures the subjective evaluation by an individual that the element belongs to the fuzzy set. Let C be a crisp set (as defined mathematically by common set theory), and let F be a fuzzy set. Let μ denote the membership function of an element x. For set C, $\mu_C(x) = 0$ or 1, i.e., x is either an element of set C or it is not. However, for the fuzzy set F, $\mu_F(x) = [0,1]$. When $\mu_F(x) = 0$, x is not an element of F, and similarly when $\mu_F(x) = 1$, x is an element of F. For $(0 < \mu_F(x) < 1)$, the closer μ_F is to 1, the stronger the subjective assessment that x is likely to be an element of F. Going back to the mine safety example, there are unsafe mines ($\mu_F(x) = 0$), safe mines ($\mu_F(x) = 1$) and mines whose safety is not well defined $(0 < \mu(x) < 1)$. On this illustration F is assumed to be the fuzzy set of safe mines.

In the next section the radionuclide application is detailed, along with the sensitivity analysis using contrast intensification and blurring techniques performed on the subjective data generated. These two operations have opposite effects on the original subjective memberships $\mu_F(x)$. Contrast intensification (INT) reduces the grayness between the elements by pulling them closer to either nonmembership ($\mu_F(x) = 0$), or full membership ($\mu_F(x) = 1$). Blurring (BLR) moves the elements closer to the middle (0.5) of the interval.

4. WASTE MANAGEMENT APPLICATION - RADIONUCLIDE RELEASES

The four-compartment (barrier) isolation system (Figure 1), through which radionuclides must pass before reaching the accessible environment, is shown in Figure 1. The four barriers consist of:

(1) The waste form in which the radionuclides are immobilized (spent fuel rods or glass logs),
(2) The remaining waste package components (canister and overpack) and the proximal salt,
(3) The salt along the release path from barrier two to barrier four and
(4) The geologic strata surrounding barrier 3 to the border of the "accessible environment" as defined in Figure 1.

Within each barrier, a number of mechanisms act to retard radionuclides, and each barrier in turn contributes to the retention ability of the total system. The mechanisms for each barrier are listed in Table 1, and the radionuclides used in these analyses are uranium (U), plutonium (Pu), americium (Am), technetium (Tc), radium (Ra), neptunium (Np), and cesium (Cs). Based on estimates of radionuclide behavior in each compartment of the isolation system, the fuzzy set mathematics are applied to perform a sensitivity analysis.

4.1 RANKING SCALES

Data for the analyses are generated for each radionuclide mechanism pair in each barrier by

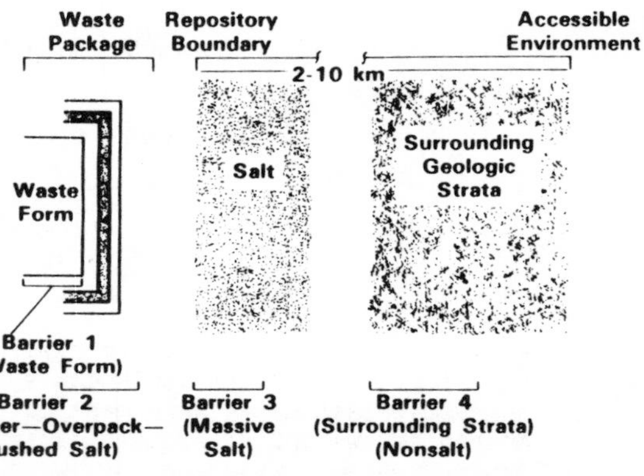

FIGURE 1. SCHEMATIC DIAGRAM OF THE FOUR COMPARTMENT (BARRIER) ISOLATION SYSTEM

making subjective rankings of the predictability and efficiency scales as follows. The predictability of each radionuclide's behavior, with respect to each mechanism in a given barrier, is judged on a scale from 0 (unpredictable) to 1 (completely predictable). The efficiency of retention for each pair is also ranked from 0 to 1 in terms of the absolute retention due to that mechanism. For example, the predictability of a given radionuclide-mechanism pair in a barrier may be high (close to 1), while the absolute degree of retention expected may be low (closer to 0). The efficiency scale can also be thought of as a "goodness-badness" scale since a judgment is made as to how well or poorly radionuclides are retained by a given mechanism. Needless to say, radionuclide behavior is a function of many variables and, consequently, the rankings are subjective, to a degree. The predictability-efficiency estimates for each radionucide-mechanism pair are given in Table 1. The products of predictability and efficiency generate an additional fuzzy set for further analyses.

Total retention in each barrier is the sum of each operative mechanism, and the total system performance is the sum of each barrier's contribution. Subjective weighting factors were also estimated for the contributions of each mechanism to a barrier's performance and each barrier to the total system performance (Table 2). By applying fuzzy set mathematics to the weighted sums, a sensitivity analysis can be performed to determine where the predictability of each component in the total system should be improved to increase the predictability of the total system. Blurring and contrast intensification techniques applied to both the scale estimates and weighting factors show the effects of varying these estimates on individual barrier and total system performance for each radionuclide, and the relative performance of each barrier in the system. By identifying areas where decreasing uncertainty can increase total performance most

Table 1. Predictability and efficiency scale rankings for retention mechanisms in the four barrier system for seven radionuclides

	Barrier 1		Barrier 2		Barrier 3		Barrier 4	
	pred.	eff.	pred.	eff.	pred.	eff.	pred.	eff.
Pu								
Leachability	0.60	0.50	1.00	0.00	1.00	0.00	1.00	0.00
Solubility	1.00	0.00	0.60	0.60	0.60	0.60	0.60	0.60
Ion Exchange	1.00	0.00	0.70	0.40	0.70	0.40	0.70	0.50
Adsorption	1.00	0.00	0.80	0.50	0.80	0.50	0.80	0.60
Reactions	1.00	0.00	0.60	0.50	0.50	0.50	0.50	0.50
Decay	1.00	0.10	1.00	0.10	1.00	0.20	1.00	0.30
Tc								
Leachability	0.50	0.20	1.00	0.00	1.00	0.00	1.00	0.00
Solubility	1.00	0.00	0.60	0.30	0.60	0.70	0.60	0.70
Ion Exchange	1.00	0.00	0.80	0.10	0.80	0.10	0.80	0.10
Adsorption	1.00	0.00	0.80	0.20	0.80	0.10	0.80	0.10
Reactions	1.00	0.00	0.50	0.30	0.50	0.30	0.50	0.20
Decay	1.00	0.10	1.00	0.10	1.00	0.20	1.00	0.40
U								
Leachability	0.80	0.40	1.00	0.00	1.00	0.00	1.00	0.00
Solubility	1.00	0.00	0.60	0.50	0.60	0.70	0.60	0.70
Ion Exchange	1.00	0.00	0.50	0.40	0.50	0.20	0.50	0.30
Adsorption	1.00	0.00	0.60	0.50	0.60	0.30	0.60	0.40
Reactions	1.00	0.00	0.70	0.40	0.40	0.20	0.40	0.30
Decay	1.00	0.10	1.00	0.10	1.00	0.20	1.00	0.50
Cs								
Leachability	0.80	0.20	1.00	0.00	1.00	0.00	1.00	0.00
Solubility	1.00	0.00	0.80	0.10	0.80	0.10	0.80	0.10
Ion Exchange	1.00	0.00	0.70	0.30	0.70	0.30	0.70	0.40
Adsorption	1.00	0.00	0.80	0.20	0.80	0.20	0.80	0.30
Reactions	1.00	0.00	0.50	0.30	0.60	0.20	0.60	0.30
Decay	1.00	0.10	1.00	0.30	1.00	0.50	1.00	0.60
Ra								
Leachability	0.50	0.60	1.00	0.00	1.00	0.00	1.00	0.00
Solubility	1.00	0.00	0.60	0.60	0.60	0.50	0.60	0.60
Ion Exchange	1.00	0.00	0.60	0.50	0.60	0.60	0.60	0.50
Adsorption	1.00	0.00	0.60	0.50	0.60	0.60	0.60	0.50
Reactions	1.00	0.00	0.60	0.50	0.70	0.50	0.70	0.60
Decay	1.00	0.10	1.00	0.10	1.00	0.10	1.00	0.10
Np								
Leachability	0.60	0.60	1.00	0.00	1.00	0.00	1.00	0.00
Solubility	1.00	0.00	0.60	0.60	0.60	0.60	0.60	0.60
Ion Exchange	1.00	0.00	0.20	0.40	0.70	0.50	0.70	0.50
Adsorption	1.00	0.00	0.40	0.40	0.80	0.60	0.80	0.60
Reactions	1.00	0.00	0.60	0.40	0.50	0.60	0.50	0.60
Decay	1.00	0.10	1.00	0.10	1.00	0.20	1.00	0.30
Am								
Leachability	0.50	0.50	1.00	0.00	1.00	0.00	1.00	0.00
Solubility	1.00	0.00	0.60	0.60	0.60	0.60	0.60	0.60
Ion Exchange	1.00	0.00	0.60	0.50	0.60	0.50	0.60	0.70
Adsorption	1.00	0.00	0.60	0.50	0.60	0.50	0.60	0.70
Reactions	1.00	0.00	0.70	0.50	0.60	0.50	0.60	0.60
Decay	1.00	0.10	1.00	0.10	1.00	0.30	1.00	0.50

significantly, research areas can be prioritized for more effective allocation of limited research resources.

4.2 BARRIERS, MECHANISMS, AND WEIGHTING FACTORS

In barrier 1, radioactive decay and waste form leach resistance (leachability) act to limit releases from this barrier. Once in barrier 2, which consists of the salt, brine, and metallic components of the waste package, radionuclides can be retained by solubility constraints, adsorption, ion exchange processes on the solid phases, and reactions between the solid and liquid phases which entrain radionuclides. In the remaining barriers, the same mechanisms are present. Decay is also included as a retention mechanism since it accounts for decreasing releases as a function of the radionuclide residence time within each compartment.

Assigning efficiency estimates to the decay mechanism and barrier weights generates two different situations (cases) which must be considered, an expected and an unexpected condition. Under expected conditions, the waste package (waste form-canister and overpack) is expected to contain the waste for a specified period, while for the unexpected case the package is prematurely breached accidently. Also, under expected conditions, releases through the salt (barrier 3) should be minimal to nonexistent and, therefore, the weighting factor for this barrier is high. For the unexpected situation where releases from the waste package (barriers 1 and 2) to the nonsalt strata (barrier 4) above or below are much more rapid, a lower weighting factor is used for barrier 3 and a higher factor for barrier 4 (Table 2).

4.3 MATHEMATICAL SETUP

The basic variables used in this study are as follows:

p_{imb} = predictability membership value of nuclide i for mechanism m in barrier b; i =1,2,..., 7; m=1,2,...6; b=1,2,3,4

e_{imb} = efficiency membership value of nuclide i for mechanism m in barrier b; 1=1,2,..., 7; m= 1,2...,6; b=1,2,3,4

α_{mb} = weight of mechanism m in barrier b;m=1,2,..., 6; b= 1,2,3,4 such that $\sum_m \alpha_{mb} = 1$ for all b

β_b = weight of barrier b; b = 1,2,3,4 such that $\sum_b \beta_b = 1$

c_{ib} = score of nuclide i in barrier b; i=1,2,...7; b=1,2,3,4 $\sum_m \alpha_{mb}\ e_{imb}\ p_{imb}$

r_i = overall rating of nuclide i $\sum_b\sum_m \beta_b\ \alpha_{mb} e_{imb} p_{imb} = \sum_b \beta_b c_{ib}$

Two distinct data sets are used for expected and unexpected cases (Table 2). While the above mathematics will allow an overall nuclide ranking, it also provides complete traceability. Once the nuclides are ranked, one can work backwards to find the contributing factors that led to the overall ranking as illustrated in the next section.

The overall rating r_i provides a rating value for nuclide i over the 6 mechanisms and 4 barriers. The product $p_{imb}\ e_{imb}$ is analogous to the method of first order second moment uncertainty analyses used for quantitative data. In these methods (ignoring correlation), the contribution of a parameter to the uncertainty of the performance measure is a function of the performance measure's sensitivity to that parameter and the parameter's uncertainty. While the sensitivity will not change unless the modeled process is changed, the parameter uncertainty can be reduced by additional allocation of resources to further study that parameter. The parameter uncertainty is similar to the predictability p_{imb}, and the efficiency e_{imb} is not unlike the sensitivity of the performance measure to that parameter.

Ranking the 7 r_i values can be used to highlight future research areas which would give the best payoff in terms of overall systems safety, i.e., geochemical areas are prioritized to indicate where efforts to reduce uncertainty should be focused. Any allocation of resources should employ a global performance measure such as done here to maximize the benefit obtained from the limited resources.

It is important to emphasize that the data, while based on expert opinion, are nonetheless subjective. How robust the overall rankings are can be tested via the fuzzy set sensitivity techniques, contrast intensification and blurring. The middle of the [0,1] interval for the predictability and efficiency fuzzy measures is 0.5. A membership value of 0.5 indicates indifference between the two extremes 0 and 1. Contrast intensification is used to transform the initial predictability and efficiency values toward a more "black" or "white" score by moving the initial membership values closer to the 0 and 1 scale extremes, effectively removing some of the "grayness." Blurring introduces additional grayness by moving the values further away from the extremes. Contrast intensification (INT) and blurring (BLR) for the predictability and efficiency values are defined below, where $\mu_A(x)$ is a generic membership function in fuzzy set A used to represent either p_{imb} or e_{imb}.

Table 2. Weighting Factors for Retention Mechanisms in Each Barrier and for Each Barrier in the Total System (Expected and Unexpected Cases)

Weighting Factors - Mechanisms within Barriers (α_{mb})

	Barrier 1	Barrier 2	Barrier 3	Barrier 4
Leachability	0.70	0.00	0.00	0.00
Solubility	0.00	0.50	0.50	0.20
Ion Exchange	0.00	0.10	0.10	0.20
Adsorption	0.00	0.10	0.10	0.10
Reactions	0.00	0.20	0.10	0.10
Decay	0.30	0.10	0.20	0.40

Weighting Factors - Barriers in the Total System (β_b)

	Barrier 1	Barrier 2	Barrier 3	Barrier 4
Expected Case	0.10	0.20	0.60	0.10
Unexpected Case	0.20	0.10	0.10	0.60

$$INT(A)=\begin{cases}\mu_A^2(x) & \text{for all } x \text{ such that } \mu_A(x) < 0.5\\ \mu_A^{.5}(x) & \text{for all } x \text{ such that } \mu_A(x) \geq 0.5\end{cases}$$

$$BLR(A)=\begin{cases}\mu_A^{.5}(x) & \text{for all } x \text{ such that } \mu_A(x) < 0.5\\ \mu_A^2(x) & \text{for all } x \text{ such that } \mu_A(x) \geq 0.5\end{cases}$$

Additionally, the sensitivity of the subjective weights for the mechanisms (α_{mb}) and barriers (β_b) may be considered by weight contrast intensification (WINT) and weight blurring (WBLR) described below. The rationale behind WINT and WBLR is based on two points. First, the average weight of k categories is 1/k; thus, 1/k is the pivotal value used. Secondly the new weights must still sum to 1. Below, $w_i \varepsilon W$ is a generic weight for i=1,2...,k.

$$WINT(W)=\begin{cases}w_i' = \frac{w_i^2}{c} & \text{for all } w_i < {}^1/k\\ w_i' = \frac{w_i^{.5}}{c} & \text{for all } w_i \geq {}^1/k\end{cases}$$

where c normalizes the new weights such that

$$\sum_i w_i' = 1$$

$$WBLR(W)=\begin{cases}w_i' = \frac{w_i^{.5}}{c} & \text{for all } w_i < {}^1/k\\ w_i' = \frac{w_i^2}{c} & \text{for all } w_i \geq {}^1/k\end{cases}$$

where c normalizes the new weights such that

$$\sum_i w_i' = 1$$

The software developed for this application is in FORTRAN 77 on a VAX 11/780. These "fuzzy" algorithms are coded such that the subjective values may be left as they were initially evaluated (designated N for normal in the output), blurred (designated B), or contrast intensified (designated I). The data are broken into the following categories:

1. predictability and efficiency data (p_{imb}, e_{imb})
2. mechanisms weights (α_{mb})
3. barrier weights (β_b)

Each of the 3 categories may be designed N, B, or I separately. Thus 27 different combinations are possible for either the expected or unexpected case. Additionally there is user control of the quantity of output generated, including such items as data echoing choices. An output example is provided in the appendix.

5. RESULTS

Rankings for the seven radionuclides under expected and unexpected cases are listed in Table 3, for the normal data (N N N) as well as combinations of blurred (B) and contrast intensified (I) variations of p_{imb}, e_{imb}, β_b, and α_{mb}.

The radionuclides are listed in order of least predictable (lowest r_i) to most predictable (highest r_i). For this application, the relative values of r_i are of importance. Some generalizations are apparent after inspecting the rankings.

1. For both the expected and unexpected cases, the relative differences between highest and lowest r_i values do not change drastically for equivalent combinations of p_{imb}, e_{imb}, β_b, and α_{imb}.
2. Cesium changes relative position in the listing for expected vs. unexpected conditions.
3. Technetium has the least predictable retention under both expected and unexpected conditions.

Table 3. Radionuclide Rankings (r_i) for Expected and Unexpected Cases for Normal (N), Blurred (B) and Contrast Intensified (I) Combinations of ($p_{imb} e_{imb}$, β_b, α_{mb})

Expected Case

N N N	N B B	B B B	B N N	N I I	I I I	I N N
Tc 0.18	Tc 0.14	Ra 0.16	Ra 0.20	Ra 0.12	Tc 0.05	Tc 0.09
Ra 0.22	Cs 0.21	Am 0.17	Cs 0.25	Tc 0.20	U 0.07	U 0.18
U 0.23	U 0.23	Pu 0.21	Pu 0.28	U 0.21	Ra 0.07	Np 0.29
Pu 0.27	Ra 0.27	Tc 0.23	Am 0.28	Pu 0.21	Np 0.09	Pu 0.29
Np 0.27	Np 0.27	Np 0.24	Np 0.29	Np 0.21	Pu 0.09	Cs 0.31
Cs 0.29	Pu 0.29	U 0.26	Tc 0.30	Am 0.30	Am 0.14	Ra 0.31
Am 0.31	Am 0.29	Cs 0.29	U 0.30	Cs 0.46	Cs 0.63	Am 0.37
D=0.13	D=0.15	D=0.13	D=0.10	D=0.34	D=0.58	D=0.28

Unexpected Case

N N N	N B B	B B B	B N N	N I I	I I I	I N N
Tc 0.23	Tc 0.14	Am 0.13	Am 0.18	Ra 0.24	Tc 0.24	Tc 0.16
Ra 0.25	Cs 0.19	Ra 0.14	Ra 0.18	Tc 0.30	Cs 0.34	Cs 0.24
Cs 0.27	U 0.24	Pu 0.18	U 0.25	Pu 0.33	Ra 0.35	U 0.35
Pu 0.31	Ra 0.29	Tc 0.20	Pu 0.25	Np 0.33	Np 0.39	Ra 0.39
U 0.32	Am 0.30	Np 0.20	Np 0.26	Cs 0.34	Pu 0.39	Pu 0.40
Np 0.32	Pu 0.30	U 0.27	Cs 0.28	U 0.36	U 0.47	Np 0.40
Am 0.37	Np 0.31	Cs 0.28	Tc 0.29	Am 0.42	Am 0.64	Am 0.57
D=0.14	D=0.17	D=0.15	D=0.11	D=0.18	D=0.40	D=0.41

D=highest r_i-lowest r_i

4. Actinide elements (U, N_p, Pu, Am) tend to show similar behavior under both expected and unexpected conditions.

6. DISCUSSION AND CONCLUSIONS

The most useful observation from these analyses is that the relative separation in r_i values for both expected and unexpected cases does not vary significantly. This constancy indicates that retention mechanisms within barriers 3 and 4 function to compensate for the large changes in barrier weights. Consequently, demonstrating containment under expected or unexpected conditions can rely on the retention mechanisms within the respective major barriers, although the relative weightings of the barriers in the total system will vary considerably. For the expected case, the major barrier (barrier 3) is the salt, while for the unexpected case the ground water/rock system in barrier 4 provides the retardation.

The remainder of this discussion centers on implications of the fuzzy set results for increasing radionuclide behavior predictability in the overall isolation system. Closer examination of the algorithm output shows that radioactive decay plays a very significant role in both barriers 3 and 4. This is a direct consequence of the long transport times assumed for movement through the salt (barrier 3) under expected conditions, and the long (slow) ground water travel paths through barrier 4 under unexpected conditions. Nothing can be done to increase the predictability (p_{imb}) or efficiency (e_{imb}) of the decay process. Therefore, increasing system level predictability requires refinements in predictability (p_{imb}) of other retention mechanisms.

Solubility limits are subjectively identified in Table 1 as a major component of the retention in barriers 2-4. Increases in the predictability of solubility behavior both in these barriers would increase overall system predictability. Since actinide elements (U, Np, Pu, Am) tend to behave in a similar manner, additional information on solubility relationships would increase the predictability of all these radionuclides. Technetium behavior would also become more predictable by increasing p_{imb} for the solubility mechanism, particulary since the ion exchange and adsorption mechanisms provide little effective retention (lower e_{imb} values).

Quantifying reactions between radionuclides in solution and solids which result in the entrainment of radionuclides may also increase system predictability for some radionuclides, notably U, Np, Am, Ra, in barrier 2, for both expected and unexpected cases. Quantifying these reactions more thoroughly may be more difficult than improving solubility behavior predictability, largely due to experimental difficulties. Therefore, given limited research resources, higher priority would be given to increasing predictability of solubility relationships in barriers 2-4.

In summary, these analyses show that retention mechanisms in barriers 3 and 4 function to keep the overall system predictability relatively consistent under both expected and unexpected cases. Radioactive decay plays a prominent role in system retention behavior, but as a first priority increasing system predictability could be achieved by improving predictability (p_{imb}) estimates for radionuclide solubility. As a second priority, increased predictability of the effects of water/rock reactions on the entrainment of radionuclides would also increase total system predictability.

Continued work in this application of fuzzy set mathematics will comprise the following. Additional "fuzzy" analyses will be performed to determine the results of varying values of p_{imb} and e_{imb} while maintaining constant barrier and mechanism weights. This exercise should help focus the research area prioritization further. In addition, the p_{imb} and e_{imb} estimates will be sought from a number of sources and combined for a further refinement of these analyses.

REFERENCES

Chameau, J.L.A., Altschaeffl, A., Michael, H. L., and Yao, J.T.P., Potential Application of Fuzzy Sets in Civil Engineering, ASCE Journal of Structural Engineering, 109 (1983) 7-24.

Dubois, D., and Prade, H., Fuzzy Sets and Systems: Theory and Applications (Academic Press, New York, NY, 1979).

Freund, J. E., Mathematical Statistics, 2nd edn. (Prentice-Hall, Inc., Englewood Cliffs, NJ, 1971).

Gupta, M. M. (Ed.), Ragade, R. K., and Yager, R. R. (Assoc. Eds.), Advances in Fuzzy Set Theory and Applications (North-Holland, Amsterdam, 1979).

Gupta, M. M., 1983. Fuzzy Set Theory, in Kotz, S., Johnson, N. L., and Read, C. B. (Eds.), Encyclopedia of Statistical Sciences.

ACKNOWLEDGEMENTS

This work was supported by the U.S. Department of Energy on a contract (contract no. DE-AC06-76-RL01830-ONWI) with Battelle Memorial Institute.

APPENDIX - EXAMPLE COMPUTER OUTPUT

EXPECTED CONDITIONS

DATA N   BARRIER WTS N   MECH. WTS N

FUZZY RESULTS

Pu				
Leachability	0.30	0.00	0.00	0.00
Solubility	0.00	0.36	0.36	0.36
Ion Exchange	0.00	0.28	0.28	0.35
Adsorption	0.00	0.40	0.40	0.48
Reactions	0.00	0.30	0.25	0.25
Decay	0.10	0.10	0.20	0.30

The above 6 x 4 matrix contains the p_{imb} e_{imb} products for the 6 mechanisms and 4 barriers for this nuclide

0.22	0.31	0.25	0.34

The above are the 4 c_{ib} values for this nuclide

0.27

Above is the r_i value for this nuclide

Tc				
Leachability	0.10	0.00	0.00	0.00
Solubility	0.00	0.18	0.42	0.42
Ion Exchange	0.00	0.08	0.08	0.08
Adsorption	0.00	0.16	0.08	0.08
Reactions	0.00	0.15	0.15	0.10
Decay	0.10	0.10	0.20	0.40
	0.10	0.15	0.19	0.28
	0.18			

U				
Leachability	0.32	0.00	0.00	0.00
Solubility	0.00	0.30	0.42	0.42
Ion Exchange	0.00	0.20	0.10	0.15
Adsorption	0.00	0.30	0.18	0.24
Reactions	0.00	0.28	0.08	0.12
Decay	0.10	0.10	0.20	0.50
	0.23	0.26	0.20	0.35
	0.23			

Cs				
Leachability	0.16	0.00	0.00	0.00
Solubility	0.00	0.08	0.08	0.08
Ion Exchange	0.00	0.21	0.21	0.28
Adsorption	0.00	0.16	0.16	0.24
Reactions	0.00	0.15	0.12	0.18
Decay	0.10	0.30	0.50	0.60
	0.14	0.14	0.36	0.35
	0.29			

	DATA N	BARRIER WTS N	MECH. WTS N	
Ra				
Leachability	0.30	0.00	0.00	0.00
Solubility	0.00	0.36	0.30	0.36
Ion Exchange	0.00	0.30	0.36	0.30
Adsorption	0.00	0.30	0.36	0.30
Reactions	0.00	0.30	0.35	0.42
Decay	0.10	0.10	0.10	0.10
	0.22	0.30	0.20	0.24
	0.23			
Np				
Leachability	0.36	0.00	0.00	0.00
Solubility	0.00	0.36	0.36	0.36
Ion Exchange	0.00	0.08	0.35	0.35
Adsorption	0.00	0.16	0.48	0.48
Reactions	0.00	0.24	0.30	0.30
Decay	0.10	0.10	0.20	0.30
	0.26	0.25	0.27	0.34
	0.27			
Am				
Leachability	0.25	0.00	0.00	0.00
Solubility	0.00	0.36	0.36	0.36
Ion Exchange	0.00	0.30	0.30	0.42
Adsorption	0.00	0.30	0.30	0.42
Reactions	0.00	0.35	0.30	0.36
Decay	0.10	0.10	0.30	0.50
	0.19	0.32	0.31	0.43
	0.31			

Summary of r_i values for the 7 nuclides

1	Tc	0.18
2	Ra	0.23
3	U	0.23
4	Pu	0.27
5	Np	0.27
6	Cs	0.29
7	Am	0.31

COMPUTER SCIENCE AND STATISTICS:
The Interface, L. Billard (ed.)

BIPLOT FOR EXPLORATION AND DIAGNOSIS - EXAMPLES AND SOFTWARE

K.R.Gabriel and C.L. Odoroff
University of Rochester

Rochester, New York 14642

The biplots of several data sets are presented to illustrate uses of this method of display. Data on thirty 1977 car models are displayed (the biplot having been fitted by a resistant algorithm). U.S. cars are clearly seen to be distinct from almost all imported models, being heavier, larger and more expensive; the foreign cars are seen to have beter repair records and lower mpg. Anderson's well-known Iris data are shown to group into three well separated clusters ordered along the axis of three out of four variables. Data on density of alcohol in water solution are classified by concentration and temperature biplot in a distinctive geometric structure which diagnoses an additive model (temperature effect plus concentration effect). More detailed inspection of the 3D biplot suggests that these effects should be modeled by quadratic functions. Various available computer programs for fitting and displaying biplots are tested.

1. WHAT IS A BIPLOT?

A biplot is an approximate graphical representation of a matrix of numbers by means of markers for its rows and its columns. If a[i] denotes the (vector) marker for row i and b[j] the (vector) marker for column j, then biplot representation ensures that the inner-product

$\langle a[i], b[j]\rangle$ approximates $y[i,j]$, (1)

the [i,j]-th element of Y, the matrix represented (Gabriel, 1983).

For a least squares approximation, the biplot markers are obtained by means of the singular value decomposition of Y. If this is written

$$Y = \Sigma_e \ \ell[e]\ p[e]\ q'[e], \qquad (2)$$

with $\ell[1] \geq \ell[2] \geq \dots > 0$, then one computes matrices

$$A = (p[1],\ p[2])R' \qquad (3)$$

and

$$B = (\ell[1]\ q[1],\ \ell[2]\ q[2])S \qquad (4)$$

for a suitable non-singular matrix R(2x2) and its inverse S. The two-dimensional biplot is then constructed (Gabriel, 1971) by plotting the rows of A as row markers a[i] and the rows of B as column markers b[j]. (For a 3D-biplot one would add ℓ[3], p[3] and q[3] in (3) and (4), above and use a (3x3) non-singular matrix R).

Resistant approximations can be obtained by algorithms which are multiplicative analogues of median polish (Gabriel and Odoroff, 1983). These are insensitive to outliers but can be scaled in a manner similar to (3) and (4).

Biplots with special properties -- in addition to the inner-product representation (1) -- can be obtained by suitable choice of R. Thus, the principal component biplot (or GH-biplot) is obtained by using R = I for a matrix Y, each of whose columns has been centered by subtracting its mean. In this biplot

length (b[j]) approximates St. Dev. (column j,) (5)

cos (b[j], b[j']) approximates Corr(column j, column j'), (6)

distance (a[i], a[i']) approximates Mahalanobis distance (rows i and i'). (7)

Another biplot of this type of matrix is the JK biplot with R = Diag(ℓ[1],ℓ[2]). In that biplot

distance (a[i], a[i']) approximates Euclidean distance (rows i and i'). (8)

A third type of biplot allows for easy plotting by allocating the ℓ's evenly to both sets of markers. Thus, in the SQ-biplot $R = \mathrm{Diag}(\sqrt{\ell[1]}, \sqrt{\ell[2]})$.

Another way of looking at biplots is to consider the scatter of the rows of matrix Y with respect to a set of orthogonal axes defined by the columns of Y. The biplot can then be viewed as the projection of this higher dimensional scatter onto a well chosen plane as well as the projection of vectors along its axes onto the same plane - the scatter being projected as the a[i]'s, the axis vectors as the b[j]'s.

2. THREE BIPLOT EXAMPLES

2.1 Data on automobiles (Chambers et. al., 1983, Appendix Table 7) were summarized in a matrix of 30 models by 12 characteristics, centered on each characteristic's mean. A rank 3 approximation was fitted by a resistant algorithm to avoid undue influence of any one (or a few) unusual models, and the GH-biplot is displayed in Figure 1. (The third dimension is indicated by the size of the labels. A few of the labels were omitted to avoid crowding the display)

Figure 1

3D-BIPLOT OF DATA ON 1977 MODEL AUTOMOBILES

Biplot fitted by resistant methods

(Gabriel and Odoroff, 1983)

30 models of cars

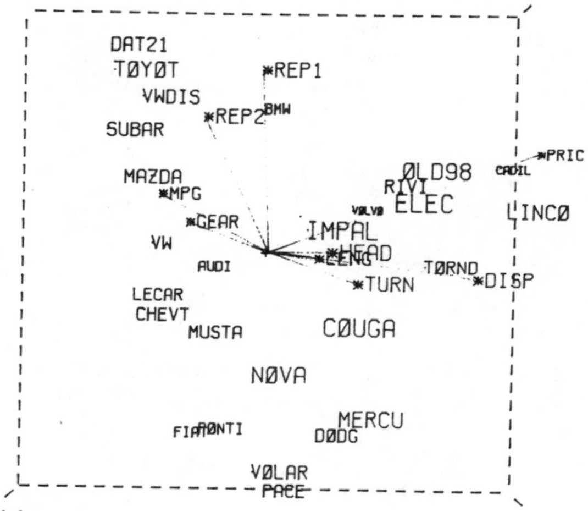

Variables:

PRIC	Price ($)
MPG	
REP 1	Repair record 1978 (5 point scale)
REP 2	Repair record 1977
HEAD	Headroom (in clearance)
REAR	Rearseat (in)
TRUN	Trunk space (cu ft.)
WEIT	Weight (lbs)
LENG	Length (in)
TURN	Turn circle (ft)
DISP	Displacement (cu in)
GEAR	Gear ratio (high gear)

The configuration of the column markers in Figure 1 shows a sheaf of variables which are highly correlated with length and displacement (and negatively correlated with miles per gallon and gear ratio). The repair records stand out as a separate sheaf, having slight negative correlation with length and displacement. Price is also distinct, uncorrelated (90^{0} angle) with repair record, but positively correlated with length and displacement.

The scatter of row markers shows that the high priced models (i.e., those with row markers in the direction of the price column marker) are US makes such as the Cadillac and Lincoln and to a lesser degree Olds 98, Buick Electra, Riviera and Toronado. The only foreign car in that group is the Volvo. Cars with good repair records and low price are exclusively foreign, especially Japanese. Cars with poor repair records are mostly US made medium priced models such as the Pacer, Volare, Pontiac and Dodge. Note, however, that the Fiat is one foreign car in this group.

2.2 Anderson's well known data on 150 iris flowers of three species (Chambers et. al., 1983, Appendix Table 14) have four variable observations. The least squares GH-biplot of these data is shown in Figure 2 with distinct symbols for the row markers corresponding to flowers of the distinct species.

The separation of the three species' markers is very evident, especially that of the *Iris setosa* sample. The configuration of the column markers (here shown by lines from the origin so as to accentuate the vector character of the representation) shows high correlations between petal length and width and sepal length, but sepal width varies independently, or at least with low and possibly negative correlation to the first three measures. The scatter of the flowers' row markers and the configuration of the measures' column markers are related by the inner-product relation (1). This indicates that *Iris setosa* are much smaller on the first three measures than *Iris versicolor* and *Iris virginica* and the latter is the largest, though not by much. It shows no such ordering of species for the fourth measure.

Figure 2

2D-BIPLOT OF IRIS DATA
4-Variable observations on 150 irises

Variety:		
• IRIS SETOSA	PETLN	petal length
o IRIS VIRGINICA	PETWD	petal width
x IRIS VERSICOLOR	SEPLN	sepal length
	SEPWD	sepal width

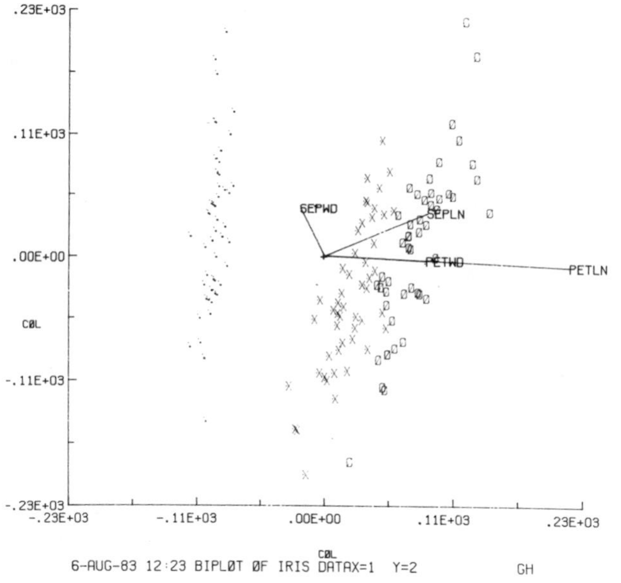

Figure 3

3D-BIPLOT OF IRIS DATA

Rotation chosen to emphasize variety differences. Ellipses are 1 st. dev. concentration ellipses which summarize the scatter of the 50 observations of each variety.

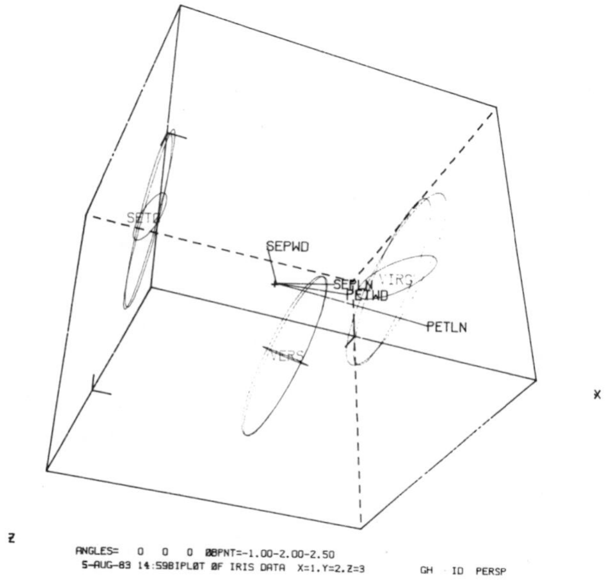

To explore the data further , a 3D biplot was generated and the row markers of each species summarily described by a concentration ellipse. The 3D biplot was then rotated to highlight the separation between the three species. This is shown in Figure 3.

The rotated 3D biplot reproduces the picture of species differentiation on the first three measures. It further indicates that there may also be some ordering by sepal width (setosa> virginica> versicolor) but that there is much overlap on that measure.

2.3 Finally, consider a 6 by 7 matrix of data on alcohol density (Bradu and Gabriel, 1978), centered on the overall mean. Its SQ-biplot is shown in Figure 4 with the markers labelled by concentration (3 to 8) and column markers labelled by temperature (10° to 40°).

Figure 4

3D BIPLOT OF DENSITY

Black markers - concentrations
Red markers - temperatures (centigrade)

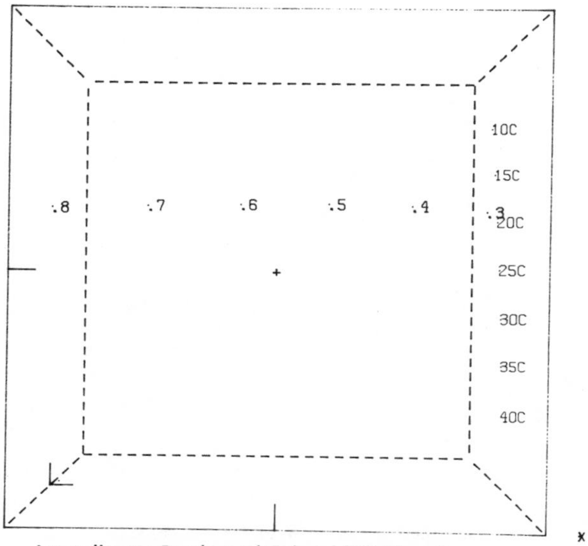

According to Bradu and Gabriel (1978) such a pattern diagnoses an additive model

y[i,j] = m + a[i] + b[j].

Indeed such a plot has goodness of fit .999594

This biplot shows a striking pattern: the row markers and column markers lie very close to two mutually orthogonal straight lines. Bradu and Gabriel (1978) have shown that this implies that the data are very closely fitted by an additive model. Indeed that model was found to have a goodness-of-fit of 99.96%.

However, the residuals from this fit still exhibited considerable regularity. This can be explored further by a variant of the 3D biplot in which the scales of the higher dimensions are inflated - Figure 5.

Figure 5

ANOTHER VIEW OF THE DENSITY BIPLOT IN 3D

(2nd and 3rd dimensions expanded relative to the first)

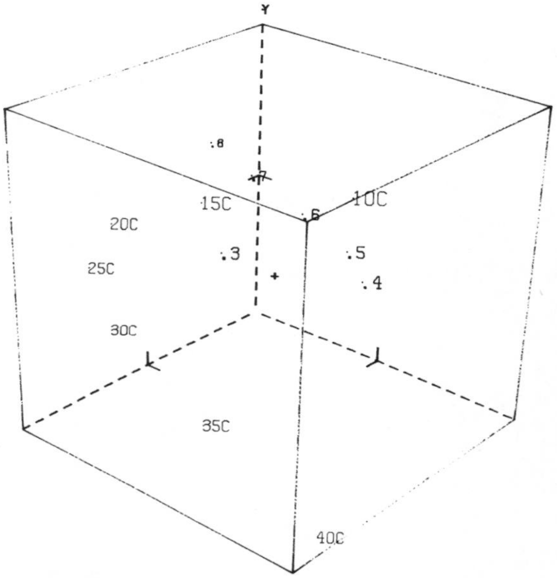

DIAGNOSIS

(1) Quadratic effects in temperature
(2) Unusual effect at concentration of 0.3.

Model taking such features into account has goodness of fit 0.9999995

This shows that the column markers appear to follow a parabolic curve. That observation was used to deduce (by a number of algebraic steps) a more complex model involving a quadratic in temperature. Fitting such a model reduced the residuals dramatically and led to a total goodness-of-fit of 99.9995%.

3. THE BIPLOT IN THE INTERFACE

Biplot display is a statistical or data analytic tool, as illustrated by the examples which show it to facilitate the inspection of data and to allow the diagnosis of closely fitting models. Biplot display is an exercise in computing and computer graphics, as evidenced by the extensive computations needed, especially for resistant fits, and by the problems of display and manipulation of rotations and data summarizations such as concentration ellipses.

The statistical uses of the biplot may dictate the computations and displays that are required, but the computer hardware and software will determine what can be done and how it will be done. Thus, 3D biplots may be useful in revealing statistical phenomena, but our ability to perceive these depend on computer facilities and methods of display. For example, certain diagnoses of models depend on our ability to perceive coplanarity of markers (or subsets of markers) and the orthogonality (or parallelism) of different planes which contain such markers. For any configuration of hardware (CRTs, graphics terminals, etc.) and suitable software, the statistician may have to learn how much diagnosing can be achieved; the computer scientist may have to strive to provide more powerful tools for these purposes.

The statistician's ability to diagnose depends on learning to use the available computing tools. The computer scientist's ability to provide suitable tools depends on his or her ability to anticipate the statistician's capacity to exploit these tools. There is no prior need or prior tool. In this interface of computer science and statistics a synergism between the two is needed in order to provide the tools that can be used to good effect.

4. BIPLOT COMPUTER PROGRAMS

4.1. Any Eigenvalue Program can be used in the following manner:
(1) Center data to obtain matrix Y,
(2) Compute Y'Y and its eigenvalues {ℓ[e]}**2 and eigenvectors q[e], e=1,2,...,
(3) Compute p[e] = Yq[e]/ℓ[e], e=1,2,...,
(4) Assemble matrices G = (p[1], p[2]) and H = (ℓ[1]q[1], ℓ[2]q[2]),
(5) Plot rows of G as row markers and rows of H as column markers.

SCALES: Different scales can be used for the set of G-rows and for the set of H-rows, but for each set the vertical and horizontal scales must be the same.

3-D: Three dimensional biplots are obtained by solving the above for e = 1,2,3 and adding the appropriate columns to G and to H.

4.2. MINITAB macro 'BIPLOT' (Available from the Division of Biostatistics)
(1) Center data and read into M10; set K1, K2 numbers of rows and columns,
(2) Exec 'BIPLOT' will provide options for GH- JK- or SQ-biplots; (3)Output can be a MINITAB printer plot or coordinates for manual plotting.

4.3 APL program BIPLOT (Available from Dr. E. Weber Krebsforschungszentrum, Heidelberg, West Germany).

4.4 SAS TSO CLIST BIPLOT (Available from Dr. Michael C. Tsianco, Merck, Sharp and Dohme Research Laboratories, Rahway, N.J.)

4.5 BIPLOTV, Macro No. 24, GENSTAT MACRO LIBRARY (Available from Numerical Algorithms Group, 1101 31st Street, Downers Grove, IL 60515)

4.6 BIPLOT program (Available from Division of Biostatistics)
FORTRAN batch program with many options, including MANOVA, contingency tables, and others. Fits lower rank approximation by least squares and produces printer plots of two biplots with other very detailed output.

4.7 LORANK package (Available from the Division of Biostatistics)
Interactive FORTRAN program that produces lower rank (up to 3) approximation to matrices by least squares or resistant methods. Also allows weighted least squares fit with arbitrary weights. Outputs biplot coordinates which can be (i) used for manual plotting, or (ii) input into a package BGRAPH for computer plots.

4.8 BGRAPH package (Available from the Division of Biostatistics)
Interactive package based on National Center for Atmospheric Research System Plot Package (or on ISSCO DISSPLA) which reads in 2 or 3 dimensional biplot coordinates and plots biplots on a variety of graphical display devices. Allows 3-D display through perspective views, stereo views or analglyphs. Permits rotation and windowing as well as such visual aids as labels and concentration ellipses.

ACKNOWLEDGEMENTS

This work has been supported by the office of Naval Research under Contract No. N 00014-80-C-0387. We gratefully acknowledge the assistance of Gangaji Magaluri with the computer graphics and of Patricia Petrovick with the preparation of the paper for print.

REFERENCES

(1) BRADU, D. and GABRIEL, K.R. (1978). The biplot as a diagnostic tool for models of two-way tables. Technometrics, 20, 47-68.

(2) CHAMBERS, J.M., CLEVELAND, W.S., KLEINER, B. and TUKEY, P.A. (1983) Graphical Methods for Data Analysis. Belmont: Wadsworth

(3) COX, C. and GABRIEL, K.R. (1982) Some comparisons of biplot display and pencil-and-paper E.D.A. methods, in Modern Data Analysis (eds. A.L. Launer and A.F. Siegel). New York: Academic Press, 103-122.

(4) GABRIEL, K.R. (1971). The biplot-graphic display of matrices with application to principal component analysis. Biometrika, 58, 453-467.

(5) GABRIEL, K.R. (1981). Biplot display of multivariate matrices for inspection of data and diagnosis. Interpreting Multivariate Data (V. Barnett, ed.). London: Wiley, 147-173.

(6) GABRIEL, K.R. (1983) Biplot in Encyclopedia of Statistical Science Vol. III (N.L. Johnson and S. Kotz, eds.). New York: Wiley, 263-271.

(7) GABRIEL, K.R. and ZAMIR, S. (1979). Lower rank approximation of matrices by least squares with any choice of weights. Technometrics, 21, 489-498.

(8) GABRIEL, K.R. and ODOROFF, C.L. (1983). Resistant lower rank approximation of matrices. Computer Science and Statistics: Proceedings of the Fifteenth Symposium on the Interface (ed. J.E. Gentle). Amsterdam: North Holland, 304-308.

(9) TSIANCO, M.C. and GABRIEL, K.R. (1984) Modeling temperature data: An illustration of the use of biplots in non-linear modeling. J. Climate and Appl. Meteor. (To appear).

COMPUTER SCIENCE AND STATISTICS:
The Interface, L. Billard (ed.)
© Elsevier Science Publishers B.V. (North-Holland), 1985

STATISTICAL AND DATA DIGITIZATION TECHNIQUES APPLIED TO AN ANALYSIS OF LEAF INITIATION IN PLANTS

Colin R. Goodall

Department of Statistics
Princeton University

This paper aims to exemplify how a problem in an applied area, the development of plants, generates new and interesting questions at the interface between statistics and computing. Sufficient biological background is presented to motivate the data collection and its analysis outlined here, and to suggest additional approaches and problems.

The computing issues center on efficient, high-volume, input of a temporal sequence of two-dimensional maps of cells from photographs. As an alternative to a fully automatic procedure, the emphasis is on user-friendly, interactive, image-processing programs for fast and accurate data digitization and correlation. The two explicit statistical problems are to describe the growth of each cell, using the stain cross representation, and to estimate the position of newly-apparent cell walls at the earlier time of their initiation. Generally, the goal is to measure, estimate, and correlate local changes in geometry (cell shape, growth and division direction), directional reinforcement of cell walls, and changes involving shape of the plant and the initiation of new leaves.

The results are summarized in rules of cell behavior, which may be genetically-programmed into each cell, and provide the basis of an algorithm for locally-regulated plant development, with minimal global control.

1. INTRODUCTION

Biologically, the intent is to investigate the manner by which cells co-ordinate their developmental activities, in particular, during leaf and stem initiation in plants. At the present time, development is one of the major mysteries in biology. The research is facilitated by digital analysis of photographs of cell patterns, seen over time. We outline elementary techniques in image analysis, and a general technique in the statistical analysis of growth. The context of the analysis is the biophysical theory discussed in Green (1980), Green and Lang (1981), Green and Poethig (1982), and Green (1984). This theory, with the cell and its biomechanical properties as basic unit, provides an algorithmic model for shoot regeneration. It is intermediate between theories of explicit genetic control (Horvitz, 1982) and field theories (Gierer, 1981; Meinhardt, 1982, Goodwin, 1980).

For animal cells, Steinberg (1963) and others have promoted the theory of cell adhesion to model cell sorting and morphogenetic movements. Odell et al (1980) model the mechanical properties of a cell to simulate invagination and evagination occuring in epithelial morphogenesis. Childress and Percus (1981) suggest that cell adhesion properties alone are sufficient for this. By contrast, in plant morphogenesis the cells are immobile. Neighborhood relations between cells are preserved in the progeny of the cells. Therefore, in place of cell adhesion, governing contacts between cells, we consider a model of stress and the resulting (directional) strains, i.e. a deformation analysis of all cells, in a manner shortly to be elaborated.

For both animal and plant development, however, the emphasis is on global morphology arises from the behavior of individual cells according to their given properties, which we may term rules of behavior, with the minimum requirement for morphogenetic fields or a genetic program of development. Development, in this case the repeated initiation of new leaves, should be as far as possible self-sustaining, in terms of the (biomechanical) parameters considered.

In a cylinder containing fluid under pressure, circumferential stress is double axial stress. The circumferential lines of cellulose reinforcement, from parallel polar cells, (Fig.2) more than compensate, so that growth is predominantly axial.

Some remarks help clarify the relation between stress, strain, and reinforcement. (1) For any tissue, a mosaic of reinforcement patterns, mediates the relationship between stress and strain. The microfibirils in each cell are parallel, but the orientations in neighboring cells may differ.

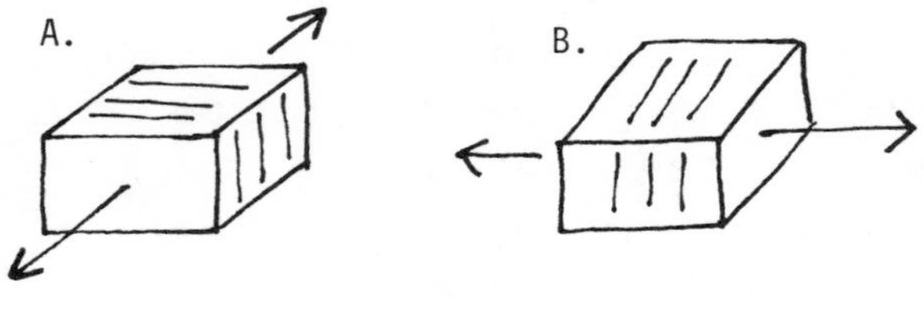

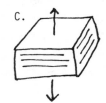

FIG.1 *Orientation of cellulose in plant cell walls, and corresponding polarity. With the surface uppermost, C. is not found.*

The driving force for growth in plant cells is turgor pressure (Ray et al, 1972), some 6-10 atmospheres. The epidermis has a predominant role in controlling growth, since turgor pressure largely counterbalances across internal walls, but must be contained as tangential stress in the thickened outer epidermal wall. Thus a simplified model considers tangential stresses to be those in a membrane enclosed pressure vessel with the same outer form. The actual stress depends on the geometry of the surface, i.e. the curvatures. Directional cellulose reinforcement in the cell walls, together with the stresses imposed from neighboring cells, govern the direction of growth of a cell. The reinforcement has the form of hoops of cellulose microfibrils (Fig.1). The hoops impose polarity (strictly, bipolarity) on the cell. To contain tangential stress, the polarity, perpendicular to the plane of the hoops, must be tangential to surface. A straightforward example is the elongation of a cylindircal organ, for example the shoot.

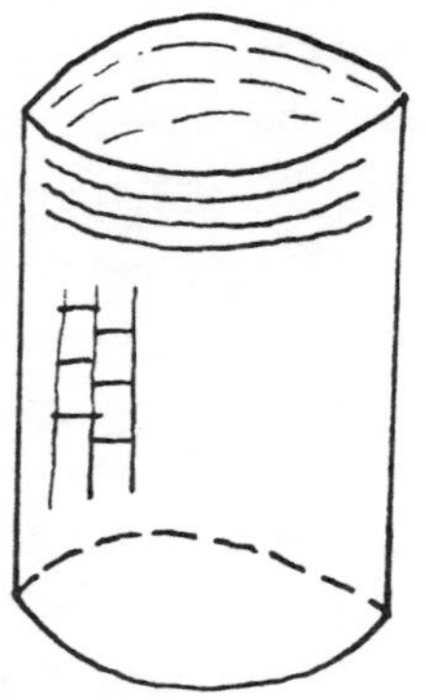

FIG.2 *Ladders of cell files and aggregate circumferential cellulose in plant stem.*

(2) Following mitosis, a cell synthesizes a new layer of microbibrils, with potentially different orientation. This layer is structurally predominant over previous layers (Richmond et al, 1981).

We now turn to the reorganization of tissue at the intiation of a lateral organ, namely a leaf from a stem or residual meristem, or a stem from a residual meristem. Topographically, a lateral organ is first apparent as a bump in the approximately flat epidermis. The protrusion extends to become a cylindrical organ with parallel symmetry (Figure 3A), the primordium when viewed from above (on the axis) has the radial symmetry appropriate to its later extension. Thus the initiation of a lateral organ implies a conversion of symmetry, from a parallel to a radial symmetric pattern.

The simplest account of reorganization states that cell division spontaneously reorients in a patch of cells, giving a radial pattern about some site, the axis of the lateral organ. Reinforcement direction, obligated to be parallel to the new cell wall, shifts spontaneously. This has not been observed (Green and Lang, 1981). Instead, first there is a 90 degree flip in cell division and reinforcement directions in a transverse band of cells, termed the *reorientation band* (Figure 3B). The contrast in growth tendencies generates the protrusion. Subsequently, there is a smoothing of the discontinuity to a radial pattern, partly accomplised by the inclination of the epidermis as the organ grows.

Furthermore, cell polarity is not invariably perpendicular to the new cell ware. A well-tested empirical rule (Green, 1984) is the following. When a cell divides transversely with respect to the existing polarity, polarity is unchanged. When the cell divides longitudinally, the cell polarity flips through 90 degrees, provided that the daughter cells are relatively elongate parallel to the new cross wall. Thus in stems, whereas most new cell walls are transverse to the axis, occasional longitudinal (parallel to the axis) division occur in broad cells to compensate for the transverse minor component of growth.

The goal is to first *describe* the reorganization of tissue at organ initiation in terms of change in cell geometry, cell division and reinforcement. The second step is to infer rules of cell behavior from the observations. These rules are the basis for algorithms that model (by simulation) plant development.

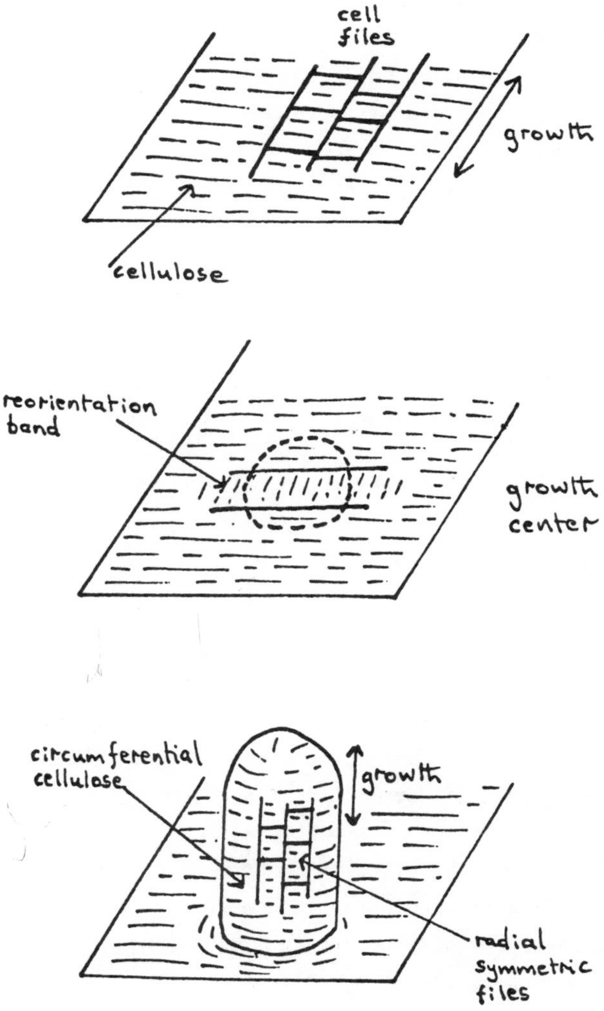

FIG.3 *First appearance of a leaf bump.*

The longitudinal observations necessary for this study are obtained from *Graptopetalum paraguayense*, a desert succulent, for which the apical meristem, the site of leaf initiation, is revealed with minimal non-lethal, surgery (Green and Brooks, 1978, Green and Lang, 1981). This contrasts with the destructive peeling of layers of protective leaves to uncover the apical meristem of a conventional shoot.

A key element is a new non-toxic ink stain (Green and Lang, 1981). The ink, applied to the surface with a brush, collects in the crevices between cells caused by turgor pressure acting against the anchoring anticlinal (interior) walls. With the aid of a light microscope, periodic (daily, or more frequent) sets of polaroid photographs of ink-stained epidermis are a permanent record of development, complete for cell growth and cell division. Each set of overlapping photographs, constituting a *frame*, capture the geometry of cell outlines in the curved epidermis.

Reinforcement pattern is available only by destructive sampling, in which a thin epidermal peel is viewed in polarized light. The deficiency (cross-sectional data only) is not critical: initial cell polarity is longitudinal, and changes can be inferred using the empirical rule above.

A limited analysis is possible using the photographs directly. For example, the overall geometry of the cell pattern provides useful indication of developmental events, especially when compared to reinforcement data for the same stage of development. Furthermore, individual cells or groups of cells may be followed through several time periods by simply coloring the photographs. However, no precise data may be obtained on cell division direction and growth. Visual determination of the principal axes of growth for an irregularly shaped cell may not be straightforward. The solution is to digitize the data. There is a tradeoff between high volume, lesser quality data directly from photographs, and low volume, high quality digital data. The digital data are analized for growth and cell division directions.

2. DIGITAL DATA COLLECTION

The protocol for data digitization, implemented on the PDP11/45 and peripherals at the Remote Sensing Laboratory, Stanford University, is diagrammed in Figure 4. A Hammatsu C100 vidicon camera encodes each photograph into a 1024x1024 pixel array with 8 bits (256 intensity levels) at each pixel. The image is written directly to tape. To ensure equal magnification, all photographs in a given series of frames are scanned, with focus constant, in a single session. Under light additional load on the host, each digitization takes approximately 200 seconds. Thus a series of 5 photographs may be digitized in 30 minutes. Each image occupies 1MB. In practice 10 image files fill a tape at 1600 b.p.i. One or two 1MB image files are kept on disc for the subsequent steps, digitizing and correlating maps of cell outlines.

The image file is used as background for a Grinnell color raster graphics display, of 512x256 pixels, with 32 bit planes. The entire image file is first displayed by pixel averaging, to locate the co-ordinates of the areas of interest, before display of the portion of interest at full magnification. Larger vertical slices are viewed using the scrolling feature.

By means of a joyswitch-controlled cursor, the user digitizes the vertices of each succesive cell in clockwise sequence. With a distance bound to determine whether a new vertex is intended, a given vertex may be common to several adjacent cells. The current digitized map, superimposed on the image of the photograph, provides a simultaneous record of the digitization. This visual over-

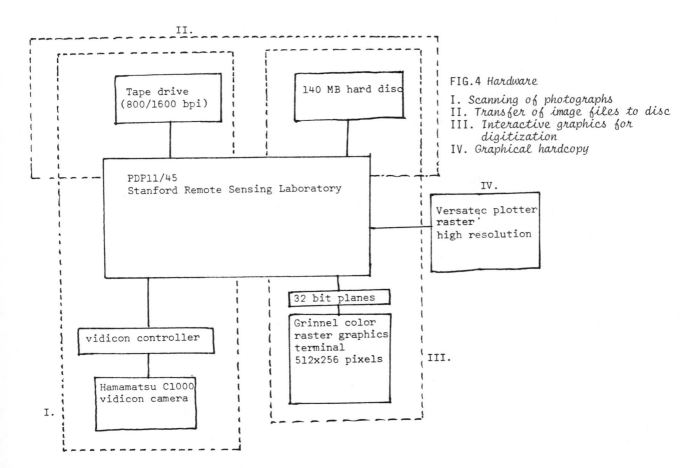

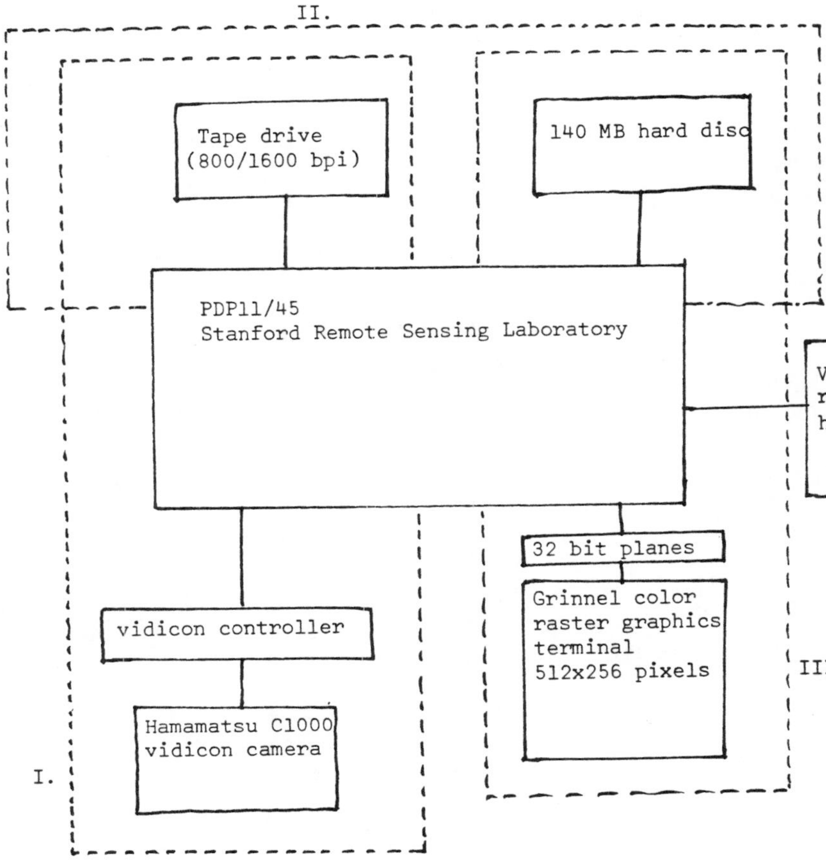

FIG.4 *Hardware*

I. *Scanning of photographs*
II. *Transfer of image files to disc*
III. *Interactive graphics for digitization*
IV. *Graphical hardcopy*

lay is very important, given the sometimes indistinct quality of the ink stain on newly initiated cell walls. However, the magnification provided in the image file is more than adequate--the ink in each cell wall has minimum width approximately 10 pixels. Program control is by a pair of function switches, by cursor selection of screen menu items, and by key board selection of a VDT menu. Options include vertex enter, end-of-cell, vertex edit, cell edit, and control of video configuration.

Furthermore cell maps from two overlapping photographs may be splice together (a simple alternative to sterogrammetry). The best, i.e. most normal, projection for each region of tissue is the photograph in which each cell is largest. Ambiguities, for which a given cell is longer in one photograph, but broader in the other, are resolved "sensibly". Operationally, the pre-existing cell and vertex map is transformed by a translation and rotation to its appropriate position on the newly displayed digitized photograph, with callibration points along the splice. The leaf surface tends to be convex so that the compound map is split adjacent to the splice--vertices and edges along the split appear twice.

Two further interactive graphics programs are used to specify th temporal correspondences between maps on successive days. The first program is for cell lineages. Although we are researching an automatice pattern matching procedure, the preliminary approach emphasized convenient interactive, but accurate, data input. A split screen display shows two successive maps simultaneously, with the background images included to clarify cell lineages. Each cell has a unique ancestor (if any) in the previous frame. Thus the program cycles through the cells in the later frame while the user moves the cursor around the cells in the previous frame.

The second program uses a similar scheme to input point ancestry. Much vertex lineage information is deduced from cell lineages, using the fact that in two-dimensions a vertex is uniquely determined by any three adjacent cells. Biologically, no more than three cells have a vertex in common. However, within the resolution of the ink staining and data input, four or more cells may share a vertex. Since, as the tissue dilates, resolution improves with successive frames, vertices tend to split rather than merge. A unique ancestor assumption is practicable, whereas a unique successor assumption, though biologically true, is not. More sophisticated algorithms take into account the spatial (metric) as well as topological relations between cells and vertices.

The data for each frame has four component files: (1) An array of vertex co-ordinates. (2) An array of lists of vertices for each cell, with each entry a pointer to the vertex co-ordinates array. (3) An array of cell ancestors, with each entry a pointer to the cell array of the previous frame, and a 0 entry if there is no ancestor in the previous frame. (4) An array of vertex ancesotrs, with each entry a pointer to the vertex array co-ordinates array of the previous frame, and, again, a 0 entry if there is no ancestor in the previous frame.

Foley and van Dam (1982, Section 13.2) discuss a number of data structures for the representation of polygonal meshes (files 1 and 2 above), including storage of edges. The one used here is not necessarily optimal. However, it is convenient to program (in FORTRAN), and gives adequate flexibility for the subsequent analyses, including calculation of growth and the determination of cell division direction.

3. STRAIN CALULATION BY LEAST-SQUARES

The strain ellipse representation

The deformation of the surface is continuous and locally affine. Tissot's theorem (Tissot, 1881) states that in the deformation of an infinitesimal circle to an ellipse there is a unique pair of perpendicular diameters of the circle that remain perpendicular after deformation, unless the tranformation is isotropic. After deformation, the diameters become the principal axes of the ellipse.

Thus Tissot's indicatrix, a *strain ellipse*, describes the spatially homogeneous deformation of a two-dimensional region, Fig.6. The major and minor axes of the ellipse correspond to the perpendicular maximum and minimum strain, i.e. the singular values of the affine transformation (below) or strain tensor. Although the metrics in the original and deformed regions are the same, there is in general no natural choice of base direction (and origin). Therefore there are two orientations of the major axis, and the deformation is represented by a pair of crosses, the principal axes, drawn in the region before and after deformation. Richards and Kavanagh (1945), Erickson (1966, 1976), Bookstein (1977, 1978, 1980, 1982, 1984), Erickson and Silk (1980) and Green and Poethig (1982) are among those who use the strain ellipse, or strain cross, representations in morphometric and plant growth contexts.

We have available as landmarks the vertices of each cell before and after deformation. Our specific application is to summarize and contrast the deformations of a group of cells. Therefore we approximate the tensor field by an ensemble of strain ellipses, one for each cell between each successive pair of frames. The *strain rate* form substitutes rates for finite strains and facilitates comparison of strain in consecutive intervals of time of different durations.

Affine transformation and its singular value decomposition

We obtain the parameters of the strain crosses from the singular value decomposition (SVD) of the affine transformation fitted by least squares to the vertex co-ordinates.

Let X and Y be the nx2 matrices of n vertices before and after deformation respectively. Let the matrix A by 2x2 and M be nx2, with each row of M equal to μ^T. Then (A,μ) specifies an affine transformation of R^2. Our model is

(1) $Y = XA^T + M + E,$

where the elements of E are i.i.d., with zero mean and common variance. The least-squares estimates of A and μ may be obtained by two separate, three-carrier regressions. Cell centroid before deformation maps to cell centroid after deformation. Centering the vertex arrays X and Y, to X' and Y' respectively, eliminates the translation term M. The normal equations are then

(2) $\hat{A} = Y'^T X'(X'^T X')^{-1}.$

When n = 3 and the vertices are noncollinear both before and after deformation (X and Y have full rank, 2), the affine transformation is uniquely defined and maps triangle exactly to triangle. For $n \geqslant 3$, the residual sum of squares has 2n - 6 degress of freedom.

Let R_θ denote the 2x2 matrix of positive (anti-clockwise) rotation around θ,

(3) $$R_\theta = \begin{matrix} \cos\theta & -\sin\theta \\ \sin\theta & \cos\theta \end{matrix} \quad .$$

Let $D_{p,q}$ be the dilation matrix

(4) $$D_{p,q} = \begin{matrix} p & 0 \\ 0 & q \end{matrix} \quad .$$

Then the SVD of A is

(5) $$A = R_\psi D_{p,q} R_{-\theta}.$$

The SVD is calculated explicitly as given in Goodall (1984). Our preferred solution has the dilations,

$$p \geqslant |q| \geqslant 0$$

and the orientation θ in $(-\pi/2, \pi/2)$, ψ in $(-\pi/2, 3\pi/2)$ See Fig. 5. A single binary symbol distinguished the 2 intervals of length π for ψ (after deformation). Goodall & Green (1984) contains numerical examples and step-by-step interpretation.

Statistical issues arising in growth analysis

The statistical issues divide into two parts. The first is methods for fitting locally-affine transformations to the growth data, for a single cell or for several cells simultaneously, including subclasses of transformations and

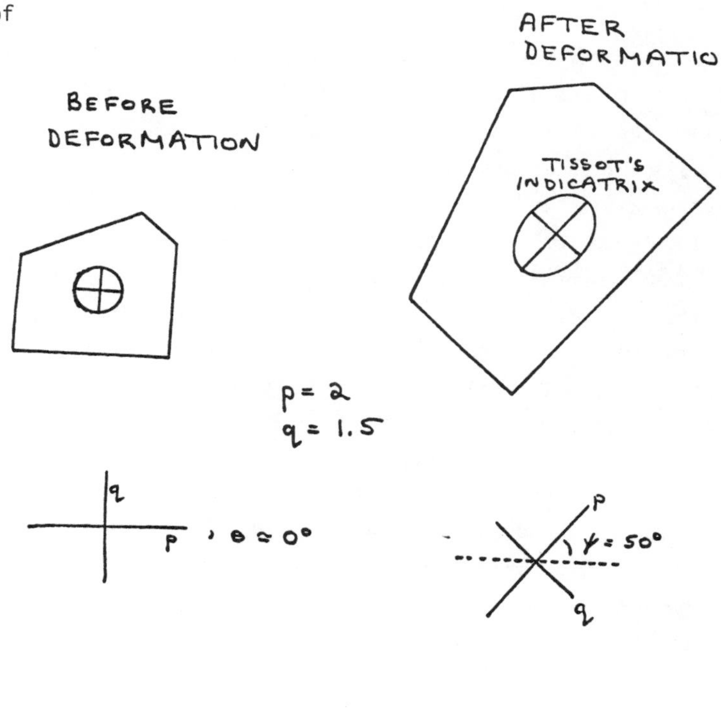

FIG.5 *Homogeneous deformation of a five-sided cell, with Tissot's indicatrix showing transformation of a small circle to an ellipse. The greatest increase in dimension is doubling (p=2) in the horizontal (θ=0°) direction, the smallest a 50% vertical increase. The orientation of the major axis after deformation (ψ) is 50°. Cell rotation (ψ-θ) is 50°.*

associated hypothesis tests. The second part is to understand the nonlinear SVD to the strain ellipse estimates, and their statistical properties.

The fitted affine transformation summarizes the deformation, whereas the residuals reveal the inhomogeneity. The residuals may be plotted as vectors originating in the vertices of the cell, either before or after deformation (Fig.10). The model error has two components, input error and inhomogeneity error. Input error arises in recording and digitizing the data. The inhomogeneity is less conventional, since it reflects predictable failure of the underlying model, namely that there is homogeneous deformation within a given cell. Bookstein (1984) draws the extreme conclusion from this that the landmarks must first be triangulated, and the affine transformation fit exactly. Input error can be separated into three components:

(1) Measurement error stems from the finite width of the ink lines and the error in digitization.
(2) Mapping error corresponds to misspecification of vertex ancestry.
(3) Projection error arises from curvature of the plant surface.

The vertex co-ordinates both before and after deformation are subject to input error. Moreover, input error at a given vertex is common to all adjacent cells. On the other hand, we arbitrarily assign inhomogeneity error to the vertices after deformation only. Therefore the conventional regression model of equation (1) is satisfactory when input error is a small fraction of inhomogeneity error. Repeated input of some data (Goodall, 1983) suggest that measurement error is approximately 20% of the total. More generally, the geometrical dependencies among the deformations of adjacent cells are expressed in the error decomposition. Similar issues arise in assembling a photomontage. We are led to a mixed model variant of the errors-in-variables approach (Gleser and Watson, 1973, Gleser, 1981). This is solved using the EM-algorithm (Dempster et al, 1977), by iteration between separate parameter estimation for each cell and separate input error estimation for vertices before and after deformation. See Goodall (1985). Procrustes analysis (Gower, 1975, Sibson, 1978) is a variant in which a similarity (orthogonal) transformation is fit to the data.

We now sketch the second part of the statistical investigations. The SVD induces a map from the affine transformation matrix A to the strain ellipse parameters p, q, θ and ψ. A Gaussian error assumption in equation (1) induces a Gaussian distribution on A. The distributional properties of the strain ellipse estimates are discussed in Goodall (1983). Of particular importance are confidence intervals: to assess the pattern in a field of strain crosses (Fig.7) we need estimates of angular variability (Goodall, 1984).

4. CROSS WALL INTERPOLATION

The second basic element of the analysis of the temporal sequence of cell maps is cross wall interpolation. A new anticlinal wall (cross wall) acts against the turgor pressure in the two daughter cells to create a depression. Only then does the ink stain indicate a cell division. Therefore we anticipate the position of cross walls in the frame previous to their first appearance--the dashed lines in Fig.7--using an interpolation technique. This facilitates direct comparison of strain and new cell wall directions during cell wall formation.

The procedure for cross wall interpolation is as follows. Define the *boundary cycle* to be the combined progeny of the original, mother, cell. Each vertex of the boundary cycle is *mapped* or *unmapped* according to whether or not it is a landmark. We assume that the mother cell divides one or more times, to give a set of cross walls partially ordered by temporal order of mitoses. See Fig. 6. First we con-

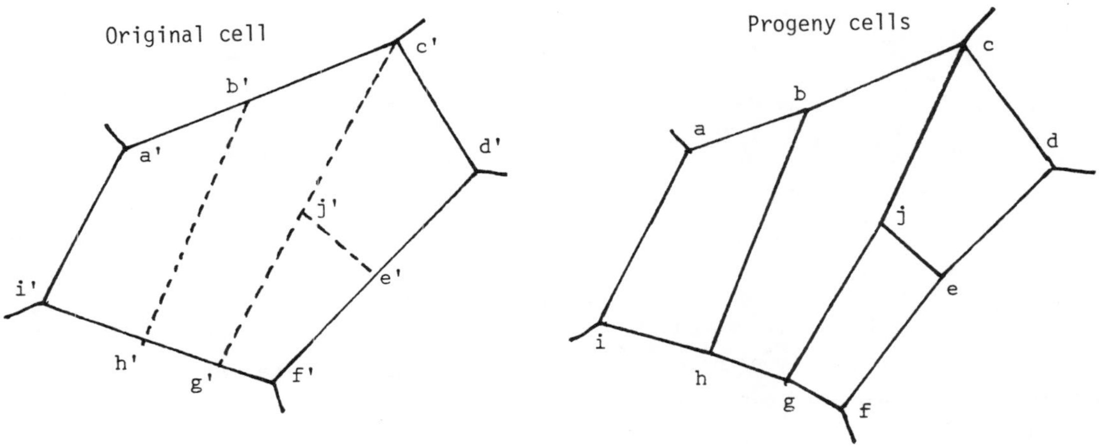

FIG.6. *Cross wall interpolation from progeny to original cell. Boundary cycle is abc...i. Vertices a, c, d, f & i are mapped. The three cross walls are (partly subjectively) bh, cjg and je, with cjg before je. Vertex c is mapped, i & f anchor g, and g & c anchor j. c' is an original vertex, interpolation of i' and f' gives g', and subsequent interpolation of g' and c' gives j'.*

sider each cross wall vertex on the boundary cycle. No interpolation of a mapped vertex is necessary. Each unmapped vertex has two *anchor vertices*. These are the closest mapped vertices on the boundary cycle in respectively the clockwise and anti-clockwise directions. The estimated point in the previous frame ancestral to the cross wall vertex interpolates the boundary of the mother cell on one of the (straight) already-interpolated cross walls.

This method for interpolation is consistent with an homogeneous deformation of the cell, except that a cross wall can be curved, whereas its interpolated image is straight. The naive remedu is to interpolate vertex positions with a fitted affine transformation, for example the inverse of the least-squares transformation. However, the interpolated cross wall may then lie outside (!) the parent cell. Furthermore, cross walls that initiate at different times whould be mapped back to different times. Also the time interval between succesive frames need not be constant, and indeed need not correspond to the best interval bewteen cross wall initiation and the first appearance of that wall. Therefore we are developing a more flexible mapping procedure, together with an algorithm for interpolating the configuration of a given graph between two time points. Such a procedure, in which also strain rate is calculated from several frames and is interpolated between frames, permits comparison of cross wall initiation with strain rate at any arbitrary time.

5. DATA ANALYSIS

The data set focuses on the smoothing of the perpendicular discontinuity at the reorientation band to radial symmetry during leaf initiation.

The data consists of four frames at daily intervals of the proximal left quadrant of the midline leaf. A small sketch on the plot for days 2 and 3 (Figs. 7 & 8) shows the development of the leaf bump. The leaf apex is the upper and right of each plot, the stem tissue is to the lower and left. By swelling of the leaf primordium, the horizontal top edge (day 2, viewed from above), the site of the reorientation band, rotates to vertical (day 3, oblique view) as the region approaches a spherical segment.

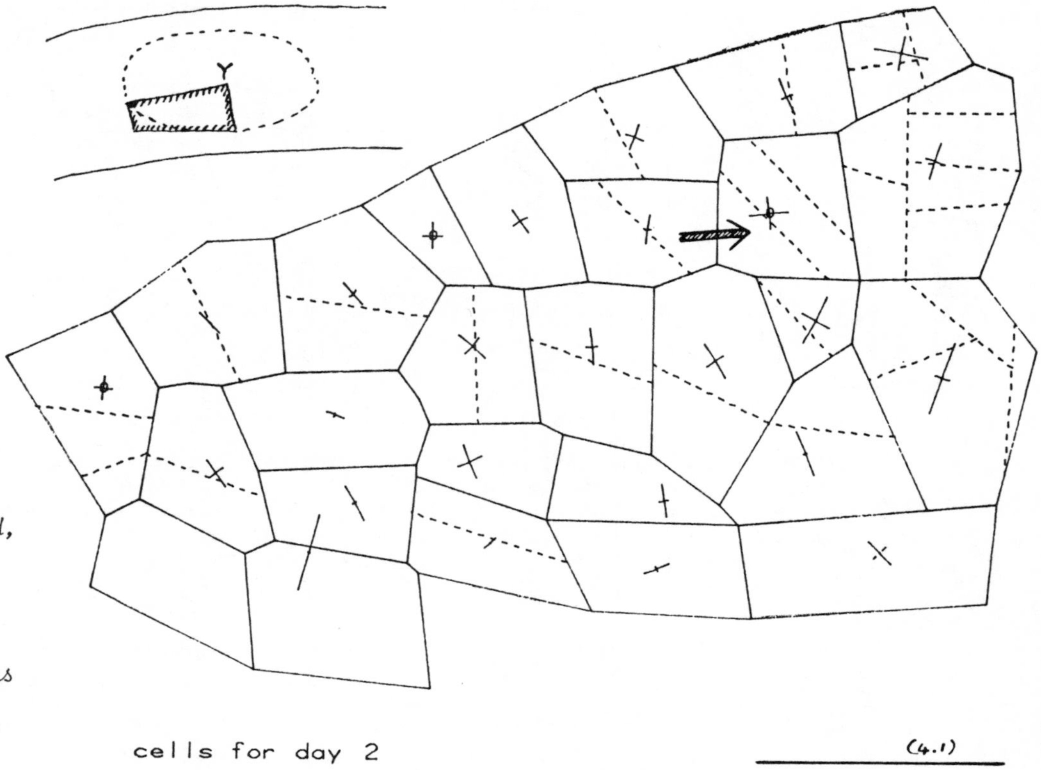

FIG.7. *Growth for day 2 to day 3, shown on day 2. The small sketch shows the quadrant of the leaf bump that is mapped, with leaf apex of Y. Dashed lines show interpolated cross walls first apparent at day 3. The 0 on the crosses indicates nearly anisotropic strain.*

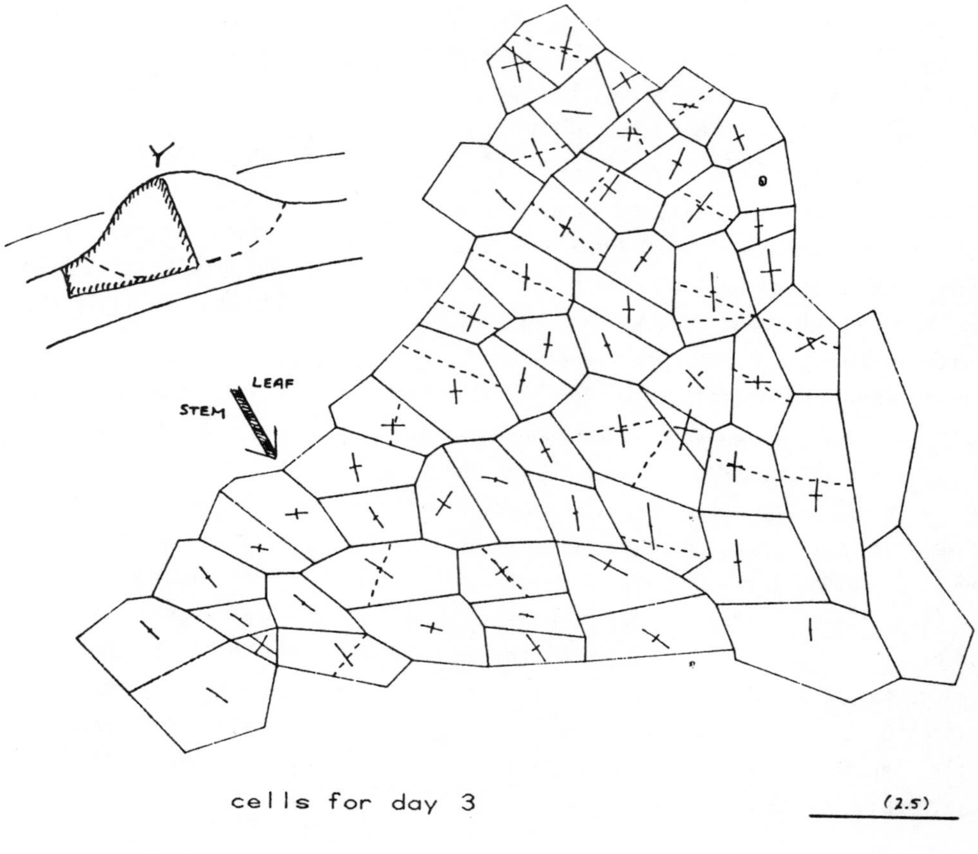

FIG.8. *Growth for day 3 to day 4, shown on day 3, and accompanying sketch. Growth and new cell walls are both predominantly radial. The arrow indicates the boundary between stem and leaf.*

The predominant direction of growth from day 1 to day 2, and from day 2 to day 3 (Fig. 7) is unchanged from growth previous to leaf initiation (i.e. vertical major axes in Fig. 7). However, growth from day 3 to day 4 (Fig. 4) is radical about the leaf apex, characteristic of a new leaf. Notice the boundary between leaf and stem (unchanged growth direction) arrowed in Fig. 8. The cell division patterns on days 2 and 3 are *both* radial. The empirical rule for reinforcement direction shows that the reinforcement established from day 2 to day 3 is parallel to the new cell walls, and therefore has an overall radial pattern also. Subsequent growth, Figure 8, corresponds to the radial reinforcement. The arrowed cell, Figure 7, is a particularly strong indicator of smoothing.

6. DISCUSSION

Rules of cell behavior governing strain and reinforcement direction are well-established. Strain results from turgor pressure mediated by the cellular mosaic of cellular reinforcement. Reinforcement is governed by the empirical rule given in 1. Rules governing cell division direction are harder to realize: strain direction does not solely govern division direction, but is implicated along with the aspect ratio of the cell (Goodall, 1983, Green, 1984). Moreover, cells have a tendency to divide so that the subsequent cellulose microfibrils coalign across anticlinal walls (consider Fig.7). We are unable to eliminate a global variable governing division directrion, namely "prosperity to leaf inittiation", corresponding to substrate levels.

The analysis of a sequence of maps involves interpolating cell division, growth, and estimated reinforcement direction, within the context of the overall development of the organism. To reiterate, growth is a function of the global geometry, via the stress, and the reinforcement mosaic. The flip rule for reinforcement allows confident deduction of the reinforcement direction given the initial configuration. Therefore the cell maps alone are adequate for analysis. The strain cross is a powerful tool for summarizing deformation, with the cell by cell resolution required for biological interpretation and modelling. New cross wall interpretation is another part. Within a region, growth and division are quite variable, although overall patterns are evident. Close attention to the photographs enhances the quality of the data. We have explicitly and quantitatively described the inition of leaf. An algorithm for plant development is based on (tentative) rules of cell behavior expressed in terms of cell division, growth and polarity. In association with Green & Baxter, the author is investigating the predictive ability of the rules by finite element simulation.

The availability of multi-dimensional growth data must increase through the wide adoption of image analysis devices: NMR, video technology, ultrasound, Moiré optics. This calls for new tools in the analysis of multidimensional longitudinal data, and expertise in computer graphics, in image analysis, and in computational geometry.

ACKNOWLEDGEMENTS

This is an account of joint research at Stanford University, with Paul Green, Professor of Botany at the Department of Biological Sciences, while the author was a graduate student in the Harvard University Department of Statistics. This work was supported in part by U.S. National Science Foundation grants MCS81-20495 and PCM81-02330 to Stanford University (Paul B. Green, principal investigator). Additional support came from the Higgins fund of Princeton University and from a visiting fellowship to the Institute of Advanced Studies, the Australian National University.

REFERENCES

Bookstein, F.L. 1977. "The study of shape transformations after D'Arcy Thompson." Mathematical Biosciences, 34: 177-219.

____________ 1978. The Measurement of Biological Shape and Shape Change. Lecture Notes in Biomathematics, 24. Berlin: Springer-Verlag.

____________ 1980. "When one form is between two others: an application of biorthogonal analysis." American Zoologist, 20: 627-641.

__________ 1982. "Foundations of morphometrics." Annual Reviews of Ecology and Systematics, 23: 451-470.

__________ 1984. "A statistical method for biological shape comparisons. "Journal of Theoretical Biology, 107: 475-520.

Childress, S. and Percus, J.K. 1981. "Modeling of cell and tissue movements in the developing embryo." Lectures on Mathematics in the Life Sciences 14: 59-88.

Dempster, A.P., Laird, N.M. & Rubin, D.B. 1977. "Maximum likelihood from incomplete data via the EM algorithm." With Discussion. Journal of the Royal Statistical Association, Series B, 39: 1-38.

Erickson, R.O. 1966. "Relative elemental rates and anistropy of growth in area: a computer program." Journal of Experimental Botany, 17: 390-403.

__________ 1976. "Growth in two-dimensions, descriptive and theoretical studies." In: Automata, Languages, Development (A. Lindenmayer and G. Rozenberg, Eds.). Amsterdam: North Holland.

__________ and Silk, W.K. 1980. "The kinematics of plant growth." Scientific American. 242(5): 134-151.

Foley, J.D. and van Dam, A. 1982. Fundamentals of Interactive Computer Graphics. Reading, Mass. Addison-Wesley.

Gierer, A. 1981. "Generation of biological patterns and form: some physical, mathematical and logical aspects." Prog. Biophys. Molec. Biol., 37: 1-47.

Gleser, L.J. 1981. "Estimation in a multivariate 'errors-in-variables'' regression model: large sample results." Annals of Statistics, 9: 24-44.

__________ & Watson, G.S. 1973. "Estimation of a linear transformation". Biometricka, 60: 525-534.

Goodall, C.R. 1983. "The statistical analysis of growth in two dimensions." Harvard University, Department of Statistics: doctoral dissertation.

__________ 1984. "The growth of a two-dimensional figure: strain crosses and confidence regions." American Statistical Association: Proceedings of the Statistical Computing Section.

__________ 1985. "Multivariate morphometric analysis of a cellulated region, via the EM algorithm. In preparation.

__________ & Green, P.B. 1984. "Quantitative characterization of surface growth". Developmental Biology: submitted .

Goodwin, B.C. 1980. "A field description of the cleavage process in embryogenesis." Journal of Theoretical Biology, 86: 757-770.

Gower, J.C. 1975. "Generalised Procrustes analysis". Psychometrika, 40: 33-51.

Green, P.B. 1980. "Organogenesis--a biophysical view." Annual Reviews of Plant Physiology, 31: 51-82.

Green, P.B. 1984. "Shifts in plant cell axiality: histogenetic influences on cellulose orientation in the succulent, Graptopetalum" Devel. Biol. 103: 18-27.

__________ and Brooks, K.E. 1978. "Stem formation from a succulent leaf: its bearing on theories of axiation." American Journal of Botany, 65: 13-26.

__________ and Lang, J.M. 1981. "Towards a biophysical theory of organogenesis: birefringence observations on regenerating leaves in the succulent Graptopetalum paraguayense E. Walther." Planta, 151: 413-426.

__________ and Poethig, R.S. 1982. "Biophysics of the extension and initiation of plant organs." In: Developmental Order: Its Origin and Regulation (S. Subtelny and P.B. Green, Eds.). New York: Alan Liss.

Horvitz, H.R. 1982. "Nematode post-embryonic cell lineages." J. Nematol., 14: 240-248.

Lintilhac, P.M. and Vesecky, T.B. 1980. "Mechanical stress and cell wall orientation in plants. I. Photoelastic derivation of principal stresses.: With a discussion of the concept of axillarity and the significance of the "arcuate shell zone." Am. J. Bot., 67: 1477-1483.

Meinhardt, H. 1982. Models of Biological Pattern Formation. New York: Academic Press.

Odell, G., Oster, G., Burnside, B. and Alberch, P. 1980. "A mechanical model for epithelial morphogenesis." Journal of Mathematical Biology, 9: 291-295.

Rao, C.R. 1973. Linear Statistical Inference and Its Applications. New York: John Wiley.

Ray, P.M., Green, P.B. and Cleland, R. 1972. "Role of turgor in plant cell growth." Nature, 239: 163-164.

Richards, O.W. and Kavanagh, A.J. 1943. "The analysis of the relative growth gradients and changing form in growing organisms, illustrated by the tobacco leaf." American Naturalist, 77: 385-399.

Richmond, P.A., Corey, A., Huun, P. and Metraux, J.P. 1981. "Cellulose synthesis inhibition and cell expansion in Nitella internodes." J. Cell Biology, 91: A153.

Sibson, R. 1978. "Studies in the robustness of multidimensional scaling. Procrustes statistics." J. Roy. Statist. Soc., B, 40: 234-238.

Steinberg, M. 1963. "Reconstruction of tissues by dissociated cells." Science, 141: 401-408.

Tissot, M.A. 1881. Memoire sur la representation des surfaces. Paris: Gauthier Villars.

COMPUTER SCIENCE AND STATISTICS:
The Interface, L. Billard (ed.)

AN ALTERNATIVE TEST FOR NORMALITY

Thomas R. Gulledge, Jr. and Stephen W. Looney

Department of Quantitative Business Analysis
Louisiana State University
Baton Rouge, Louisiana 70803

A new normal probability plot correlation coefficient test for normality is proposed. The test uses the Benard and Bos-Levenbach plotting position (i-.3)/(n+.4), which is based on an estimate of the i'th order statistic median. Monte Carlo results indicate that this test is superior in terms of 5% power to Filliben's test, which is also based on an estimate of the order statistic median. Empirically constructed percentage points for the test are provided.

1. INTRODUCTION

This paper presents a goodness-of-fit test for normality that is based on the information contained in a probability plot. In particular, the research follows the lead of Filliben [4] and uses a plotting position that is based on an estimate of the order statistic median. Monte Carlo results indicate that the proposed test is more powerful than Filliben's test. As a standard of comparison, it is noted that the test is at least as powerful as the Shapiro-Francia [7] test.

2. HISTORICAL PERSPECTIVE

Let $W=(Y-\mu)/\sigma$ denote the standardized variate from some hypothesized distribution, and let $W_{(i)}=[Y_{(i)}-\mu]/\sigma$ denote its i'th order statistic. Let $M[W_{(i)}]$ denote the median of the i'th order statistic, and consider the following plotting position:

$$p_i=F[M(W_{(i)})], \tag{2.1}$$

where F denotes the distribution function of some hypothesized distribution. If $x_i=F^{-1}(p_i)$, an estimate of $M[W_{(i)}]$, is plotted against the sample order statistic $y_{(i)}$, and if the resulting graph appears to be linear, then the hypothesized distribution is not rejected. However, a visual summary of the information contained in the probability plot may not be appropriate since the researcher must make a subjective determination of what constitutes nonlinearity. In short, an objective criterion for evaluating linearity in probability plots is needed.

Filliben [4] proposes the correlation coefficient as a measure of the linearity of the plot since it is conceptually easy to understand and it is easy to compute. Various authors have suggested that Filliben's test be used in testing for normality; for example, see Johnson and Wichern [5, Chapter 4]. This research follows the lead of Filliben, and the correlation coefficient is used to objectively assess linearity in the probability plot. However, this research differs from Filliben in the selection of an estimate of the median of the i'th order statistic. In particular, if the normal distribution is the hypothesized distribution, the estimate of $F[M(W_{(i)})]$ presented by Benard and Bos-Levenbach [2] is used. This estimate is

$$p_i=(i-.3)/(n+4), \tag{2.2}$$

where n is the sample size. Alternatively, Filliben [4, p. 116] proposes his own approximation of $F[M(W_{(i)}]$, namely,

$$p_i = \begin{cases} 1-m_n & i=1 \\ (i-.3175)/(n+.365) & i=2,\ 3,\ \ldots,\ n-1 \\ .5^{(1/n)}. & i=n. \end{cases}$$

As demonstrated in the Monte Carlo results that follow, the selection of (2.2) as an estimate of the order statistic median leads to a test that is more powerful than Filliben's test in terms of 5% power.

3. NUMERICAL METHODS

Since the order statistics are heteroscedastic and correlated, empirical sampling is used to derive the null distribution of the test statistic. For the plotting position given in (2.2), a test statistic for the composite test of normality is constructed using the Pearson product-moment correlation coefficient between the sample order statistics $y_{(i)}$ and $x_i=F^{-1}(p_i)$, where F is the standard normal cumulative distribution function. Hasting's approximation is used to invert the distribution function (see Abramowitz and Stegun [1, p. 933, formula 26.2.23]). The empirical percentage points of the test statistic under normality were constructed for n=3(1)50(5)100 by generating N=10,000 normal random samples using the GRAND generator [3]. The run length of 10,000 was selected because longer run lengths affected the percentage points only in the fourth decimal place. The percentage points were smoothed by replicating each experiment twelve times and taking the average, i.e., 120,000 samples were generated for each sample size. The percentage points are presented in Table 1.

4. POWER COMPARISONS

To compare the power of the test based on (2.2) with the Filliben and Shapiro-Francia tests, an empirical sampling study was conducted. Samples of sizes n=20, 50, 100 were generated from each of the 25 alternative distributions for n=50 used in Filliben's [4] study. The required uniform numbers were generated using the algorithm presented by Wichmann and Hill [8], and the normal random numbers were generated using the GRAND generator [3].

Since only N=1,000 normal random samples were used in generating the published percentage points for the Shapiro-Francia test for n=50 [7, p. 215], and since percentage points are not given in their paper for n=20 and n=100, the procedure described in Section 3 was used to determine the percentage points for the Shapiro-Francia test. The algorithm published by Royston [6] was used to compute the order statistic means. Published percentage points [4, p. 113] were used for the Filliben test.

One thousand samples were generated for each of the 25 alternative distributions, and the power calculations were smoothed by replicating the experiment twelve times and taking the average. The results of the study are presented in Table 2. The distributions are divided into three groups in Table 2: Group A are symmetric alternatives that are shorter-tailed than the normal, group B are symmetric alternatives that are longer-tailed than the normal, and group C are skewed alternatives. The values for the skewness measure ρ and the tail length measure τ_2 are both taken from Filliben [4, Table 2].

n	.000	.005	.010	.025	.050	.100	.250	.500	.750	.900	.950	.975	.990	.995
3	.866	.867	.869	.872	.879	.891	.924	.966	.992	.999	1.000	1.000	1.000	1.000
4	.784	.812	.823	.845	.867	.894	.931	.958	.979	.992	.996	.998	.999	1.000
5	.727	.807	.824	.855	.880	.903	.934	.960	.977	.988	.992	.995	.997	.998
6	.684	.815	.836	.865	.887	.910	.939	.962	.977	.986	.990	.993	.996	.997
7	.649	.827	.848	.875	.897	.917	.943	.964	.978	.986	.990	.992	.995	.996
8	.620	.839	.859	.885	.905	.923	.948	.966	.979	.986	.989	.992	.994	.995
9	.596	.852	.870	.894	.912	.929	.952	.968	.980	.987	.990	.992	.994	.995
10	.575	.861	.878	.900	.917	.934	.954	.970	.981	.987	.990	.992	.994	.995
11	.556	.869	.885	.907	.923	.938	.957	.972	.982	.987	.990	.992	.994	.995
12	.540	.877	.892	.912	.927	.941	.960	.973	.982	.988	.990	.992	.994	.995
13	.525	.883	.897	.917	.931	.945	.962	.975	.983	.988	.991	.992	.994	.995
14	.512	.888	.903	.922	.935	.948	.964	.976	.984	.989	.991	.993	.994	.995
15	.500	.894	.908	.923	.938	.950	.965	.977	.985	.989	.991	.993	.994	.995
16	.489	.898	.912	.929	.941	.953	.967	.978	.985	.989	.992	.993	.994	.995
17	.479	.904	.916	.932	.943	.954	.968	.979	.986	.990	.992	.993	.994	.995
18	.470	.908	.919	.934	.946	.956	.970	.980	.986	.990	.992	.993	.994	.995
19	.461	.912	.923	.937	.948	.958	.971	.980	.987	.990	.992	.993	.995	.995
20	.453	.914	.925	.940	.950	.960	.972	.981	.987	.991	.992	.994	.995	.996
21	.445	.919	.929	.942	.952	.961	.973	.982	.987	.991	.993	.994	.995	.996
22	.438	.922	.932	.945	.954	.963	.974	.982	.988	.991	.993	.994	.995	.996
23	.431	.923	.934	.946	.955	.963	.975	.983	.988	.992	.993	.994	.995	.996
24	.425	.927	.936	.948	.957	.965	.975	.983	.989	.992	.993	.994	.995	.996
25	.419	.928	.938	.950	.958	.966	.976	.984	.989	.992	.993	.994	.995	.996
26	.413	.932	.940	.951	.960	.967	.977	.984	.989	.992	.994	.994	.995	.996
27	.407	.933	.942	.953	.961	.968	.978	.985	.989	.992	.994	.995	.996	.996
28	.402	.936	.944	.954	.962	.969	.978	.985	.990	.993	.994	.995	.996	.996
29	.397	.938	.946	.956	.963	.970	.979	.986	.990	.993	.994	.995	.996	.996
30	.392	.939	.946	.956	.964	.971	.979	.986	.990	.993	.994	.995	.996	.996
31	.388	.939	.946	.956	.964	.971	.979	.986	.990	.993	.994	.995	.996	.996
32	.384	.924	.950	.959	.966	.972	.980	.987	.991	.993	.994	.995	.996	.996
33	.379	.944	.951	.960	.967	.973	.981	.987	.991	.993	.994	.995	.996	.996
34	.375	.945	.952	.961	.967	.974	.981	.987	.991	.993	.994	.995	.996	.997
35	.371	.946	.953	.962	.968	.974	.982	.987	.991	.994	.995	.995	.996	.997
36	.368	.947	.955	.963	.969	.975	.982	.988	.991	.994	.995	.996	.996	.997
37	.364	.949	.955	.964	.969	.975	.983	.988	.992	.994	.995	.996	.996	.997
38	.361	.950	.957	.965	.970	.976	.983	.988	.992	.994	.995	.996	.996	.997
39	.357	.951	.957	.965	.971	.976	.983	.988	.992	.994	.995	.996	.996	.997
40	.354	.952	.959	.966	.972	.977	.983	.989	.992	.994	.995	.996	.996	.997
41	.351	.953	.960	.967	.972	.977	.984	.989	.992	.994	.995	.996	.997	.997
42	.348	.954	.960	.967	.973	.978	.984	.989	.992	.994	.995	.996	.997	.997
43	.345	.955	.961	.968	.973	.978	.984	.989	.992	.994	.995	.996	.997	.997
44	.342	.956	.962	.969	.974	.979	.985	.989	.993	.995	.995	.996	.997	.997
45	.339	.957	.962	.969	.974	.979	.985	.990	.993	.995	.996	.996	.997	.997
46	.337	.957	.963	.970	.975	.979	.985	.990	.993	.995	.996	.996	.997	.997
47	.334	.959	.964	.970	.975	.980	.986	.990	.993	.995	.996	.996	.997	.997
48	.331	.959	.964	.971	.976	.980	.986	.990	.993	.995	.996	.996	.997	.997
49	.329	.960	.965	.971	.976	.980	.986	.990	.993	.995	.996	.996	.997	.997
50	.327	.961	.966	.972	.976	.981	.986	.990	.993	.995	.996	.996	.997	.997
55	.315	.964	.968	.974	.978	.982	.987	.991	.994	.995	.996	.997	.997	.997
60	.305	.966	.971	.976	.983	.988	.992	.994	.996	.996	.997	.997	.997	.998
65	.297	.969	.973	.978	.981	.985	.989	.992	.995	.996	.997	.997	.997	.998
70	.289	.971	.975	.979	.982	.966	.990	.993	.995	.996	.997	.997	.998	.998
75	.289	.973	.976	.980	.983	.986	.990	.993	.995	.996	.997	.997	.998	.998
80	.275	.974	.978	.981	.984	.987	.991	.993	.995	.997	.997	.997	.998	.998
85	.268	.975	.979	.982	.985	.988	.991	.994	.995	.997	.997	.998	.998	.998
90	.263	.977	.980	.983	.986	.988	.992	.994	.996	.997	.997	.998	.998	.998
95	.257	.978	.981	.984	.987	.989	.992	.994	.996	.997	.997	.998	.998	.998
100	.252	.979	.982	.985	.987	.989	.992	.995	.996	.997	.998	.998	.998	.998

Table 1. Percentage Points for the Normal Probability Plot Correlation Coefficient Test for Normality Using the Benard and Bos-Levenbach Plotting Position as an Estimate of the Order Statistic Median.

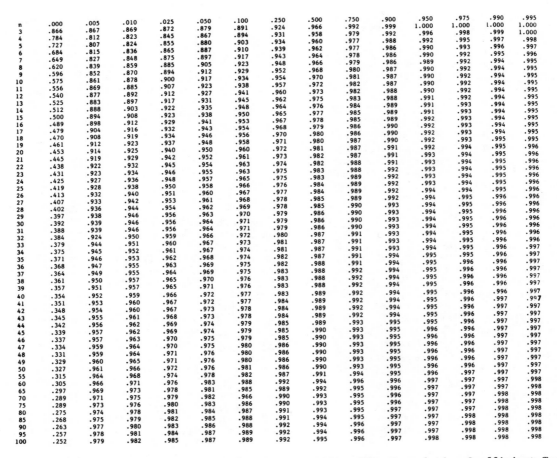

Group A	$\sqrt{\beta_1}$	ρ	β_2	τ_2	Power n=20 BB	F	SF	n=50 BB	F	SF	n=100 BB	F	SF
Arcsine	0	.5	1.500	.035	46	43	47	99	99	99	100	100	100
Johnson bounded JSB(0,.5)	0	.5	1.627	.136	22	20	23	87	86	88	100	100	100
Tukey λ(1.5)	0	.5	1.753	.150	10	9	10	60	57	60	99	98	99
Uniform	0	.5	1.800	.167	8	7	8	48	44	48	97	95	97
Tukey λ(.75)	0	.5	1.890	.214	5	4	5	28	25	58	85	79	85
Anglit	0	.5	2.194	.331	2	2	2	4	4	4	17	12	17
Triangular	0	.5	2.400	.352	2	2	2	2	1	2	4	3	4
Group B													
Logistic	0	.5	4.200	.579	15	14	14	27	26	24	42	37	36
LaPlace	0	.5	6.000	.617	34	32	32	63	62	60	87	84	84
Johnson unbounded JSU(0,1)	0	.5	36.188	.728	50	48	48	83	82	81	97	97	97
Tukey λ(-.5)	0	.5	-	.827	68	67	67	96	95	95	100	100	100
Cauchy	0	.5	-	.941	89	89	89	100	100	100	100	100	100
Tukey λ(-1.5)	0	.5	-	.982	98	98	98	100	100	100	100	100	100
Group C													
Weibull (10)	-.638	.392	3.570	.507	16	15	15	37	35	34	65	60	62
Weibull (3)	.168	.527	2.729	.454	4	4	4	5	4	4	7	5	6
Skewed: λ(1.5,.5)	.497	.655	2.209	.268	21	19	21	74	72	73	100	99	100
Extreme Value Type 1	1.140	.664	5.400	.554	32	31	31	70	68	68	94	93	93
Half-Normal	.995	.709	3.869	.467	39	37	38	89	88	89	100	100	100
Power log-normal:PLN(.5)	1.750	.727	8.898	.590	52	50	51	92	91	91	100	100	100
Extreme Value Type 2(5)	3.535	.768	48.092	.667	65	64	64	97	97	97	100	100	100
Exponential	2.000	.818	9.000	.579	80	79	80	100	100	100	100	100	100
Pareto (10)	2.811	.844	17.829	.638	87	86	86	100	100	100	100	100	100
Lognormal	6.185	.877	113.936	.728	92	91	91	100	100	100	100	100	100
Chi-Square (1)	2.828	.910	15.000	.631	97	97	97	100	100	100	100	100	100
Extreme Value 2(1)	-	.970	-	.942	99	99	99	100	100	100	100	100	100

BB = Benard and Bos-Levenbach Position F = Filliben Position SF = Shapiro-Francia Position

Table 2. Empirical 5% Power in (%) for the Correlation Coefficient Test for Normality.

An examination of Table 2 indicates that the test based on the Benard and Bos-Levenbach plotting position is in general more powerful than the test based on Filliben's plotting position. Also, it is at least as powerful as the Shapiro-Francia test.

5. CONCLUSION

A new correlation coefficient test for normality is proposed. Like Filliben's [4] test, it is based on an estimate of the i'th order statistic median from a standard normal distribution. However, instead of the estimate proposed by Filliben, it uses the estimate proposed by Benard and Bos-Levenbach [2]. Empirical percentage points of the new test are presented. Empirical power comparisons indicate that the new test is generally more powerful than Filliben's test against a wide variety of alternative distributions. The test also compares favorably in terms of power with the Shapiro-Francia [7] test, a correlation coefficient test based on the order statistic means.

6. REFERENCES

[1] Abramowitz, M. and Stegun, I. A. (eds.). Handbook of Mathematical Functions (U.S. Government Printing Office, Washington, 1964).

[2] Benard, A. and Bos-Levenbach, E. C., The plotting of observations on probability paper, Statistica. 7 (1953), 163-173.

[3] Brent, R. P., A Gaussian pseudo-random number generator (G5), Comm. ACM. 17 (1974), 704-706.

[4] Filliben, J. J., The probability plot correlation coefficient test for normality, Technometrics. 17 (1975), 111-117.

[5] Johnson, R. A. and Wichern, D. W., Applied Multivariate Statistical Analysis (Prentice-Hall, Englewood Cliffs, N.J., 1982).

[6] Royston, J. P. Expected normal order statistics (exact and approximate), App. Stat. 31 (1982), 161-165.

[7] Shapiro, S. S. and Francia, R. S., An approximate analysis of variance test for normality, J. Amer. Stat. Assoc. 67 (1972), 215-216.

[8] Wichmann, B. A. and Hill, I. D., An efficient and portable pseudo-random number generator, Appl. Stat. 31 (1982), 188-190.

COMPUTER SCIENCE AND STATISTICS:
The Interface, L. Billard (ed.)

COMPUTER GENERATED DISTRIBUTIONS FOR A RANDOM STATISTIC OF MIXTURES OF GAMMA POPULATIONS

K. J. Kapoor, Henry Ford Hospital, Detroit
D. S. Tracy, University of Windsor, Windsor

Random number generator routines available in existing software are important tools to generate data with different standard (known) distributions. Sampling from mixtures of gamma populations is simulated utilizing such routines in SAS. The ratio of the population mixture was insured by the routine RANTBL. Sampling distributions of a random statistic (skewness coefficient for example) are obtained for different mixtures of different gamma (and exponential) populations.

1. INTRODUCTION

Gamma distributed populations often occur in engineering and industrial applications. We say that a random variable x has the $\Gamma(\alpha,\beta)$ density, $\alpha>0$, $\beta>0$, if

$$f(x) = \frac{1}{\beta^{\alpha}\Gamma(\alpha)} x^{\alpha-1} e^{-x/\beta}, \quad x \geq 0.$$

Here α is the shape parameter and β the scale parameter.

When α is 1, we have the exponential density

$$f(x) = \frac{1}{\beta} e^{-x/\beta}, \quad x \geq 0.$$

It occurs frequently in practice as a lifetime distribution. For events recurring at random in time, it is the most used density. Mixtures of exponential distributions have become important through their applications in life testing and failure time data. Such mixtures have density

$$\frac{p}{\beta_1} e^{-x/\beta_1} + \frac{1-p}{\beta_2} e^{-x/\beta_2}, \quad x \geq 0$$

where the two populations are mixed in the proportion p, 1-p. Petigny (1966) has applied it to distances between elements in traffic and called it the Schuhl distribution. Such mixtures are also used to represent demographic distributions, e.g. Susara and Pathala (1965). Thomas (1966) fits an exponential mixture to the discharges of brain's neurons.

One may be interested in the sampling distribution of a random statistic for samples drawn from such mixtures. Often such sampling distributions become mathematically intractable. In this paper, for example, we consider the distributions of the coefficient of skewness for samples from mixed exponential populations. We generate such distributions by computer methods. In fact, we tackle the more general case of mixed gamma populations. Mixtures of two gamma populations with the same shape parameter are studied by John (1970). Ashton (1971) uses such mixtures in studying the distribution of time gap in road traffic flow.

2. COMPUTER GENERATION

The sampling is done using random number generator routines available in Statistical Analysis System (SAS). It is required to initialize a random number stream with a seed in this method. One can use the function routine in an assignment statement, e.g., X = FUNCTION (ARGUMENT LIST) or a call statement as CALL FUNCTION (ARGUMENT LIST). The latter provides greater control over the seed stream and the random number stream than the former.

The function RANTBL which generates deviates from a tabled probability mass function has been used to ensure the randomness in the population ratios. The statement X = RANTBL (SEED, P1, P2); (P1 + P2 = 1) will assign X = 1 with probability P1 and X = 2 with probability P2. To generate gamma distributions, the function RANGAM has been used. The statement X = RANGAM (SEED, ALPHA); will assign X with values from a gamma distribution with shape parameter ALPHA and scale parameter 1. And X = BETA* RANGAM (SEED, ALPHA); provides a gamma distribution with shape parameter ALPHA and scale parameter BETA. The following algorithm can be used to generate a sample of size 10, say, from mixed gamma populations with proporations P1 to P2, with P1 + P2 = 1, and parameter ALPHA, BETA, and ALPHA1, BETA1.

```
SAMPLE (10) - a vector of 10 elements
DO I = 1 to 10;
   X = RANTBL  (SEED, P1, P2);
   IF X = 1 THEN
      SAMPLE(I)=BETA*RANGAM(SEED1,ALPHA);
ELSE
   SAMPLE(I) = BETA1*RANGAM(SEED2,APLHA1);
END;
```

3. EXPONENTIAL MIXTURES

We draw 5000 samples of size 10 each from each of the mixtures

$$\frac{p}{\beta_1} e^{-x/\beta_1} + \frac{1-p}{\beta_2} e^{-x/\beta_2}$$

of exponential populations, letting β_1 be 1, $\beta_2 = 1(1)5$, $p = 0.1(0.1)0.5$. The case of $\beta_2=1$ is one of the "unmixed" populations, and we have samples from a standard exponential. The sampling distribution of the coefficient of skewness $g_1 = k_3/k_2^{3/2}$ is as below.

$0.1\Gamma(1,1) + 0.9\Gamma(1,1)$

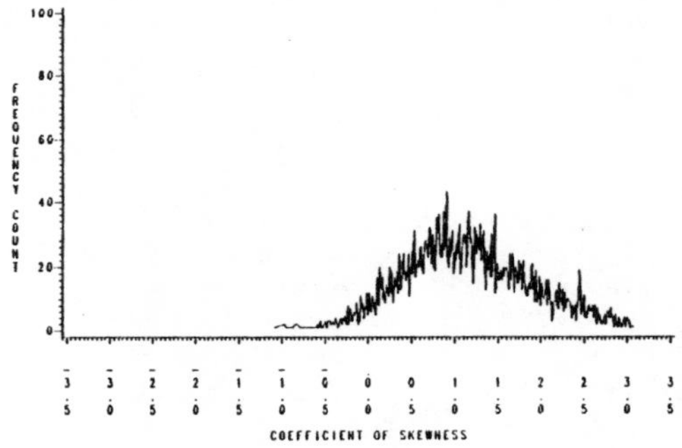

We obtain the mean $\bar{x}$ of g_1 as 1.15 and its standard deviation as 0.74.

Holding p at 0.1, we let β_2 change gradually from 1 to 5. The skewness first decreases and then starts increasing. A typical distribution is presented below.

$0.1\Gamma(1,1) + 0.9\Gamma(1,5)$

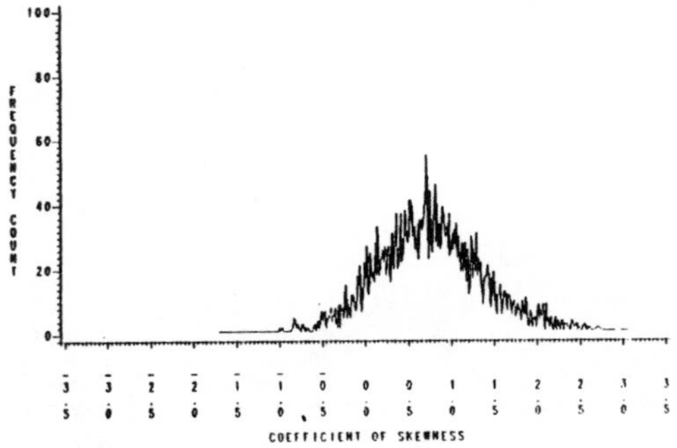

The means and standard deviations of g_1 as well as the relative frequencies in the intervals $\bar{x} \pm s$, $\bar{x} \pm 2s$, $\bar{x} \pm 3s$ are presented in the table below.

$\alpha_1 = 1$, $\beta_1 = 1$, $\alpha_2 = 1$ $p = 0.1$

			RF in interval		
β_2	$\bar{x}$	s	$\bar{x} \pm s$	$\bar{x} \pm 2s$	$\bar{x} \pm 3s$
1	1.15	0.74	0.6766	0.9588	0.9998
2	0.60	0.62	0.7042	0.9498	0.9942
3	0.59	0.60	0.6940	0.9506	0.9946
4	0.68	0.61	0.6972	0.9482	0.9962
5	0.76	0.62	0.6954	0.9458	0.9978

We now change p to 0.2, 0.3, 0.4 and 0.5, and change β_2 also. We present the sampling distributions for p = 0.3 and 0.5 and $\beta_2 = 2$.

$0.3\Gamma(1,1) + 0.7\Gamma(1,2)$

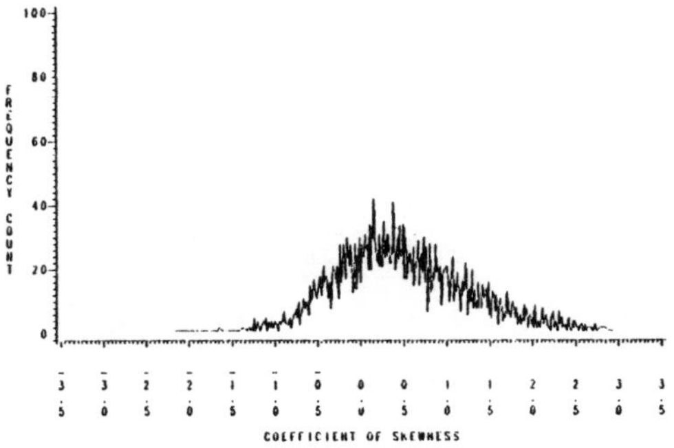

$\alpha_1 = 1,\ \beta_1 = 1,\ \alpha_2 = 1$					$p = 0.3$
			RF in interval		
β_2	$\bar{X}$	s	$\bar{X} \pm s$	$\bar{X} \pm 2s$	$\bar{X} \pm 3s$
1	1.15	0.74	0.6766	0.9588	0.9998
2	0.49	0.79	0.6866	0.9492	0.9990
3	0.34	0.66	0.7142	0.9446	0.9934
4	0.43	0.61	0.7066	0.9506	0.9938
5	0.56	0.61	0.6950	0.9526	0.9934

$0.5\Gamma(1,1) + 0.5\Gamma(1,2)$

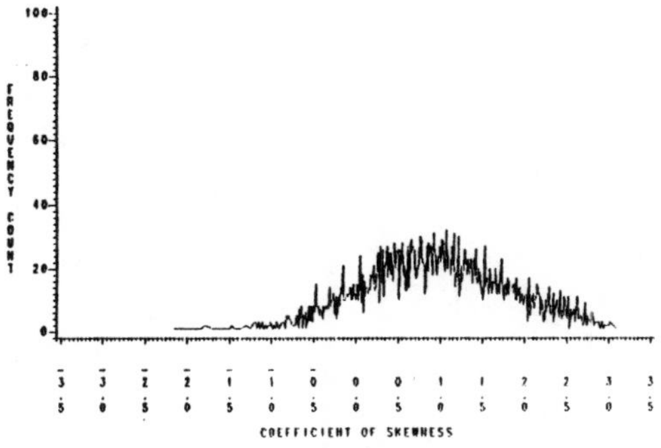

$\alpha_1 = 1,\ \beta_1 = 1,\ \alpha_2 = 1$					$p = 0.5$
			RF in interval		
β_2	$\bar{X}$	s	$\bar{X} \pm s$	$\bar{X} \pm 2s$	$\bar{X} \pm 3s$
1	1.15	0.74	0.6766	0.9588	0.9998
2	0.95	0.85	0.6686	0.9598	0.9988
3	0.71	0.85	0.6666	0.9554	0.9998
4	0.60	0.77	0.6942	0.9462	0.9992
5	0.60	0.70	0.7086	0.9514	0.9960

As β_2 increases, the distributions get more spread out. We present tables for changing values of β_2 when p = 0.3 and p = 0.5.

We also present tables arranged differently to bring out the effect of changing the proportion p, while holding the two exponential populations fixed. We let $\beta_1=1$, $\beta_2=3$, 5 and vary p in the tables below.

$\alpha_1 = 1,\ \beta_1 = 1,\ \alpha_2 = 1,\ \beta_2 = 3$					
			RF in interval		
p	$\bar{x}$	s	$\bar{x} \pm s$	$\bar{x} \pm 2s$	$\bar{x} \pm 3s$
0.1	0.59	0.60	0.6940	0.9506	0.9946
0.2	0.38	0.60	0.7104	0.9464	0.9940
0.3	0.34	0.66	0.7142	0.9446	0.9934
0.4	0.48	0.78	0.7066	0.9488	0.9988
0.5	0.71	0.85	0.6666	0.9554	0.9998

$\alpha_1 = 1,\ \beta_1 = 1,\ \alpha_2 = 1,\ \beta_2 = 5$					
			RF in interval		
p	$\bar{x}$	s	$\bar{x} \pm s$	$\bar{x} \pm 2s$	$\bar{x} \pm 3s$
0.1	0.76	0.62	0.6954	0.9458	0.9978
0.2	0.63	0.61	0.7118	0.9544	0.9954
0.3	0.56	0.61	0.6950	0.9526	0.9934
0.4	0.56	0.64	0.7084	0.9512	0.9950
0.5	0.60	0.70	0.7086	0.9514	0.9960

3. GAMMA MIXTURES

Same Shape Parameter

We now consider mixtures of gamma populations. First, we take the same shape parameter 2 for both populations. We let β_1, the scale parameter for the first population, remain 1, and vary β_2 from 1 to 5. When $\beta_2 = 1$, we again have an "unmixed" population. The sampling distribution of the skewness coefficient is as below

$0.3\Gamma(2,1) + 0.7\Gamma(2,1)$

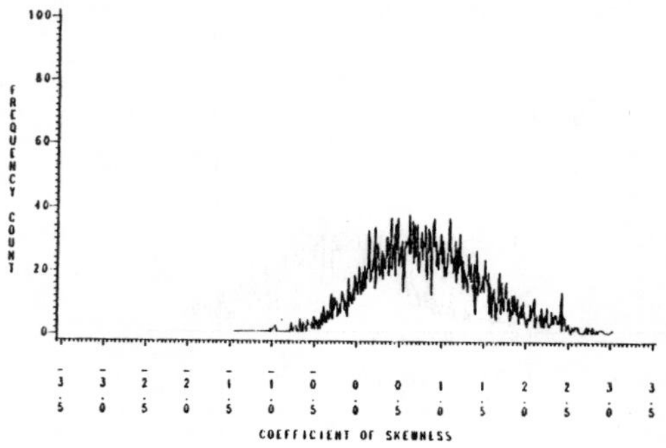

The mean of g_1 is 0.84 and its standard deviation 0.71.

For low p, there is not much change on increasing β_2, except the mean of g_1 shifts to about 0.88. This is depicted in the table below.

$\alpha_1 = 2,\ \beta_1 = 1,\ \alpha_2 = 2$					p = 0.1
			RF in interval		
β_2	$\bar{x}$	s	$\bar{x} \pm s$	$\bar{x} \pm 2s$	$\bar{x} \pm 3s$
1	0.84	0.71	0.6914	0.9498	0.9992
2	0.88	0.71	0.6940	0.9504	0.9992
3	0.89	0.71	0.6948	0.9542	0.9994
4	0.88	0.70	0.6906	0.9502	0.9988
5	0.87	0.70	0.6890	0.9520	0.9988

However, as p increases, the mean of g_1 keeps going up with increasing β_2, while its standard deviation remains remarkably stable. We see this in the tables for p = 0.3 and p = 0.5.

$0.5\Gamma(2,1) + 0.5\Gamma(2,5)$

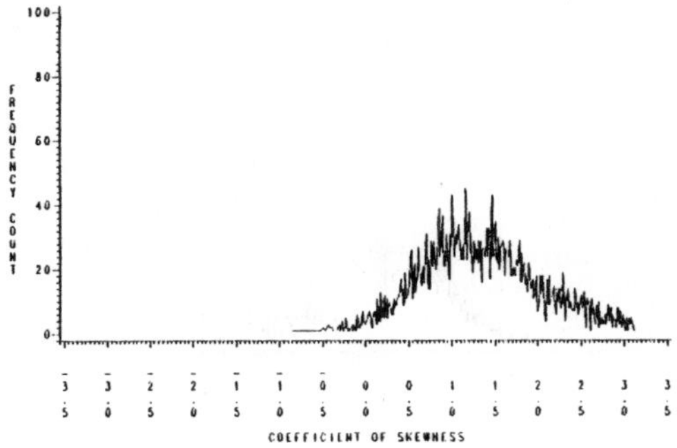

$0.5\Gamma(2,1) + 0.5\Gamma(4,4)$

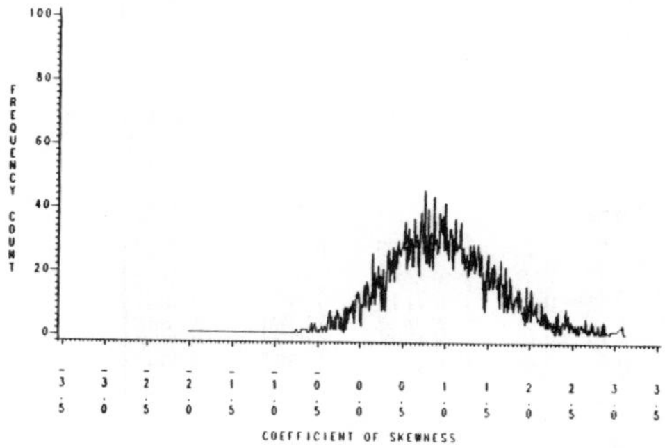

Different Shape Parameters

We now mix a $\Gamma(2,1)$ population with a $\Gamma(4,4)$ population. The sampling distributions for $p = 0.1$ and $p = 0.5$ are shown below.

$0.1\Gamma(2,1) + 0.9\Gamma(4,4)$

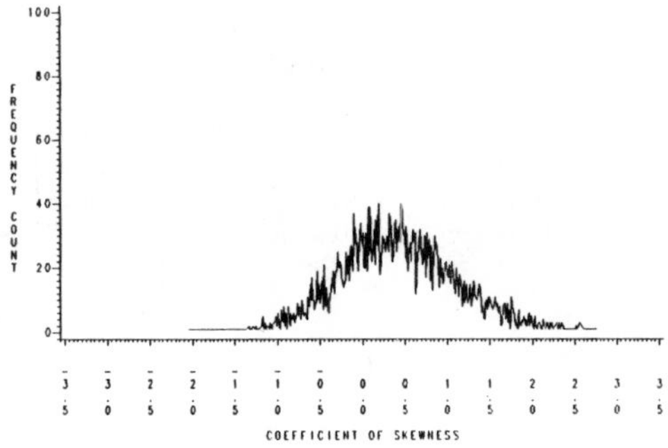

The effect of mixing a $\Gamma(2,1)$ population with a $\Gamma(4,\beta_2)$ population is studied next. We let β_2 range from 1 to 5, and the proportion p from 0.1 to 0.5. We see a marked change from the case of low p to the case of $p = 0.5$ in the tables below.

$\alpha_1 = 2,\ \beta_1 = 1,\ \alpha_2 = 4$				$p = 0.1$	
			RF in interval		
β_2	$\bar{x}$	s	$\bar{x} \pm s$	$\bar{x} \pm 2s$	$\bar{x} \pm 3s$
1	0.59	0.69	0.6886	0.9548	0.9980
2	0.52	0.69	0.6934	0.9542	0.9980
3	0.47	0.69	0.6966	0.9536	0.9974
4	0.44	0.69	0.6928	0.9532	0.9986
5	0.41	0.69	0.6920	0.9522	0.9962

$\alpha_1 = 2, \beta_1 = 1, \alpha_2 = 2$				p = 0.3	
			RF in interval		
β_2	$\bar{x}$	s	$\bar{x} \pm s$	$\bar{x} \pm 2s$	$\bar{x} \pm 3s$
1	0.84	0.71	0.6914	0.9498	0.9992
2	0.96	0.72	0.6868	0.9494	0.9990
3	1.03	0.71	0.6856	0.9528	0.9990
4	1.05	0.70	0.6896	0.9531	0.9990
5	1.04	0.69	0.6888	0.9516	0.9990

$\alpha_1 = 2, \beta_1 = 1, \alpha_2 = 2$				p = 0.5	
			RF in interval		
β_2	$\bar{x}$	s	$\bar{x} \pm s$	$\bar{x} \pm 2s$	$\bar{x} \pm 3s$
1	0.84	0.71	0.6914	0.9498	0.9994
2	1.04	0.74	0.7588	0.9516	0.9994
3	1.21	0.73	0.6882	0.9541	1.0000
4	1.29	0.71	0.6836	0.9534	1.0000
5	1.33	0.70	0.6786	0.9522	0.9998

It is also interesting to compare the above tables with those for the corresponding exponential mixtures.

We also present a table for changing p while mixing a $\Gamma(2,1)$ population with a $\Gamma(2,5)$ population.

$\alpha_1 = 2, \beta_1 = 1, \alpha_2 = 2, \beta_2 = 5$					
			RF in interval		
p	$\bar{x}$	s	$\bar{x} \pm s$	$\bar{x} \pm 2s$	$\bar{x} \pm 3s$
0.1	0.87	0.70	0.6890	0.9520	0.9988
0.2	0.94	0.69	0.6868	0.9524	0.9984
0.3	1.04	0.69	0.6888	0.9516	0.9990
0.4	1.18	0.70	0.6944	0.9546	0.9992
0.5	1.33	0.70	0.6786	0.9522	0.9998

The sampling distribution when p = 0.3 is as below.

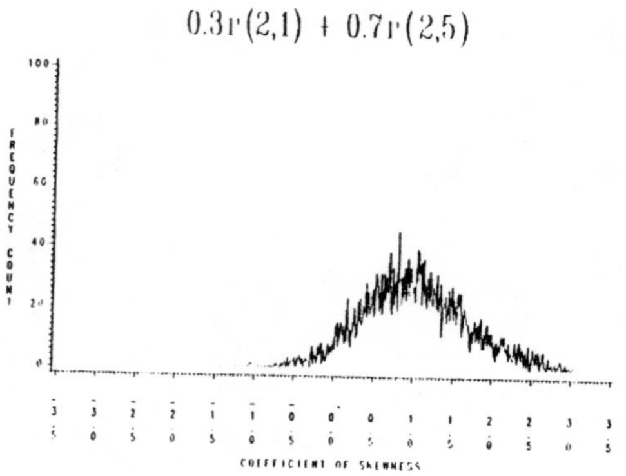

For an even mixture of the two populations, the sampling distributions is:

$\alpha_1 = 2, \beta_1 = 1, \alpha_2 = 4$					$p = 0.5$
			RF in interval		
β_2	$\bar{x}$	s	$\bar{x} \pm s$	$\bar{x} \pm 2s$	$\bar{x} \pm 3s$
1	0.73	0.68	0.6894	0.9424	0.9982
2	0.93	0.66	0.6940	0.9520	0.9982
3	0.98	0.66	0.6942	0.9498	0.9976
4	0.98	0.67	0.7012	0.9486	0.9964
5	0.98	0.68	0.7052	0.9490	0.9958

REFERENCES

[1] Ashton, W.D. (1971). Distribution for gaps in road traffic. J. Inst. Math and Its Applns. 7, 37-46.

2 John, S. (1970). On identifying the population of origin of each observation in a mixture of observations from two gamma populations. Technometrics 12, 565-568.

3 Petigny, B. (1966). Extension de la distribution de Schuhl. Ann des Ponts et Chaussées 136, 77-84.

4 SAS User's Guide: Basics (1982). Cary, North Carolina. SAS Institute, Inc.

5 Susara, V. and Pathala, K. S. (1965). A probability distribution for the time of first birth. J. Sci. Res. 16, 59-62.

6 Thomas, E. A. C. (1966). Mathematical models for the clustered firing of single cortical neurons. Brit. J. Math. Stat. Psych. 19, 151-162.

COMPUTER SCIENCE AND STATISTICS:
The Interface, L. Billard (ed.)

QUALITY CONTROL ON MICROCOMPUTERS

T. Bruce McLean

Mathematics and Computer Science Dept.
Georgia Southern College, Statesboro, Georgia 30460-8093

McElrath and Associates Inc.
600 France Ave. South, Minneapolis, Minnesota 55435

This is a collection of quality control programs that can be executed on an Apple II under the UCSD Pascal operating system. They consist of a 1) Shewhart x bar and r chart, 2) sequential sampling based upon the Wald sequential probability ratio test, and 3) commulative sum and r chart. They include data entry, saving to diskette, using Turtlegraphics to display the charts, reading data from diskette, printing the data, printing the graphics screen, and they provide for data analysis. If the user needs the power of SPSS, a simplified file creation program is also included. The user answers questions supplied by the program and the SPSS file is then prepared for them. Data for the created SPSS file may also be entered from the microcomputer if desired. The completed file would then be uploaded to a mainframe for execution.

I. INTRODUCTION

This collection of programs is designed to be implemented in a quality control environment on an Apple IIe or Apple II+ with 64K of main memory, one disk drive, an 80 column screen, and a dot matrix printer. They were prepared under the UCSD Pascal operating system that incorporates Turtlegraphics. The UCSD Pascal operating system was selected because of the ease in maintaining and improving programs and because Turtlegraphics is supplied by the system. Two of the programs have identical structures. These are the x bar and r chart [1] and the cummulative sum chart [4].

2. X BAR AND R CHART

This program is menu driven and the menus follow the design of the operating system where selections can be made with the touch of one key. Once deciding to create a new file and supplying a title, the user can enter data. The data is displayed in column format with the default sample titles of S-1 through S32767 as displayed in Figure 1. On the screen, there is space for two rows of samples with ten samples per row. After the twentieth sample has been entered, the top row scrolls off the screen leaving the last ten samples still visible. The title of each sample can be changed to the user's choice at any time data is being entered from the keyboard by preceding the title with a slash. The data can be entered in sample sizes from two through eight and can display from one to five decimal digits to the right of the decimal.

After a complete sample has been entered, the mean and range is displayed below the sample data in customary control chart fashion. The data can be edited until the return key is pushed. If there are any syntax problems with the last number entered, the user will be requested to reenter it. Even if a complete sample has not been entered, the user may interrupt the data entry by entering a carriage return with no data. At this time the program will return to the main menu.

From the main menu, you can ask for help, calculate limits, look at the graphs, change an existing entry or title, delete a sample, save the data, or print the data onto a printer connected to the microcomputer. On the graphics page, a x bar and r control chart is displayed cutting the graph off at the limits as shown in figure 2. This graph can be expanded or shrunk. It displays everyother sample title due to space limitations. A maximum of thirty-two samples can be shown on the graph at one time, but it can be moved left or right to display the rest. You can ask for help or dump the screen to a dot matrix printer. The program uses the Western Electric [3] guidelines of marking any mean that is the second of three farther than two standard errors from the mean on the same side of x-double bar, the fourth mean out of five that is more than one standard error from the mean on the same side, and eight in a row on the same side of x-double bar. It also marks means and ranges that are outside of the control limits.

Control limits may be calculated on the last n samples, on all data that is in the circular queue, or can be entered by the user. Once the data has been saved from the main menu, the user may recall it at another time and continue the process. The same command checks to see if there is sufficient space on the diskette and then writes the data.

March 16, 1984

S-1	S-2	S-3	S-4	S-5	S-6	S-7	S-8	S-9	S10
1.25	3.00	2.82	1.84	2.23	2.10	2.10	3.00	1.75	2.25
3.45	1.75	2.45	1.65	2.67	2.90	3.10	2.60	2.50	3.00
2.30	2.25	3.00	2.21	2.30	3.40	1.80	2.40	2.25	2.35
3.00	2.00	3.00	2.50	3.10	3.20	2.00	2.78	2.58	3.40
2.500	2.250	2.818	2.050	2.575	2.900	2.250	2.695	2.270	2.750
2.20	1.25	0.55	0.85	0.87	1.30	1.30	0.60	0.83	1.15

S11	S12	S13	S14	S15	S16	S17	S18	S19	TITLES
1.55	1.35	2.35	4.25	3.22	3.70	2.29	2.00	2.20	1
1.95	2.35	3.12	3.28	3.00	2.73	2.92	2.30	3.20	2
2.45	3.25	2.75	2.45	3.00	3.00	3.20	3.10		3
2.20	3.25	2.20	3.10	3.10	3.23	2.67	2.60		4
2.037	2.550	2.605	3.270	3.080	3.165	2.770	2.500	2.700	----MEAN
0.90	1.90	0.92	1.80	0.22	0.97	0.91	1.10	1.00	RANGE

Figure 1: Data being entered

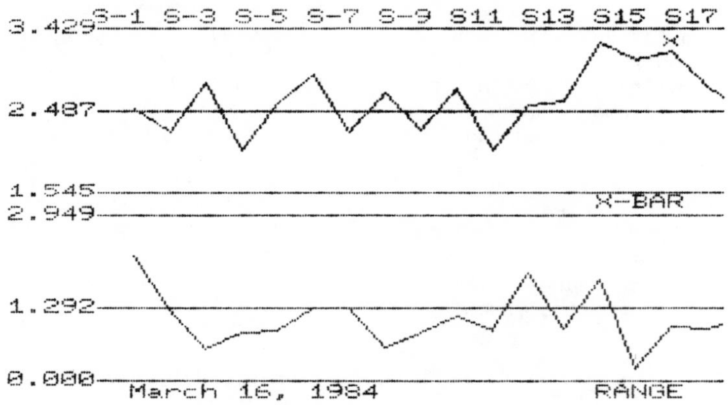

Figure 2: x bar r chart

3. CUMMULATIVE SUM AND R CHART

Figure 3 shows a commulative sum and r chart. This program has all of the features that the x bar and r chart has and runs a two sided chart. This is equivalent to the mask as explained in the Western Electric manual [4]. The commulative limits need to be entered by the user at least once. The range limits can be calculated by the program exactly as before. Once a commulative sum indicates the process is out of control, that sum is marked and reset to zero. Either of the above programs can read data that has been saved by the other making it possible to run a x bar and r chart until the limits have been established, and then switch to a cummulative sum chart. In addition to the lower and upper cummulative sum, the mean and range are also displayed if there is room on the screen.

4. SEQUENTIAL SAMPLING

The user enters the title, alpha, AQL, beta, and RQL for a sequential sampling plan based upon the Wald sequential probability ratio test [2]. The equations of the rejection and acceptance lines are calculated and displayed as shown in Fig. 4. All of the data is entered while observing the graphics screen. Multiple numbers of conforming or non conforming parts can be entered and the graph of the total parts inspected is plotted versus the number of nonconforming parts If the graph breaks one of the decision lines, the program gives you the opportunity to save the title and a record of the data entered. The window that displays the graph of the incoming data can be expanded, shrunk, moved left, right, up, or down.

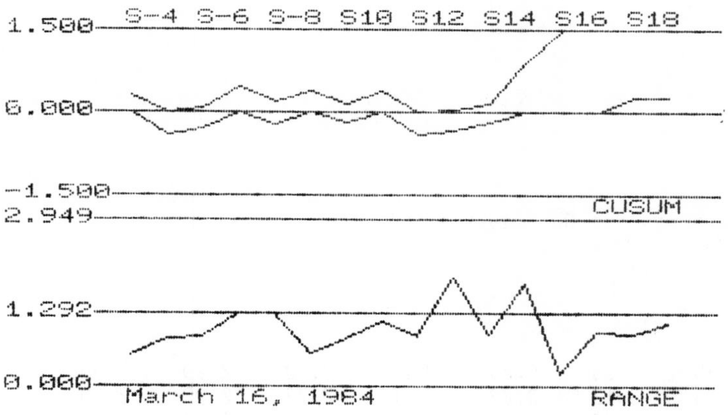

Figure 3: Commulative sum chart

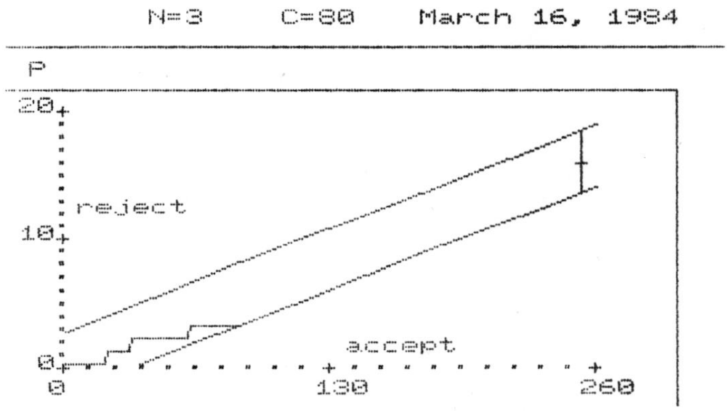

Figure 4: Sequential sampling plan

5. SPSS

A user answers questions supplied by the program concerning the run name and the status of the system files. Variable names, value labels, variable labels, and missing values must conform to SPSS standards. The program checks for invalid responses, and asks the user to reenter if there are any. If the user forgets, commas and slashes are placed into their file automatically by the program and the data list card is created based upon the information supplied. The program uses a data structure called a bag that permits more of main memory to be utilized and makes it possible for all of the information on one variable to be entered at one time. Then the program distributes it to the correct SPSS line after all of the variables have been entered.

After the initial format of the data is decided upon, the program moves to a modest selection of procedure cards that includes frequency, condescriptive, t-test, oneway, anova, scattergram, and crosstabs. The options and statistics available for each procedure card will be displayed upon request and error checking prevents the user from reusing variables or using incorrect variable names. The user may enter the data from the program or attach it later. If it is entered from the keyboard, column headers are provided to ensure the data is in the correct column. Once the completed file is prepared, it is then uploaded to a main frame computer that has SPSS and executed. There is a high probability that the program will execute the first time it is submitted. It has been class tested under SPSS, version 8 on the Cyber 750 in Athens, Georgia in the Spring of 1983 before SPSS-X was available.

6. ACKNOWLEDGEMENTS

We are grateful to the suggestions of Dr. Robert A. McLean, Statistics Department, University of Tennessee, for suggestions on the first three programs and to Georgia Southern College for supplying peripheral equipment to support the last program under a college research grant.

7. REFERENCES

[1] Grant, E.L. and Leavenworth, R.S., Statistical Quality Control, 37-356, (McGraw-Hill, New York 1972).

[2] Ibid, 456-459.

[3] Western Electric, Statistical Quality Control Handbook 24-28, (Mack Printing, Easton, Pennsylvania 1977).

[4] Ibid, 464-484.

BIOGRAPHY

T. Bruce McLean received his Ph.D. in Mathematics from the University of Kentucky in 1971. He teaches mathematics, computer science, and statistics at Georgia Southern College and quality engineering courses for McElrath and Associates Inc.

COMPUTER SCIENCE AND STATISTICS:
The Interface, L. Billard (ed.)

SAMPLING DISTRIBUTION OF SKEWNESS COEFFICIENT FOR NORMAL MIXTURES

Derrick S. Tracy, University of Windsor, Windsor
Kunwar J. Kapoor, Henry Ford Hospital, Detroit

Sampling distributions of the skewness coefficient are studied when sampling from mixtures of two normal populations. Five thousand random samples of size 10 each are generated, using a computer, from mixtures $pN(\mu_1, 1.5^2) + (1-p)N(\mu_2, 1.5^2)$ of two normal populations, for various values of p, μ_1, and μ_2. Representative graphs and tables are presented and certain conclusions are drawn about the distributions.

1. INTRODUCTION

Skewness coefficient measures the lack of symmetry of a frequency distribution. Denoted by g_1, it is defined as the ratio statistic $k_3/k_2^{3/2}$ in terms of k-statistics or $m_3/m_2^{3/2}$ in terms of moments (Kendall and Stuart, 1977, p. 316), (Cramér, 1946, p. 356). Cramér provides its mean and variance, for sample size n, as:

$$E(g_1) = \gamma_1 + O(\tfrac{1}{n})$$

$$V(g_1) = \frac{1}{4n\mu_2^5}\{4\mu_2^2\mu_6 - 12\mu_2\mu_3\mu_5 - 24\mu_2^3\mu_4 + 9\mu_3^2\mu_4 + 35\mu_2^2\mu_3^2 + 36\mu_2^5\} + O(\frac{1}{n^{3/2}})$$

where γ_1 denotes the population skewness coefficient and μ's the population moments. When sampling from a normal population, the exact expressions are:

$$E(g_1) = 0$$
$$V(g_1) = \frac{6(n-2)}{(n+1)(n+3)}$$

Even when sampling from a large population, the sampling distibution of g_1 can only be very approximately determined by theoretical methods.

Tracy and Conley (1982) provided a computer approach to obtain the exact sampling distributions of g_1 for small samples drawn from a discrete, uniform population. Their method, however, was general enough for sampling from any underlying distribution.

Often a practice, the underlying distributions are mixtures of two populations. We study here the case of mixtures of two normal populations. Mixtures of such populations have been extensively studied, e.g. Teichroew (1957). Also, Everitt and Hand (1981) give a detailed account, indicating how the parameters of the mixture determine its shape. Behboodian (1972) gives some general results on the distribution of the sample mean and the sample variance when sampling from normal mixtures with a common variance. Bowman and Shenton (1973) do a Monte Carlo study for the distribution of skewness from a normal mixture when sample size is large, and investigate the power of g_1 in testing skewed departures from normality using the Cornish-Fisher normal expansion.

We generate the sampling distributions of the skewness coefficient for small samples from a normal mixture.

2. SAMPLING DISTRIBUTIONS

Two independent normal populations with means μ_1, μ_2 and same standard deviation 1.5 are considered. μ_1 is held at 5, while μ_2 takes the values 5, 10, 15, 20, 40, 60, 80, 100, and 200. The populations are mixed in proportions p and 1-p, where p takes the values 0.1(0.1)0.9. From each such mixture, 5000 simple random samples of size 10 are generated using a computer. The skewness coefficient is computed for each sample, and the values plotted. Representative graphs are reproduced below.

3. THE EFFECT OF VARYING μ_2

We let $p = 0.1$, $\mu_1 = 5$, and study the effect of varying μ_2 from 10 to 200. Here 90% observations are drawn from the second population. The sampling distribution of the skewness coefficient gradually moves from symmetry for low values of μ_2 to highly negatively skew for large values of μ_2.

$0.1N(5,1.5^2) + 0.9N(10,1.5^2)$

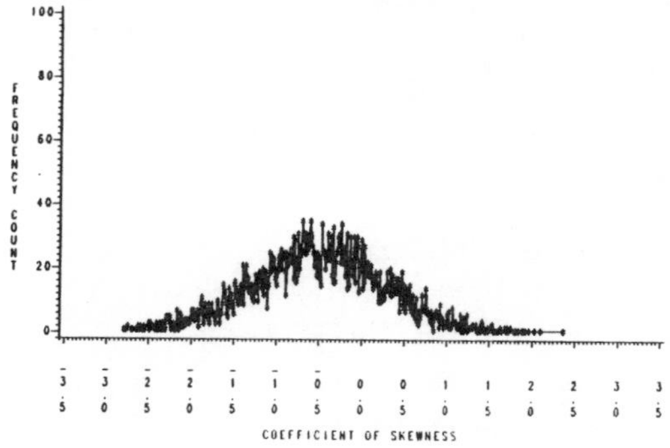

$0.1N(5,1.5^2) + 0.9N(200,1.5^2)$

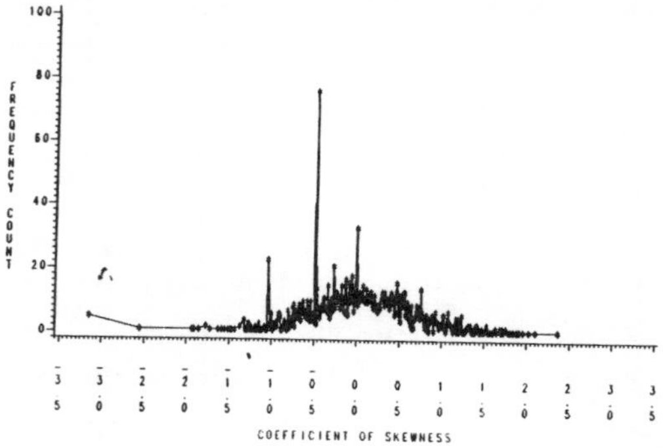

$0.1N(5,1.5^2) + 0.9N(20,1.5^2)$

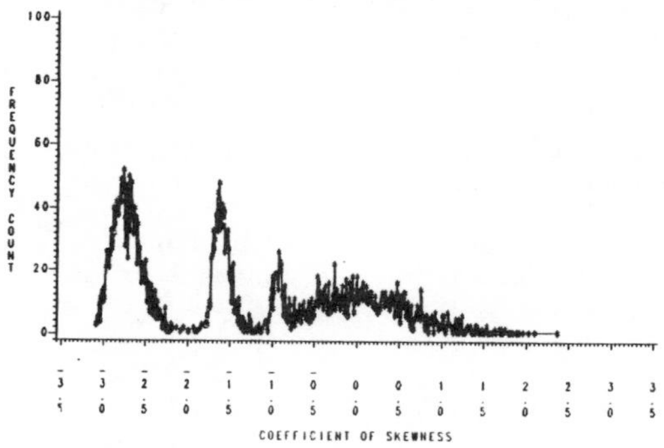

$0.1N(5,1.5^2) + 0.9N(80,1.5^2)$

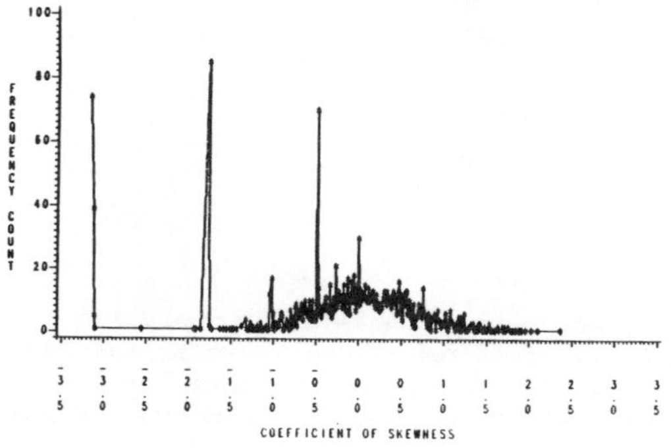

Also, the mean value of g_1 shifts from 0 gradually to -1.57. In fact, this value is achieved near $\mu_2 = 60$ and stays there for larger μ_2. The standard deviation of g_1 also stablizes at 1.47.

The following table, where μ stands for μ_2, summarizes the situation. It also shows the proportions of relative frequencies in the intervals $\bar{x} \pm cs$, $c = 1, 2, 3$, where $\bar{x}$ and s denote the mean and standard deviation of g_1.

p = .1

			RF in interval		
μ	$\bar{x}$	s	$\bar{x} \pm s$	$\bar{x} \pm 2s$	$\bar{x} \pm 3s$
5	0.01	0.69	0.6964	0.9526	0.9954
10	-0.51	0.85	0.6834	0.9526	0.9996
15	-1.14	1.12	0.6000	0.9780	0.9898
20	-1.36	1.28	0.5310	0.9834	1.0000
40	-1.53	1.43	0.3976	0.9882	1.0000
60	-1.56	1.45	0.3932	0.9886	1.0000
80	-1.57	1.46	0.3932	0.9892	1.0000
100	-1.57	1.46	0.3932	0.9892	1.0000
200	-1.57	1.47	0.3944	0.9896	1.0000

As another representative situation, we present graphs for $p = 0.4$, with the same values of μ_2 as considered earlier. The skewness is not so marked now, since the proportions of the mixture are more homogeneous, p and 1-p being not so far apart. In fact, the sampling distributions are quite similar to those for an equal mixture (p=0.5). The sampling distributions are presented below.

$0.4N(5,1.5^2) + 0.6N(80,1.5^2)$

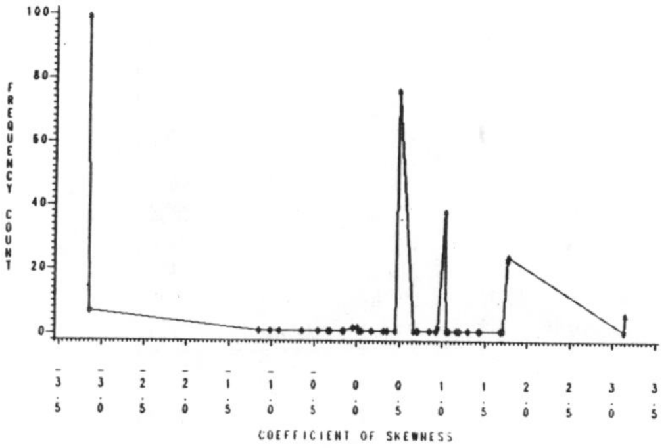

$0.4N(5,1.5^2) + 0.6N(10,1.5^2)$

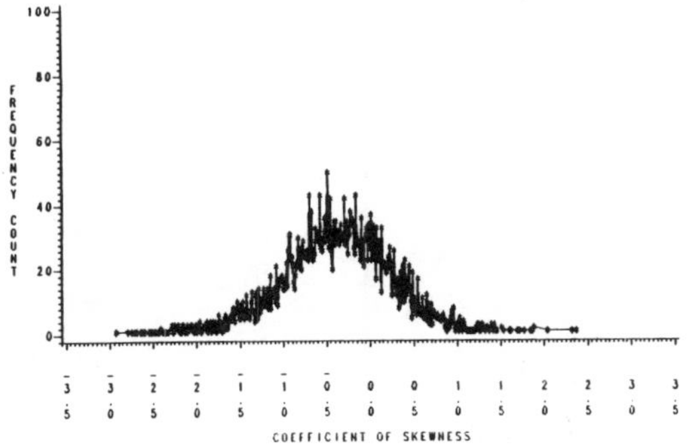

$0.4N(5,1.5^2) + 0.6N(200,1.5^2)$

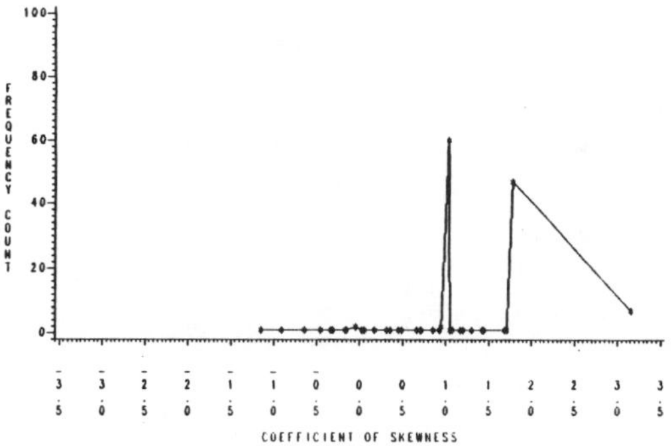

$0.4N(5,1.5^2) + 0.6N(20,1.5^2)$

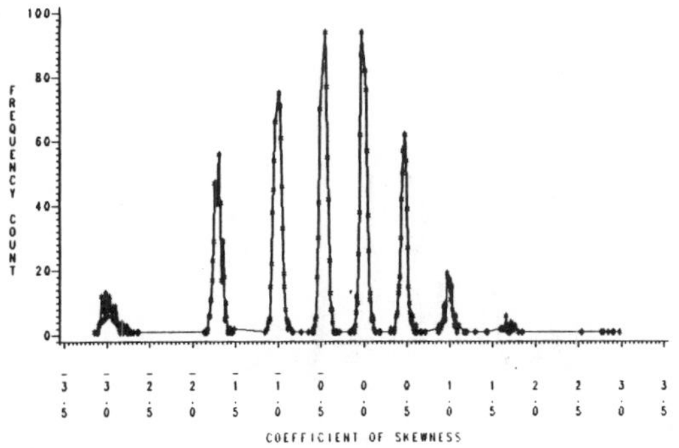

We also present the table of sampling means and standard deviations, and the relative frequencies in various intervals for $p = 0.4$.

p = .4

μ	$\bar{x}$	s	RF in interval: $\bar{x} \pm s$	$\bar{x} \pm 2s$	$\bar{x} \pm 3s$
5	0.01	0.69	0.6964	0.9526	0.9954
10	-0.64	0.64	0.7128	0.9498	0.9936
15	-0.61	0.79	0.7028	0.9436	0.9970
20	-0.60	0.87	0.6836	0.9452	0.9988
40	-0.58	0.92	0.6782	0.9458	0.9986
60	-0.58	0.93	0.6784	0.9458	0.9986
80	-0.58	0.93	0.6784	0.9458	0.9986
100	-0.58	0.93	0.6782	0.9458	0.9986
200	-0.58	0.93	0.6784	0.9458	0.9986

$0.1N(5,1.5^2) + 0.9N(15,1.5^2)$

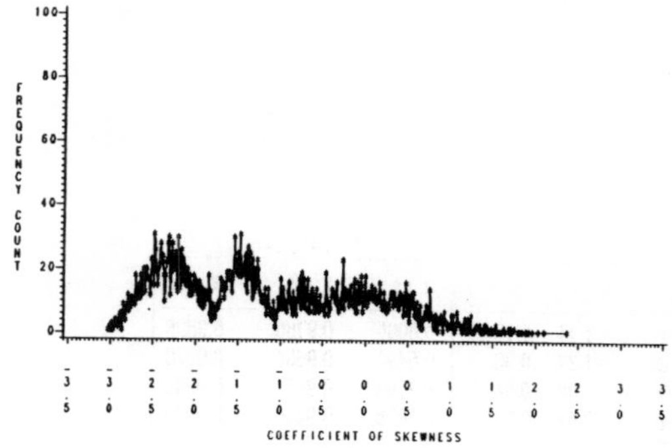

For an interesting comparison, we present a similar table for p = 0.5. Here the samples are drawn evenly from both populations.

$0.3N(5,1.5^2) + 0.7N(15,1.5^2)$

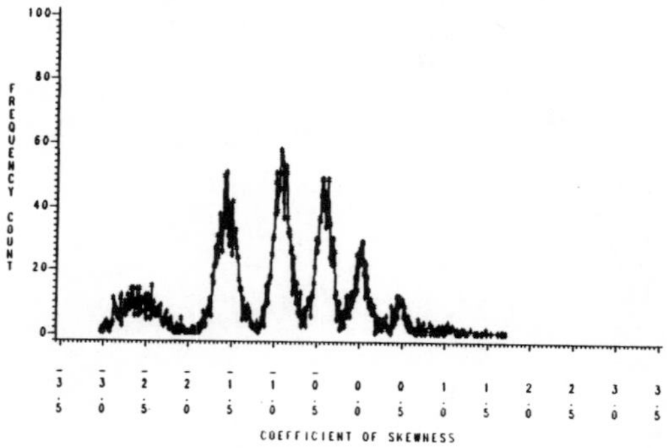

p = .5

μ	$\bar{x}$	s	RF in interval: $\bar{x} \pm s$	$\bar{x} \pm 2s$	$\bar{x} \pm 3s$
5	0.01	0.69	0.6964	0.9526	0.9954
10	-0.42	0.59	0.7128	0.9520	0.9914
15	-0.15	0.74	0.7080	0.9420	0.9880
20	-0.08	0.82	0.7078	0.9402	0.9832
40	-0.03	0.89	0.6696	0.9710	0.9790
60	-0.02	0.90	0.6696	0.9590	0.9590
80	-0.02	0.89	0.6696	0.9590	0.9590
100	-0.02	0.89	0.6696	0.9590	0.9590
200	-0.02	0.90	0.6696	0.9590	0.9590

4. THE EFFECT OF VARYING THE PROPORTIONS

We look at sampling distributions from a different viewpoint now. With μ_1 fixed at 5, we let μ_2 be 15. We let p vary from 0.1 to 0.9. The behavior of distributions reverses at p = 0.5, when negative skewness gives way to positive skewness. The degree of skewness is marked for low and high values of p, and is very moderate between 0.4 and 0.6. The distributions for p = 0.1, 0.3, and 0.5 are presented below.

$0.5N(5,1.5^2) + 0.5N(15,1.5^2)$

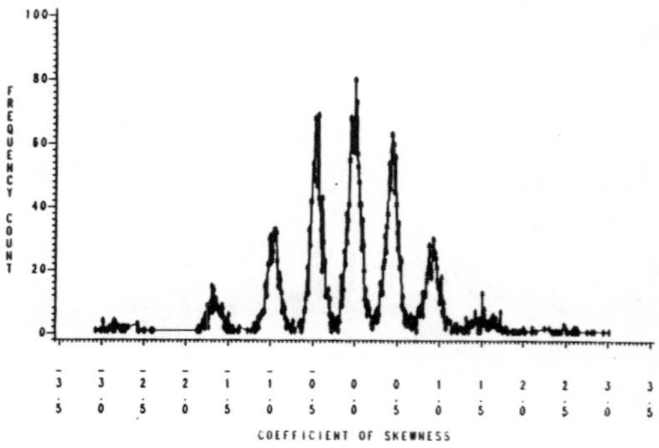

The table for sampling means and standard deviations is as below.

$\mu = 15$

p	$\bar{X}$	s	RF in interval $\bar{X} \pm s$	$\bar{X} \pm 2s$	$\bar{X} \pm 3s$
0.1	−1.14	1.12	0.6000	0.9780	0.9898
0.2	−1.27	0.93	0.6490	0.9684	0.9972
0.3	−1.02	0.84	0.7198	0.9474	0.9992
0.4	−0.61	0.79	0.7028	0.9436	0.9970
0.5	−0.15	0.74	0.7080	0.9420	0.9880
0.6	0.33	0.70	0.7036	0.9568	0.9952
0.7	0.76	0.70	0.6894	0.9458	0.9970
0.8	1.11	0.77	0.6892	0.9594	0.9968
0.9	1.11	1.04	0.6034	0.9778	0.9996

The sampling distributions get much more spread out when μ_1, μ_2 differ by a large amount. We present some typical distributions for $\mu_1 = 5$, $\mu_2 = 200$.

$0.1N(5,1.5^2) + 0.9N(200,1.5^2)$

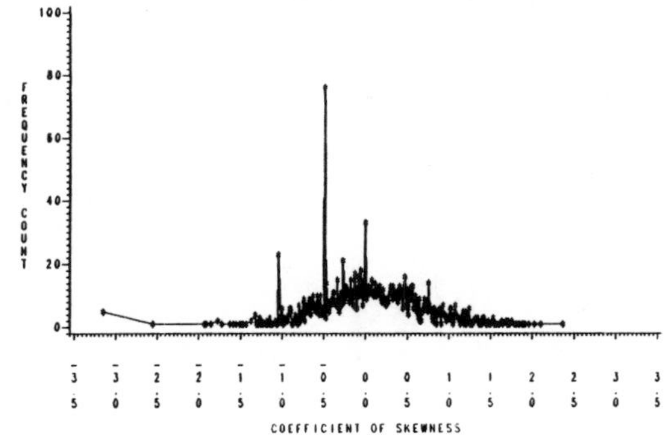

$0.3N(5,1.5^2) + 0.7N(200,1.5^2)$

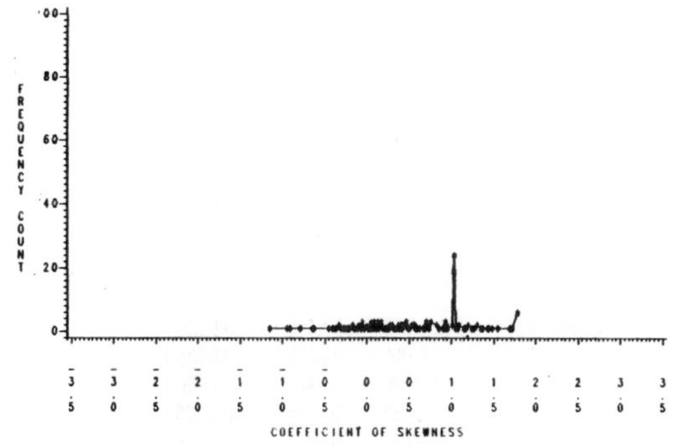

$0.5N(5,1.5^2) + 0.5N(200,1.5^2)$

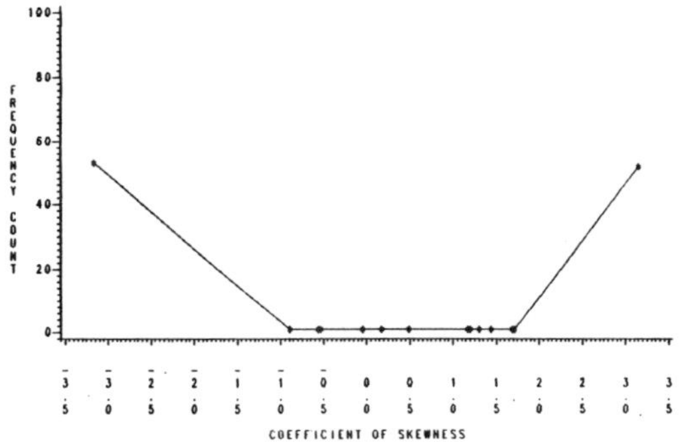

The table for sampling means and standard deviation is as below.

$\mu = 200$

p	$\bar{X}$	s	RF in interval $\bar{X} \pm s$	$\bar{X} \pm 2s$	$\bar{X} \pm 3s$
0.1	−1.57	1.47	0.3944	0.9896	1.0000
0.2	−1.60	1.17	0.5940	0.9764	0.9998
0.3	−1.15	1.02	0.7070	0.9838	1.0000
0.4	−0.58	0.93	0.6784	0.9458	0.9986
0.5	−0.02	0.90	0.6696	0.9590	0.9590
0.6	0.55	0.94	0.6760	0.9470	0.9980
0.7	1.12	1.00	0.7124	0.8696	0.9998
0.8	1.60	1.11	0.5452	0.9800	0.9900
0.9	1.60	1.43	0.4766	0.9926	1.0000

4. CONCLUSION

The sampling distribution of skewness coefficient is difficult, almost intractable, to obtain theoretically. With computer methods, we study such distributions when sampling from a mixture of two normal populations. The effects of varying proporations of the mixture, and of the distance between the two means, for homoscedastic populations, are considered and demonstrated.

REFERENCES

[1] Behboodian, J. (1972). On the distribution of a symmetric statistic from a mixed population. Technometrics 14, 919-923.

[2] Bowman, K.O. and Shenton, L.R. (1973). Remarks on the distribution of b_1 in sampling from a normal mixture and normal type A distribution. J. Amer. Statist. Asso. 68, 998-1003.

[3] Cramér, H. (1946). Mathematical Methods of Statistics. Princeton: Princeton University Press.

[4] Everitt, B.S. and Hand, D.J. (1981). Finite Mixture Distributions. London: Chapman and Hall Ltd.

[5] Kendall, M.G. and Stuart, A. (1977). The Advanced Theory of Statistics, Vol. 1, 4th Edition. London: Charles Griffin and Co., Ltd.

[6] Teichroew, D. (1957). The mixture of normal distributions with different variances. Ann. Math. Statist. 28, 510-512.

[7] Tracy, D.S. and Conley, W.C. (1982). Exact sampling distributions of two measures of skewness--a computer approach. Computer Science and Statistics: Proc. 14th. Symp. Interface, Ed. K.W. Heiner, R.S. Sacher and J.W. Wilkinson. New York: Springer Verlag, 262-265.

COMPUTER SCIENCE AND STATISTICS:
The Interface, L. Billard (ed.)

DIAGNOSTICS FOR ASSESSING MULTIMODALITY

M. Anthony Wong and Christian Schaack

Sloan School of Management
Massachusetts Institute of Technology
Cambridge, Massachusetts, U. S. A.

Diagnostics based on the kth nearest neighbor density estimates are proposed for assessing multimodality. The sampling distributions of the proposed statistics for various sample sizes and for a range of unimodal, bimodal, and trimodal populations are obtained approximately by computer simulations. The results indicate that these diagnostics are useful in discriminating populations with different modality. A procedure for determining the number of modes is developed and is shown to be an effective tool for investigating multimodality.

1. INTRODUCTION

We assume in this study that the statistical data consist of a sample from a distribution F with density function f. Our aim is to develop procedures that are useful for investigating the number of modes present in f. It will be shown that the kth nearest neighbor density estimator is useful in providing diagnostics for assessing the modality of f.

A brief review of the literature on investigating and testing multimodality will be given in Section 2. In Section 3, the kth nearest neighbor density estimator will first be reviewed and then it will be shown how diagnostic statistics based on this procedure can be constructed to investigate multimodality. The sampling distributions of the proposed statistics for sample sizes N = 50, 70, and 100 and for a range of unimodal, bimodal, and trimodal populations are obtained approximately by computer simulations and the results are presented in Section 4. In Section 5, a simple diagnostic procedure is proposed and is shown to be a useful tool for assessing multimodality.

2. LITERATURE REVIEW

Wertz and Schneider (1979) recently presented a bibliography of the extensive literature on statistical density estimation. The problem of investigating the number of modes in a density or its derivative has, however, only been considered by a few authors, for example Cox (1966), Good and Gaskins (1980), and Silverman (1981). As pointed out in Silverman (1980), most existing methods of assessing modality seem to depend on some arbitrary implicit or explicit choice of the scale of the effects being studied. Silverman (1981) therefore proposed the use of the "M-critical window width" $h_{crit}(M)$ statistics to test the null hypothesis that the density f has M or fewer modes against the alternative that f has more than M modes, where $h_{crit}(M) = \inf\{h;\ \hat{f}(.,h)$ has at most M modes$\}$, M = 1,2,3,...; and $\hat{f}(.,h)$ is the kernel density estimate of f using window width h. Since $h_{crit}(M)$ is a natural choice for the amount of smoothing needed to obtain an M-modal density estimate, Silverman also suggested that a conservative assessment of the significance of a sample $h_{crit}(M)$ statistic can be obtained approximately by Efron's (1979) bootstrap method using $\hat{f}(.,\ h_{crit}(M))$ as the null distribution.

Although the $h_{crit}(M)$ statistics are useful for examining multimodality, it is too conservative to use $\hat{f}(.,\ h_{crit}(M))$ as the null distribution. Hence, Silverman's test of unimodality against multimodality has been shown to have very low power even when the underlying distribution is strongly trimodal and the sample size is moderate (N = 100). (See Wong and Schaack, 1982.) In this paper, diagnostic statistics based on the kth nearest neighbor density estimates are proposed for investigating multimodality, and it will be shown that these statistics are useful in discriminating populations with different multimodality.

3. DIAGNOSTICS FOR INVESTIGATING MULTIMODALITY

In this section, it is shown that the kth nearest neighbor density estimates given in Loftsgaarden and Quesenberry (1965) can be used to provide diagnostics for investigating the modality of f using some sample data $x_1, x_2, \ldots, x_N$ from f.

This density estimation procedure can be described as follows: the estimated density at point x is $f_N(x) = k/(NV_k(x))$, where $V_k(x)$ is the volume of the smallest sphere centered at x containing k sample observations. Such a density estimate is uniformly consistent with probability one if f is uniformly continuous and if k = k(N) satisfies $k(N)/N \to 0$ and $k(N)/\log N \to \infty$. (See Devroye and Wagner, 1977.) It is, however, difficult to choose k in practice and it has been suggested that a range of values of k near $N^{1/2}$ should be tried.

Clearly, the value of k controls the amount by which the data are smoothed to give the density estimate. When k increases from 1 to N, the density estimate becomes smoother or less bumpy. If we denote the number of sample modes identified in the density estimate by M(k), then M(.) is a non-increasing discrete-valued function of k. It is proposed here that S(m), the number of values of k with M(k) = m, for m = 2,3,... should be used as diagnostic statistics for investigating the multimodality of f because S(m) can be viewed as the number of observations in the smallest modal cluster among the m sample modes. And if the data are strongly bimodal, for example, then S(2)/N will be significantly greater than zero. The results of a Monte Carlo study performed to examine the sampling distributions of these diagnostics for various sample sizes and for a range of multimodal distributions will be reported next.

4. SAMPLING DISTRIBUTIONS OF S(m)

4.1 Sampling Distributions of S(2) and S(3) for N = 100

One hundred samples, each with 100 observations, were generated from the following normal mixtures:

Unimodal: [1] N(0,1); [2] 1/2N(0,1) + 1/2N(2,1)
Balanced Bimodal: [3] 1/2N(0,1) + 1/2N(3,1); [4] 1/2N(0,1) + 1/2N(4,1); [5] 1/2N(0,1) + 1/2N(5,1)
Unbalanced Bimodal: [6] 2/3N(0,1) + 1/3N(4,1); [7] 3/4N(0,1) + 1/4N(4,1)
Trimodal: [8] 1/3N(-4,1) + 1/3N(0,1) + 1/3N(4,1); [9] 1/3N(-6,1) + 1/3N(0,1) + 1/3N(6,1)

The sampling distributions of S(2) and S(3) for samples from these populations are given in Figure 1, and the parallel box-plots shown there are constructed as follows: the lower and upper extremes depict respectively the 5th and 95th percentile of the distribution, and the box itself is delimited by the lower and upper quartiles. The median, which is very close to the mean for all the sampling distributions, is used as the measure of central location.

In Figure 1a, the sampling distribution of S(2) for the various populations are shown. Clearly, S(2) is large only when the population is strongly bimodal, and this diagnostic is therefore useful for detecting bimodal distributions even when the sample size is moderate (N = 100). It should be noted, however, that S(2) is not particularly effective in identifying unbalanced bimodal distributions; this can be expected because S(2) is a measure of the size of the smallest modal group of observations. Similarly, in Figure 1b, it can be observed that S(3) is large only when the population is strongly trimodal, and that the sampling distributions of S(3) for the two populations N(0,1) and 1/3N(-4,1) + 1/3N(0,1) + 1/3N(4,1) do not overlap when the sample size is equal to 100. The distributions of S(4) were also computed and it was found that the 95th percentiles of these distributions were all very similar, again suggesting that S(4) would be useful in distinguishing quadri-modal populations from other multimodal distributions.

4.2 Sampling Distributions of S(2) and S(3) for N = 50 and 70

One hundred samples, each with 50 (and 70) observations, were generated from the following normal mixtures:

Unimodal: [1] N(0,1); [2] 1/2N(0,1) + 1/2N(2,1)
Bimodal: [3] 1/2N(0,1) + 1/2N(4,1); [4] 1/2N(0,1) + 1/2N(6,1); [5] 1/2N(0,1) + 1/2N(8,1)
Trimodal: [6] 1/3N(-4,1) + 1/3N(0,1) + 1/3N(4,1); [7] 1/3N(-6,1) + 1/3N(0,1) + 1/3N(6,1)

The sampling distributions of S(2) and S(3) for samples of size N = 50 from these populations are given in Figure 2. Again, S(2) and S(3) are found to be useful in detecting bimodal and trimodal distributions respectively. For example, the sampling distributions of S(2) for the two populations N(0,1) and 1/2N(0,1) + 1/2N(4,1) have less than 20% overlap (see Figure 2a). Similar results can be observed in Figure 3, where the sampling distributions of S(2) and S(3) for samples of size 70 from the various populations are shown.

5. A DIAGNOSTIC PROCEDURE FOR DETECTING MULTIMODALITY

Since S(m) is the number of observations in the smallest modal cluster among the m sample modes and is bounded from above by N/m, a simple decision rule would be to let m-modality be indicated by the relationship $S(m) > 0.1N/(m-1) + (m-1)$. This is equivalent to saying, for example, that if the smaller of two modal clusters contain more than 10% of the observations, bimodality is indicated. We decided to use 10% because we would like to use a simple and easy-to-interpret diagnostic decision rule, especially if we can demonstrate its effectiveness.

The following diagnostic procedure is therefore suggested for use in investigating multimodality:

STEP 1: For m = 2,3,4,... compute S(m)
STEP 2: Let $D(m) = S(m) - 0.1N/(m-1) - (m-1)$; m = 2,3,4,...
STEP 3: Use the largest value of m with $D(m) > 0$ as an estimate of the underlying modality. (This follows from considerations of parsimony, because all values of m with $D(m) > 0$ are plausible estimates of the underlying modality.) Moreover, unimodality is indicated by $D(m) \leq 0$ for all $m > 1$.

The effectiveness of this diagnostic procedure will be illustrated next, using generated data which are obtained by repeating the computer simulations described previously in Section 4. However, only fifty samples of each sample size N(N = 50, 70, and 100) were generated here. The estimation, or classification, results obtained when the above procedure is applied to the various generated samples of size N = 100, 70, and 50 are given respectively in Table 1a, 1b and 1c. These results indicate that the proposed procedure is a useful diagnostic tool for investigating multimodality. For example, when N = 50, the procedure correctly indicates (i) unimodality for 68% of the samples from the flat-top unimodal distribution 1/2N(0,1) + 1/2N(2,1), (ii) bimodality for 90% of the samples from the distinctly bimodal distribution 1/2N(0,1) + 1/2N(4,1), and (iii) trimodality for 82% of the samples from the trimodal distribution 1/3N(-4,1) + 1/3N(0,1) + 1/3N(4,1). Although the present procedure is not particularly effective in detecting unbalanced multimodal distributions (see Table 1a), its demonstrated utility in investigating multimodality cannot be overlooked.

6. REFERENCES

Cox, D. R. (1966). Notes on the analysis of mixed frequency distributions. British Journal of Mathematical and Statistical Psychology, 19, 39-47.

Devroye, L. P. and Wagner, T. J. (1977). The strong uniform consistency of nearest neighbor density estimates. Annals of Statistics, 5, 536-540.

Efron, B. (1979). Bootstrap methods--another look at the jack-knife. Annals of Statistics, 7, 1-26.

Good, I. J. and Gaskins, R. A. (1980). Density estimation and bump-hunting by the penalized likelihood method exemplified by scattering and meteorite data. Journal of the American Statistical Association, 75, 42-56.

Loftsgaarden, D. O. and Quensenberry, C. P. (1965). A nonparametric estimate of a multivariate density function. Annals of Mathematical Statistics, 36, 1049-1051.

Silverman, B. W. (1980). Comment on Good and Gaskins (1980). Journal of the American Statistical Association, 75, 67-68.

Silverman, B. W. (1981). Using kernel density estimates to investigate multimodality. Journal of the Royal Statistical Society, B, 43, 97-99.

Wertz, W. and Schneider, B. (1979). Statistical density estimation: a bibliography. International Statistical Review, 47, 155-175.

Wong, M. A. and Schaack, C. (1982). Using the kth nearest neighbor clustering procedure to determine the number of subpopulations. Proceedings of the Statistical Computing Section, American Statistical Association, 40-48.

Table 1a Classification Matrix for N = 100

Population*	Modality	Estimated Modality [1]	[2]	[3]	[4]
1	[1]	39	9	2	0
2	[1]	39	10	1	0
3	[2]	7	37	5	1
4	[2]	1	46	1	2
5	[2]	0	48	1	1
6	[2]	31	9	10	0
7	[2]	44	2	4	0
8	[3]	0	1	48	1
9	[3]	0	0	49	1

* See Section 4.1 in text for a full description of these populations.

Table 1b Classification Matrix for N = 70

Population**	Modality	Estimated Modality [1]	[2]	[3]	[4]
1	[1]	41	6	3	0
2	[1]	23	24	3	0
3	[2]	1	47	2	0
4	[2]	0	48	1	1
5	[2]	0	45	4	1
6	[3]	1	7	42	0
7	[3]	0	0	49	1

Table 1c Classification Matrix for N = 50

Population**	Modality	Estimated Modality [1]	[2]	[3]	[4]
1	[1]	38	10	2	0
2	[1]	34	13	3	0
3	[2]	2	45	2	1
4	[2]	0	44	5	1
5	[2]	0	46	3	1
6	[3]	0	9	41	0
7	[3]	0	4	46	0

** See Section 4.2 in text for a full description of these populations.

Figure 1a. Sampling Distributions of S(2) when N = 100

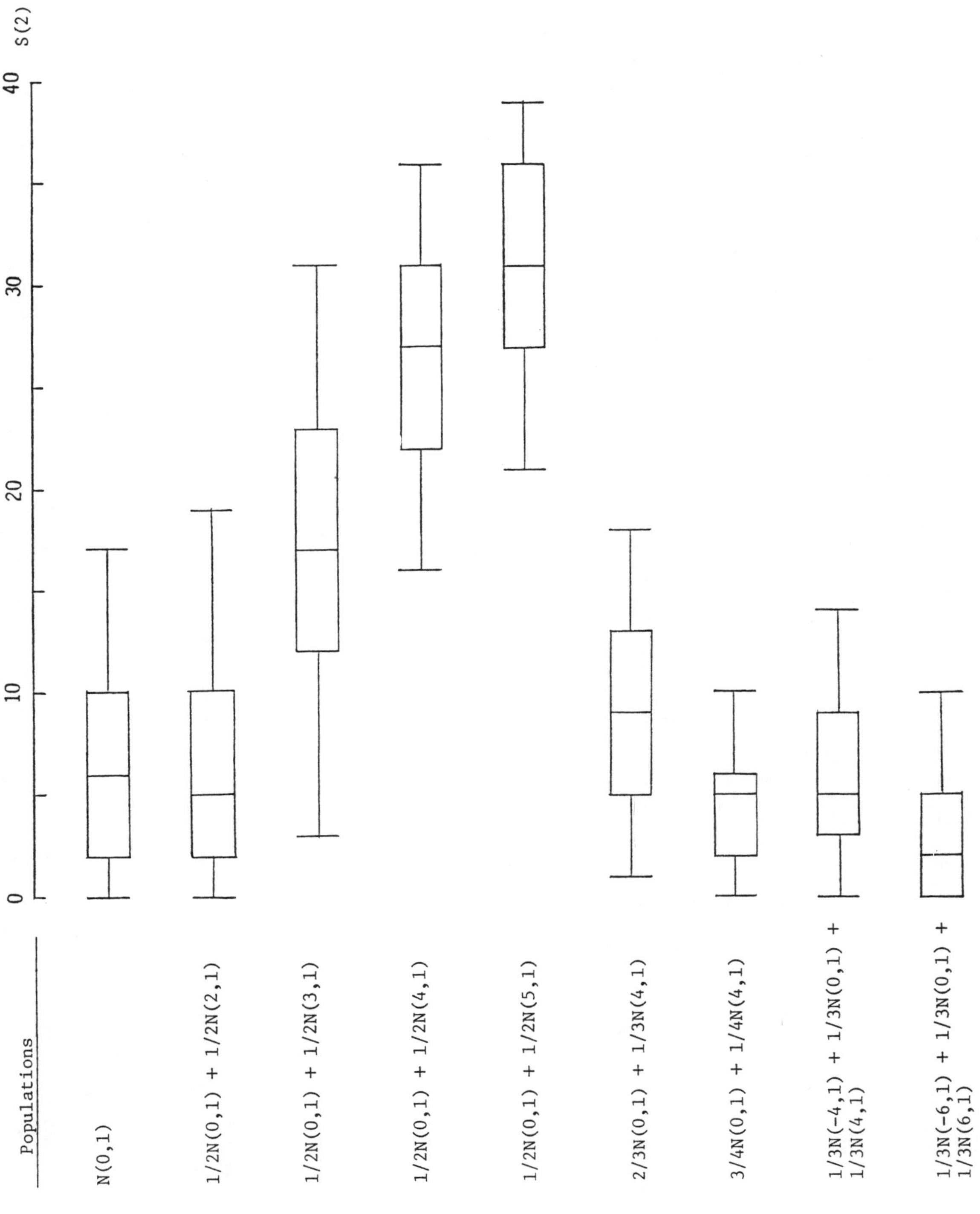

Figure 1b. Sampling Distributions of S(3) when N = 100

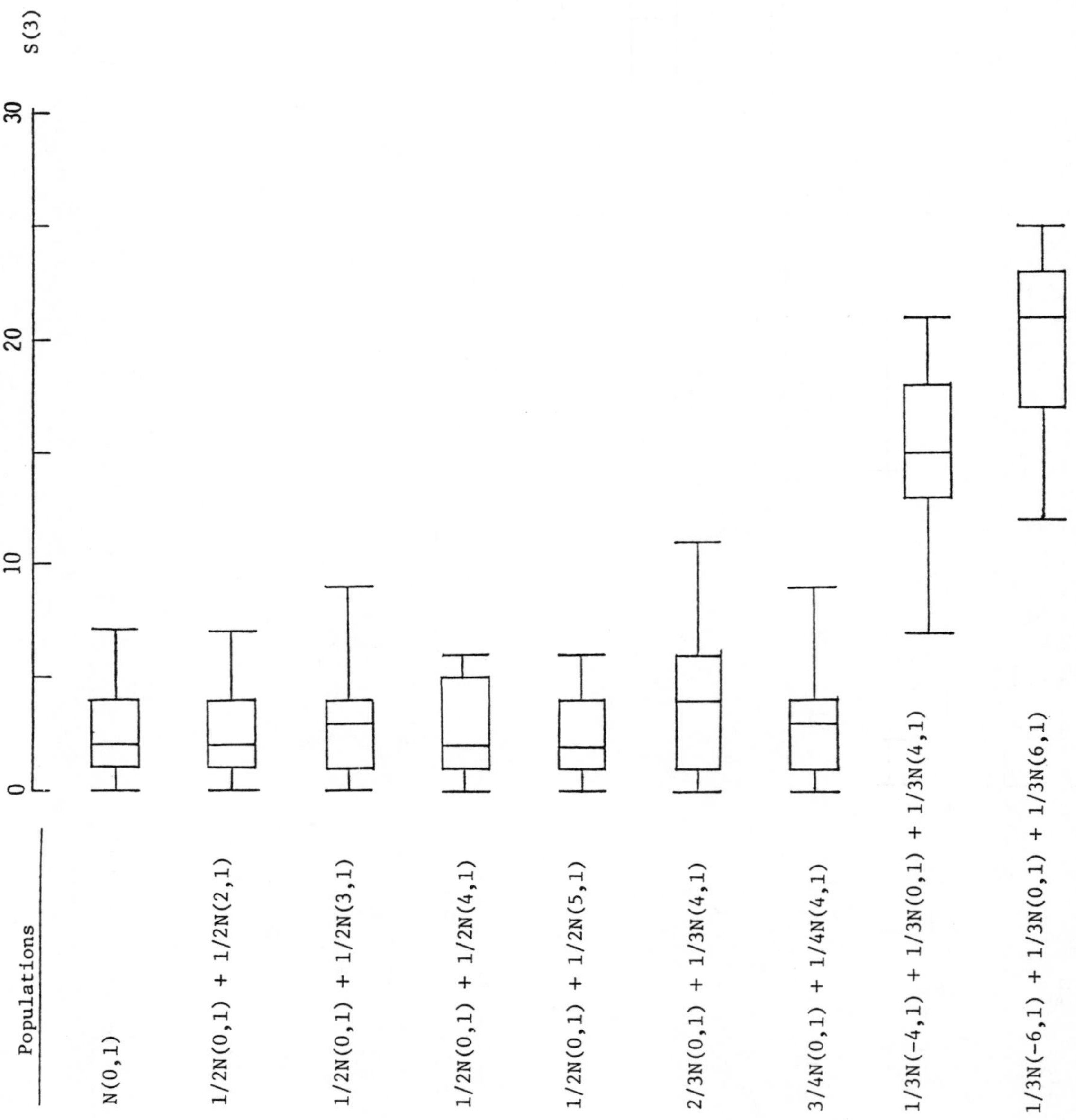

Figure 2a. Sampling Distributions of S(2) when N = 50

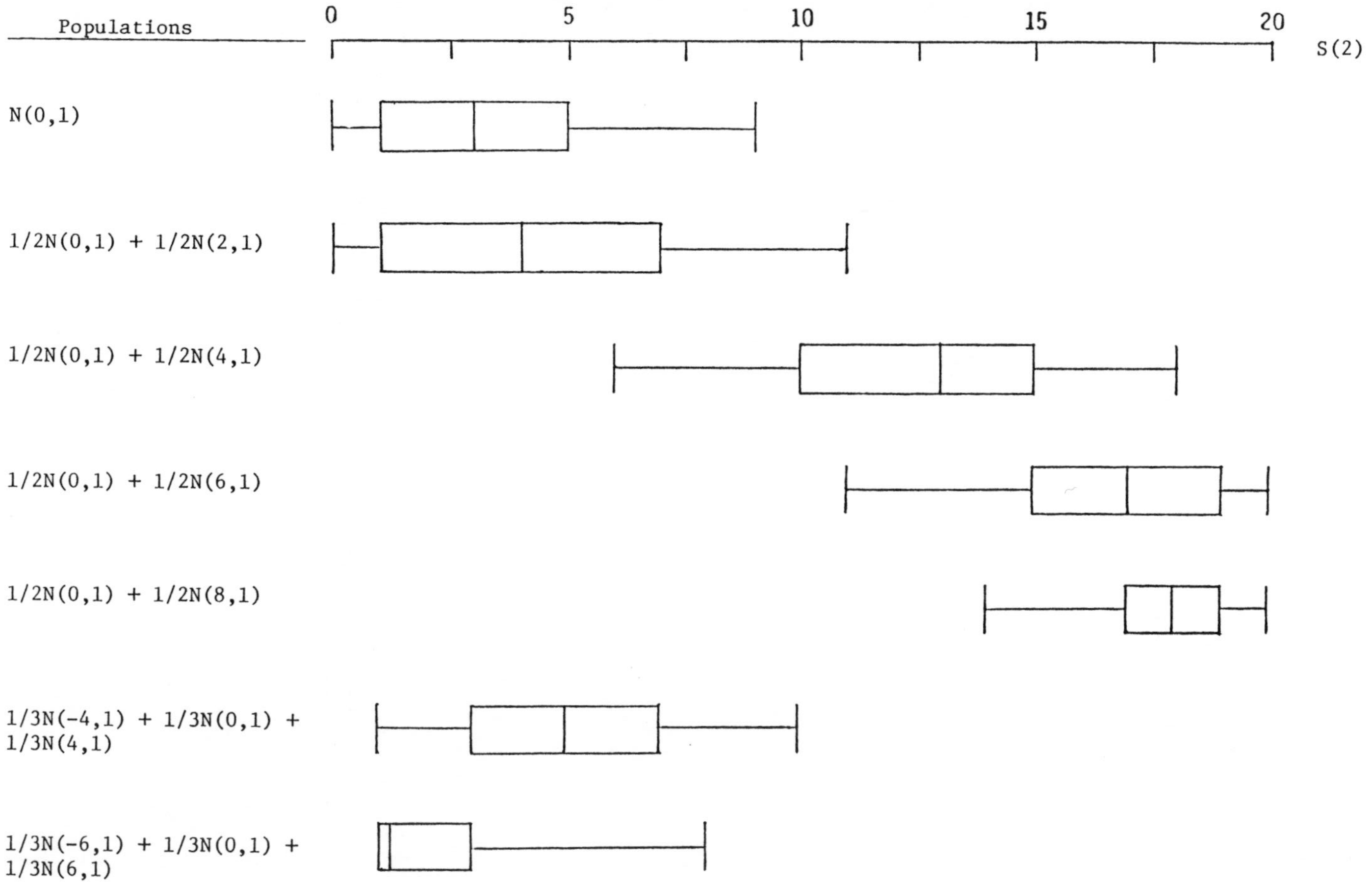

Figure 2b. Sampling Distributions of S(3) when N = 50

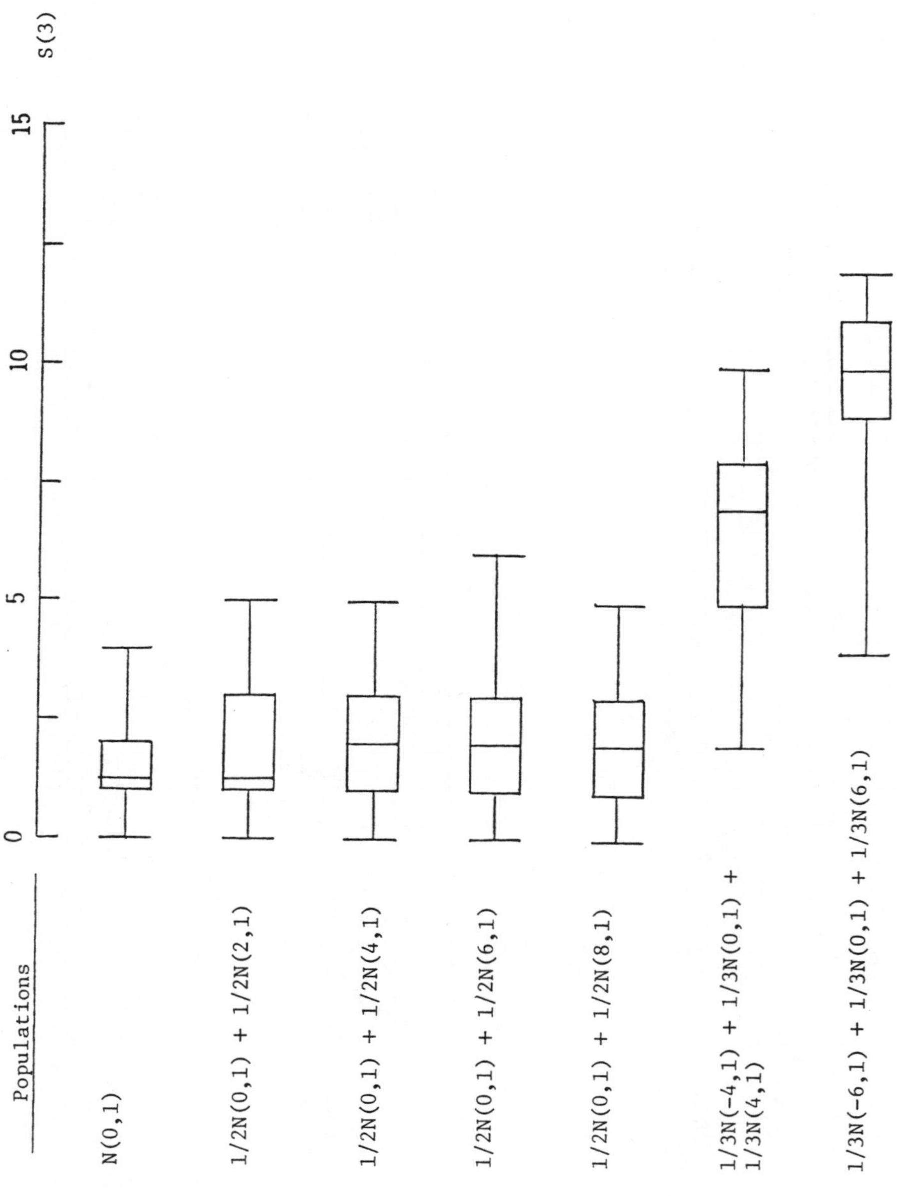

Figure 3a. Sampling Distributions of S(2) when N = 70

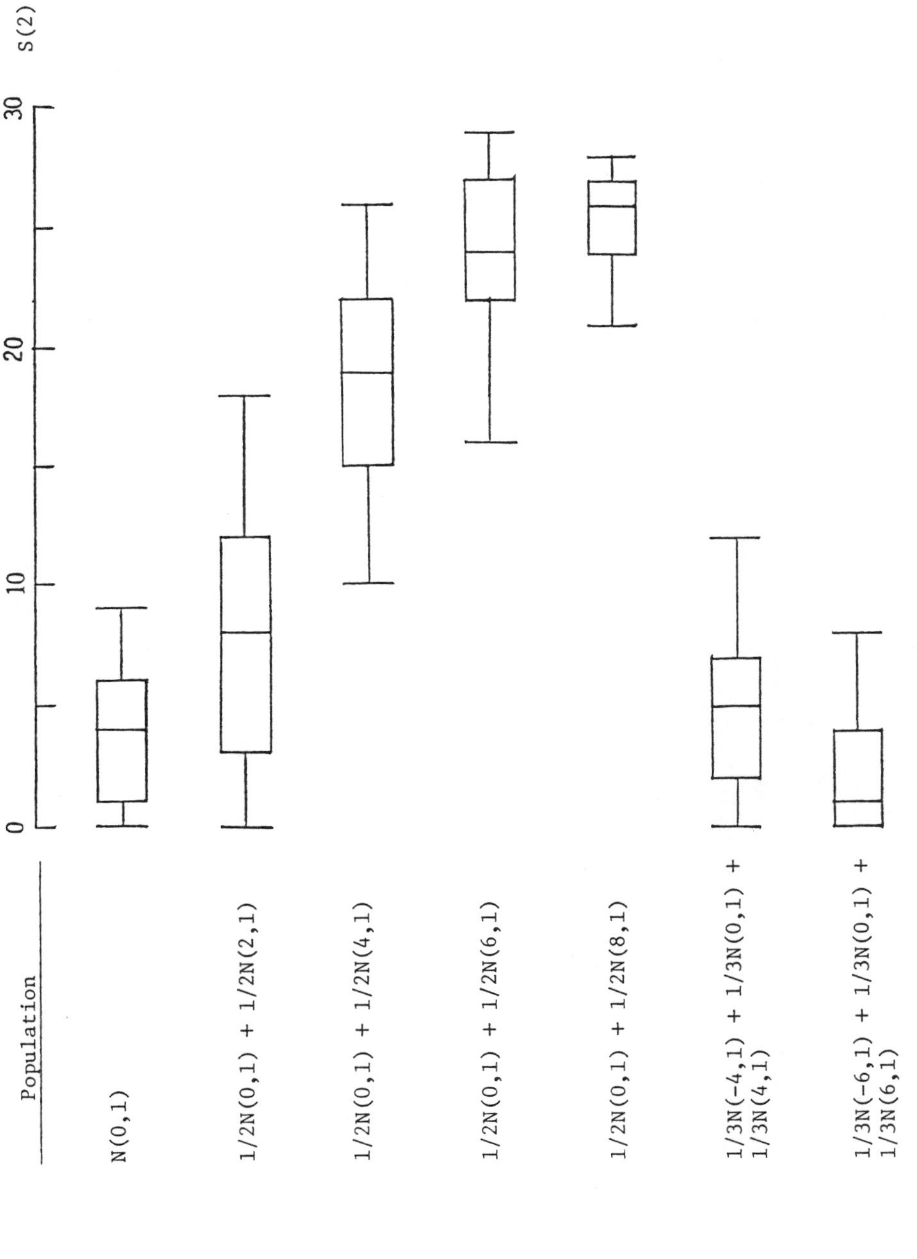

Figure 3b. Sampling Distributions of S(3) when N = 70

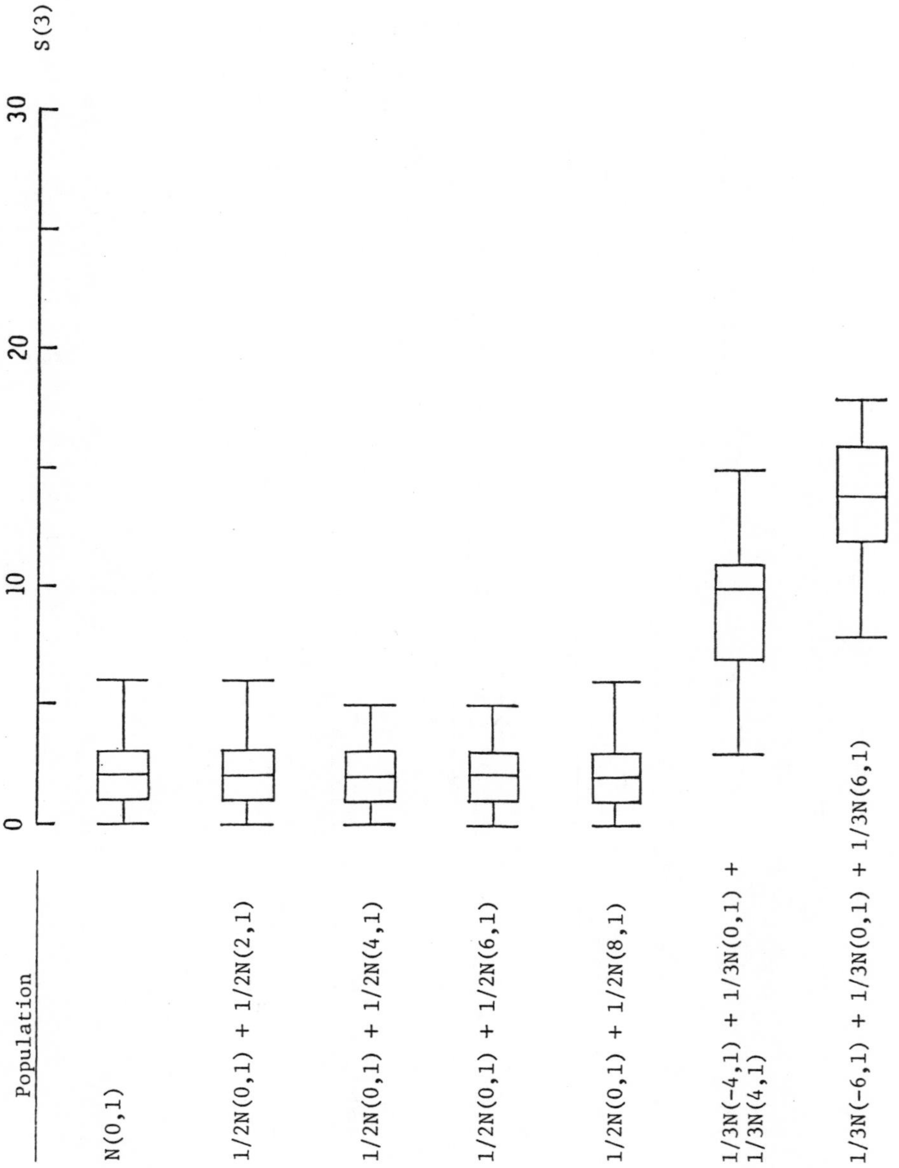